Essential Property Law and Practice for SQE1

Eliza Hakes and Martin George

Routledge
Taylor & Francis Group
LONDON AND NEW YORK

Designed cover image: DragonTiger/Getty Images®

First published 2026
by Routledge
4 Park Square, Milton Park, Abingdon, Oxon OX14 4RN

and by Routledge
605 Third Avenue, New York, NY 10158

Routledge is an imprint of the Taylor & Francis Group, an informa business

British Library Cataloguing-in-Publication Data
A catalogue record for this book is available from the British Library

Library of Congress Cataloging-in-Publication Data
Names: Hakes, Eliza author | George, Martin (Law teacher) author
Title: Essential property law and practice for SQE1 / Eliza Hakes and Martin George.
Description: Abingdon, Oxon [UK] ; New York, NY : Routledge, 2026. | Series: Routledge essential law for SQE1 | Includes bibliographical references and index.
Identifiers: LCCN 2025038837 | ISBN 9781032711485 hardback | ISBN 9781032711447 paperback | ISBN 9781032711508 ebook Subjects: LCSH: Property—Great Britain—Examinations, questions, etc. | Real property—Great Britain—Examinations, questions, etc. | Solicitors Qualifying Examination | LCGFT: Study guides
Classification: LCC KD810 .H35 2026 | DDC 346.4204—dc23/eng/20250820 LC record available at https://lccn.loc.gov/2025038837

ISBN: 978-1-032-71148-5 (hbk)
ISBN: 978-1-032-71144-7 (pbk)
ISBN: 978-1-032-71150-8 (ebk)

DOI: 10.4324/9781032711508

Typeset in The Sans
by Apex CoVantage, LLC

Access the SQE1 Series Companion Website: www.routledge.com/cw/sqe

Essential Property Law and Practice for SQE1

Essential Property Law and Practice for SQE1 explains the key principles of property law and practice in a clear, concise, and easy-to-understand style. Principles are introduced and illustrated with reference to realistic practical examples.

Written specifically for SQE study, this book provides an overview of five types of property transaction, with a coherent and structured approach to dealing with these from start to finish. It also includes a range of supportive features:

- *Transaction overview.* A flowchart guiding you through the stages of each type of transaction, with signposts to the relevant chapters. Appendices also include examples of key documents and forms needed for different types of transaction.
- *Revision points.* Each chapter concludes with a concise list of key revision points.
- *Multiple-choice questions.* Each section of the book provides multiple-choice questions following the SQE1 question format (with answers to enable you to test your knowledge). Further multiple-choice questions and answers are also provided on the companion website.

Part of Routledge's Essential Law for SQE1 series, this concise and accessible text provides a clear understanding of the property law and practice element of SQE1 and will enable you to test your assessment skills. Without the assumption of any prior knowledge of property law and practice, it is suitable for any SQE candidate, whether a law or non-law graduate.

Eliza Hakes is a Lecturer in Law at Aston University. Eliza worked as a solicitor before moving to work in higher education, where she has experience designing materials and teaching on the LLB, GDL, LPC, SQE, and Bar Training Course.

Martin George is Professor of Land Law and Executive Dean of the School of Law and Social Sciences at Aston University. He is an academic fellow of the Inner Temple, and an academic associate member of Gatehouse Chambers.

Essential Law for SQE1
Series editor: Wendy Laws

Essential Law for SQE1 is a series of concise textbooks aligned to the latest SQE1 curriculum. Providing candidates with an accessible summary of the core principles in each area of law, the style of each book is precise, with bullet-point lists summarizing key information and revision points concluding each chapter. The books also feature multiple choice questions with answers, example problem questions, and a glossary of key cases.

Essential Tort Law for SQE1
Wendy Laws

Essential Dispute Resolution for SQE1
Ben Waters

Essential Business Law and Practice for SQE1
Bill Davies

Essential Land Law for SQE1
Mohammad Sabuj

Essential Legal System and Legal Services for SQE1
Ian Bowden and Zaman F. Kala

Essential Criminal Law and Criminal Practice for SQE1
James Thornton, Amanda Parker and Orla Slattery

Essential Constitutional and Administrative Law for SQE1
Zaman F. Kala and Ian Bowden

Essential Contract Law for SQE1
Fred Motson and Stephen Bunbury

Essential Property Law and Practice for SQE1
Eliza Hakes and Martin George

For more information about this series, please visit: www.routledge.com/Essential-Law-for-SQE1/book-series/SQE1

Contents

Table of cases

Table of legislation

Introduction

This book provides a clear, concise explanation of key principles of property law and practice.

It focuses on those areas which fall within the assessment specification for the Solicitors Qualifying Examination (**SQE1**) Functioning Legal Knowledge Part 2 (**FLK2**), namely:[1]

1. The key elements of a freehold or leasehold residential or commercial property transaction.
2. Investigation of a registered or an unregistered freehold and leasehold title.
3. Pre-contract searches and enquiries undertaken when acquiring a freehold or leasehold property.
4. Steps in progressing a freehold or leasehold property transaction to exchange of contracts.
5. Pre-completion steps relevant to a freehold or leasehold property transaction.
6. Completion and post-completion steps relevant to a freehold or leasehold property transaction in each of England and Wales including remedies for delayed completion.
7. The grant and the assignment of a commercial lease or underlease.
8. The key lease covenants in a commercial lease and the law relating to their breach.
9. Security of tenure under the Landlord and Tenant Act 1954 Part II.
10. Taxation of property transactions through Stamp Duty Land Tax for land in England, Land Transaction Tax for land in Wales, Value Added Tax and Capital Gains Tax.

The style of the book reflects the SQE1 assessment specification:

- The SQE1 assessment requires knowledge and understanding of fundamental legal principles and the ability to apply them.

1 See: SQE1 Functioning Legal Knowledge Assessment Specification, updated April 2024, published by the Solicitors Regulation Authority, available via www.sqe.sra.org.uk/exam-arrangements/assessment-information/sqe1-assessment-specification.

- Candidates are not required to recall specific case names or statutory provisions (except where they are normally used in practice to describe a legal principle).
- Candidates will be tested on the current law and will not be tested on the historical development of the law.

In order to effectively cover the requisite functioning legal knowledge in a way which reflects the assessment specification, principles are introduced and illustrated with reference to realistic practical examples by following five property transactions from start to finish from the perspective of both the buyer's and the seller's solicitor. Each practical phase of a transaction has its own section in the book, complete with its own revision summary and set of practice questions.

This approach enables the book to provide a clear and accessible account of key principles in a practical context, making it easy for the reader to understand the principles, remember them, and apply them to practical scenarios in an assessment.

Key features to assist learning:

- *Transaction overview.* Each of the five transactions begins with a flowchart guiding the reader through the various stages of that transaction, with signposts to the relevant chapters. This enables the reader to learn transaction by transaction.
- *Revision points.* Each chapter concludes with a concise list of key revision points, and there is a more detailed revision summary included at the end of each section of the book.
- *Multiple-choice questions.* The SQE1 assessment uses multiple-choice questions to test understanding of key principles. Multiple-choice questions, following the SQE format, are provided at the end of each section of the book (with answers in the final chapter). A further set of review multiple-choice questions and answers is provided at www.routledge.com/cw/sqe.

Whilst the SQE does not require candidates to recall specific case names or statutory provisions, references to key cases and statutes are provided to serve as an additional resource for those readers who wish to cement their understanding of the key principles by reference to the original source of law.

We endeavour to state the law as of 31 January 2025, but some later additions have been possible.

1 Using this book

1.1 Chapter overview

This book explores the SQF1 Property Practice syllabus using practical illustrations by following five transactions (the **Transactions**) from start to finish.

The Transactions are:

- the purchase of freehold land which is registered, for residential purposes;
- the purchase of freehold land which is registered, for commercial purposes;
- the purchase of freehold land which is unregistered, for commercial purposes;
- the grant of a commercial lease; and
- the assignment of a commercial registered lease.

This chapter sets out the key background information about each Transaction and provides an individual roadmap through the book for each.

1.2 The scenario
- 1.2.1 André's purchase of the House
- 1.2.2 Style&Go Ltd's purchase of the Salon
- 1.2.3 Style&Go Ltd's purchase of the Car Park
- 1.2.4 Grant of the Nail Bar Lease to Polished Perfection Ltd
- 1.2.5 Assignment of the Nail Bar Lease to Gemma's Gels Ltd

1.3 Phases of the transaction

1.4 Roadmaps
- 1.4.1 André's purchase of the House
- 1.4.2 Style&Go Ltd's purchase of the Salon
- 1.4.3 Style&Go Ltd's purchase of the Car Park
- 1.4.4 Grant of the Nail Bar Lease to Polished Perfection Ltd
- 1.4.5 Assigning the Nail Bar Lease
- 1.4.6 Granting a commercial sub-lease

1.2 The scenario

Throughout this book, we will follow each of the Transactions from start to finish, examining the relevant steps taken by the solicitors for each party. There are

DOI: 10.4324/9781032711508-1

accompanying documents for each Transaction enclosed at Appendices 1–5, and you will be cross-referred to them in the relevant chapter so that you can read them at the appropriate moment.

1.2.1 André's purchase of the House

In September 2025, André Gomez moves to Westshire to set up a business. He is purchasing a house to live in, called The Old Bakery, in a village called Torton (the **House**) as shown in Figures 1.1 and 1.2. The House, including its grounds, used to be part of a bigger parcel of land comprising a wheat farm and mill. It is now a four-bedroom house with a main bathroom upstairs and a recently-added downstairs toilet. The House has a large garden.

André's purchase of the House completes in December 2025.

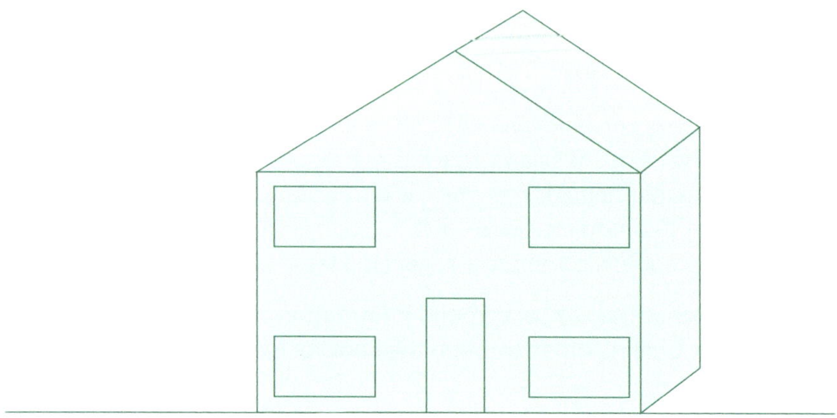

Figure 1.1 The House.

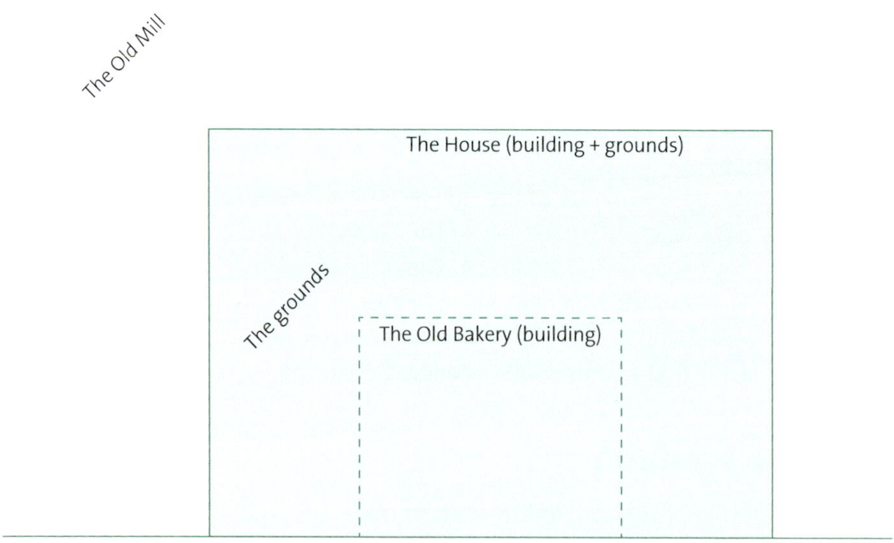

Figure 1.2 A bird's-eye view of the House.

1.2.2 Style&Go Ltd's purchase of the Salon

In January 2026, André sets up a company, Style&Go Ltd, and looks to purchase a building to run as a hair salon and a piece of land close to it to use as a car park for his customers.

André finds a building on the High Street of a local town called Barnford which is currently residential but which André thinks would make an appropriate commercial premises, as lots of other buildings on the same terrace are commercial. The building has a large extended ground floor which André thinks would be a great size for his hair salon. We will refer to this property as the **Salon** and it is shown in Figure 1.3.

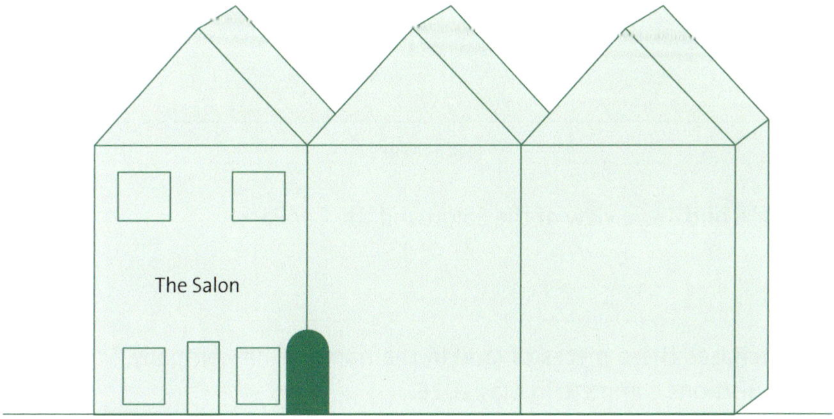

Figure 1.3 The Salon.

1.2.3 Style&Go Ltd's purchase of the Car Park

There is a piece of land for sale behind the Salon which looks as though it has been used to sell cars. There is a disused office building on the site, but it is otherwise clear and looks to be in good condition. André thinks this will work well as an on-site car park for customers using the Salon. We will refer to this land as the **Car Park** and it is shown in Figure 1.4.

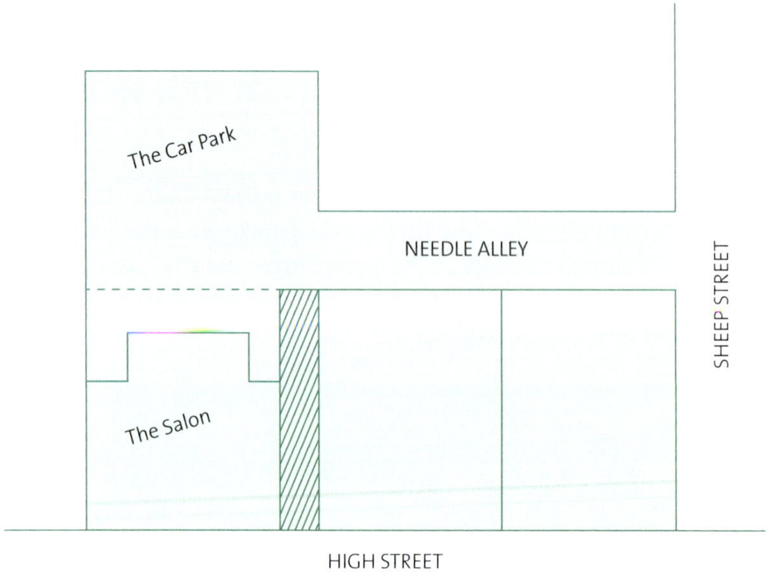

Figure 1.4 A bird's-eye view of the Salon and the Car Park.

André purchases these pieces of land in the name of his company, Style &Go Ltd. These acquisitions complete in May 2026.

1.2.4 Grant of the Nail Bar Lease to Polished Perfection Ltd

In June 2026, Style&Go Ltd looks to generate some extra income whilst also expanding their customer base, by inviting a complementary business to operate from their building (as Style&Go Ltd only uses the ground floor for the hair salon). They decide to grant a lease over the first floor of their building to a local nail technician, Meena Kasih, who runs a business called Polished Perfection Ltd, to operate as a nail bar (the **Nail Bar**). This is shown in Figures 1.5 and 1.6.

The lease (the **Nail Bar Lease**) is granted in September 2026.

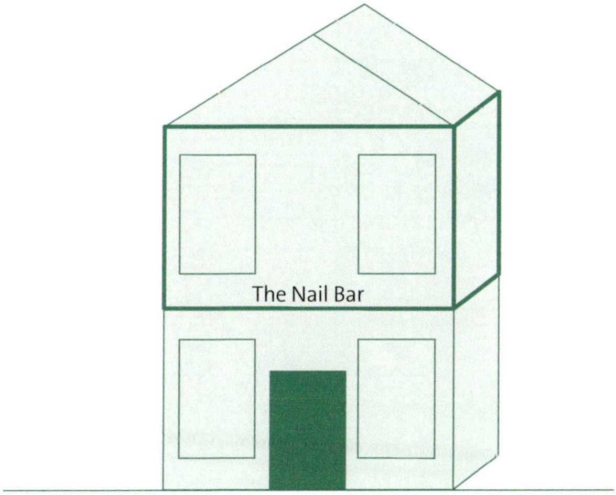

Figure 1.5 The Nail Bar.

Figure 1.6 Illustrating the grant of the Nail Bar Lease.

1.2.5 Assignment of the Nail Bar Lease to Gemma's Gels Ltd

Shortly after completion of the lease, Meena needs to take a step back from the business to care for her mother and does not know when she will be able to return. She explores the possibility of assigning or sub-letting the Nail Bar. In the end, she decides to assign the Nail Bar Lease to Gemma's Gels Ltd. This is shown in Figure 1.7.

The assignment completes in February 2027.

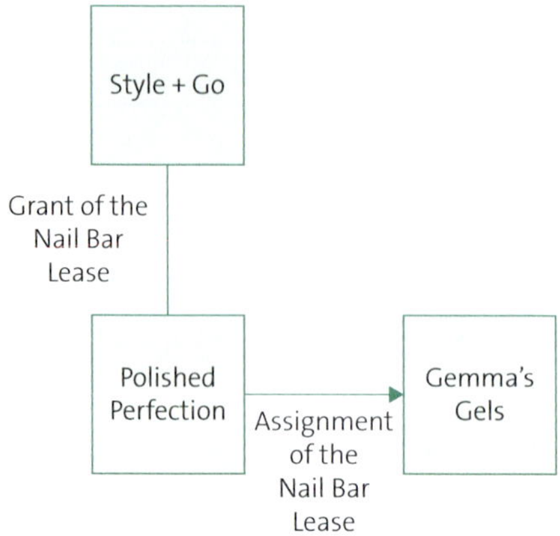

Figure 1.7 The assignment of the Nail Bar Lease.

1.3 Phases of the transaction

Each property transaction includes the following basic phases:

- **Phase 0: commercial considerations and taking instructions.** This phase is about finding out about your client and the transaction, ensuring you can act for them, and advising them on commercial matters such as tax.
- **Phase 1: due diligence.** This is usually done by the buyer's solicitor and is their opportunity to find out about the land. It comprises investigating the title to the land, making searches and enquiries about the land, and considering planning permission.
- **Phase 2: the documentation.** There are three categories of documentation typically seen in a property transaction: documentation relating to the landlord's consent to the transaction, documentation binding the parties contractually to enter into the transaction, and documentation effecting the disposition.
- **Phase 3: preparing for completion.** Once the documentation is agreed upon and the parties are ready, contracts are exchanged and the parties become bound to complete the transaction. The buyer's solicitor will undertake some final searches to check that nothing about the property has changed, and the solicitors will make practical arrangements ahead of completion.
- **Phase 4: completion.** This is the phase in which the solicitors complete the transaction and the legal interest in the land is transferred from one party to the other. For the seller, this is the final stage.

- **Phase 5: post-completion.** After completion, the buyer must pay any taxes due and register the transaction with HM Land Registry. For the buyer of freehold land, this is the final stage.
- **Phase 6: leasehold management.** For leasehold land, there are further considerations even once the transaction has completed; for example, the landlord may be required to consent to something the tenant wishes to do with the premises, or either party may need to deal with a breach of covenant by the other or may wish to bring the lease to an end.

This book is structured to work through each phase and can simply be read from start to finish. If you wish to revise on a transaction-by-transaction basis, not all chapters will be relevant to each transaction, and so please use the roadmaps in Section 1.4 to guide you through the relevant transaction.

Chapter 2 provides a reminder of some important Land Law concepts in the context of Property Practice, and we recommend that everyone read this chapter.

Each Phase ends with a revision summary of all relevant topics and a set of practice questions relevant to the topics in that Phase.

1.4 Roadmaps

In this section you will find a roadmap for each of our Transactions, giving you an overview of the broad stages involved and signposting you to the relevant chapters to work through each one.

Whilst we do not grant a sub-lease within our scenario, there is an additional roadmap included at Section 1.4.6 for this type of transaction.

1.4.1 André's purchase of the House

Solicitors acting for a buyer or seller of residential property often follow the Law Society Conveyancing Protocol (the **Protocol**). This guides the conveyancing process for residential property, whether freehold or leasehold, and sets out the steps which should be taken by each party's solicitor in the sale and purchase of a home. The Protocol is available from the Law Society.

You may wish to refer to the Protocol as you work through André's purchase of the House.

The documents relevant to André's purchase of the House are in Appendix 1.

André's purchase of the House will follow these five phases set out in Figure 1.8 (the relevant chapters you need to read have been noted):

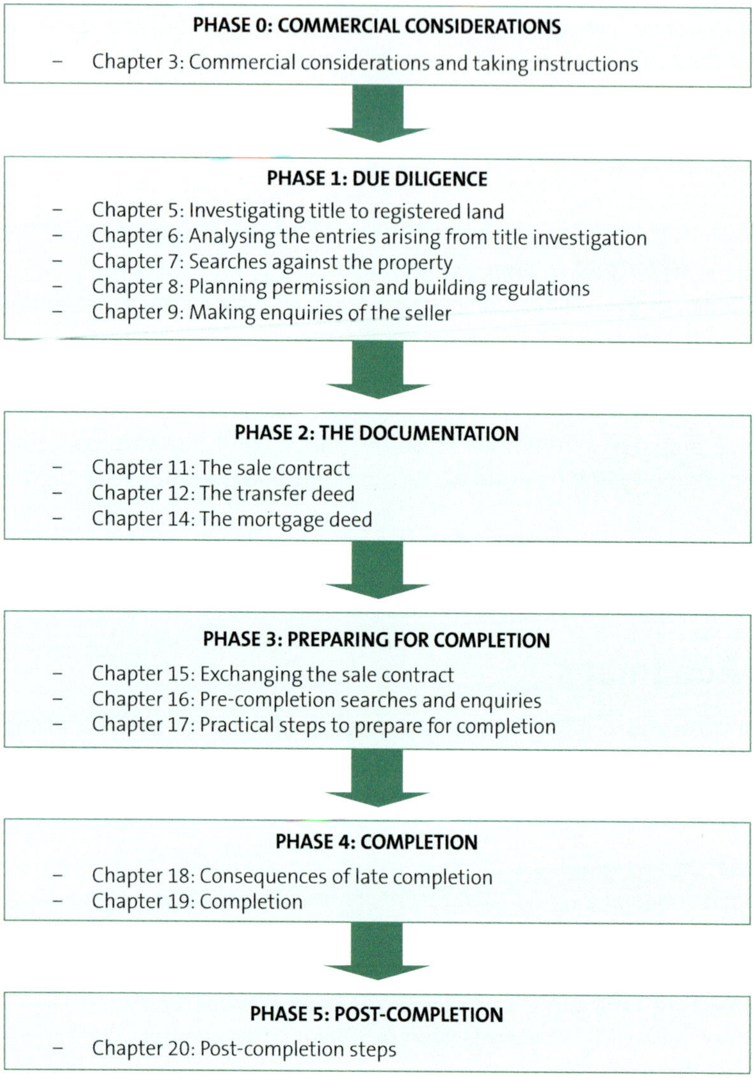

Figure 1.8 Roadmap of André's purchase of the House.

1.4.2 Style&Go Ltd's purchase of the Salon

As the Salon is currently being used as a residence, the solicitors for the buyer and seller may follow the Protocol when conveying the Salon; you may wish to refer to this as you work through Style&Go Ltd's purchase of the Salon.

The documents relevant to Style&Go Ltd's purchase of the Salon are in Appendix 2.

Style&Go Ltd's purchase of the Salon will follow these five phases as set out in Figure 1.9 (the relevant chapters you need to read have been noted):

PHASE 0: COMMERCIAL CONSIDERATIONS

- Chapter 3: Commercial considerations and taking instructions

↓

PHASE 1: DUE DILIGENCE

- Chapter 5: Investigating title to registered land
- Chapter 6: Analysing the entries arising from title investigation
- Chapter 7: Searches against the property
- Chapter 8: Planning permission and building regulations
- Chapter 9: Making enquiries of the seller

↓

PHASE 2: THE DOCUMENTATION

- Chapter 11: The sale contract
- Chapter 12: The transfer deed

↓

PHASE 3: PREPARING FOR COMPLETION

- Chapter 15: Exchanging the sale contract
- Chapter 16: Pre-completion searches and enquiries
- Chapter 17: Practical steps to prepare for completion

↓

PHASE 4: COMPLETION

- Chapter 18: Consequences of late completion
- Chapter 19: Completion

↓

PHASE 5: POST-COMPLETION

- Chapter 20: Post-completion steps

Figure 1.9 Roadmap of Style&Go Ltd's purchase of the Salon.

1.4.3 Style&Go Ltd's purchase of the Car Park

The purchase of the Car Park is a commercial transaction because the land is currently being used for commercial purposes. Therefore, the solicitors will not follow the Protocol when conveying the Car Park.

The documents relevant to Style&Go Ltd's purchase of the Car Park are in Appendix 3.

Style&Go Ltd's purchase of the Car Park will follow these five phases as set out in Figure 1.10 (the relevant chapters you need to read have been noted):

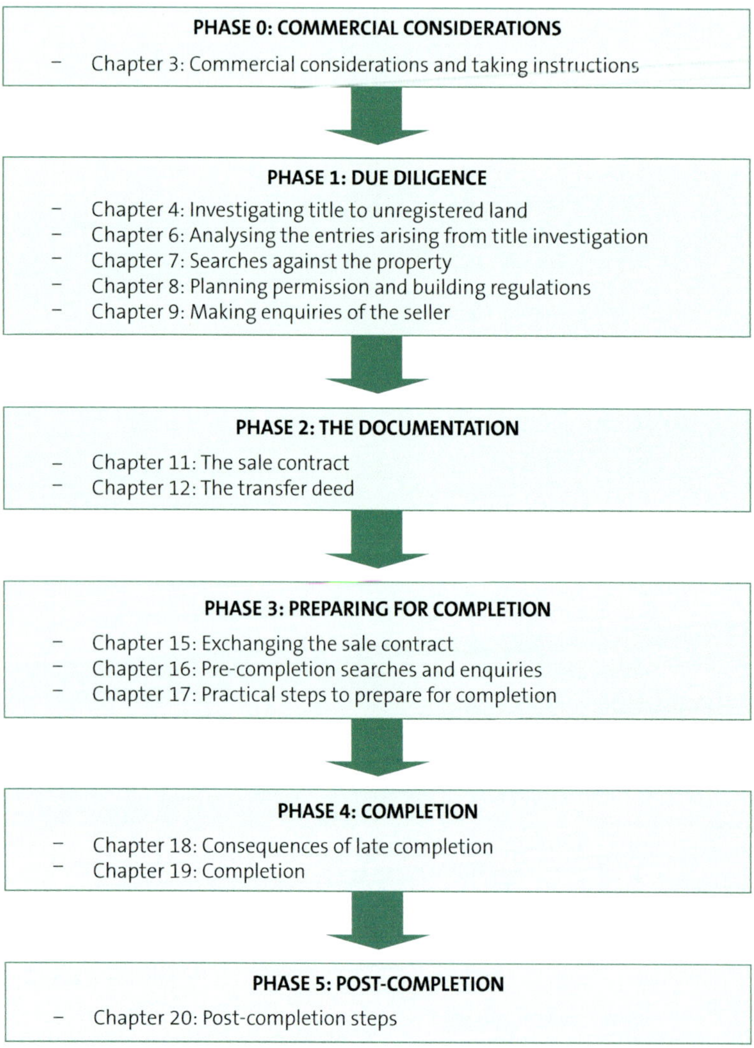

Figure 1.10 Roadmap of Style&Go Ltd's purchase of the Car Park.

1.4.4 Grant of the Nail Bar Lease to Polished Perfection Ltd

The process of granting a lease is very similar to that of the transfer of freehold land. For the purposes of this book, the parties have not entered into a contract in respect of the grant of the Nail Bar Lease, and so the chapters relating to the contract, exchange, and delayed completion are not relevant for the grant of the Nail Bar Lease.[1]

The documents relevant to the grant of the Nail Bar Lease to Polished Perfection Ltd are in Appendix 4.

The grant of the Nail Bar Lease will follow these six phases as set out in Figure 1.11 (the relevant chapters you need to read have been noted):

1 It is possible to enter into a contract to grant a lease – this is known as an agreement for lease and is noted briefly in Chapter 11.

PHASE 0: COMMERCIAL CONSIDERATIONS

- Chapter 3: Commercial considerations and taking instructions

↓

PHASE 1: DUE DILIGENCE

- Chapter 5: Investigating title to registered land
- Chapter 6: Analysing the entries arising from title investigation
- Chapter 7: Searches against the property
- Chapter 8: Planning permission and building regulations
- Chapter 9: Making enquiries of the seller

↓

PHASE 2: THE DOCUMENTATION

- Chapter 13: The lease

↓

PHASE 3: PREPARING FOR COMPLETION

- Chapter 16: Pre-completion searches and enquiries
- Chapter 17: Practical steps to prepare for completion

↓

PHASE 4: COMPLETION

- Chapter 19: Completion

↓

PHASE 5: POST-COMPLETION

- Chapter 20: Post-completion steps

↓

PHASE 6: LEASEHOLD MANAGEMENT

- Chapter 21: Consent under a lease
- Chapter 22: Enforcing leasehold covenants
- Chapter 23: Ending a lease

Figure 1.11 Roadmap of the grant of the Nail Bar Lease.

1.4.5 Assigning the Nail Bar Lease

The process of assigning a lease begins with an analysis of whether the landlord's consent is required for the assignment. From that moment, the process is similar to that of the transfer of freehold land, with the additional consideration of those matters relevant to the landlord/tenant relationship once the assignment has been completed.

The documents relevant to the assignment of the Nail Bar Lease to Gemma's Gels Ltd are in Appendix 5.

The assignment of the Nail Bar Lease will follow these stages as set out in Figure 1.12 (the relevant chapters you need to read have been noted):

PHASE 0: COMMERCIAL CONSIDERATIONS

- Chapter 3: Commercial considerations and taking instructions

↓

PHASE 6: LEASEHOLD MANAGEMENT

- Chapter 21: Consent under a lease

↓

PHASE 1: DUE DILIGENCE

- Chapter 5: Investigating title to registered land
- Chapter 6: Analysing the entries arising from title investigation
- Chapter 7: Searches against the property
- Chapter 8: Planning permission and building regulations
- Chapter 9: Making enquiries of the seller

↓

PHASE 2: THE DOCUMENTATION

- Chapter 10: the licence
- Chapter 11: the sale contract
- Chapter 12: the transfer deed

↓

PHASE 3: PREPARING FOR COMPLETION

- Chapter 15: Exchanging the sale contract
- Chapter 16: Pre-completion searches and enquiries
- Chapter 17: Practical steps to prepare for completion

↓

PHASE 4: COMPLETION

- Chapter 18: Consequences of late completion
- Chapter 19: Completion

↓

PHASE 5: POST-COMPLETION

- Chapter 20: Post-completion steps

↓

PHASE 6: LEASEHOLD MANAGEMENT

- Chapter 21: Consent under a lease
- Chapter 22: Enforcing leasehold covenants
- Chapter 23: Ending a lease

Figure 1.12 Roadmap of the assignment of the Nail Bar Lease.

1.4.6 Granting a commercial sub-lease

This book does not contain a transaction for the grant of a sub-lease. However, you can still use this book to guide the process.

The process of granting a sub-lease begins with an analysis of whether the landlord's consent is required for the grant (just like for an assignment). From that moment, the process is the same as when granting a lease.

The grant of a sub-lease would follow these stages as set out in Figure 1.13 (the relevant chapters you need to read have been noted):

PHASE 0: COMMERCIAL CONSIDERATIONS

- Chapter 3: Commercial considerations and taking instructions

PHASE 6: LEASEHOLD MANAGEMENT

- Chapter 21: Consent under a lease

PHASE 1: DUE DILIGENCE

- Chapter 5: Investigating title to registered land
- Chapter 6: Analysing the entries arising from title investigation
- Chapter 7: Searches against the property
- Chapter 8: Planning permission and building regulations
- Chapter 9: Making enquiries of the seller

PHASE 2: THE DOCUMENTATION

- Chapter 10: the licence
- Chapter 13: the lease

PHASE 3: PREPARING FOR COMPLETION

- Chapter 16: Pre-completion searches and enquiries
- Chapter 17: Practical steps to prepare for completion

PHASE 4: COMPLETION

- Chapter 19: Completion

PHASE 5: POST-COMPLETION

- Chapter 20: Post-completion steps

PHASE 6: LEASEHOLD MANAGEMENT

- Chapter 21: Consent under a lease
- Chapter 22: Enforcing leasehold covenants
- Chapter 23: Ending a lease

Figure 1.13 Roadmap of the grant of a commercial sub-lease.

2 The context of a property transaction

2.1 Chapter overview

Whilst this is not a Land Law textbook, it is necessary to have a good understanding of Land Law in order to follow this book. This chapter recaps some of the key Land Law principles which are relevant to this book.

This chapter is relevant to all freehold and leasehold transactions.

2.2 Estates and interests

2.2.1 Ownership of land: estates

When we talk about ownership of land, we are really talking about the ownership of rights over a piece of land for a period of time: this temporal relationship of ownership rights is known as an ***estate***. When we own an estate in land, a key right we own is the right of ***possession*** over that land for the duration of the estate.

In this book we will be considering both ***freehold estates***, which is land which is owned for perpetuity,[1] and ***leasehold estates***, which is land which is owned for a specified duration.

There are three key types of lease, categorised by the period of time they last for:

- ***a periodic tenancy***: this is a tenancy for a set period (e.g. a week, a month, a quarter, or a year) which keeps renewing/rolling over until determined by one

1 It is, in fact, more nuanced a definition than this, but to think of it as 'perpetuity' will suffice for the purposes of this book. Please consult a more specialist Land Law text for a deeper discussion.

DOI: 10.4324/9781032711508-2

of the parties. Either party can terminate the tenancy by giving notice of the same duration as the period;

- ***a tenancy at will***: this can be terminated by either party at any time; and
- ***a fixed-term tenancy***: the parties agree in advance the duration of the lease and the lease will automatically expire at the end of the term.

2.2.1.1 Statutory regimes

Ownership of an estate in land is not an absolute power to do whatever we want to with the land; instead, it is a bundle of rights and powers over a piece of land. Our powers over a piece of land are subject to various statutory controls, such as planning law. We will consider how these impact a property transaction in Chapter 8.

2.2.1.2 Legal and equitable ownership

Equity emerged during the late middle ages as a supplement to the harshness of the common-law rules and was subsequently developed in the courts of Chancery, while the common law was applied in the King's (or Queen's) Bench. The courts were merged towards the end of the nineteenth century, but the two systems of law remained. This would have been unworkable without an understanding of which system would take priority where the two come to different answers, and so it came to be understood that equity would take priority over the common law.

2.2.1.2.1 THE RECOGNITION OF RIGHTS AND INTERESTS

One feature of equity is that it recognises rights and interests that the common law does not. For example, a ***restrictive covenant*** does not require a response in the common law, because obligations cannot be enforced in law against people who did not agree to them.[2] Equity takes a different view of that obligation (it acts against the conscience of the person, or *in personam*), and this is why restrictive covenants are only recognised in equity.

For this reason, some interests are termed 'equitable' rights and interests (those which are recognised in equity), and others 'legal' rights and interests (being those which are recognised in the common law). In general terms, an equitable interest in land will be created because of one of three reasons:

- *A lack of formality.* Legal property rights will usually require formalities to create them, but if these are not satisfied, then equity may intervene to specifically enforce the contract to create that interest.
- *The right recognised only in equity.* Some interests in land can only exist in equity, such as the restrictive covenant mentioned above.
- *Time.* Legal interests can only exist for the length of either a freehold or a leasehold, which means that any attempt to create an interest for any other length – an easement for life, for example – can only be equitable.

2 See Section 2.2.2.1.

2.2.1.2.2 REMEDIES

A further feature of equity is that it may supply a different response to a complaint than would be provided under the common law. If one party breaches a contract, then the common law allows the other party to sue for damages. In equity, however, because it acts on the person, it may issue an order for that person to do something (specific performance) or to refrain from doing something (an injunction).

These equitable remedies are particularly important in the context of land disputes, because often damages are inadequate to compensate for the loss. Instead, it should be the case that non-performance of a contract for sale of land, for example, is enforced by specific performance of the contract, or the blocking of a right of way (easement) should be remedied with an injunction. It will be remembered that a maxim of equity is that it sees as done that which should have been done, and this is why the availability of specific performance is so central to the creation of equitable property rights. The caveat is that equitable remedies are discretionary, and this is why it is not always a simple answer as to whether an equitable interest in land has been created in a particular case.

2.2.2 Rights affecting the land of another: third-party interests

Other people may have rights over a piece of land, known as ***third-party rights*** or ***third-party interests***.

2.2.2.1 The nature of proprietary rights: enforcement and remedies

When a party grants rights to another, this is known as a personal right. The doctrine of ***privity of contract*** provides that the rights are only enforceable between the original parties: generally, the burden of these rights cannot be enforced against a third party. Further, any breach of or interference with a personal right is typically remedied using damages to compensate the innocent party for any losses they have suffered.

Proprietary rights, on the other hand, attach to the land itself. This means that they can be enforced against a third party – a purchaser of the land benefitting from the right will gain that right when they purchase the land, and a purchaser of the land burdened by the right will have to respect the right when they become the owner of the burdened land. Proprietary rights can be enforced by an action *in rem* – meaning, the remedy may be the right itself, rather than compensation. For example, the holder of an easement[3] which is interfered with may be awarded the right to exercise the easement as a remedy, rather than damages to compensate him for the inconvenience of the interference.

3 See Section 2.2.2.2.2 for an explanation of an easement.

2.2.2.2 Types of third-party interest

The third-party interests in land we will examine in this book are as follows:

2.2.2.2.1 CHARGES

A ***charge*** or ***mortgage*** is a proprietary interest which is granted over an estate in land in exchange for the advancement of a loan. Charges can exist in law and in equity.[4]

2.2.2.2.2 EASEMENTS

An ***easement*** is a right to use land belonging to another. The most obvious of these is the right of way: for example, a landowner has a right of way over his next-door neighbour's land in order to access the public highway. Easements can be created expressly (e.g. one person grants such a right using a deed), or they can arise by implication or prescription. Easements can exist in law and in equity.[5]

2.2.2.2.3 FREEHOLD COVENANTS

A ***freehold covenant*** is a promise relating to land. These can be positive or restrictive in nature. Positive covenants remain personal: they are enforceable between the original parties, and the burden of a positive covenant will generally not bind a purchaser of the affected land.[6] Restrictive covenants, on the other hand, have become a proprietary right which can be enforced against a purchaser of the affected land. Restrictive covenants can only exist in equity.[7]

2.2.2.2.4 ESTATE CONTRACTS

Contracts for the sale of land (known as ***estate contracts***) are also proprietary rights one has over a piece of land. There are formalities for creating these, which we will discuss in Chapter 11. Estate contracts can only exist in equity.[8]

2.2.2.2.5 INTERESTS ARISING UNDER A TRUST

An interest in land can arise under a trust. A common example of when land is subject to an equitable interest held under a trust is when land is co-owned. Where there is an equitable interest arising under a trust, the legal owners of the property are the trustees, and they hold the land on trust for the beneficiaries, who are the equitable owners.

2.2.2.3 Priority of interests

The concept of ***priority*** between proprietary rights is very important in Property Practice. It deals with the question of when an existing interest in land (e.g. an

4 s1 Law of Property Act 1925 (**LPA 1925**).
5 Ibid.
6 There are some exceptions, such as the circumstances arising in *Halsall v Brizell* [1957] Ch 169.
7 s1 LPA 1925.
8 Ibid.

easement) will take priority over (e.g. will bind) a subsequent disposition of that land. In other words, if A has the benefit of a right of way over B's land and B sells that land, will the purchaser (C) acquire B's land subject to A's right of way, or will A lose their right of way once the sale to C completes? The rules of priority are different depending on whether the land is unregistered or registered.

We consider each of these interests in this book. We will examine the question of priority of interests during the due diligence phase of the transaction (Phase 1) in order to advise on which interests will bind a purchaser of the land. We will also examine the relevant formalities to ensure that an interest in land is properly protected against subsequent dispositions – this is in the post-completion phase of the transaction (Phase 5). We will be considering how priority operates on the disposal of an unregistered estate (the Car Park), and on a number of dispositions of registered estates (the House, the Salon, and the grant and assignment of the Nail Bar Lease).

2.3 The land registration system

It used to be the case that all land in England and Wales was unregistered. A buyer of land would be reliant on any available documentation about the land as well as his own investigations (e.g. inspecting the land and making enquiries of the seller) to get to know the land.

The distinction between those estates and interests which operated in law and those which operated in equity[9] was very important in enforcing a proprietary right and determining priority between competing interests over land.

Legal interests could be enforced against anyone purchasing the land. Equitable interests, however, were enforceable according to the ***doctrine of notice***: they would bind everyone *except* a purchaser for value who did not have notice of the interest. Notice included things the purchaser *was* aware of, but also things he *should* have been aware of (thus, proper inspections and enquiries were essential). This was to protect purchasers from becoming bound by interests they did not and could not have discovered.

There were two key flaws with this system:

1. purchasers of a legal estate could be bound by legal interests, even if they did not know about them (if the law determined they *should* have known about them – ascertaining this was complicated in practice); and
2. owners of an equitable interest could easily lose their interest if the law decided that the purchaser did not have notice of it.

9 See Section 2.2.1.2.

2.3.1.2.2.3 COMPULSORY REGISTRATION OF TITLE

As noted above, the Land Registration Act 1925 (**LRA 1925**, subsequently replaced by the **LRA 2002**) introduced a system of registration whereby the title to land would not be proved by the title deeds but instead by registration. Registration would be conclusive as to the title to land and to interests affecting that land; as per the insurance principle, HMLR would provide compensation to parties affected by errors, but the legal position would remain as per the register.[20]

In order to move from a system where no land was registered to one where all land was registered, the LRA 1925 made it compulsory to register each estate in land, the requirement to do so being triggered by certain dispositions of unregistered land. If one of these dispositions occurred to an unregistered estate in land, that would trigger the requirement to register that estate in land for the first time: this is known as compulsory first registration.

The events triggering compulsory first registration which are relevant for this book are:[21]

1. the conveyance or transfer of a freehold interest;
2. the grant of a lease of more than seven years; and
3. the grant of a legal mortgage.

If one of these triggering events occurs today, the purchaser in respect of that triggering event must apply to HMLR to register the title within two months of the completion of the disposition.[22] This is known as an application for first registration.

Failure to apply for first registration within the required timeframe means that the purchaser (now the legal owner by virtue of the completion of the deed)[23] loses the legal title to the land – instead, the legal title reverts back to the previous owner (the seller of the land), who holds it on trust for the purchaser, who now only holds an equitable title until they are registered as the legal proprietor.[24]

We look at the process of first registration in detail in Chapter 20, but in brief, the purchaser (under the triggering event) will supply all the relevant deeds and documentation relating to the land to HMLR.

20 With some minor exceptions for which rectification of the register is possible; these are beyond the scope of this book.
21 The full list can be found at s4 Land Registration Act 2002 (LRA 2002).
22 s6 LRA 2002.
23 See Section 2.3.1.2.2.2.4.
24 s7 LRA 2002.

2.3.1.2.2.3.1 Investigation of title by HMLR

Upon receipt of the application for first registration and the relevant documentation, the Land Registrar will do its own investigation of the title, considering the title deeds and any interests registered on the Land Charges Register.

It will then create an official copy ***register of title*** for the estate, giving each estate in land its own unique ***title number***.

2.3.1.2.2.3.1.1 The legal proprietor Provided that the Land Registrar is satisfied by the title deeds, the purchaser (now the legal owner, following completion of the conveyance) will be registered as the legal proprietor.

2.3.1.2.2.3.1.2 Noting the interests benefitting the land Any interests benefitting the property which are contained within the title deeds will be added to the register by the Land Registrar.

2.3.1.2.2.3.1.3 Noting the interests burdening the land The Land Registrar will note on the title register any interests burdening the land. The Land Registrar knows about the interests burdening the land because they will be:

- contained in the documentation supplied to it;
- revealed in a search of the register kept pursuant to the Land Charges Act; or
- specifically disclosed to it by the purchaser.

These interests can be noted on the title register as ***notices*** or ***restrictions***.

2.3.1.2.2.3.1.3.1 Notices A notice will be entered on the title register to note:

- leases the land is subject to;
- easements the land is subject to;
- restrictive covenants the land is subject to; and
- estate contracts relevant to the land.

A notice is informative for a buyer of registered land.

2.3.1.2.2.3.1.3.2 Restrictions Restrictions on the title can prevent the relevant estate from being disposed of (e.g. a transfer of the freehold, the grant of a lease, or the grant of a mortgage) unless certain conditions have been complied with. They are typically used to protect mortgages, to protect interests arising from a trust, and to indirectly enforce positive covenants. They appear on the Proprietorship Register of the register of title.

2.3.1.2.2.3.1.4 Interests overriding first registration Section 11(4) of the LRA 2002 states that upon first registration, the purchaser will take the land subject to interests which will not appear on the register but nonetheless override; it refers to a list of these interests contained in Schedule 1 of the LRA 2002.

Schedule 1 contains the following interests:

- a lease of seven years or less;
- the interest of a person in actual occupation; and
- a legal easement.

We introduced the concept of an overriding interest in Section 2.3.1.1.1. The wording of section 11(4) appears to suggest that these Schedule 1 interests are overriding interests. However, for a conveyance of unregistered land, priority is determined on completion of the conveyance according to the rules noted in Section 2.3.1.2.2.2, and there are no other interests which can 'override' the disposition and take priority.

The writers understand[25] this wording in section 11(4) to instead relate to any interests falling in those categories in Schedule 1 which:

- are known about by the proprietor and notified to the Land Registrar (as per Section 2.3.1.2.2.3.1.3); or
- are not known about by the proprietor but which have only arisen in the short period between completion and registration.

2.3.1.2.2.3.2 Creating a register of title

The register of title is split into three sections:

2.3.1.2.2.3.2.1 Section A: the property register This contains information about the land itself, including a description, whether the land is freehold or leasehold, and any rights or interests which benefit the land.

If mines and minerals are excluded from the land (e.g. they belong to someone else), then this will be noted in this section of the register.

2.3.1.2.2.3.2.2 Section B: the Proprietorship Register This contains information about the ownership of the land, including the class of title, the registered proprietor, and anything preventing disposal, for example, restrictions.

The registrar can assign different quality of title to the property.

Absolute title This means that the registered proprietor owns the legal estate in the property, and that legal estate is only subject to:
  - entries registered;
  - unregistered interests such as those noted in Schedule 1 or 3;
  - (if the land is leasehold) express and implied covenants under the lease; and

25 But note there is a distinct lack of clarity on this issue.

- third party rights of which they have notice, if they hold the land as a trustee.

Possessory title. The Proprietor is also subject to adverse interests existing at the date of first registration.

Qualified title. HMLR's guarantee of title does not extend to a specified defect.

Good leasehold title. HMLR are satisfied that title to the leasehold interest is sound, but not prepared to guarantee the lease against defects in the freehold title or guarantee that the freeholder has the right to grant the lease. This is typically allocated to an estate when HMLR have no access to the superior reversionary interest, for example, if the freehold title is unregistered or the freehold title is registered with less than absolute title and the new leaseholder does not give evidence of the freehold title when applying to register the lease.

2.3.1.2.2.3.2.3 Section C: the Charges Register This contains information about encumbrances affecting the land, for example, charges, restrictive covenants or easements burdening the land, and leases the land is subject to. This is where notices will appear.

2.3.1.2.3 DEALINGS WITH A REGISTERED ESTATE OR INTEREST

Once an estate in land is registered, any subsequent dealings with that land must be registered in order to maintain the accuracy of the register.

We discussed in Section 2.3.1.2.1 that the LPA 1925 reduced the list of estates and interests which could operate at law. The LRA 2002 restricted this even further by requiring these 'potential' legal estates and interests to be registered in order to be legal – these are known as ***registrable dispositions*** and includes:[26]

- transfers of land;
- the grant of a lease for more than seven years;
- the express grant or reservation of a legal easement;
- the express grant or reservation of a landlord's right of re-entry; and
- the grant of a legal charge.

This means that any transfer of a registered estate (or granting a lease over it, or undertaking any of the other actions listed in section 27 of the LRA 2002) is a registrable disposition, and that disposition in itself must be registered in order to take effect in law. Failure to register a registrable disposition of a registered estate renders it equitable only.[27]

26 Please see s27 LRA 2002 for the full list.
27 Ibid.

2.3.1.2.3.1 PRIORITY

Once an estate is registered, a purchaser for value (which is a registrable disposition) of that estate will take it subject to:[28]

1. interests which are protected in the register by way of a charge or a notice; and
2. interests which are not registered but which nonetheless override.

2.3.1.2.3.1.1 Registered interests

Once land is registered, the Land Charges Act is no longer relevant. The title register created by HMLR will reflect the status of the land and all the interests affecting it, whether legal or equitable. Anything noted on the register will bind a subsequent purchaser for value.

2.3.1.2.3.1.2 Interests which override a registered disposition

As noted briefly earlier in Section 2.3.1.1.1, there are some special categories of interest which will still bind the purchaser even if they do not appear on the register. These largely reflect the interests which cannot be discovered (because they themselves are not subject to registration and therefore do not appear on the title register) or which require protection.

These are listed in Schedule 3 of the LRA 2002 and are as follows:

- a legal lease not exceeding seven years;
- the equitable interests of a person in actual occupation; and
- implied legal easements.

The detail of these overriding interests is a matter for your Land Law studies; for the purposes of Property Practice, you need to be aware of overriding interests and the fact that they will bind a purchaser for value, and, when acting for a buyer, ensure you make sufficient enquiries of the seller to discover any which could impact your client.

28 s29 LRA 2002. There are some minor exceptions, but these are beyond the scope of this book.

PHASE

0 Commercial considerations

Once a property has been marketed, and an offer made and accepted, each party will instruct a solicitor to conduct the conveyancing. Before the conveyancing process begins, a solicitor will ensure that they can act for the client. They will also gather information about how the transaction will be financed and provide initial advice on some of the additional costs of a property transaction, such as tax.

It is these initial conversations which form the content of this Phase 0, considered in Chapter 3.

DOI: 10.4324/9781032711508-3

3 Commercial considerations and taking instructions

3.1 Chapter overview

Before a solicitor can begin the conveyancing process on behalf of a buyer or seller, they will undertake certain checks to ensure they can accept the instruction. Next, a solicitor needs to ensure that their client understands the costs of the transaction and has made sufficient arrangements to finance it.

This chapter explores some of the costs associated with a property transaction, including the three key taxes:

1. Stamp Duty Land Tax and Land Transaction Tax;
2. Value Added Tax; and
3. Capital Gains Tax.

It also examines how a buyer might use a mortgage to finance their purchase.

This chapter is relevant to all freehold and leasehold transactions.

This chapter in the context of our Transactions

These topics are examined in the context of each of the Transactions. You may wish to refer to the heads of terms for each Transaction whilst working through this chapter.

DOI: 10.4324/9781032711508-4

3.2 Instructing solicitors

Upon being contacted by a prospective client about undertaking the conveyancing for a property transaction, a solicitor will need to undertake checks to ensure that it can act for the relevant party, such as whether there is a conflict of interest with an existing client or if the solicitor has been asked to act on behalf of two parties to the transaction (such as buyer and lender – see Section 3.4.4), and anti-money laundering checks to ensure that the source of funds being used to pay for the transaction is legitimate. For more information on professional conduct issues, please see *Essential Legal System and Legal Services for SQE1*.[1]

The prospective client will provide relevant details of the transaction. Sometimes these can be found in a ***heads of terms*** document.

The solicitor will assess the complexity of the matter and provide an initial fee quote. Once the prospective client is happy with the fee quote and has signed up to the solicitor's terms of business, the solicitor can proceed to act for the client.

3.3 Costs of a property transaction

Property transactions can be expensive, and solicitors must ensure at the outset that their clients have considered all costs associated with the transaction. The buyer of property may incur the following costs:

- purchase price;
- tax;
- legal fees and disbursements;
- surveyor fees; and
- refurbishment or redevelopment costs.

The purchase price is likely to be the most significant cost, but parties must also factor in any taxes they may be liable to pay, as these could be considerable.

The acquisition of property attracts Stamp Duty Land Tax (**SDLT**) or Land Transaction Tax (**LTT**). Disposals of property can attract Capital Gains Tax (**CGT**) for the seller (see Section 3.3.3), and both parties to commercial transactions need to consider Value-Added Tax (**VAT**).

1 Ian Bowden, Zaman F. Kala, *Essential Legal System and Legal Services for SQE1*, Routledge, 2024.

3.3.1 SDLT and LTT

Stamp Duty Land Tax and ***Land Transaction Tax*** are taxes payable on all types of property transaction.[2] SDLT applies to property in England, and LTT applies to property in Wales (from April 2018. Before this date, SDLT operated in Wales). SDLT replaced Stamp Duty on 1 December 2003.

For each land transaction, there are two key requirements:

1. submit a land transaction return;[3] and
2. pay any SDLT or LTT due.

We will examine this in detail in Chapter 20, but before the transaction commences, it is useful for the buyer to know how much SDLT or LTT they will be liable to pay, so that they can budget for this.

3.3.1.1 Amount payable

The amount of tax payable depends on the type and value of the transaction. We will explore some of the key rates below.

3.3.1.1.1 RESIDENTIAL PROPERTY

The classification of land as 'residential' or 'non-residential' occurs at the moment the land is acquired. This means that the purchase of the House and the Salon will both be considered 'residential' for tax purposes, because at the moment of completion those properties are both capable of being occupied as a dwelling. There are general rates of SDLT and LTT and special rates for specific categories of buyer.

3.3.1.1.1.1 GENERAL RATES OF SDLT

Where the transaction is the transfer of a residential property, no SDLT will be payable if the value of the property is less than £125,000. For transactions over £125,000, SDLT is applicable at different rates according to the value of the transaction.

The general rates are shown in Table 3.1:[4]

2 s43 Finance Act 2003 (**FA 2003**); s2 Land Transaction Tax and Anti-avoidance of Devolved Taxes (Wales) Act 2017 (**Devolved Taxes Act 2017**)

3 s76 FA 2003; s44 Devolved Taxes Act 2017. We look at how to do this this in Chapter 20.

4 s55 FA 2003. Valid from 1 April 2025.

Table 3.1 The general rates of SDLT applicable on the acquisition of residential property

Value of the transaction	Rate of SDLT applicable to that portion
The portion up to £125,000	0%
The portion between £125,001 and 250,000	2%
The portion between £250,001 and £925,000	5%
The portion between £925,001 and £1,500,000	10%
The portion over £1,500,000	12%

The value of the transaction will be the price paid for the property. If the property is a lease, the value of the transaction for the purposes of the SDLT rates will be the lease premium. In addition, the total rent over the life of the lease is calculated by multiplying the Annual Rent by the length of the lease – this is known as the **NPV** (or Net Present Value). If the NPV exceeds £125,000, then an additional SLT charge is payable at 1% on the portion of the NPV which exceeds £125,000.

The general rates of SDLT will apply to André's purchase of the House because it is situated in England and André is not a first-time buyer, nor is he purchasing it as a second home, and he is not a corporate buyer.[5] André is purchasing the House for £350,000. André will be liable to pay £7,500 in SDLT for the purchase of the House, calculated as follows:

- 0% on the first £125,000 (the portion up to £125,000) = £0;
- 2% on the second £125,000 (the portion between £125,001 and £250,000) = £2,500; and
- 5% on the final £100,000 (the portion between £250,001 and £350,000) = £5,000.

3.3.1.1.1.2 GENERAL RATES OF LTT

Where the transaction is the transfer of a residential property, no LTT will be payable if the value of the property is less than £225,000. For transactions over £225,000, LTT is applicable at different rates according to the value of the transaction.

The general rates are as shown in Table 3.2:[6]

5 See Sections 3.3.1.1.1.3 and 3.3.1.1.1.4.

6 Schedule to The Land Transaction Tax (Tax Bands and Tax Rates) (Wales) Regulations 2018 (**LTT Regulations 2018**).

Table 3.2 The general rates of LTT applicable on the acquisition of residential property

Value of the transaction	Rate of LTT applicable to that portion
The portion up to and including £225,000	0%
The portion over £225,000 and up to and including £400,000	6%
The portion over £400,000 and up to and including £750,000	7.5%
The portion over £750,000 and up to and including £1,500,000	10%
The portion over £1,500,000	12%

For residential leases, LTT is not paid on the rent.

3.3.1.1.1.3 FIRST-TIME BUYER WHOSE HOME IS VALUED UP TO £500,000: SDLT

If the purchaser is a first-time buyer and the value of the property being purchased does not exceed £500,000, a different set of rates are applicable, as shown in Table 3.3:[7]

Table 3.3 The rates of SDLT applicable on the acquisition of residential property by a first-time buyer

Value of the transaction	Rate of SDLT applicable to that portion
The portion up to £300,000	0%
The portion between £300,001and £500,000	5%

This means that first-time buyers where the property is less than £300,000 will not pay any SDLT.

There is no first-time buyer relief in Wales applicable to LTT.

3.3.1.1.1.4 SECOND HOMES AND CORPORATE BUYERS

Where the purchaser is buying the property as a second home, or where the purchaser is a company, a higher set of rates applies. These higher rates of SDLT and LTT are only chargeable on property transactions where the property is valued at more than £40,000. The higher rates are set out below in Tables 3.4 and 3.5.

7 FA 2003 Schedule 6ZA.

3.3.1.1.1.4.1 SDLT

The higher SDLT rates[8] are as shown in Table 3.4:

Table 3.4 The rates of SDLT applicable on the acquisition of second homes or by corporate buyers

Value of the transaction	Rate of SDLT applicable to that portion
The portion up to £125,000	5%
The portion between £125,001 and £250,000	7%
The portion between £250,001and £925,000	10%
The portion between £925,001 and £1,500,000	15%
The portion over £1,500,000	17%

Further, companies purchasing residential land costing more than £500,000 must pay a special rate of 17% SDLT on the entire purchase price. This is the rate which will apply to Style&Go Ltd's purchase of the Salon, because the Salon is being purchased for £525,000. This means Style&Go Ltd will pay £89,250 in SDLT for the Salon (being 17% on £525,000).

3.3.1.1.1.4.2 LTT

Table 3.5 The rates of LTT applicable on the acquisition of second homes or by corporate buyers[9]

Value of the transaction	Rate of LTT applicable to that portion
The portion up to and including £180,000	5%
The portion over £180,000 and up to and including £250,000	8.5%
The portion over £250,000 and up to and including £400,000	10%
The portion over £400,000 and up to and including £750,000	12.5%
The portion over £750,000 and up to and including £1,500,000	15%
The portion over £1,500,000	17%

8 These rates will apply from 1 April 2025. The Finance Bill (which is currently passing through Parliament) will amend FA 2003 Schedule 4ZA.

9 Schedule to LTT Regulations 2018.

3.3.1.1.1.5 NON-UK RESIDENT: SDLT

Where the purchaser is not a UK resident (someone who has not been present in the UK for at least six months in the previous 12 months), an additional 2% is added to the relevant set of SDLT rates.[10]

3.3.1.1.2 COMMERCIAL PROPERTY

Where the transaction is for property which is commercial in nature or a mixture of commercial and residential, a different set of rates applies.

3.3.1.1.2.1 GENERAL RATES OF SDLT

The general rates of SDLT for commercial property are as shown in Table 3.6:[11]

Table 3.6 The general rates of SDLT applicable on the acquisition of commercial property

Value of the transaction	Rate of SDLT applicable to that portion
The portion up to £150,000	0%
The portion between £150,001 and £250,000	2%
The portion over £250,000	5%

The value of the transaction will be the price paid for the property.

3.3.1.1.2.1.1 Style&Go Ltd's purchase of the Car Park

The Car Park is situated in England, so SDLT will be the applicable tax. The general rate will apply. The Car Park is being purchased for £85,000, and therefore, Style&Go Ltd will not need to pay any SDLT on this, as the total value falls within the 0% rate.

3.3.1.1.2.1.2 The assignment of the Nail Bar Lease

When a lease is assigned, the value for SDLT purposes is the consideration paid for the lease (in other words, the premium). There is no SDLT payable on the rent. The Nail Bar Lease is being purchased for a premium of £1, and therefore, Gemma's Gels Ltd will not need to pay SDLT on this as it falls within the 0% rate.

3.3.1.1.2.1.3 Grant of new lease

When a lease is granted, the value of the transaction for the purposes of the general SDLT rates above[12] will be the lease premium. Polished Perfection Ltd are not paying a premium for the grant of the Nail Bar Lease, and therefore, no SDLT is payable on this.

10 FA 2003 s75ZA.
11 s55 FA 2003.
12 The general rates at Section 3.3.1.1.2.1.

In addition, when a lease is granted, SDLT is charged on the NPV as shown in Table 3.7:[13]

Table 3.7 The SDLT applicable on the NPV when a commercial lease is granted

Value of the NPV	Rate of SDLT applicable to that portion
The portion up to £150,000	0%
The portion between £150,001 and £5,000,000	1%
The portion over £5,000,000	2%

The NPV of the Nail Bar Lease is £100,000 (because the Annual Rent is £10,000 for a term of ten years), and therefore, there will be no SDLT payable on the NPV because this falls within the 0% rate.

3.3.1.1.2.2 GENERAL RATES OF LTT

For properties in Wales, the general rates of LTT for commercial property are as shown in Table 3.8:[14]

Table 3.8 The general rate of LTT applicable on the acquisition of commercial property

Value of the transaction	Rate of LTT applicable to that portion
The portion up to and including £225,000	0%
The portion over £225,000 and up to and including £250,000	1%
The portion over £250,000 and up to and including £1,000,000	5%
The portion over £1,000,000 and up to and including £750,000	6%

3.3.1.1.2.2.1 GRANT OF A NEW LEASE

If the property is a lease, the value of the transaction for the purposes of the general LTT rates will be the lease premium. Please note that if the Annual Rent is more than £13,500, the 0% band does not apply and LTT will be charged at 1% on the portion of the premium up to and including £250,000.

In addition, LTT is charged on the NPV as shown in Table 3.9:[15]

13 FA 2003 Schedule 5.
14 Schedule to LTT Regulations 2018.
15 Ibid.

Table 3.9 The LTT applicable on the NPV when a commercial lease is granted

Value of the NPV	Rate of LTT applicable to that portion
The portion up to and including £225,000	0%
The portion over £225,000 and up to an including £2,000,000	1%
The portion over £2,000,000	2%

3.3.2 VAT

3.3.2.1 What is VAT?

Value-Added Tax is a tax which is chargeable on goods or services made in the course of a business. It is the *supply* of those goods or services which attracts VAT; this means that goods or services which are subject to VAT will have this tax added on to the purchase price.[16]

All goods or services are categorised by His Majesty's Revenue and Customs (**HMRC**) as follows:

1. ***Exempt supplies***. These are not subject to VAT, so no VAT is added to the price for these goods or services.[17] Often, exempt supplies come with an ***option to tax***, which we discuss at Section 3.3.2.3;
2. ***Zero-rated supplies***. These supplies are subject to VAT, but the applicable tax is charged at a rate of 0%[18] (which means, in practice, no additional money is charged for these goods or services); and
3. ***Standard-rated supplies***. These supplies are subject to VAT, and such VAT is chargeable at the standard rate – this is currently 20%.[19]

3.3.2.2 The VAT categorisation of supplies made as part of a property transaction

We will now consider the different goods and services which are supplied in a typical property transaction and the VAT categorisation for each of those supplies.

3.3.2.2.1 THE SALE OF THE LAND FROM SELLER TO BUYER

There are different rules for residential property and commercial property, and the analysis of whether property is residential or not occurs at the moment of supply; therefore, the sale of the House and the Salon would be (if the supply was being made in the course of a business) assessed for VAT purposes as residential prop-

16 s1 Value Added Tax Act 1994 (**VAT Act 1994**).
17 Schedule 9 VAT Act 1994.
18 Schedule 8 VAT Act 1994.
19 s2 VAT Act 1994.

erty because, at the moment of supply (the sale), those properties are both dwellinghouses. This would be the case even though Style&Go Ltd is a commercial purchaser and intends to use the Salon for commercial purposes.

3.3.2.2.1.1 RESIDENTIAL PROPERTY

There are different categories of residential property, the supply of which attracts different rates of VAT.

3.3.2.2.1.1.1 SALE OF A NEW HOUSE BY THE DEVELOPER: ZERO-RATED SUPPLY

Once a developer has constructed a house, if they sell it within three years, then it is categorised as zero-rated.[20] This means the transaction is subject to VAT, but the purchaser does not pay any additional money.

The onward sale of this house by a private individual (whether within three years or otherwise) will not attract VAT because the sale is not being made in the course of a business. This is the case for the sale of the House from Michael's estate to André and the sale of the Salon from Neeta to Style&Go Ltd.

3.3.2.2.1.1.2 SALE OF A BUY-TO-LET PROPERTY: EXEMPT SUPPLY

A buy-to-let property which is sold constitutes an exempt supply and is not subject to VAT.[21]

3.3.2.2.1.2 COMMERCIAL TRANSACTIONS

There are different categories of commercial property, the supply of which attracts different rates of VAT.

3.3.2.2.1.2.1 SALE OF A NEW FREEHOLD BUILDING: STANDARD-RATED SUPPLY

The sale of a freehold commercial property which is less than three years old is a standard-rated supply.[22] This means the VAT is applicable at a rate of 20%. The wording of the contract is important in ensuring whether the purchase price includes this VAT or whether 20% must be added to the purchase price.[23]

3.3.2.2.1.2.2 SALE OF AN 'OLD' FREEHOLD BUILDING: EXEMPT SUPPLY (WITH OPTION TO TAX)

The sale of freehold commercial properties which are more than three years old constitutes an exempt supply.[24] This means no VAT is applicable. However, the seller has the option to charge VAT on this supply;[25] this is the case for the Car Park.

20 Schedule 8 VAT Act 1994.
21 Schedule 9 VAT Act 1994.
22 Ibid.
23 Please see Chapter 11.
24 Schedule 9 VAT Act 1994.
25 Schedule 10 VAT Act 1994.

3.3.2.2.1.2.3 GRANT OR ASSIGNMENT OF A LEASE: EXEMPT SUPPLY (WITH OPTION TO TAX)

The grant or assignment of a commercial lease is an exempt supply which is not subject to VAT.[26] However, the grantor or assignor has the option to charge VAT on this supply.[27] This is the case for the grant of the lease over the Nail Bar and the assignment of the Nail Bar Lease.

3.3.2.2.1.3 SALE OF GREENFIELD SITES: EXEMPT SUPPLY (WITH OPTION TO TAX)

If a greenfield site is being purchased (e.g. perhaps a developer purchases a piece of land for the purposes of development), this is exempt from VAT[28] but carries with it an option to tax.[29] This is the case whether the proposed development is to be used for residential or commercial purposes once built.

3.3.2.2.2 CONSTRUCTION WORKS UNDERTAKEN ON THE PROPERTY

3.3.2.2.2.1 CONSTRUCTING A NEW RESIDENTIAL DWELLING: ZERO-RATED SUPPLY

Where a new dwelling is being built as part of a residential development, the construction works will be zero-rated[30] – meaning that VAT is applicable but no additional money is charged.

3.3.2.2.2.2 CONSTRUCTING A NEW COMMERCIAL PROPERTY: STANDARD-RATED SUPPLY

Where a new commercial property is being built, the construction works will be standard-rated[31] – meaning that VAT is applicable at a rate of 20%.

3.3.2.2.2.3 BUILDING OR CONSTRUCTION SUPPLIES: STANDARD-RATED SUPPLY

The goods needed to undertake building or construction work for both residential and commercial properties are usually standard-rated,[32] meaning that VAT is applicable at a rate of 20%. For example, if you (or a contractor on your behalf) purchase building materials for the construction of a downstairs toilet, you will usually pay VAT at 20% on top of the cost of the goods.

3.3.2.2.2.4 BUILDING OR CONSTRUCTION WORKS ON OTHER PROPERTIES: STANDARD-RATED SUPPLY

For most building or construction works, VAT is applicable on the supply at the standard rate,[33] meaning that the contractor will charge 20% VAT in addition to their labour costs.

26 Schedule 9 VAT Act 1994.
27 Schedule 10 VAT Act 1994.
28 Schedule 9 VAT Act 1994.
29 Schedule 10 VAT Act 1994.
30 Schedule 8 VAT Act 1994.
31 Schedule 9 VAT Act 1994.
32 Ibid.
33 Ibid.

3.3.2.2.3 PROFESSIONAL SERVICES: STANDARD-RATED SUPPLY

Most property transactions require some professional services, for example:

1. estate agency fees;
2. legal fees; and
3. surveyor fees.

These services are usually standard-rated,[34] meaning that 20% VAT will be charged on top of the cost of the service.

3.3.2.3 *Recovering input tax: the option to tax*

We noted in Section 3.3.2.1 that some exempt supplies carry an option to tax.

We will explore the option to tax in the context of Style&Go Ltd's plans for the Salon. Style&Go Ltd intend to do refurbishment works to turn the Salon into a hair salon, and once it has been refurbished, they plan to grant a lease over the first floor to Polished Perfection Ltd.

3.3.2.3.1 WHAT IS *INPUT TAX*?

A business will pay VAT on supplies made to it. For example, when Style&Go Ltd's contractor purchases construction materials for the refurbishment, the shop selling those construction materials adds VAT to the price of the materials amounting to £200, and this will have been paid by the contractor: this is called ***input tax***, and is shown in Figure 3.1.

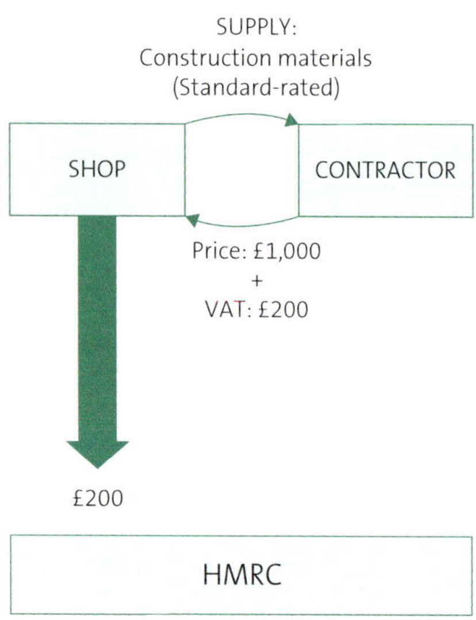

Figure 3.1 Input tax charged on the supply of goods.

34 Ibid.

3.3.2.3.2 WHAT IS *OUTPUT TAX*?

Output tax is the name for the VAT charged by the supplier, so in our example in Figure 3.1, the VAT charged by the shop. It is the output tax which must be paid to HMRC (by the shop).

You will notice that the input and output tax are not separate charges; the terminology changes depending on whether the tax is being paid or received.

3.3.2.3.3 OFFSETTING INPUT AND OUTPUT TAX

Where a business both pays and receives VAT, the input tax and output tax of that business can be offset against each other to enable it to recover from HMRC any input tax incurred whilst making taxable supplies (supplies which are not exempt, meaning standard-rated or zero-rated supplies).

This means that the contractor who purchases the construction materials to enable it to perform the refurbishment for Style&Go Ltd can recover from HMRC the £200 VAT paid on the materials, because the refurbishment services are themselves a taxable supply (being a standard-rated service attracting VAT at 20%). In Figure 3.2, you can see how the contractor only needs to pay £1,800 to HMRC rather than the full £2,000 received from Style&Go Ltd, as the £200 already paid to the shop has been offset against the £2,000 received.

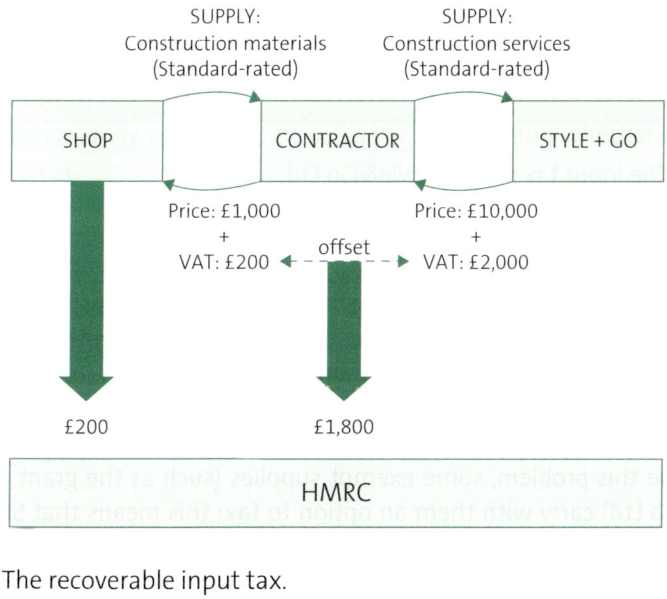

Figure 3.2 The recoverable input tax.

This also means that a business who pays input tax but does *not* do so in the provision of taxable supplies cannot recover that input tax. This provides an incentive for business to ensure that, wherever they have paid input tax, any supplies they

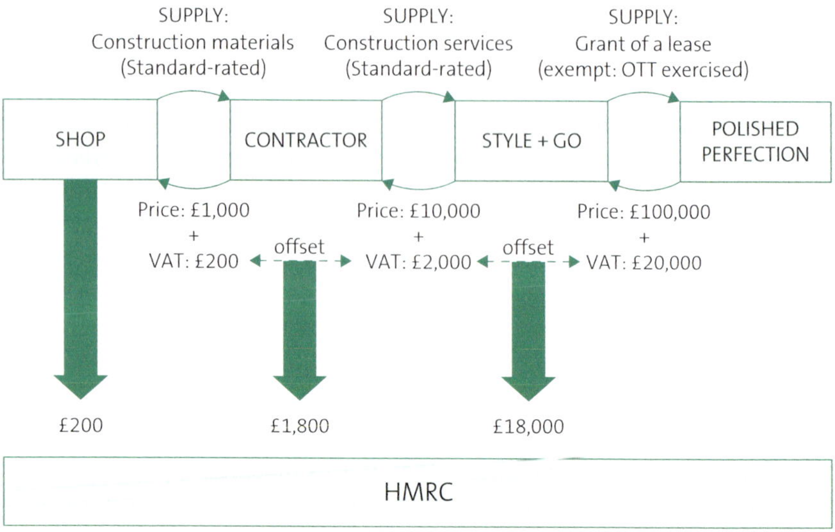

Figure 3.4 Style&Go Ltd exercising its option to tax.

Polished Perfection Ltd paid input tax on fit-out works and on the rent paid to Style&Go Ltd but has recovered a lot of this already by offsetting it against the taxable services it provides to clients; it has not opted to tax the assignment of the Nail Bar Lease because it is only charging a premium of £1 for the assignment.[37]

Urban Spaces Ltd has decided not to exercise its option to tax when transferring the Car Park.

The agreed VAT position for each Transaction can be found in the heads of terms document.

3.3.3 Capital Gains Tax

3.3.3.1 What is Capital Gains Tax

Capital Gains Tax is a tax levied on the profit made when disposing of an asset which has increased in value.[38] The price of the asset when purchased[39] is subtracted from the price of the asset upon disposal. The difference in those two prices is the ***capital gain***, and tax is paid on this gain: this is Capital Gains Tax. The rate of CGT, and therefore the amount of tax to pay on the gain, depends on the type of person making the disposal and the type of asset. A detailed discussion of

37 Polished Perfection Ltd cannot charge VAT to Gemma's Gels Ltd on the rent due under the Nail Bar Lease because it is Style&Go Ltd as the landlord who will receive the rent from Gemma's Gels Ltd, not Polished Perfection Ltd.

38 s1 Taxation of Chargeable Gains Act 1992 (**TCGA 1992**).

39 Or if purchased before 1982, its value in 1982.

the rates is beyond the scope of this book, but please see the Taxation of Chargeable Gains Act 1992, or associated Government guidance, for the full detail.

There are three requirements to CGT:

- the asset is a ***chargeable asset***;
- the disposal is a ***chargeable disposal***; and
- the disposal is made by a ***chargeable person***.

3.3.3.2 Chargeable assets

Not all assets are subject to CGT.[40] The key type of chargeable asset relevant for this book is an interest in land.

3.3.3.3 Chargeable disposals

CGT is payable when a chargeable disposal is made in respect of a chargeable asset.

A chargeable disposal can include the sale of an asset, the exchange of one asset for another, and the gift of an asset.
The transfer of assets from the deceased to the personal representatives (the **PRs**) on death is *not* a chargeable disposal.[41] This means the transfer of the House to the personal representatives on Michael's death would not have counted as a chargeable disposal, and any gains since Michael acquired the House are disregarded. The PRs would be liable only for any gain in value occurring between their acquisition of the House on Michael's death and their disposal of it to André (but any such gain is unlikely if selling at market value).

3.3.3.4 Chargeable persons

The following can be liable to CGT:

- individuals;
- trustees; and
- personal representatives.

Companies pay tax on any gains arising from chargeable assets: this forms part of their ***Corporation Tax*** liability.[42]

3.3.3.5 Relevance to Property Practice

3.3.3.5.1 ADVISING THE SELLER

As the sale of land and that of rights over land are chargeable disposals of chargeable assets, when advising on the disposal of a property, solicitors for the seller must advise that the disposal could give rise to a tax liability if the property has

40 See TGCA 1992.
41 s62(1) TCGA 1992.
42 A detailed discussion of Corporation Tax is beyond the scope of this book.

increased in value since it was acquired. For individuals, this liability will take the form of CGT, and for companies, Corporation Tax.

3.3.3.5.2 ADVISING THE BUYER

Although the buyer will not incur a CGT liability upon *acquiring* the property, it is important to advise them that this liability may be incurred if they subsequently dispose of the property.

The solicitors for Style&Go Ltd should advise Style&Go Ltd that any increase in value of the Salon or the Car Park could be taxed as Corporation Tax if they disposed of either of these assets, for example, when Style&Go Ltd grants the lease over the Nail Bar.

Similarly, Polished Perfection Ltd's solicitors should advise Polished Perfection Ltd that if they later dispose of their interest in the Nail Bar (e.g. by assignment or sub-lease), then they may be liable to pay Corporation Tax on any increase in value.

3.3.3.5.3 RELEVANT RELIEFS: PRIVATE RESIDENCE RELIEF

If the property being disposed of was a person's ***only or main residence*** for ***the period of their ownership***, then ***Private Residence Relief*** (**PRR**) is available, meaning that CGT is not chargeable.[43]

This relief is likely to be relevant for Neeta, meaning that if the Salon has increased in value since she acquired it, she is unlikely to pay CGT on that increase.

Similarly, André's solicitors should advise him that if in the future he sells the House and it has increased in value, he could be liable to pay CGT on that gain, but that PRR is likely to be available provided he complies with the relevant conditions.

There are a number of conditions affecting the applicability of this relief:

3.3.3.5.3.1 ONLY OR MAIN RESIDENCE

The relief requires the property being disposed of to have been the only or main residence of the seller.[44] Residence takes the ordinary meaning, being whether the property was the seller's home.

3.3.3.5.3.1.1 GROUNDS SOLD WITH THE RESIDENCE

Grounds or gardens which are included in the sale of the main residence (e.g. a house with a garden) may attract a CGT liability if they exceed 0.5 hectares,[45] unless it can be shown that the excess is required for the reasonable enjoyment of the main residence.[46]

43 S223 TCGA 1992.
44 S222 TCGA 1992.
45 This liability will only be levied on the excess.
46 S222(3) TCGA 1992.

3.3.3.5.3.1.2 Grounds sold without the residence

Grounds or gardens of the main residence can be sold separately from the residence and still benefit from the relief, provided they do not exceed 0.5 hectares.

3.3.3.5.3.1.3 Part business use

Properties which are used for business as well as residence may incur a deduction in the relief available in proportion to the size of the business area of the property when compared to the size of the residential area.[47] This will not apply to people working from home and will only be relevant if some of the property is used *exclusively* for business purposes.

3.3.3.5.3.1.4 Properties acquired with the intention to make a gain

PRR is not available where the property being disposed of has been acquired with the intention to make a gain, for example, a buy-to-let property or a house which is converted into flats and sold on.[48]

3.3.3.5.3.2 PERIOD OF OWNERSHIP

The relief only applies if the property was the seller's main residence during his or her **period of ownership**. The period of ownership typically commences when the seller acquired the property (e.g. completion of his acquisition) and ends when he disposes of it (completion of the disposal).

3.3.3.5.3.2.1 Permitted absences

The seller is allowed to have had a number of ***permitted absences*** during this period of ownership, during which the property may not have been his main residence, without losing the relief. These include:[49]

1. the last nine months of ownership, as residence elsewhere may have been required to enable him to purchase another property;
2. the first two years of ownership, for example, if the property had been acquired but could not be occupied as construction or renovation hadn't yet been completed;
3. a period of three years at any point during the ownership (or separate periods not exceeding three years in total) for any reason;
4. a period of any duration in which the owner worked abroad;
5. a period of four years (or separate periods not exceeding four years in total) during which the owner had to reside elsewhere for work; or
6. a period of four years (or separate periods not exceeding four years in total) during which the owner lived with a spouse or civil partner.

Any absences which do not fall within this list of permitted absences will not benefit from the relief.

47 S224(1) TCGA 1992.
48 S224(3) TCGA 1992.
49 S223 and s223ZA TCGA 1992.

The proportion of the absence in relation to the whole duration of ownership will be established. If the seller has owned the property for 20 years and has been absent for five years, three of these would be permitted absences,[50] but two would not. So the seller has been absent for 2 of the 20 years of ownership, amounting to 10% of the duration of his ownership.

CGT will then be payable on this proportion of the gain (so in our example, the seller will have to pay CGT on 10% of the gain). If the gain is £100,000, the seller will need to pay CGT on £10,000.

3.3.3.5.3.2.2 Letting the property

If the property is let during the period of ownership, then it will not constitute the owner's only or main residence during this period of letting. If the period of letting does not qualify as a permitted absence (see Section 3.3.3.5.3.2.1), then CGT will be chargeable on any gain proportionate to the period of letting.

To take our example above, let's assume that during the seller's absence (which was five years), he let the property out. Three of those years would have been a permitted absence, leaving a letting period of two years. The duration of ownership was 20 years, and so the letting period constitutes 10% of the duration of ownership.

For properties which have been let out, CGT is only payable on a proportion of the gain which is in excess of:

- the non-chargeable gain (in this case, 90% of the gain is non-chargeable, amounting to £90,000); and
- – £40,000.[51]

In our example, the chargeable gain is £10,000, which is lower than both the non-chargeable gain and £40,000, and so no CGT is payable on this.

If the chargeable gain had been £50,000 (let's say the letting period was 13 years, three of which were a permitted absence and ten of which were not, leaving an absence of 50%), then £10,000 of this (being the amount in excess of £40,000) would be liable to CGT, and the seller would have to pay CGT on £10,000.

3.3.3.5.3.3 SPOUSES AND CIVIL PARTNERS

PRR is not available to both individuals in a marriage or civil partnership: they are only permitted one main residence between them,[52] and the relief applies to that

50 As per category 3 above.
51 S223B TCGA 1992.
52 S222(6) TCGA 1992.

residence. Any other properties owned by the couple will not attract the relief, and CGT will be chargeable.

Couples can choose which property benefits from PRR.

3.4 Financing a property transaction

We have discussed above some of the key costs which can be incurred during property transactions. Because of the number of potentially high costs involved, solicitors must ensure at the outset that their clients have considered how to finance the transaction.

The seller may incur fees, such as legal fees and disbursements and estate agent fees and, potentially, Capital Gains Tax. It is common for these fees to be paid out of the sale proceeds, and financing options are not usually required.

In the remainder of this chapter, we will focus on the finance options available to the buyer. Some buyers may finance their purchase by selling another asset, such as a different property. Some may have financial assistance from family members or be funding the purchase using savings or inheritance money. Some buyers may require financial assistance to facilitate their purchase of the property.

3.4.1 What is a mortgage?

The buyer may require a loan to assist with the purchase of the property: this is called a ***mortgage***.

A mortgage is a loan from a lender to the borrower, in exchange for which the borrower transfers to the lender an interest in land. This interest in land is typically a charge over the property for which the loan is required. Mortgages are available for residential and commercial transactions.

A legal mortgage provides security for the loan because it provides the lender (the mortgagor) with various powers if the borrower (the mortgagee) defaults on the loan, the most important of which is the power of sale. This power of sale arises as soon as the mortgage is entered into but (under section 103 of the Law of Property Act 1925) only becomes exercisable if:

- the borrower has default in a repayment of capital for three months;
- a repayment of interest due is two or more months in arrears; or
- the borrower has broken a provision in the mortgage.

The exercise of the power of sale allows the mortgagor to dispose of the property to a buyer, who will acquire the legal title to the property from the borrower.

3.4.2 Types of mortgage

Most mortgages are provided by banks and building societies. The lender will loan an agreed amount to the borrower, and the borrower agrees to pay this amount back, plus interest, within a certain amount of time.

3.4.2.1 Repayment mortgages

Under a ***repayment mortgage***, the borrower makes monthly payments which comprise interest and an amount of the capital. By the end of the mortgage term, the borrower has paid off the amount of the loan and the interest.

3.4.2.2 Interest-only mortgages

Under an ***interest-only mortgage***, the borrower makes monthly payments which only go towards paying off the interest on the loan. At the end of the term, the capital remains outstanding, and the borrower must pay this off. Some borrowers simultaneously invest in another financial product alongside the mortgage to save up enough money to repay the capital at the end of the term.

3.4.2.3 Commercial mortgages

Commercial mortgages tend to have shorter terms and higher interest rates than residential mortgages because they are considered by lenders to be higher risk.

3.4.2.4 Types of interest rate

The interest rate on a mortgage can be fixed for a set number of years (usually 2, 3, 5, or 10), or it can be variable – meaning, it rises and falls in line with the UK base rate. For borrowers who desire certainty over how much their monthly payments will be, a fixed-rate mortgage may be the best option.

3.4.3 The mortgage offer

If a buyer needs to rely on a mortgage in order to finance the property, they will approach a lender or lenders to find out about the amount they could borrow and the interest rates.

If a lender is happy to lend funds to a borrower, they will produce what is known as a ***mortgage offer***, stipulating the amount they are willing to lend. In commercial transactions, this is called a ***commitment letter*** and ***term sheet***.

The mortgage offer may include the following information set out in Table 3.10:

Table 3.10 The key types of information contained in a mortgage offer

Information about the property	• Address • Price • Tenure[53]
Information about the mortgage	• The amount being loaned • The term of the mortgage • The type of mortgage, for example, interest-only or repayment • The interest rate • The monthly repayments
Details of retentions	• Occasionally, the lender may retain some of the mortgage funds in case future expenditure is required. For example, the lender may require repairs to be made to the property, and so they may retain some of the mortgage funds until those repairs are complete. The client will need to ensure that they still have sufficient funds to complete, without whatever amount has been retained by the lender.
Details of guarantee premium	• If the loan-to-value ratio is particularly high, the lender may require the borrower to take out an insurance policy to cover the risk that the lender may not recover the full amount of the loan on resale if the borrower defaults.
Common conditions of the offer	• Existing mortgages held by the borrower must be discharged on or before completion. This is so that the lender can be confident that upon default by the borrower, the lender will be paid back first. • Prohibition on letting the property without the lender's consent. • Prohibition on making alterations to the property without the lender's consent. This is to ensure that the property does not decrease in value, affecting the value of the lender's security.

The buyer's solicitor must advise the buyer on the terms of the mortgage offer before the client accepts it.

53 This means whether it is freehold or leasehold.

It is common for most borrowers to have approached a lender before they commence the conveyancing process, and so it is likely that a prospective buyer will already have received a mortgage offer from a lender before approaching their solicitor about undertaking the conveyancing; however, this *must* be in place before exchange of contracts.

3.4.4 The lender's solicitor

Upon making a mortgage offer, the lender will appoint a solicitor to act for it. The lender will need to achieve the following:

- undertake due diligence on a property, to ensure that it is structurally sound and has a good and marketable legal title. This is because the lender wishes to ensure it will recoup the money it has loaned, if it needs to exercise its power of sale;
- enter into documentation in respect of the mortgage;
- undertake pre-completion searches to ensure that the due diligence position does not change; and
- register the mortgage to ensure that the lender gets priority over other forms of security.

You may notice that this process and the aims of the lender are very similar to those of the buyer. This is because both the buyer and the lender are acquiring a proprietary interest in the property. For this reason, it is common in residential transactions for the buyer's solicitor to also act for the lender. The solicitor must, of course, be cognisant of the possibility for a conflict of interest to arise, and act appropriately if it does.

In commercial transactions, there tends to be more negotiation on the terms of the mortgage between the lender and the borrower, which would give rise to a conflict of interest for a solicitor acting for both parties; therefore, lenders and borrowers in commercial transactions are usually represented separately.

For a deeper analysis of professional conduct, please see *Essential Legal System and Legal Services for SQE1*.[54]

When acting for the lender in a residential transaction, the solicitor must follow the UK Finance Mortgage Lenders' Handbook for Conveyancers (the **Lenders' Handbook**), which is a set of standard mortgage instructions.[55] Some lenders have adopted the Building Societies Association Mortgage Instructions as an alternative, and a solicitor must use this if the lender it represents wishes to use these instructions instead of the Lenders' Handbook.

54 Available from Routledge.
55 This is available from UK Finance.

3.4.5 The House

André is purchasing the House with the assistance of a mortgage from Country Funding Building Society (**CFBS**). He is borrowing £165,000 and has received a mortgage offer. André's solicitors have advised him on the terms of this offer and have agreed to act for CFBS.

Chapter 3 revision points

- Before acting for a client, a solicitor must undertake a 'conflict of interests' check, and a money laundering check.
- Buyers of land may need to pay Stamp Duty Land Tax or Land Transaction Tax. The rate of tax varies according to whether the property is residential or commercial. Relief may be available for first-time buyers. Corporate buyers, those purchasing a second home, and overseas residents generally pay higher rates.
- Value-Added Tax is chargeable on the supply of goods or services made in the course of a business. In a property transaction, it could be added to the price of the land, to construction services, or to professional services. Supplies are designated as standard-rated, zero-rated, or exempt from VAT. Sometimes a seller will choose to charge VAT on an otherwise-exempt supply in order to offset any VAT they have already paid.
- Capital Gains Tax is a tax levied against the gain in the value of an asset. Sellers of land need to be advised about any CGT liability, and buyers need to be aware that subsequent disposals of that land may give rise to a future CGT liability if the land increases in value. Private Residence Relief may be available for sellers of residential land.
- A buyer may grant a mortgage over property in exchange for a loan. The lender will provide a mortgage offer containing key information about the mortgage. The buyer's solicitor may sometimes act for the lender, as their objectives are aligned.

Revision Summary

PHASE 0

Commercial considerations

Financing a property transaction

- A buyer may need a ***mortgage*** to assist with buying a property.
- A buyer will usually have approached a lender and received a ***mortgage offer*** before instructing a solicitor. An offer must be in place before exchange of contracts.
- A solicitor will advise a buyer on the terms of the mortgage.
- A ***repayment mortgage*** requires a monthly payment of interest and capital, and by the end of the term, the borrower has paid off the full loan and interest.
- An ***interest-only mortgage*** requires a monthly payment of interest; by the end of the term, the borrower has paid off the interest, but the capital remains outstanding and must be paid off.
- Interest rates can be fixed or variable.

Instructing a solicitor

- Once a property has been marketed, and an offer made and accepted, each party will instruct a solicitor to conduct the conveyancing.
- A solicitor will need to undertake 'conflict of interest' checks and anti-money laundering checks before it can act for the client.
- A buyer's solicitor may sometimes act for the lender, as the aims of the lender match that of the buyer:
  - to ensure that the property is sound and has a good and marketable title;
  - to enter into documentation to secure the purchase of the property and the loan; and
  - to register the purchase and mortgage to secure priority over subsequent dispositions.
- A solicitor cannot act for both buyer and lender if there is a conflict of interest between the two: this is likely to be the case in commercial transactions.
- Solicitors acting for a lender must follow the UK Finance Mortgage Lenders' Handbook for Conveyancers or the Building Societies Association Mortgage Instructions, as instructed by the lender.

Stamp duty land tax

- ***Stamp Duty Land Tax*** is payable by the buyer of land in England purchased after 1 December 2003.
- The tax is a percentage of the purchase price or lease premium.

Rates for residential land:

General rates:

Table 3.1 The general rates of SDLT applicable on the acquisition of residential property

Purchase price or lease premium	Rate of SDLT applicable to that portion
The portion up to £125,000	0%
The portion between £125,001 and 250,000	2%
The portion between £250,001 and £925,000	5%
The portion between £925,001 and £1,500,000	10%
The portion over £1,500,000	12%

Higher rates for second homes or commercial purchasers of property valued at more than £40,000:

Table 3.4 The rates of SDLT applicable on the acquisition of second homes or by corporate buyers

Value of the transaction	Rate of SDLT applicable to that portion
The portion up to £125,000	5%
The portion between £125,001 and £250,000	7%
The portion between £250,001 and £925,000	10%
The portion between £925,001 and £1,500,000	15%
The portion over £1,500,000	17%

For the general rates and the higher rates, if the land is leasehold, an additional 1% SDLT is paid on the portion of the NPV (Annual Rent × length of lease) exceeding £125,000.

Rates for a first-time buyer of property not exceeding £500,000:

Table 3.3 The rates of SDLT applicable on the acquisition of residential property by a first-time buyer

Value of the transaction	Rate of SDLT applicable to that portion
The portion up to £300,000	0%
The portion between £300,001 and £500,000	5%

- Rates for companies purchasing residential land costing more than £500,000: 17% on the entire purchase price.
- Rates for non-UK residents: additional 2% on the relevant set of SDLT rates.

Rates for commercial land
General rates:

Table 3.6 The general rates of SDLT applicable on the acquisition of commercial property

Value of the transaction	Rate of SDLT applicable to that portion
The portion up to £150,000	0%
The portion between £150,001 and £250,000	2%
The portion over £250,000	5%

If the land is leasehold, an additional amount is payable as follows:

Table 3.7 The SDLT applicable on the NPV when a commercial lease is granted

Value of the NPV	Rate of SDLT applicable to that portion
The portion up to £150,000	0%
The portion between £150,001 and £5,000,000	1%
The portion over £5,000,000	2%

Land transaction tax

- ***Land Transaction Tax*** is payable by the buyer of land in Wales purchased after April 2018.
- The tax is a percentage of the purchase price or lease premium.

Rates for residential land

General rates:

Table 3.2 The general rates of LTT applicable on the acquisition of residential property

Value of the transaction	Rate of LTT applicable to that portion
The portion up to and including £225,000	0%
The portion over £225,000 and up to and including £400,000	6%
The portion over £400,000 and up to and including £750,000	7.5%
The portion over £750,000 and up to and including £1,500,000	10%
The portion over £1,500,000	12%

Higher rates for second homes or commercial purchasers of property valued at more than £40,000:

Table 3.5 The rates of LTT applicable on the acquisition of second homes or by corporate buyers

Value of the transaction	Rate of LTT applicable to that portion
The portion up to and including £180,000	5%
The portion over £180,000 and up to and including £250,000	8.5%
The portion over £250,000 and up to and including £400,000	10%
The portion over £400,000 and up to and including £750,000	12.5%
The portion over £750,000 and up to and including £1,500,000	15%
The portion over £1,500,000	17%

For the general and higher rates, if the land is leasehold, no additional LTT is paid on the rent.

Rates for commercial land

Table 3.8 The general rate of LTT applicable on the acquisition of commercial property

Value of the transaction	Rate of LTT applicable to that portion
The portion up to and including £225,000	0%
The portion over £225,000 and up to and including £250,000	1%
The portion over £250,000 and up to and including £1,000,000	5%
The portion over £1,000,000 and up to and including £750,000	6%

If the property is leasehold:

- if the Annual Rent is more than £13,000: LTT at 1% on the portion of the premium up to and including £250,000; and
- LTT is charged on the NPV as follows:

Table 3.9 The LTT applicable on the NPV when a commercial lease is granted

Value of the NPV	Rate of LTT applicable to that portion
The portion up to and including £225,000	0%
The portion over £225,000 and up to an including £2,000,000	1%
The portion over £2,000,000	2%

VAT

- ***Value-Added Tax*** is chargeable on the supply of goods or services made in the course of a business.
- Categories of supply:
  - ***Exempt supplies***. Not subject to VAT but sometimes come with an option to tax.
  - ***Zero-rated supplies***. Subject to VAT at a rate of 0%.
  - ***Standard-rated supplies***. Subject to VAT at the standard rate (currently 20%).
- Categories of supply common in a property transaction:

Table R0.1 The VAT categorisation of supplies common to property transactions

Supply	VAT category
Sale of new residential house by developer within first three years	Zero-rated
Sale of buy-to-let property	Exempt
Sale of new commercial freehold building	Standard-rated
Sale of old commercial freehold building	Exempt with option to tax
Grant or assignment of lease	Exempt with option to tax
Sale of greenfield site	Exempt with option to tax
Constructing a new residential building	Zero-rated
Constructing a new commercial property	Standard-rated
Other building or construction works	Standard-rated
Building or construction supplies	Standard-rated
Professional services	Standard-rated

- ***Input tax*** is the VAT paid by a business on a supply made to it.
- ***Output tax*** is the VAT received by a business when making a supply.
- A business can offset input tax and output tax to recover input tax incurred whilst making taxable supplies.
- A business may elect to exercise an ***option to tax***, charging VAT on an otherwise-exempt supply to enable it to receive output tax to offset against the input tax it has already paid.Instructing a solicitor

CGT

- ***Capital Gains Tax*** is a tax levied on the capital gain of an asset.
- The ***capital gain*** is the difference in price between when the asset was purchased and when it was disposed of.
- A seller of land should be advised as to whether there is any CGT to pay.
- CGT arises when there is a ***chargeable disposal*** of a ***chargeable asset*** made by a ***chargeable person***.
- Interests in land are chargeable assets.
- Selling, exchanging, and gifting are chargeable disposals.
- Individuals, trustees, and personal representatives are chargeable persons. Companies are not chargeable persons.
- CGT is not chargeable where ***Private Residence Relief*** is available.
- Private Residence Relief is available where the property disposed of is a person's ***only or main residence*** for the ***period of their ownership***.

Multiple-choice practice questions

Question 1

A solicitor is acting for the buyer of a freehold property in Wales to be used as a residence. The solicitor is advising the buyer of the potential costs of the transaction. Which of the following is the best estimation of the costs likely to be payable by the buyer?

A. The purchase price, LTT, legal fees, and disbursements.
B. The purchase price, SDLT, legal fees, and disbursements.
C. The purchase price, VAT, legal fees, and disbursements.
D. The purchase price, CGT, legal fees, and disbursements.
E. The purchase price, LTT, VAT, legal fees, and disbursements.

Question 2

A solicitor is acting for the seller of a freehold property who has resided in the property for 50 years. The seller acquired it for £10,000 and is selling it for £200,000.

The solicitor advises the seller that no Capital Gains Tax is due on the transaction. Which of the following best explains the solicitor's advice?

A. The property is not a chargeable asset.
B. The seller is not a chargeable person.
C. The property has not increased in value since it was acquired.
D. Private Residence Relief is available.
E. CGT is only relevant on the purchase of an asset.

Question 3

A solicitor is acting for the buyer of a commercial lease.

After acquiring the lease, the buyer plans to renovate the leasehold property. The buyer asks for advice about VAT on the transaction. Which is the best advice the solicitor can give?

A. VAT may be payable on the construction supplies and works.
B. VAT may be payable on the price of the property, the construction supplies and works, and the professional services.
C. VAT cannot be charged on the price of the property because it is an exempt supply.
D. VAT cannot be charged on the price of the property because it is a zero-rated supply.
E. VAT may be charged on the price of the property and the professional services.

PHASE 1 Due diligence

The solicitors have agreed to work for their respective clients, taken instructions on the transaction, and given initial advice relating to finance and tax. The next phase is to undertake due diligence relating to the property and transaction.

1 Why do we do due diligence?

Due diligence is undertaken when an interest in land is being acquired. According to the principle of ***caveat emptor*** (meaning 'buyer beware'), the buyer takes the property as they find it, even if there is something wrong or undesirable about it. For this reason, their solicitor will investigate the property and try to find out as much as possible about it. Any issues that are discovered may be used to re-negotiate the purchase price, or in extreme circumstances, the buyer may decide not to proceed with the purchase of the property.

1.1 Who does due diligence?

Due diligence is primarily the responsibility of the buyer's solicitor (owing to the principle of caveat emptor), but the seller's solicitor will also need a good understanding of the land in order to get all the relevant documents ready for the buyer's solicitor. If a lender is loaning money and taking a mortgage over the property, the lender's solicitor will carry out title investigation and searches on the property in the same way the buyer's solicitor does to ensure that the lender is satisfied with the security they are taking in exchange for their loan.

DOI: 10.4324/9781032711508-5

2 What due diligence do we do?

Due diligence primarily takes the following forms:

2.1 Title investigation

This seeks to:

- establish whether the current seller has the right to sell the estate in land and can convey a legal title to the buyer;
- establish whether any other estates exist over the same piece of land, or whether a third party has a valid interest in the land, and advise on whether the buyer will take the land subject to these; and
- ascertain whether the buyer requires any rights over a third party's land in order to use the land it is purchasing.

We look at how to investigate title in unregistered land (Chapter 4) and registered land (Chapter 5), and we analyse some common entries revealed and how to deal with them (Chapter 6).

2.2 Searches over the property

These tell a solicitor practical information about the property, such as whether the nearby roads are adopted, and whether the property is susceptible to flooding. We examine the key searches in Chapter 7.

2.3 Planning status and compliance with Building Regulations

Some of the searches will reveal information about the planning status of the property; it is essential to consider whether there have been any breaches of planning control (which your client could become liable for), and whether your client's plans for the property may require planning permission – this is examined in Chapter 8 along with a consideration of the building regulations regime.

2.4 Making enquiries of the seller

This enables the buyer's solicitor to find out specific information about the property based on the seller's knowledge. Some enquiries are standard, but the buyer's solicitor can also raise specific enquiries to confirm or clarify issues which have come up elsewhere during the due diligence process. Enquiries of the seller are considered in Chapter 9.

We have split these into individual chapters for ease of understanding, but in practice the entire due diligence process will take place simultaneously, and there may be lots of crossover between the different stages. The solicitor will assess all the information gathered and compile it into a report for their client (and, if relevant, the lender) and create an 'issues list' to ensure that any issues discovered are appropriately dealt with. We have included a summary of due diligence for each of our Transactions, available in the relevant Appendix.

3 What do we do with the information we discover?

In almost all cases, the buyer's solicitor will produce a ***report on title*** for their client, flagging the key information about the property. This is produced during the due diligence process, noting the key features benefitting or affecting the property, and is provided to the buyer before contracts are exchanged. The purpose of the report on title is to provide the buyer with a clear understanding of what they are purchasing before the buyer is contractually bound to proceed with the purchase; on occasion, a buyer may decide not to proceed with a purchase. The content of a report on title will vary depending on the type of transaction and what has been agreed with the client. A residential buyer may simply require an explanation of matters affecting the title; a commercial client may require a full report additionally covering search results and reporting on the key terms of documentation (such as the sale contract and financial documents).

The lender's solicitor will produce a certificate of title for the lender. A copy of the Law Society's certificate of title, which is required in residential transactions, is available from the Law Society.

The purpose of the certificate of title is:

- To confirm that the property is adequate security for the loan, namely:
  - that the title to the property is good and marketable, meaning that the buyer will acquire the legal title and that this can be passed on by the lender if it exercises a power of sale;
  - that any adverse encumbrances are reported which could reduce the value of the property, making it less valuable than the amount of the loan; and
- to confirm that the mortgage will be registered as a first legal charge.

The certificate of title contains a request for the loan to be advanced. It therefore is formally sent to the lender between exchange and completion so that the funds are available on completion. However, in practice, any issues which may arise during the due diligence process should be discussed with the lender prior to exchange, in case the issue is fundamental enough that it may result in the mortgage offer being withdrawn.

4 Investigating title in unregistered land

4.1 Chapter overview

Title investigation seeks to:

- establish whether the current seller has the right to sell the estate in land and can convey a legal title to the buyer;
- establish whether any other estates exist over the same piece of land or whether a third party has a valid interest in the land, and advise on whether the buyer will take the land subject to these; and
- ascertain whether the buyer requires any rights over a third party's land in order to use the land it is purchasing.

This chapter explores how to investigate title to a parcel of unregistered land. This chapter is relevant to all freehold and leasehold transactions relating to unregistered land.

This chapter in the context of our Transactions

Solicitors have been instructed on Style&Go Ltd's acquisition of the Car Park from Urban Spaces Ltd, and Style&Go Ltd's solicitors have advised their client on tax and related matters. The Car Park is currently unregistered; Style&Go Ltd's solicitors now need to examine title to the Car Park.

You may wish to refer to the following documentation for the Car Park whilst working through this chapter:

- Epitome of title
- Conveyance dated 29 September 1989
- Central Land Charges Search dated 4 September 1989
- Conveyance dated 1 June 1956
- Lease dated 30 September 1989
- Change of name certificate dated 20 May 2020
- Mortgage deed dated 29 September 1989

DOI: 10.4324/9781032711508-6

4.2 Establishing that the current seller can transfer the legal and beneficial ownership to the buyer

The way in which we establish that the current seller can transfer legal and beneficial title to the property when we are dealing with unregistered land is by inspecting the ownership history of the property. Remember, the buyer's solicitor is trying to get comfortable that the current seller has the legal and beneficial title to the property the buyer plans to buy.

The seller is required[1] to supply a document which evidences their ownership of the property, and then the buyer's solicitor will check that there is an unbroken chain of ownership between the owner in that document and the current seller. The document proving ownership is known as the ***root of title***.

The buyer's solicitor is looking for a document which:

- *is over 15 years old, but hasn't triggered first registration*;
- *describes the property*: the rationale for this is so that the buyer's solicitor can ensure that the document concerns the property that the buyer intends to purchase;

1 This requirement comes from the standard conditions governing the sale contract and has a specific timeframe attached to it, which we examine in Chapter 11. In practice, a seller will deduce title before they are contractually obligated to.

- *deals with the ownership of the whole legal and equitable interest*: this is to ensure that the seller (and no one else) holds the legal and equitable title to the property, and that there is no one else who may have a competing claim against the buyer; and
- *casts no doubt on the seller's title*: again, this is to ensure that no one else has a competing claim to the property and may defeat the buyer's title.

A document satisfying these criteria is known as a *good* root of title.

4.2.1 Type of document

The key feature of a root document is that it must evidence ownership of the property.

Usually, the root of title document will be a conveyance on sale or a mortgage (although it doesn't have to be). The rationale for this is that when land is sold or when a mortgage is taken over land, the purchaser or mortgagee will have investigated the title before completing the relevant document and acquiring the interest. The buyer then gets the benefit of his own title and investigation *and* that of the current seller or mortgagee. We can contrast this with an assent of property.[2] Because assents deal with gifts of land (e.g. no consideration is paid), title investigation is not typically carried out.

4.2.2 The root document must be at least 15 years old

The root of title should be at least 15 years old.[3] First registration became compulsory on 1 December 1990 for most types of conveyance,[4] so conveyances after this date would have triggered registration of the land. This means that many root documents will be over 30 years old, as they will not have changed hands since before December 1990.

The root document must also be dated before compulsory registration (for that type of disposition); otherwise, it would have triggered first registration. We discussed in Chapter 2[5] that the effect of failing to register a disposition that is subject to first registration is that the purchaser under that conveyance would not hold the legal title to the property. This conveyance, therefore, would not evidence the legal ownership of the property and cannot form a good root of title. In practice, it would be sent back to the seller's solicitor to register the land (which would transfer the legal title to the seller) before it could be transferred to a buyer.

2 An assent is the document used to transfer property from the estate of a deceased to a beneficiary of the estate.

3 s44 LPA 1925 and s23 LPA 1969. This ties in with the limitation period for bringing claims in land: If we investigate title going back 15 years and find no issues, then anyone with a claim dating back earlier than that 15 years will not be able to bring a claim.

4 This is the relevant date for conveyances by sale; for conveyances by gift and assent, registration became compulsory on 1 April 1998.

5 In Section 2.3.1.2.2.3.

Compulsory registration occurred in different parts of England and Wales at different times. Make sure you check the date of compulsory registration for the area of England and Wales you are dealing with.[6]

If the root document is a conveyance on sale or a legal mortgage, then the purchaser under that conveyance or the mortgagee under that mortgage will also have reviewed a root document of at least 15 years before taking their interest in the property. This achieves the 'double guarantee' of title investigation noted in Section 4.2.1.

There are two conveyances supplied by Urban Spaces Ltd's solicitor. They are dated 29 September 1989 (which we shall refer to as the **1989 Conveyance**) and 1 June 1956 (which we shall refer to as the **1956 Conveyance**), respectively. Therefore, both conveyances satisfy the 15-year rule and are both dated before compulsory registration, which occurred on 1 December 1990 for conveyances by sale.

4.2.3 The root document must adequately describe the property being transferred

This description can be by way of:

- an address;
- a description; or
- a plan.

The 1989 Conveyance describes the property and supplies an address and postcode. It does not contain a plan but refers to a plan contained in the 1956 Conveyance. The plan does not need to be included in the root of title document in order for that document to constitute a good root of title. It is sufficient that the root of title refers to an older document which contains a plan of the land, provided you have a copy of that older document for inspection.

The 1956 Conveyance describes the property, supplies an address, and includes a plan.

Both of these conveyances, therefore, adequately describe the property being transferred.

4.2.4 The root document must be properly executed as a deed

The buyer's solicitor must check that the conveyance transfers both the legal *and* the beneficial interest in the land. You will recall from Chapter 2 that certain formalities are required in order to create or convey a legal interest in land. If the rel-

6 HMLR Practice Guide 1: First Registration has a useful summary.

evant formalities have not been complied with, then the current seller will only hold the beneficial interest in the land, but not the legal interest. This means that the current seller will not be able to pass the legal interest on to the buyer, because the seller themselves does not hold it.

In order to properly create or convey the legal interest in the land, the document must be executed as a deed.[7] Traditionally, the common law required a deed to be sealed. This requirement was removed,[8] and now, instead of sealing a deed, the parties must clearly indicate their intention to create a deed.

In order to be a deed, the document must now:

- be in writing;
- make clear on its face that it is intended to be a deed;
- be validly executed as a deed; and
- be delivered: for companies, this is deemed on execution unless a contrary intention can be shown.

Table 4.1 sets out the various requirements for creating a deed, and an example of how this might look.

Both conveyances of the Car Park are dated pre-31 July 1990; therefore, we need to apply the set of rules in application before 1 July 1990.

Urban Developments Ltd is a company and purchased the Car Park from another company, FPC Storage Ltd, so each needed to execute the 1989 Conveyance either in accordance with its own articles of association or by applying its company seal in the presence of a director and secretary. We can see that both parties executed the 1989 Conveyance by applying their company seal in the presence of a director and a secretary. This deed has therefore been properly executed by both parties.

The 1956 Conveyance was made between an individual and a company. Kristjan and Miranda Norris have both signed the document in the presence of Maurice McGraw, and the document has been sealed and delivered as a deed. It has therefore been executed properly by the seller. It has also been executed correctly by Regener8 Ltd according to the rules above by the application of a company seal in the presence of a director and a secretary.

7 s52 LPA 1925. There are exceptions, such as the grant of a lease of less than 3 years.
8 By the Law of Property (Miscellaneous Provisions) Act 1989 (**LP(MP)A 1989**).

Table 4.1 The execution requirements for creating a deed

Date	Who is signing	Requirements	Example
Pre–31 July 1990	Individual	A deed had to be: • Signed by the maker • Sealed by the maker • Delivered as a deed	SIGNED SEALED AND DELIVERED by [FULL NAME OF PARTY] .... [SIGNATURE OF PARTY] [SEAL] in the presence of: .... [SIGNATURE OF WITNESS] [NAME OF WITNESS] [ADDRESS OF WITNESS] [OCCUPATION OF WITNESS]
	Company[9]	EXECUTION UNDER COMPANY'S ARTICLES OF ASSOCIATION The relevant formalities were whatever the articles of association required. EXECUTION UNDER COMMON SEAL • Company seal affixed • In the presence of a director and secretary This was a valid method of execution even if it didn't accord with the company's articles of association.	Executed as a deed by affixing the common seal of [NAME OF COMPANY] in the presence of: [COMMON SEAL] .... Director .... [Director **OR** Secretary]

9 s74 LPA 1925.

31 July 1990 onwards	Individual[10]	A deed has to be: ● Signed by the maker* ● In the presence of a witness who attests that signature *It is permitted for another person to sign on their behalf if there are two attesting witnesses.	Signed as a deed by [FULL NAME OF PARTY] .... [SIGNATURE OF PARTY] in the presence of: .... [SIGNATURE OF WITNESS] [NAME OF WITNESS] [ADDRESS OF WITNESS] [OCCUPATION OF WITNESS]
	Company[11]	<u>EXECUTION BY TWO AUTHORISED SIGNATORIES</u> Signed by two directors (or director and company secretary)	[Executed as a deed] by [NAME OF EXECUTING COMPANY] acting by [NAME OF DIRECTOR], a Director .... Director and [NAME OF DIRECTOR OR SECRETARY] [a Director **OR** its secretary] .... [Director **OR** Secretary]

(Continued)

10 s1 LP(MP)A 1989.
11 s36 Companies Act 1985 (**CA 1985**) and s44 Companies Act 2006 (**CA 2006**).

Table 4.1 (Continued)

Date	Who is signing	Requirements	Example
		EXECUTION UNDER COMMON SEAL ● Company seal affixed; ● witnessed by two directors (or director and company secretary).	Executed as a deed by affixing the common seal of [NAME OF COMPANY] in the presence of: [COMMON SEAL] …………………………… Director …………………………… [Director **OR** Secretary]
6 April 2008 onwards	Company[12]	EXECUTION BY ONE DIRECTOR BEFORE A WITNESS ● Execution by a single director ● In the presence of a witness who attests that signature	Executed as a deed by [NAME OF EXECUTING COMPANY] acting by [NAME OF DIRECTOR], a Director, …………………………… in the presence of: [SIGNATURE OF DIRECTOR] …………………………… Director [SIGNATURE OF WITNESS] [NAME OF WITNESS [IN BLOCK CAFITALS]] [ADDRESS OF WITNESS] [OCCUPATION OF WITNESS]

12 s44 CA 2006.

4.2.5 The root document must not contain a title defect

The disposal of land triggered certain administrative requirements. The buyer was required to:

- pay stamp duty; and
- produce documentation to the Inland Revenue.

Undertaking each of these actions resulted in a stamp being applied to the documentation.

A document omitting the required stamps constitutes a title defect. It will not be able to be produced in court proceedings, and the Land Registrar will not accept an incorrectly stamped document as a good root of title.

For this reason, it is necessary when conducting title due diligence on unregistered land to check that the root of title document has been properly stamped. If it hasn't, prospective buyers can raise a requisition with a seller to rectify the defect and can seek to obtain defective title indemnity insurance if the defect cannot be rectified. If there is an alternative good root of title without defects, a buyer is likely to simply rely on this instead.

4.2.5.1 Ad valorem duty

The payment of stamp duty was triggered by the transfer of land.[13] Upon payment of stamp duty, stamps were placed on the deed, evidencing that the duty had been paid. These stamps look like this:

Figure 4.1 Ad valorem stamps.

Solicitors need to check that the correct amount of ***ad valorem stamp duty*** was paid on the relevant conveyance.

Occasionally, a transaction was exempt from stamp duty because the consideration was below the threshold to be liable for stamp duty. In these cases, a certificate of value was included in the conveyance, evidencing that stamp duty was not payable. Such a certificate is worded like this:

13 s1 Stamp Act 1981.

> It is hereby certified that the transaction hereby effected does not form part of a larger transaction or of a series of transactions in respect of which the amount or value or the aggregate amount or value of the consideration exceeds . . .[14] pounds.

A conveyance which does not contain either ad valorem stamps *or* a certificate of value (some conveyances have both, which is fine) has not been correctly stamped; as noted above, this constitutes a title defect, and the document cannot form a good root of title.

We can see that the 1989 Conveyance has three stamps totalling £300. The value of the transaction was £30,000, and the stamps reflect that the correct amount of stamp duty has been paid.[15] This has therefore been stamped correctly in respect of ad valorem duty.

The 1956 Conveyance does not contain any stamps, but it does contain the certificate of value noted above. This satisfies the requirements for ad valorem duty.

4.2.5.2 Particulars Delivered

Upon:

- the conveyance on sale of the freehold;
- the grant of a lease of 7+ years; or
- the transfer on sale of a lease of 7+ years;

documentation had to be provided to the Inland Revenue (now HMRC) together with a form giving particulars of the documents and any consideration received.[16] The document was stamped with a '***PD stamp***' as proof that the document had been provided to the Inland Revenue.

The PD stamp looks like this:

Figure 4.2 PD stamp.

The three types of document listed above will not form a good root of title unless they contain this stamp.

14 The amount entered here would reflect the stamp duty threshold at the date of the conveyance.
15 The rate on the date of the 1989 Conveyance was £1 per every £100 consideration.
16 s28 Finance Act 1931.

Some conveyances were exempt from having a PD stamp. They would have contained a ***certificate of exemption***:

> IT IS CERTIFIED that this instrument falls within category . . .[17] in the Schedule to the Stamp Duty (Exempt Instruments) Regulations 1987.

A conveyance which does not contain a PD stamp or a certificate of exemption has not been stamped properly and cannot form a good root of title.

The 1956 Conveyance and the 1989 Conveyance are both conveyances on the sale of the freehold and therefore require a PD stamp. The 1989 Conveyance contains this stamp; the 1956 Conveyance does not. The 1956 Conveyance, therefore, cannot form a good root of title, but the 1989 Conveyance can.

4.2.6 The chain of documents showing title passing to the current seller must cast no doubt on the seller's title

The buyer's solicitor must be confident that, from the root of title until now, there are no gaps in the seller's ownership; a gap would cast doubt on the seller's title and must be investigated. The key issue which may cast doubt on the seller's title is when the legal owner in the root title document is not the same as the individual or entity listed as the seller in the heads of terms. There are some common reasons for this, which must be investigated with the seller's solicitor and appropriate documentary evidence obtained:

- the seller has changed their name;
- the legal title was held by more than one party, one of whom has died; or
- the root title document was executed under a power of attorney.

The first of these examples has occurred in respect of the 1989 Conveyance. We have ascertained that this conveyance to Urban Developments Ltd forms a good root of title. However, we have been told that the seller of the Car Park is Urban Spaces Ltd. On face value, this could point to a gap in the seller's ownership. However, there is a certificate of incorporation included in the ***epitome of title***, and this shows that on 20 May 2020, Urban Developments Ltd changed its name to Urban Spaces Ltd. Therefore, Style&Go Ltd's solicitor can be confident that Urban Developments Ltd and Urban Spaces Ltd are the same company.

Applying the rules above, it is clear that the 1989 Conveyance will form a good root of title for the Car Park, evidencing that Urban Spaces Ltd can transfer the legal and beneficial title to the Car Park to Style&Go Ltd.

17 There are categories A–E in the Schedule to the Stamp Duty (Exempt Instruments) Regulations 1987, and the relevant one for the transaction would be included here.

4.3 Establishing which other rights and interests affect the land and will bind the buyer

We noted in Chapter 2 the estates and interests which a piece of land could be subject to and how these could bind a purchaser for value. It is essential for solicitors to be able to navigate these interests and work out, when the land is sold to a buyer, which of these rights and interests will bind the buyer and which they will take the land free from. Please note this book is concerned with the priority rules post-1925 and deals with the rules as they apply to a purchaser for value.

4.3.1 The priority rules in unregistered land

The priority rules are summarised below, but please see Chapter 2 for the full explanation of these rules.

4.3.1.1 Legal interests

In unregistered land, a *legal* interest binds the world. As a reminder, a legal interest is one which:

1. is capable of being legal in nature under section 1(2) the LPA 1925; and
2. has been properly created (e.g. by complying with the formalities required under section 52 of the LPA 1925).

A legal estate or interest will be binding on a subsequent purchaser even if they did not know about it.

4.3.1.2 Equitable interests

Equitable interests, however, will not bind the world.

4.3.1.2.1 EQUITABLE INTERESTS REGISTRABLE AS A LAND CHARGE

Some equitable interests are registrable as a land charge.[18] In order for these interests to bind a subsequent purchaser for value, they must be registered in the Land Charges Register.

4.3.1.2.2 OTHER EQUITABLE INTERESTS

Other equitable interests which are not registrable as a land charge are subject to the doctrine of notice. They will bind a purchaser for value who knew or should have known of their existence.

4.3.1.3 Overriding interests

We noted in Chapter 2 the concept of an overriding interest. For a conveyance of unregistered land, priority is determined on completion of the conveyance accord-

18 s10 LCA 1925.

ing to the rules noted above,[19] and there are no other interests which can 'override' the disposition and take priority.

However, you will recall that the LRA 2002[20] contains a list of interests which 'override first registration'. The writers understand[21] this to relate to any interests falling in those categories in Schedule 1, which:

- are known about by the proprietor and notified to the Land Registrar; or
- are not known about by the proprietor but which have only arisen in the short period between completion and registration.

In practice, a solicitor will make sufficient enquiries of the seller to discover any and all interests which would fall under Schedule 1 anyway, and these would then need to be disclosed to the Land Registrar on first registration (or, for non-triggering dispositions, the purchaser would be bound by them by virtue of the doctrine of notice).

4.3.2 Checking for legal rights: reviewing the other documents in the epitome of title

As legal rights will automatically bind the purchaser for value, the documents in the epitome of title must be reviewed to see if any legal rights affect the property; for example, perhaps there is a deed of easement in the epitome of title detailing a legal easement over the property enjoyed by the neighbouring land.

There is a lease contained in the epitome of title, dated 30 September 1989 and made between (1) Urban Developments Ltd and (2) Revolution Autos Ltd. Legal leases are capable of binding everyone. However, we can see that this was a 15-year lease which expired on 29 September 2004. It was contracted out of the Landlord and Tenant Act 1954 provisions on security of tenure,[22] so there should be no tenant holding over. Style&Go Ltd's solicitor will make enquiries of Urban Spaces Ltd's solicitor to get confirmation that the Car Park will be conveyed with vacant possession, and this will be written into the contract for sale. This lease will therefore not bind Style&Go Ltd as a purchaser for value of the Car Park.

There is a mortgage dated 20 September 1989 contained in the epitome of title; as a legal interest this will take priority over Style&Go Ltd's acquisition, and so Style&Go Ltd's solicitor must ensure that this is discharged on completion.

There are no easements contained in the epitome of title. However, as a legal interest will bind Style&Go Ltd even if they do not know about it, it is important to

19 In Sections 2.3.1.2.2.2.
20 At Schedule 1.
21 But note there is a distinct lack of clarity on this issue.
22 See Chapter 23 for an explanation of this.

do additional due diligence to discover whether there could be any other legal interests not reflected in the documentation. Style&Go Ltd's solicitor will therefore raise an enquiry with Urban Spaces Ltd's solicitor to ensure any other interests are disclosed.[23]

A review of the 1956 Conveyance shows that a legal easement was created giving a right of way over Sheep Street for the benefit of the Car Park. Style&Go Ltd will acquire the Car Park with the benefit of this right of way.

4.3.3 Checking for equitable rights: searching the Land Charges Register

Before land itself was registered, the only way to register encumbrances against land was to register those encumbrances against the *owners* of the land. Therefore, the Land Charges Register (introduced in 1926) contains a list of previous owners of the land and notes whether there are any encumbrances registered against their names.

As noted above, equitable interests which are registrable as land charges will bind a purchaser for value if they are registered on the Land Charges Register.

Style&Go Ltd's solicitor will conduct a search of the Land Charges Register (a search can be made via HMLR website) to ascertain whether any encumbrances affect it. This search will be made against Urban Spaces Ltd as the current proprietor of the Car Park, and against any previous owners for the period of time that each owned the land.

Occasionally, a seller's solicitor will provide in the epitome of title a copy of the results of the Land Charges Search that was conducted when the seller acquired what they are now selling.[24] We can see that Urban Spaces Ltd's solicitor has included one dated 4 September 1989, which would have been undertaken as part of the due diligence just before Urban Spaces Ltd acquired the Car Park in 1989. Before relying on a search result provided by the Urban Space's solicitor, it is necessary for Style&Go Ltd's solicitor to review this search to ensure that it is thorough and complete and can be relied upon. If Style&Go Ltd's solicitor identifies any problems with the search result, then they will repeat the search against the previous proprietors of the Car Park in addition to conducting a search against Urban Spaces Ltd.

We discuss below the requirements for a thorough and reliable search.

23 See Chapter 9.
24 Please note it is not essential for the seller's solicitor to supply a copy of past searches.

4.3.3.1 Creating a chronology of ownership

The starting point for conducting a Land Charges Search and reviewing an existing result is to put together a chronology of the known ownership of the property.

All we know from the epitome of title is that:

- Kristjan Norris and Miranda Norris sold the land to Regener8 Ltd in 1956 (in the 1956 Conveyance); and
- FPC Storage Ltd sold the land to Urban Developments Ltd in 1989 (in the 1989 Conveyance).

Therefore, the ownership of the Car Park (in reverse chronological order) is shown in Table 4.2:

Table 4.2 A chronology of ownership

Document	Owner	Acquired	Sold
1989 Conveyance	Urban Spaces Ltd (previously known as Urban Developments Ltd)	1989	[TBC, but expected 2026]
	FPC Storage Ltd	unknown	1989
UNKNOWN	UNKNOWN	UNKNOWN	UNKNOWN
1956 Conveyance	Regener8 Ltd	1956	Unknown
	Kristjan Norris and Miranda Norris	Unknown	1956

We do not know what happened between 1956 and 1989. It is possible that Regener8 Ltd sold the land directly to Urban Developments Ltd during that period, but it is also possible that Regener8 Ltd sold the land to someone else, who then sold it on to Urban Developments Ltd; in fact, there could have been any number of transactions during that time period which we simply have no information on.

This is a significant weakness of the land charges system from the buyer's perspective: as we saw above,[25] Style&Go Ltd will be bound by *any and all* equitable rights which are registered on the Land Charges Register, even if Style&Go Ltd does not (and cannot) discover them. This means that there may well be individuals or companies who owned the Car Park between 1956 and 1989 that Style&Go Ltd's solicitor is unaware of and therefore cannot conduct a search against their names. Style&Go Ltd will be bound by any land charges registered against these individuals or companies, even though they cannot discover them.

25 At Section 4.3.1.2.1.

4.3.3.2 Identifying which names to search against

HMLR will only conduct the search against the exact version of the name stated on the application form submitted to it, so it is important to search against common variations of names in case an entry has been registered under a variation of the estate owner's name.

Style&Go Ltd's solicitor will need to conduct a search against Urban Spaces Ltd. We understand from the heads of terms that the current proprietor is Urban Spaces Ltd; *Ltd* can also be written as *Limited* sometimes, but the search automatically searches against both. We also know that Urban Spaces Ltd was previously called Urban Developments Ltd.[26] Therefore, the search should be made against:

- Urban Spaces Ltd; and
- Urban Developments Ltd.

Style&Go Ltd's solicitor will also need to review the search result relating to the previous owners of the Car Park and re-do these searches if the search was not thorough enough. The name of one of the sellers in the 1956 Conveyance is 'Kristjan Norris', and we can see that a search has been conducted against this name. However, a search should also have been conducted against common variations of this name, such as 'Kris Norris', 'Kristian Norris', and 'Christian Norris'. The current search result is therefore not thorough enough; there could be registered land charges which relate to the Car Park which have been registered against a variation of the name 'Kristjan Norris' and therefore have not been revealed by the current search. Style&Go Ltd's solicitor will re-do this search against other iterations of the name 'Kristjan Norris'.

4.3.3.3 Identifying which date to search against

The search will need to be made against all iterations of the relevant estate owner's name for the period of time they owned the land. You can find out this information from the title deeds and epitome of title. Creating a chronology like the one in Table 4.2 may assist.

The epitome of title shows that Urban Spaces Ltd (then named as Urban Developments Ltd) purchased the land in 1989 from FPC Storage Ltd. Style&Go Ltd's solicitor will need to search against Urban Spaces Ltd (in all the iterations noted above) from 1989 until today, as we know these are the dates they owned the Car Park.

As demonstrated above,[27] it is possible that you will not know the duration of ownership of every previous owner of the land. We set out below the approach to deal with any gaps in ownership, which helps to ensure that, for the owners we know about, we do not miss any land charges registered against them.

26 See Section 4.2.6.
27 See Section 4.3.3.1.

4.3.3.3.1 DEALING WITH A MISSING ACQUISITION DATE

We know that FPC Storage Ltd disposed of the Car Park in 1989 (in the 1989 Conveyance), but we do not know when they acquired it, because we do not have a copy of the conveyance under which FPC Storage Ltd acquired it. In this case, we would search against the earliest possible date that FPC Storage Ltd could have acquired the land: in this case, it would be 1956, as this is the only date prior to 1989 that we *know* the Car Park was owned by someone else (Regener8 Ltd). Regener8 Ltd could have sold the Car Park directly to FPC Storage Ltd in 1956. We can see from the search results that FPC Storage Ltd has been searched against between 1980 and 1989. Therefore, Style&Go Ltd's solicitor will need to re-do this search against FPC Storage Ltd using the dates 1956 and 1989 instead.

For Kristjan and Miranda Norris, all we know is that they disposed of the land in 1956. We do not know when they acquired it, nor do we have any information about previous owners. In this case, a search should be done against their names from 1926 (which is when the register was opened) until the year they disposed of the land. We can see from the search results that this has been done.

4.3.3.3.2 DEALING WITH A MISSING DISPOSAL DATE

Similarly, when the search is made against Regner8 Ltd, the start date for the search should be 1956, as we know this was when they acquired the Car Park. However, we do not know when they disposed of it, and so we will search against the latest possible date that Regener8 Ltd could have disposed of it: in this case it will be 1989, as this is the only date after 1956 that we *know* the land was owned by someone else (FPC Storage Ltd). Regener8 Ltd could have sold the Car Park directly to FPC Storage Ltd in 1989. The search results show us that Regener8 Ltd has been searched against between 1956 and 1976. Therefore, Style&Go Ltd's solicitor will need to re-do this search using the dates 1956 and 1989 instead.

4.3.3.4 Securing priority: completion within 15 working days

The search result confers a ***priority period***, which ensures that any land charges registered after the date of the search result but before the date the disposition is completed do not bind the purchaser for value. This protection lasts for 15 working days.[28] This means that in order to ensure priority of the purchaser for value, the relevant transfer of land must be completed within 15 working days from the date of the search result.

The transfer from Urban Spaces Ltd to Style&Go Ltd must therefore be completed within 15 working days of the new Land Charges Search result. In practice, Style&Go Ltd's solicitor is likely to conduct a Land Charges Search against Urban Spaces Ltd in the early stages of the transaction to gain an understanding of any

28 s11 Land Charges Act 1972 (**LCA 1982**).

encumbrances on the land so that these can be dealt with, and then repeat the search when completion is imminent, to ensure that the transfer has priority.[29]

Regarding the Land Charges Search result which has been provided by Urban Space's solicitor, Style&Go Ltd's solicitor must check that the relevant conveyance (being the conveyance from FPC Storage Ltd to Urban Developments Ltd) was completed in time. If it wasn't, the Land Charges Search results in respect of the then seller (being FPC Storage Ltd) cannot be relied upon, and the search against that name will need to be repeated. The search result was dated 4 September 1989. Fifteen working days from this date would be 25 September 1989. The 1989 Conveyance was not completed until 29 September 1989, which means that the search results against FPC Storage Ltd are not reliable – a third party could have registered a land charge against FPC Storage Ltd after 4 September, and Style&Go Ltd would still be bound by that interest. Therefore, Style&Go Ltd's solicitor will need to repeat the Land Charges Search against FPC Storage Ltd.

4.3.3.5 *Results of the search*

As set out in Chapter 2, some of the most common[30] land charges you may come across are:

- C(i): puisne mortgage;
- C(iv): estate contract;
- D(ii): restrictive covenants; and
- D(iii): equitable easements.

Style&Go Ltd's solicitor has done a new Land Charges Search. We can see from the search results that previous owners of the Car Park have the following land charges registered against them:

- Urban Spaces Ltd: D(ii) restrictive covenants;
- FPC Storage Ltd: D(ii) restrictive covenants;
- Regener8 Ltd: D(ii) restrictive covenants;
- Kristjan Norris: no subsisting entries; and
- Miranda Norris: no subsisting entries.

Viewing these search results alongside the conveyances, it is likely that the entries relate to the restrictive covenants contained within clause 2 of the 1956 Conveyance, notably restricting the use of the Car Park and building on the Car Park, but this point will need to be verified. Style&Go Ltd's solicitor will request a copy of these D(ii) land charges to check what they relate to.

29 See Chapter 16 for pre-completion searches.

30 A full list is available in section 10 LCA 1925.

4.3.4 Checking for overriding interests

We noted in Section 4.3.1.3 that when dealing with unregistered land, priority is determined according to the rules noted above,[31] and there are no other interests which can 'override' the disposition and take priority, but that a solicitor will, in any event, make sufficient enquiries of the seller to discover any and all interests which would fall under Schedule 1 of the LRA 2002.

In order to identify any additional interests affecting the land, the buyer's solicitor may use a combination of methods:

- requesting information from the seller, by way of pre-contract enquiries;
- undertaking a Local Land Charges Search (an **LLC Search**); and
- recommending that the buyer undertakes a physical inspection of the land, for example, to ensure that there is no one in actual occupation.

These will be explored further in Chapters 7 and 9.

Summary

We have explored the process for investigating title in unregistered land, and we have established that:

- Urban Spaces Ltd has the right to convey the legal and beneficial title to the Car Park to Style&Go Ltd by virtue of the 1989 Conveyance, which forms a good root of title;
- there are restrictive covenants affecting the Car Park; and
- the Car Park benefits from a right of way over Sheep Street.

In Chapter 6, we explore the rights and interests affecting the Car Park and how to deal with these.

Chapter 4 revision points

- A buyer of unregistered land must establish that the seller can transfer the legal and beneficial ownership to the buyer by identifying a good root of title which is at least 15 years old, properly describes the property, is executed as a deed, is properly stamped, and casts no doubt on the seller's title.
- A buyer of unregistered land will take the land subject to all existing legal interests, relevant equitable interests which are registered as a land charge, and other equitable interests of which the buyer is aware or should have been aware.
- A buyer can discover land charges by searching the Land Charges Register for charges registered against the current and previous owners of the property. The search certificate will provide a priority period of 15 working days within which the buyer's transaction must be completed.

31 In Sections 4.3.1.1 and 4.3.1.2.

5 Investigating title in registered land

5.1 Chapter overview

When transferring a parcel of registered land, investigating title is an examination of the official copy register of title and the official copy plan, alongside any additional documents which have not been extracted in that register.

This chapter explores the process of investigating title to registered land.

This chapter is relevant to all freehold and leasehold transactions relating to registered land.

This chapter in the context of our Transactions

Solicitors have been instructed on:

- André's acquisition of the House from Michael's estate;
- Style&Go Ltd's acquisition of the Salon from Neeta;
- Style&Go Ltd's grant of a lease over the Nail Bar to Polished Perfection Ltd; and
- Gemma's Gels Ltd's purchase of the Nail Bar Lease from Polished Perfection Ltd.

The House, the Salon, and the Nail Bar are all registered. Solicitors for each buyer now need to examine title to the various properties.

You may wish to refer to the official copies for each of the above Transactions whilst working through this chapter.

DOI: 10.4324/9781032711508-7

5.2 Establishing that the current seller can transfer the legal and beneficial ownership to the buyer

In registered land, it is the ***register of title*** which states who has the legal title to the land, and the register is conclusive on that point.[1] Therefore, a buyer's solicitor simply needs to check that the name of the ***registered proprietor*** on the register of title matches the name of the seller. Details of the registered proprietor are recorded in register B of the register of title – the ***Proprietorship Register***.

5.2.1 André's acquisition of the House

André's solicitor is reviewing the ***official copies*** for the House. The register of title in Section B shows that Michael Tomlinson is the proprietor of the House. We already know from the heads of terms that Michael has passed away, and therefore, the House will be transferred to André by Michael's personal representative. André's solicitor will need to ensure that they request a copy of the grant of probate, and that the personal representative is listed as the seller in both the sale contract and the transfer deed.

5.2.2 Style&Go Ltd's acquisition of the Salon

Style&Go Ltd's solicitor is reviewing the official copies for the Salon. The register of title in Section B shows that Ansar Mukhtar and Neeta Mukhtar are the proprietors of the Salon. The seller, as far as we are aware from the heads of terms, is just Neeta. Therefore, Style&Go Ltd's solicitor will need to explore why the registered proprietors do not match the name of the seller and ensure that Neeta can transfer the legal and beneficial ownership to Style&Go Ltd.

One possible explanation for the discrepancy is that Ansar and Neeta owned the Salon together but Ansar has passed away. Style&Go Ltd's solicitor can verify this by asking Neeta's solicitor for more information and, if this is indeed the case, requesting a copy of the death certificate.

5.2.3 The grant of a lease over the Nail Bar to Polished Perfection Ltd

Polished Perfection Ltd's solicitor is reviewing the official copies for the Salon because the lease over the Nail Bar will be granted out of this freehold title. The

1 s58 LRA 2002.

register of title in Section B shows that Style&Go Ltd is the proprietor of the Salon. This is as expected from the heads of terms, so no further investigation is required.

5.2.4 The assignment of the Nail Bar Lease to Gemma's Gels Ltd

Gemma's Gels Ltd's solicitor is reviewing the official copies for the Nail Bar. The register of title in Section B shows that Polished Perfection Ltd is the proprietor of the Nail Bar and that the Nail Bar has been registered with title absolute. You will recall from Chapter 2 that this means the leasehold title is guaranteed by HMLR and the freehold title does not need to be investigated.

5.3 Establishing which other rights and interests affect the land and will bind the buyer

We noted in Chapter 2 the estates and interests which a piece of land could be subject to and how these could bind a purchaser for value. It is essential for solicitors to be able to navigate these interests and work out, when the land is sold to a new purchaser, which of these rights and interests will bind the new purchaser and which they will take the land free from.

5.3.1 The priority rules in registered land

The priority rules are summarised below, but please see Chapter 2 for the full explanation of these rules. Please note that this book is concerned with the application of the priority rules to purchasers for value.[2]

Where the land is registered, any interest, whether legal or equitable, which is registered on the register of title for the land will bind a subsequent purchaser for value of the land.[3] Registered interests take priority in the order in which they are registered, so an interest registered before another takes priority over it even if it was created afterwards.

Further, an overriding interest under Schedule 3 of the LRA 2002 will bind a subsequent purchaser for value.[4]

All other interests, for example, an interest:

- which is not registered on the register of title for the land; and
- is not an overriding interest under Schedule 3 of the LRA 2002;

will *not* bind a purchaser for value of the land.

2 For other acquisitions, the priority rules are different; please see s28 LRA 2002.
3 s29 LRA 2002.
4 Ibid.

5.3.2 Checking for registered interests

As registered interests will automatically bind the purchaser for value, the register of title must be carefully reviewed to see if any interests affect the property. Where documents are referenced in the register of title but rights are not extracted, the underlying document will need to be obtained and reviewed.

Below, you will find a list of the interests registered against each of our registered titles, which will bind the purchaser for value. In Chapter 6, we will discuss how each of these issues should be dealt with.

5.3.2.1 André's acquisition of the House

The official copies reveal the following registered entries:

- B2: there is a restriction relating to a positive covenant.
- C1: there are unknown rights and covenants which affect the property.
- C2: there is a positive covenant in respect of maintenance payments relating to boundary features.[5]

5.3.2.2 Style&Go Ltd's acquisition of the Salon

The official copies reveal the following registered entries:

- B2: there is a restriction preventing the sale by a sole proprietor.
- B3: there is a restriction relating to a mortgage.
- B4: there is an indemnity covenant relating to the performance of a positive covenant.
- C1: the property is subject to a right of way.
- C2: the property is subject to a positive covenant to maintain a section of the land.
- C3: there is a restrictive covenant preventing building on the property.
- C4 and C5: there is a mortgage against the property.

5.3.2.3 The grant of a lease over the Nail Bar to Polished Perfection Ltd

The official copies reveal the following registered entries:

- B2: a restriction in respect of the performance of a positive covenant.
- C1: the property is subject to a right of way.
- C2: the property is subject to a positive covenant to maintain a section of the land.
- C3: the property is subject to a restrictive covenant preventing building on the property.

5 According to the Land Registration Rules 2003 (rule 64(1)), positive covenants should be noted in the Proprietorship Register (Register B). In practice, they are often noted in the Charges Register (Register C).

As the Nail Bar will only be on the first floor of the Salon, not all these entries will be relevant to the Nail Bar. This will be discussed in Chapter 6.

5.3.2.4 Assignment of the Nail Bar Lease to Gemma's Gels Ltd

The official copies reveal the following registered entries:

- C1: the property is subject to a restrictive covenant preventing building on the property.

5.3.3 Checking for overriding interests

Interests which are not registered on the official copy register of title can still bind a purchaser for value if they are ***overriding interests*** under Schedule 3 of LRA 2002.

Some of the key[6] overriding interests for the purposes of this book are:

- leases of seven years or less;
- interests of people in actual occupation of the land; and
- legal easements.

In order to identify any overriding interests affecting the land, the buyer's solicitor may use a combination of methods:

- requesting information from the seller, by way of pre-contract enquiries;
- undertaking an LLC1 search; and
- recommending that the buyer undertakes a physical inspection of the land, for example, to ensure that there is no one in actual occupation.

These will be explored further in Chapters 7 and 9.

Chapter 5 revision points

- The buyer of registered land must establish that the seller can transfer the legal and beneficial title to the land by checking that the seller is registered as the proprietor of the estate on the title register.
- The buyer will take the land subject to any interests already registered against the estate and any overriding interests contained within Schedule 3 of the LRA 2002.

6 The full list can be found at Schedule 3 LRA 2002.

6 Analysing the entries arising from title investigation

6.1 Chapter overview

Chapters 4 and 5 explored the process of how to investigate title to land. This chapter examines some of the key issues and entries which may arise during an investigation of title, what they mean for a buyer and how a buyer's solicitor can deal with them.

This chapter is relevant to all freehold and leasehold transactions.

This chapter in the context of our Transactions

Now that title to the properties has been investigated by the buyer's solicitor, the solicitors for the various buyers must analyse the issues identified during that process in respect of each Transaction and take any necessary action.

You may wish to refer back to the title documentation you used in Chapters 4 and 5 whilst working through this chapter.

DOI: 10.4324/9781032711508-8

6.2 Excluded rights

The deeds or title register may indicate that mines and minerals located under the land do not form part of the property. This means they belong to someone else. This should be reported to your client so that their surveyor can investigate further and advise whether this is likely to impact their development plans.

6.3 Rights benefitting the land

The deeds or title register may indicate that the land benefits from rights over someone else's land. Common examples of rights benefitting the land include easements, for example:

- a right of way over neighbouring property;
- a right to light; or
- a right to lay or use pipes or cables under neighbouring land.

In unregistered land, these will usually be clear from the title deeds. In registered land, anything benefitting the property is registered in the ***Property Register*** of the register of title.

The deeds to the Car Park contain a right of way over Sheep Street for the benefit of the Car Park. This right of way will need to be investigated to:

- ensure that it is adequate for Style&Go Ltd's requirements. For example, is it the only access to the Car Park, and are there any restrictions on access? This can be ascertained by making enquiries of the seller and by doing a highways search;
- check whether there are any maintenance responsibilities which come with the right, for example, a responsibility to contribute towards annual upkeep costs. This can be ascertained by making enquiries of the seller; and
- check that the right of way is registered against the land it burdens, by doing a SIM search against the burdened land and reviewing the relevant title register. If the burdened land is not registered, the buyer's solicitor should check that there is a caution against first registration by doing an OS1 search against the burdened land, and apply to register a caution if one is not registered.

Once Style&Go Ltd's solicitors have a better understanding of the right of way, they will be able to report on it to Style&Go Ltd.

6.4 Rights burdening the land

The deeds or register of title may indicate that the land is burdened by rights or interests which benefit other pieces of land. Common examples of rights burdening the land include easements, for example:

- a piece of neighbouring land has a right of way over the land; or
- neighbouring land has the right to run pipes and cables under the land.

6.4.1 The House

The House is burdened by unknown rights[1] contained in a conveyance which HMLR does not have a copy of – see entry C1 of the register of title. This means that someone could have rights over the House, but the nature and extent of the rights are unknown.

This could be problematic because:

1. a previous proprietor of the House may have interfered with one or more of these rights. Once André becomes the proprietor, he will be liable for any interferences, even if they occurred in the past; or
2. André may do something with the land which unknowingly interferes with someone else's right; they may take action against him to prevent the interference, or they may try to recover compensation from him.

In order to find out more about what these rights could be, André's solicitor could raise an enquiry with Michael's estate's solicitor. André's solicitor will need to report this title defect to him and explore obtaining insurance to protect André from the financial implications of enforcement.

6.4.2 The Salon

The Salon is burdened by a right of way on foot over the land hatched grey on the registered plan, for the benefit of the building next door, 19 High Street – see entry C1 on the title register.

Style&Go Ltd's solicitor will need to make enquiries of Neeta's solicitors about the nature of this right of way, but it can be assumed for now that this is an alleyway running between the two buildings. According to the title plan, the alleyway belongs to the Salon, but the next-door neighbours at number 19 have a right to use it (e.g. to bring bins to the front of the property). Style&Go Ltd's solicitor will need to report this to Style&Go Ltd so that they are aware of it.

This right of way will not affect the Nail Bar as it does not overlap with the Nail Bar demise, which is limited to the first floor of the building.

6.5 Restrictive covenants

A restrictive covenant is one which prevents a landowner from doing something on their land. The burden of restrictive covenants runs with the land, which means that when a piece of land is sold which is subject to a restrictive covenant – for example, not to use the land for any purpose involving the sale of alcohol – that obligation will automatically bind the buyer. Upon completion of the purchase by

1 And covenants – see Section 6.5.1.

the buyer, they will become liable for any breaches of that covenant, whether past or future, and can be sued by the person with the benefit of that covenant (the person who owns the land which benefits from the covenant).

6.5.1 The House

The House is burdened by unknown covenants[2] contained in a conveyance which HMLR does not have a copy of – see entry C1 of the register of title. This means that André will be obliged to comply with covenants, but the content of those covenants is unknown.

This could be problematic for the following reasons:

1. a previous proprietor of the House may have breached one of the covenants – upon completion of his purchase, André will become liable for this breach and could be pursued by the person with the benefit of the covenant; and
2. André may himself unwittingly breach one or more of the covenants, again leaving him vulnerable to action from the person with the benefit of the covenant.

In order to find out more about what these covenants could be, André's solicitor could raise an enquiry with Michael's estate's solicitor. André's solicitor should also enquire about whether these covenants have ever been enforced by the person with the benefit. André's solicitor will need to report this title defect to him and explore the possibility of insuring against enforcement of an unknown breach.

6.5.2 The Salon

The Salon is subject to a restrictive covenant not to build – see entry C3 in the register of title. We know that this has been breached because an extension has been constructed on the land. Upon completion of Style&Go Ltd's purchase, Style&Go Ltd will become liable for this breach of covenant, and the owner of the land benefitting from the covenant (in this case, Charles Bainbridge or his successor in title (if he has disposed of the land)) can take action against Style&Go Ltd in respect of the breach.

Sometimes it is possible for the current proprietor to rectify the breach before completion. Short of removing the extension (which is not desirable for a number of reasons), the breach most likely cannot be rectified in this scenario. One option for Style&Go Ltd would be to procure insurance to cover the financial risk of being sued for the breach. Style&Go Ltd could request that Neeta pay for this insurance, as the breach was committed during her ownership of the land. As Style&Go Ltd intends to keep the extension, this means that they will continue to breach the

2 And rights – see Section 6.4.1.

restrictive covenant not to build. Neeta's solicitor may therefore negotiate that Style&Go Ltd contribute to the cost of insurance on the basis that Style&Go Ltd will continue to breach the covenant.

Regarding past and future breaches of restrictive covenants, as an alternative to insurance, the person with the benefit of the covenant can be approached to release the land from the burden of the covenant. This could be an option in respect of the restrictive covenant not to build on the title to the Salon because we know that Charles Bainbridge (or his successor in title) has the benefit of this covenant. Please note that once the person with the benefit has been approached, insurance will no longer be available (as this approach would constitute 'tipping off'), so this must be considered carefully. As a last resort, an application can be made to the Upper Tribunal (Lands Chamber) to modify or discharge a covenant, but please note that the time and expense (and lack of certainty as to a particular outcome) are likely to make this an impractical option for most clients.

If Neeta is willing to pay for the insurance policy, then this is likely the lowest-risk option for Style&Go Ltd. Style&Go Ltd's solicitors should open negotiations with Neeta's solicitors about her paying for the policy and, if Neeta agrees to pay, this should be included as a special condition in the contract; this will give Style&Go Ltd a contractual remedy against Neeta if it is not complied with.

The existing breach of the restrictive covenant on the Salon title will not affect the Nail Bar as the extension does not overlap with the Nail Bar demise. However, Polished Perfection Ltd and Gemma's Gels Ltd' solicitors should inform them that the restrictive covenant prohibiting building does affect the Nail Bar demise, and therefore, they are not permitted to build on the Nail Bar.

6.5.3 The Car Park

The Land Charges Search against previous owners of the Car Park revealed that Urban Spaces Ltd, FPC Storage Ltd, and Regener8 Ltd all have D(ii) land charges (restrictive covenants) registered against them, as noted in Chapter 4. These are likely to be the restrictive covenants contained within clause 2 of the 1956 Conveyance, which restricted the use of the Car Park and restricted building on the Car Park. There is nothing on the land to suggest that these covenants have previously been breached, and Style&Go Ltd is not planning to build on the Car Park so is unlikely to breach these restrictive covenants in the future.

Style&Go Ltd's solicitor will request a copy of the land charges to verify that they do relate to those restrictive covenants. An enquiry should be raised with Urban Spaces Ltd's solicitor to confirm that there has not been a breach of these covenants in the past. The covenants should be reported to Style&Go Ltd so that they are aware of them.

6.6 Positive covenants

A ***positive covenant*** is one which requires a landowner to undertake some sort of positive action on the land, for example, to construct a fence or to pay towards the upkeep of a wall. Generally, the burden of positive covenants does not run with the land, which means when a piece of land is sold which is subject to a positive covenant, that obligation will not automatically bind the prospective purchaser.[3] We will examine below two different mechanisms for ensuring that positive covenants do bind a subsequent purchaser of the land.

6.6.1 The House: positive covenants protected by a restriction

At entry C2 of the title register for the House, we are told that clause 11.1 of the transfer on 1 November 1991 from Joanne Bates to Alan Wright contained a positive covenant to 'observe and perform the stipulations and conditions set out in Schedule 1'.

Schedule 1 is extracted in the title register, and we can see that it contains a list of covenants. The first is a positive covenant to contribute up to 25% of the annual costs of maintaining boundary features. It is likely that the House and the land adjoining it used to be one property owned by Joanne Bates, that the land was divided and Alan Wright purchased the House. Upon doing so, Alan Wright agreed to contribute to the cost of maintaining boundary features between the House and the land retained by Joanne Bates.

One common mechanism[4] to ensure that any existing positive covenants will bind future purchasers of the land is to place a restriction on the register of title, which prevents dispositions of the land from being registered unless the prospective purchaser has entered into a deed of covenant, with the beneficiary of the positive covenant, covenanting to perform the positive covenant.

We can see this on the title register for the House: entry B2 contains a restriction preventing the registration of a disposition of the House without a certificate confirming that clause 11.1 of the Transfer dated 1 November 1991 between Joanne Bates and Alan Wright (the **1991 Transfer**) has been complied with.

In order to understand the obligations contained within clause 11.1 of the 1991 Transfer and ensure compliance with them, André's solicitor will request a copy of this document to carefully review clause 11.1; the details of this clause are also replicated in the ***Charges Register*** (at entry C2).

3 There are some exceptions – please see 'Essential Land Law for SQE1', available from Routledge.
4 The other common mechanism is to create a chain of indemnity, which is discussed in Section 6.6.2.

Entry C2 tells us that when Alan Wright purchased the Property from Joanne Bates, he covenanted to the following:

1. to contribute up to 25% of the annual cost of maintaining the boundary features between the House and Joanne's retained land[5];
2. not to dispose of the House without first ensuring that a new purchaser entered into the same covenants directly with Joanne Bates or with the successors in title to her property; and
3. to enter a restriction on the register of title, which would prevent him from disposing of the property without first ensuring that a new purchaser entered into the same covenants.

Importantly, it is not *just* the covenant to contribute to maintenance costs which Alan Wright had to ensure that prospective purchasers signed up to; it is all three of the above covenants. This means that every new purchaser promises to make sure that the next is on the hook for these covenants, which essentially creates a chain and means that it is impossible to dispose of the House without a new purchaser entering into a deed of covenant directly with Joanne Bates or her successors in title. This is shown in Figure 6.1.

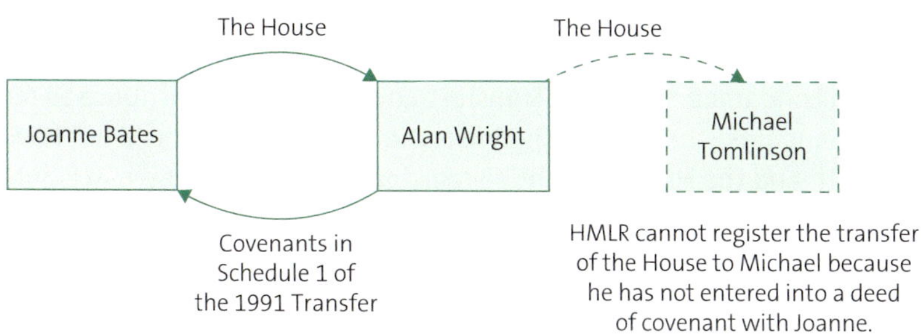

Figure 6.1 Illustrating how the House could not have been registered to Michael if he did not enter into a deed of covenant with Joanne.

The restriction was registered on the title on 12 August 1994, which means Michael must have entered into a deed of covenant directly with Joanne Bates or her successors in title when he purchased the House. This can be seen in Figure 6.2.

5 Interestingly, even if this weren't protected with a restriction, this could fall within the *Halsall v Brizell* [1957] Ch 169 exception to the rule that the burden of positive covenants cannot run with the land.

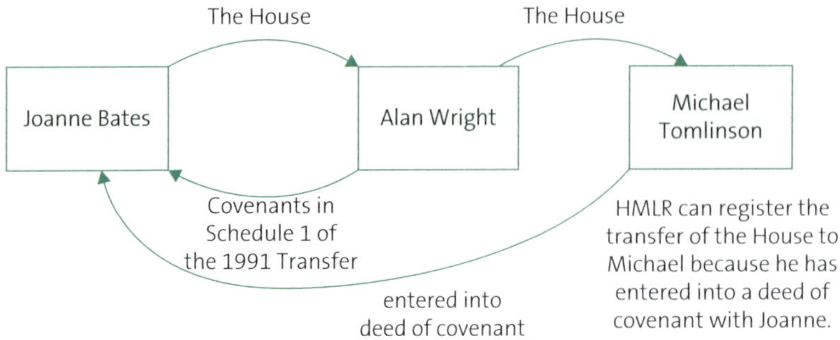

Figure 6.2 Illustrating how the House was registered to Michael because he entered into a deed of covenant with Joanne.

André will be liable for all breaches of the covenant, whether past or future, once he becomes the proprietor of the House. It is therefore important that his solicitor find out whether there have been any breaches of that covenant to date (e.g. perhaps Michael Tomlinson has missed one or more annual maintenance payments) and ensure that this is rectified before completion. André's solicitor will need to report the covenant to André to ensure he understands his obligation to contribute towards this cost.

André will need to enter into a deed of covenant with Joanne Bates (who still owns the Retained Land under the 1991 Transfer), covenanting to contribute as required under Covenant 1 in Schedule 1; otherwise, the restriction at B2 will not have been complied with and the House cannot be registered to him, as shown in Figure 6.3.

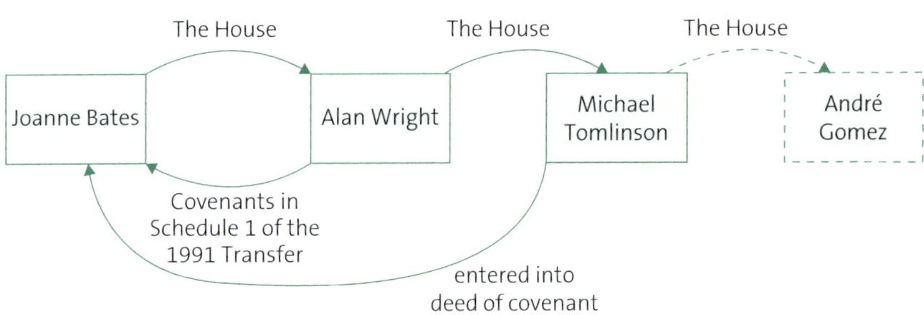

Figure 6.3 Illustrating how the House cannot be registered to André if he does not enter into a deed of covenant with Joanne.

In order for André's purchase of the House to be registered, a conveyancer will need to produce a certificate certifying that the restriction has been complied with. The effect of this is shown in Figure 6.4.

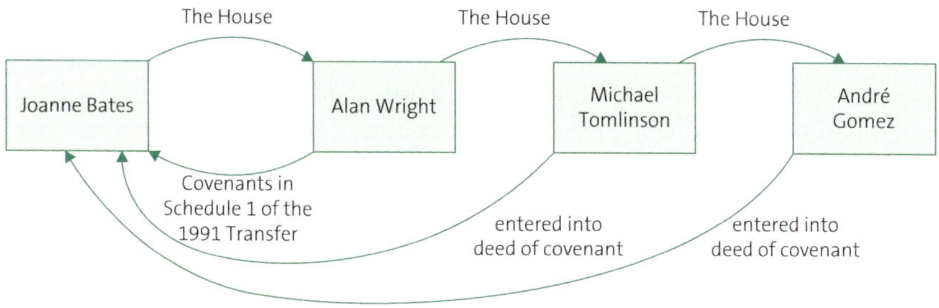

Figure 6.4 Illustrating how the House can be registered to André if he enters into a deed of covenant with Joanne.

In addition, the transfer from Michael's estate to Andre will need to include a covenant from André to Michael's estate covenanting to observe and perform the covenants contained in C2 of the Charges Register. This will then require André to pass on the covenant to a future buyer if he sells the House (as required under covenant 2 of Schedule 1), as the restriction will remain on the title register (as per covenant 3 of Schedule 1). André's requirement to enter into this covenant will be included in the contract for sale.

6.6.2 The Salon: positive covenants protected by an indemnity covenant

There is a positive covenant at entry C2 of the title register to the Salon which requires the strip of land coloured brown (hatched grey on the title plan) to be kept in good repair so that it remains safely passable on foot. This covenant was imposed in 1956 in the conveyance from Vince Francis Moon to Norman Jones, and complements the right of way which was created by this conveyance.[6] There is privity of contract between Vince and Norman, and Vince (or his successors in title) can pursue Norman for compensation if this covenant is breached. This is shown in Figure 6.5.

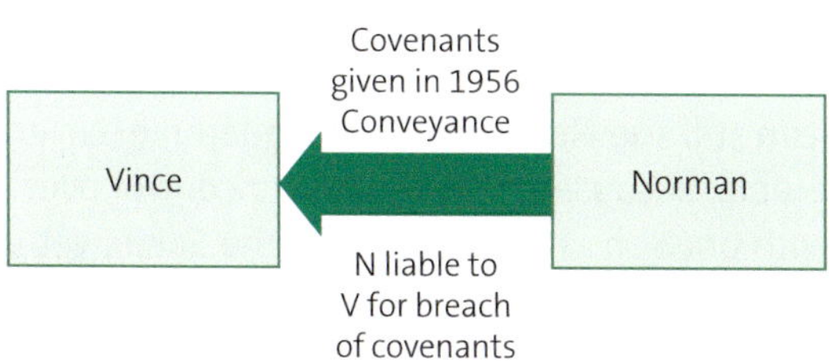

Figure 6.5 Privity of contract between Vince and Norman.

6 The relevant strip of land subject to the covenant is the same strip of land subject to the right of way discussed in Section 6.4.2.

When Norman disposed of the Salon, the conveyance effecting this disposal must have contained an indemnity covenant: a promise to indemnify Norman if the new owner (let's assume this was Charles Bainbridge) breached the covenant and Vince sued Norman in respect thereof. This is shown in Figure 6.6.

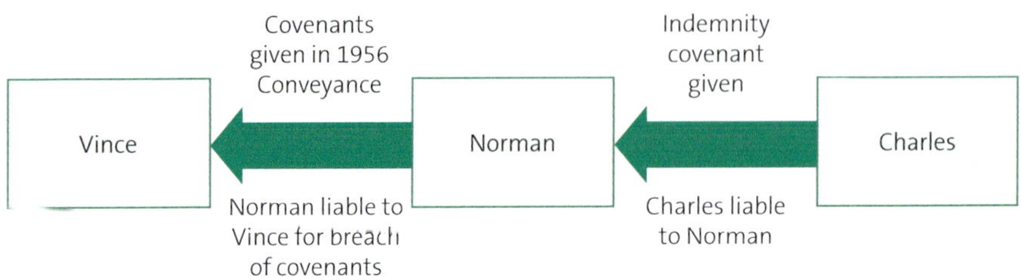

Figure 6.6 How Norman can recover from Charles if Vince sues Norman for a breach of the positive covenant.

This indemnity covenant created the chain of indemnity that we can now see at entry B4 of the Salon's title register, which requires Ansar and Neeta to perform the positive covenant at entry C2 of the title register and to indemnify Charles Bainbridge if they fail to do so. This is shown in Figure 6.7.

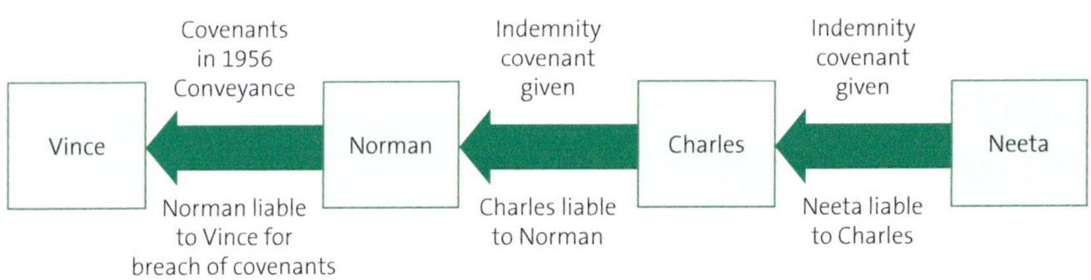

Figure 6.7 The chain of indemnity from Neeta to Norman.

Under the doctrine of privity of contract, when Neeta sells the Salon to Style&Go Ltd, she will remain contractually liable to Charles. If Style&Go Ltd breaches the covenant, Charles can still sue Neeta under the indemnity covenant she gave. This leaves Neeta vulnerable, because she will have no control over whether the covenant is complied with once she has disposed of the Salon, yet she will be financially liable to Charles if it isn't. This is shown in Figure 6.8.

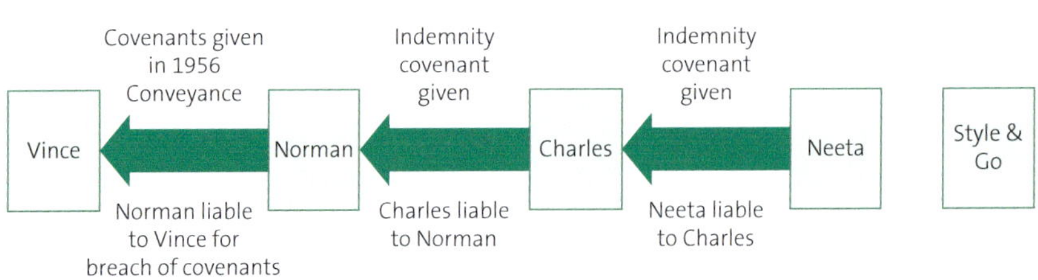

Figure 6.8 Illustrating Neeta's ongoing liability to Charles.

Therefore, Neeta will want to ensure that the responsibility for compliance with the covenant and the obligation to indemnify her if it is breached is passed on to Style&Go Ltd. This way, if Charles pursues Neeta, she can recover any monies paid out to Charles from Style&Go Ltd, as shown in Figure 6.9. If Style&Go Ltd ever sells the Salon, they are likely to require the same from a future buyer.

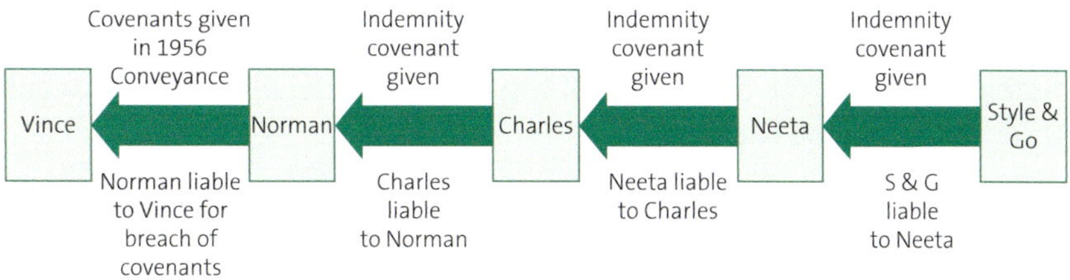

Figure 6.9 The chain of indemnity extended to include Style&Go Ltd.

Style&Go Ltd will be liable for all breaches of the covenant, whether past or future, once they are the proprietor of the Salon. It is therefore important that their solicitor find out whether there have been any breaches of that covenant to date (e.g. perhaps Neeta has allowed the accessway to fall into disrepair) and ensure that these are rectified before completion.

Style&Go Ltd's solicitor will need to report the covenant to Style&Go Ltd to ensure they understand their obligation to keep the accessway in good repair and safely passable on foot. Style&Go Ltd's solicitor will also need to consider whether their client's plans for the property will likely result in a breach of that covenant. In this situation, there are three options:

1. Style&Go Ltd could insure against their likely breach of the covenant;
2. Style&Go Ltd could ask Charles Bainbridge (as the person who has the right to sue if it is breached) to release the land from that covenant; or[7]
3. Style&Go Ltd could apply to the Upper Tribunal (Lands Chamber) for modification or discharge of the covenant.[8]

In this case, Style&Go Ltd intends to keep the accessway passable; as well as its being used by the occupiers of number 19, Style&Go Ltd will use it to access the front of the property, for example, for taking out refuse.

As the positive covenant relates to the land outside the Salon, it does not overlap with the demise of the Nail Bar.

7 But note that this step should only be explored if insurance has been ruled out. Once the person with the benefit has been approached, insurance is unlikely to be available.
8 But note that the time and expense of doing so are likely to make this an impractical option.

6.7 Mortgages

Many purchasers will acquire land with the assistance of a loan, known as a mortgage. The mortgagee (the lending institution, for example, the bank) will take a charge over the land, which gives it powers of sale if the owner defaults on the loan.

For unregistered land, the bank would take physical possession of the title deeds in respect of the first mortgages (e.g. those ranking highest). This gives the bank absolute control over the disposition of the land. Subsequent mortgages would be registered as a C(i) land charge.[9]

For registered land, all mortgages will be registered in the Charges Register of the title register. They also typically appear as a restriction in the Proprietorship Register, preventing registration of any disposition without the consent of the lending bank.

Ansar and Neeta purchased the Salon in July 1993 with the assistance of a mortgage. This is registered against the property in the Charges Register (entries C4 and C5) and as a restriction in the Proprietorship Register (entry B3) on the title register.

Before the transfer to Style&Go Ltd can be registered, Neeta's mortgage must be discharged, and the restriction must be removed from the register. This is done by way of a DS1 form, which is sent to HMLR along with the application to register the transfer of the property from Neeta to Style&Go Ltd. The DS1 form confirms that the mortgage has been discharged and permits the entries to be removed from the register of title.

In practical terms, the mortgage most likely cannot be paid off until the day of completion as Neeta will need the money she receives from Style&Go Ltd in order to give this to the bank to discharge the mortgage. However, Style&Go Ltd will not wish to pay that sum of money to Neeta without some reassurance that she will use it to discharge the mortgage. Therefore, Neeta's solicitors will give an ***undertaking*** to Style&Go Ltd's solicitors to cover the following points:

1. on receipt of the money from Style&Go Ltd upon completion, to pay to Secure Trust Bank the money required by them to discharge the mortgage; and
2. to send to Style&Go Ltd's solicitors a signed DS1 Form as soon as possible.

See Chapter 20 for more details on discharging this mortgage.

9 See Chapter 4 for a discussion of the effect of land charges.

6.8 Interests arising under a trust

Where the equitable interest in land is held under a trust, this interest can constitute an overriding interest which will bind a purchaser for value, under Schedule 3 LRA 2002.[10] However, if a purchaser buys the land from two trustees, any equitable interests in the property which were being held on trust by those trustees will transfer into the proceeds of sale. The beneficiaries under the trust will receive proceeds of sale to the value of their equitable interest, and the buyer will take the property free from the trust. This is known as overreaching.

Overreaching is usually ensured by the inclusion of a restriction on the title register. Where co-owners hold the equitable interest in the land as tenants-in-common,[11] you will see the following restriction on the Proprietorship Register:

> No disposition by a sole proprietor of the registered estate (except a trust corporation) under which capital money arises is to be registered unless authorised by an order of the court.

We can see this restriction on the title register for the Salon (entry B2). We discussed at Section 5.2.2 of Chapter 5 that Neeta appears to be the sole seller, despite the Salon being registered to both her and Ansar, and that one possible explanation for this was that Ansar had passed away. This restriction prevents Neeta from disposing of the Salon alone.

Chapter 6 revision points

- Interests affecting the property should be investigated and reported to the buyer.
- The Property Register, or the title deeds, may show that mines and minerals are excluded from the title.
- The Property Register, or the title deeds, may show that the property benefits from rights over neighbouring land. Enquiries of the seller can provide information about the nature of these rights.
- The Charges Register may show rights burdening the land which will bind the buyer. Enquiries of the seller can provide information about the nature of these rights.
- A restrictive covenant may be registered in the Charges Register or the Land Charges Register and will bind a buyer of the affected land. A buyer may require insurance to mitigate against the risk of being pursued for a breach committed by a previous owner. If a buyer cannot ensure future compliance

10 Also, please note Schedule 1 LRA 2002, which has been discussed in Chapter 4 in Section 4.3.1.3.

11 In fact, this wording is automatically applied by HMLR when land is purchased by more than one person, unless those co-purchasers expressly declare that they are to hold it as beneficial joint tenants.

with a covenant, then they could explore insurance, seeking release by the person with the benefit of the covenant, or discharging the covenant in court.

- Positive covenants cannot bind third parties as a matter of law, but it is common to see in the Proprietorship Register either an indemnity covenant or a restriction relating to a deed of covenant, both of which indirectly require the buyer to comply with the positive covenant. Any indemnity covenant will need to be replicated in the transfer to the buyer, and any restriction will need to be satisfied before the transfer to the buyer can be registered.
- A mortgage over registered land will appear in the Charges Register and is commonly protected by a restriction in the Proprietorship Register. In unregistered land, a lender may hold the title deeds, or a mortgage may be registered as a land charge. Buyers will seek an undertaking from the seller's solicitor to discharge the mortgage on completion and provide the relevant paperwork to enable the buyer to register the transfer.
- Trust interests in property do not appear on the title register or title deeds but can constitute an overriding interest. Payment to two trustees ensures these interests are overreached, and it is common to see a restriction in the Proprietorship Register requiring this.

7 Searches against the property

7.1 Chapter overview

Undertaking due diligence on a property includes undertaking searches against the property. Searches are undertaken by the buyer's solicitor and help reveal information about the land which is not discovered by the title investigation process.

This chapter explores the key searches which are undertaken during a property transaction. Some general information about each search is provided, followed by an analysis of the various search results and a discussion of any required follow-up action.

This chapter is relevant to all freehold and leasehold transactions.

This chapter in the context of our Transactions

Solicitors for each buyer have now completed the title investigation; they must now conduct and analyse searches against the relevant property and take any necessary action as a result of such searches.

You may wish to refer to the following documentation as relevant for each Transaction whilst working through this chapter:

- SIM
- LLC1
- CON29
- Highways search
- Drainage and water search
- Environmental search
- Flood search
- Chancel repair search
- Company search
- Utilities search
- Telecoms search

DOI: 10.4324/9781032711508-9

7.2 Search of the index map

The index map is a map of all the land which is registered or due to be registered. Prospective purchasers can send a plan of the land they are planning to buy, and HMLR will check it against the index map. This is known as a search of the index map (or **SIM**). HMLR will confirm whether any of the land identified on the plan is:

- registered, including the relevant title number and type of tenure;
- unregistered;
- subject to an application for first registration; or
- subject to a caution against registration.

A SIM should be conducted in all transactions. In practice, the SIM is often conducted at the start of the transaction as it informs which register of title needs to be reviewed as part of the title investigation, or whether the land is unregistered. However, it can also be conducted after title investigation to confirm that the correct register has been deduced and reviewed.

It can be applied for using the application form available online, which is sent to HMLR. A plan can be supplied as part of the application if the property does not have a recognised postal description or if there is any doubt regarding the extent of the property.[1]

Please review the SIM result for each Transaction in the relevant Appendix.

The SIM results for our Transactions relating to registered land revealed the following:

- *André's acquisition of the House*. The House is freehold and registered under title number EG132465.
- *Style&Go Ltd's acquisition of the Salon*. The Salon is freehold and registered under title number EG576798.
- *The grant of a lease to Polished Perfection Ltd*. The Nail Bar is going to be located on the first floor of the Salon. It is not yet registered with its own leasehold title. The Salon is freehold and registered under title number EG576798.
- *Assignment of the Nail Bar Lease to Gemma's Gels Ltd*. The Nail Bar is leasehold and registered under title number WX727338.

In all cases above, the title number reflects the extent of the property expected by the solicitor and which has already been reviewed, and there are no parts of the property the buyer is expecting to acquire which are registered under a different title number or are unregistered. The solicitor will note this in the report on title.

1 See HMLR Practice Guide 10: Official search of the index map.

The SIM result for the Car Park revealed that the land is unregistered and there are no applications for first registration. This is as expected, and Style&Go Ltd's solicitor will note this in the report on title.

7.3 Local Land Charge Search: the LLC1

A Local Land Charges Search is a search of the Local Land Charges Register. This reveals local land charges on the land, which are restrictions on the use of land which are imposed under statutory powers (such as planning permission). A local land charge is not the same as a land charge, and the Local Land Charges Register is not the same as the Land Charges Register.[2]

A Local Land Charges Search should be undertaken in every transaction. The Local Land Charges Registers used to be kept and maintained by each local authority. These registers are now gradually being transferred to HMLR, and eventually, local authorities will no longer maintain them; instead, HMLR will be solely responsible for these. Currently, whilst this process of transferring maintenance is ongoing, the search may need to be made with HMLR or with the relevant local authority.[3]

We discuss below some of the key information you may see on an LLC1 search result.[4]

Please review the LLC1 search result for each Transaction in the relevant Appendix.

7.3.1 Planning information

7.3.1.1 Planning permission granted

An LLC1 search result will give information about any planning permission that has been granted in respect of the land. This is the case for the Salon, Car Park, and Nail Bar, and these are explored in Chapter 8.

7.3.1.2 Article 4 Directions

An LLC1 search result will also note if there is an Article 4 Direction in place affecting the property. An Article 4 Direction disapplies parts of the permitted development legislation. We can see this on the LLC1 result for the Car Park, and this is explored fully in Chapter 8.

7.3.1.3 Modifications and revocations

Sometimes, planning permission is granted and is then modified or entirely revoked. If property has already been developed or if there are development plans,

2 For land charges and their register, see Chapter 4.

3 You can check where to make a search using the Government website.

4 We have selected the key entries for the purposes of this book. Please see the Government website for the 12 categories of local land charge noted on the Local Land Charges Register.

information about modifications or revocations of the permission is essential to understand the status of the planning permission. Solicitors acting for the buyer will need to obtain a copy of the planning permissions and review these carefully against completed developments or development plans.

7.3.2 Tree Preservation Orders

The LLC1 search results will indicate if there is a Tree Preservation Order (**TPO**) affecting the property. A TPO prevents a tree on the land from being felled. The search result for the House reveals that there is a TPO affecting the House. André's solicitor will need to do further investigations (such as raising enquiries with the seller) to identify the relevant tree and then report this to André so that he knows he must not remove the tree as part of any garden maintenance work.

7.3.3 Smoke Control Orders

A Smoke Control Order (**SCO**) restricts the use of non-smokeless fuels in fireplaces. If an SCO is in place affecting the property, then this will be revealed by the LLC1 search; this was the case for the House. André's solicitor will report this to him so that he knows only to burn certain fuels in the fireplace in the House.

7.3.4 Financial charges

There may be financial charges payable in relation to the property. For example, they may relate to the adoption of an estate road, and your client may be liable to pay this charge once they are the proprietor of the property.

All future charges should be reported to the client, and enquiries should be raised with the seller to check whether the payment of charges is up to date. If a current or past charge is unpaid, the seller should be required to pay this before completion (and this should be a condition of the contract) or reduce the purchase price accordingly.

7.3.5 Compulsory purchase orders

Compulsory purchase orders (**CPO**s) allow the local authority to acquire the land. It is helpful for prospective purchasers to know if the local area has been subject to CPOs, as this can indicate whether the land is being developed and the likelihood of a future CPO being made. Solicitors must report any CPOs to the client.

7.3.6 Conservation area designation orders

Conservation area designation orders made since 31 August 1974 will appear on the LLC1 search result. These are orders which specify that property is located within a conservation area. Additional restrictions apply to land which is within a conservation area, which may make future development of the property more challenging. These must therefore be reported to the client.

7.3.6.1 *Listed building status*

If property is a listed building, it will appear on the LLC search result. Additional restrictions apply to land which is designated as a listed building, which may make future development of the property more challenging. These must therefore be reported to the client.

7.4 Standard enquiries of the local authority: the CON29

Standard enquiries of the local authority ask the local authority a standard set of questions about the property and the local area. They are undertaken in all transactions. They can be made directly to the local authority using form CON29.

We discuss below some of the key information you may see on a CON29 search result.[5]

Please review the CON29 search result for each Transaction in the relevant Appendix.

7.4.1 Planning permission

The CON29 search discloses information about the planning status of the property.

7.4.1.1 *Planning and building decisions and applications*

Question 1.1 of the CON29 result tells us information about planning and building decisions and pending applications affecting the property. There are relevant entries on the result for each of our Transactions, and these are explored in Chapter 8.

7.4.1.2 *Notices, orders, directions, and proceedings*

We already know from the Car Park LLC search result that there is an Article 4 Direction in place in respect of the Car Park. Question 3.9(j) of the CON29 result also reveals this information. This is explored in Chapter 8.

7.4.1.3 *Whether any planning permission or building regulation applications have been refused*

A refusal of planning permission or building regulations applications indicates that there may be restrictions on how the land can be used. This is important information for all types of buyer, as it may limit how they can use or develop the property. A solicitor acting for the buyer should report this to their client and check

5 We have selected the key entries for the purposes of this book. Please see a CON29 (available from the Law Society) for the full list of possible entries.

whether this could interfere with the buyer's plans for using or developing the property.

7.4.1.4 Whether any enforcement action for breach of planning permission has been commenced

This reveals whether enforcement action has been taken in respect of a breach of planning control. This is important to know because once a purchase is complete, the new proprietor becomes liable for any breaches of planning control. A solicitor for the buyer must find out what the breach was and what enforcement action has been taken. If instructed to do so, they may lead relevant negotiations to reduce the purchase price in order to compensate for the fact that the enforcement action may be expensive.

7.4.1.5 Whether any enforcement action for a contravention of building regulations has been commenced

This enquiry tells us whether enforcement action has been taken in respect of a breach of building regulations. This is important to know, because once a purchase is complete, the new proprietor becomes liable for any contraventions of building regulations, and alterations to the property may be required in order to rectify the problem, which could be costly. A solicitor for the buyer must find out what the breach was, and what enforcement action has been taken. If instructed to do so, they may lead relevant negotiations to reduce the purchase price in order to compensate for the fact that the enforcement action may be expensive.

7.4.2 Roads and public rights of way

Question 2.1 of the CON29 search tells us about roads close to the property, such as whether they are adopted. Adopted roads are maintainable by the local authority at its own expense and can be used by anyone, as opposed to private roads, which must be maintained by and at the expense of the relevant landowner.

The CON29 for the House revealed that Cob Lane is adopted; André's solicitor will do a highways search to confirm that Cob Lane abuts the House and that there aren't any private roads in between Cob Lane and the House, and then report to André on the access.

The CON29 for the Transactions on the High Street, Barnford, revealed that the High Street is adopted. Again, solicitors will check that the High Street directly abuts the Salon and report to their client on access.

We know that access over Sheep Street and Needle Alley is required in order to access the Car Park. The fact that neither of these roads appears on the search as having been adopted tells us that they are likely private.

Private roads require a right of way for any third party wishing to use it – we know from the title investigation that the Car Park has the benefit of a right of way over Sheep Street. Needle Alley is a private road forming part of the Car Park; therefore, a right of way is not required, but Needle Alley will be maintainable by Style&Go Ltd at its own expense. If Needle Alley were to be adopted, it would be revealed by this enquiry. This would be relevant to Style&Go Ltd because owners of private roads which are subject to adoption can incur the costs of bringing the road up to an adoptable standard.

Style&Go Ltd's solicitor will undertake a highways search to make sure that the High Street directly abuts Sheep Street, and will report to Style&Go Ltd on the access. They will need to raise an enquiry with Urban Spaces Ltd's solicitor in respect of the current maintenance arrangements and costs relating to Needle Alley and report on these to Style&Go Ltd.

7.4.3 Nearby railway schemes

Question 3.5 tells us about nearby railway schemes and reveals that there is to be a new railway built close-by to the properties on the High Street, Barnford. This can affect noise and pollution levels and could therefore be off-putting for residential purchasers. However, it may be good for commercial clients because it may make the hair salon and nail bar more accessible by public transport, bringing in more customers. The solicitors will report this to their clients.

7.4.4 Traffic schemes

Question 3.6 tells us about traffic schemes affecting the property and reveals that Main Street, near to the properties on the High Street, Barnford, is going to be pedestrianised. This is relevant for our buyers because pedestrian-only zones may affect how customers can access the hair salon and nail bar. Each buyer's solicitor will check the traffic scheme plans to ensure that vehicular access to the property will still be possible and will report to their client on these proposed traffic schemes.

7.4.5 Public rights of way

The CON29 also reveals whether members of the public have access rights over the property. Residential purchasers in particular may be put off by the prospect of a right of way running through their land. It may also restrict the development potential of the land. A solicitor for the buyer must report to their client about any current or proposed public rights of way abutting or crossing property and check whether this interferes with their client's plans for use or development of the property.

7.4.6 Community Infrastructure Levy

Community Infrastructure Levy (**CIL**) is a levy applied to new developments. If the buyer is planning to develop the land, it is helpful for them to know whether this levy will be payable. The solicitor for the buyer will need to report to the client and check whether this interferes with their plans for use or development of the property, and negotiate that any unpaid charges be paid by the seller before completion (or the purchase price reduced) – this agreement should be drafted into the sale contract.

7.4.7 Whether the land is in a conservation area

The CON29 will tell us whether the property is situated in a conservation area. As we saw in Section 7.3.6, this can limit or restrict the future development of the property, and the buyer's solicitor will need to report to client and check whether this interferes with their plans for use or development of the property.

7.4.8 Compulsory purchase orders

As noted in Section 7.3.5, CPOs allow the local authority to acquire the land. The response to this enquiry will indicate the likelihood of a future CPO being made which will affect the property. The solicitor for the buyer will need to report to client and check whether this interferes with their plans for use or development of the property.

7.4.9 Contaminated land

The CON29 will disclose whether there are any contaminated land notices or remediation notices attached to the land. A contaminated land notice or remediation notice indicates that contaminants have been found on the land. Liability for cleaning up the land could pass to the buyer and can be extremely costly. The buyer's solicitor will need to make further enquiries of the seller and undertake an environmental search to ascertain the scale of the issue. This will then need to be reported to and discussed with the buyer.

7.4.10 Whether the property is in a radon-affected area

Land in certain parts of the country contains high levels of radon, which can be harmful to health. This enquiry is helpful for ascertaining whether the property is likely to have high levels of radon. If property is in a high-radon area, the buyer's solicitor will need to undertake a radon search in respect of the property and report on this to the client.

7.5 Optional enquiries of the local authority: CON29O

When requesting the standard enquiries of the local authority, there are a number of optional enquiries which can be raised at the same time. These include enquiries about parks and countryside, urban development areas, and common land or town/village greens. The full list of questions is available from the Law Society. The search can be made through a local authority or private search provider using form CON29O.

The additional enquiries do not need to be raised in every transaction; it will depend on what is relevant. No additional enquiries were raised in respect of any of our Transactions.

7.6 Highways search

A highways search will reveal whether the named roads in the vicinity of the property are adopted or private. We know some of this information from the enquiries of the local authority, but the highways search includes a plan showing the precise location of these roads. This enables the buyer's solicitor to ascertain whether the adopted highway abuts the property or whether a right of way over private land is required in order to access the property.

A highways search should be undertaken in all transactions and can be made directly with the local authority, or by using a private search provider.

Please review the highways search result for each Transaction in the relevant Appendix.

The highways search for the House revealed that Cob Lane is an adopted highway and directly abuts the House. This means that André can access the House via the adopted highway without requiring access over any private roads. André's solicitor will report to him on the access.

The highways search for the properties on the High Street, Barnford, revealed that the High Street is an adopted highway which abuts the Salon. This means that staff and customers of the hair salon and nail bar can access the premises directly from the High Street.

It also confirms that Sheep Street and Needle Alley, both of which are required in order to access the Car Park, are not adopted. The High Street directly abuts Sheep Street, and Sheep Street directly abuts the Car Park. This means that the current right of way[6] enjoyed by the Car Park over Sheep Street is sufficient to enable users of the Car Park to access it from the High Street. If the plan had shown a gap between the High Street and Sheep Street (or between Sheep Street and the Car Park), then Style&Go Ltd's solicitors would have needed to find out who owned the land in that gap and arranged an additional right of access over it.

Style&Go Ltd intend for their staff and customers to be able to park in the Car Park, which would mean using the right of way. The right of way over Sheep Street was granted in 1956; unless there has been a radical change in the character of the Car Park, which has led to a substantial increase in the burden on Sheep Street, then staff

6 See Section 6.3 in Chapter 6.

and customers of the Salon and the Nail Bar will also be able to use the right of way to access the Car Park without any additional permission from the owners of Sheep Street. Style&Go Ltd's solicitors will need to make enquiries of Urban Spaces Ltd as to the extent of the use of Sheep Street to access the Car Park and then advise on whether additional permission is likely to be required from the owners of Sheep Street.

7.7 Drainage and water

A drainage and water search will reveal information about the supply of water to the property and the drainage of surface (rainwater) and foul water from the property into sewers. Solicitors for the buyer will look for the following information:

7.7.1 Whether surface water drains to a public sewer

If surface water does not drain to a public sewer, then the owner of the property is liable for the costs of maintaining the drains and sewers. They may also be liable for the costs of bringing the drains and sewers to an adoptable standard if they are adopted by the water authority in the future.

7.7.2 Whether foul water drains to a public sewer

If foul water does not drain to a public sewer, then the owner of the property is liable for the costs of maintaining the drains and sewers. They may also be liable for the costs of bringing the drains and sewers to an adoptable standard if they are adopted by the water authority in the future.

7.7.3 Whether there are public drains or sewers in the boundary of the property

Where there are public drains or sewers in the boundary of the property, the water authority has a right of access over the property to access the drains it owns, and the water authority's consent will be needed if development is to occur near to these drains.

7.7.4 Whether the property is connected to the mains water supply

Where property is not connected to the mains supply, water is supplied from a private natural source, such as a well or a spring. The water authority is not responsible for the quality of this water, but the local authority is responsible for ensuring that the water is of a drinking standard.

7.7.5 Our Transactions

Please review the drainage and water search for each Transaction in the relevant Appendix, which reveal that:

- surface water and foul water drain to a public sewer;
- there are no public drains or sewers in the boundaries of the property; and
- the property is connected to the mains water supply.

Each buyer's solicitor will report to their client that Westshire Water is responsible for maintaining the drains and sewers and for the quality of the water supplied to the relevant property.

7.8 Environmental searches

An environmental search can help assess the risk of there being contaminants on the land. This is an important issue for any prospective buyer because:

- it may be impossible to use or develop the land if it is contaminated, especially if planning permission is required (as any planning permission is likely to be conditional upon the remediation of the land);
- the land may be difficult to sell or mortgage if it is contaminated; and/or
- the buyer may be liable to clean up the land under the Contaminated Land Regime.

Cleaning up contaminated land can be very expensive. Therefore, it is essential for prospective buyers that they are informed if there is a risk that the land is contaminated.

A desktop environmental search is a computer-based search which reviews the past use of the land and reports on the likelihood of the land being contaminated based on its past use. If the desktop search identifies the property as being at risk of contaminants, a more detailed environmental survey can be undertaken, which can include a site visit and the testing of soil extracts to establish whether contaminants are present on the land.

The standard enquiries of the local authority can indicate whether there is an issue with contamination, but a desktop environmental search should be undertaken in all transactions. The search can be made using a dedicated search provider and is often made in combination with a flood search.

Please review the desktop environmental search result for each Transaction in the relevant Appendix, which reveals that for each property the risk of contaminants being present on the land is low based on its historical usage. Each buyer's solicitor will report the results to their client and will not recommend any further environmental surveys.

7.9 Flood searches

A flood search can inform the buyer as to whether the property is at risk of flooding. Flooding can occur in coastal areas and in properties close to rivers, but also when rainfall overwhelms the drainage capacity in an area, or when sewers become blocked. Therefore, the flood risk should always be considered.

There are a number of ways to assess the flood risk of an area:

- *Government agency information*: the Land Registry and the Environment Agency both provide flood risk assessments for areas based on postcode;
- *Desktop search*: some desktop searches will comment on the flood risk in addition to the risk of contaminants on the land; and
- *Specialist flood surveys*: if the initial options above indicate that flooding may be a concern, a specialist flood risk survey can be undertaken.

Please review the flood search results for each Transaction in the relevant Appendix.

The search results for the House revealed that the local area and the House have been unaffected by flooding. This will be reported to André, and no further flood surveys will be recommended.

The search results for the properties on the High Street, Barnford, revealed that the surrounding village has been affected by flooding previously but that the properties were unaffected. This will be reported to each client, and no further flood surveys will be recommended.

As the Nail Bar is on the first floor of the building, it is unlikely to suffer property damage from flooding; however, flooding of the ground floor of the building could impact the cost of insurance for the building and could affect the accessibility of the business to customers. Therefore a flood search was still useful to Polished Perfection Ltd and Gemma's Gels Ltd.

7.10 Chancel repair search

Some properties carry an obligation to pay the cost of repairing the chancel of the parish church. These costs can be considerable. A screening search can help determine the risk of a repair liability by confirming whether the property is located in an area where repair liability is likely.

The rules governing whether a repairing liability will bind a purchaser vary depending on the type of land.

7.10.1 Unregistered land

A purchaser for value of unregistered land will be bound if the liability is referred to in the title deeds or protected by a caution against first registration. Therefore, a buyer should always check for cautions against first registration.

It is possible that a caution could be lodged after completion of the purchase but before first registration, so reliance on checking for cautions is not sufficient, and a screening search is recommended.

The Car Park is unregistered. Style&Go Ltd's solicitors have checked the title deeds and checked for a caution against registration; nothing was discovered, but they conducted a chancel repair search to mitigate the risk of a caution against registration being entered after completion but before registration of the transfer to Style&Go Ltd.

The search results revealed that the Car Park is not located within the boundary of a parish, which potentially has chancel repair liability. Insurance is therefore not required. Style&Go Ltd's solicitor will report this to their client.

7.10.2 Registered land where the previous transfer for value occurred before 13 October 2013

The chancel repair liability will bind a buyer of registered land where the previous transfer of that land occurred before 13 October 2013 if it is protected by a notice against the title of the burdened land, so a buyer should always check the register of title.

However, a notice could be entered onto the burdened land after completion of the purchase but before registration of the land to the buyer, so reliance on checking for notices is not sufficient, and a screening search is recommended.

The last sale of the House was in 1994. There is nothing registered on the register of title, but André's solicitor does a chancel repair search to mitigate the risk of a notice being registered after completion but before registration of the transfer to André. The search revealed that the House is located within the boundary of a parish which potentially has chancel repair liability; this means that a notice could be entered on the register of title before the House is registered to André. André's solicitor will report this to him and discuss obtaining chancel repair insurance from completion to cover the risk of André being required to pay the maintenance costs.

The last sale of the Salon was in 1993. There is nothing registered on the register of title, but Style&Go Ltd's solicitor conducts a chancel repair search to mitigate the risk of a notice being registered after completion but before registration of the transfer to Style&Go Ltd. The search revealed that the Salon is not located within the boundary of a parish which potentially has chancel repair liability. Insurance is therefore not required. Style&Go Ltd's solicitor will report this to their client.

7.10.3 Registered land where the previous transfer for value occurred on or after 13 October 2013

The liability will only bind subsequent buyers of registered land where the previous transfer of the land occurred on or after 13 October 2013 if it is already protected by a notice against the burdened land; therefore, a buyer should always check the register of title.

It is not possible for a notice to be entered between completion and registration of the transfer, which means that whatever the register of title reveals during title investigation will reflect with accuracy what the prospective buyer will acquire, and a screening search is not necessary.

However, HMLR will not assess the validity of a unilateral notice relating to chancel repair liability. Therefore, it is possible for a notice to be lodged even though there has been a transfer for value since 13 October 2013. For this reason, many practitioners will do a chancel repair search even when dealing with registered land where there has been a transfer for value since 13 October 2013, as the presence of a notice may not be determinative and may alert a buyer to a liability which is not valid.

Style&Go Ltd acquired the Salon (out of which the Nail Bar Lease is to be granted) in 2026. Nothing relating to chancel repair liability is registered against the title to the Salon, and therefore, Polished Perfection Ltd's solicitor and Gemma's Gels Ltd's solicitor do not conduct a chancel repair search in respect of the Nail Bar.

7.10.4 Transfers for no consideration

For transfers for no consideration, the liability will bind subsequent purchasers until a transfer for value occurs after 13 October 2013, and so a screening search is recommended in most cases.

7.11 Company search

A search of relevant documentation held at Companies House should be undertaken when the seller is a company. The search can be made directly with Companies House.

A company search can reveal whether the company is in administration or has been wound up. This is relevant for a buyer, because the buyer will not be able to deal with the seller, only the administrator, receiver, or liquidator.

A company search can also reveal whether there are any fixed or floating charges against the property. Where the land being purchased is registered, fixed and floating charges will bind a purchaser if they are registered on the register of title. If the property is unregistered, all fixed or floating charges may bind a purchaser; fixed charges must be discharged before completion, and a certificate of non-crystallisation is required from the lender in respect of floating charges.

Style&Go Ltd is purchasing the Car Park from Urban Spaces Ltd. Style&Go Ltd's solicitor has therefore conducted a company search against Urban Spaces Ltd. The search has revealed that there is a fixed charge against the Car Park held by Barnford Bank. This must be discharged before completion.

Polished Perfection Ltd is purchasing the Nail Bar from Style&Go Ltd, and so Polished Perfection Ltd's solicitor has conducted a company search against Style&Go Ltd. The search has revealed that there are no charges or insolvency issues or administration events.

Gemma's Gels Ltd is purchasing the Nail Bar Lease from Polished Perfection Ltd, and so Gemma's Gels Ltd's solicitor has conducted a company search against Polished Perfection Ltd. The search revealed no charges and no insolvency or administration events.

7.12 Utilities search

A utilities search will reveal which utility connections benefit the land, for example, electricity and gas, as well as what equipment utility providers have in the area – this is relevant when developing the land as interference with this equipment is to be avoided.

Style&Go Ltd wishes to install lighting and a charging point for electric vehicles in the Car Park. Style&Go Ltd's solicitor therefore does a utilities search over the Car Park. This search reveals that the nearest electricity connection is under the High Street. Cables connecting the Car Park run underneath the Salon; as Style&Go Ltd will owns the Salon, they will not require permission to connect into these cables.

In our other Transactions, it is clear from other searches and physical inspections that the relevant property has the benefit of gas and electricity, and so no utilities search is conducted.

7.13 Telecoms search

A telecoms search will reveal which telecoms connections benefit the land, for example, phone lines and broadband, as well as what equipment telecoms providers have in the area – this is relevant when developing the land, as interference with this equipment is to be avoided.

Telecoms connections are not required for the Car Park, but as Style&Go Ltd plans to do re-surfacing works, their solicitor has carried out a telecoms search to ensure that the works will not interfere with any equipment under the surface. The results show that no telecoms providers hold equipment under the Car Park.

In our other Transactions, it is clear from other searches and physical inspections that the relevant property has the benefit of telecoms connections.

Chapter 7 revision points

- A buyer will carry out searches to find out about the land.
- A search of the index map will reveal whether the land is registered or unregistered.
- A Local Land Charges search will reveal local land charges affecting the land, such as planning orders, Tree Preservation Orders, Smoke Control Orders, financial charges, compulsory purchase orders, and conversation area designation orders.
- Standard enquiries of the local authority will reveal information about planning applications affecting the property and information about the local area, such as local roads, railways, and traffic schemes.
- Optional enquiries of the local authority can be raised to gather additional information about the local area, such as whether the land is designated as a village green.
- A highways search will give precise information about the adopted status of nearby roads.
- A drainage and water search will confirm whether water drains to a public sewer and whether the property is connected to the mains water supply.
- Environmental searches advise on whether the land is likely to be contaminated.
- Flood searches advise on whether the land is likely to flood.
- Chancel repair searches confirm whether the land is in an area which is subject to chancel repair liability.
- A company search reveals information about a company seller, such as whether the company has granted a charge over the land.
- A utilities search provides information about utilities infrastructure close to the land.
- A telecoms search provides information about telecoms infrastructure close to the land.

8 Planning permission and building regulations

8.1 Chapter overview

This chapter focuses on investigating the status of planning permission and building regulations approval in respect of the property being acquired.

For the buyer's solicitor, the reasons for verifying the status of these matters are twofold:

- First, to check that the land as it currently stands has all the relevant permissions. If it doesn't, the buyer will take on liability for any breach of planning or building control.
- Second, the buyer's solicitor will need to make sure that upon acquisition of the land, the buyer will be able to do with the land what it plans to. It is important that the buyer is informed as to any permissions it is likely to need to obtain before acquiring the land.

This chapter begins with an examination of the planning permission rules, followed by a detailed analysis of:

- things already done on the land which could constitute a breach and how to deal with this; and
- requiring planning permission for future activities and how to go about obtaining this.

This chapter is relevant to all freehold and leasehold transactions.

This chapter in the context of our Transactions

Solicitors for each buyer have now completed title investigation and conducted searches against the relevant property. They must now consider the planning position for the relevant property. For some, like the House, this may be simple. For the Salon, which Style&Go Ltd wishes to change from a residence to a commercial premises, it will require a deeper analysis to ensure Style&Go Ltd can use the Salon in their intended manner.

You may wish to refer to the LLC1 and CON29 search results for each Transaction whilst working through this chapter.

DOI: 10.4324/9781032711508-10

8.2 Planning permission

Planning permission is concerned with:

- works done to the land; and
- how the land is used.

8.2.1 Overview of the planning permission regime

We begin with an overview of the regime before we look at the provisions in more detail.

8.2.1.1 Development

Planning permission is required for any '***development***',[1] which is defined[2] as:

- the carrying out of building, engineering, minor or other operations in, on, over or under land; or
- the making of any material change in the use of any buildings or other land.

Some activities are expressly excluded from the definition of 'development',[3] which we examine in detail in Sections 8.2.2.1.1.2 and 8.2.2.2.1.2.

8.2.1.2 Permitted Development

If an activity constitutes 'development', then planning permission is required. However, not all activities which require planning permission need to be the subject of an express application for such permission. This is because the Town and Country Planning (General Permitted Development) Order 2015 (**GPDO**) automatically grants planning permission to certain types of activity, to remove the requirement to make an express application for planning permission. It is, in effect, a rubber-stamping of certain activities.

1 s57 Town and Country Planning Act 1990 (**TCPA 1990**).
2 s55 TCPA 1990.
3 s55(2) TCPA 1990.

8.2.1.2.1 IS THE ACTIVITY OF A TYPE PERMITTED BY THE GPDO?

Only certain types of activity can be 'permitted' under the GPDO. Some of the key categories of activity[4] which may be 'permitted' are:

- Part 1: development within the curtilage of a dwellinghouse
- Part 2: minor operations
- Part 3: changes of use
- Part 4: temporary buildings and uses
- Part 7: non-domestic extensions and alterations

Within each part, there are a number of more specific activities listed (each labelled with a letter) – these are the activities which constitute ***permitted development***.

8.2.1.2.2 IS THE ACTIVITY EXCLUDED FROM THE SCOPE OF THE GPDO?

For each specific permitted development activity, there is a list of circumstances under which the development will not be automatically permitted, for example, if the height restriction on a building is exceeded.

8.2.1.2.3 HAVE ALL RELEVANT CONDITIONS WITHIN THE GPDO BEEN COMPLIED WITH?

There are conditions attached to each type of activity which must be complied with in order for the development to be permitted under the GPDO. For example, the materials used in construction must be of a similar appearance to those used in the rest of the building.

8.2.1.2.4 HAS THE GPDO BEEN DISAPPLIED BY AN ARTICLE 4 DIRECTION?

Whilst the GPDO generally applies to automatically grant planning permission for certain types of activity, the effects of the GPDO can be disapplied in respect of specific pieces of land. For example, whilst a small downstairs extension to a dwellinghouse may be unproblematic, additional protections and approvals may be required before an extension is built on a property of historical significance.

8.2.1.3 Breaches of planning control

A buyer of land will become liable for breaches of planning control, even if those breaches were committed by a previous owner of the land.

A breach of planning control is either where:

- 'development' has taken place without planning permission; or
- a condition or limitation of planning permission has been breached.

4 Schedule 2 GPDO.

A buyer's solicitor will therefore carefully review works done to a property and changes of use to a property, to ensure that 'development' has not taken place without planning permission. Where planning permission has been granted, a buyer's solicitor must review that planning permission carefully to ensure that all conditions or limitations have been complied with.

8.2.1.3.1 WHAT ENFORCEMENT ACTION CAN BE TAKEN IN RESPECT OF THE BREACH OF CONDITION?

Where there has been a breach of planning control, the options open to the local planning authority (**LPA**) are as follows:[5]

- ***Enforcement notice.*** This sets out the nature of the breach of planning control and the steps which need to be taken in order to remedy or cease the breach. The recipient is given 28 days to either restore the land to the condition it was in before the development or to comply with any conditions imposed by planning permission.
- ***Stop notice.*** This can mandate that the activity comprising the breach of planning control must stop before the deadline for compliance set out in the enforcement notice. An enforcement notice must therefore necessarily precede a stop notice.
- ***Temporary stop notice.*** This can mandate the immediate cessation of the activity comprising the breach of planning control. No enforcement notice is required, but it can only be used to prohibit certain activities.[6]
- ***Breach of condition notice.*** This requires compliance with terms of a planning condition and can be used as an alternative to an enforcement notice.
- ***Injunction.*** The planning authority can apply to the courts for an injunction to restrain a breach of planning control. This remedy is discretionary for the court.

8.2.1.3.2 WHAT ARE THE TIME LIMITS FOR BRINGING ENFORCEMENT ACTION?

The local planning authority must bring enforcement action within a certain timeframe.[7] The timeframes for enforcement[8] vary depending on the type of breach and whether the property is located in England or Wales and are set out in Table 8.1:

5 TCPA 1990 Part VII.
6 See s171F TCPA 1990 for more information.
7 Unless the development has been concealed, according to *Fidler v Secretary of State for Communities and Local Government* [2010] EWHC 143 (Admin).
8 Contained within s171B(1) TCPA 1990, as amended by the Levelling Up and Regeneration Act 2023.

Table 8.1 The time limits for enforcement action

Type of breach	Time limit for enforcement action
Building works carried out without planning permission	• Ten years from substantial completion of the works, for properties in England where the operations were substantially completed on or after 25 April 2024 • Four years from substantial completion of the works, for properties in Wales, or for properties in England, where the operations were substantially completed before 25 April 2024.
Breach of a planning condition	• Ten years from the breach of the condition (NB some conditions are ongoing).
Material changes of use without planning permission	In the case of changes of use to single dwellinghouses: • Ten years from the date of the change of use, for properties in England where the change to a dwellinghouse began after 24th April 2024. • Four years from the date of the change of use, for properties in Wales., or for properties in England, where the change began on or before 24 April 2024. • In all other cases: ten years from the date of the change of use.

We will now examine the planning permission rules in more detail in respect of:

1. Building operations.
2. Material changes of use.

in the context of our Transactions.

8.2.2 Carrying out building operations

All ***building operations*** will constitute 'development'[9] and, therefore, will require planning permission, unless the work is within the exceptions listed in s55(2) TCPA 1990.

'Building operations' includes:[10]

- demolition;
- rebuilding;

9 s57 TCPA 1990.
10 S55(1A) TCPA 1990.

- structural alterations or additions to buildings; and
- other operations normally undertaken by a person carrying on business as a builder.

Building operations has been interpreted quite widely and can even include things like putting in new windows.

8.2.2.1 The House

We know that the space under the stairs was converted into a downstairs toilet in 2020. As André will become liable for any breaches of planning control once he acquires the House, his solicitors will need to check whether planning permission was required for this work and, if it was, ensure that it was obtained and adhered to.

8.2.2.1.1 DEVELOPMENT

André's solicitor will consider whether this work constitutes 'development' and, therefore, required planning permission.

8.2.2.1.1.1 ARE THE WORKS 'BUILDING OPERATIONS'?

The installation of a toilet downstairs will likely have included the following types of work:

- plumbing, to ensure a working toilet and sink, and radiator;
- re-wiring to ensure adequate lighting;
- plastering;
- tiling; and
- fitting a floor.

These types of work are all likely to be in the category of 'operations normally undertaken by a person carrying on business as a builder'. The work as a whole could be considered a 'structural alteration' to the building if it involved the addition or removal of walls.

The installation of the toilet, therefore, will constitute 'building operations'.

8.2.2.1.1.2 ARE THE WORKS EXCLUDED FROM BEING 'DEVELOPMENT' UNDER S55(2)?

Section 55(2) TCPA 1990 excludes a number of matters from the definition of 'development', including the maintenance, improvement, or alteration of a building where works affect the interior of the building only, or do not materially affect the external appearance of the building.[11]

11 Works which provide additional space underneath the building do not benefit from this exclusion and are classed as 'development'.

This is likely to apply to the works to the House, meaning that the conversion of the toilet will not be considered 'development' and therefore does not require planning permission. André's solicitors will report to him that the conversion into a toilet did not require planning permission.

8.2.2.2 The Salon

We already know that an extension to the Salon was built in 1996. As Style&Go Ltd will become liable for any breaches of planning control once they acquire the Salon, their solicitors will need to check whether planning permission was required for this work and, if it was, ensure that it was obtained and adhered to.

8.2.2.2.1 DEVELOPMENT

Style&Go Ltd's solicitors will consider whether this work constitutes 'development' because, if it does, it will have required planning permission.

8.2.2.2.1.1 ARE THE WORKS 'BUILDING OPERATIONS'?

The extension to the property will almost certainly constitute making a 'structural alteration or addition' to the building. It could also have included demolition and rebuilding, for example, if outhouses were knocked down and the extension built in their place. The extension, therefore, will constitute 'building operations'.

8.2.2.2.1.2 ARE THE WORKS EXCLUDED UNDER S55(2) TCPA?

The s55(2) exclusion is unlikely to apply to the extension because the extension will have altered the exterior of the building. These works will therefore still constitute 'development' and require planning permission.

8.2.2.2.2 PERMITTED DEVELOPMENT

Now that is has been established that the extension required planning permission, Style&Go Ltd's solicitors will need to consider whether the extension would have been a 'permitted development'.

The extension will fall within Part 1 of Schedule 2: Development within the curtilage of a dwellinghouse. The specific activity relevant to the extension is: 'A – the enlargement, improvement or other alteration of a dwellinghouse'. In respect of these specific activities, Schedule 2 Part 1 A1 (f)(i) states that an enlarged part of a dwellinghouse which has a single storey and extends beyond the rear wall of the original dwellinghouse by more than 4 metres (in the case of detached dwellinghouses) will not be a permitted development.

Style&Go Ltd's surveyor has inspected the property and informed Style&Go Ltd and their solicitors that the extension is a single-storey extension and extends beyond the rear wall of the original dwellinghouse by 4.7 metres. The extension is therefore excluded from the scope of the GPDO. This means that the extension will not automatically be given planning permission, and an express application for planning permission was required. The local searches[12] revealed that this planning permission was granted.

8.2.2.2.3 DEALING WITH PAST BREACHES OF PLANNING CONTROL

Style&Go Ltd's solicitors have reviewed a copy of the planning permission, which shows that it was conditional on the following:

> [T]he development must be carried out in accordance with the approved plans submitted with the application.

The plans submitted with the application (which have not been reproduced here) show that the extension as designed was supposed to have one large window on the rear wall. The information from Style&Go Ltd's surveyor shows that the rear wall has two small windows instead of one large one. There has therefore been a breach of planning control in respect of the extension.

8.2.2.2.3.1 WHAT ENFORCEMENT ACTION CAN BE TAKEN IN RESPECT OF THE BREACH OF CONDITION?

Now that Style&Go Ltd's solicitor has discovered that the extension was constructed in breach of the conditions stipulated in the planning permission, they must consider what action the local planning authority could take to enforce that condition, as this will become Style&Go Ltd's problem on completion of the purchase.

The extension was completed in 1994. This was longer than ten years ago; therefore, the time limit for the LPA to bring enforcement action in respect of the breach of a planning condition has expired.

Style&Go Ltd's solicitor should report to Style&Go Ltd that there has been a breach of a planning condition regarding the design of the windows in the extension, but that this breach cannot be enforced against Style&Go Ltd by the LPA as the time-limit for doing so has expired.

8.2.2.2.4 STYLE&GO LTD'S FUTURE PLANS FOR THE SALON AND THE CAR PARK

We will consider Style&Go Ltd's future plans for the Salon and the Car Park together, because they constitute one 'planning unit' and Style&Go Ltd will make any necessary planning applications for both parcels together.

Style&Go Ltd wants to do the following works to the Salon:

- *Reconfigure the internal layout*. This will require the removal and installation of some internal walls; and

12 See the LLC1 and CON29 search results.

- *Fit out the building with the required equipment to enable it to be used as a hair salon.*

These works are internal, and so it is likely that they will fall within the exclusions under s55(2) TCPA 1990 and, therefore, will not constitute 'development' and will not require planning permission.

Style&Go Ltd wants to do the following works to the Car Park:

- *demolish the disused building;*
- *level the land so that it can be used as a car park; and*
- *install barriers and fencing.*

These works are likely to constitute 'development'. 'Building operations' include 'demolition', and levelling the land and installing barriers and fencing are all types of work that would usually be undertaken by a builder. None of the exclusions in s55(2) appear relevant to these types of works. Planning permission will therefore be required.

Some demolition falls within the GPDO (Part 11 Class B), and provision of a hard surface within the curtilage of a building used for commercial purposes also falls within the GPDO (Part 7 Class E), so provided the conditions are met, an express application for planning permission may not be required as these works may constitute 'permitted development'. However, the LLC search shows that there is an Article 4 Direction in place in respect of the Car Park. This indicates that the General Permitted Development Order has been disapplied in respect of the Car Park for permitted development falling within Schedule 2 Part 7. The Article 4 Direction means that, although Style&Go Ltd's development proposals would ordinarily be a 'permitted development' under Schedule 2 Part 7, an express application will still need to be made.

Style&Go Ltd's solicitor must inform them that the work to the Car Park will require planning permission and that it is likely an express application will need to be made.

8.2.2.3 The Nail Bar

The local searches undertaken against the Nail Bar (in respect of both the initial grant of the lease and the subsequent assignment) revealed the conditional planning permission for the rear extension. The enforceability of this has already been discussed;[13] in addition, the extension does not form part of the Nail Bar demise.

Any internal fit-out works undertaken by Polished Perfection Ltd or Gemma's Gels Ltd would not constitute 'development' as they would fall under the s55(2) exceptions, being internal-only.

13 At Section 8.2.2.2.3.

8.2.3 Changing the use of a building

'Development' includes the making of any ***material change in the use*** of any buildings or other land.[14]

8.2.3.1 *Use classes*

The different ways in which land can be used are known as ***use classes***. The use classes can be found in the Town and Country Planning (Use Classes) Order 1987 (the **Order**). Within the Order, there are different classes of use categorised using a letter and a number. Various, more specific uses falling within this broad categorisation are then listed within that class.

For example, the broad category 'Class C3. Dwellinghouses' includes the following specific uses:

1. use as a dwellinghouse by a single person or people forming a single household (e.g. a family);
2. use as a dwellinghouse by not more than six residents living together as a single household, where care is provided; and
3. use as a dwellinghouse by not more than six residents living together as a single household, where care is not provided.

There are some uses which are not given a class. These are called ***sui generis*** uses, and a list can be found in s3(6) of the Order. It includes use as a theatre, a taxi firm, and a cinema.

Please note the Order was amended in 2020. For all *future* changes of use, the list in the amended Order will be the correct one to refer to when assessing whether a change of use is 'material'. For *past* changes of use, please see Table 8.2 to guide you as to which version of the Order to refer to.

Table 8.2 Which use classes order to refer to

When was the change of use?	Which use classes order to refer to?
Before 1 September 2020	The old use classes order
After 31 July 2021	The new use classes order
Between 1 September 2020 and 31 July 2021	Both. If the change is only material under one of them, then planning permission will not be required.

8.2.3.2 *What counts as 'material'?*

All *material* changes of use fall within the definition of 'development' and therefore require planning permission.

14 S57 TCPA 1990.

Any change from one use class to another, for example, from a hotel (C1) to a hospital (C2), constitutes a 'material change of use'. Each sui generis use constitutes its own use class, and so any changes to or from that use also constitutes a material change of use, for example, a theatre to a laundrette (different sui generis uses), a theatre to a hospital (sui generis use to Class C2 use), or a hospital to a theatre (C2 use to a sui generis use). Changes within a use class – for example, from a post office (A1(b)) to a travel agency (A1(c)) – do not constitute a 'material change of use'.

8.2.3.3 Permitted Development

Just like with building works, some changes of use can be automatically granted planning permission by the GPDO. These can be found in Part 3 of Schedule 2 GPDO.

8.2.3.4 Enforcement in respect of material changes of use

The LPA can take enforcement action in respect of material changes of use which occur without planning permission, as this constitutes 'development' without planning permission.[15] The timeframes for bringing enforcement action are set out above.[16]

8.2.3.5 The House

Upon physical inspection, the House appears to have been used as a residence. The local searches[17] have not revealed any information about the use of the House, so André's solicitor will make enquiries of the seller to confirm the permitted use of the House and ensure that there have been no breaches of this permitted use.[18]

André intends to use the House as a residence; provided the House has permission to be used as a residence, he will not need planning permission for this.

8.2.3.6 The Salon and the Car Park

8.2.3.6.1 PAST USE

The local searches for the Salon reveal that the Salon has planning permission to be used as a residence (after permission was given in 1991 for the use to be changed from commercial to residential). Style&Go Ltd's solicitor will request a copy of the planning permission, and they will need to ensure that the current planning permission (to use the Salon as a residence) has not been breached, by making enquiries of Neeta's solicitors.

The local searches for the Car Park show that, in 1989, the permitted use of the land was changed from business use to the sale or display for sale of motor vehi-

15 See Section 8.2.1.3 for enforcement action.
16 See Section 8.2.1.3.2.
17 The LLC2 and CON29.
18 See the responses to these enquiries in Chapter 9.

cles. Style&Go Ltd's solicitors will need to ensure that the current planning permission (to use the Car Park for the sale of motor vehicles) has not been breached, by making enquiries of Urban Spaces Ltd's solicitors.

8.2.3.6.2 FUTURE USE

As above, we will consider Style&Go Ltd's future plans for the Salon and the Car Park together because they constitute one 'planning unit', and Style&Go Ltd will make any necessary planning applications for both parcels together.

Style&Go Ltd wishes to use the Salon as a hair salon and to use the Car Park as a car park for their employees and customers. As the Car Park is not going to be a commercial car park but, rather, will form part of the hair salon and be used only for customers of the hair salon, it is unlikely that the Car Park will have its own use class. We will therefore consider the planning requirements to change the use of the Salon and the Car Park to a hair salon with onsite parking.

According to the amended Order,[19] the change from C3: Dwellinghouses to E: Commercial, Business, and Service would constitute a material change of use, and therefore, Style&Go Ltd will need planning permission for this change of use. Changing from a dwellinghouse to a hair salon is not a permitted development under the GPDO, so Style&Go Ltd will need to submit an express application for planning permission to change the Salon and the Car Park into a hair salon with parking for staff and customers. If Style&Go Ltd fails to obtain planning permission for this change of use, the LPA will have ten years in which to bring any enforcement action.

8.2.3.7 The Nail Bar

The local searches show that the whole building has planning permission for Use Class E: Commercial, Business, and Service. It is likely[20] that this is sufficient for both parties' proposed use of the property to provide nail services. Therefore, neither party will need to apply for any changes with respect to the Nail Bar.

Both parties' solicitors will request a copy of the planning permission from their seller's solicitors and raise an enquiry with their seller's solicitor to confirm that there have not been any breaches of this planning permission.

8.3 Building regulations

Building regulations (the **Regulations**) are a statutory regime to regulate health and safety aspects of undertaking building works, for example, the structural integrity of the building.

19 Which was used because the change is a future change of use.
20 Though not certain, as there have been conflicting decisions on this issue.

We begin with an overview of the regime before we look at the provisions in more detail.

8.3.1 Overview of the building regulation regime

Building regulations consent is required prior to undertaking any ***building work*** covered by the Regulations. The type of work covered includes extending or altering a building.[21] Once work has commenced, the work is inspected by a building control inspector. Once work has been completed, if it meets the standards of the regulations, a certificate of compliance is issued.

8.3.1.1 Enforcement of building regulations

Breach of the Regulations is a strict liability offence. There are three primary methods of enforcement action open to the local authority, if it discovers a breach of the Regulations:

- ***Prosecution.*** The local authority can prosecute the person responsible for the breach (e.g. the contractor) in the magistrates court;
- ***Enforcement notice.*** This gives the property owner notice of the breach and requirements to remedy it, with a deadline of 28 days for compliance; and
- ***Injunction.*** The local authority can apply to court for an injunction to stop the breach.

8.3.1.1.1 WHAT ARE THE TIME LIMITS FOR BRINGING ENFORCEMENT ACTION?

The time limits for bringing enforcement action depend on the method of enforcement. These are set out in Table 8.3.

Table 8.3 The time limits for enforcement action for non-compliance with the Regulations

Method of enforcement	Time limit for enforcement action
Prosecution	Six months from discovery of the breach
Enforcement notice	Ten years after completion of the building work
Injunction	No time limit

8.3.2 House

The installation of the toilet in the House would constitute 'building work' and, therefore, would require consent. The CON29 search confirmed that there is a building regulation approval and completion certificate which appear to relate to the conversion of the downstairs toilet. André's solicitor will request a copy of the building regulation approval certificate from Michael's estate's solicitor.

21 The full list of work can be found in Section 3 of the Building Regulations 2010.

8.3.3 Salon

The extension to the Salon would constitute 'building work' and, therefore, would require consent. The CON29 search did not reveal any approvals or completion certificates. This is a concern because all building works should have Regulations approval, and the absence of a Regulations approval certificate in respect of the extension implies that this work was not approved by building control. Once their purchase of the Salon is complete, Style&Go Ltd will be liable for any breaches of the Regulations.

Although an enforcement notice can no longer be issued because the building work was completed in 1996, there is no time limit for bringing an injunction in respect of a breach of the Regulations. Therefore, when Style&Go Ltd's purchase of the Salon is complete Style&Go Ltd may still face enforcement action in respect of the extension. Style&Go Ltd's solicitor will need to raise enquiries with Neeta's solicitor to find out more about the missing approval.

In order to protect Style&Go Ltd, there are two options for their solicitor to explore with them:

8.3.3.1 Insure against the risk

Style&Go Ltd may be able to obtain insurance to cover the risk of the LPA taking enforcement action in respect of the breach of building control. They could require Neeta to obtain or pay for this, as she should have ensured the correct certificates were obtained at the time the work was completed.

8.3.3.2 Obtain a regularisation certificate

Style&Go Ltd could obtain a regularisation certificate from the LPA to approve the work retrospectively. One point to note about this is that if Neeta contacts the LPA about this but is unable to obtain such a certificate, the authority has been tipped off about the breach, and it may make enforcement much more likely. This will therefore make insurance more difficult (and more expensive) to obtain.

Style&Go Ltd's solicitor will need to report to them on the past breach and advise on the options available, explore insurance policies, and engage in any negotiations with Neeta about her paying for these. Whichever option Style&Go Ltd chooses (insurance or regularisation certificate) will require action from Neeta, and so this should be cemented in the contract.

The lack of Regulations approvals for the extension likely would not be enforced against Polished Perfection Ltd or Gemma's Gels Ltd because the extension does not fall within the Nail Bar demise.

Chapter 8 revision points

- Planning permission is required for all types of development, which includes building operations and materially changing the use of a building. Some types of development are automatically granted planning permission as they constitute 'permitted development'; others require an express application to the local planning authority.
- Developing without planning permission or in breach of a planning condition enables the local planning authority to take enforcement action. In England, these enforcement powers last for ten years from the breach.
- Building work requires consent or approval under the building regulations regime. The local authority can take enforcement action for ten years in respect of a failure to obtain consent for building work.
- When purchasing land which does not have the requisite planning or building regulations approvals, the buyer will take responsibility for this and so may wish to obtain insurance against the risk of the local planning authority taking enforcement action.

9 Making enquiries of the seller

9.1 Chapter overview

The buyer's solicitor will need to ask a number of questions of the seller as part of the process of finding out about the property.

Some questions which are relevant to many transactions are captured in a standard form. These lists of questions differ depending on the nature of the transaction. In addition to making standard enquiries, the buyer's solicitor will also ask of the seller's solicitor anything else they need to know about the property. Many of these questions may arise during the title investigation process or when examining search results or considering the position as regards planning permission or building regulations.

This chapter outlines the content of the standard enquiries and explores some additional enquiries raised as part of the due diligence process.

This chapter is relevant to all freehold and leasehold transactions.

This chapter in the context of our Transactions

This is the final stage of due diligence for our Transactions. Each buyer's solicitor will raise enquiries with the seller's solicitor to ensure they have all the required information about the property and to resolve any queries arising as a result of their title investigation or searches.

You may wish to refer to the TA6 or CPSE responses and the responses to the additional enquiries for each Transaction and remind yourself of the other issues arising throughout the due diligence process whilst working through this chapter.

DOI: 10.4324/9781032711508-11

9.2 Overview of making enquiries

The purpose of making enquiries of the seller is to find out any relevant information about the property which has either not been discovered during title investigation or searches or which requires further clarification.

9.2.1 Standard form enquiries

Some questions which are relevant to many transactions are captured in a standard form. These lists of questions differ depending on the nature of the transaction, but some of the key ones for the purposes of this book are as follows:

- ***TA6 Property Information Form***. This is used where the property being disposed of is residential in nature. This will be the case for the House and the Salon, as they are both currently being used for residential purposes and the sellers are not companies.
- ***Commercial Property Standard Enquiries***. These are used where the property being disposed of is commercial in nature, and includes:
  - CPSE1: general enquiries for all commercial property transactions;
  - CPSE3: supplemental enquiries for commercial property on the grant of a new lease – this will be relevant for the grant of the Nail Bar Lease;
  - CPSE4: supplemental enquiries for commercial leasehold property on the assignment of the lease – this will be relevant for the assignment of the Nail Bar Lease; and.
  - CPSE7: general short-form enquiries for all property transactions – this can be used instead of CPSE1 if the level of detail in CPSE1 is not required.

Sometimes multiple enquiry forms will be used.

9.2.2 Additional enquiries

Throughout the due diligence process, the buyer's solicitor will collate a list of things they require more information on, much as we did throughout earlier chapters. This is then assembled into a list of questions for the seller to respond on. In practice, a bit of back-and-forth between the buyer and the seller's solicitors is common in order for the buyer's solicitor to gather all the information they require.

9.3 Enquiries relevant to our Transactions

We will now examine the enquiries in respect of each of our Transactions. For each Transaction, we examine the standard enquiry form used and what the responses received tell us about the property. We then use this information, together with the rest of the information gained throughout the due diligence process, to assemble a list of additional enquiries for each seller. The responses to these enquiries can be found in the relevant Appendix.

9.3.1 André's purchase of the House

9.3.1.1 Standard enquiries

André's solicitor asked Michael's estate's solicitor to complete a TA6 Property Information Form. This tells us the following key pieces of information about the House, summarised in Table 9.1:

Table 9.1 A summary of the information provided in the TA6 form from Michael's estate

Type	Information provided
Boundaries	It will be André's responsibility to maintain the boundary at the front of the House. The neighbour is responsible for the remainder.
	The owner of the House is required to contribute financially towards the maintenance of boundary features.
Amenities	The House has its own driveway.
Planning and building regulations	The space under the stairs was converted into a toilet in 2020.
	This didn't require planning permission.
	Buildings regulations approvals and certificates have been enclosed by the seller's solicitor.
Encumbrances	There is no mortgage on the property.
	There are other unknown rights or covenants affecting the House.
	There is a tree subject to a TPO, and this TPO has been complied with and has been enclosed by the seller's solicitor.
Water and utilities	The electrics were tested in 2022, and a certificate has been supplied.
	The House has a mains gas system which was installed in 1995 and was serviced in 2022; a certificate has been supplied.

Table 9.1 (Continued)

Type	Information provided
	The House is connected to mains electricity and gas and receives these from Octopus Energy.
	The House is connected to the mains water and sewerage system and receives water from South West Water.
	The House receives telephone and cable from BT.
Warranties, insurance, and documentation	The House has warranties for the following, which have been supplied by the seller's solicitor: 1. damp proofing; 2. windows; 3. electrical work; 4. roofing; and 5. central heating.
	The seller's solicitor has enclosed an EPC.
	The House is insured, and there have not been any issues obtaining insurance in the past.

9.3.1.2 Additional enquiries

André's solicitor specifically asked some additional enquiries which were not covered by the TA6 form and which arose whilst undertaking due diligence on the House. These are set out in Table 9.2:

Table 9.2 The additional enquiries raised by André's solicitor about the House

Type	Enquiry from André's solicitor
Documentation	Please provide a copy of the grant of probate.
	Please provide a copy of the transfer, dated 1 November 1991, between Joanne Bates and Alan Wright.
Title queries	Due diligence has revealed unknown rights and covenants contained in a conveyance dated 27 January 1929. Please provide a copy of the conveyance. Please confirm: • what these rights and covenants are; • who has the benefit of these rights and covenants; • whether they have been breached; and • whether the rights and covenants have been enforced.

Table 9.2 (Continued)

Type	Enquiry from André's solicitor
	There is a covenant on the title in respect of the contribution towards the maintenance of boundary features. Please confirm: • Whether the covenant has been breached. • Whether there are outstanding costs. • How much this charge has been, on average, annually.
Searches	The property is subject to a TPO. Please identify the relevant tree.
Use	Please confirm the current use of the property.
Overriding interests	Please confirm whether there are any overriding interests affecting the property.

9.3.2 Style&Go Ltd's purchase of the Salon

9.3.2.1 Standard enquiries

Style&Go Ltd's solicitor asked Neeta's solicitor to complete a TA6 Property Information Form. Even though Style&Go Ltd plan to use the property for commercial purposes, it is currently a residence and doesn't yet have planning permission for any other use, and so TA6 is the appropriate form. Neeta, the seller, is also an individual as opposed to a company, and so lots of the commercial enquiries in the CPSE forms are not relevant to her.

The TA6 tells us the following key pieces of information about the Salon, as set out in Table 9.3:

Table 9.3 A summary of the information provided in the TA6 form from Neeta

Type	Information provided
Amenities	The Salon does not have any parking.
Planning and building regulations	An extension was made on the ground floor; this was completed in 1996, and: • planning permission was obtained. The documentation has been provided; • the planning conditions were not complied with, but the deadline for enforcement action has passed; and. • building regulations approval and certification are missing in respect of the extension.
Encumbrances	There is a mortgage on the property.
	The property next door enjoys a right of way over the alleyway forming part of the property.

Table 9.3 (Continued)

Type	Information provided
Water and utilities	The electrics were tested in 2022, and a certificate has been supplied.
	The Salon has a mains gas system which was serviced in 2024; a certificate has been supplied.
	The Salon is connected to the mains water and sewerage system and receives water from Westshire Water.
	The Salon is connected to mains electricity and gas and receives these from Scottish Power.
	The Salon receives telephone and cable from Virgin Media.
Warranties, insurance, and documentation	The Salon is insured, and there have not been any issues obtaining insurance in the past.
	The seller's solicitor has enclosed an EPC.

9.3.2.2 *Additional enquiries*

Style&Go Ltd's solicitor specifically asked some additional enquiries, noted in Table 9.4, which were not covered by the TA6 form:

Table 9.4 The additional enquiries raised by Style&Go Ltd about the Salon

Type	Enquiry from Style&Go Ltd's solicitor
Title queries	The registered proprietors are Ansar Mukhtar and Neeta Mukhtar, and there is a restriction preventing the disposal by a sole trustee. Please confirm why Ansar is not a seller, and the arrangements for sale by a sole trustee.
	There is a restrictive covenant prohibiting building any structure on the property. An extension has been built in breach of that covenant. Please confirm that your client will obtain and pay for a restrictive covenant insurance policy to cover my client in respect of the risk of enforcement action.
	There is a positive covenant at entry C2 and an indemnity in respect thereof. Please confirm: • whether there have been any breaches of this covenant to date; • what work has been done to ensure compliance with this covenant; and • the average annual cost of maintaining the land referred to.

Table 9.4 (Continued)

Type	Enquiry from Style&Go Ltd's solicitor
	The property is subject to a right of way. Please provide the following details: • the nature of the right of way; • who uses it; and • how regularly is it used.
Mortgage	There is a mortgage registered against the property and an associated restriction. Please provide an undertaking that you will: • pay the completion monies towards the mortgage; and • immediately send a DS1 to us.
Planning and building regulations	There is no building regulations certificate for the extension. Please confirm that your client will obtain and pay for a building regulations insurance policy to cover my client in respect of the risk of enforcement action.
Overriding interests	Please confirm whether there are any overriding interests affecting the property.

9.3.3 Style&Go Ltd's purchase of the Car Park

9.3.3.1 Standard enquiries

Style&Go Ltd's solicitor asked Urban Spaces Ltd's solicitor to complete a CPSE7 form because this is a commercial transaction. Style&Go Ltd did not need the additional detail contained in the CPSE1 form, and so the shorter version was sufficient. The CPSE7 form tells us the following key pieces of information about the Car Park, as set out in Table 9.5:

Table 9.5 A summary of the information provided in the CPSE7 form from Urban Spaces Ltd

Type	Information provided
Access	Sheep Street is a private road which is required for access to and from the property.
Encumbrances	There are covenants affecting the property.
	Urban Spaces Ltd has complied with the restrictive covenants contained in the 1956 Conveyance.
Utilities	The property has: • electricity; • gas; • broadband/telephone; and • water.

Table 9.5 (Continued)

Type	Information provided
	Connections are direct to a mains supply.
	Connections are not metered.
	Services pass under the Salon to connect into the mains under the High Street.
	Copies of latest bills are enclosed.
Planning permission and building regulations	There was a change of use in 1989 from business use to use for the sale or display for sale of motor vehicles. Planning permission was obtained. Copy enclosed.
	The seller has had no difficulty obtaining insurance for the Car Park.
	EPC enclosed.
	A hard-copy health and safety file will be provided on completion.
Occupiers	The lease expired on 29 September 2004, and the property is now vacant.
VAT	Seller is registered for VAT under number GB987654321. The supply is exempt from VAT, and the seller has not opted to tax.

9.3.3.2 Additional enquiries

Style&Go Ltd's solicitor specifically asked some additional enquiries, set out in Table 9.6, which were not covered by the CPSE form:

Table 9.6 The additional enquiries raised by Style&Go Ltd about the Car Park

Type	Enquiry from Style&Go Ltd's solicitor
Title	Please confirm there has not been a breach of the restrictive covenants (D(ii) land charges) registered against Urban Spaces Ltd.
	Please confirm whether there are any overriding interests affecting the property.
	A company search has revealed that Barnford Bank has a fixed charge against the property. Please provide an undertaking that you will: • pay the completion monies towards the mortgage; and • send a copy of the receipted mortgage deed to us as evidence that the charge has been discharged.

Table 9.6 (Continued)

Type	Enquiry from Style&Go Ltd's solicitor
Access	We note the property is accessed via Sheep Street, which we understand is private. Please confirm: • how much the right of way is used; • whether there are any restrictions on access; and • whether there are any maintenance requirements or obligations to contribute towards maintenance costs.
	We understand that a private road (Needle Alley) forms part of the property. Please confirm the current maintenance arrangements and costs for this.

9.3.4 Polished Perfection Ltd's lease over the Nail Bar

9.3.4.1 Standard enquiries

Polished Perfection Ltd's solicitor asked Style&Go Ltd's solicitor to complete CPSE3 and 7 forms. These tell us the following key pieces of information about the Nail Bar, as summarised in Table 9.7:

Table 9.7 A summary of the information provided in the CPSE3 and 7 forms from Style&Go Ltd

Type	Information provided
Accessing the premises	Access is through the hair salon on the ground floor.
Rights benefitting the premises	The lease comes with a right to park in car park behind the building, accessed via Sheep Street.
Covenants affecting the premises	Restrictive covenants affect the property – the seller has not breached these during their ownership.
Overriding interests affecting the premises	None known.
Planning permission	The Nail Bar has planning permission for Class E.
	No works have been done to the Nail Bar in the last ten years. An extension was constructed in 1996, but it doesn't overlap with the Nail Bar demise.
Service charge and managing agent	There is no service charge payable. There is no managing agent.

Table 9.7 (Continued)

Type	Information provided
Utilities	The Nail Bar benefits from: • electricity; • gas; • broadband; and • water. All utilities are supplied direct from the mains. These utilities are not metered. The latest copies of all bills are enclosed.
	The services reach the Nail Bar, which is situated on the first floor, from the High Street via the rest of building.
	The heating and hot water are shared with the rest of the building.
Documentation	The seller has or will supply: • Digital Health and Safety file (to be supplied on completion). • EPC (enclosed). • Air conditioning inspection report (enclosed).
Insurance	The main building is insured, and the seller will continue to insure the whole building. A copy of the policy is enclosed. The insurers have waived their subrogation rights, and the tenant's interest will be noted on the policy.
VAT	The seller is VAT-registered with number GB654567814. The seller is opting to tax and has enclosed a notice.

9.3.4.2 *Additional enquiries*

Polished Perfection Ltd's solicitor specifically asked some additional enquiries, set out in Table 9.8, which were not covered by the CPSE forms:

Table 9.8 The additional enquiries raised by Polished Perfection Ltd in respect of the Nail Bar

Type	Enquiry from Polished Perfection Ltd's solicitor
Title	There is a restrictive covenant prohibiting building any structure on the property. An extension has been built. Please confirm that this structure does not overlap with the demised premises.
	There is a positive covenant at entry C2 and an indemnity in respect thereof. Please confirm this does not affect the demised premises.
	The property is subject to a right of way. Please confirm that this does not affect the demised premises.

9.3.5 Gemma's Gels Ltd's assignment of the Nail Bar Lease

9.3.5.1 Standard enquiries

Gemma's Gels Ltd's solicitor asked Polished Perfection Ltd's solicitor to complete CPSE4 and 7 forms. These tell us the following key pieces of information about the Nail Bar, as summarised in Table 9.9:

Table 9.9 A summary of the information provided in the CPSE4 and 7 forms from Polished Perfection Ltd

Type	Information provided
Accessing the Nail Bar	Access to the Nail Bar is through the hair salon on the ground floor.
Rights benefitting the Nail Bar	The lease comes with a right to park in the car park behind the premises. This right is noted against the title to the car park.
Covenants affecting the Nail Bar	Covenants affect the property. The seller has not breached these.
Overriding interests affecting the Nail Bar	None known.
Planning permission	The Nail Bar has planning permission for Class E.
	No works have been done to the Nail Bar in the last ten years. An extension was constructed in 1996, but it does not overlap with the Nail Bar demise.
Service charge and managing agent	There is no service charge payable. There is no managing agent.
Utilities	The Nail Bar benefits from: • electricity; • gas; • broadband; and • water.

Table 9.9 (Continued)

Type	Information provided
	All utilities are supplied direct from the mains. These utilities are not metered. The latest copies of all bills are enclosed.
	The services reach the Nail Bar, which is situated on the first floor, from the High Street via the rest of the building.
	The heating and hot water are shared with the rest of the building.
Documentation	The seller has or will supply: • Digital Health & Safety file to be supplied on completion; • EPC enclosed • Air conditioning inspection report enclosed.
Insurance	The main building is insured, and the seller will continue to insure the whole building. A copy of the policy is enclosed.
	The insurers have waived their subrogation rights, and the tenant's interest is noted on the policy.
VAT	The seller is not exercising the option to tax.
The Lease	The current landlord is Style&Go Ltd. There have been no former landlords.
	The lease gives access to the common areas (kitchen and bathroom), as detailed in the leases.
	The tenant is entitled to uninterrupted use of the Nail Bar.
	A schedule of fixtures and fittings belonging to the landlord is enclosed.
	Polished Perfection Ltd did fit-out works to the Nail Bar in October 2026.
	Polished Perfection Ltd decorated the Nail Bar internally in October 2026.
	The current rent is £10,000. There are no arrears.
	Rent review has taken place in accordance with the lease.

9.3.5.2 Additional enquiries

Gemma's Gels Ltd's solicitor specifically asked some additional enquiries, as set out in Table 9.10, which were not covered by the CPSE forms:

Table 9.10 The additional enquiries raised by Gemma's Gels Ltd about the Nail Bar

Type	Enquiry from Gemma's Gels Ltd's solicitor
Title	Please confirm whether the property is currently occupied.
	There is a restrictive covenant prohibiting building any structure on the property. Please confirm this has not been breached.
Security of tenure	Please confirm that the notice procedure required under the LTA 1954 was properly followed.

9.4 Collating the information

As noted in the Introduction to Phase 1, it is usual to prepare a report for your client (and for the lender, if acting for the lender as well). This report will usually contain relevant information arising from the due diligence process (title investigation, searches and enquiries, and planning matters).

Once the seller's solicitor has provided answers to all the buyer's solicitor's questions, the buyer's solicitor will compile everything they have learned about the property into a report for their client(s).

In the relevant Appendix, you can find a summary of the due diligence for each Transaction, to be used by the buyer's solicitor to produce a report on title.

Chapter 9 revision points

- The buyer will make enquiries of the seller to find out information about the land.
- For transactions of residential land, standard enquiries can be made using the TA6 Property Information Form.
- For transactions of commercial land, standard enquiries can be made using one of the Commercial Property Standard Enquiries forms.
- The buyer can also raise any additional bespoke enquiries with the seller.

Revision Summary

PHASE 0 Due diligence

Process and purpose of due diligence

- Due diligence is normally undertaken by the buyer's solicitor and the lender's solicitor.
- The purpose of due diligence is to find out as much as possible about the property, as the buyer will take the property as they find it.
- Due diligence usually comprises:
  - investigating title to the property;
  - undertaking searches over the property; and
  - making enquiries of the seller.
- Usually, the information discovered during the due diligence process is collated into a ***report on title*** for the client and a ***certificate of title*** for the lender.

Investigating title

- Title investigation is undertaken by the buyer's solicitor and the lender's solicitor.
- We investigate title to:
  - Ensure that the seller holds the legal and beneficial title to the property and can pass this to the buyer.
  - Find out about other rights and interests affecting the property which may bind the buyer.

- Some common rights and interests:

Table R1.1 Some common rights and interests, how to find them, and what action is required

Entry	Where it can be found	Action required by buyer's solicitor
Things excluded from the property, for example, mines and minerals	Unregistered land: deeds Registered land: Property Register (A)	Report it to the client.
Rights benefitting the property	Unregistered land: deeds Registered land: Property Register (A)	Report it to the client, and check that the right will be sufficient for their needs.
Rights burdening the property	Unregistered land: deeds Registered land: Charges Register (C)	Check with the seller whether the right has been interfered with in the past. Report to client and check whether their future plans for the property may lead them to interfere with the right. Explore insurance for a past or future interference.
Restrictive covenants	Unregistered land: deeds Registered land: Charges Register (C)	Check with the seller whether the covenant has been breached in the past. Report to client and check whether their future plans for the property may lead them to breach the covenant. Explore insurance for a past or future breach. For a future breach, explore: • Release from the person with the benefit • Release or modification from the Upper Tribunal (Lands Chamber)

Table R1.1 (Continued)

Entry	Where it can be found	Action required by buyer's solicitor
Positive covenants	Unregistered land: deeds Registered land: the covenant is likely to be noted on the Charges Register (C), with either a restriction or an indemnity covenant on the Proprietorship Register (B)	Check with the seller whether the covenant has been breached in the past. Past breaches may be rectified. Report to client and check whether their future plans for the property may lead them to breach the covenant. Explore insurance for a past breach which cannot be rectified, or a future breach. A deed of covenant or indemnity covenant may be required in order to register the transfer with HMLR.
Mortgages	Unregistered land: deeds Registered land: noted on the Charges Register (C), with a restriction on the Proprietorship Register (B)	Obtain an undertaking from the seller that the mortgage funds will be discharged on completion and a DS1 form or receipted mortgage deed supplied. This will need to be supplied to HMLR in order to register the transfer with HMLR.
Trust interests	Unregistered land: deeds show if multiple proprietors Registered land: proprietor and a restriction on the Proprietorship Register (B)	Require two trustees to be a party to the transfer deed in order to overreach any beneficial interests.

How to investigate title to unregistered land

- Identify a ***good root of title***:
  - *Type of document*. Any document which deals with the legal and beneficial title, but preferably a conveyance or a mortgage deed.
  - *Date of document*. At least 15 years old, and must be dated before compulsory registration.
  - Content of document:
    - Adequate description of the property.
    - Properly executed as a deed.
    - Stamped properly.
      - ***Ad valorem***. Stamp duty paid or certificate of value.
      - ***Particulars delivered***. PD stamp or certificate of exemption.
  - Cast no doubt on the seller's title:
    - Account for changes of name.
    - Account for death of a co-owner.
    - Account for executions under a power of attorney.
- Conduct a search of the ***Land Charges Register*** against the names of all previous owners of the property, for their duration of ownership.
- ***Priority*** rules:

Table R1.2 The priority rules applicable on a disposition of unregistered land

Type of interest	Key examples	Who it will bind	How to discover it
Legal	• Freehold and leasehold estates • Easements for the duration of a freehold or leasehold estate • Legal mortgages	Everyone	Inspection of documents in the ***epitome of title***

Table R1.2 (Continued)

Type of interest	Key examples	Who it will bind	How to discover it
Equitable interests subject to registration as a land charge, under s10 LCA 1925	• Puisne mortgage • Estate contract • Restrictive covenants • Equitable easements	A purchaser only if it has been registered as a land charge; everyone else (even if not registered as a land charge)	Search of the Land Charges Register. • Search for entries registered against current and previous owners of the property: ○ Search against all common iterations of names. ○ Search against each name for the dates they owned or could have owned the land. • Priority protection period: 15 working days from the date of the search result. • Key results: ○ C(i) Puisne mortgage ○ C(iv) Estate contract ○ D(ii) Restrictive covenants ○ D(iii) Equitable easements
Other equitable interests		A purchaser for value only if they had notice of it; everyone else	Searches, inspections, enquiries

How to investigate title to registered land

- Review the register of title to ascertain the legal ownership. This is conclusive as to the ***legal ownership*** of the property. This will be in the ***Proprietorship Register***.
- Details about the property and any rights which benefit it are noted on the ***Property Register*** (A).
- ***Restrictions*** are noted on the Proprietorship Register (B).
- ***Notices***, including covenants and rights burdening the property, are noted on the ***Charges Register*** (C).
- Priority rules:
  - All interests, whether legal or equitable, will bind a purchaser for value only if they are noted on the register of title.
  - ***Overriding interests*** in Schedule 3 LRA 2002 will bind everyone even if not noted on the title.
  - Other interests which are not noted will not bind a purchaser for value but will bind all others.

Conducting searches

Table R1.3 The key searches over land

Search	What it tells us	When it should be done	How to do it
Index map search	Whether the land is registered or unregistered, and the title number	All transactions	Submit SIM form to HMLR
Local Land Charge Search	Restrictions on the land imposed by statutory powers, for example, planning permissions	All transactions	Submit LLC1 form to HMLR or local authority
Standard enquiries of the local authority	Information about the local area, such as planning permission, roads, and railways	All transactions	Submit CON29 form to local authority

Table R1.3 (Continued)

Search	What it tells us	When it should be done	How to do it
Optional enquiries of the local authority	Additional information about the local area, such as common land and village greens, and urban development areas	Only if any of the questions asked are relevant to the transaction	Submit CON29O form to the local authority
Highways search	Adoption status of roads in the vicinity, including their precise location	All transactions	Submit form to the local authority or request via private search provider
Drainage and water search	Information about the supply of water to the property and the drainage of surface and foul water to sewers	All transactions	Request direct to the water company or via private search provider
Desktop environmental search	Assessment of risk as to the likely contamination of the land	All transactions	Usually via a private search provider
Desktop flood search	Assessment as to the likely flood risk of the land	All transactions	Usually via a private search provider
Chancel repair search	Whether the property is located in an area where chancel repair liability is likely	Unregistered land; registered land where the previous transfer for value occurred before 13 October 2013; Transfers for no consideration	Usually via a private search provider

Table R1.3 (Continued)

Search	What it tells us	When it should be done	How to do it
Company search	Whether the seller is in administration, and whether there are any charges (fixed or floating) over the company	Where the seller is a company	Via Companies House
Utilities search	Which utility connections benefit the property and equipment in the area	Where utility connections are required or where development of the land may interfere with equipment	Usually via a private search provider
Telecoms search	Which telecommunications connections benefit the property and equipment in the area	Where telecoms connections are required or where development of the land may interfere with equipment	Usually via a private search provider

Planning permission

Development

- Planning permission is required for any '***development***' under s57 TCPA 1990.
- An activity will constitute 'development' if:
  - It involves:
    - the carrying out of ***building operations*** in, on, over, or under land; or
    - the making of any ***material change in the use*** of any buildings or other land; and
  - it is not expressly excluded under section 55(2) TCPA.

Building operations

'Building operations' includes:

- demolition;
- rebuilding;

- structural alterations or additions to buildings; and
- other operations normally undertaken by a person carrying on business as a builder.

Material change of use

- The use classes can be found in the Town and Country Planning (Use Classes) Order 1987, which was amended in 2020.
- 'Material change of use' includes:
  - any change from one use class to another; and
  - any changes to or from a specified ***sui generis*** use.
- Changes within a use class do not constitute a 'material change of use'.
- Use the relevant version of the Order depending on when the change of use occurred:

Table R1.4 Which use classes order to refer to

When was the change of use?	Which use classes order to refer to?
Before 1 September 2020	The old use classes order
After 31 July 2021	The new use classes order
Between 1 September 2020 and 31 July 2021	Both. If the change is only material under one of them, then planning permission will not be required.

Permitted development

- Some activities which require planning permission are automatically granted it; this is known as ***permitted development***.
- Where an activity is a permitted development, it still requires planning permission, but an express application for planning permission is not required.
- Permitted development activities can be found in Schedule 2 of the GPDO. There are categories relevant to:
  - building works; and
  - changes of use.
- To work out whether an activity is a permitted development, you need to check that:
  - The activity is of a type permitted by GPDO (consult Schedule 2).
  - The activity is not excluded from the scope of the GDPO (consult Schedule 2).
  - All relevant conditions have been complied with (consult Schedule 2).
  - The GPDO has not been disapplied by an Article 4 Direction (consult the LLC search result).

Enforcement of planning control

- A breach of planning control is either where:
  - 'development' has taken place without planning permission; or
  - a condition or limitation of planning permission has been breached.
- A breach can be enforced against the current owner of the property even if the breach was committed by a previous owner.
- The remedies available to the local planning authority are as follows:

Table R1.5 The types of enforcement action for a breach of planning control

Remedy	Key features
Enforcement notice	• The notice sets out: ○ the nature of the breach of planning control and ○ the steps which need to be taken in order to remedy or cease the breach. • The recipient is given 28 days to either: ○ restore the land to the condition it was in before the development; or ○ comply with any conditions imposed by planning permission.
Stop notice	• Can only be used in conjunction with an enforcement notice. • Requires the breaching activity to stop until the deadline for compliance set out in the enforcement notice. • Can only be used to prohibit certain activities – see s183 TCPA.
Temporary stop notice	• Does not have to be used in conjunction with an enforcement notice. • Mandates the immediate cessation of the breaching activity. • Can only be used to prohibit certain activities – see s171F TCPA 1990.
Breach of condition notice	• Requires compliance with terms of a planning condition. • Can be used as an alternative to an enforcement notice.
Injunction	• An injunction can restrain a breach of planning control. • Injunctions are discretionary for the court.

- The time limit for taking enforcement action depends on the type of breach:

Table R1.6 The time limit for enforcement action for a breach of planning control

Type of breach	Time limit for enforcement action
Building works carried out without planning permission	Four years from substantial completion of the works
Breach of a planning condition	Ten years from the breach of the condition
Material changes of use without planning permission	For changes of use to single dwellinghouses: four years from the date of the change of use In all other cases: ten years from the date of the change of use

Building regulations

- ***Building regulations*** are a statutory regime to regulate health and safety aspects of undertaking building work.
- The regime applies to any ***building work***, as defined in Section 3 of the Building Regulations 2010.
- Before work starts, consent is required.
- During work, inspections occur.
- Once work has been completed, a certificate of compliance is issued (if the work meets the required standard).
- Breach is a strict liability offence, and enforcement can take the following forms:
  - ***Prosecution*** *of the responsible contractor.* This must be done within six months of discovery of the breach;
  - ***Enforcement notice*** *requiring the property owner to remedy the breach within 28 days.* This must be served within 12 months from completion of the building work; and
  - *An* ***injunction*** *to stop the breach.* There is no time limit for this.
- For a buyer of property in breach, insurance may be available, or a regularisation certificate could be obtained from the local planning authority.

Making enquiries of the seller

- The purpose of making enquiries of the seller is to find out any relevant information about the property which has either not been discovered during title investigation or searches or which requires further clarification.
- Some standard enquiries are made – these differ depending on the nature of the transaction:

Table R1.7 The forms of standard enquiry

Form	Type of transaction
TA6 Property Information Form	Disposals of residential property
CPSE1	General enquiries for all commercial property transactions (alternative to CPSE7)
CPSE3	Supplemental enquiries on the grant of a new lease
CPSE4	Supplemental enquiries on the assignment of the lease
CPSE7	General short-form enquiries for all property transactions (alternative to CPSE1)

- Additional enquiries are made to cover everything which has not been resolved by the standard enquiries.Investigating title

PHASE 1

Multiple-choice practice questions

Question 1

A solicitor is acting for the seller of a freehold property with unregistered title.

The solicitor is preparing for deduction of title to the property to a solicitor acting for the buyer. He examines the deeds and documents relating to the property.

Which of the following is the best candidate for a good root of title when deducing title to the property?

A. A conveyance of the property, dated 2009.
B. A 3-year lease over the property, dated 2020.
C. A conveyance of the property, dated 2024.
D. A mortgage deed of the property, dated 2014.
E. A conveyance of the property, dated 1985.

Question 2

A solicitor is acting for the seller of a freehold property with unregistered title.

The solicitor is preparing for deduction of title to the property to a solicitor acting for the buyer. He examines the deeds and documents relating to the property.

Which of the following is the best candidate for a good root of title when deducing title to the property?

A. A lease for five years which contained no stamps.
B. A lease for eight years which contained a certificate of value in respect of ad valorem stamp duty.

C. A conveyance for the sale of freehold land which contained a certificate of value in respect of ad valorem stamp duty and a certificate of exemption in respect of particulars delivered.
D. A conveyance for the sale of freehold land which contained no stamps.
E. A conveyance for the sale of freehold land which contained a particulars delivered stamp.

Question 3

A solicitor is acting for the purchaser of a freehold property with unregistered title. The property is to be purchased for £300,000. Whilst investigating the title, the solicitor discovers a number of encumbrances potentially affecting the property.

The epitome of title contains the following documents:

- A deed of easement relating to a right of way (in fee simple absolute).
- A lease for six years.
- A contract for sale.

A Land Charges Search reveals a D(ii) restrictive covenant registered against the current proprietor.

Which of the above will bind the purchaser?

A. The easement, the restrictive covenant, and the lease.
B. The contract for sale and the restrictive covenant.
C. The easement and the restrictive covenant.
D. The restrictive covenant only.
E. The restrictive covenant and the lease.

Question 4

A solicitor is acting for the seller of a freehold property with unregistered title.

The solicitor is preparing for deduction of title to the property to a solicitor acting for the buyer. He examines the deeds and documents relating to the property and identifies a conveyance dated 1 August 1990 which makes a good candidate for a good root of title to deduce to the solicitor acting for the buyer.

The conveyance was executed by the seller of the property, a company.

Which of the below is the execution block required in this conveyance?

A. Executed as a deed by affixing THE COMMON SEAL of [*company name*] in the presence of [*director*].
B. EXECUTED as a DEED by [*company name*] acting by a director in the presence of [*witness name and address*].
C. Executed as a deed by affixing THE COMMON SEAL of [company name] in the presence of [*director*] and [*director*].
D. SIGNED, SEALED, AND DELIVERED by the said [*person name*] in the presence of [*witness name and address*].
E. SIGNED AS A DEED AND DELIVERED by the said [*person name*] in the presence of [*witness name and address*].

Question 5

A solicitor is acting for the buyer of a freehold property with registered title.

The seller's solicitor tells the buyer's solicitor that the property is subject to a legal right of way on foot exercisable by a neighbour.

What will the buyer's solicitor look for when examining the Land Registry official copy of the title to the property?

A. An entry referring to an easement in the Property Register.
B. An entry relating to an easement in the Proprietorship Register.
C. An entry referring to an easement in the Charges Register.
D. A restriction on dealings in the Proprietorship Register.
E. An entry referring to a restrictive covenant in the Charges Register.

Question 6

A solicitor is acting for the buyer of a freehold property with registered title.

The seller's solicitor tells the buyer's solicitor that the property is subject to a promise to contribute towards the maintenance costs of a shared pathway.

What will the buyer's solicitor look for when examining the Land Registry official copy of the title to the property, to check whether this promise will bind their client?

A. An entry referring to a positive covenant in the Property Register.
B. An entry relating to a restrictive covenant in the Proprietorship Register.
C. An entry referring to a positive covenant in the Charges Register.
D. An indemnity covenant in the Proprietorship Register.
E. An entry referring to a restrictive covenant in the Charges Register.

Question 7

A solicitor is acting for the buyer of a freehold property with registered title.

The seller's solicitor tells the buyer's solicitor that the property was owned by two tenants-in-common in unequal shares, and that one of the tenants-in-common of the property has died.

What is the most likely way in which this would be reflected on the register of title?

A. The register of title would be silent on the matter because the estate of the deceased co-owner will have an overriding interest.
B. The Proprietorship Register will contain a restriction preventing a disposal of the property by a sole legal owner.
C. A restriction on the Proprietorship Register preventing a disposal without the consent of all the tenants-in-common.
D. A notice on the Charges Register detailing the equitable interest.
E. A notice on the Property Register detailing the equitable interest.

Question 8

A solicitor is acting for a developer who is purchasing a freehold property.

The seller has disclosed that in January 2021 the use of the property changed from a shop to a financial services provider.

Was planning permission required for this change of use?

A. No, because the change was not a material change of use under either version of the Order.

B. Yes, because the change was a material change of use under both versions of the Order.
C. Yes, because the change was a material change of use under the 1987 version of the Order.
D. No, because the change was a material change of use under one version of the Order.
E. Yes, because the change was a material change of use under the 2020 version of the Order.

Question 9

A solicitor is acting for a local authority client who is the sole owner of a freehold property.

The property has been used as a library.

The client plans to build a large double-storey extension on the property and use it instead as a museum.

The client has asked for the solicitor's advice about whether their plans constitute 'development' and, therefore, whether they will need to obtain planning permission.

Will the client require planning permission for their plans for the property?

A. Yes, they will require planning permission for both the change of use and the extension.
B. Yes, they will require planning permission for the extension, but not for the change of use.
C. Yes, they will require planning permission to change the use, but the extension will not constitute 'development'.
D. No, they will not require planning permission because neither constitutes 'development'.
E. No, they will not require planning permission because the change of use is not 'material' and the extension is 'permitted development'.

Question 10

A solicitor is acting for a purchaser of a freehold building.

The property has previously been used as office premises. The client plans to carry out internal works to the property so that she can let it as a single private dwellinghouse.

She has asked for the solicitor's advice about whether her plans constitute 'development' and, therefore, whether she will need to obtain planning permission.

Will the client need to apply for planning permission for her plans for the property?

A. No, because the internal works do not constitute development, and the change of use is permitted under Schedule 2 Part 3 GPDO.
B. No, the internal works do not constitute development, nor does the change of use, because it is permitted under Schedule 2 Part 3 GPDO.
C. No, the internal works do not constitute development, nor does the change of use, because it is a change to a single private dwellinghouse.
D. Yes, she will need to apply for planning permission for both the internal works and the change of use because they are developments which are not permitted.
E. No, the internal works do not constitute development, nor does the change of use, because the change is not material.

Question 11

A solicitor is acting for a local planning authority (LPA).

Conditional planning permission was granted six years ago for the construction of a building. The building works were completed a year later.

It has been discovered that the building was not constructed in accordance with the plans approved by the LPA.

What is the most appropriate action the LPA could take?

A. Serve a stop notice on the owner of the property.
B. Apply for an injunction to restrain the breach of planning control.
C. The LPA cannot take any action because the building works were completed five years ago.
D. Serve a breach of condition notice on the owner of the property.
E. Serve temporary stop notice on the owner of the property.

PHASE

2 The documentation

The solicitors have completed their due diligence on the various properties and have reported to their respective clients. In Phase 2, we will be examining the documentation used in land transactions.

The documentation primarily serves four functions:

1 Documentation relating to the landlord's consent to a transaction

In leasehold land, the landlord's consent is required for some actions, for example, assigning the lease or granting a sub-lease. This consent is documented in a ***licence***. In Chapter 10 we will explore the key features of a ***licence to assign*** and a ***licence to underlet***.

2 Contractual documentation

The process following on from an offer being accepted on a property to that property actually being transferred from the seller to the buyer can be lengthy, and there can be significant expense incurred before the land is transferred. For example, a buyer may incur legal and surveyor fees in conducting due diligence on the property, and a seller may turn down other interested buyers.

The consequences of one party withdrawing from the transaction during this process (e.g. if a seller receives a higher offer on the property, they may decide to sell to that buyer instead) can be significant, especially if the parties are in a chain

DOI: 10.4324/9781032711508-12

(e.g. if the seller withdraws and sells to a higher bidder, the delay may cause the buyer to lose their own buyer).

In order to mitigate the risk of one party withdrawing from the transaction after time and expense have been committed, it is common for the parties to enter into a contract requiring them to proceed to completion. This formalises the process, gives both parties clear obligations and timeframes for completing the transaction, and importantly, provides them with a contractual remedy if the other party withdraws from the transaction.

In freehold transactions, and where a lease is being assigned, a ***sale contract*** is used. Where parties agree to grant or take a lease, an ***agreement for lease*** is entered into. A contractual agreement to buy or sell land is considered of such value that it constitutes an equitable interest in land which can be registered.

In Chapter 11, we look in detail at sale contracts in the context of a freehold purchase and the assignment of a lease.

3 Documentation effecting the disposition of an estate in land

The sale contract and agreement for lease noted above simply set out the agreement between the parties, and although they are an interest in land, these documents are not capable of transferring the legal estate from one party to another. The transfer of freehold land and the assignment of a lease is effected with a ***transfer deed*** (also known as a ***deed of assignment***, where the interest being transferred is leasehold), and the grant of a lease is effected by the lease itself.

We examine the use of a transfer deed to transfer a freehold estate and to assign a lease in Chapter 12, and the use of a lease to create a leasehold estate in Chapter 13.

4 Finance documentation

If the buyer is purchasing property with the assistance of a loan from the bank, mortgage documentation needs to be entered into in order to create the security. In Chapter 14, we examine the ***mortgage deed*** in the context of a freehold purchase.

10 The licence

10.1 Chapter overview

Some activities relating to leasehold property require the consent of the landlord. Where the landlord's consent is required for a particular activity, that consent takes the form of a licence. This chapter focuses on two key licences:

- Licence to assign
- Licence to underlet

Another key licence that you may come across in practice is a licence for alterations, which is used where the tenant wishes to make alterations to the premises. A detailed examination of this type of licence is beyond the scope of this work.

This chapter is relevant to commercial leases.

> **This chapter in the context of our Transactions**
>
> Polished Perfection Ltd has decided to assign the Nail Bar Lease (the **Lease**) to Gemma's Gels Ltd, and Style&Go Ltd has provisionally agreed to this. The Lease requires Style&Go Ltd's consent to take the form of a licence to assign, which Style&Go Ltd's solicitors will draft.
>
> You may wish to refer to the licence to assign in Appendix 5 (the **Nail Bar Licence**) whilst working through this chapter.

DOI: 10.4324/9781032711508-13

10.2 Licence to assign

Polished Perfection Ltd is assigning their lease over the Nail Bar to Gemma's Gels Ltd. We will examine the process and key provisions in a licence to assign in the context of this Transaction.

10.2.1 Terminology

The parties relevant to a licence to assign are:

- *The landlord under the lease which is being assigned.* In our case, this is Style&Go Ltd;
- *The tenant under the lease which is being assigned.* This party is selling the lease and is also known as the ***assignor***. In our Transaction, this is Polished Perfection Ltd; and
- *The party purchasing the lease.* This party is known as the incoming tenant (as once the lease has been assigned, they will become the tenant under that lease) or the ***assignee***. In our Transaction, this is Gemma's Gels Ltd.

In this book we refer to these parties as the **landlord**, the **tenant**, and the **assignee**.

10.2.2 Process

Usually, the landlord prepares the licence to assign and provides it to both the tenant and the assignee to review and agree. If either party wishes to amend any of the terms, negotiations take place at this stage.

Once agreed, the licence will be signed by:

- the landlord;
- the tenant; and
- the assignee.

The licence can be completed at any point after it has been duly executed by the relevant parties, but in practice, this usually happens shortly before completion of the deed of assignment.

10.2.3 Key provisions of the licence

We will now examine some of the key terms of a licence to assign.

10.2.3.1 Transaction details

The licence will contain basic details about the transaction, such as:

- *Details of the parties to the licence.* This will be the landlord, tenant, and assignee (in our case, Style&Go Ltd, Polished Perfection Ltd, and Gemma's Gels Ltd);
- *Details of the lease which is being assigned.* In our case, this is the lease over the Nail Bar granted by Style&Go Ltd to Polished Perfection Ltd on 21 September 2026; and
- Details of the premises under the lease (so in our case, the Nail Bar).

In the Nail Bar Licence, these details are included as defined terms.

10.2.3.2 The permission

The licence will contain provisions which relate to the landlord's consent to the assignment. In the Nail Bar Licence, this is at clause 2.

Some common provisions relating to the landlord's consent are as follows:

10.2.3.2.1 LANDLORD'S CONSENT AND CONDITIONS

The licence will state the landlord's consent to the assignment. It is common to see a clause that this consent will become void if the relevant assignment is not completed within a certain amount of time, even though in practice the licence is usually completed just before the assignment is completed. You can see this in clause 2.2 of the Nail Bar Licence.

The licence will list any conditions of the landlord's consent. Common conditions of consent include:

*10.2.3.2.1.1 THE REQUIREMENT FOR THE TENANT TO ENTER INTO AN AUTHORISED GUARANTEE AGREEMENT (AN **AGA**) WITH THE LANDLORD*

A tenant will often be required under the licence to enter into an AGA with the landlord. An AGA is a contract between the landlord and the tenant (so between Style&Go Ltd and Polished Perfection Ltd) in which the tenant guarantees the assignee's performance of the tenant covenants under the lease.

Style&Go Ltd requires this as a condition of their consent – please see clause 2.3 and Schedule 1 of the Nail Bar Licence. Polished Perfection Ltd will be financially liable to Style&Go Ltd if Gemma's Gels Ltd breaches any of the tenant covenants under the Nail Bar Lease.

10.2.3.2.1.2 RECEIPT OF A RENT DEPOSIT DEED FROM THE ASSIGNEE

An assignee is often required to enter into a rent deposit deed. A ***rent deposit deed*** is an agreement between the landlord and the assignee (so between Style&Go Ltd and Gemma's Gels Ltd) which:

- requires the assignee to pay a deposit for the assignment of the lease;
- sets out how the landlord will hold that deposit as security for non-performance of the tenant covenants; and
- details the circumstances in which the landlord can draw upon that deposit.

Style&Go Ltd requires this from Gemma's Gels Ltd – please see clause 2.4 of the Nail Bar Licence.

10.2.3.2.1.3 THE RECEIPT OF SATISFACTORY REFERENCES FOR THE ASSIGNEE

An assignee may be required to provide references to the landlord. These could be from previous landlords, and they serve to reassure the landlord that the assignee will make a reliable tenant.

10.2.3.2.2 ASSIGNEE COVENANTS IN RESPECT OF THE TENANT COVENANTS UNDER THE LEASE

The licence may contain direct covenants from the assignee to the landlord in respect of the tenant covenants in the lease. This creates privity of contract between the landlord and the assignee and overcomes some of the challenges of enforcing covenants.[1]

Style&Go Ltd has imposed direct covenants on Gemma's Gels Ltd at clause 3 of the Nail Bar Licence to:

1. perform the tenant covenants under the Nail Bar Lease; and
2. pay rent due under the Nail Bar Lease.

10.2.3.2.3 ADDITIONAL ASSIGNEE OBLIGATIONS

There are often additional obligations on the assignee, such as:

1. an obligation to notify the landlord of completion of the assignment; and
2. an obligation to register the assignment at HMLR.

These are contained within the Nail Bar Licence and can be found at clause 11.

10.2.3.2.4 TENANT COVENANTS TO PAY LANDLORD COSTS

The licence may require the tenant to pay the landlord's costs associated with preparing the licence, by way of a covenant. In our transaction, Style&Go Ltd requires Polished Perfection Ltd to pay its costs for preparing the Nail Bar Licence, at clause 5.

10.2.3.2.5 LANDLORD'S RIGHT OF RE-ENTRY

The licence will often include a provision allowing the landlord to exercise their right of re-entry under the lease in cases where the licence has been breached. This is the case under clause 6 of the Nail Bar Licence and allows Style&Go Ltd to re-enter the Nail Bar if Gemma's Gels Ltd breaches any of the licence terms.

10.2.4 The AGA

If it is a condition of the landlord's consent that the tenant enter into an ***authorised guarantee agreement*** (which it is in our Transaction – see clause 2.3 and

1 See Chapter 22.

Section 10.2.3.2.1.1), then it is common that this AGA is incorporated into the licence. It can alternatively be entered into as a separate deed which is completed at the same time as the licence. In our Transaction, the AGA is incorporated into the Nail Bar Licence at Schedule 1.

We will now examine some of the key provisions in an AGA.

10.2.4.1 The guarantee

The AGA will set out the extent of the tenant's guarantee. In clause 1 of the AGA in the Nail Bar Licence, we can see that Polished Perfection Ltd guarantees the performance by Gemma's Gels Ltd of the following covenants in the Nail Bar Lease:

1. the payment of rent; and
2. the performance of tenant covenants.

Polished Perfection Ltd gives a covenant to Style&Go Ltd that if Gemma's Gels Ltd fails to perform either of the aforementioned, Polished Perfection Ltd will indemnify Style&Go Ltd and will perform those covenants itself.

10.2.4.2 Time limit on tenant's liability

It is common to see a clause which states the duration for which the tenant will remain liable under the AGA. This is typically for the term of the lease, including any continuation under the 1954 Act, unless the landlord expressly releases the tenant from this liability. We can see this at clause 2.1 of the AGA in the Nail Bar Lease.

10.3 Licence to underlet

A licence to underlet is used to document the landlord's consent to the tenant granting an ***underlease*** (or sub-lease) over the lease premises. As explained in Chapter 1, our Transactions do not include a sub-lease; however, we discuss the process and key provisions of a licence to underlet in general terms, and this can be combined with the roadmap in Section 1.4.6 of Chapter 1 to guide you through the process for sub-letting a leasehold property.

10.3.1 Process

Just like with the licence to assign, the landlord will prepare the licence to underlet and provide it to the tenant and the ***subtenant*** to review and agree.

The licence will be signed by:

1. the landlord;
2. the tenant; and
3. the subtenant.

The licence can be completed at any point after it has been duly executed by the relevant parties, but in practice, this usually happens shortly before completion of the sub-lease.

10.3.2 Key provisions of the licence

We detail some of the key provisions you may see in a licence to underlet. Many of these are similar to those we looked at in Section 10.2.3 relating to the licence to assign.

10.3.2.1 Transaction details

Just like in the licence to assign, the licence to underlet will contain basic details about the transaction, such as:

1. details of the parties to the licence, namely, the landlord, the tenant, and the subtenant;
2. details of the lease to which the licence relates; and
3. details of the premises under the lease.

10.3.2.2 Landlord's consent

The licence will state the landlord's consent to the sub-lease. The consent will be given specifically to a particular sub-lease to a specific subtenant, the terms of which will be annexed to the licence. The tenant will not be permitted to vary these terms without the landlord's consent.

In practice, the licence is usually completed just before the sub-lease is completed, but it is still common to see a clause stating that this consent will become void if the relevant sub-lease is not completed within a certain amount of time.

10.3.2.3 Obligations relating to the sub-lease

In addition to the terms of the sub-lease being annexed to the licence, the licence will set out additional obligations of the tenant in respect of the sub-lease. Some of the most common obligations are:

10.3.2.3.1 SUB-LEASE IS CONTRACTED OUT OF LTA

The tenant must ensure that the sub-lease is contracted out of the LTA 1954 and the relevant notice procedure has been followed. This is to make sure that the sub-tenant does not have security of tenure.[2]

10.3.2.3.2 NO OCCUPATION BEFORE GRANT OF SUB-LEASE

The tenant must ensure that the sub-tenant does not occupy the premises before the sub-lease is granted. This is because the covenants given by the sub-tenant do

2 See Chapter 23.

not come into force until the sub-lease is granted, so the landlord needs to protect itself against breaches which occur before the sub-tenant becomes liable for them.

10.3.2.3.3 ENFORCING COVENANTS IN SUB-LEASE

The tenant must enforce the tenant covenants of the sub-lease against the sub-tenant and cannot release or waive any breaches of them.

10.3.2.3.4 RENT REVIEW IN SUB-LEASE

Some of the processes under the sub-lease cannot be completed without the landlord's approval; for example, the tenant must seek the landlord's approval of any revised rent for the sub-lease.

10.3.2.4 Subtenant covenants

The licence will require the subtenant to enter into direct covenants with the landlord. This creates privity of contract between the landlord and the subtenant and overcomes some of the challenges of enforcing covenants.[3]

Common subtenant covenants include:

1. the payment of rent and performance of tenant covenants in the sub-lease;
2. the performance of tenant covenants in the lease; and
3. in the case of a future assignment of the sub-lease, a requirement to ensure that a future assignee enters into a direct covenant with the landlord on the same terms.

10.3.2.5 Rights of re-entry

The licence will usually include a provision allowing the landlord to exercise his right of re-entry under the lease in cases where the licence has been breached.

10.3.2.6 Landlord's costs

The licence may require the outgoing tenant to pay the landlord's costs associated with preparing the licence, by way of a covenant.

10.3.2.7 Formalities

The licence will usually require the tenant to notify the landlord upon completion of the grant of the underlease and require the subtenant to register the sub-lease at HMLR.

The licence also usually requires the subtenant to give a direct indemnity to the landlord against breaches of the licence terms by the subtenant.

3 See Chapter 22.

Chapter 10 revision points

- A licence is used to document the landlord's consent to a particular activity under the lease. Where a tenant wishes to alienate the property, a licence to assign or licence to underlet may be required.
- A licence to assign may contain conditions to the landlord's consent, such as a requirement that the tenant enter into an authorised guarantee agreement, acting as guarantor of the assignee's obligations, and a requirement that the assignee enter into direct covenants with the landlord.
- The landlord's consent under a licence to underlet will be limited to a specific sub-tenant on specific terms, noted in the licence. It is common for the sub-tenant to enter into direct covenants with the landlord.

11 The sale contract

11.1 Chapter overview

When an interest in land is disposed of, it is common for the parties to enter into a contract for the disposal of that land, before the land itself is transferred.

When the estate is being transferred from one party to another – for example, the transfer of the freehold or the assignment of a lease – this is done by way of the sale contract. On the grant of a lease or sub-lease, this is done by way of an agreement for lease.

This chapter examines some of the key provisions in a sale contract. Agreements for lease are not looked at in detail.

This chapter in the context of our Transactions

The following Transactions require a sale contract, which is prepared by the relevant seller's solicitor for review by the relevant buyer's solicitor:

- André's acquisition of the House;
- Style&Go Ltd's acquisition of the Salon;
- Style&Go Ltd's acquisition of the Car Park; and
- Polished Perfection Ltd's assignment of the lease to Gemma's Gels Ltd.

You may wish to refer to the sale contract for each of the aforementioned Transactions and the set of standard conditions relevant to that Transaction (in Appendix 6) whilst working through this chapter.

DOI: 10.4324/9781032711508-14

11.2 Purpose of the contract

11.2.1 Sale contract

A sale contract is a contract between the prospective seller and the prospective buyer whereby the parties are contractually bound to transfer the land on a future date. If the land is not later transferred in accordance with the terms of the contract, the innocent party will have a contractual remedy against the breaching party. They are typically used in all transfers of freehold land and commonly on assignment of a lease.

A sale contract will be relevant for:

- André's acquisition of the House;
- Style&Go Ltd's acquisition of the Salon and the Car Park; and
- Polished Perfection Ltd's assignment of the Nail Bar Lease to Gemma's Gels Ltd.

11.2.2 Agreement for lease

An agreement for lease is a contract between the prospective landlord and the prospective tenant whereby the parties are contractually bound to enter into a lease (or sub-lease) on a future date.

The agreement for lease creates a set of contractual obligations relating to the entry into the lease. If the lease is not entered into under the terms of the agreement for lease, then the innocent party will have a contractual remedy against the breaching party.

They are not used in all situations where a lease is to be granted, but they are used when the parties want the contractual certainty of knowing a lease will be entered into but cannot enter into the lease immediately. Some examples of when an agreement for lease could be useful are:

- the tenant knows that its lease of a different property is coming to an end in 12 months. It has identified a new property and wishes to ensure that it can take a lease in 12 months' time, when its current lease expires;
- the parties wish to enter into a lease, but this cannot be granted immediately because planning permission is outstanding; or
- the parties wish to enter into a lease, but this cannot be granted immediately because construction work is outstanding – for example, the landlord is undertaking building work on the property, or the tenant is carrying out fit-out works.

In our scenario, an agreement for lease could be entered into between Style&Go Ltd and Polished Perfection Ltd, obliging Polished Perfection Ltd to take a lease of the Nail Bar on a future date once they have completed the fit-out works, but the parties have agreed that this will not be necessary. We therefore do not consider agreements for lease further.

11.3 Process

It is the seller's solicitor who prepares the first draft of the sale contract, and the buyer's solicitor reviews it.

Once negotiations on the draft contract are complete, each solicitor must ensure their client understands the terms of the contract and is happy with them. Once both parties are happy with the wording of the contract and are comfortable to proceed to exchange, the parties must each sign the contract (either both parties sign one version of the contract or they each sign an identical version). If there is an occupier in the property who is not an owner and vacant possession is being provided on completion, the occupier will usually be a party to the contract and will need to sign it; this is so that the buyer has a direct contractual remedy against that occupier if the occupier does not vacate the property on completion.

Sometimes a client will sign a contract in person in the presence of their solicitor, but the most common method of execution is for solicitors to send the contract to their client, indicating where the client must sign.

As Style&Go Ltd is a company, a director or secretary will need to be authorised to sign on behalf of the company.

Execution of the contract must comply with the statutory formalities for transferring land.[1] Wet ink remains the 'safest' method of execution because there has been no formal guidance on whether electronic signatures satisfy the statutory requirements. However, some practitioners do allow electronic signatures based on guidance from the Law Commission and HMLR about executing other types of document electronically, and drawing inferences from case law.[2]

11.4 Terms of the contract

Broadly speaking, agreements for lease and sale contracts will both comprise a set of standard conditions, plus some bespoke provisions which are used to deviate from the position set out under those standard conditions and to cover anything additional which is not covered by them.

1 Set out in s2 LP(MP)A 1989.
2 Such as *Nucleolus v Rees* ([2019] EWHC 2462 (Ch)).

Typically, sale contracts comprise three parts:

- the ***particulars of sale.*** This is where key details about the transaction are recorded;
- the ***standard conditions;*** and
- the ***special conditions.*** These 'disapply' any of the standard conditions which are deemed inappropriate for the particular transaction, and they cover any additional obligations which aren't covered by the standard conditions.

We will look at these in turn.

11.4.1 Particulars of sale

The particulars of sale appear on the first page of the contract and will typically cover the following information:

11.4.1.1 Date of the contract

The contract will be dated upon exchange.

11.4.1.2 Seller

The name and address of the seller must be included.

If the title deeds show that the property was owned by tenants-in-common and one has since died, a second trustee will need to be a party to the transfer deed in order to overreach any beneficial interests. As the sellers under the sale contract must match those in the transfer deed, that trustee must also be a party to the contract. You will recall that this was the case for the Salon – a second trustee, Samir Mukhtar, is listed as a seller in the sale contract for the Salon.

If the proprietor, according to the title deeds, has died and a personal representative is disposing of the property on behalf of the estate, the personal representative(s) will need to be a party to the contract as well as the transfer deed. This was the case for the House, and you will see in the **House Contract** that Paul Thompson is the seller.

The seller may be a company, provided that the company has the power to deal with land (as per its articles of association or memorandum of association). This is the case in respect of the assignment of the Nail Bar Lease by Polished Perfection Ltd.

The seller may be a mortgagee (lender) if the borrower has defaulted on the loan and the lender's power of sale has become exercisable.

11.4.1.3 Buyer

The name and address of the buyer must be included in the particulars of sale.

11.4.1.4 Description of the property

The particulars of sale will identify the property by way of the following information:

- an address;
- a plan showing the location and boundaries of the property, if necessary;
- whether the property is freehold or leasehold; and
- the title number (relevant for registered land only).

11.4.1.5 Specified encumbrances

Encumbrances affecting the property should be listed by the seller. The effect of the seller failing to disclose an encumbrance is not that that encumbrance doesn't bind the buyer – as we have seen, certain types of encumbrance will attach to the land itself, so the buyer will still purchase the property subject to those encumbrances. However, if the seller has failed to disclose a particular encumbrance, the buyer will have a contractual remedy against the seller.

Some encumbrances are already listed in the standard conditions[3] and are therefore deemed to have been disclosed by the seller. Any encumbrances which are not automatically disclosed under the standard conditions will need to be specifically disclosed by the seller.[4]

11.4.1.6 Title guarantee

The particulars of sale will specify whether the land will be sold with full title guarantee or limited title guarantee.

Full title guarantee means that the seller makes the following covenants:

1. the seller has the right to dispose of the land;
2. the seller will do all they reasonably can to transfer the title;
3. (in leasehold land) the lease is subsisting, and the lease is not liable to forfeiture by virtue of a breach of covenant; and
4. the land is disposed of free from encumbrances other than those the seller does not know about and could not reasonably know about.

Limited title guarantee means that the seller makes the covenants above except as regards to the encumbrances: when giving a limited title guarantee, the seller will covenant that they have not encumbered the land and they are not aware that anyone else has encumbered the land during the seller's period of ownership.

3 see Section 11.4.2.
4 With the exclusion of those which will not bind the buyer under the usual priority rules.

If this is left blank in the particulars of sale, the default position under the standard conditions will apply.[5]

11.4.1.7 Completion date

The ***completion date*** will be agreed by the parties upon exchange of contracts and filled in at that time. If a date for completion is not entered into the particulars of sale on exchange, the position under the standard conditions applies.[6]

11.4.1.8 Contract rate

The ***contract rate*** specified in the particulars of sale relates to the compensation which is payable as a penalty for late completion, to compensate the innocent party for losses caused by that delay. In practice, parties typically use a rate of 4% above the base lending rate of a particular bank. If this is left blank, the standard conditions will impute a rate.[7]

11.4.1.9 Purchase price

The particulars of sale will state the agreed purchase price for the property that the buyer is to pay to the seller. In the case of the assignment of the Nail Bar Lease, Gemma's Gels Ltd is only paying a premium of £1 to purchase the lease, so the purchase price is £1.

11.4.1.10 Deposit

The deposit to be paid for the purchase of the property, payable on exchange, will be included in the particulars of sale, and if it is left blank, the deposit required under the standard conditions will be imputed.[8]

11.4.1.11 Balance

The balance to be paid by the buyer upon completion (which is the purchase price minus the deposit) will be noted in the particulars of sale.

11.4.2 Standard conditions

The standard conditions used to govern the contract for the disposal of land are drafted by the Law Society and are a set of standard contract terms and conditions which are incorporated into most sales of land. There are separate sets for residential and commercial land: the Standard Conditions of Sale (the **SCS**s), used for sales of residential land, and the Standard Commercial Property Conditions (the **SCPC**s), used for sales of commercial land.

5 See Section 11.4.2.4.2.
6 See Section 11.4.2.6.1.
7 See Section 11.4.2.7.3.
8 See Section 11.4.2.2.1.

Below are some of the key provisions contained in both sets of standard conditions. If the position under any of the standard conditions is deemed inappropriate for the particular transaction, the parties can use special conditions[9] to disapply the relevant standard condition.

We set out below the position in the standard conditions of some of the key provisions.[10]

11.4.2.1 VAT

The VAT position under the standard conditions for residential transactions is that the sale price is inclusive of VAT.[11]As we saw in Chapter 3,[12] the supply of the House and the Salon are not being made in the course of a business and so do not attract VAT, but if they were (e.g. if the seller was a company), then the standard conditions tell us that, because of their residential nature, the purchase price would be inclusive of VAT.

The VAT position under the standard conditions for commercial transactions is that the sale attracts VAT;[13] this means that the buyer must pay VAT on top of the agreed purchase price. If the seller has decided not to opt to tax,[14] Special Condition A1 of Part 2 must be specifically incorporated to disapply the standard position and ensure that no VAT will be payable on top of the purchase price. This is the case for the transfer of the Car Park to Style&Go Ltd – Urban Spaces Ltd has not opted to tax and so has incorporated Special Condition Part 2 A1.

If the VAT arrangements are to differ from the aforementioned, they must be amended by way of special condition.

11.4.2.2 Formation

The standard conditions contain provisions about the formation of the sale contract, including when a contract will be deemed to have been formed and the deposit payable.

11.4.2.2.1 DEPOSIT

If this section is left blank in the particulars of sale, a 10% deposit will be imputed.[15] This is acceptable for the House and the Salon, but Style&Go Ltd and Urban Spaces Ltd have agreed that only 5% deposit will be paid for the sale of the

9 See Section 11.4.3.
10 We cover those which are most relevant to this book, but we encourage readers to familiarise themselves with the entire content of the standard conditions.
11 SCS 1.4.1.
12 Section 3.3.2.2.1.
13 SCPC 2.
14 Please see Chapter 3 for a reminder of why a seller might opt to tax.
15 SCS 2.2 and SCPC 3.2.

Car Park, and no deposit at all is payable on the assignment of the Nail Bar Lease. The standard conditions are therefore not sufficient for these Transactions, and the agreed positions must be included in the particulars of sale.

The standard conditions also dictate that this deposit is held as ***stakeholder*** for the seller. This means the deposit cannot be given to either party without the consent of the other (but if the seller requires the money for another purchase in the chain of transactions, this is permitted).

To amend this so that the deposit is held as ***agent*** for the seller, which means the deposit can be given to the seller before completion, requires a special condition.

11.4.2.3 Matters affecting the property

The standard conditions set out any matters affecting the property, such as encumbrances, the physical state of the property, and any breaches of repair covenant (if the property is leasehold), and any leases affecting the property.

11.4.2.3.1 SPECIFIED ENCUMBRANCES

As noted above,[16] encumbrances affecting the property should be disclosed by the seller.

Some encumbrances are already listed in the standard conditions (and are therefore deemed to have been disclosed automatically by the seller). The encumbrances which are listed in the standard conditions vary depending on whether the SCSs or the SCPCs are used and, in summary, are as follows in Table 11.1:[17]

Table 11.1 The specified encumbrances as per the standard conditions

	SCS	SCPC
1	Matters discoverable by inspection of the property before the contract. *This includes obvious encumbrances. In practice, these are specifically disclosed to avoid any dispute as to the 'discoverability' of the encumbrance.*	
2	Matters the seller does not and could not have reasonably known about. *The seller must show that they did not know about the encumbrance and could not have reasonably known about it. Title due diligence would likely reveal anything that the seller could 'reasonably' have known about.*	

16 In Section 11.4.1.5.
17 The wording in italics in this table is the authors' commentary.

Table 11.1 (Continued)

	SCS	SCPC
3	Matters, other than mortgages, which the buyer knows about. *Any information which the buyer already has will be deemed to have been disclosed, even if this information did not come from the seller.*	Matters, other than mortgages, disclosed or which would have been disclosed by the searches and enquiries which a prudent buyer would have made before entering into the contract. *This means that the seller will be deemed to have disclosed anything which the buyer should have discovered during its title due diligence, for example, anything registered on the title at the Land Registry. In practice, sellers will specifically disclose these entries even though it is not strictly necessary to.*
4	Entries made before the date of the contract in any public register except those maintained by the Land Registry or the Land Charges Registry or by Companies House. *Entries registered at Companies House, the Land Registry, or the Land Charges Registry will need to be disclosed by the seller. The seller may wish to restrict this disclosure to those encumbrances listed on the title register at a particular date and time to mitigate against potential liability under breach of contract.*[18] *Any entries in other public registers will be deemed to have been disclosed by the seller.*	N/A. *Note that no entries made in a public register will be deemed to have been disclosed by the seller.*
5	Public requirements. *This includes notices, orders, proposals made by bodies acting on statutory authority (e.g. matters revealed by the standard enquiries of the local authority).*	

18 See Chapter 16, Section 16.2.1.2.

11.4.2.3.2 COVENANTS FOR TITLE

If the buyer is buying a lease (e.g. the seller is a tenant under a lease and is assigning it to the buyer, as Polished Perfection Ltd is to Gemma's Gels Ltd), it is common for the covenants for title to be amended. The position under the standard conditions[19] is that the seller has complied with the covenants under the lease, including repair covenants. This is at odds with the position under the doctrine of ***caveat emptor***, which puts the onus on the buyer to do investigations and purchase the property as it is. The standard conditions are therefore commonly amended to exclude references to repair. This is the case for the contract to assign the Nail Bar Lease to Gemma's Gels Ltd.

11.4.2.4 Title and transfer

The standard conditions set out provisions relating to the seller's deduction of title, the buyer's right to raise requisitions, the timetable for deducing and investigating title, and the effect of the transfer and title guarantee.

11.4.2.4.1 DEDUCTION OF TITLE

The seller must provide certain documentation to the buyer according to the standard conditions,[20] for example, the register of title, or an epitome of title and associated deeds. As title investigation usually occurs long before exchange of contracts, this will likely have already been complied with by the date of exchange, and indeed, this is the case for all our Transactions. However, if the seller has not provided all the relevant documentation, then their solicitor should amend this standard condition to instead refer to the documentation they have provided.

In assignments of a lease, the seller (the current tenant) is not obliged under the standard conditions to deduce title to the superior title. The reason for this is that, where the leasehold title is registered with title absolute, HMLR guarantees against defects in the superior title.[21] If the buyer (the assignee) requires the seller to deduce title to the superior title, for example, if the leasehold estate is only registered with good leasehold title, then this must be included as a special condition.

11.4.2.4.2 TITLE GUARANTEE

If the particulars of sale do not specify the level of title guarantee to be provided by the seller, then the default position under the standard conditions will apply, which is that full title guarantee will be given.

19 See SCS 3.2.2 and 4.6.3, and SCPC 4.2.2 and 7.6.4.
20 SCS 4.1 and SCPC 7.1.
21 See Chapter 2.

11.4.2.4.3 INDEMNITY COVENANTS

As discussed in Chapter 6, any positive covenants which the seller entered into when purchasing the property will continue to bind them once they have disposed of the property. To protect itself, the seller may require the buyer to enter into an indemnity covenant to indemnify the seller if the seller is sued for a breach of the positive covenant. The standard conditions already provide for this,[22] but it is common for this to be entered as a special condition as well.

You will recall that this is the case for the Salon, and Style&Go Ltd will be providing an indemnity covenant to Neeta.

11.4.2.5 Risk and insurance

The standard conditions set out when risk in the property passes from the seller to the buyer and any obligations on either party to insure the property.

The position under the standard conditions is that from the date of the contract (which is the date the contracts are exchanged),[23] the property is at the risk of the buyer. This means that it is the buyer's responsibility to insure the property (although there is no obligation to do so). Although unlikely, if the parties decide that the property should be at the risk of the seller even once contracts have been exchanged, or that it is the seller's responsibility to insure the property, the standard position must be disapplied or amended by special condition.

11.4.2.6 Completion

The standard conditions set out key information about completion, including the date and time for completion, the practical arrangements, provisions about apportionments and the amount payable by the buyer, provisions relating to the title deeds after completion, and the process and effect of serving a notice to complete.

11.4.2.6.1 COMPLETION DATE

If a date for completion is not entered into the particulars of sale on exchange, the standard conditions[24] require completion to occur 20 working days after the date of the contract (so 20 working days from exchange).

Where a contract is to be conditional on a particular event, for example, upon planning permission being obtained, or upon obtaining the consent of the landlord to an assignment, this must be drafted in as a special condition because the parties will not wish to incur liability for failing to complete if circumstances outside of their control make it impossible to do so. This is the case for the

22 SCS 4.6.4 and SCPC 7.6.5.
23 See Section 11.4.1.1.
24 SCS 6.1.1 and SCPC 9.1.1.

assignment of the Nail Bar Lease – see Special Condition 1, which makes completion conditional on Style&Go Ltd's consent.

11.4.2.6.2 TIME FOR COMPLETION

According to the standard conditions,[25] completion can occur at any time, but the completion monies must be received by 2:00 p.m.; otherwise, completion is considered to be 'late', and compensation is payable. In chain transactions, it is common practice to include a special condition to bring that time even earlier; the reason for this is to ensure that later transactions in the chain have sufficient time for the necessary funds to be transferred ahead of completion on that same day.

You will recall that André is in a chain and needs to complete on the sale of his current property on the same day as he completes the purchase of the House, and Special Condition 5 requires the completion monies for the House to be received by 12:00 p.m.

11.4.2.7 Remedies

The standard conditions set out the remedies available under the contract for errors and omissions in the contract, and for late completion. This is discussed briefly below and in more detail in Chapter 18.

11.4.2.7.1 WHO CAN BE COMPENSATED IF COMPLETION IS DELAYED?

If completion does not occur by the specified date and time, the standard conditions require the defaulting party to pay compensation to the innocent party at the specified contract rate.[26] In residential transactions, either party can be the innocent or defaulting party. Conversely, the SCPCs only envisage the buyer being the defaulting party, and so the buyer has no right to compensation if the seller delays completion. This can be amended by special condition so that both parties have the right to compensation if the other defaults and delays completion.

11.4.2.7.2 WHAT CONSTITUTES 'DELAYED COMPLETION'?

As noted above,[27] if completion monies are received after 2:00 p.m., this constitutes delayed completion under the standard conditions. This means that if the buyer transfers completion monies to the seller on 31 March and they are received at 2:30 p.m., actual completion will still occur on 31 March, but the buyer will have to pay a day's worth of compensation to the seller at the

25 SCS 6.1.2 and SCPC 9.1.2.

26 See Sections 11.4.1.8 and 11.4.2.7.3.

27 In Section 11.4.2.6.2.

specified contract rate. It is common practice for this cut-off time to be amended by special condition.

11.4.2.7.3 CONTRACT RATE

If the definition of Contract Rate is left blank in the particulars of sale, the standard conditions[28] will impute '[t]he Law Society's interest rate from time to time in force'.

11.4.2.8 Leasehold property

In contracts for the sale of an existing lease, the standard conditions set out that the buyer accepts the lease terms. For the assignment of the Nail Bar Lease from Polished Perfection Ltd to Gemma's Gels Ltd, it is therefore an important part of the due diligence process that Gemma's Gels Ltd's solicitor reviews the lease terms and reports on them to their client.

Where the landlord's consent is required for an assignment, the standard conditions[29] require the seller of a lease to apply for the landlord's consent at its own expense.

11.4.3 Special conditions

The function of the special conditions in the sale contract is threefold:

1. *To incorporate the standard conditions into the contract.* This is usually the first special condition. Note, the SCPCs come in two parts. If the SCPCs are incorporated generally, Part 1 will automatically apply, but the conditions in Part 2 must be specifically incorporated into the contract by special condition or they will not apply;
2. *To amend the standard position set out by the SCSs or SCPCs.* We have noted above some of the key provisions, and when these might need to be amended; and.
3. *To address other matters which are not covered by the SCSs or the SCPCs.* For example, any matter which was discovered during title investigation and that needed to be addressed by way of a contractual obligation on one of the parties.

Solicitors drafting the contract therefore need a good understanding of their client's instructions and to keep a list of issues arising during the due diligence process which are likely to need addressing.[30]

28 SCS 7.2 and SCPC 10.3.
29 SCS 8.3 and SCPC 11.3.2.
30 Such as the summaries produced for each of our Transactions.

11.4.3.1 Using special conditions to address matters which are not covered by the standard conditions

Special conditions can also be added to address any matters which haven't been covered by the standard conditions. Some common amendments include:

11.4.3.1.1 VACANT POSSESSION

The special conditions should specify whether the property is sold with ***vacant possession*** or subject to leases (which should then be listed). The buyer's solicitor will wish to review a copy of the terms of any occupational leases which the property will be sold subject to. All our properties are being sold with vacant possession, and this is reflected in the sale contracts.

If the property is currently occupied by someone who is not the seller but the buyer is to take the property with vacant possession, it is common practice to ensure that the current occupier sign a statement in the sale contract agreeing to vacate the property on the relevant date. The SCSs contain a form of wording which can be inserted as a special condition, but the SCPCs do not, and so parties using the SCPCs will need to draft some appropriate wording to include as a special condition.

11.4.3.1.2 CONTENTS TO BE INCLUDED WITH THE SALE, OR FIXTURES TO BE EXCLUDED FROM THE SALE

Fixtures, which are items attached to the land, will automatically pass with the land, but a special condition can be inserted to allow the seller to remove them if this has been agreed between the parties.

Fittings, which are items not attached to the land, will not automatically pass with the land and will need to be removed by the seller, but a special condition can be inserted if these are included in the sale.

Both parties' solicitors will need to ascertain from their client which items are to be removed from the property and which are to remain, and whether any additional consideration will be paid for fittings included with the sale. For residential sales, a **Fittings and Contents Form** is typically used to document this information.

11.4.3.1.3 DEALING WITH DEFECTS IN TITLE

Any defects in title should be disclosed by special condition. A defect in title (as opposed to an encumbrance) may include a conveyance which has not been stamped correctly. The buyer may wish to include a special condition requiring the seller to rectify this defect before completion, as a defective conveyance cannot form a good root of title, as we saw in Chapter 4.

11.4.3.1.4 INDEMNITY INSURANCE

Where the buyer's investigation of the title has revealed that a covenant has been breached and the buyer wishes to insure against the risk of enforcement, it may be appropriate for the seller to pay for this insurance. If agreed between the parties that the seller will arrange and/or pay for this, this should be included in a special condition. You will recall that this is the case for the Salon, as constructing the extension has breached the restrictive covenant not to build. Neeta has agreed to pay for an insurance policy, and this has been included as a special condition.

Chapter 11 revision points

- A sale contract contractually binds the seller and the buyer to transfer the land at a date in the future.
- The seller's solicitor will prepare the contract for review by the buyer's solicitor.
- Sale contracts comprise three sections: particulars of sale, a set of standard conditions, and special conditions.
- Particulars of sale set out key information about the specific transaction.
- Standard conditions are a set of standard terms and conditions applicable to property transactions. The Standard Conditions of Sale apply to residential transactions, and the Standard Commercial Property Conditions apply to commercial transactions.
- Special conditions can be used to address matters which are not covered in the standard conditions and to amend the position under the standard conditions if it is not suitable for the particular transaction.
- Once the sale contract is agreed, both parties must execute it in accordance with the statutory formalities.

12 The transfer deed

12.1 Chapter overview

In order to create or transfer a legal estate in land, a deed must usually be used. This chapter focuses on the process for drafting and agreeing the transfer deed, which is the deed for transferring a freehold estate and assigning a lease, as well as the key provisions contained within.

This chapter is relevant to transactions involving the transfer of a freehold or leasehold estate.

This chapter in the context of our Transactions

A transfer deed is required to transfer:

- the House from Michael's estate to André;
- the Salon from Neeta to Style&Go Ltd;
- the Car Park from Urban Spaces Ltd to Style&Go Ltd; and
- the Nail Bar Lease from Polished Perfection Ltd to Gemma's Gels Ltd.

The buyer's solicitor drafts the transfer deed for review by the seller's solicitor.

You may wish to refer to the TR1 for each of the above Transactions whilst working through this chapter.

DOI: 10.4324/9781032711508-15

12.2 Process

You will recall from Chapter 2 that in order to transfer land, the LPA 1925 requires certain formalities to be complied with. We will examine the process of producing and agreeing a document which satisfies these formalities and is capable of transferring the relevant legal estate.

12.2.1 Drafting the transfer deed

12.2.1.1 Format of the deed

For transfers of land which is already registered, the legal estate must be transferred using a specific form:[1]

- ***Form TR1*** for transfers of whole; and
- ***Form TP1*** for transfers of part.

When transferring land which is not yet registered, the TR1 is not a specific requirement; it is possible to draft a conveyance (relevant for unregistered freehold land) or a deed of assignment (for unregistered leases) which satisfies the relevant formalities. However, in practice, the TR1 is commonly used on account of the fact that the transfer of the land will likely trigger first registration.

12.2.1.2 Practicalities

The buyer's solicitor will draft the transfer deed and send it to the seller's solicitor for review and approval.

According to the Conveyancing Protocol, this can be drafted at the same time as the sale contract and reviewed prior to exchange of the sale contract, and this is often what happens in practice. However, it is not essential: the standard conditions simply require it to be drafted and sent to the seller's solicitor 12 working days before the completion date.[2]

12.2.2 Approving the transfer deed

Once received from the buyer's solicitor, the seller's solicitor will review the transfer deed carefully. Any necessary amendments will be discussed and agreed

1 Rule 58 of the Land Registration Rules 2003.
2 See Chapter 11.

upon between the parties before being made to the document. According to the standard conditions, this must be done within four working days of receipt from the buyer's solicitor; in practice, timeframes tend to be governed by the parties' requirements.

12.2.3 Producing engrossments

Once both parties are happy with the drafted transfer deed, the buyer's solicitor will prepare an ***engrossment*** of the transfer deed – this is a clean copy for execution. This will be sent to the seller's solicitor to arrange for their client to sign it. According to the standard conditions, this must be done at least five working days before the completion date.

12.3 Content of the transfer deed

The buyer's solicitor will use the contract and the official copies to draft the transfer deed. The deed will contain the following key information.

12.3.1 Title number

The title number of the property being transferred is stated. Where the land being transferred is unregistered land, this will be left blank.

12.3.2 Property

The address or description of the property is included and, in the case of registered land, should match the register of title. It is not usually necessary to refer to a plan in the case of registered land, but if the contract refers to a plan, or if the land is unregistered, this should be replicated in the transfer deed.

12.3.3 Date

This is left blank until completion occurs.

12.3.4 Transferor

The name of the seller must be included, and this must match the name of the registered proprietor, or the proprietor according to the title deeds if the land is unregistered.

12.3.4.1 Change of name

If the proprietor has changed their name, then the amended name is the name which must appear in the transfer deed as the seller, and the change of name must be evidenced to HMLR upon registration.

You will recall that Urban Developments Ltd is listed on the title deeds for the Car Park but changed their name to Urban Spaces Ltd in 2020. The seller listed in the TR1 is therefore Urban Spaces Ltd, as that is their current name, and Style&Go Ltd's solicitors will need to submit a copy of the change of name certificate from Companies House to HMLR when applying to register the transfer of the Car Park to Style&Go Ltd.

12.3.4.2 Sale by personal representative

Where a personal representative is selling the land (e.g. if the proprietor has died), then the personal representative's name and address will need to appear in the transfer deed as the seller (notwithstanding they are not the legal proprietor), and the grant of probate will need to be evidenced to HMLR upon registration.

This is the case for the sale of the House, as Michael has died, and Paul Thompson, his personal representative, is selling the House on behalf of Michael's estate. You can see at panel 4 of the TR1 that Paul is listed as the transferor.

12.3.4.3 Sale by surviving owner

Where the beneficial estate of registered land is held by more than one owner as tenants-in-common, the title register will contain a restriction preventing a sole surviving co-owner from selling the property alone (e.g. if other co-owners pass away). In this situation, a second trustee must be appointed as a seller along with the surviving co-owner to ensure that overreaching occurs.[3] The trustee can be appointed using the TR1[4] or using a deed of appointment. The second trustee's name and address will appear in the transfer deed as one of the sellers, and the death certificate will need to be evidenced to HMLR upon registration.

This was the case for the sale of the Salon; you can see at panel 11 of the TR1 that Samir Mukhtar has been appointed as a trustee and listed in panel 4 as a transferor along with Neeta.

12.3.5 Transferee for entry in the register

The name of the buyer must be noted. This is the name which will appear as the 'registered proprietor' once the transfer is registered.

12.3.6 Transferee's intended address for service

The buyer's address must be noted. This is the address at which any notices will be served. For companies, this is usually a registered office. For residential buyers, it is often the address of the property being acquired, if it is going to be their main residence.

12.3.7 Transferring the property

The transfer deed will include a statement that the transferor transfers the property to the transferee.

12.3.8 Consideration

The total consideration being paid for the property, including VAT (if any), must be included. This should match what is contained in the contract.

3 See Chapter 6, Section 6.8.
4 Panel 11.

12.3.9 Title guarantee

The transfer deed must specify the level of title guarantee being provided, and this must match whatever is specified in the contract.

Where the interest being transferred is a lease, the contract may have modified the covenants for title to ensure that the seller is not giving a covenant that they have complied with the tenant's repair covenants in the lease.[5] If this is the case, the covenants for title must be amended in Panel 9 or 11 of the TR1 as well, by including wording as follows:

> The covenants set out in section 4 of the Law of Property (Miscellaneous Provisions) Act 1994 will not extend to any breach of the tenant's covenants in the lease relating to the physical state of the property.

You will recall from Chapter 11 that this was addressed in the sale contract for the assignment of the Nail Bar Lease and so has been replicated in panel 9 of the transfer deed assigning the Nail Bar Lease to Gemma's Gels Ltd.

12.3.10 Declaration of trust

If there is more than one buyer, an implied statutory trust will be created in respect of the equitable interest. The buyers must state in the transfer deed whether they will hold that equitable interest as joint tenants, or as tenants-in-common, and if the latter, the division of shares between them. If the equitable interest is to be held as tenants-in-common, HMLR will enter a restriction on the register preventing disposal by a sole co-owner, in order to ensure the equitable interests are overreached on a subsequent disposal. We saw this restriction on the title to the Salon.

12.3.11 Additional provisions

Any additional provisions relevant to the transaction should be included in the transfer deed. In the TR1, this will be in panel 11.

12.3.11.1 Covenants

Any new covenants agreed between the parties must be noted in the transfer deed, whether they are positive or restrictive in nature. This is most common on a sale of part.

André has given a covenant to comply with the positive covenant on the title register requiring him to contribute towards the costs of maintaining the boundary – this is noted in Panel 11 of the TR1.

As discussed in Chapter 6, the burden of positive covenants does not pass with the land, and these can be made to bind a buyer by way of an indemnity covenant. The

5 See Chapter 11, Section 11.4.2.3.2.

wording of indemnity covenants must be noted in the transfer deed. Style&Go Ltd has agreed to give a covenant to indemnify Neeta in the case of a breach of the positive covenant to maintain the alleyway at the side of the Salon – this is noted in panel 11 of the TR1.

If the covenants for title are amended,[6] the required wording can be included in panel 11 rather than panel 9.

12.3.11.2 Declarations

If a second trustee is being appointed to facilitate the sale by a sole surviving co-owner, a declaration of their appointment can be included in the TR1. This is the case for the sale of the Salon, and you can see Samir's appointment in panel 11.

12.3.11.3 Restrictions

If the buyer is entering a new restriction on the title, the wording of this will be entered on the transfer deed.

12.3.12 Execution

The seller must always execute the transfer: This is required to transfer the legal estate.[7]

The buyer will only need to execute the transfer deed if:

1. *They are giving a covenant to the seller*. This only applies to *new* covenants. There is no need for the buyer to execute the transfer simply because there are existing restrictive covenants registered against or affecting the title. This is the case for the transfer of the House (André is covenanting to perform the positive covenant) and the Salon (Style&Go Ltd is giving an indemnity covenant to Neeta), and so these buyers will need to execute the respective transfers.
2. *The transfer deed contains a declaration of trust*. This will be the case if there are multiple buyers.
3. *They are applying for a restriction*. Again, this is only for new restrictions and will not be the case just because there are existing restrictions on the title register.

12.3.12.1 How to validly execute

In Chapter 4 we examined the formalities required to execute a deed. These apply equally here, and the requirements for validly executing a new purchase deed are included at Table 12.1.[8]

6 See Section 12.3.9.
7 s53 LPA 1925.
8 We have included the rules for execution by an individual and a registered company. For the rules relating to other types of entity, please see HMLR Practice Guide 8.

Individual[1]	A deed has to be: • Signed by the maker* • In the presence of a witness who attests that signature *It is permitted for another person to sign on their behalf if there are two attesting witnesses.	Signed as a deed by [FULL NAME OF PARTY] in the presence of: .... [SIGNATURE OF WITNESS] [NAME OF WITNESS] [ADDRESS OF WITNESS] [OCCUPATION OF WITNESS]	.... [SIGNATURE OF PARTY]
Company[2]	<u>EXECUTION BY TWO AUTHORISED SIGNATORIES</u> Signed by two directors (or a director and company secretary)	[Executed as a deed] by [NAME OF EXECUTING COMPANY] acting by [NAME OF DIRECTOR], a director and [NAME OF DIRECTOR OR SECRETARY] [a director **OR** its secretary]	.... Director .... [Director **OR** Secretary]

(Continued)

(Continued)

	<u>EXECUTION UNDER COMMON SEAL</u> • Company seal affixed • Witnessed by two directors (or director and company secretary).	Executed as a deed by affixing the common seal of [NAME OF COMPANY] in the presence of: [COMMON SEAL] .... Director .... [Director **OR** Secretary]
	<u>EXECUTION BY ONE DIRECTOR BEFORE A WITNESS</u> • Execution by a single director • In the presence of a witness who attests that signature	Executed as a deed by [NAME OF EXECUTING COMPANY] acting by [NAME OF DIRECTOR], a director, ... [SIGNATURE OF DIRECTOR] Director in the presence of: .... [SIGNATURE OF WITNESS] [NAME OF WITNESS [IN BLOCK CAPITALS]] [ADDRESS OF WITNESS] [OCCUPATION OF WITNESS]

1 s1 LP(MP)A 1989.
2 s44 CA 2006.

Chapter 12 revision points

- A deed is usually required to transfer land from one party to another.
- The format of this deed must be a form TR1 for transfers of an entire parcel of registered land. Transfers of unregistered land often use form TR1, though this is not a requirement.
- The buyer's solicitor will produce the transfer deed, and the seller's solicitor will review it.
- The seller always needs to execute the transfer deed. The buyer will need to execute if they are giving new covenants to the seller, applying for a new restriction on the land, or making a declaration of trust.
- Individuals must sign the deed in the presence of an attesting witness. Companies can execute a deed by two authorised signatories signing the deed, by one director signing the deed in the presence of an attesting witness, or by affixing the company seal in the presence of two witnesses.

13 The lease

13.1 Chapter overview

In order to create a legal estate in land, a deed must usually be used. A lease is the deed required to create a leasehold estate.

This chapter covers the process of drafting and agreeing a lease, and the key provisions contained within. The information in this chapter is also relevant to the grant of a sub-lease.

This chapter is relevant to transactions involving the grant of a lease or sub-lease.

This chapter in the context of our Transactions

A lease is required for Style&Go Ltd to grant a lease over the Nail Bar to Polished Perfection Ltd. Style&Go Ltd's solicitor prepares a first draft of this, for review by Polished Perfection Ltd's solicitor.

You may wish to refer to the Nail Bar Lease whilst working through this chapter.

DOI: 10.4324/9781032711508-16

13.2 Structure of a lease

A typical lease is structured as follows:

13.2.1 Land registry–prescribed clauses

Where a lease is registrable with HMLR,[1] there are a set of clauses which must be included at the start of the lease. These contain key information about the lease, and the information in these clauses is used by the Land Registrar to register the lease.

The list of prescribed clauses required by HMLR is as follows:

Table 13.1 The HMLR-prescribed clauses

No.	Clause
LR1	Date of lease
LR2	Title number(s)
LR3	Parties to the lease
LR4	Property
LR5	Prescribed statements
LR6	Term for which the property is leased
LR7	Premium
LR8	Prohibitions or restrictions on disposing of the lease
LR9	Rights of acquisition
LR10	Restrictive covenants given by the landlord in respect of land other than the property
LR11	Easements
LR12	Estate rent charge burdening the property
LR13	Application for standard form of restriction
LR14	Declaration of trust where there is more than one person comprising the tenant

1 Leases over 7 years are registrable – see Chapter 2, Section 2.3.1.2.3, for a reminder about registrable dispositions.

The Nail Bar Lease is for a 10-year term and so is registrable and contains prescribed clauses.

13.2.2 Lease provisions

After the prescribed clauses, the main body of the lease will contain the key terms agreed by the parties, often divided into the following sections:

- parties;
- background or recitals;
- defined terms; and
- main clauses.

13.2.3 Schedules

In order to keep the main body of the lease as concise and simple as possible, some information is commonly added into a schedule at the end of the lease. Some common clauses to be added as schedules include:

- the description of the premises demised by the lease;
- rights granted with the lease;
- rights reserved to the landlord;
- third party rights over the premises;
- rent review provisions; and
- insurance provisions.

13.3 Process for agreeing a lease

It is the landlord's solicitor who prepares the first draft of the lease and sends it to the tenant's solicitor for review and approval.

Once received from the landlord's solicitor, the tenant's solicitor will review the lease carefully. Any necessary amendments will be discussed and agreed between the parties before being made. Where there are provisions which are heavily negotiated between the parties, the RICS Code for Leasing Business Premises (**the Code**) sets out a recommended 'best practice' position for achieving fairness and balance between the parties.

13.4 Key provisions of a lease

We will now examine some key provisions commonly included as defined terms, main clauses, and schedules.[2]

13.4.1 Commencement date

The commencement date under the lease is the date the lease is granted, which is entered on completion of the lease. It is not necessarily the same date that the

2 We focus on the key provisions for the purposes of this book.

term of the lease commences; landlords often wish to align the expiry of a lease term with other leases, for ease of administration of rent payments, or renewal. For this reason, the term of a lease is often back- or forward-dated from the defined commencement date.

The date of the Nail Bar Lease will be entered on the day of completion.[3]

13.4.2 Term of the lease

The length of the lease is included as a defined term. Terms which state that they run 'from [ ]' will start the day *after* the date stated and will end on the anniversary of the date stated. Terms stated to run 'from and including [ ]' will commence *on* the stated date and will end on the day before the anniversary of the stated date.

The Nail Bar Lease is a fixed-term lease running for ten years from and including the date it is completed.

13.4.3 The grant

13.4.3.1 Description of the property

The lease will describe the property being let to the tenant. This is often included as a defined term which refers to a schedule containing more information. Where the premises is located in a larger building, the description must be precise as to where the demise starts and ends. The Nail Bar is situated on the first floor of the Salon, and Schedule 1 makes it clear who owns the ceiling, walls, and floors of the Nail Bar.

13.4.3.2 Rights granted

The lease will need to specify which rights are granted along with the grant of the premises, for example, any rights of way needed to access the premises, rights to use common parts of a larger building, and rights to use water, gas, and electricity.

Schedule 2 of the Nail Bar Lease includes rights to use water and other utilities coming into the main building. The toilet and kitchen facilities are situated on the ground floor in the Salon, and therefore, Polished Perfection Ltd's employees (and customers, in the case of the toilet) have been granted a right to use these facilities. The Nail Bar is situated on the first floor, so Polished Perfection Ltd's employees and customers have a right of access from the front door of the Salon, through and up the stairs, to reach the Nail Bar. Polished Perfection Ltd and their customers have also been granted a right to use the Car Park.

13.4.3.3 Rights reserved

Landlords often wish to reserve rights over the premises for the benefit of other parts of the building, for example, rights of support, or rights of access to the premises to enable them to carry out repairs which affect other parts of the building.

3 See Chapter 19.

In Schedule 3 of the Nail Bar Lease, Style&Go Ltd has reserved themselves a number of rights, including a right of entry over the Nail Bar, in order to repair other parts of the building and service media serving the building.

13.4.3.4 Third-party rights

The grant of the lease must be subject to any third-party rights over the property as revealed by the title due diligence. There were no third-party rights affecting the Nail Bar, and so none are comprised in the Nail Bar Lease.

13.4.4 Alienation[4]

Alienation provisions typically cover those scenarios whereby the tenant parts with possession of the premises (e.g. assignment and sub-letting) or shares occupation of the premises (e.g. by granting a licence to occupy).

A landlord may wish to control or restrict the tenant's ability to alienate under the lease because the landlord will want to ensure that its tenants are able to pay the rent and will keep the premises in good repair. The different types of alienation covenant are as follows:

13.4.4.1 Absolute prohibition on alienation

An ***absolute prohibition*** on alienation prohibits the tenant from assigning or sub-letting the lease in any circumstance. This does not prevent the tenant from requesting permission to do so, and the landlord could waive the covenant and grant permission, but the landlord is free to refuse to do this and can refuse for any reason.

13.4.4.2 Qualified prohibition on alienation

A ***qualified prohibition*** on alienation prohibits the tenant from assigning or sub-letting the lease without the landlord's consent. Statute[5] implies a term into qualified covenants that the landlord's consent cannot be withheld unreasonably.

Style&Go Ltd and Polished Perfection Ltd have agreed that the Nail Bar Lease will contain a qualified prohibition on alienation (see clauses 6–9). Style&Go Ltd will be permitted to refuse to give consent to alienation if the covenant strength of the assignee or subtenant is not satisfactory. The parties have also agreed that it will be a pre-condition to Style&Go Ltd's consent that Polished Perfection Ltd enter into an authorised guarantee agreement if they assign the lease and that the assignee enters into a rent deposit deed.

13.4.4.3 Fully qualified prohibition on alienation

A ***fully qualified prohibition*** on alienation prohibits the tenant from assigning or sub-letting the lease without the landlord's consent, and the lease expressly states that the landlord cannot withhold consent unreasonably.

4 We discuss alienation covenants and consents in more detail in Chapters 10 and 21.

5 s19(1)(a) of the Landlord and Tenant Act 1927 (**LTA 1927**).

13.4.5 Repair and decoration

Leases will usually require the tenant to keep the premises in good repair. Similarly, there will usually be a covenant on the landlord to keep the rest of the building in good repair. The extent of the obligation must be clear: for example, if a landlord wants a tenant to decorate the premises every five years, this must be stated in a covenant.

The tenant will usually be responsible for the costs associated with their own repairing obligation, and it is usual for the landlord to pass on some of the costs of keeping the structural or common parts of the rest of the building to the tenant via a service charge. For this reason, the extent of the landlord's repair obligation must also be clear to the tenant so that the tenant does not find themselves paying for work they had not anticipated (e.g. if the landlord replaces the door with a much improved, double-glazed version, effectively improving the state of the building, then the tenant may be required to contribute towards this door).

Style&Go Ltd and Polished Perfection Ltd have agreed that Polished Perfection Ltd will keep the Nail Bar in 'good repair and condition', with an obligation to decorate every five years and during the last year of the term – this is reflected in clauses 10 and 11 of the Nail Bar Lease.

13.4.6 Alterations[6]

The tenant may wish to make alterations to the premises. Landlords usually wish to retain some control over what can be done to the premises, for two key reasons: ensuring the safety of the building as a whole and ensuring that the premises do not lose value as a result of the alterations. The lease will therefore need to set out which alterations (if any) the tenant is permitted to make to the premises.

Some common provisions are:

13.4.6.1 An absolute prohibition on alterations

An absolute prohibition on alterations prohibits the tenant from making alterations to the premises. The tenant can still request permission for alterations, but the landlord has absolute discretion over whether or not to approve the request.

13.4.6.2 A qualified prohibition on alterations

A qualified prohibition on alterations prohibits the tenant from making alterations to the premises without the landlord's consent.

6 We discuss alterations and associated consents in more detail in Chapters 10 and 21.

If the alteration amounts to an improvement (which is viewed solely from the tenant's perspective[7]), then the landlord cannot unreasonably withhold consent.[8] If the alteration does not amount to an improvement to the premises, the landlord can withhold consent regardless of whether he or she is acting reasonably. In reality, alterations which the tenant does not view as an improvement to the premises are likely to be rare.

13.4.6.3 A fully qualified prohibition on alterations

A fully qualified prohibition on alterations prohibits the tenant from making alterations to the premises without the landlord's consent but expressly requires the landlord to act reasonably when deciding whether or not to consent.

Style&Go Ltd and Polished Perfection Ltd have agreed that the alteration covenant in the lease of the Nail Bar will be fully qualified in respect of internal non-structural alterations. Structural alterations will not be permitted. This can be reviewed at clause 12 of the Nail Bar Lease.

13.4.7 Permitted user

In addition to the planning controls on the use of land we examined earlier in this book,[9] it is common for the landlord to limit the use of the property by way of a clause in the lease.

Style&Go Ltd and Polished Perfection Ltd have agreed that the Nail Bar must be used for the provision of commercial beauty services. This would include using it as a nail salon or for other beauty services, such as tanning or eyebrow shaping. This is referenced in the definition of 'Permitted Use' and in clause 14 in the Nail Bar Lease, which together restrict the use of the property to the provision of beauty services within Use Class E.

13.4.8 Insurance

Leases must specify which party is responsible for insuring the property. This is usually the landlord, who has the most to lose if the property is damaged and so wishes to make sure that adequate insurance is in place in order to protect their building. The cost of this can be recouped from tenants by way of service charge or insurance rent.

The insurance clauses in a lease will specify which risks are covered, which should accord with what is specified in the policy itself. The risks are usually set out in a defined term – this is often '**Insured Risks**'. Damage caused by an uninsured risk (e.g. anything not covered by the definition of 'Insured Risks') will be the responsib-

7 *Lambert v FW Woolworth & Co Ltd* ([1938] Ch 883).
8 s19(2) LTA 1927.
9 In Chapter 8.

ility of the tenant to rectify at its own cost, because the insurance policy will not cover any such damage.

The landlord will usually covenant to make sure that the policy insures the premises to their full reinstatement value, which will ensure that the premises can be rebuilt if destroyed by one of the specified 'Insured Risks'.

The following landlord covenants are also common in insurance clauses:

1. the proceeds of the insurance policy must be used to reinstate the premises;
2. the rent should be suspended during any period of time during which the premises cannot be occupied because of damage by an Insured Risk; and
3. the parties can terminate the lease if the premises cannot be reinstated.

Style&Go Ltd and Polished Perfection Ltd have agreed (see Schedule 5 of the Nail Bar Lease) that Style&Go Ltd will insure the building, but that Polished Perfection Ltd will contribute to this financially by paying the Insurance Rent. They have agreed to a market-standard definition of 'Insured Risks'. Style&Go Ltd will covenant to insure the Nail Bar to the full reinstatement value, and the above covenants will be incorporated.

13.4.9 Landlord and Tenant Act 1954

The Landlord and Tenant Act 1954 (the **LTA 1954**) gives protection to commercial tenants by automatically renewing fixed-term leases. The lease will specify whether or not the LTA 1954 will apply to the lease. The detail of the LTA 1954 provisions is covered in depth in Chapter 23.

Clause 23 of the Nail Bar Lease confirms that Style&Go Ltd and Polished Perfection Ltd have agreed that the provisions of the LTA 1954 will not apply to the Nail Bar Lease.

13.4.10 Rent

The lease will require the tenant to pay the '**Annual Rent**', a term which will be defined in the lease and which is the yearly amount the tenant pays for the lease. The parties will agree this with the assistance of their surveyors, and the rent clauses will cover when and how that rent is to be paid by the tenant. The Annual Rent agreed between Style&Go Ltd and Polished Perfection Ltd for the Nail Bar is £10,000 per annum, payable in four quarters per year.

If a tenant is to contribute to the cost of insurance by paying insurance rent, or to the cost of services provided by the landlord by paying a service charge, this is also noted in the lease. Polished Perfection Ltd will contribute a fair proportion towards the cost of insuring the Nail Bar by paying a specified 'Insurance Rent'.

13.4.11 Rent review

The value of property changes rapidly, and landlords want to ensure that the rent charged under a lease increases with inflation and in accordance with other changes in the market, to ensure that the rent received on a premises which has been let out on a long-term basis is not lower than would be obtained from a new tenant. For this reason, many leases contain a ***rent review*** clause, setting out how the landlord can adjust the rent in longer-term leases.

Rent review commonly occurs every five years from the commencement of the term of the lease (in leases where the term commencement date is backdated to fall in line with other leases in the block, tenants should be aware that this will mean their review occurs sooner than five years into the term of the lease).

The revised rent can be ascertained in a number of ways:

1. the lease states what the revised rent will be, for example, £45,000 for the first five years, £55,000 for the second five years, and so on. This is known as a ***fixed increase***. The certainty of this is attractive to both parties, but the fixed amounts may not reflect the reality of the market;
2. the revised rent may be linked to an index and increase (or decrease) in line with that index. This is known as an ***index-linked review***;
3. the revised rent may be linked to the tenant's turnover, for example, by being an agreed percentage of the tenant's turnover. This is known as a ***turnover rent***; or
4. the revised rent may be linked to the current property market. This is known as an ***open market rent review*** and is the most common method of dealing with rent review.

We will be focusing on an open market rent review. This process is often an informal negotiation between the landlord and the tenant, but if they cannot agree a revised rent by the review date they have specified in the lease, a valuer can be appointed to determine the revised rent, and that determination is binding on both parties.

The valuer will create a hypothetical lease of the premises and then value this hypothetical lease in order to determine the market value of the premises. The rental value of the hypothetical lease then becomes the revised rent of the actual lease.

The hypothetical lease needs to be as similar as possible to the actual lease of the premises so that the value of the premises is not artificially inflated or deflated. The rent review clause therefore typically includes a list of assumptions to be included in the hypothetical lease, and a list of disregards to be disregarded from the hypothetical lease; this is often a point for negotiation between the parties.

Style&Go Ltd and Polished Perfection Ltd have agreed that the rent of the Nail Bar shall be reviewed every five years based on an open market rent review. The rent review provisions agreed by Style&Go Ltd and Polished Perfection Ltd are in Schedule 4 of the Nail Bar Lease and reflect as closely as possible the terms of the actual Nail Bar Lease. We recommend that you review these alongside reading the explanations below.

We will now examine some of the key terms of the hypothetical lease.[10]

13.4.11.1 The property

The 'Property' (or 'Premises') as defined in the hypothetical lease (including any rights and easements) needs to be identical to those in the actual lease so that the valuation is accurate. A definition of the premises which has a smaller footprint than the actual property under the actual lease, or which does not contain the same rights (e.g. right to use common areas), is likely to be less valuable on the open market and therefore attract a lower rent.

There will therefore usually be an assumption that the 'Property' in the hypothetical lease is identical to that defined in the actual lease. The valuer will consider the rent paid for comparable properties in the area when doing the valuation.

13.4.11.2 The parties

The valuer will need to make an assumption that there is a willing landlord, and a willing tenant, for the hypothetical lease. This addresses the problem whereby the premises are so unique that only the current tenant would consider renting them – if there were not another willing tenant who wanted to lease the property, then that tenant would have the upper hand in negotiations and be able to negotiate a very low rent for the hypothetical lease. This would have the effect of making the revised rent under the actual lease very low.

13.4.11.3 Vacant possession

Even though the tenant under the actual lease will occupy the property, the valuer will need to make an assumption for rent review purposes that the property comes with vacant possession. This is because the value of a hypothetical lease which the hypothetical tenant cannot possess is very low, and of course, the actual tenant *will* be able to occupy the property.

10 Key for the purposes of this book.

This approach may be contested by the landlord if the actual tenant has sub-let the premises, because a hypothetical tenant may be willing to pay more for a lease which brings in a good rent from a sub-tenant. This would have the effect of pushing up the hypothetical rent and the actual revised rent, which is good for the landlord.

13.4.11.4 Fit-out

When a tenant vacates premises, they usually remove all their fixtures. This leaves an incoming tenant with the need to do fit-out works before they can take occupation. During this fit-out period, the tenant cannot occupy or trade from the premises, which can make the premises less attractive to prospective tenants and therefore may make the hypothetical lease less valuable. This can be dealt with by including an assumption that the premises are fully fitted out and ready for immediate occupation.

13.4.11.5 Premium

On occasion, a tenant will pay a premium at the start of the lease in exchange for a lower rent, or the landlord will offer a period of months 'rent-free' in exchange for a higher rent.

In order to address this distortion of the actual rental value, the valuer can make an assumption that no premium or rent-free period is offered with the lease. This may be contested by either party, for example, where the tenant has paid a premium in exchange for a lower rent, it is this lower rent that he will wish to see reflected in the hypothetical lease (because this will lead to a lower revised rent in his actual lease). Where the landlord has negotiated a higher rent in exchange for a rent-free period, he will wish to see this higher rent reflected in the hypothetical lease, so that the revised rent under the actual lease is higher.

13.4.11.6 Alienation

Restrictive alienation clauses in the hypothetical lease (e.g. which prohibit all forms of alienation) will make the open market value of the hypothetical lease lower than a hypothetical lease with more flexibility around alienation.

A landlord, therefore, may wish to make the alienation clause in the hypothetical lease less restrictive than in the actual lease in order to make the hypothetical lease more valuable. A tenant will wish to resist this, as they will be paying (via revised rent) for the benefit of flexibility as regards alienation that they do not have in the actual lease.

13.4.11.7 Permitted use

A restricted user clause in the hypothetical lease is likely to make the open market value of the hypothetical lease lower than that of a hypothetical lease with more flexibility, because tenants typically pay more for the flexibility of being able to change the use of the premises.

A landlord may attempt to overcome this by altering the user clause in the hypothetical lease to allow for increased flexibility. Again, a tenant will wish to resist this; otherwise, they will end up paying a higher revised rent which reflects the benefit of a flexibility they do not actually have.

13.4.11.8 Rent and rent review

The hypothetical lease will disregard the actual rent paid under the actual lease to avoid distorting the rental figure achieved under the review process.

The hypothetical lease should also include a rent review clause in order to match the actual lease. The reason for this is that a hypothetical lease without a rent review clause will be much more valuable to hypothetical tenants than one containing a rent review clause, as it guarantees a rent which is likely on a long-term basis to be lower than the market rent. This will therefore push up the revised rent.

13.4.11.9 Length of term

The hypothetical lease will need to include a term. Depending on the market, longer- or shorter-term leases may be more valuable, and so the fairest approach is for the term of the hypothetical lease to match as closely to the remaining term under the actual lease, but this may be negotiated between the parties.

The hypothetical lease should also accurately reflect the actual lease as regards to whether it is contracted out of the provisions of the LTA 1954. A lease which is contracted out will give less certainty and statutory protection to prospective tenants and will therefore be less valuable, which would drive the revised rent down.

13.4.11.10 Compliance with covenants

A hypothetical lease where the tenant covenants have not been complied with – for example, if the tenant has allowed the property to fall into disrepair – is likely to be less valuable to hypothetical tenants, and the actual tenant should not benefit from this by gaining a lower revised rent. The landlord, therefore, will want the hypothetical lease to include an assumption that all tenant covenants have been complied with.

Similarly, a hypothetical lease whereby the landlord has not complied with its covenants – for example, if the landlord has not kept the common parts of the building in good repair – will be less valuable to hypothetical tenants. A tenant, therefore, will not want to include an assumption that the hypothetical landlord has complied with its covenants, because it will result in the actual tenant paying revised rent reflective of a property which is more valuable than it actually is.

13.4.11.11 VAT

A premises which the landlord has opted to tax will be less attractive to some hypothetical tenants who may not be able to offset any tax paid.[11] These tenants may request a lower rent to ensure they are not left out of pocket. The landlord, therefore, may wish to include an assumption that the hypothetical tenant will be able to recover its VAT in full. The tenant is likely to resist this, as again it would make the hypothetical lease more attractive than the actual lease if the actual tenant cannot recover its VAT.

13.4.11.12 Goodwill

The tenant may have generated goodwill at the premises, which will make the premises more valuable. The tenant is likely to want this goodwill to be disregarded from the hypothetical lease, to avoid their paying a financial penalty via revised rent for having generated goodwill.

13.4.11.13 Occupation

A hypothetical tenant who is currently in occupation of a premises is likely to be willing to pay a higher amount of rent to avoid the hassle of having to move. It is therefore common to disregard the actual tenant's occupation from the hypothetical lease.

13.4.11.14 Improvements

The actual tenant may have done works at their own expense to improve the premises, and these are likely to increase the rental value of the premises. The tenant may request for these to be disregarded from the hypothetical lease, on the basis that it is not fair and reasonable for the landlord to benefit and the tenant to suffer (via a higher revised rent) for an improvement undertaken and paid for by the tenant.

13.5 Executing the lease

Once both parties are happy with the contents of the lease, the landlord's solicitor will produce engrossments. The lease must be signed by both parties, and so the landlord's solicitor will send it to their own client for execution and to the tenant's solicitor to arrange for the tenant to sign it.

The lease will most likely be a deed and so must comply with the execution requirements already discussed, which we have reproduced in Table 13.2 for ease of reference.

11 See Chapter 3, Section 3.3.2.3.3.

Table 13.2 The requirements for executing a deed

Individual[1]	A deed has to be: • Signed by the maker* • In the presence of a witness who attests that signature *It is permitted for another person to sign on their behalf if there are two attesting witnesses.	Signed as a deed by [FULL NAME OF PARTY] in the presence of: .... [SIGNATURE OF PARTY] .... [SIGNATURE OF WITNESS] [NAME OF WITNESS] [ADDRESS OF WITNESS] [OCCUPATION OF WITNESS]
Company[2]	<u>EXECUTION BY TWO AUTHORISED SIGNATORIES</u> Signed by two directors (or director and company secretary)	[Executed as a deed] by [NAME OF EXECUTING COMPANY] acting by [NAME OF DIRECTOR], a director .... Director and [NAME OF DIRECTOR OR SECRETARY] [a director **OR** its secretary] .... [Director **OR** Secretary]

	<u>EXECUTION UNDER COMMON SEAL</u> ● Company seal affixed; ● Witnessed by two directors (or director and company secretary)	Executed as a deed by affixing the common seal of [NAME OF COMPANY] in the presence of: .... Director .... [Director **OR** Secretary]	[COMMON SEAL]
	<u>EXECUTION BY ONE DIRECTOR BEFORE A WITNESS</u> ● Execution by a single director ● In the presence of a witness who attests that signature	Executed as a deed by [NAME OF EXECUTING COMPANY] acting by [NAME OF DIRECTOR], a director, in the presence of: .... [SIGNATURE OF WITNESS] [NAME OF WITNESS [IN BLOCK CAPITALS]] [ADDRESS OF WITNESS] [OCCUPATION OF WITNESS]	.... [SIGNATURE OF DIRECTOR] Director

1 s1 LP(MP)A 1989.
2 s44 CA 2006.

Chapter 13 revision points

- The landlord's solicitor will usually prepare the first draft of the lease and send this to the tenant's solicitor for review.
- A lease will include key details, including the commencement date, the term of the lease, the details of the grant, the permitted use of the premises, and the rent payable.
- A lease will specify whether the tenant is permitted to dispose of the lease by way of assignment or underletting, and whether the tenant is permitted to make alterations to the premises.
- A lease will specify who is responsible for insuring the premises and which risks are to be insured against.
- A lease will specify whether the protections under the LTA 1954 are applicable.
- A lease will specify whether the rent will be reviewed during the term of the lease and, if so, the mechanism for ascertaining the revised rent.
- A lease must usually be made by deed. Individuals must sign the lease in the presence of an attesting witness. Companies can execute a deed by two authorised signatories signing the deed, by one director signing the deed in the presence of an attesting witness, or by affixing the company seal in the presence of two witnesses.

14 The mortgage deed

14.1 Chapter overview

When a buyer purchases property with the assistance of a loan and grants a mortgage to a lender, the mortgage documentation must be prepared ahead of completion so that it can be completed at the same time as the transfer of the property to the buyer.

This chapter provides a brief overview of the key terms of the mortgage and the process for agreeing a mortgage deed.

This chapter is relevant to all transactions which are being financed by way of a mortgage.

This chapter in the context of our Transactions

André is purchasing the House with the assistance of a mortgage from Country Funding Building Society, who has produced a mortgage deed which André's solicitor will review and explain to André.

You may wish to refer the mortgage deed (Form CH1) in Appendix 1 when working through this chapter. Please note, the terms of the mortgage have not been reproduced in Form CH1, as the details are beyond the scope of this book; however, we provide some general information about the key terms commonly found in a mortgage deed, which will be relevant for André's mortgage over the House.

DOI: 10.4324/9781032711508-17

14.2 Format of the mortgage

A legal mortgage must be made by deed.[1] The following formats are common:

- For residential transactions:
  - the lender's standard form ***mortgage deed***, incorporating the lender's standard terms and conditions;
  - HMLR Form CH1; or
  - a mortgage deed drafted by the lender's solicitor.
- For commercial transactions:
  - a loan agreement (facility letter or credit agreement) and separate charge; or
  - a debenture incorporating a charge.

14.3 Key terms of the mortgage

The lender will draft the mortgage deed and provide this to the borrower.

The mortgage deed will typically contain the following types of terms, as contained within Table 14.1, which must be explained to the borrower:

Table 14.1 The types of clauses contained in a mortgage deed

Type of clause	Details of the clause
Commercial terms	• The value of the loan. • The repayment date. • The interest rate. • The repayment amount and the due date of the first repayment.
Security	• The lender will take a legal mortgage over the property. *Commercial borrowers:* • The lender may additionally take a fixed charge over fixtures, plant and machinery belonging to the borrower. • The lender may additionally take a floating charge over other assets of the borrower.

1 s85 LPA 1925.

Table 14.1 (Continued)

Type of clause	Details of the clause
Borrower's liabilities	• The borrower is liable to repay the loan and interest by the repayment date. • The lender can use its power of sale (if the borrower defaults on the mortgage) to pay off other loans from the lender to the borrower (e.g. if the borrower had a credit card from the same bank as the mortgage) – this is known as an ***all-monies charge***.
Borrower's covenants	• The borrower must keep the property in good repair. • The borrower must not let the property without consent from the lender. • The borrower must not invalidate the insurance policy on the property. • The borrower must not make alterations to the property without the lender's consent.
Events of default by the borrower	• Failure to make repayments. • Breach of covenant. • Insolvency.
Lender's rights (statutory powers)	• Selling the property. • Leasing the property. • Insuring the property and recovering premiums from the buyer.
Penalty charges	The borrower must pay a charge for early repayment of the loan.
Negative pledge	The borrower cannot take out an additional loan on the property, as this may reduce the borrower's ability to make repayments under the mortgage.

14.4 Executing the mortgage deed

Once the terms have been explained by the borrower's solicitor and the borrower is comfortable and happy to proceed with the mortgage, the deed must be executed by the borrower. It does not need to be executed by the lender. As it is a deed, it must be executed as set out in Table 14.2:

Table 14.2 The execution requirements to create a deed

Individual[1]	A deed has to be: • Signed by the maker* • In the presence of a witness who attests that signature *It is permitted for another person to sign on their behalf if there are two attesting witnesses.	Signed as a deed by [FULL NAME OF PARTY] in the presence of: .... [SIGNATURE OF WITNESS] [NAME OF WITNESS] [ADDRESS OF WITNESS] [OCCUPATION OF WITNESS]	.... [SIGNATURE OF PARTY]
Company[2]	<u>EXECUTION BY TWO AUTHORISED SIGNATORIES</u> Signed by two directors (or director and company secretary)	[Executed as a deed] by [NAME OF EXECUTING COMPANY] acting by [NAME OF DIRECTOR], a director and [NAME OF DIRECTOR OR SECRETARY] [a director **OR** its secretary]	.... Director .... [Director **OR** Secretary]

	EXECUTION UNDER COMMON SEAL • Company seal affixed • Witnessed by two directors (or director and company secretary)	Executed as a deed by affixing the common seal of [NAME OF COMPANY] in the presence of: .... Director .... [Director **OR** Secretary]	[COMMON SEAL]
	EXECUTION BY ONE DIRECTOR BEFORE A WITNESS • Execution by a single director • In the presence of a witness who attests that signature	Executed as a deed by [NAME OF EXECUTING COMPANY] acting by [NAME OF DIRECTOR], a director, in the presence of: .... [SIGNATURE OF WITNESS] [NAME OF WITNESS [IN BLOCK CAPITALS]] [ADDRESS OF WITNESS] [OCCUPATION OF WITNESS]	.... [SIGNATURE OF DIRECTOR] Director

1 s1 LP(MP)A 1989.
2 s44 CA 2006.

Chapter 14 revision points

- Mortgages are granted to a bank or building society in exchange for the provision of a loan to purchase the property with.
- Residential mortgages usually take the form of the lenders standard T&Cs, or form CH01.
- Commercial mortgages take the form of a loan agreement and charge, or a debenture incorporating a charge.
- The mortgage deed will usually detail the commercial terms and type of security, the borrower's covenants and liability, and the lender's rights.
- A legal mortgage must be made by deed and must be executed by the borrower. Individuals must sign the deed in the presence of an attesting witness. Companies can execute a deed by two authorised signatories signing the deed, by one director signing the deed in the presence of an attesting witness, or by affixing the company seal in the presence of two witnesses.

Revision Summary

PHASE 2 The documentation

Documents relating to the landlord's consent

- Where the landlord's consent is required before the tenant can undertake a particular activity on property which is subject to a lease, that consent is captured in a licence.
- Common licences include:
  - a ***licence to assign***;
  - a ***licence to underlet***; and
  - a ***licence for alterations***.
- The parties to the licence will be:
  - the landlord;
  - the tenant; and
  - the ***assignee*** or ***subtenant***.
- The landlord will draft the licence, and it will be reviewed by the other parties.
- The consent given under the licence may be time-limited, but in practice, the licence is completed just before completion of the deed of assignment or the sub-lease to minimise the risk of the consent expiring.
- The tenant may be required to pay the landlord's costs of preparing the licence.
- A breach of the licence may entitle the landlord to exercise their right of re-entry under the lease.

Key features of a licence to assign

- The landlord's permission may be conditional upon:
  - the tenant entering into an *AGA*;
  - the assignee entering into a ***rent deposit deed***; and/or
  - satisfactory references in respect of the assignee.
- The licence may require the assignee to covenant directly with the landlord to perform the tenant covenants in the lease.

Key features of an authorised guarantee agreement

- An AGA requires the tenant to indemnify the landlord if the assignee does not perform the tenant covenants in the lease.
- An AGA typically requires the tenant to be liable for the remainder of the lease term, unless released by the landlord.

Key features of a licence to underlet

The licence may impose requirements relating to the sub-lease, such as:

- the sub-lease must be ***contracted out*** of LTA 1954;
- the subtenant must not occupy the premises before the sublease is granted;
- the tenant must enforce the ***tenant covenants*** of the sublease; and/or
- the tenant must seek the landlord's approval for any ***rent review***;
- The subtenant may be required to enter into direct covenants with the landlord relating to:
  - the payment of rent and performance of tenant covenants in the sub-lease; and
  - the performance of tenant covenants in the lease.

Contractual documents

The sale contract

- Sale contracts are made between the prospective seller and the prospective buyer.
- The effect of a sale contract is that the parties are contractually bound to transfer the land on a future date. If the land is not later transferred in accordance with the terms of the contract, the innocent party will have a contractual remedy against the breaching party.
- Sale contracts are typically used in all transfers of freehold land and commonly on the assignment of a lease.
- Process:
  - the seller's solicitor drafts the sale contract;
  - the buyer's solicitor reviews the sale contract;
  - any required amendments are made; and
  - both parties sign it.

- Key terms of the sale contract:
  - The ***particulars of sale*** record key details about the transaction.
  - The ***standard conditions*** are a set of contract terms which are usually incorporated into the sale contract:
    - the ***Standard Conditions of Sale*** are used for residential transactions; and
    - the ***Standard Commercial Property Conditions*** are used for commercial transactions;
  - The ***special conditions*** are used to:
    - incorporate the standard conditions;
    - disapply any standard conditions which are not appropriate; and/or
    - cover additional obligations which aren't covered by the standard conditions.

The agreement for lease

- An agreement for lease is made between the prospective landlord and the prospective tenant.
- The effect of an agreement for lease is that the parties are contractually bound to enter into a lease (or sub-lease) on a future date. If the lease is not entered into under the terms of the agreement for lease, then the innocent party will have a contractual remedy against the breaching party.
- Agreements for lease are used when the parties want the contractual certainty of knowing a lease will be entered into but cannot enter into the lease immediately, for example, because planning permission is outstanding.

The *transfer deed*

- The transfer of a legal estate in land must be made by deed.
- For registered land, this deed must be in ***Form TR1***.
- For unregistered land, a conveyance can be used instead, but often the TR1 is used.

Process for producing a transfer deed

- The process and timeframe for producing a transfer deed is as set out in Table R2.1:

Table R2.1 Summarising the process for producing a transfer deed

Step	Process	Timeframe in Conveyancing Protocol	Timeframe under the standard conditions
1	The buyer's solicitor drafts the purchase deed.	At the same time as the sale contract is drafted	At least 12 working days before the completion date in the sale contract
2	The seller's solicitor reviews the purchase deed and makes necessary amendments.	Before exchange of the sale contract	Within four working days of receipt from the buyer's solicitor
3	The buyer's solicitor produces ***engrossments***.	At same time as sale contract	At least five working days before the completion date in the sale contract

Contents of the transfer deed

- The TR1 includes the following information noted in Table R2.2:

Table R2.2 Summarising the information contained in a TR1

Panel no.	Description	Notes
1	Title number	Leave this panel blank when the land is unregistered.
2	Property	• An address or description of the land must be included. • In registered land, this must match the register of title. There is no need to include a plan unless the contract refers to one. • In unregistered land, the location of the property must be shown on a plan.
3	Date	This is filled in on completion.

4	Transferor	The seller's name entered here must match that of the legal proprietor. • Changes of name must be evidenced to HMLR. • If the registered proprietor has died, the personal representatives must be stated as the transferor, and the death certificate and grant of probate must be supplied to HMLR. • If the transferor is the sole surviving owner, appoint a second trustee as transferor.
5	Transferee	This is the buyer's name.
6	Transferee's address	This can match the address of the property if it is to be the main residence of the transferee.
8	Consideration	The figure entered in this panel must: • include VAT; and • match the contract.
9	Title guarantee	• The level of ***title guarantee*** specified must match the contract. • If you are amending the ***covenants for title*** upon assigning a lease, include an amended covenant in this panel.
10	Declaration of trust	This must be completed when there are multiple purchasers.
11	Additional provisions	Include in this panel details of: • new covenants being given by the transferee (e.g. positive, restrictive or indemnity covenants); • declarations (e.g. if appointing a trustee); and • new restrictions affecting the property.

Executing the transfer deed

- The seller must always execute the transfer deed.
- The buyer must execute the transfer deed if:
  - they are giving a new covenant;
  - the transfer contains a ***declaration of trust***; or
  - they are applying for a ***restriction***

The lease

- The grant of a lease must usually be made by deed.
- The landlord's solicitor will prepare the lease, and the tenant's solicitor will review it.
- A registrable lease must contain the Land Registry–prescribed clauses.
- Both parties must sign the lease.

Common lease terms

Table R2.3 Summarising common lease terms

Term	Details
Commencement date	This will be filled in on completion and is the date the lease is entered into.
Term of the lease	The duration of the lease will be specified: • A term described as 'from [date]' starts the day after the date stated and ends on the relevant anniversary of the date stated. • A term described as 'from and including [date]' starts on the stated date and ends the day before the relevant anniversary of the stated date.
Grant	An overview of what the lease is granting will include: • a precise description of the premises; • details of any rights granted to the tenant over other property; • details of any rights over the premises reserved to the landlord; and/or • details of any third-party rights over the premises
Alienation	The lease will state whether the tenant can dispose of their interest. This may be: • an ***absolute prohibition***; • a ***qualified prohibition***, which requires the landlord's consent. Statute requires consent not to be unreasonably withheld; or • a ***fully qualified prohibition***, which requires the landlord's consent, expressed in the lease not to be unreasonably withheld.

Repair and decoration	The lease will set out: • the extent of the tenant's responsibility to maintain the premises at its own cost; and • the extent of the landlord's responsibility to maintain the building. These costs may be recovered via service charge.
Alterations	The lease will state whether the tenant can make alterations to the property. This may take the form of: • an absolute prohibition; • a qualified prohibition, which requires the landlord's consent. Statute requires consent not to be unreasonably withheld to alterations which amount to improvements from the tenant's perspective; or • a fully qualified prohibition, which requires the landlord's consent, expressly stated in the lease not to be unreasonably withheld.
Permitted user	The use of the property is restricted to that which is defined.
Insurance	Insurance provisions will set out: • which party is responsible for insuring the property. • which risks are covered by the policy. The insuring party often gives a covenant: • to use the proceeds of insurance to reinstate the premises; and • to suspend the requirement to pay rent during any non-occupiable periods. It is usually possible to terminate the lease if the premises cannot be reinstated.
LTA 1954	The lease will specify whether the parties have contracted out of the provisions of the LTA 1954.
Rent	The lease will specify the: • 'Annual Rent'; • 'Insurance Rent'; and • 'Service Rent' payable by the tenant.

Rent review	The lease will give details of the basis for ***rent review***. This is usually: • ***fixed-increase***; • ***index-linked***; • ***turnover rent***; or • ***open market rent review***. It will also list the assumptions and disregards relevant to open market rent review, if relevant.

Open market rent review

- If the landlord and tenant cannot agree a revised rent by the agreed review date, a valuer can be appointed to determine the revised rent. The valuer's review is binding.
- The valuer will create a ***hypothetical lease*** of the premises and value it: this rental value becomes the revised rent.
- The hypothetical lease must be as similar as possible to the actual lease.
- The lease will set out a list of ***assumptions*** and ***disregards***: these are often negotiated as they can affect the rental value of the hypothetical lease.
- The effect of key terms of the hypothetical lease when negotiating the rent review provisions is as follows:

Table R2.4 Summarising the effect of lease clauses during rent review

Lease term	Effect on hypothetical rent	Fairest approach
The premises	The size of premises and the rights granted with it can change the value of a property, affecting its rental value.	Replicate the position under the actual lease.
The parties	If only one party is 'willing' to enter into the lease, the other has a monopoly and can push the rental value up or down to suit them.	Assume there is a willing landlord and a willing tenant.
Vacant possession	The value of a premises which cannot be possessed because it is already occupied is low.	Assume the hypothetical lease has vacant possession.

Lease term	Effect on hypothetical rent	Fairest approach
Fit-out	Fully fitted-out premises are more valuable than empty premises, as the tenant does not need to spend time and money undertaking works.	Assume the hypothetical premises are fitted out.
Premium	Payment of a premium can reduce the rent paid on a property.	Replicate the position under the actual lease.
Alienation	A lease with more flexibility to alienate will be more valuable.	Replicate the position under the actual lease.
Permitted use	A lease with more flexibility around use will be more valuable.	Replicate the position under the actual lease.
Rent and rent review	A lease without rent review will be more valuable than one with rent review, as the rent will not increase throughout the term.	Replicate the position under the actual lease.
Length of term	The term of a lease can affect its value depending on market conditions. A lease which has been contracted out of the LTA 1954 will be less valuable to prospective tenants than one offering security of tenure.	Replicate the remaining term of the actual lease as well as the position as to the LTA 1954.
Compliance with covenants	Non-compliance with tenant or landlord covenants will make the property less valuable, reducing the hypothetical rental value.	Assume there has been compliance with the leasehold covenants.
VAT	A guarantee of VAT recovery will make the hypothetical lease attractive and increase the hypothetical rental value.	Replicate the position for the actual tenant.
Goodwill	Goodwill generated by a tenant will make the property more valuable and push up the hypothetical rent.	Disregard goodwill generated by the tenant.

Lease term	Effect on hypothetical rent	Fairest approach
Occupation	A tenant in occupation will pay a higher rent to avoid moving.	Disregard the actual tenant's occupation.
Tenant improvements	Improvements to the property made by the tenant will make the property more valuable.	Disregard any improvements made by the tenant to the property.

The mortgage deed

- A legal mortgage must be made by deed.
- In residential transactions, it is common for the lender to use their standard-form ***mortgage deed*** or ***Form CH1***.
- In commercial transactions, a loan agreement and a charge or debenture are commonly used.
- The lender's solicitor prepares the mortgage deed, and the borrower's solicitor reviews it.
- The mortgage deed will include clauses covering:
    - the value of the loan and repayment provisions;
    - the type of security being granted;
    - the borrower's liabilities;
    - the borrower's covenants;
    - events constituting default by the borrower;
    - rights of the lender;
    - penalty charges; and
    - negative pledges.
- Only the borrower needs to execute the mortgage deed.

Valid execution of a deed

Individuals

- An individual must execute a deed by signing it in the presence of an attesting witness.

Companies

- A company must execute a deed by:
    - two authorised signatories signing the deed. This can be two directors, or one director and one company secretary;
    - affixing the company seal in the presence of two authorised signatories; or
    - one director signing the deed in the presence of an attesting witness.

Multiple-choice practice questions

Question 1

A landlord's solicitor is drafting a licence to underlet. She is drafting the covenant to govern future liability under any tenant covenants in the lease.

Which one of the following possible covenants should the landlord's solicitor include in the draft licence to underlet?

A. The tenant covenants with the landlord to provide the landlord with an authorised guarantee agreement (in an agreed form) on the grant of the sublease.
B. The tenant covenants with the landlord that the subtenant will perform the covenants in the lease during the remainder of the term of the lease.
C. The tenant covenants with the landlord that the subtenant will perform the covenants in the lease until the next valid assignment of the lease made with the landlord's consent.
D. The subtenant covenants with the landlord to perform the covenants in the lease during the remainder of the term of the lease.
E. The subtenant covenants with the landlord to perform the covenants in the lease until the next valid assignment of the lease made with the landlord's consent.

Question 2

A solicitor is acting for a client who is selling a residential freehold property.

The solicitor is drafting the sale contract. The parties have agreed that a deposit of 10% is to be paid by the buyer, to be held as stakeholder for the seller.

Which of the below best represents how this agreement can be reflected?

A. Add it into the particulars of sale.
B. The Standard Conditions of Sale already cover the position

C. The Standard Commercial Property Conditions already cover the position
D. Add it as a special condition
E. Add it into the transfer deed.

Question 3

A solicitor is acting for a client who is selling a residential freehold property.

The solicitor is drafting the sale contract. The parties have agreed that a deposit of 10% is to be paid by the buyer, to be held as agent for the seller.

Which of the below best represents how this agreement can be reflected?

A. Add it into the particulars of sale.
B. The Standard Conditions of Sale already cover the position
C. The Standard Commercial Property Conditions already cover the position
D. Add it as a special condition
E. Add it into the transfer deed.

Question 4

A solicitor is acting for a client who is selling a commercial freehold property.

The solicitor is drafting the sale contract. The parties have agreed that the seller will provide full title guarantee.

Which of the below best represents how this agreement can be reflected?

A. Add it into the particulars of sale.
B. The Standard Conditions of Sale already cover the position
C. The Standard Commercial Property Conditions already cover the position
D. Add it as a special condition
E. Add it into the transfer deed

Question 5

A solicitor is acting for a client who is selling a residential freehold property.

The solicitor is drafting the sale contract. There is a restrictive covenant on the official copy register of title to the property.

Which of the below best represents how this should be reflected in the contract?

A. Add it into the particulars of sale.
B. The Standard Conditions of Sale already cover the position
C. The Standard Commercial Property Conditions already cover the position
D. Add it as a special condition
E. Add it into the transfer deed

Question 6

A solicitor is acting for a client who is selling a commercial freehold property.

The solicitor is drafting the sale contract. There is a D(ii) Land Charge registered against the current owner of the property (the seller).

Which of the below best represents how this should be reflected in the contract?

A. Add it into the particulars of sale.
B. The Standard Conditions of Sale already cover the position
C. The Standard Commercial Property Conditions already cover the position
D. Add it as a special condition
E. Add it into the transfer deed

Question 7

A solicitor is acting for a client who is buying a commercial freehold property. The sale contract states that completion is to take place on 20 December. The sale contract is exchanged on 1 December.

The buyer is ready to complete on 18 December. The seller is ready to complete at 3:00 p.m. on 20 December.

What best describes the position?

A. Completion can occur on 20 December. The buyer will be entitled to compensation for delayed completion because completion occurred after 2:00 p.m.
B. Completion can occur on 21 December, and the buyer will be entitled to compensation for delayed completion.
C. Completion can occur on 20 December. The buyer is not entitled to compensation for delayed completion under the SCPCs.
D. Completion can occur on 20 December. The buyer will not be entitled to compensation because completion is not delayed.
E. Completion can occur on any time up to 30 December according to the SCPCs.

Question 8

A solicitor is acting for a client who is purchasing a lease. The solicitor is drafting the TR1 to assign the lease to their client.

The sale contract contains the following special conditions:

1. The seller agrees to pay all outstanding maintenance costs before completion.
2. The property is being transferred with vacant possession.
3. The covenants set out in Section 4 of the LP(MP)A will not extend to any breach of the tenant's covenants in the lease relating to the physical state of the property.

Which of these will the solicitor need to draft into the TR1?

A. All.
B. None.
C. (3) only.
D. (1) and (3).
E. (1) and (2).

Question 9

A solicitor is acting for a tenant who is taking a lease over a shop. The tenant is not paying a premium for the lease.

The solicitor is reviewing the lease drafted by the landlord's solicitor. The solicitor is amending the rent review provisions.

Which of the following amendments should the solicitor make?

A. Disregard any goodwill generated by the tenant, improvements made by the tenant, and the tenant's occupation of the premises.
B. Disregard compliance with the tenant covenants and landlord covenants.
C. Include assumptions relating to any goodwill generated by the tenant, improvements made by the tenant, and the tenant's occupation of the premises.
D. Include assumptions that the tenant covenants and landlord covenants have been complied with.
E. Include an assumption that the tenant paid a premium for the lease.

Question 10

A solicitor is acting for a tenant. The tenant wishes to assign the lease.

The lease contains an alienation clause as follows:

The Tenant may assign the whole of the Property with the consent of the Landlord.

What advice should the solicitor give the tenant?

A. The landlord can refuse consent for any reason because the lease contains an absolute prohibition on alienation.
B. The landlord can refuse consent for any reason because the lease contains a qualified prohibition on alienation.
C. The landlord can refuse consent but must act reasonably in doing so because the lease contains a fully qualified prohibition on alienation
D. The landlord can refuse consent because the lease contains a qualified prohibition on alienation but must act reasonably in doing so under s19(1)(a) LTA 1927.
E. The landlord cannot refuse consent.

Question 11

A solicitor acts for a purchaser of a house. The purchaser is buying the house with the assistance of a loan from the bank, to whom he will grant a mortgage over the house.

Which of the following best describes the documentation the client's solicitor should expect to receive from the bank?

A. A facility agreement and charge containing clauses requiring the borrower to repay the loan by a specified date.
B. A debenture including a charge containing a covenant requiring the borrower to keep the property in good repair.
C. A mortgage deed on the bank's standard terms and conditions containing clauses requiring the borrower to repay the loan by a specified date, and covenants requiring him to keep the property in good repair.
D. A mortgage deed on the bank's standard terms and conditions enabling the bank to take an additional floating charge over the other assets of the buyer.
E. A facility agreement and charge containing clauses requiring the borrower to repay the loan by a specified date and a covenant requiring the borrower to keep the property in good repair.

PHASE

3 Preparing for completion

The solicitors have now drafted and/or reviewed all documentation associated with the transaction, and their respective clients have executed these documents.

In Phase 3, we will be examining the remaining steps required to get ready for completion.

Once documents are signed, there are three key steps before completion occurs:

1. **Exchanging the sale contract.** First, the sale contract or agreement for lease which has been signed by the parties must be exchanged. We discuss the methods of exchange and the effects of exchanging contracts in Chapter 15.
2. **Pre-completion searches.** Once contracts have been exchanged, the buyer's solicitor will undertake some final searches to check that nothing has changed since the due diligence was undertaken. We discuss the key pre-completion searches in Chapter 16.
3. **Practical preparations.** The parties' solicitors will make practical arrangements for completion, such as ensuring that they are holding the necessary funds and documentation and agreeing how keys will be provided to the buyer upon completion. This is examined in Chapter 17.

DOI: 10.4324/9781032711508-18

15 Exchanging the sale contract

15.1 Chapter overview

In Chapter 11 we explored the key provisions contained in a sale contract. This chapter focuses on the process and effect of the parties exchanging that contract.

The chapter begins by examining the effect of exchanging contracts, and some practical steps which necessarily must be completed before the parties consider exchanging contracts.

Next, it explores the different methods of exchanging contracts and their associated requirements, followed by the steps that must be taken by solicitors immediately after contracts have been exchanged.

This chapter is relevant to all transactions in which a sale contract has been agreed.

This chapter in the context of our Transactions

A sale contract has been drafted and agreed for the following Transactions:

- André's acquisition of the House;
- Style&Go Ltd's acquisition of the Salon;
- Style&Go Ltd's acquisition of the Car Park; and
- Polished Perfection Ltd's assignment of the lease to Gemma's Gels Ltd.

Each buyer's solicitor must first ensure their client is ready to exchange, and then both parties' solicitors will exchange contracts.

You may wish to refer to the memorandum of exchange for each of the earlier Transactions whilst working through this chapter.

DOI: 10.4324/9781032711508-19

15.2 The effect of exchanging contracts

15.2.1 A binding contract

Exchanging contracts creates a binding obligation for the buyer to purchase the property on the completion date which has been agreed upon by the parties and entered into the particulars of sale.[1] The obligation to transfer the property from the seller to the buyer on the agreed-upon completion date is absolute and remains binding even if one party dies between exchange and completion.[2] For this reason, the buyer's solicitor must ensure that the buyer will be able to purchase the property on the completion date.[3]

15.2.1.1 Practical steps

Because of this effect, there are a number of matters for the buyer's solicitor to consider before proceeding to exchange.

15.2.1.1.1 IS THE BUYER HAPPY TO PROCEED WITH PURCHASING THE PROPERTY?

15.2.1.1.1.1 TITLE INVESTIGATION

The buyer's solicitor will need to ensure that the title investigation process is complete and that there are no outstanding searches, enquiries, or surveys. Most solicitors will keep a list of title issues in order to check that these have all been adequately dealt with.

15.2.1.1.1.2 SALE CONTRACT

The buyer's solicitor will need to ensure that the buyer is happy with the sale contract in its agreed form and has signed it.

1 See Chapter 11.
2 In this situation, the obligation to complete passes to their personal representative.
3 For the consequences of not being able to complete on time, please see Chapter 18.

15.2.1.1.2 ARE THE FINANCES IN PLACE TO ENABLE THE BUYER TO PURCHASE THE PROPERTY?

The buyer's solicitor will need to ensure that the buyer has the necessary funds to proceed with the purchase on the completion date.

15.2.1.1.2.1 MORTGAGES

The buyer may be purchasing the property with the assistance of a mortgage. This is the case for André's purchase of the House. André's solicitor will need to ensure that the mortgage is agreed before contracts are exchanged, so that those funds are available from the lender in time for completion. This will mean making sure that André has received a mortgage offer and has accepted this by signing it. The mortgage offer contains the terms and conditions of the loan.

We saw in Chapter 3 that the mortgage offer is typically received by a buyer before solicitors are instructed, and in Chapter 14, we looked at the content and execution requirements of a mortgage deed. André has done everything he needs to in respect of the mortgage on the House.

15.2.1.1.2.2 DEPOSIT

The buyer's solicitor will need to transfer the deposits to the seller's solicitor immediately after exchange occurs and will give an undertaking to do so to the seller's solicitor.[4] This means that, upon exchange of contracts, the funds must already be in the solicitor's client account, ready for sending on to the seller's solicitor (otherwise, the buyer's solicitor cannot comply with the undertaking they have given[5]). When transferring money to a solicitor's client bank account, it can take a few days for this money to be checked and become available for the solicitor to send on. This process is known as 'clearing', and the deposit will need to be in the solicitor's account in 'cleared funds' before exchange occurs.

André's solicitor must ensure that André sends a 10% deposit amounting to £35,000 for his purchase of the House and wait for these funds to clear before proceeding to exchange.

Style&Go Ltd's solicitor will need to ensure that Style&Go Ltd send a 10% deposit (amounting to £52,500) for their purchase of the Salon, and a 5% deposit (£4,250) for their purchase of the Car Park, and will wait for these funds to clear before proceeding to exchange on these Transactions.

There is no deposit payable on the assignment of the Nail Bar Lease to Gemma's Gels Ltd.

4 See Section 15.4.3.

5 For the impact of not complying with an undertaking, see Essential Legal System and Legal Services for SQE1, available from Routledge.

15.2.2 Title and risk

15.2.2.1 Title

Legal title to the property remains with the seller after the sale contracts are exchanged. The seller can stay in occupation of the property and is still responsible for outgoings, etc., until completion occurs, which triggers the transfer of the legal title to the buyer.

Beneficial title to the property passes to the buyer upon exchange. Any increases in the value of the property after contracts have been exchanged will benefit the buyer, but any losses in value are also borne by the buyer.

15.2.2.2 Risk

The risk position after exchange of contracts is set out in the standard conditions and confirms that the risk of accidental damage to the property passes to the buyer from the date of exchange of contracts.

15.2.2.3 Practical steps: insurance

Because the risk passes to the buyer on exchange, it is important for the buyer that the property is insured from exchange of contracts and that the buyer can benefit from this insurance policy.

Under the sale contract, the seller usually has no contractual responsibility for insuring the property once contracts have been exchanged, except in certain situations or when agreed between the parties.[6] In some situations, it will make sense for the seller to insure the property between exchange and completion; for example, if the seller has a mortgage, it is likely to be a term of this mortgage that the seller insures the mortgaged property. It may even be the case that both the buyer and the seller have an insurance policy over the property during the period between exchange and completion. If damage occurs to the property before completion, the sale contract governs how the proceeds of the insurance policy are to be used.[7]

André and Style&Go Ltd will need to have insurance in place from exchange of contracts because, as explained earlier, they will be bound to proceed with their respective purchases even if the relevant property is damaged between exchange and completion and is no longer a worthwhile purchase.

Their solicitors will need to ensure that André and Style&Go Ltd are aware that the properties will be at their risk from exchange, and that insurance is likely to

6 See Chapter 11, Section 11.4.2.5.
7 There are standard conditions covering this matter.

be available. In practice, this means making sure that André and Style&Go Ltd have selected an insurance policy and are comfortable that it meets their needs, so that they can quickly effect the policy after exchange. The Nail Bar is already insured by Style&Go Ltd (and the tenant contributes to this cost by paying 'Insurance Rent'), and so Gemma's Gels Ltd does not need to arrange insurance from exchange.

Solicitors are not permitted to provide advice on regulated matters, and so providing advice on insurance policies or arranging an insurance policy would require authorisation from the Financial Conduct Authority, or for the solicitor to fall under an exemption and comply with the conditions relating to that exemption.[8]

15.3 Obtaining authority to exchange

Because of the binding nature of exchanging contracts, each solicitor must obtain their client's express authority before exchanging the contract. This is usually required to be given in writing. Once the solicitors have authority from their clients, they can proceed to exchanging the contract.

15.4 Methods of exchanging the contract

There are three ways that the contract can be exchanged:

- in person;
- by post or document exchange; or
- by telephone.

It is not possible to exchange contracts via email or fax.

15.4.1 In person

To exchange contracts in person, the seller and the buyer's solicitor meet and physically exchange the contracts, each handing their client's signed contract to the other solicitor. The contracts become binding immediately. This is uncommon in practice due to the lack of proximity between offices. The standard conditions as drafted do not allow for exchange in person and so will need to be amended by special condition if exchange is to happen this way.

8 For a discussion on this matter, please refer to Essential Legal System and Legal Services for SQE1, available from Routledge.

15.4.2 By post or document exchange

It is possible to exchange contracts by post. The buyer's solicitor will post their client's part of the contract and a cheque for the deposit to the seller's solicitor. Upon receipt, the seller's solicitor will post their client's part of the contract to the buyer's solicitor. The contracts are formally 'exchanged' and become binding the moment the seller's solicitor posts their client's part of the contract. There is inevitably a delay when exchanging by post and a period of uncertainty for the buyer. For this reason, postal exchange is not used in a chain of transactions, where certainty and immediacy are paramount.

Document exchange service can be used to exchange contracts in the same way as by post, and the standard conditions make it clear that the contract becomes binding when the seller's solicitor deposits their client's part at the document exchange.

15.4.3 Telephone

By far, the most common method of exchanging contracts is by telephone. The Law Society has devised three formulae which govern the exchange by telephone and which must be followed by solicitors exchanging by telephone.

15.4.3.1 Formula A

When using ***Formula A***, one solicitor (usually the seller's solicitor) holds both parties' signed part of the contract. (Necessarily, therefore, the buyer's solicitor will have already posted their client's signed contract and deposit to the seller's solicitor in advance of exchange.)

A phone call then ensues in which:

1. A completion date is agreed by the two solicitors.
2. The solicitor holding both parts of the contract checks and confirms that they are identical and both signed.
3. The solicitor holding both parts confirms that they will insert the agreed completion date in both contracts.
4. The solicitors agree that exchange occurs.
5. The solicitor holding both parts confirms that they now hold their client's part to the order of the other solicitor and gives an undertaking to send this to the other solicitor that day. This can be by first-class post, document exchange, or hand delivery.
6. If the solicitor holding both parts is the buyer's solicitor, they give an undertaking to send the deposit along with the contract.

Following the telephone call, both parties shall make a note of the telephone call recording the following information in a ***memorandum of exchange***:

1. The date and time of exchange.
2. The formula used and any agreed variations (e.g. if the contract is going to be posted the next morning rather than the same day).
3. The completion date.
4. The deposit to be paid (if the solicitor holding the documents is the buyer's solicitor).
5. The names of both solicitors.

15.4.3.2 Formula B

When using ***Formula B***, each solicitor holds their own client's signed part of the contract.

A phone call occurs between the solicitors, in which:

1. A completion date is agreed by the two solicitors.
2. Each solicitor confirms that they are holding the agreed form of contract, signed by their client.
3. Each solicitor confirms they will insert the agreed completion date.
4. The solicitors agree that exchange occurs.
5. Each solicitor gives an undertaking to the other that they hold their client's part to the order of the other solicitor.
6. Each solicitor undertakes to send their client's part of the contract to the other solicitor that day. This can be by first-class post, document exchange, or hand delivery.
7. The buyer's solicitor also gives an undertaking to send the deposit along with the contract.

Following the telephone call, both parties shall make a memorandum of exchange recording the following information:

1. The date and time of exchange.
2. The formula used and any agreed variations (e.g. if the contract is going to be posted the next morning rather than the same day).
3. The completion date.
4. The deposit to be paid.
5. The names of both solicitors.

Formula B is the most common method of telephone exchange in practice. A common variation is that the buyer's solicitor will transfer the deposit to the seller's solicitor before the telephone call occurs, to be held by the seller's solicitor to the buyer's solicitor's order.

Formula B was used to exchange contracts on:

- The Salon.
- The Car Park.
- The assignment of the Nail Bar Lease.

Please review the memorandum of exchange in the relevant Appendix.

15.4.3.3 Formula C

Formula C occurs in two stages and is only used in transactions which are part of a larger chain.

In the first stage, the two solicitors agree that they will exchange contracts later that same day, provided one solicitor contacts the other by a specified cut-off time. This gives the solicitors the time to line up exchange for any dependent transactions (e.g. if their client needs to exchange on the sale of a property before exchanging on the purchase of another). If the dependent transactions are not lined up, exchange won't happen.

The second stage, therefore, only kicks in if the parties are in a position to exchange before the agreed cut-off time. If the second stage is activated, the contracts are exchanged and the solicitors give undertakings in respect of sending the contracts and paying the deposit.

A client must expressly agree to its solicitor using Formula C.

Part 1

A telephone call occurs in which:

1. a completion date is agreed by the two solicitors;
2. the final time for exchange is agreed by the two solicitors;
3. the two solicitors agree whom the deposit is to be paid to.
4. each solicitor confirms that they are holding the agreed form of contract, signed by their client;
5. each solicitor gives an undertaking to the other that they will hold their client's part until the agreed final time for exchange;
6. each solicitor gives an undertaking to the other that they will comply with Part 2 of the formula if the seller's solicitor notifies the buyer's solicitor by the cut-off time; and
7. the buyer's solicitor gives a further undertaking that someone will be available to comply with Part 2 until the final time for exchange.

Following the telephone call, both parties shall make a note of the telephone call recording the following information:

1. the date and time the solicitors agreed to use Formula C;
2. the wording of any agreed variations;
3. the final time for exchange;
4. the agreed completion date;
5. the name of the solicitor to whom the deposit is to be paid; and
6. the names of both solicitors.

Part 2

A telephone call occurs in which:

1. Each solicitor undertakes to hold their client's part of the contract to the order of the other.
2. The solicitors agree that exchange occurs.
3. Each solicitor undertakes to send their client's part of the contract to the other solicitor that day. This can be by first-class post, document exchange, or hand delivery.
4. The buyer's solicitor undertakes to send (or arrange to send) to the seller's solicitor (or other nominated solicitor) a banker's draft or a solicitor's client account cheque for the deposit. This deposit must be held as stakeholder or as agent for the seller (but is only permitted to pass it to another solicitor as a deposit in an onward purchase).

Following the telephone call, both parties shall make a note of the telephone call recording the request to activate Part 2, from the seller's solicitor to the buyer's solicitor.

15.5 Steps immediately following exchange

Once exchange has occurred, it is imperative that each solicitor comply with the undertakings they have given.

15.5.1 Informing the client

Each solicitor will inform their client that contracts have been exchanged.

15.5.2 The documents

Depending on the method of exchange, the solicitors will need to ensure that they send their client's part of the contract to the solicitors for the other party.

As the contracts for the Salon and the Car Park were both exchanged using Formula B, Style&Go Ltd's solicitor will need to send:

- Style&Go Ltd's signed part of the contract for the Salon to Neeta's solicitor; and
- Style&Go Ltd's signed part of the Car Park contract to Urban Space Ltd's solicitor

The contract for the assignment of the Nail Bar Lease was also exchanged using Formula B, and so Gemma's Gels Ltd's solicitor will need to send their client's signed part of the contract for the assignment to Polished Perfection Ltd's solicitor.

The contract for the House was exchanged using Formula C, so André's solicitor will need to send his signed part of the contract to Michael's estate's solicitor.

15.5.3 The deposit

The buyer's solicitor will transfer the deposit to the seller's solicitor immediately after exchange, if this hasn't already been done. The seller's solicitor will usually hold these as ***stakeholder***, which means that the money cannot be transferred to any party without the consent of the other.[9]

For each of our Transactions requiring a deposit, this was sent to the seller's solicitor ahead of exchange, so this step is not necessary.

15.5.4 Insurance

Because the risk in the property has now passed to the buyer following exchange, the solicitor for the buyer will need to ensure that an insurance policy is in place to cover the risk of accidental damage occurring.

Further, if the chancel search[10] revealed that the property is in an area with potential chancel repair liability, a buyer may wish to insure a property against this risk from the moment contracts are exchanged, even if a notice is not present on the title when the initial due diligence is conducted. This is because if a notice is entered once the contracts have been exchanged but before the transaction is protected by a priority search,[11] that notice will bind the buyer.

André's and Style&Go Ltd's solicitors will need to ensure that the insurance policies they previously selected are now put in place.

9 This can be compared with the position when holding a deposit as agent for the seller, which permits the solicitor to give the money to the seller before completion – this is clearly risky for the buyer, who will struggle to recover their deposit if the seller defaults on completion.

10 See Chapter 7.

11 See Chapter 16.

Chapter 15 revision points

- Exchanging contracts creates a binding obligation for the buyer to purchase the property on the agreed completion date.
- Before exchanging contracts, the buyer's solicitor will need to ensure that title investigation is complete and the buyer is happy to purchase the property, that the solicitor has received the deposit from the buyer and is holding this in cleared funds, and that any mortgage documentation is signed.
- Upon exchange, risk in the property will pass to the buyer, so the buyer will need to arrange insurance to be effective from exchange.
- The buyer's solicitor will need their client's express authority to proceed with exchanging contracts.
- Contracts can be exchanged in person, by post, or by telephone. Telephone exchange Formula B is the most common method of exchanging contracts – by this method, each solicitor holds their own client's documents, and these are swapped after the telephone call. Formula C is a two-part process used when the transaction is part of a chain.
- After exchange, solicitors will inform their clients, post relevant documentation to the other side, transfer the deposit (if this hasn't been done before exchange), and effect any insurance policy.

16 Pre-completion searches and enquiries

16.1 Chapter overview

Once contracts have been exchanged, some final due diligence is undertaken before completion of the transaction occurs. This is to make sure that nothing concerning the land or the parties has changed since the due diligence was undertaken.

This chapter examines the different types of search, including those revealing entries which affect the land itself and those revealing information about the parties. Some common search results are reviewed, with a discussion of any additional steps which must be taken before completion can occur.

This chapter is relevant to all freehold and leasehold transactions.

This chapter in the context of our Transactions

For each of our Transactions, the buyer's solicitor must conduct pre-completion searches before proceeding to completion.

You may wish to refer to the priority search for each Transaction whilst working through this chapter.

DOI: 10.4324/9781032711508-20

16.2 Searches revealing entries affecting the land

In Chapters 4, 5, and 6, we examined how to investigate title to land, and we explored the types of encumbrances which can affect land; some of these affected the land in our Transactions. Once contracts have been exchanged, it is necessary to repeat some of these searches to make sure that no additional encumbrances have been registered against the land since we last checked.

These searches also have the benefit of conferring priority on a purchaser. This means that a buyer will take the land free of any encumbrances which are registered after the date they lodge a search.[1]

16.2.1 Registered land: the priority search

When dealing with registered land, the relevant search is made with HMLR using ***Form OS1*** (for purchases of the whole title of land) or ***OS2*** (for purchases of part of a title of land). The purchaser's solicitor enters the details of the register of title they reviewed when investigating the land (e.g. the date and time of the register), and HMLR will search the register of title for new entries made since this date.

If the solicitor is acting for a buyer and a lender, the search should be made in the name of the lender: this will protect both the buyer and the lender.

An OS1 search has been made by the buyer's solicitor in each of our Transactions relating to registered land. Please review those OS1 search results, located in the relevant Appendix.

16.2.1.1 Effect of the search

The search has three key effects.

16.2.1.1.1 REVEALING NEW ENTRIES

The search reveals whether any entries have been registered against the title since the date of the register initially reviewed. This is essential for buyers, who will take the property subject to any interests which are registered against the title.[2] This is shown in the 'Result' section in the middle of the search certificate.

16.2.1.1.2 CONFERRING PRIORITY

The search also confers priority on the purchaser. The search result will contain a ***priority period***, specifying the date on which priority ends. You can see this date on the top right-hand side of the search certificate. The priority period is 30 working days from the date the search was ordered.

1 Provided certain conditions are met – see Sections 16.2.1.1.2 and 16.2.2.1.2.
2 See the priority rules for registered land set out in Chapters 2 and 5.

Provided that the purchase of the land is completed and an application to register the purchase is lodged with HMLR by noon on the date this priority period expires, the buyer's acquisition will have priority over any applications lodged during the priority period.[3] This means that the buyer will take the land free from any encumbrances which someone had applied to register during that time period. Without priority, the buyer would take the land subject to any encumbrances for which an application to register them had been made before the buyer's application for registration of the purchase was made.

The solicitor for each of our buyers will note the expiry of the priority period noted on the OS1; the relevant transaction must complete, and an application to register that transfer must be lodged with HMLR by this date in order to benefit from the priority period. If it isn't, the buyer will lose priority and any entries affecting the property which are subject to an application for registration during this period will take priority over the buyer's purchase.

A search conducted in the name of the lender will confer priority on the lender and the buyer, provided that both applications for registration (the application to register the transfer to the buyer and the application to register the mortgage) are made before the expiry of the priority period. This is the case for the OS1 search against the House, which was conducted in the name of André's lender, Country Funding Building Society.

16.2.1.1.3 FREEZING THE REGISTER

The search also ***freezes the register*** for the priority period. This means that it is impossible for third parties to register interests against the title during the priority period; if a third party submits an application to register an interest against the title during the priority period, this interest will not be registered until the day after the priority period expires.

This becomes relevant in the event that completion and the application to register with HMLR do not occur before the priority period expires and means that if the buyer's solicitor needs to re-do the priority search, the expiry of the priority period should be used as the 'search from' date, because the first date that new entries could be registered is the day after this date (as it is not possible for new entries to have been registered during the priority period).

If any of our buyers is not in a position to complete before the priority period expires, their solicitor will re-do the priority search, using the day the priority period expires as the 'search from' date, knowing that no entries could have been registered before this date.

3 s72 LRA 2002.

16.2.1.2 Results of the search

Most commonly, the searches reveal "no new entries" and the transaction can proceed to completion. You can see from the OS1 results that this is the case for the searches conducted in respect of our Transactions.

On occasion, a new entry will be revealed by the search. In this situation, the buyer's solicitor will need to make enquiries with the seller's solicitor about what this entry relates to and request that the entry be removed on or before completion. It is the person who benefits from the entry who must give their consent to it being removed from the register of title. If an entry cannot (or will not) be removed, the buyer will be bound by this entry when they acquire the property (and they are obliged to acquire the property as a result of having exchanged contracts). However, this may constitute a breach of contract on the part of the seller if it is not one of the specified encumbrances listed by the seller in the contract.[4]

One entry which may come up on the OS1 result is a notice of chancel repair liability. The seller is unlikely to be able to make sure that this entry is removed from the title upon completion, and as we saw in Chapter 7, chancel repair liability can be very expensive. This, therefore, may be something the buyer chooses to insure against from exchange of contracts.[5]

HMLR does not guarantee that the results of an OS search are accurate. In the rare event that a result is inaccurate and there are entries affecting a title which the search fails to flag to a purchaser, these rights will still bind the buyer and take priority over their purchase, but HMLR may offer compensation to the buyer if this error causes loss.

16.2.2 Unregistered land: the Land Charges Search

When dealing with unregistered land, there is no OS1, and instead the central Land Charges Search against the seller's name must be repeated. A search against previous owners is not necessary as it is not possible to register entries against previous owners once they have disposed of the land. The search should be made in the same way as when title was investigated. You will recall from Chapter 4 that when we conduct this search, we need to enter the year we wish to search from and to; for the pre-completion search, the 'from' date will be the same year as the 'to' date in the initial search (because all entries pre-dating that will already have been revealed). The 'to' date will be the current year.

4 See chapter 11. To mitigate the risk of liability in breach of contract, a seller may restrict the definition of 'specified encumbrances' to those encumbrances registered against the title on a specific date, and at a specific time.
5 See Chapter 15, Section 15.5.4.

16.2.2.1 *Effect of the search*

16.2.2.1.1 REVEALING NEW ENTRIES

The search reveals whether any land charges have been registered against the seller's name between the 'from' and 'to' dates. This means the search will reveal any land charges registered against the seller since the 'search from' date.

16.2.2.1.2 CONFERRING PRIORITY

The search also confers priority on the purchaser. The search result will contain a priority period, specifying the date on which priority ends. The priority period is 15 working days from the date of the search.[6]

Provided the transfer of the land is completed before this priority period expires, the buyer will have priority over any applications lodged during the priority period and will not take subject to these. If the transfer of the land is not completed before the expiry of the priority period, the buyer will take subject to any interests registered during the priority period. The search against Urban Spaces Ltd confers a priority period expiring on 22 May 2026. Style&Go Ltd's purchase of the Car Park must complete their purchase of the Car Park by 22 May 2026 in order to benefit from this priority period; otherwise, they lose priority, and any entries affecting Urban Spaces Ltd which are registered during this period will bind them on their purchase of the Car Park.

Note the distinction here between registered land and unregistered land: in registered land, it is *registration* of the disposition which transfers the legal title, and so it is the application for registration which must occur within the priority period; in unregistered land, the legal title transfers on *completion* of the deed, and so it is completion which must occur within the priority period.

16.2.2.1.3 NO FREEZING OF THE REGISTER

The search *does not* freeze the Land Charges Register for the priority period. This means that if a third party submits an application to register a land charge against the owner of the property during the priority period, this interest will be registered against that person on the day it was lodged (but it will not bind the buyer, provided completion occurs within the priority period).

This is relevant in instances where the buyer does not complete the transaction within the priority period. You will recall that in registered land, no interests could be registered against the title during the priority period, and therefore, if the application for registration wasn't made during the priority period, the search only needed to be repeated from the expiry of the priority period. In unregistered land,

6 s11 LCA 1925.

land charges can be registered against the owner during the priority period, and so any search which needs to be re-done needs to search the whole of the priority period to ensure that any land charges registered during this period are picked up.

If Style&Go Ltd's purchase of the Car Park does not complete before 22 May 2026, their solicitor will need to re-do the priority search using 1 May 2026 as the 'search from' date to ensure they discover any entries made during the priority period.

16.2.2.2 Results of the search

Mostly, the searches don't reveal new entries and the transaction can proceed to completion, and indeed, this is the case for the search against Urban Spaces Ltd

However, on occasion, a new entry will be revealed by the search. Just like with registered land, in this situation the buyer's solicitor will need to make enquiries about what this entry relates to, by obtaining an official copy of the entry and by making enquiries with the seller's solicitor. The buyer's solicitor can then request that this entry be removed on or before completion. It is the person who benefits from the entry who must give their consent to it being removed from the Land Charges Register.

Just like in registered land, if an entry cannot (or will not) be removed, the purchaser will be bound by this land charge when they acquire the property (which they are now contractually obliged to do) and may have a claim for breach of contract against the seller.

Unlike the situation with registered land, if an official certificate of search doesn't reveal any entries, then this is considered conclusive, and the buyer will not be bound by any entries which were on the register but not revealed by the search.

16.3 Searches revealing information about the parties

16.3.1 Searches against the seller

Where the seller is an individual, a buyer does not normally need to check that the seller is not bankrupt.

In unregistered land, if a seller was bankrupt, it would be revealed by the central Land Charges Search made against the seller, which has already been undertaken during the due diligence phase and repeated close to completion. In registered land, a purchaser for value acting in good faith will take good title from a bankrupt seller, provided that the title register, which has already been reviewed during due diligence, contains no notice or restriction relating to the bankruptcy. Further, the interest of the trustee in bankruptcy would appear on the OS1 search which has been undertaken even more recently. Therefore, a separate bankruptcy search is not normally conducted.

If the seller is a company, the buyer's solicitor will repeat the company search already undertaken to make sure that the information has not changed and to make sure that there is no pending insolvency or crystallisation of a floating charge – these do not appear on the title to registered land and so would not be picked up by any of the other pre-completion searches. Company searches don't confer priority, and so this search should be done as close to completion as possible.

In each of our Transactions where the seller is a company, the buyer has repeated the company search, and this has confirmed in all cases that the information has not changed since the due diligence was initially undertaken.[7]

16.3.2 Searches against the borrower

Before transferring the mortgage funds, a lender will want to do a search against the borrower to make sure that they are not bankrupt. This is to minimise the risk of lending money to a borrower who is unlikely to repay the loan. The lender will not advance the mortgage funds if the search reveals an adverse entry relating to the borrower unless the borrower's solicitor certifies that the entry, in fact, does not relate to the borrower.

If the borrower is an individual, the lender's solicitor will usually do this search via HMLR using ***Form K16***. If a borrower is a corporate entity, the lender will do a company search and, on the day of completion, will do a telephone search at the Registry of Winding Up Petitions at Companies Court, to check for orders, applications, and petitions which are not yet appearing on the company search.

Chapter 16 revision points

- Before completion, the solicitor may undertake searches against the land and against the parties, to ensure that nothing has changed since the due diligence was undertaken.
- Where the land is registered, the buyer's solicitor will undertake an OS1 search with priority; this will reveal whether there have been any new entries registered against the title since the title register was reviewed. The search has a priority period of 30 working days; provided the buyer applies to register their transaction before that period ends, they will not take subject to any new entries registered in the interim.

7 Repeat company searches have not been reproduced in the Appendices.

- Where the land is unregistered, the buyer's solicitor will repeat the Land Charges Search; this will reveal whether there have been any new land charges registered against the owner since the last search. The search has a priority period of 15 working days; provided the buyer completes their transaction before that period ends, they will not take subject to any new land charges registered in the interim.
- Where the seller is a company, the buyer's solicitor may repeat the company search to check that the seller has not become insolvent.
- A lender will undertake a bankruptcy search against a borrower before transferring the loan, to ensure that the borrower is not bankrupt.

17 Practical steps to prepare for completion

17.1 Chapter overview

Before completion can occur, the solicitors for both parties will need to agree practical arrangements and ensure they are holding correctly executed on documentation.

This chapter explores the key steps which must be taken to prepare for completion, including:

- the completion information provided by the seller's solicitor covering practical matters such as when and where keys and alarm codes will be handed over; and
- how the buyer's solicitor can ensure that they are holding the relevant funds to complete the transaction, both from the buyer and from a lender (if relevant).

This chapter is relevant to all freehold and leasehold transactions.

> **This chapter in the context of our Transactions**
>
> For each of our Transactions, the buyer's solicitor must ensure that they are practically ready for completion. We have not reproduced a bespoke TA13 or SCR form for each Transaction because the detail of these forms is beyond the scope of this book, but you will find a sample SCR form in Appendix 6 which you may wish to refer to whilst working through this chapter.

DOI: 10.4324/9781032711508-21

17.2 Completion information from the seller

Before completion can occur, the solicitors for both parties will need to agree the practical arrangements for completion. The buyer's solicitor will request completion information from the seller's solicitor. The following standard-form requests are commonly used:

- For residential transactions or those using the Protocol: Law Society ***Form TA13***
- For commercial transactions: ***Solicitors Completion Requirements***

Just as we saw in Chapter 11, the transfer of the Salon constitutes a residential transaction, notwithstanding Style&Go Ltd's long-term plans to use the property for commercial purposes, because it is currently being used as a residence. The House also constitutes a residential transaction. These two transactions, therefore, would use Form TA13 to capture the completion information.

The remainder of the Transactions are considered commercial and would use the Solicitors Completion Requirements to capture the completion information.

Both forms cover basic information, such as:

1. the practical arrangements for handing over keys and alarm codes from the seller to the buyer;
2. confirmation of the documents to be provided by the seller to the buyer on completion;
3. how and where completion is to occur;
4. the amount of money required to be sent from the buyer to the seller on completion, and the account details to send this to; and
5. details of any mortgages burdening the property which need to be discharged on completion, along with relevant undertakings in respect thereof.

Upon returning the form to the buyer's solicitor, the seller's solicitor will also usually include a ***completion statement*** which details the total amount due from the buyer on completion and a breakdown of how that figure has been calculated.

If the property is mortgaged, the seller's solicitor must also obtain a ***redemption figure*** from the seller's lender, which will confirm the amount required to pay off the mortgage on the completion date. There is a mortgage on the Salon. The seller's solicitor has provided an undertaking to the buyer's solicitor to discharge this mortgage on completion,[1] and so it is imperative before completion that Neeta's solicitors make sure the sale proceeds are sufficient to discharge the mortgage (and if they are not, they must request additional funds from her).

1 See Chapter 9.

17.3 Obtaining funds

The buyer's solicitor will need to ensure that they have the relevant funds to complete the transaction.

17.3.1 Financial statement

Ahead of completion, the buyer's solicitor will put together a ***financial statement*** which shows the amount due from the buyer. This will include the balance of the purchase price as well as SDLT and any legal fees due. The buyer's solicitor will need to be in cleared funds before completion can occur.

17.3.2 Obtaining funds from the lender

If acting for the lender as well as the buyer (as is the case for the purchase of the House), the buyer's solicitor will release the final certificate of title and pre-completion search results to the lender and request the mortgage monies ahead of completion.

17.4 Documentation

Ahead of completion, solicitors for both parties will ensure they are holding the correct documentation, executed by their client.

17.4.1 Seller's documentation

The seller's solicitor will ensure that they are holding the deed to create or transfer the legal estate, signed by their client. This will (for the purposes of our Transactions) be the TR1 or the lease.

17.4.2 Buyer's documentation

The buyer's solicitor will ensure that they are holding:

- the deed to create or transfer the legal estate, signed by their client. This will (for the purposes of our Transactions) be either the TR1 or the lease; and
- if relevant, a mortgage deed signed by their client.

Chapter 17 revision points

- Before completion can occur, the solicitors for both parties will need to agree practical arrangements and ensure they are holding correctly executed documentation.
- For residential transactions, Law Society Form TA13 is used to agree practical arrangements; in commercial transactions, the Solicitors Completion Requirements are used.

- The seller's solicitor will obtain a redemption amount from the lender and will send a completion statement to the buyer's solicitor.
- The buyer's solicitor will compile a financial statement requesting funds from their client, which it will need to hold in cleared funds before completion can occur.
- The lender's solicitor will send the certificate of title to the lender and request the mortgage funds.
- Both solicitors will ensure they are holding the relevant documentation, signed by their client.

Revision Summary

PHASE 3 Preparing for completion

Exchange of contracts

- ***Exchanging contracts*** creates a binding obligation for the buyer to purchase the property on the completion date which has been agreed by the parties.
- ***Legal title*** to the property remains with the seller after exchange.
- ***Beneficial title*** to the property passes to the buyer upon exchange.
- Risk in the property passes to the buyer from the date of exchange, unless amended in the contract.

Pre-exchange checklist for the buyer's solicitor

Table R3.1 A checklist of pre-exchange steps for the buyer's solicitor

Category	Checklist	Reason
Title investigation and searches	Are all queries arising out of title investigation and/ or searches resolved?	The buyer is contractually bound to complete the purchase once contracts have been exchanged, so it is important that the client is happy to buy the property.
Contract	Is the contract approved by the buyer and signed?	The buyer is contractually bound to complete the purchase on the terms stated in the contract, once exchanged, so it is important that the client has approved these terms.
Mortgage	Has the mortgage offer documentation been accepted and signed by the buyer?	The buyer is contractually bound to complete the purchase once contracts have been exchanged, so it is important that the buyer has the funds to do so.
Deposit	Has the buyer sent the deposit to the solicitor, and have these funds cleared?	The solicitor must send the deposit to the other side immediately following exchange so must have this in cleared funds before exchanging.
Insurance	Have insurance options been explored and any appropriate policies identified?	Risk in the property will pass to the buyer following exchange, so the buyer should be in a position to insure the property from the moment contracts are exchanged.
Authority	Has the client's authority to complete been obtained?	The solicitor cannot exchange without the client's express authority.

Methods of exchange

Table R3.2 Methods of exchanging contracts

Method	Key features	When does exchange occur?	Undertakings
In person	The contracts are exchanged in person.	Immediately.	None required.
By post	The buyer's solicitor posts their client's contract first; the seller's solicitor posts their client's contract on receipt of the buyer's part.	When the seller's solicitor posts the seller's part of the contract to the buyer's solicitor.	None, unless the buyer's solicitor posts last. In this case, the buyer's solicitor must give an undertaking to send the deposit to the seller's solicitor.
Telephone ***Formula A***	The seller's solicitor holds both parts of the contracts.	Immediately.	The solicitor holding both parts of the contract undertakes that they hold their client's part to the order of the other solicitor. That solicitor undertakes to send their client's part to the other solicitor the same day. The buyer's solicitor undertakes to send the deposit to the seller's solicitor (if this has not already been done).
Telephone ***Formula B***	Each solicitor holds their own client's part of the contract.	Immediately.	Each solicitor undertakes to hold their client's part to the order of the other solicitor. Each solicitor undertakes to send their client's part to the other solicitor. The buyer's solicitor undertakes to send the deposit to the seller's solicitor.

Method	Key features	When does exchange occur?	Undertakings
Telephone ***Formula C***	This is used for chain transactions only. Special authority from the client is required before it can be used. Exchange happens in two stages. Each solicitor holds their own client's part of the contract.	During the second telephone call, once Part 2 is activated.	<u>Part 1</u> Each solicitor gives an undertaking to the other that they will hold their client's part of the contract until the agreed final time for exchange. Each solicitor gives an undertaking to the other that they will comply with Part 2 of the formula if the seller's solicitor notifies the buyer's solicitor by the cut-off time. The buyer's solicitor gives a further undertaking that they will be available to comply with Part 2 until the final time for exchange. <u>Part 2:</u> Each solicitor undertakes to hold their client's part of the contract to the order of the other. Each solicitor undertakes to send their client's part of the contract to the other solicitor that day. The buyer's solicitor undertakes to send the deposit to the seller's solicitor.

Post-exchange checklist

Table R3.3 A post-exchange checklist for both solicitors

Step	Which solicitor
Inform client that exchange has occurred.	Both
Send the documents as required by the undertakings.	Both
Transfer the deposit if required.	Buyer's solicitor
Ensure insurance policies are put in place.	Buyer's solicitor

Pre-completion searches

- Before completion, the buyer's solicitor will do a search against the land to ensure that no encumbrances have been registered since the title due diligence was undertaken. If the buyer's solicitor also acts for the lender, this search will be made in the lender's name.
- If the seller is a company, the buyer's solicitor will do a company search to check for fixed or floating charges affecting the property. This must be done as close to completion as possible.
- The lender's solicitor will do a bankruptcy search against the borrower.

Searches revealing information about the land

Table R3.4 A summary of pre-completion searches against the land

Type of land	Undertaking the search	Conditions for conferring priority	Freezing the register
Registered	***OS1***: search of whole with priority ***OS2***: search of part with priority Search from the date of the register of title reviewed during the due diligence stage	• The disposition must be completed; and • an application to register it must be made at HMLR, both within 30 working days of the search being made. The expiry date will be specified on the search result.	The register freezes during the ***priority period***, and no new interests can be registered against the title during the priority period. Any applications lodged during the priority period are registered the day after the expiry of the priority period.

Type of land	Undertaking the search	Conditions for conferring priority	Freezing the register
Unregistered	***Central Land Charges Search*** against the seller. Search date: • 'from' the 'to' date in the initial search conducted during title investigation; and • 'to' the current date.	The disposition must be completed within 15 working days of the search being made. The expiry date will be specified on the search result.	The register does not freeze during the priority period – new interests can be registered during the priority period, but these will not bind the buyer if priority is conferred as per the previous column.

Practicalities

- The seller's solicitor will complete a questionnaire containing practical information about the completion process:
  - For residential transactions, this is ***Form TA13***.
  - For commercial transactions, this is the ***Solicitors Completion Requirements***.
- The seller's solicitor will send a ***completion statement*** detailing the outstanding funds payable by the buyer on completion.
- The buyer's solicitor will send a ***financial statement*** to the buyer detailing the funds necessary for completion, including SDLT and fees.
- If the property is mortgaged, the seller's solicitor will obtain a ***redemption statement*** from the lender detailing the sum required to discharge the mortgage.
- If acting for the lender as well as the buyer, the buyer's solicitor will send the final certificate of title to the lender and request the mortgage monies.
- Solicitors for both parties will need to ensure they are holding the relevant documentation, signed by their client. This could include a TR1, a lease, and a mortgage deed.

PHASE 3

Multiple-choice practice questions

Question 1

A solicitor acts for a company purchasing a lease.

The company is not paying a premium for the lease, and so there is no deposit to be paid. The lease contains a provision requiring the landlord to insure the premises. The solicitor holds the contract signed by their client.

What checks should the solicitor do before exchanging contracts with the seller?

A. After exchange, the buyer will be contractually bound to purchase the lease, so the solicitor must ensure that all title queries are resolved and they have their client's authority to exchange contracts.
B. After exchange, the buyer will be contractually bound to purchase the lease, so the solicitor must ensure that all title queries are resolved, that the client has signed the contract, and that they have their client's authority to exchange.
C. After exchange, the buyer will be contractually bound to purchase the lease, so the solicitor must ensure that the buyer's mortgage offer has been signed and the solicitor is holding the buyer's deposit for the property in cleared funds.
D. After exchange, the buyer will be contractually bound to purchase the lease even if the premises become damaged, so the solicitor must ensure that the buyer has taken out an insurance policy in respect of the premises.
E. After exchange, the buyer will be contractually bound to purchase the lease even if the premises become damaged, so the solicitor must ensure that all title queries are resolved, that the buyer has taken out an insurance policy in respect of the premises, and that they have their client's authority to exchange contracts.

Question 2

A solicitor is acting for a purchaser of a freehold property. The parties have agreed to complete using Formula B.

Which of the following best describes the process the solicitor must follow to exchange contracts?

A. Each solicitor holds their own client's signed part of the contract. Each solicitor undertakes to hold their client's part to the order of the other solicitor until the agreed time for exchange and undertakes to send their client's part to the other solicitor immediately after exchange.
B. The seller's solicitor holds both parts of the contract and undertakes to hold their client's signed part to the order of the buyer's solicitor and undertakes to send their client's part to the buyer's solicitor immediately after exchange.
C. The buyer's solicitor posts their client's contract; seller's solicitor posts their client's contract on receipt of buyer's part.
D. The buyer's solicitor emails their client's contract; the seller's solicitor emails their client's contract on receipt of the buyer's part.
E. Each solicitor holds their own client's signed part of the contract. Each solicitor undertakes to hold their client's part to the order of the other solicitor and undertakes to send their client's part to the other solicitor immediately after exchange.

Question 3

A solicitor is acting for the purchaser of a registered freehold property. The purchaser is acquiring the property from an individual.

Which searches should the solicitor do before completing the purchase?

A. An OS1 to discover encumbrances affecting the property.
B. An OS2 to discover encumbrances affecting the property.
C. A Land Charges Search against the seller to discover encumbrances affecting the property.
D. An OS1 to discover encumbrances affecting the property, and a bankruptcy search against the seller.
E. A Land Charges Search against the seller to discover encumbrances affecting the property, and a bankruptcy search against the seller.

Question 4

A solicitor is acting for the purchaser of an unregistered freehold property. The purchaser is acquiring the property from a company.

Which searches should the solicitor do before completing the purchase?

A. An OS1 to discover encumbrances affecting the property and a company search against the seller.
B. An OS2 to discover encumbrances affecting the property and a company search against the seller.
C. A Land Charges Search against the seller to discover encumbrances affecting the property.
D. An OS1 to discover encumbrances affecting the property and a bankruptcy search against the seller.
E. A Land Charges Search against the seller to discover encumbrances affecting the property and a company search against the seller.

Question 5

A solicitor acts for a purchaser of registered freehold property.

The solicitor has conducted a priority search over the property. It revealed that no further entries have been registered against the property since the solicitor's title investigation.

How can the solicitor ensure that no new entries are registered which will bind his client?

A. The solicitor must complete the transfer within 30 working days of the OS1 search result.
B. The solicitor must apply to register the transfer within 30 working days of the OS1 search result.
C. The solicitor must complete the transfer within 15 working days of the date the OS1 was undertaken.
D. The solicitor must apply to register the transfer within 30 working days of the date the OS1 was undertaken.
E. The solicitor must apply to register the transfer within 30 days of the expiry date specified on the OS1.

PHASE 4 Completion

In Phase 3, the solicitors exchanged contracts, which made it contractually compulsory for both parties to complete the transaction to transfer the land. The solicitors then got everything ready for ***completion***: the buyer's solicitor conducted searches to ensure that nothing had changed which might affect the buyer's interest in the land, both solicitors ensured they were holding signed copies of all relevant documentation, and the buyer's solicitor arranged for funds to be sent to them from the buyer and, if relevant, from the lender.

In Phase 4 we focus on completing the transfer of the land from the seller to the buyer. We will first examine what happens under the sale contract if one of the parties is not able to complete on the agreed completion date (Chapter 18), and then we discuss the process of completion (Chapter 19).

DOI: 10.4324/9781032711508-22

18 Consequences of late completion

18.1 Chapter overview

Once contracts have been exchanged, the parties are contractually bound to complete the transaction on the agreed completion date. However, occasionally, things don't go to plan and parties may exchange contracts only for one of them to find themselves unable to complete on the agreed date.

It is possible for parties to deal informally with delays, for example, simply by communicating and rearranging the completion date, or to formally vary the completion date in the contract using a deed of variation.

Where the parties do not deal with a delay informally, the standard conditions contained in the contract for sale set out a process for managing the situation. This chapter focuses on the position and formal processes under the standard conditions.

This chapter is relevant to all transactions in which a sale contract has been exchanged.

This chapter in the context of our Transactions

A sale contract was exchanged in respect of:

- André's acquisition of the House;
- Style&Go Ltd's acquisition of the Salon;
- Style&Go Ltd's acquisition of the Car Park; and
- Polished Perfection Ltd's assignment of the Lease to Gemma's Gels Ltd.

Solicitors for both parties in these Transactions must understand the consequences of late completion, as governed by that sale contract.

You may wish to refer to the sale contract for each of the above Transactions and the set of standard conditions relevant to that Transaction in Appendix 6 whilst working through this chapter.

DOI: 10.4324/9781032711508-23

18.2 Financial remedies

When completion is delayed, the most commonly used mechanism under the standard conditions is that the innocent party will proceed with completion of the transaction once the delayed party is in a position to complete but will seek a financial remedy to compensate them for having suffered a delay.

18.2.1 Contractual compensation

Completion will be considered to be delayed if completion monies are not received by the time set out in the contract (regardless of whether completion actually occurs later that day or not). The standard time for sending completion monies is 2:00 p.m., but this may have been amended by special condition.

Often, a delay in completion will occur as a result of a delay earlier in the process. When completion is delayed and there has been a default under the contract, the standard conditions[1] require the payment of ***compensation***, even if the delay has not actually caused any losses.

Compensation will be payable at the ***contract rate*** defined in the contract applied to the outstanding balance (which is the purchase price minus any deposit paid) and will apply for each day that completion is delayed. In the situation above (where the completion monies are received after 2:00 p.m.), this will constitute the first day of the delay.

18.2.1.1 Residential transactions

In residential transactions, the standard conditions require compensation to be paid by the delaying party who is most at fault.[2] As we saw in Chapter 11, the standard conditions[3] contain timeframes within which the pre-completion steps

1 SCS 7.2 and SCPC 10.3.
2 SCS 7.2.1.
3 SCS 4.3.

must be completed.[4] This means, for example, that if André is not in a position to complete his purchase of the House on the agreed completion date but the reason for this is that Michael's estate's solicitors took longer than they should have in reviewing and approving the draft transfer deed, then Michael's estate will be required to pay compensation to André for late completion even though they are ready to complete and André isn't, because they are the party who is most at fault by causing the initial delay.

18.2.1.2 Commercial transactions

In commercial transactions, however, the seller has a contractual entitlement to compensation caused by a delay from the buyer,[5] but the buyer does not have a reciprocal right to compensation if the seller causes the delay in completion. This means that if Style& Go are not in a position to complete the purchase of the Car Park on the agreed completion date, they must pay compensation to Urban Spaces Ltd, but if Urban Spaces Ltd defaults in performing their obligations under the sale contract and this leads to a delay in completion (e.g. perhaps they have not vacated the Car Park by the agreed date and time for completion), Style&Go Ltd has no right to be compensated.

18.2.2 Damages for breach of contract

A delay in completion is a breach of contract and entitles the innocent party to damages for their loss caused by the delay. This remedy is available to all parties under the common law so would mean that, in the above example, Style&Go Ltd could seek ***common law damages*** from Urban Spaces Ltd to compensate them for any losses suffered as a result of their delay.

Common law damages are available even where a party has already been compensated under the contractual compensation provisions, but any contractual compensation paid will be subtracted from the calculation of common law damages so that the party is not compensated twice for the same loss.

18.3 Revising the completion date

Where completion has not occurred by the contractual completion date, there are mechanisms in the standard conditions for revising this completion date. Where a completion date is formally revised and completion does not occur by the revised date, additional remedies become available.[6]

4 We recommend that you take note of these timeframes. You will notice that they set deadlines for doing things between exchange and completion, which ordinarily would have been done before exchange (such as title investigation).

5 Under SCPC 10.3.

6 Which we discuss in Section 18.4.

18.3.1 Delaying the completion date in commercial assignments

Where the transaction is an assignment and that assignment is conditional upon the landlord's consent, then, clearly, completion cannot go ahead on the completion date if the landlord's consent is still outstanding.

In commercial assignments,[7] such as the assignment of the Nail Bar Lease, if the landlord's consent has not been provided by the completion date, then, initially, the completion date is simply postponed until that consent is obtained. The revised completion date is the date falling five working days after the seller notifies the buyer in writing that the consent has been given by the landlord.[8]

If, six months after the original completion date the consent has still not been provided by the landlord, either party can[9] ***rescind*** the contract, provided that both parties have performed their respective obligations associated with obtaining that consent.

18.3.2 Serving a notice to complete

For other types of transaction, once the agreed date and time for completion have passed, either party is entitled[10] to serve on the other what is known as a ***notice to complete***. This notice operates on the basis that a party is 'ready, willing, and able to complete'.

The notice requires completion to occur within ten working days (excluding the date of service of the notice). The notice also requires that if a deposit of less than 10% was paid on exchange, then the buyer is required to now pay an extra deposit to bring the total amount paid to 10% of the purchase price.[11] You will recall that this was the case for the Car Park: the parties agreed that a deposit of 5% would be paid. If completion was delayed and Urban Spaces Ltd served a notice to complete on Style&Go Ltd, then Style&Go Ltd would need to pay an additional 5% of the purchase price to Urban Spaces Ltd.

Non-compliance with the revised completion date gives the innocent party the right to rescind the contract.

7 In residential assignments, there is no formal process to postpone the completion date. If the landlord's consent has not been obtained three working days before the completion date, then the parties have the option to rescind the contract.

8 SCPC 11.3.5.

9 Though, of course, they do not have to.

10 Again, they do not have to.

11 SCS 6.8.3 and SCPC 9.8.3.

18.4 Rescinding the contract

Recission can only occur in limited circumstances, and we have seen above the processes which must be followed (and must have failed to bring the parties to completion) before rescission becomes an option for the parties.

When a contract is rescinded, the parties walk away from the transaction as they are no longer contractually bound to perform it. The seller is permitted to sell the property to someone else, and the buyer may choose to purchase an alternative property.

18.4.1 Recission following a delay caused by lack of consent to an assignment

Where a party opts to rescind the contract relating to an assignment because the landlord's consent is outstanding, the deposit is to be repaid to the buyer, and the buyer must return any documents and cancel registration of the contract.

18.4.2 Recission following a notice to complete

Where an innocent party opts to rescind a contract following the notice to compete process, then what happens to the deposit depends on who the defaulting party is.

If the buyer is the defaulting party, then the seller may keep the deposit paid by the buyer as well as any accrued interest, but if the seller is the defaulting party, then the deposit will be repaid to the buyer with interest.

The innocent party will also have a right to claim damages, as noted above.[12]

Chapter 18 revision points

- Occasionally, parties may exchange contracts only for one of them to find themselves unable to complete on the agreed date.
- In residential transactions, the sale contract may enable the innocent party to claim compensation from the party causing the delay. In commercial transactions, only the seller is entitled to compensation for a delay by the buyer. The rate of compensation will be specified in the contract.
- The parties may be able to revise the completion date; if completion does not occur by the revised completion date, then the parties can rescind the contract and walk away from the transaction.
- An innocent party who suffers loss as a result of delayed completion can claim damages for breach of contract.

12 See Section 18.2.2.

19 Completion

19.1 Chapter overview

Once contracts have been exchanged, the parties are contractually bound to complete the transaction on the agreed completion date.

As we saw in Chapters 12 and 13, the document which creates or transfers the estate in land is likely to be a TR1 or a lease. There may be associated documentation which requires completing at the same time as the TR1 or the lease, such as consent documentation (e.g. a licence to assign) or mortgage documentation.

This chapter outlines the method and process for completing the various documents to effect the creation of a leasehold estate or the transfer of a freehold or leasehold estate from one party to another.

This chapter is relevant to all freehold and leasehold transactions.

This chapter in the context of our Transactions

All our Transactions are now ready to complete. Solicitors for both parties in each of our Transactions will need to complete the relevant Transaction on the agreed completion date.

You may wish to refer to the terms of the sale contract for each Transaction (if relevant), along with the relevant deed for that Transaction, any consent or mortgage documentation, and the Law Society's Code for Completion by Post.[1]

1 Available to download from the Law Society website: www.lawsociety.org.uk/topics/property/code-for-completion-by-post.

DOI: 10.4324/9781032711508-24

19.2 Methods of completion

Completion can occur in person, by post, or over the telephone. The solicitors will need to have agreed this in advance of the completion date.

19.2.1 In person

Where completion happens in person, the buyer's solicitor will attend the offices of the seller's solicitor, where completion will occur.

19.2.2 By post

This is the most common method for residential transactions and is being used to complete André's acquisition of the House and Style&Go Ltd's acquisition of the Salon. The Law Society's ***Code for Completion by Post*** should be used to guide the completion process. When completing by post, the seller's solicitor acts as agent for the buyer's solicitor and effects completion at the agreed time.

19.2.3 By telephone

This is the most common method for commercial transactions. The solicitors for each party will agree on the telephone that completion has occurred. The remainder of our Transactions will complete by telephone.

19.3 Date and time of completion

19.3.1 Date

In most circumstances, the parties will have agreed the completion date and written this on the contract at exchange, and indeed, this is the case for our Transactions which used a sale contract. If the parties have not agreed on a date, the standard conditions state that completion shall occur on the 20th working day after exchange.[1]

19.3.2 Time

The standard conditions do not require completion to occur at a specified time,[2] but the parties can make this a term by including it as a special condition. If it is not a term of the sale contract, the solicitors can arrange between themselves a convenient time to complete.

The appropriate time for completion to occur will depend on whether the transaction is part of a chain. If the funds to purchase the property are coming from the proceeds of sale of a different property, then completion of the purchase cannot occur until the first sale has completed and proceeds have been paid to the seller in that transaction. This is the case for André, who must complete the sale of another property before he can complete the purchase of the House, as he will be using those proceeds of sale to part-fund his purchase of the House.

The restrictions of the relevant banks for transmitting funds must also be considered.

19.4 What happens on the completion date

19.4.1 Immediately preceding completion

If the transfer is conditional upon obtaining the consent of the landlord, that consent documentation (such as a licence to assign) must be completed before the transfer documents are completed.

Once completion of the main transaction is imminent, the solicitors for each party to the licence (e.g. the landlord, tenant, and assignee) will liaise to complete this

1 SCS 6.1.1 and SCPC 9.1.1.
2 Although they do require the payment of interest if completion monies are received after 2:00 p.m.

document. Each will hold their client's executed part of the licence and will date the document upon agreement with the other solicitors, usually over the telephone.

19.4.2 Process of completion

There are several key steps which form part of the completion process.

19.4.2.1 The buyer's solicitor sends the completion monies to the seller's solicitor

The buyer's solicitor will send the outstanding completion monies to the seller's solicitor. The completion monies will be sent to the account specified in the TA13 or SCR form.[3] The money must be sent electronically in same-day cleared funds.[4]

The outstanding completion monies may be made up of cash, a loan being secured by a mortgage, or proceeds of sale from completion of another transaction.

If the transfer is being funded by proceeds from the sale of another property and those two transactions are completing on the same day, it is common for the sale proceeds from the first transaction to be sent directly to the solicitor of the seller in the second transaction (the purchase) so that completion of the purchase can occur. This is the case for André, whose purchase of the House is reliant on the sale of another property. Michael's estate's solicitor will receive the sale proceeds from André's sale to hold until completion of the House occurs.

19.4.2.2 The documents are checked one last time

Before completion occurs, key documentation will be checked one last time:

- the transfer deed is reviewed to ensure that it is the version agreed and executed by the parties, and that it has been executed properly;
- if dealing with unregistered land, the original documents are compared against the abstract or epitome to ensure that it is a true copy. This is called ***verification of title***;
- if the buyer has purchased chattels or fittings with the property they should obtain a receipt for these items signed by the seller's solicitor; and
- if payments of outgoings have been apportioned on the completion statement, the buyer's solicitor should check any receipts to ensure that the correct apportionments have been applied.

If completion is occurring in person, the buyer's solicitor will undertake these checks.

3 See Chapter 17.
4 SCS 6.7 and SCPC 9.7.

Where completion is taking place by post (like for André's acquisition of the House and Style&Go Ltd's acquisition of the Salon), the seller's solicitor will act as agent to perform these checks on behalf of the buyer's solicitor, provided the buyer's solicitor has given instructions on what to do and will hold the documentation to the order of the buyer's solicitor for release after completion.

If completion is occurring over the telephone, each solicitor will check their own client's documents and hold these to the order of the other solicitor, for release after completion.

19.4.2.3 The transfer documents are dated

Once the seller's solicitor is holding the completion monies in cleared funds and the documents have been checked, completion of the transfer deed or lease can occur. Completion occurs when the solicitor writes the date onto the relevant document.

Michael's estate's solicitor will date the TR1 to transfer the House to André. For the other Transactions, each solicitor will date their client's executed copy of the relevant document.

19.4.3 Immediate steps following completion

19.4.3.1 Complete associated documentation

There may be additional documentation to complete, such as a mortgage deed. This must be dated immediately following completion of the main transaction.

19.4.3.2 Inform clients

Each solicitor will inform their client that the transaction has completed.

19.4.3.3 Discharge the seller's mortgage

If the property was subject to a mortgage, an undertaking will have been supplied by the seller's solicitor to pay this off using the sale proceeds and provide the relevant forms to enable the buyer's solicitor to have the charge removed from the title register (see Chapter 9, where Neeta's solicitor provided an undertaking to Style&Go Ltd's solicitor in respect of the mortgage over the Salon).

Once completion has occurred, the seller's solicitor will send the redemption amount to the seller's lender, who, in response, sends a ***Form DS1*** (if the land is registered) or the receipted deed (if the land is unregistered). In commercial transactions, the DS1 may already have been signed by the lender and sent to the seller's solicitor, who holds it and dates it upon completion.

Some lenders prefer to use HMLR's electronic discharge system, whereby they send an electronic message to HMLR to remove the charge from the title register. If this is the case, there will be no DS1 form.

There was a mortgage registered against the Salon, and so Neeta's solicitors will use the sale proceeds to redeem this mortgage and obtain a Form DS1.

There was also a mortgage against the Car Park; Urban Spaces Ltd's solicitors will use the sale proceeds to redeem this and obtain a ***receipted mortgage deed***.

19.4.3.4 Sale proceeds disseminated

Once any mortgages have been discharged, any remaining proceeds of sale are sent to the seller. If the sale proceeds are to be used to fund an onward purchase which is completing on the same day, the sale proceeds will be sent to the solicitor of the seller in the onward transaction so that completion of the onward purchase can occur.

19.4.3.5 Relevant documents

In the completion information form,[5] the parties agreed the documentation to be provided to the buyer upon completion. These will be either handed to the buyer's solicitor, if completion occurs in person, or posted immediately following completion, if completion occurs by post or telephone. The seller's solicitor may have produced a schedule of deeds and documents and require the buyer's solicitor to sign to confirm that everything has been received.

Common documentation to be sent to the buyer's solicitor includes:

- The completed transfer deed or lease.
- Mortgage discharge documentation, for example, DS1 or receipted mortgage deed.
- If the land is unregistered, like the Car Park, originals of the documents in the epitome of title.

Where completion occurs by telephone, the buyer's solicitor will post their client's executed and completed the TR1 or lease to the seller's solicitor.

19.5 Effect of completion

19.5.1 Unregistered land

Once completion of a disposal of unregistered land has occurred, the ***legal title*** to the property passes to the buyer.

19.5.2 Registered land

Upon completion of a disposal of registered land, it is the ***equitable title*** which passes to the buyer. The legal title to the property does not pass to the buyer until the disposal is registered by HMLR.

5 See Chapter 17.

19.6 Our Transactions

A summary of the completion process for each of our Transactions follows.

19.6.1 Transfer of the House from Michael's estate to André: 4 December 2025

19.6.1.1 Before completion

The solicitors agreed that completion would occur by post, governed by the Law Society's Code for Completion by Post.

André's solicitor sent André's signed the TR1 to Michael's estate's solicitor along with instructions to review and confirm that the TR1 was the same version as agreed by the parties and had been executed properly. Michael's estate's solicitor checked this and confirmed.

The sale of André's other property completed early on 4 December 2025, and the proceeds were sent directly to Michael's estate's solicitor along with the mortgage monies from Country Funding Building Society.

19.6.1.2 Completion

Both parts of the TR1 were dated 4 December 2025 by Michael's estate's solicitor.

19.6.1.3 After completion

André's solicitor dated the mortgage deed and the deed of covenant 4 December 2025 and informed André that completion had occurred.

Michael's estate's solicitor sent the completion monies and the deposit received on exchange to Paul Thompson, personal representative for Michael's estate, and posted the part of the TR1 signed by Michael's estate to André's solicitor.

19.6.2 Transfer of the Salon from Neeta to Style&Go Ltd: 18 May 2026

19.6.2.1 Before completion

The solicitors agreed that completion would occur by post, governed by the Law Society's Code for Completion by Post.

Style&Go Ltd's solicitor sent the signed the TR1 to Neeta's solicitor along with instructions to review and confirm that the TR1 was the same version as agreed by the parties and had been executed properly. Neeta's solicitor checked this and confirmed.

Style&Go Ltd's solicitor sent £472,500 to Neeta's solicitor.

19.6.2.2 Completion
The TR1s were dated 18 May 2026 by Neeta's solicitor.

19.6.2.3 After completion
Each solicitor then informed their client that the transaction had completed.

Neeta's solicitor paid the completion monies to Secure Trust Bank to redeem the mortgage and sent the remaining proceeds of sale to Neeta. Neeta's solicitor then posted the completed the TR1 executed by Neeta and the DS1 received from the lender to Style&Go Ltd's solicitors.

19.6.3 Transfer of the Car Park from Urban Spaces Ltd to Style&Go Ltd: 18 May 2026

19.6.3.1 Before completion
The solicitors agreed that completion would occur by telephone.

Style&Go Ltd's solicitor sent £80,750 to Urban Spaces Ltd's solicitor.

Each solicitor held their own client's executed the TR1 to the order of the other and checked that this was the same version as agreed between the parties and had been executed properly.

19.6.3.2 Completion
During a telephone call, Style&Go Ltd's solicitor and Urban Spaces Ltd's solicitor dated the respective parts of the TR1 18 May 2026.

19.6.3.3 After completion
Each solicitor informed their client that the transaction had completed.

Urban Spaces Ltd's solicitor paid the completion monies to Barnford Bank to redeem the mortgage and sent the remaining proceeds of sale to Urban Spaces Ltd.

Urban Spaces Ltd's solicitor sent the completed the TR1 executed by their client and the receipted mortgage deed received from the lender to Style&Go Ltd's solicitors, along with originals of all the documents in the epitome of title.

Style&Go Ltd's solicitors sent the completed the TR1 executed by Style&Go Ltd to Urban Spaces Ltd's solicitors.

19.6.4 Grant of a lease over the Nail Bar by Style&Go Ltd to Polished Perfection Ltd: 21 September 2026

19.6.4.1 Before completion
The solicitors agreed that completion would occur by telephone.

Polished Perfection Ltd's solicitor sent the rent payable under the lease on the 'Rent Commencement Date' to Style&Go Ltd's solicitor. As per clause 4 of the Nail Bar Lease, this reflected the amount due from the 'Rent Commencement Date' (which is the same as the 'Completion Date' – 21 September 2026) until the next 'Rent Payment Date' (29 September 2026), which amounted to £82.19.

Each solicitor held their own client's executed lease or counterpart and checked and confirmed that this accorded with the agreed version and had been executed properly as a deed.

19.6.4.2 Completion

During a telephone call, Polished Perfection Ltd's solicitor and Style&Go Ltd's solicitor dated the lease and counterpart 21 September 2026.

19.6.4.3 After completion

Each solicitor informed their client that the transaction had completed.

Style&Go Ltd's solicitor transferred the advance rent to Style&Go Ltd and posted the completed lease executed by Style&Go Ltd to Polished Perfection Ltd's solicitors.

Polished Perfection Ltd's solicitors sent the completed lease executed by Polished Perfection Ltd to Style&Go Ltd's solicitors.

19.6.5 Assignment of the Nail Bar Lease from Polished Perfection Ltd to Gemma's Gels Ltd: 27 February 2027

19.6.5.1 Before completion

The solicitors agreed that completion would occur by telephone.

Ahead of completion

- Polished Perfection Ltd's solicitor, Style&Go Ltd's solicitor, and Gemma's Gels Ltd's solicitor completed the licence to assign;
- Polished Perfection Ltd's solicitor and Style&Go Ltd's solicitors completed the authorised guarantee agreement; and
- Gemma's Gels Ltd's solicitor and Style&Go Ltd's solicitors completed the rent deposit deed.

The completion monies of £1 were sent from Gemma's Gels Ltd to Polished Perfection Ltd.

Polished Perfection Ltd's solicitor held the executed the TR1 to the order of Gemma's Gels Ltd's solicitor[6] and checked and confirmed that this was the same version as agreed between the parties and had been executed properly.

6 Gemma's Gels Ltd did not execute the TR1, so there is only one part to be completed: the TR1 executed by Polished Perfection Ltd.

19.6.5.2 Completion

During a telephone call, Polished Perfection Ltd's solicitor dated the respective TR1 with 27 February 2026.

19.6.5.3 After completion

Each solicitor informed their client that the transaction had completed.

Polished Perfection Ltd's solicitor sent the completed the TR1 to Gemma's Gels Ltd's solicitor as well as the original lease between Style&Go Ltd and Polished Perfection Ltd and paid the completion monies to Polished Perfection Ltd.

Chapter 19 revision points

- Completion can occur in person, by post, or by telephone. Completion by post is common for residential transactions, and completion by telephone is common for commercial transactions.
- If the landlord's consent is required, this licence must be completed before the main transaction. The buyer's solicitor will send the completion monies to the seller's solicitor ahead of completion.
- When the parties are ready to complete, the documents will be checked and dated to effect completion.
- Immediately following completion, any associated documents (e.g. a mortgage deed) will be completed, and the clients will be informed that completed has taken place. If there is a mortgage registered against the property, this must be discharged. Sale proceeds and relevant documents will be distributed to the relevant parties.

Revision Summary

PHASE 4 Completion

Delayed completion

- If the parties do not complete on the agreed completion date specified in the contract, this is known as ***delayed completion***.
- Delayed completion is a breach of contract for which ***common law damages*** are available.
- The standard conditions also contain mechanisms for dealing with delayed completion.

Contractual compensation

- ***Contractual compensation*** is available at the rate specified in the contract for the outstanding balance owed.
- In residential transactions, whichever party is most at fault must compensate the other.
- In commercial transactions, only the seller has the right to compensation.

Notice to complete

- If one party is ready, able, and willing to complete, they can serve a ***notice to complete*** on the other party.
- A notice to complete requires completion to occur within ten working days from service.
- A notice to complete requires a 10% deposit to have been paid.
- Failure to complete by the date specified in the notice enables the innocent party to ***rescind*** the contract and permits forfeiture or recovery of the deposit with interest.

Delayed completion of assignments

- Where completion of an assignment is delayed because the landlord's consent is outstanding, a notice to complete cannot be used because neither party is 'ready, able, and willing' to complete.

- In residential assignments where the landlord's consent is outstanding three working days before the completion date, either party can rescind the contract immediately.
- In commercial assignments where the landlord's consent is outstanding, the completion date will be postponed for up to six months before recission becomes available.

Methods of completion

- **In person:**
  - The buyer's solicitor attends the seller's solicitor's offices. This is the place of completion.
  - The buyer's solicitor undertakes checks before dating the document to effect completion.
- **By post:**
  - Postal completion is used in residential transactions, guided by the Law Society's Code for Completion by Post.
  - The seller's solicitor is the agent for the buyer's solicitor.
  - The seller's solicitor undertakes checks of the documents as instructed by the buyer's solicitor and dates the documents to effect completion.
- **By telephone:**
  - Telephone completion is commonly used for commercial transactions.
  - Each solicitor holds its own client's executed documentation and undertakes necessary checks.
  - Each solicitor dates the documents whilst on a telephone call, effecting completion.

Things to check before completion can occur

- **Both solicitors must:**
  - check the completion date and time in the contract;
  - check that the documentation is executed and with the relevant solicitor ready for completion;
  - agree the method of completion; and
  - ensure arrangements are in place for the transfer of keys from the seller to the buyer.
- **The buyer's solicitor must additionally:**
  - ensure that pre-completion searches have been conducted and the priority periods noted; and
  - ensure that the buyer's completion monies are held in cleared funds, from the buyer and/or lender.

On the day of completion

1. **Steps immediately preceding completion:**
   - Conditional documents are completed (e.g. consent documents).
2. **Process of completion:**
   - the purchase monies are sent to the seller's solicitors;
   - the documentation is checked; and
   - the TR1 or lease is dated.
3. **Steps immediately following completion:**
   - complete associated documents e.g. mortgage deed;
   - inform clients that completion has occurred;
   - discharge seller's mortgage and obtain DS1 or receipted deed;
   - disseminate sale proceeds; and
   - post relevant documentation to the other side.

Effect of completion

- In registered land: completion confers the ***equitable title*** to the property to the buyer.
- In unregistered land: completion confers ***legal title*** to the property to the buyer.

PHASE 4 Multiple-choice practice questions

Question 1

A solicitor acts for a seller of a residential freehold property.

The purchase price of the property is £350,000, and the deposit under the contract is 10%. The contract rate is 4%.

Contracts were exchanged on 20 April, and the completion date in the contract is 1 May.

The buyer sends the completion monies at 3:00 p.m. on 1 May, and completion occurs at 4:00 p.m. on 2 May.

Which advice should the solicitor give the client?

A. The seller is entitled to one day's worth of compensation at 4% on £315,000.
B. The seller is entitled to one day's worth of compensation at 4% on £350,000.
C. The seller is entitled to two days' worth of compensation at 4% on £315,000.
D. The seller is entitled to two days' worth of compensation at 4% on £350,000.
E. The seller is not entitled to any compensation.

Question 2

A solicitor acts for a buyer of commercial freehold premises. The completion date in the contract is 1 May.

On 1 May, the buyer is ready to complete but the seller is not, and completion does not occur. The buyer has seen an alternative property and asks the solicitor for advice about whether it can walk away from this purchase.

What advice should the solicitor give to the buyer?

A. The buyer is entitled to compensation under the contract at the contract rate.
B. The buyer must pursue a claim for damages for breach of contract.
C. The buyer can rescind the contract immediately.
D. The buyer must serve a notice to complete; if completion does not occur by the date specified in the notice, the buyer can rescind the contract.
E. The buyer cannot rescind the contract before 1 November.

PHASE 5 Post-completion

In Phase 4, we saw the completion of each of our Transactions. For the seller's solicitor, this was the last stage of the transaction, and they will have confirmed to their client that the relevant property has been sold, sent all relevant documentation, and closed the file.

For the buyer's solicitor, there is one final stage: post-completion. There are three key steps we will be discussing in Chapter 20:

1. **Payment of SDLT/LTT and notifying HMRC/WRA.** As you will recall from Chapter 3, there are taxes payable on the acquisition of property. We discuss how and when to pay these and the consequences of not doing so.
2. **Registration of a charge with Companies House.** When a company grants a mortgage over property, this charge must be registered at Companies House in order for the charge to be enforceable against other creditors and the company's administrator or liquidator. We will discuss how and when to register this charge.
3. **Registration of the transaction with HMLR.** As you will recall from Chapter 2, registration of a registrable disposition of registered land is necessary to transfer the legal title to that land. For unregistered land which triggers first registration, the completion of the conveyance confers legal title to the purchaser, but if the transaction is not registered within the required timeframe, then the legal title reverts back to the seller and the purchaser only holds the equitable title to the land.

We will discuss how and when to register the transaction, as well as making associated applications, such as registering a mortgage.

DOI: 10.4324/9781032711508-25

By the end of these steps, the transaction is complete for the freehold buyer's solicitor, who will notify their client that the above steps have been actioned and will send any relevant documentation to the buyer before closing the file.

Where the estate transferred is leasehold, the parties must consider the ongoing landlord and tenant relationship, discussed in Phase 6.

20 Post-completion steps

20.1 Chapter overview

For the seller's solicitor, completion was the final stage of the transaction. For the buyer's solicitor, there are some key steps they must take following completion to ensure that the buyer's acquisition of the property does not lose priority to other interests and that the buyer does not incur any financial penalties, namely:

1. paying SDLT or LTT and notifying the transaction to the relevant authority (HMRC or WRA);
2. registering charges with Companies House; and
3. registering the transaction with HMLR.

This chapter examines the details of these requirements and how the buyer's solicitor can comply with them.

This chapter is relevant to all freehold and leasehold transactions.

This chapter in the context of our Transactions

Each Transaction has now completed. The buyer's solicitors will need to undertake the relevant post-completion steps on behalf of their client.

You may wish to refer to the following documentation for each Transaction whilst working through this chapter:

- the official copies initially reviewed in Phase 1 and the summary of due diligence;
- the relevant HMLR forms such as the AP1, FR1, DS1, RXCs, and CH1, along with any relevant accompanying documents; and
- the official copies post-completion, which register our buyers as the proprietors.

DOI: 10.4324/9781032711508-26

20.2 SDLT and LTT

As you know from Chapter 3, Stamp Duty Land Tax and Land Transaction Tax are taxes payable on the acquisition of property. SDLT applies to property in England, and LTT applies to property in Wales.

20.2.1 What is required?

As set out in Chapter 3, for each land transaction, there are two key requirements:

1. submit a ***land transaction return***[1]; and
2. pay any SDLT or LTT due.

The buyer in the transaction is responsible for submitting the land transaction return and paying any tax due, but their solicitor will usually complete the land transaction return on their behalf and submit it along with payment to HMRC or the Welsh Revenue Authority (**WRA**).

Once a return is submitted, HMRC or the WRA will send a certificate in response; this needs to be submitted along with the application to register the transaction with HMLR. For this reason, the SDLT or LTT requirements must be actioned before the transaction can be registered with HMLR.

20.2.1.1 When is a return not required?

In very limited circumstances, a land transaction return is not required.[2] These include the following:

1. transactions for no consideration;
2. property acquired under a will;
3. property transferred as a result of divorce or the dissolution of civil partnership;

1 See Section 20.2.1.1 for the circumstances in which this isn't necessary.
2 See s77 and s77A FA 2003, and s44–46 Devolved Taxes Act 2017.

4. the grant of a lease of seven or more years where the premium is less than £40,000 and the annual rent is less than £1,000;
5. the grant of a lease of less than seven years where the amount of SDLT or LTT is under the threshold;
6. the assignment of a lease originally granted for seven years or more where the ***chargeable consideration*** for the assignment is less than £40,000; and
7. transactions for less than £40,000 which relate to freehold property in Wales.

Even though SDLT was not chargeable on some of our Transactions (the Car Park, the grant of the Nail Bar Lease, and the assignment of the Nail Bar Lease), only the assignment of the Nail Bar Lease falls within one of the categories above (that category being 6, because consideration of only £1 was paid for the assignment of the lease); a land transaction return is required for all the other Transactions.

20.2.2 What is the deadline?

For transactions in England, the land transaction return and payment must be made to HMRC within 14 days of the '***effective date***' of the transaction;[3] for the purposes of this book, the effective date is completion. All of our Transactions relate to property in England, and so the 14-day deadline will be relevant for each of them.

For transactions of land in Wales, the land transaction return and payment must be made to WRA within 30 days of the effective date of the transaction.[4]

There are financial penalties for failing to file a return on time, or failing to pay tax on time, and interest is added to these penalties.

20.2.3 Amount payable

We have already calculated the SDLT payable on our Transactions.[5] For ease of reference, these are repeated here:

- André's purchase of the House: £7,500
- Style&Go Ltd's purchase of the Salon: £89,250
- Style&Go Ltd's purchase of the Car Park: £0
- Grant of the Nail Bar Lease to Polished Perfection Ltd: £0
- Assignment of the Nail Bar Lease to Gemma's Gels Ltd: £0

For André and Style&Go Ltd, these amounts will need to be paid to HMRC within 14 days of their relevant completion date, along with the submission of

3 s76(1) FA 2003.
4 s44 Devolved Taxes Act 2017.
5 See Chapter 3.

the relevant return. In practice, the SDLT amount will have been requested by their solicitor on the financial statement requested before completion, so the buyer's solicitor will already be holding this amount, ready to pay to HMRC.[6]

20.3 Registering the company charge

If the buyer is a company and has purchased the property with the assistance of a mortgage, it must register this charge at Companies House within 21 days of its creation.[7] Failure to comply with this timeframe renders the charge void against the company's liquidator or administrator and against other creditors.[8]

The charge must be registered using form MR01 and accompanied by a fee, a certified copy of the mortgage deed, and a statement of particulars which contains the information specified at s859D Companies Act 2006.

Companies House will provide a certificate of registration which must be supplied to HMLR when registering the transaction. For this reason, this step must be completed before the application is made to HMLR to register the disposition.

None of our Transactions involve a company purchasing with the assistance of a mortgage, so this is not explored further.

20.4 Registering the disposition

As you will recall from Chapter 2, once a '***trigger event***' occurs in respect of unregistered land, such as a conveyance or the grant of a lease, the estate must be registered with HMLR to the new owner.[9] The sale of the Car Park to Style&Go Ltd will trigger first registration.

All registrable dispositions of registered land must also be registered with HMLR.[10] The transfers of the House, Salon, and Nail Bar Lease are all registrable dispositions, as is the grant of the Nail Bar Lease (this is the case because, even though it creates a new legal estate, it is being created out of a registered title).

Once HMLR has processed the application and completed the registration,[11] the register of title will be created, in the case of first registration, or amended, in the

6 See Chapter 17, Section 17.3.1.
7 s859A CA 2006.
8 s859H CA 2006.
9 See Chapter 2, Section 2.3.1.2.2.3.
10 s27 LRA 2002. See Chapter 2, Section 2.3.1.2.3.
11 This can take several months and, at times, over 18 months – see HMLR's latest processing data available online.

case of dispositions of registered land. HMLR will supply a copy of this to the buyer's solicitor. This should be reviewed thoroughly once received.

20.4.1 Timeframe for registering the disposition

An application for first registration must be made within two months of completion of the relevant conveyance.[12] Failure to comply with this results in the transfer of the legal estate becoming void.[13] For the acquisition of the Car Park, completion occurred on 18 May 2026, and so an application for first registration must be made before 17 July 2026.

An application to register a disposition of registered land must be lodged with HMLR within 30 working days of the date of the priority search (the OS1); in other words, within the ***priority period*** specified on the search result. Failure to comply with this timeframe results in the disposition losing priority to other applications which are lodged before it. If the disposition of land is not registered at all, it will not exist at law.[14]

20.4.2 Making the application to register the disposition

For dispositions of unregistered land which have triggered first registration, the application which needs to be made is an ***application for first registration***. ***Form FR1*** is used to make this.

For dispositions of registered land, the application which needs to be made is an ***application to change the register***. ***Form AP1*** is used for this.

Documents accompanying the application must be originals or certified copies. The relevant fee must be paid when making the application, which is based on the value of the land.[15]

20.4.2.1 The applications

The application for first registration or to change the register is the main application being submitted to HMLR. However, within that main application there may be other applications being made. For example, if land is purchased with the assistance of a mortgage, not only does the transfer to the new proprietor need to be registered, but the mortgage also needs to be registered – this is a separate application.

The AP1 and FR1 forms serve as an umbrella document capturing all the applications being made in respect of the land. Within each of those forms there is a

12 s6(4) LRA 2002.

13 s7(1) LRA 2002. This is separate from the issue of priority, which has already been secured by completing the transfer deed or lease within the priority period set out in the Land Charges Search.

14 s27 LRA 2002.

15 HMLR keeps a list of fees for each type of application, available online.

section in which the solicitor will list the applications they are making relating to that land. In form FR1, this is in panel 5, and in the form AP1, it is in panel 4.

The Land Registrar will make the applications in the order they are listed in the relevant panel. The order of applications is important, as you will see below.

20.4.2.1.1 DISCHARGING MORTGAGES

If there was a mortgage on the property which has been discharged on completion, like for the Salon, then the first application for the Land Registrar to deal with is to remove that mortgage from the title register; this will be the first application noted in panel 4 of the AP1. Please note that an ***application to discharge a mortgage*** will not be required on an application for first registration, because there will be no mortgages to remove from the title register (as the title *register* does not exist yet).

To remove the charge and associated restriction from the title register, a certified copy of the DS1 form must be submitted to HMLR along with the AP1. If the lender discharged the mortgage electronically, there will be no DS1 to include.

20.4.2.1.2 REGISTERING THE DISPOSITION

The next application to make will be to register the main disposition, for example, the transfer from seller to buyer, or the grant of a lease.

20.4.2.1.2.1 EVIDENCING THE CHANGE IN PROPRIETOR

A number of documents will need to be included with the application form to evidence that the land has been transferred.

- In all cases, the solicitor must enclose:
  - the completed transfer deed or lease;
  - the ***SDLT/LTT certificate***; and
  - ***Form DI***, if there are any known overriding interests burdening the land.
- In cases where the seller is not the same person as the legal proprietor, the solicitor must enclose:
  - the death certificate and grant of probate, if a registered proprietor has died. This is the case for André's purchase of the House, and for Style&Go Ltd's purchase of the Salon;
  - the power of attorney, if the transfer has been executed under a power of attorney;
  - the change of name certificate, if the seller has changed their name. This is the case for Style&Go Ltd's purchase of the Car Park from Urban Spaces Ltd, who, according to the title deeds, used to be called Urban Developments Ltd.

Where the land is currently unregistered and is being registered for the first time, the Land Registrar will need to see additional documents to verify the title to the land. The solicitor must list these in ***Form DL*** in chronological order:

- the documents forming the evidence of title (e.g. those in the epitome of title);
- buyer's pre-contractual searches and enquiries which are relevant to the title to the land, plus any replies from the seller;
- the contract for sale;
- requisitions on title plus replies; and
- pre-completion search certificates.

If relevant, the solicitor will also supply:

- the seller's receipted mortgage;
- the lease (if the unregistered property is leasehold).

20.4.2.1.2.2 DEALING WITH RESTRICTIONS

In registered land,[16] before a disposition can be registered to a new proprietor, any restrictions on the title register will need to be dealt with. You will recall that restrictions on the title register can prevent the registration of a disposition of that land, unless a conveyancer can certify that certain conditions have been met.

The Land Registrar will need to see evidence that a restriction has been complied with *before* they will register the disposition to the new proprietor. Usually, a solicitor will complete ***Form RXC*** to certify that the restriction has been complied with and will enclose any relevant documentation.

20.4.2.1.3 RESTRICTIONS PREVENTING DISPOSITIONS BY A SOLE PROPRIETOR

When land is held by tenants-in-common, we typically see a restriction on the title register preventing the registration of a disposition by a sole trustee. We saw this on the title register for the Salon at entry B2. Neeta has complied with this restriction by appointing Samir as a second trustee, and this will be evident to the Land Registrar when they review the TR1. A ***restriction certificate*** is not required to remove this restriction – the Land Registrar will automatically do so upon seeing that there are two trustees disposing of the property.

If Samir had been appointed using a ***deed of appointment***, then a certified copy of this would need to be supplied to HMLR.

16 This is only relevant to registered land, because land which does not have a title register necessarily cannot be subject to restrictions on a title register.

20.4.2.1.4 RESTRICTIONS PREVENTING DISPOSITIONS WITHOUT THE CONSENT OF THE LENDER

As we saw in Chapter 6, where there is a mortgage secured against registered land, it is common to see a restriction preventing the registration of a disposition of that land without the consent of the lender. This is the case for the Salon, which has, at entry B3, a restriction which requires the consent of Secure Trust Bank. This restriction will have been removed as part of the Land Registrar dealing with the discharge of the mortgage,[17] and so compliance with this restriction is no longer required. This is one demonstration of why the order of applications listed in the AP1 and FR1 forms is so important.

20.4.2.1.5 RESTRICTIONS PREVENTING DISPOSITIONS WITHOUT THE ENTRY INTO A DEED OF COVENANT

You will recall that one way of requiring the burden of a positive covenant to run with the land is to place a restriction on the title register which prevents that land from being disposed of unless the new proprietor enters into a deed of covenant to perform the positive covenant. This was the case for the House, and André entered into a deed of covenant with Joanne Bates. André's solicitor will need to certify in an RXC form that André has complied with the restriction and supply a certified copy of the deed of covenant to HMLR.

20.4.2.1.5.1 AUTOMATIC REGISTRATIONS

Some rights or interests affecting the land will be automatically registered by the Land Registrar (without a specific application being required).

This will include all rights and interests which are written in the transfer deed or lease. For example:

- *The burden of* ***covenants given by the buyer*** *in the transfer.* This is the case for Style&Go Ltd, who has covenanted to indemnify Neeta in respect of their performance of the positive covenant to maintain the alleyway – this will be automatically noted on the title register to the Salon once it is registered to Style&Go Ltd.
- ***Easements granted or reserved*** *in a lease.* These will be noted against the title number they burden. The right to park in the Car Park granted in the Nail Bar Lease will be noted on the title to the Car Park, and the rights reserved by the Nail Bar Lease will be noted on the title to the Nail Bar.

For land which is being registered for the first time, this will also include all rights or interests contained within the title documents. For example, the easement over Sheep Street benefitting the Car Park will be noted on the title to the Car Park, and the burden of that easement will be noted on the title to Sheep Street. Similarly, the restrictive covenants registered on the Land Charges Register will be noted against the title to the Car Park as it is created.

17 See Section 20.4.2.1.1.

20.4.2.1.6 APPLICATION TO REGISTER A NEW LEGAL CHARGE

If the buyer has purchased the property with the assistance of a mortgage, then this will need to be registered as a new legal charge using ***Form CH1***, which is then noted on the AP1 form. This is the case for André, who purchased the House with a mortgage. André's solicitor will need to include a certified copy of the mortgage deed with the AP1.

Where the borrower is a company, a certified copy of the certificate of registration issued by Companies House, along with confirmation from the conveyancer or lender that the mortgage deed is the same as that filed at Companies House and relates to the certificate of registration,[18] must also be included with the AP1.

20.4.2.1.7 OTHER COMMON APPLICATIONS

Other common applications you may come across are:

- the registration or removal of a restriction; and
- the registration or removal of a notice noting the burden of a third-party interest, such as a restrictive covenant or easement.

20.4.2.1.8 UNAMENDED ENTRIES ON THE TITLE REGISTER

The Land Registrar will only deal with the applications listed in the AP1 or FR1 and those automatic registrations arising out of the main transfer deed or lease. All other rights and covenants which were previously on the title register and which have not been the subject of an application for removal will remain on the title register.

This means that restrictions on the title register which have been complied with (enabling registration of the disposition) but not removed, such as the restriction on title register to the House relating to the requirement to comply with the positive covenant, will remain on the title register.

Chapter 20 revision points

- After completion, tax must be paid and a tax return must be submitted, in most circumstances. HMRC requires SDLT to be paid and an SDLT return to be submitted within 14 days of the effective date; the WRA requires LTT to be paid and an LTT return to be submitted within 30 days of the effective date.
- Companies buying with the assistance of a loan must register charges with Companies House within 21 days of completion.
- The disposition must be registered with HMLR. For first registrations, an application must be made within two months of the transaction completing.

18 See Section 20.3.

For other registrations, an application must be made within the specified priority period of 30 working days.

- On the application to HMLR, existing mortgages must be discharged before the disposition is registered, and restrictions must be complied with or discharged. The buyer may also need to register a new mortgage or add a new restriction or notice to the register.

Revision Summary

PHASE 5 Post-completion

Post-completion steps

Table R5.1 Summarising the steps that must be taken after completion has occurred

Action	Deadline	Relevant documents
1. TAX		
Pay SDLT if due, and submit a return to HMRC.	14 days from the ***effective date***	***SDLT1***
Pay LTT if due, and submit a return to WRA.	30 days from the effective date	***LTT return***
2. REGISTER COMMERCIAL MORTGAGES		
Register the charge at Companies House.	21 days from completion	***MR01***
3. REGISTER THE DISPOSITION WITH HMLR		
Register the transaction at HMLR by making the following applications, where relevant: 1. remove irrelevant entries from the register of title; 2. register the disposition;	Dispositions of registered land: 30 days from end of priority period (see OS1 search result) Dispositions of unregistered land, triggering first registration: within two months from completion of conveyance	*In all cases:* • transfer deed/lease; • ***SDLT/LTT certificate***; and • ***Form DI***, if relevant. *If applying to remove a mortgage:* • ***DS1 form***; or • ***receipted mortgage***.

Action	Deadline	Relevant documents
3. register new mortgages; 4. register new restrictions; and 5. register new notices.		*Register the disposition using:* • ***Form AP1***, for registered land • ***Form FR1***, for first registration *If the seller does not match the legal proprietor, enclose relevant documentation to prove the seller's right to sell:* • grant of representation or probate; • power of attorney; • death certificate; • deed of appointment of a second trustee; and/or • change of name certificate. *If there are restrictions preventing registration of a disposition, enclose:* • ***Form RXC***, to certify compliance with the restriction; and • any relevant accompanying evidence. *Additional title documents to enclose when applying for first registration:* • documents forming the evidence of title • pre-contractual searches and enquiries, plus replies

Action	Deadline	Relevant documents
		• the sale contract • requisitions on title plus replies • pre-completion search certificates *If registering a new mortgage, enclose:* • the mortgage deed; and/or • the certificate of registration issued by Companies House plus the required confirmation.

Submitting SDLT and LTT returns

Table R5.2 Submitting SDLT and LTT returns

	SDLT	LTT
Applicable to	Properties in England	Properties in Wales (from April 2018)
Requires buyer to	• submit a ***land transaction return***; and • pay any tax due	
No return required for	• transactions for no consideration • property acquired under a will • property transferred as a result of divorce or the dissolution of civil partnership • leases of seven or more years where the premium is less than £40,000 and the annual rent is less than £1,000 • leases of less than seven years where the amount of SDLT is under the threshold	• transactions for no consideration • property acquired under a will • property transferred as a result of divorce or the dissolution of civil partnership • leases of seven or more years where the premium is less than £40,000 and the annual rent is less than £1,000 • leases of less than seven years where the amount of SDLT is under the threshold • freehold property for less than £40,000

	SDLT	LTT
Deadline for return and tax	14 days from ***effective date***	30 days from effective date
Consequences of late filing or payment	Penalties and interest	

PHASE 5

Multiple-choice practice questions

Question 1

A solicitor is acting for the purchaser of a property in England with unregistered title. The purchase will trigger first registration.

The purchaser is buying the property with the aid of a mortgage.

Contracts have been exchanged, requisitions on title made, and the solicitor has conducted a pre-completion priority search of the title.

Following completion, the solicitor will need to deal with post-completion matters involving payment of Stamp Duty Land Tax (SDLT) to HM Revenue & Customs and registration of the dealing at the Land Registry.

Registration at the Land Registry must take place within two months of which date?

A. The date contracts are exchanged, to avoid interest becoming payable on outstanding SDLT.
B. The date of completion, to avoid interest becoming payable on outstanding completion monies.
C. The date of completion, to avoid the legal title in the property reverting to the seller.
D. The date of the result of the priority search, to avoid subsequent entries being made on the title which bind the purchaser.
E. The date of completion, to avoid the mortgagee's power of sale arising under the legal charge.

Question 2

A solicitor is acting for a purchaser of a residential freehold property in England with registered title for £200,000.

Contracts have been exchanged, requisitions on title made, and the solicitor has conducted a pre-completion priority search of the title.

Following completion, the solicitor will need to deal with post-completion matters involving payment of Stamp Duty Land Tax (SDLT) to HM Revenue & Customs.

Which of the following best describes the steps the solicitor will take?

A. The solicitor must pay any SDLT due and submit a land transaction return within 14 days from completion.
B. The solicitor must pay any SDLT due and submit a land transaction return within two months from completion.
C. The solicitor must pay any SDLT due and submit a land transaction return within 30 working days from the date of the priority search.
D. A land transaction return is not required because no SDLT is payable.
E. A land transaction return is not required because the transaction is not notifiable.

Question 3

A solicitor is acting for a purchaser of a leasehold property in England with registered title for £38,000. The lease being assigned is for a term of ten years, nine of which remain.

Contracts have been exchanged, requisitions on title made, and the solicitor has conducted a pre-completion priority search of the title.

Following completion, the solicitor will need to deal with post-completion matters involving payment of Stamp Duty Land Tax (SDLT) to HM Revenue & Customs.

Which of the following best describes the steps the solicitor will take?

A. The solicitor must pay the SDLT and submit a land transaction return within 14 days from completion.
B. The solicitor must pay the SDLT and submit a land transaction return within two months from completion.
C. The solicitor must pay the SDLT and submit a land transaction return within 30 working days from the date of the priority search.
D. A land transaction return is not required because no SDLT is payable.
E. A land transaction return is not required because the transaction is not notifiable.

PHASE

6 Leasehold management

As we have seen, for freehold transactions, the story ends once the transaction completes and the post-completion steps have been carried out. For leasehold transactions, this is not the case; this final phase (Phase 6) focuses on three key aspects of the ongoing management of a commercial lease:

1. **Requiring the landlord's consent.** We will be looking in Chapter 21 at the situations in which the tenant wishes to do something to the premises which requires the landlord's consent, such as assigning or sub-letting the lease or making alterations to the premises. We will examine when the landlord can withhold consent to these requests, as well as the process for obtaining this consent.
2. **Enforcing leasehold covenants.** Whilst many landlord/tenant relationships are positive, occasionally, things go wrong and one party does not comply with their obligations under the lease. We will be looking in Chapter 22 at the rules surrounding enforcement of leasehold covenants and the remedies available to a landlord if the tenant breaches one of the tenant covenants under the lease.
3. **Ending a lease.** Finally, in Chapter 23 we will look at the ways in which a lease can come to an end, and the protections afforded to some business tenancies under the Landlord and Tenant Act 1954.

DOI: 10.4324/9781032711508-27

21 Consent under a lease

21.1 Chapter overview

Occasionally, a tenant may wish to do something with the lease premises which requires consent from the landlord, for example, parting with possession (alienation) or making alterations to the premises. In Chapter 13 we explored different types of alienation and alteration provisions and the various types of covenants which determine whether consent is required for a particular activity, and whether that consent must be given reasonably.

In this chapter we explore the consent requirements in more detail, looking at the circumstances in which a landlord can refuse consent, as well as the process the tenant must follow to obtain consent.

This chapter is relevant to commercial leases only.

This chapter in the context of our Transactions

Shortly after acquiring the Nail Bar, Meena (the director of Polished Perfection Ltd) needs to take a step back from the business because her mother is in poor health. Polished Perfection Ltd is considering two options: creating an eyebrow bar in part of the premises and sub-letting this to a local eyebrow technician (Becky's Brows Ltd), to ensure some additional income to help pay for Meena's mother's care, or assigning the Nail Bar Lease to another nail technician, Gemma's Gels Ltd, so that Meena can care for her mother herself.

Polished Perfection Ltd requires advice from its solicitor about whether these would be permitted under the Nail Bar Lease, and Style&Go Ltd requires advice from its solicitor about whether it has to consent to the proposed alienation.

You may wish to refer to the Nail Bar Lease whilst working through this chapter.

DOI: 10.4324/9781032711508-28

21.2 Alienation

The types of alienation we focus on in this book are assignment and sub-letting.

Assignment of a lease occurs when the tenant sells the lease to another party. This is what would happen if Polished Perfection Ltd sold the Nail Bar Lease to another nail company, Gemma's Gels Ltd. The original tenant, Polished Perfection Ltd, would walk away from the lease, and Style&Go Ltd would become landlord to Gemma's Gels Ltd, the new tenant. This is shown in Figure 21.1. Gemma's Gels Ltd would take the lease for whatever term remains, along with the relevant benefits, and subject to the burdens of that lease.

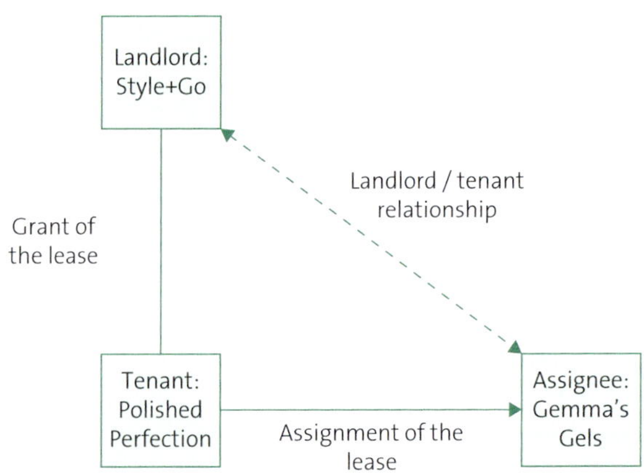

Figure 21.1 The assignment of the Nail Bar Lease.

The flexibility of being able to dispose of the lease before the expiry of the term is desirable to a tenant. However, a landlord may wish to control or restrict the tenant's ability to do so (as we saw at Section 13.4.4 of Chapter 13).

Sub-letting of a lease occurs when the tenant grants a sub-lease of the premises to another party. This would be the arrangement if Polished Perfection Ltd granted a sub-lease over part of the Nail Bar to an eyebrow technician. Polished Perfection

Ltd would remain the tenant under the Nail Bar Lease and remain bound by all the tenant covenants within that lease (e.g. repair, payment of rent, etc.), but part of the Nail Bar would be occupied by Becky's Brows Ltd, who would pay rent to Polished Perfection Ltd. This is shown in Figure 21.2.

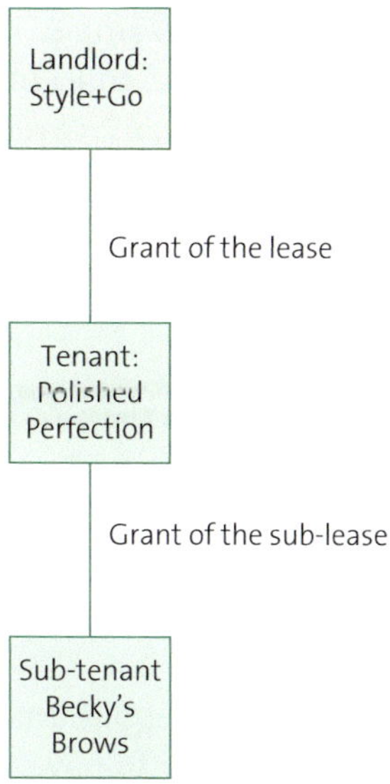

Figure 21.2 The sub-letting of the Nail Bar Lease.

As with assignment, a landlord may wish to control or restrict a tenant's ability to sub-let.

For a tenant wishing to assign or sub-let, the first step is to work out whether alienation is permitted under the lease and whether the landlord's consent is required. As we saw in Chapter 13, this information is contained within the lease.

The types of covenants have already been discussed,[1] and we already know that the Nail Bar Lease contains a ***qualified prohibition*** on alienation; this means that Polished Perfection Ltd cannot assign or sub-let the Nail Bar without Style&Go Ltd's consent, but Style&Go Ltd must act reasonably when deciding whether to provide this consent.[2]

1 See Section 13.4.4 of Chapter 13.
2 s19(1)(a) LTA 1927.

21.2.1 Complying with the alienation covenant

21.2.1.1 What constitutes 'unreasonable' when withholding consent?

In order to be 'reasonable' under a qualified prohibition or a fully qualified prohibition, the landlord's reason for refusing consent must be related to the premises or to the landlord/tenant relationship. For example, it would be reasonable for a landlord to refuse consent on the basis of concerns about an assignee or sub-tenant's ability to comply with the tenant covenants, or if an assignee or sub-tenant's proposed use of the premises would breach a tenant covenant or would disrupt the landlord's tenant mix. It would not, however, be reasonable for a landlord to refuse consent on the basis of something personal about the assignee or sub-tenant, such as their age.

21.2.1.1.1 ADDITIONAL PROVISIONS RELATING TO ASSIGNMENT ONLY

In leases created on or after 1 January 1996, the parties can agree in advance and list within the lease the possible reasons for which the landlord is permitted to withhold consent to an assignment, or any pre-conditions to that consent.[3] Any reasons listed in the lease will automatically be considered to be reasonable. These reasons can be fact-based or discretionary, but if they are at the landlord's discretion, then the lease must also expressly require that the discretion be exercised reasonably, or that the tenant is permitted to have the landlord's exercise of this discretion reviewed by an independent third party.

In clause 7.3(c) of the Nail Bar Lease, Style&Go Ltd is permitted to refuse to give consent to assignment if the covenant strength of the assignee is not satisfactory. The parties also agreed in clause 7.2 to a pre-condition to Style&Go Ltd's consent that Polished Perfection Ltd enter into an authorised guarantee agreement if they assign the lease, and that the assignee enters into a rent deposit deed.

For leases created before 1 January 1996, it was permitted to include express pre-conditions to the landlord's consent; these would be valid provided they were genuine pre-conditions as opposed to an attempt to list reasonable grounds for refusal.

21.2.1.2 Landlord must decide within a reasonable time

All fully qualified covenants (both those drafted expressly as fully qualified and those drafted as qualified which have been upgraded by s19(1)(a) LTA 1927) include an implied term that, when the tenant has applied in writing for consent, the landlord must provide a decision within a reasonable time.[4] Provided the landlord has all the relevant information to make a decision, 28 days will be considered

3 Under s19(1A) LTA 1927.

4 s1 Landlord and Tenant Act 1988 (**LTA 1988**).

to be a reasonable time.[5] The landlord must provide written notice of their decision and specify the conditions they are imposing or the reasons for which they are withholding consent.[6]

21.2.2 Process for assigning or sub-letting

21.2.2.1 Obtaining consent

As we have seen above, Polished Perfection Ltd will need to obtain the consent of Style&Go in order to assign or sub-let the Nail Bar Lease. Informal discussions with Style&Go have been positive, and Style&Go has indicated they would consent to the assignment to Gemma's Gels Ltd or sub-lease to Becky's Brows Ltd.

Consent to the alienation will take the form of a licence to assign or licence to underlet. The standard conditions[7] provide that the seller (being the current tenant, Polished Perfect) has to apply for this consent at its own expense and must use reasonable efforts to obtain it.

21.2.2.2 Phases 1 to 5

Once the tenant has established that the landlord is willing to consent to the disposal, the process of assigning the lease or sub-letting the premises constitutes a new transaction for the disposal of an interest in land. If the transaction progresses, the following steps will be taken by the prospective assignee or subtenant, just like they are undertaken by a buyer when acquiring a freehold title or by a lessee when being granted a lease:

- **Due diligence.** The prospective assignee or sub-tenant will undertake due diligence, including reviewing the title of the leasehold property, undertaking searches and enquiries, and considering the planning position (if relevant).
- **Agree the relevant documentation.** As well as entering into the relevant licence, the parties will need to enter into documentation in respect of the transfer of the interest in the relevant premises, such as a contract for sale or agreement for lease, and the relevant deed to transfer the property, such as a TR1 or a sub-lease. These will need to be drafted and agreed between the parties.
- **Prepare for completion.** The sale contract or agreement for lease will be exchanged, and the prospective assignee or sub-tenant will conduct pre-completion searches and ensure the finances are in place for completion.
- **Completion.** The deed will be dated, effecting the transfer of the interest to the assignee or sub-tenant.
- **Post-completion.** The assignee or sub-tenant will need to pay any relevant tax, register a mortgage, and ensure the transaction is registered with HMLR.

5 *Dong Bang Minerva (UK) v Davina* [1996] 2 EGLR 31.
6 s1 LTA 1988.
7 See Chapter 11.

21.3 Alterations

The tenant may wish to make alterations to the premises, just like if Meena wishes to convert part of the Nail Bar into an eyebrow bar. Landlords usually wish to retain some control over what can be done to the premises, as we saw in Chapter 13, in Section 13.4.6. For this reason, the lease will specify whether alterations are permitted, and in which circumstances, and whether the landlord's consent is required. For a tenant wishing to make alterations to the premises, the first step is to work out whether the work is permitted under the lease and whether the landlord's consent is required.

The types of covenant have already been discussed,[8] and we already know that the Nail Bar Lease contains an ***absolute prohibition*** on all types of alteration except non-structural internal alterations, which are subject to a fully qualified prohibition. It is likely that the work Polished Perfection Ltd would need to do to the Nail Bar to create an eyebrow bar would be internal and non-structural. Polished Perfection Ltd will therefore require Style&Go Ltd's consent, but Style&Go Ltd must act reasonably when deciding whether to provide this consent.

21.3.1 Complying with the alteration covenant

21.3.1.1 What is 'unreasonable' withholding of consent?

What constitutes 'unreasonable' withholding of consent will depend on the circumstances, but anything unrelated to the premises or to the landlord/tenant relationship would likely be considered unreasonable. If the landlord refused because of concerns about the impact of the works on the structure of the remainder of the building, this would likely be considered reasonable.

21.3.1.2 Conditions of consent

The landlord can impose the following conditions on giving consent (and these will usually be included as covenants in the licence):[9]

- the payment of compensation for loss in value to the reversion caused by the alterations;
- reinstatement of the premises if reasonable (at the end of the lease term); and
- payment of the landlord's expenses incurred in giving consent.

There is no requirement in the statute that the landlord provide consent within a reasonable timeframe, or that they give reasons for a refusal.

8 In Section 13.4.6 of Chapter 13.
9 Under s19(2) LTA 1927.

21.3.2 Process for making alterations

Polished Perfection Ltd will need to obtain the consent of Style&Go in order to turn the Nail Bar into an eyebrow bar. Informal discussions with Style&Go have been positive, and Style&Go has indicated they would consent to the alterations.

Consent for making alterations will take the form of a licence for alterations. We do not cover in detail the content of a licence for alterations, as it is beyond the scope of this book.

Making alterations to the premises does not involve the disposal of an interest in land, so Phases 1 to 5 of this book do not need to be followed. However, in addition to considering the position under the lease, the tenant may wish to consider:

- a review of the landlord's freehold title, as this will indicate whether there are any covenants which may mean the landlord cannot permit the alterations; and
- a review of the planning and building regulations position, which will indicate whether planning permission and building regulation consent are required for the proposed alterations.

21.4 Meena's decision about the Nail Bar

After much consideration, Meena decides to proceed with the assignment of the Nail Bar Lease to Gemma's Gels Ltd. In addition to obtaining Style&Go Ltd's formal consent to the assignment (Chapter 10), the assignment will need to progress through Phases 1 to 5 (as set out in Section 21.2.2.2). Therefore, please return to the start of this book to follow the assignment of the Nail Bar Lease from start to finish.

Chapter 21 revision points

- A tenant may wish to part with possession of the lease, by assigning the lease or granting a sub-lease. The lease will specify whether, and to what extent, the landlord's consent is required.
- A landlord must provide a decision on a request to alienate within a reasonable time, usually 28 days.
- If the lease requires the landlord to act reasonably when deciding whether to consent to alienation of the lease, the landlord's decision must be related to the landlord/tenant relationship or the premises.
- For leases created on or after 1 January 1996, the parties can agree in advance a list of possible reasons for which the landlord is permitted to withhold consent to an assignment, or pre-conditions to this consent.

- A tenant may wish to alter the lease premises. The lease will specify whether, and to what extent, the landlord's consent is required for this.
- Where the landlord is required to act reasonably in making a decision, a refusal of consent will not be reasonable unless it is related to the landlord/tenant relationship or to the premises. Concerns about the impact of works on the structure of the building will likely be considered reasonable.
- The landlord can impose conditions, such as the payment of compensation or expenses, and reinstatement of the premises at the end of the lease term.
- For alienation and alterations, the landlord's consent will take the form of a licence.

22 Enforcing leasehold covenants

22.1 Chapter overview

Covenants, being promises contained within a deed, are commonly contained within a lease, and we saw in Chapter 13 some examples of common covenants that a landlord and tenant may enter into.

We know from Chapter 2 that covenants are enforceable between the original landlord and tenant by virtue of the doctrine of privity of contract. This chapter examines the enforceability of leasehold covenants against other parties, for example, if a lease is assigned or sub-let by the tenant, and explores the remedies available to a landlord where the tenant breaches a covenant of the lease.

This chapter is relevant to commercial leases only.

This chapter in the context of the Transactions

Style&Go Ltd has provisionally agreed to permit Polished Perfection Ltd to assign the Nail Bar Lease to Gemma's Gels Ltd and requires some information and advice about whether the terms of the Nail Bar Lease will be enforceable against Gemma's Gels Ltd if the assignment goes ahead.

You may wish to refer to the Nail Bar Lease whilst working through this chapter.

DOI: 10.4324/9781032711508-29

22.2 Liability under leasehold covenants

22.2.1 Leases granted before 1 January 1996

For leases granted before 1 January 1996, in order to claim for breach of a leasehold covenant, there needed to be a direct relationship between the claiming party and the party they were pursuing. This could either be a contractual relationship – the original landlord and the original tenant would have a direct contractual relationship (known as ***privity of contract***) – or it could be a proprietary relationship – the original parties also have a direct landlord/tenant relationship (known as ***privity of estate***).

22.2.1.1 Privity of contract

The doctrine of privity of contract operates to ensure that, as the original covenantors (the landlord being the original covenantor of the landlord covenants, and the tenant being the original covenantor of the tenant covenants), the original landlord and tenant remain liable to each other for any breaches of those covenants during the term of the lease. This is shown in Figure 22.1.

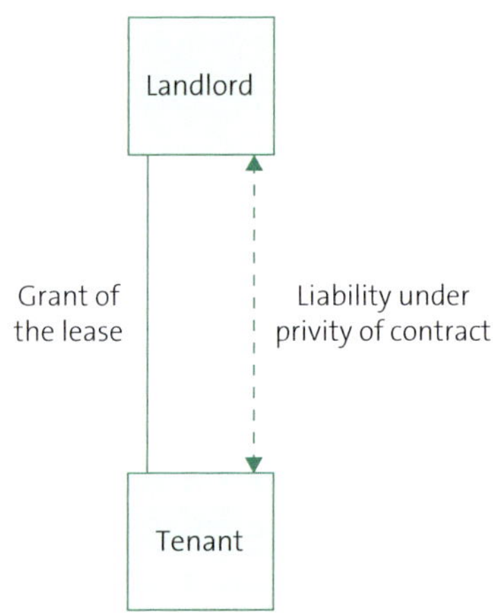

Figure 22.1 The reciprocal liability between the landlord and the tenant under privity of contract.

Statute has stepped in to ensure that if the landlord disposes of his interest by assigning the reversion, then he will not be liable to the tenant for any subsequent breaches of the landlord covenants by the assignee of the reversion. In essence, despite privity of contract, the landlord's liability for performance of the landlord covenants comes to an end when he disposes of his proprietary interest.[1] This is shown in Figure 22.2.

1 s142 LPA 1925.

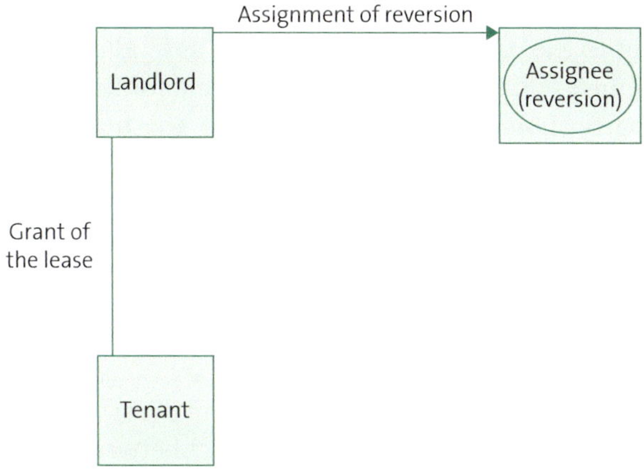

Figure 22.2 The landlord's lack of liability to the tenant under privity of contract when the assignee of the reversion breaches a landlord covenant.

However, there is no equivalent for the tenant; this means that the tenant will remain liable to the landlord for all breaches of tenant covenants, even if he has disposed of his interest (e.g. by assignment or sub-lease) and is not the breaching party, as shown in Figure 22.3.

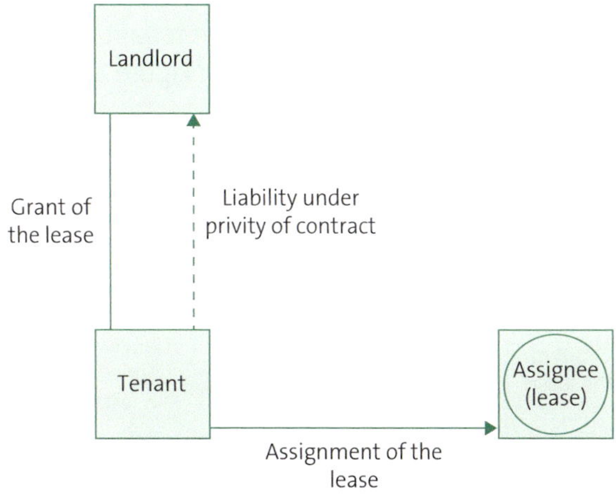

Figure 22.3 The tenant's ongoing liability to the landlord under privity of contract when the assignee of the lease breaches a tenant covenant.

22.2.1.2 Privity of estate

Under the doctrine of privity of estate, parties with a direct landlord/tenant relationship are liable to each other in respect of covenants which touch and concern the land. The requirement to touch and concern simply means that the covenant in question must not be one which is personal but instead is one which is relevant to the parties in their capacities as landlord and tenant and relevant to the premises under the lease. The rationale for this requirement is clear and simple: a party should not be able to pursue another for a breach of covenant simply because they have a landlord/tenant relationship if the covenant in question is totally unrelated to that relationship and the relevant premises under the lease.

The doctrine of privity of estate serves to fill some of the gaps left by the operation of privity of contract, as follows:

- If the original tenant has assigned the lease and the assignee has breached the tenant covenants, there is no privity of contract between the landlord and the assignee of the lease. The doctrine of privity of estate enables the landlord to pursue the assignee (instead of the original tenant under privity of contract) by virtue of the fact that the assignee has now become the tenant under the lease, and so there is a direct proprietary relationship between the landlord and the assignee (now the tenant). This is shown in Figure 22.4.
- If the landlord has assigned the reversion and the assignee of the reversion has breached the landlord covenants, there is no privity of contract between the tenant and the assignee of the reversion. The doctrine of privity of estate enables the tenant to pursue the assignee of the reversion, by virtue of the fact that the assignee of the reversion has become the landlord and there is now a direct proprietary relationship between the tenant and the assignee of the reversion (now the landlord). This is shown in Figure 22.5.

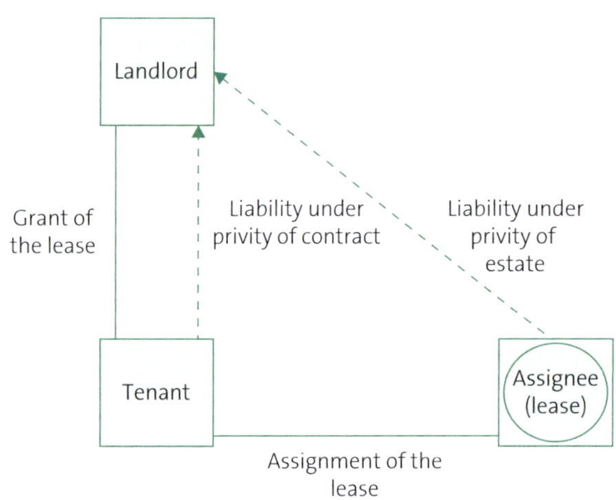

Figure 22.4 The liability of the assignee of the lease to the landlord under privity of estate.

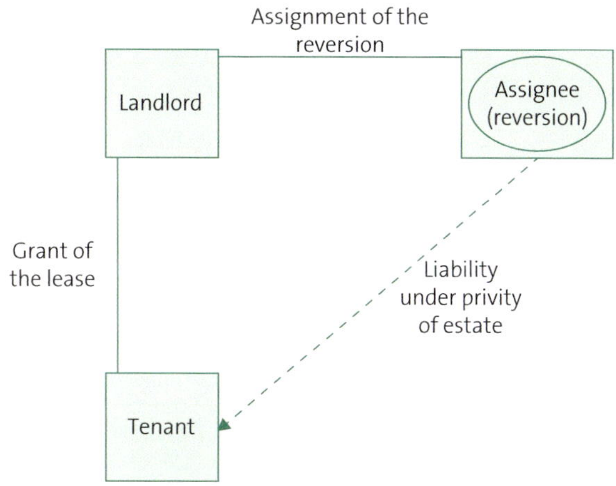

Figure 22.5 The liability of the assignee of the reversion to the tenant under privity of estate.

22.2.1.3 *Problems*

Notwithstanding the operation of both doctrines, problems remain; these primarily impact the original tenant:

22.2.1.3.1 ONGOING LIABILITY OF THE ORIGINAL TENANT

First, the original tenant remains liable for breaches of covenant by his successors in title. Although the doctrine of privity of estate enables the landlord to pursue the current tenant (assignee) for breaches, it does not require him to, and it does not release the original tenant from liability to the landlord under privity of contract, notwithstanding the fact that the original tenant no longer has a proprietary interest in the property and cannot control whether or not the current tenant complies with the tenant covenants. Figure 22.4 illustrates the ongoing liability of the tenant, even once they have disposed of the lease.

22.2.1.3.2 SUB-LEASES

Further, there is a gap in the system where the lease is sub-let rather than assigned; in this case, there is no privity of estate between the original landlord and the sub-tenant, nor is there privity of contract. This means that if the sub-tenant breaches the tenant covenants, the landlord must pursue the original tenant in respect of the breach, under either the doctrine of privity of contract or that of estate. This is shown in Figure 22.6.

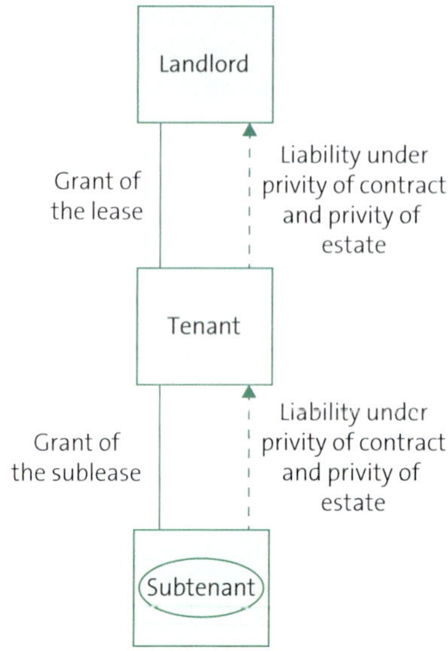

Figure 22.6 The liability position where the subtenant breaches a tenant covenant.

22.2.2 Liability under leases granted on or after 1 January 1996

The Landlord and Tenant (Covenants) Act 1995 (the **LTCA 1995**) operates to address some of these inadequacies; it applies to leases granted on or after 1 January 1996. Broadly speaking, landlord and tenant covenants can still be enforced under the doctrines of privity of contract and privity of estate, but the LTCA 1995 serves to soften some of the inequalities facing the original tenant, who found themselves perpetually liable under privity of contract for breaches they did not commit.

22.2.2.1 Original parties

Where the original landlord and tenant remain the landlord and tenant under the lease and neither party disposes of their interest, the position is simple: the parties are liable to each other for any breaches of covenant during the term of the lease, under the doctrines of privity of contract and privity of estate.

This is the same as was illustrated in Figure 22.1.

22.2.2.2 Tenant assigns the lease

We will now consider the position if the tenant assigns the lease. We will deal first with a breach of the landlord covenants, and then with a breach of the tenant covenants.

22.2.2.2.1 LANDLORD COVENANTS

If the tenant assigns the lease, the assignee (the new tenant) takes the benefit of the landlord covenants and can pursue the landlord for any breaches of these covenants which occur during the assignee's ownership of the leasehold estate and which relate to that leasehold estate; this is the same as the position pre-1996 and operates on the basis of privity of estate. This is shown in Figure 22.7.

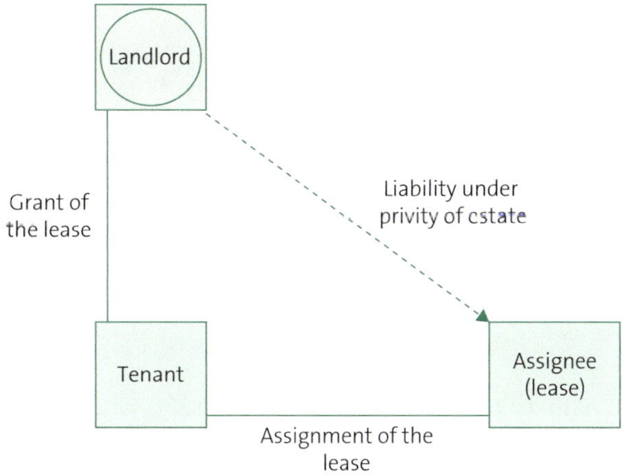

Figure 22.7 The landlord's liability to the assignee of the lease under privity of estate.

If the breach of landlord covenant occurs before the assignee takes over the lease, then the assignee cannot pursue the landlord in respect of these because there was no privity of estate at the time of the breach; instead, the tenant must pursue the landlord.

22.2.2.2.2 TENANT COVENANTS

22.2.2.2.2.1 ASSIGNEE BECOMES LIABLE FOR PERFORMANCE AFTER ASSIGNMENT

The assignee also becomes liable for performing the tenant covenants from the date of assignment and can be pursued by the landlord for any breaches of these covenants which occur during the assignee's ownership of the leasehold estate and which relate to that leasehold estate; this is the same as the position pre-1996 and operates on the basis of privity of estate.

22.2.2.2.2.2 ORIGINAL TENANT IS RELEASED FROM LIABILITY AFTER ASSIGNMENT

The key difference under the LCTA 1995 is that, upon assignment, the original tenant is released from future liability in respect of the tenant covenants.[2] This

2 s5 LTCA 1995.

means that if the assignee breaches one of the tenant covenants, the landlord cannot pursue the original tenant on the basis of privity of contract, as shown in Figure 22.8.

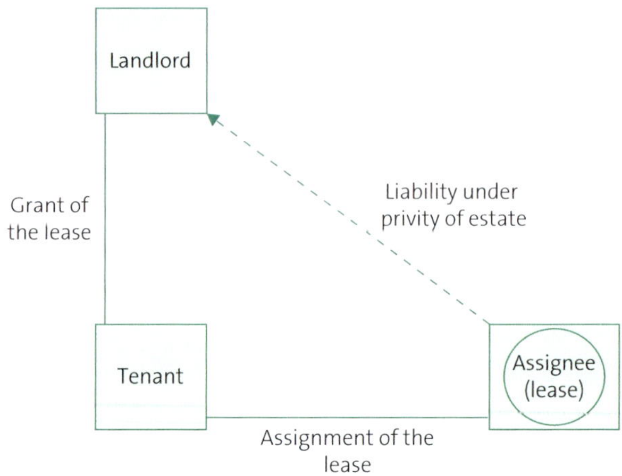

Figure 22.8 The liability position from 1 January 1996 where the assignee of the lease breaches a tenant covenant.

22.2.2.2.2.2.1 Exception – authorised guarantee agreement

There is an exception to this which operates if the tenant has entered into an authorised guarantee agreement. An AGA is a contract between the original tenant and the original landlord under which the tenant promises to the landlord that it will guarantee the performance of the tenant covenants by the assignee. In essence, the tenant is promising to be financially liable to the landlord if the assignee does not perform the tenant covenants under the lease. This liability position can be seen in Figure 22.9. You will recall that Polished Perfection Ltd entered into an AGA with Style&Go Ltd to guarantee Gemma's Gels Ltd's performance under the Nail Bar Lease.

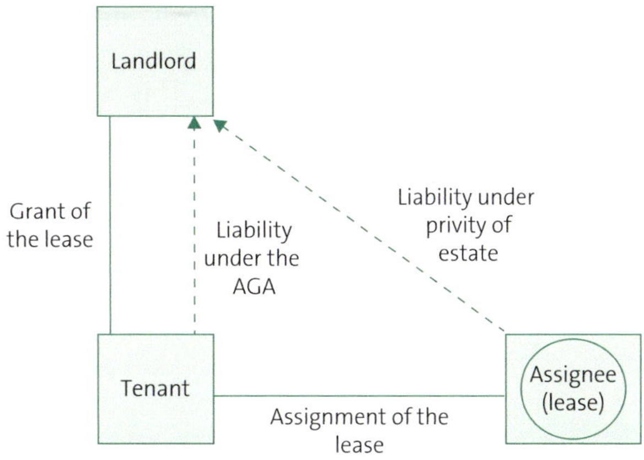

Figure 22.9 The liability position where the assignee of the lease breaches a tenant covenant and where the tenant has entered into an AGA with the landlord.

Under an AGA, the original tenant will only be liable to the landlord for breaches by its immediate successors, that is, the person it assigns the lease to. If that assignee later assigns to someone else, or sub-lets to someone else, and it is that party who breaches the tenant covenant, then the original tenant will not be liable to compensate the landlord in respect of those breaches.

In summary, a key difference with post-1996 leases is that the original tenant will only be responsible for breaches of the tenant covenants once he has disposed of his interest in the property if he has expressly agreed to be.

You might be wondering why a tenant would ever agree to enter into an AGA. Firstly, it may be a term of the lease that the tenant has to do this. For commercial leases granted on or after 1 January 1996, it can be a term of that lease that if the tenant disposes of its interest in the lease property, then he must enter into an AGA.[3]

Second, it may be that the landlord is permitted to refuse to consent to the assignment if the tenant does not enter into an AGA. This was the case for Polished Perfection Ltd – Style&Go Ltd required Polished Perfection Ltd to enter into an AGA as a condition of Style&Go Ltd's consent to the assignment of the Nail Bar Lease.

Notwithstanding the attempts made by the LTCA 1995 to improve the position, in practice, many original tenants find themselves still liable for breaches of tenant covenant by their successors, by virtue of an AGA being a requirement of the landlord granting the lease in the first place or consenting to the assignment of that lease.

3 This is not possible for residential leases.

The original tenant can take additional steps to protect itself. If assigning a lease and entering into an AGA in respect of the assignee, the original tenant can require an indemnity covenant from the assignee. This requires the assignee to indemnify the tenant if the tenant has to compensate the landlord for a breach of tenant covenant committed by the assignee. This is shown in Figure 22.10.

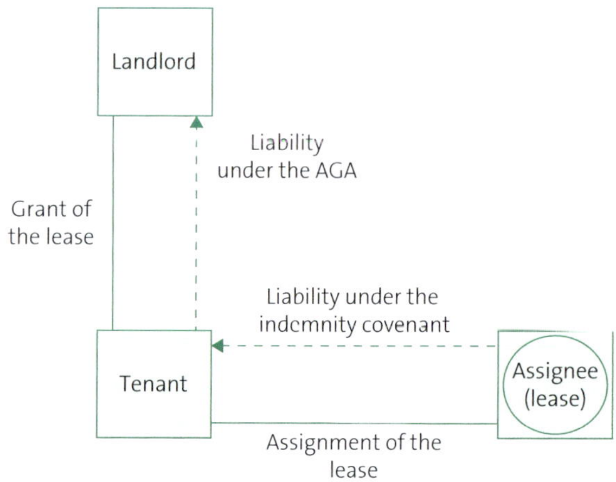

Figure 22.10 The use of an indemnity covenant from the assignee of the lease to mitigate the tenant's liability to the landlord under the AGA.

22.2.2.2.2.3 LANDLORD WISHING TO RECOVER FROM THE ORIGINAL TENANT MUST SERVE A NOTICE

Where a lease has been assigned, in order for a landlord to pursue the original tenant for breach of a covenant by a successor in title to the original tenant, the landlord must serve a notice on the original tenant.[4]

This requirement applies to all leases, regardless of when they were granted, and applies whether the landlord is pursuing the original tenant under:

- privity of contract (for leases granted before 1 January 1996); or
- an AGA (for leases granted on or after 1 January 1996).

The notice must be served within six months of the monies becoming due from the original tenant to the landlord and must specify the amount payable by the original tenant.

4 s17 LTCA 1995.

22.2.2.2.2.4 ORIGINAL TENANT IS ENTITLED TO AN OVERRIDING LEASE

The LTCA 1995 confers one further benefit for the original tenant, regardless of when the lease was granted: if the original tenant pays to the landlord any sums due under a notice, then the original tenant is entitled to an ***overriding lease*** if it requests it from the landlord.[5]

An overriding lease is a new lease which sits between the landlord's reversion and the original lease, which effectively turns the original lease into a sub-lease: the original landlord and tenant become landlord and tenant under the overriding lease, and the original tenant becomes the landlord of the assignee under the original lease. This is shown in Figure 22.11.

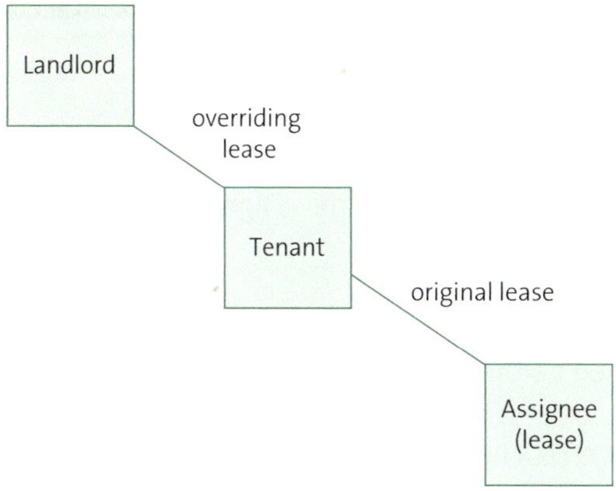

Figure 22.11 Illustrating an overriding lease.

The benefit of this for the original tenant is that he regains a proprietary interest in the property, and he regains the right to enforce the performance of the tenant covenants by the assignee. In brief, he has much better control over the performance of the tenant covenants.

22.2.2.3 Landlord assigns reversion

We will now consider the position if the landlord assigns the reversion. We will deal first with a breach of the tenant covenants, and then with a breach of the landlord covenants.

5 s19 LTCA 1995.

22.2.2.3.1 TENANT COVENANTS

If the landlord assigns the reversion, the assignee of the reversion automatically gets the benefit of the performance of the tenant covenants and can enforce these against the tenant by virtue of privity of estate, as shown in Figure 22.12.

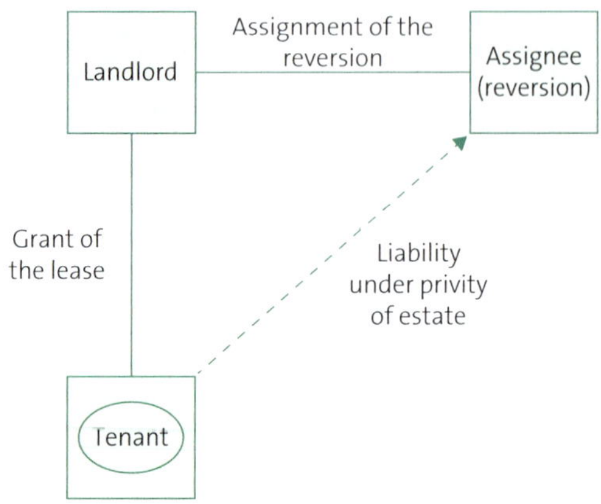

Figure 22.12 The tenant's liability to the assignee of the reversion under privity of estate.

Further, the assignee of the reversion can also enforce any breaches of tenant covenant which occurred before the reversion was assigned.[6]

22.2.2.3.2 LANDLORD COVENANTS

In respect of the landlord covenants, the pre-1996 position was that the original landlord was immediately released from these and the tenant would need to pursue the assignee of the reversion for breach of a landlord covenant which occurred once the reversion had been assigned.

The post-1996 position is slightly different. Rather than being automatically released, the original landlord must apply to the tenant for a release; the tenant has four weeks in which to respond, and unless he disputes the release within this four-week period, the original landlord will be released. If the tenant disputes the release, then the matter will be decided by the courts.

22.3 Landlord's remedies for tenant's breach of a leasehold covenant

The type of remedy available to the landlord for breach of a leasehold covenant varies depending on the nature of the breach.

6 s141 LPA 1925.

22.3.1 Generally available remedies

22.3.1.1 Forfeiture

Forfeiture is a remedy which enables the landlord to terminate the lease early and gain possession of the property (for example, by changing the locks). The right can be exercised by the landlord physically re-entering the premises and taking possession or by obtaining a court order for possession.

There are some requirements before forfeiture can be exercised:

1. the lease expressly permits forfeiture;
2. the landlord has served a notice on the tenant which complies with section 146 of the LPA 1925. The requirements are that the notice must:
   a. specify the breach;
   b. require the tenant to remedy the breach (if it is capable of remedy); and
   c. require the tenant to pay compensation; and
3. the tenant has failed to:
   a. remedy the breach within a reasonable amount of time (if it is capable of remedy); and
   b. pay compensation to the landlord's satisfaction.

Provided the requirements are met, the landlord is permitted to re-enter the premises or obtain a court order stating that the lease has been forfeited.

The tenant is entitled to apply for relief from the court to have the lease reinstated.

If relying on forfeiture for a breach of the covenant to pay rent, or a breach of the repairing covenant, slightly different rules apply. Please see Sections 22.3.2 and 22.3.3, respectively.

22.3.1.2 Common law damages

Damages for breach of contract are available for breach of a tenant covenant subject to the usual contractual rules on remoteness of damage.[7]

22.3.1.3 Equitable remedies

On occasion, equitable remedies may be awarded when damages are not adequate. These are as follows.

22.3.1.3.1 INJUNCTION

An ***injunction*** can be awarded to stop the tenant from taking an action which would breach a tenant covenant. For example, if the tenant is going to breach a

7 These rules are beyond the scope of this book, but see *Hadley v Baxendale* (1854) 9 Exch 341.

prohibition on assignment or alteration, the tenant could be injuncted from assigning a lease or making alterations to the premises.

22.3.1.3.2 SPECIFIC PERFORMANCE

Specific performance can be awarded to require a tenant to take a particular action in order to prevent or rectify a breach of a tenant covenant. For example, if the tenant has breached the requirement to repair the premises, the tenant could be ordered to put the premises into a specific state of repair.

22.3.2 Specific remedies for non-payment of rent

Where the breach in question is the non-payment of rent, the landlord has a number of options open to him.

22.3.2.1 Forfeiture

Forfeiture is available in respect of the non-payment of rent. When the covenant breached is the covenant to pay rent, the procedure is slightly different from that set out above:[8]

1. the lease must expressly permit forfeiture;
2. the rent must be unpaid. This does not simply mean that the rent has become due: rather, the forfeiture clauses will specify the duration of unpaid rent which gives rise to the landlord's right to forfeit the lease – this is commonly 21 days. The forfeiture clause will also specify whether the landlord needs to make a formal demand for rent before the forfeiture right is exercisable;
3. any requirement in the lease to serve a formal demand on the tenant must be complied with. All leases assume a formal demand is required, so this requirement must be expressly dispensed with in the lease if it isn't to be applicable;
4. there must not be any restrictions on forfeiture; and
5. the landlord must not have waived his right to forfeit.

Provided that the requirements are met, the landlord can either re-enter the premises or obtain a court order stating that the lease has been forfeited. The tenant is entitled to apply for relief from the court to have the lease reinstated.

22.3.2.2 Commercial rent arrears recovery

Commercial Rent Arrears Recovery (**CRAR**) is a remedy which enables landlords to enter the premises and seize goods owned by the tenant to the value of the sum owed in rent, in order to sell them. It is only applicable to leases of commercial premises. The procedure is governed by the Taking Control of Goods Regulations 2013 (the **2013 Regulations**).

8 At Section 22.3.1.1.

There are restrictions on its use:

1. It is only available in respect of rent arrears which have been outstanding for at least seven days.[9] It does not include service change and insurance rent payments.
2. The landlord must serve an ***enforcement notice*** on the tenant giving the tenant seven clear days' notice of entry to the premises.[10] This notice must contain the information set out in Regulation 7.[11] A tenant who receives an enforcement notice can apply for a court order to set the notice aside.
3. An enforcement agent enters the premises to seize the goods. Certain types of goods cannot be removed; these are listed in Regulation 4 and include low-value goods (under £1,350) which are required for the tenant's business.
4. The tenant must then be provided with seven clear days' notice (containing specific information set out in Regulation 30) that the goods are to be sold, and any subsequent sale must occur at a public auction.

22.3.2.3 Action in debt

Unpaid rent under a lease constitutes a debt and can be recovered as such. An ***action in debt*** is preferable for a landlord than bringing a claim for damages, as the landlord does not need to prove the various elements of a breach of contract claim: the very fact that the debt has accrued is sufficient to enable the landlord to recover the amount. The Limitation Act 1980 requires the action to be commenced within six years of the rent falling due.

22.3.2.4 Rent deposit

The landlord may be able to draw upon a ***rent deposit***. This is a sum paid by the tenant as security when the lease is granted. A rent deposit deed is usually entered into at the same time, and its terms will set out the circumstances in which the landlord can draw upon the deposit.

22.3.2.5 Pursue other parties: current guarantors and former tenants or their guarantors

If a current tenant has a guarantor, this guarantor can be pursued to indemnify the landlord in respect of the non-payment of rent by the current tenant.

9 Regulation 52(1) of the 2013 Regulations.
10 Regulation 6 of the 2013 Regulations.
11 The detail of Regulation 7 is beyond the scope of this book, but the notice must include information like the debtor's name and address and details about the debt.

The landlord may be able to pursue a former tenant for the sum on the basis of privity of contract.[12] As noted above,[13] the landlord must first serve a default notice within six months of the sum falling due.

The landlord may be able to pursue a former tenant's guarantor for the sum, provided that the guarantee agreement did not restrict the guarantor's liability to the duration of the former tenant's ownership. In practice, it is unlikely that a guarantor would agree to indemnify for future breaches not committed by the specific tenant it is acting as guarantor for.

22.3.3 Specific remedies for breaches of repair covenants

22.3.3.1 Forfeiture

Forfeiture is available as a remedy in respect of a breach of the tenant's repairing covenant, with the following requirements:

1. the lease expressly permits forfeiture;
2. the landlord has served a notice on the tenant which complies with both section 146 LPA 1925 and section 1 of the Leasehold Property (Repairs) Act 1938 (the **LP(R)A 1938**). The requirements (together) are that the notice must:
    a. specify the breach;
    b. require the tenant to remedy the breach (if it is capable of remedy);
    c. require the tenant to pay compensation; and
    d. if the lease was originally granted for seven years or more and has at least three years left to run, contain a statement informing the tenant of his right to serve a counter-notice within 28 days; and
3. the tenant has failed to:
    a. (if relevant under LP(R)A 1938) serve a counter-notice within 28 days;
    b. remedy the breach within a reasonable amount of time (if it is capable of remedy); and
    c. pay compensation to the landlord's satisfaction.

Provided the requirements are met, the landlord is permitted to re-enter the premises or obtain a court order stating that the lease has been forfeited.

If the tenant serves a counter-notice within 28 days, then the landlord is not permitted to re-enter the premises and instead must obtain a court order permitting him to do so.

12 See Section 22.2.1.1.
13 At Section 22.2.2.2.2.3.

The tenant is entitled to apply for relief from the court to have the lease reinstated.

22.3.3.2 Damages

The landlord is entitled to claim damages for breach of a tenant's repairing covenant.

If the lease is subject to LP(R)A 1938 (e.g. it is a lease of seven or more years with three years left to run), then the landlord cannot claim damages without first following the notice procedure set out in Section 22.3.1.1, serving a section 146 notice on the tenant which includes wording reminding the tenant of their right to serve a counter-notice.

Damages will be capped at the reduction in value of the landlord's reversion which has been caused by the breach.[14]

22.3.3.3 Self-help

Provided the lease contains a clause allowing it, then the landlord can enter the premises and carry out the repairs himself. Any costs incurred in doing so can be recovered from the tenant as a debt. This is known as a ***Jervis v Harris clause***.[15]

Chapter 22 revision points

- If the original parties to the lease do not dispose of their interests, they will remain liable to each other for any breaches of covenant during the term of the lease.
- If the landlord assigns the reversion, for leases granted before 1 January 1996, the original landlord will not be liable for any subsequent breaches of the landlord covenant; the assignee of the reversion will be. For leases granted on or after 1 January 1996, the original landlord will not automatically be released from liability for a breach of the landlord covenants; instead, the landlord must apply to the tenant for a release.
- If the original tenant assigns the lease, for leases granted before 1 January 1996, the original tenant remains liable for all breaches of tenant covenant, but the landlord can alternatively pursue the assignee. For leases granted on or after 1 January 1996, the original tenant will not be liable for breaches of tenant covenant by the assignee unless the tenant has provided an AGA; the landlord instead must pursue the assignee.

14 s18 LTA 1927.
15 The name being taken from the case *Jervis v Harris* [1996] Ch 195.

- If the tenant breaches a covenant of the lease, the landlord may be entitled to the following remedies:
  - Forfeiture
  - Damages
  - Specific performance
  - Injunction
  - Commercial Rent Arrears Recovery
  - A debt action
  - Drawing upon a rent deposit
  - Pursuing guarantors or former tenants
  - Self-help

23 Ending a lease

23.1 Chapter overview

A key consideration for a landlord and tenant is how a lease may come to an end. Either party may wish to end the lease before its end date, or one party may wish the lease to continue for as long as possible.

This chapter explores the key methods by which a lease may come to an end, whether after or before its specified end date. It also examines the statutory protection provided to some business tenants, enabling them to remain in the premises after the lease end date or request a new lease over the same premises.

This chapter is relevant to commercial leases only.

This chapter in the context of our Transactions

Style&Go Ltd has requested some general information about how and when a tenancy can come to an end, so that they can plan for the future of the Salon and the Nail Bar.

You may wish to refer to the Nail Bar Lease whilst working through this chapter.

DOI: 10.4324/9781032711508-30

23.2 Methods of ending a tenancy

23.2.1 Effluxion of time

This method applies to fixed-term leases and essentially means that the fixed term has come to an end. When the contractual term expires, the lease automatically ends without notice being required from either party. This is subject to the discussions below on protected tenancies in Section 23.3.

The Nail Bar Lease is a fixed-term lease expiring on 20 September 2036.

23.2.2 Surrender

The ***surrender*** of a lease occurs when a tenant surrenders (or gives back) their lease to their landlord, who accepts it. The lease merges with the landlord's – this means that the landlord owns both the freehold and the leasehold, and so the leasehold estate is extinguished. Surrender of a lease is a disposition of an estate in land and must therefore usually be effected by deed.[1] This is shown in Figure 23.1.

Figure 23.1 The surrender of a lease.

23.2.3 Merger

A ***merger*** occurs when the leasehold interest and the reversion (either the freehold reversion or a headlease) are held by the same party. For example, the tenant

1 s52 LPA 1925.

acquires the immediate reversion (the landlord's estate), or a third party acquires both the lease and the reversion. When those interests are held by the same party, the lease automatically merges and is extinguished, as shown in Figure 23.2.

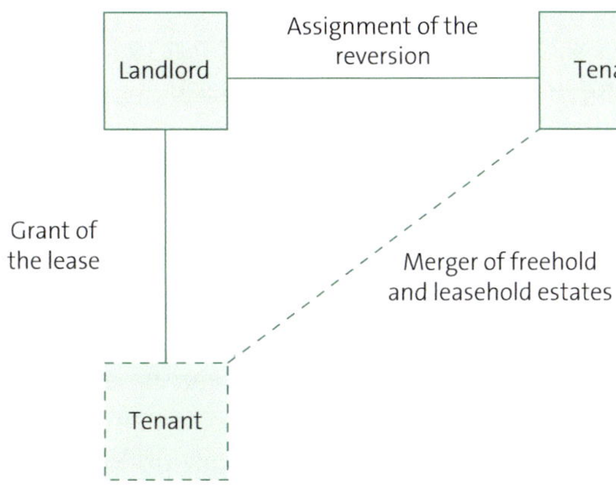

Figure 23.2 The merger of a lease upon assignment of the reversion to the tenant.

23.2.4 Notice to quit

Under a periodic tenancy, either party can give a notice to determine the tenancy. This is known as a ***notice to quit***. It is only applicable to periodic tenancies.

The required notice period depends upon the term of the tenancy. If the tenancy does not specify a notice period, then the common law will imply a notice period as follows:

- Where the tenancy is a yearly tenancy, the required notice is at least half a year (meaning 182 days or two quarters), and the notice should expire on the last day of the year of the tenancy. By way of illustration, for a tenancy running from 1 January until 31 December, the notice to quit must be served on or before 2 July, and the notice expiry date will be 31 December.
- For tenancies of other periods, one full period must be given in notice, and the notice should expire at the end of a completed period of the tenancy. For example, the notice required under a monthly tenancy commencing on the first of the month is at least one full month – the expiry date will be the last date in the month, and the notice must be served before the first of the month.

Please note the notice doesn't have to be 'clear' (meaning, the day of service and the notice expiry date do not have to be excluded from the calculation of the notice period).

23.2.5 Break clause

There may be a ***break clause*** included within the lease, which gives the parties the opportunity to end the lease before the expiry date. The lease will set out thus:

- who can operate this break clause;
- when it can be exercised (it is common for it not to kick in immediately, but rather after a proportion of the term has passed);
- the required notice; and
- any preconditions to its operation (for example it is common for it to be a pre-condition of exercising a break clause that the rent is up to date).

23.3 Protected tenancies

For business tenants, regularly moving premises can be expensive and cumbersome, and it can be beneficial for their business to remain in the same premises. By way of illustration, a coffee shop may have built up local custom during the term of a lease and may not wish to move premises and lose these customers.

The Landlord and Tenant Act 1954 (the **LTA 1954**) confers protection to some business tenants, overriding the normal mechanisms for ending a tenancy and enabling these tenants to remain in their premises beyond the expiry date of their lease. This is called ***security of tenure***.

If a tenant is protected under the LTA 1954, there are two key effects which both operate once the tenant's lease has come to an end (e.g. the contractual end date has passed):

1. the tenant can continue to occupy the premises on the same lease terms, even though their lease has expired. This is called ***holding over***; and
2. the tenant can request a new lease over the premises on different terms.

23.3.1 Effect of the LTA 1954: tenant can hold over

If the tenant decides to hold over, the tenancy will continue on the same terms until it is terminated in accordance with the LTA 1954 despite the fact that the fixed term of the lease has come to an end[2] (the tenant, of course, doesn't *have* to hold over and can vacate the premises at the end of the lease term if they don't wish to remain there).

A landlord who wishes to end the tenancy must serve a notice on the tenant. See Section 23.3.4.1 for the process. Upon receipt of such a notice, the tenant has the right to request a new lease.

2 s24 LTA 1954.

23.3.2 Effect of the LTA 1954: tenant can request a new lease

The LTA 1954 provisions also entitle the tenant to request a new lease on different terms. The tenant can do this by serving a notice on the landlord (see Section 23.3.4.2) or by making an application to the court.

23.3.2.1 Why would a tenant request a new lease?

A new lease may be requested by the tenant upon expiry of the contractual term of their lease because they want to remain in the premises but not on the same terms – this may be the case if the current lease terms are no longer favourable (e.g. perhaps the market rent has fallen and the tenant thinks it is paying too much under the original lease).

Alternatively, a new lease may be requested by a tenant who is already holding over, in response to the landlord taking steps to terminate the current lease.

23.3.2.2 Can the landlord refuse to grant a new lease?

If the tenant requests a new lease, the landlord is only entitled to refuse to grant one in certain circumstances – these are set out in section 30 of the LTA 1954 and discussed in Section 23.3.5.1.

23.3.2.3 Who decides?

It is up to the court to decide whether one of the relevant grounds has been satisfied by the landlord. If the court decides that the landlord has not satisfied one of the relevant grounds and must grant a new tenancy, the court will also rule upon the terms of that tenancy (if there is no agreement between the parties).

23.3.3 When does the LTA 1954 apply?

The protective provisions of the LTA 1954 apply to:

> "any tenancy where the property comprised in the tenancy is or includes premises which are occupied by the tenant and are so occupied for the purposes of a business carried on by him or for those and other purposes".[3]

We will examine the components of this in turn.

23.3.3.1 There must be a tenancy

This can include a lease, an agreement for lease, and an underlease but will not extend to licences. You will recall from your Land Law studies that, as per *Street v Mountford*,[4] leases confer exclusive possession and last for a certain period of time.[5]

3 s23(1) LTA 1954.
4 [1985] UKHL 4.
5 Please see Essential Land Law for SQE1, available from Routledge, for a reminder of these principles.

23.3.3.1.1 EXCLUDED TENANCIES

Some tenancies are excluded from the protective provisions of the LTA 1954.[6] These are as follows:

23.3.3.1.1.1 TENANCIES AT WILL

Tenancies at will can be terminated by the landlord or tenant at any time and have been held by the courts[7] in to be outside of the LTA 1954 protection.

23.3.3.1.1.2 FIXED-TERM TENANCIES NOT EXCEEDING SIX MONTHS

Fixed-term tenancies which do not exceed six months are excluded from the protective provisions, unless:

- they can be renewed or extended beyond six months; or
- the tenant has been in occupation for 12 or more months.

23.3.3.1.1.3 CONTRACTED-OUT TENANCIES

Parties can agree to ***contract out*** of the security of tenure provisions.[8] This is only applicable to fixed-term lettings, not periodic tenancies. You will recall from Chapter 13 that Style&Go Ltd and Polished Perfection Ltd contracted out of the security of tenure provisions under the Nail Bar Lease.

The contracting-out rules were changed in June 2004, and so we will examine the two sets of rules separately.

23.3.3.1.1.3.1 Leases prior to 1 June 2004

Before 1 June 2004, a court had to approve all contracting-out before a lease was granted. When dealing with a 'contracted-out' lease which was granted before 1 June 2004, you must check that a court order was obtained approving the contracting out.

23.3.3.1.1.3.2 Leases granted on or after 1 June 2004

For leases granted on or after 1 June 2004, a court order is no longer required in order to contract out of the security of tenure provisions. Instead, a notice procedure must be followed – when dealing with a 'contracted-out' lease which was granted on or after 1 June 2004, you must check that the notice procedure has been complied with.

The notice procedure is as follows:

1. The landlord gives the tenant a notice in a prescribed form warning the tenant that the lease does not benefit from security of tenure.

6 s43 LTA 1954.
7 *Wheeler v Mercer* [1957] AC 416.
8 s38A LTA 1954.

2. The tenant makes a declaration in a prescribed form that they have received the landlord's notice and they agree to contract out of the security provisions in the lease. The tenant must give this notice more than 14 days before the grant of the lease (or before they are contractually bound to take the lease, if entering into an agreement for lease); if the tenant does not comply with this notice period, they must make the declaration before an independent solicitor in the form of a ***statutory declaration***.

The lease itself must contain reference to the service of the notice and the tenant's declaration.

As the Nail Bar Lease was contracted out of the security of tenure provisions, during their due diligence process, Gemma's Gels Ltd required Polished Perfection Ltd's solicitor to confirm that notice procedure had been complied with.

23.3.3.1.1.4 RESIDENTIAL TENANCIES

Residential tenancies (including 'home business' operated from the house) are excluded from the LTA 1954 provisions.

23.3.3.1.1.5 BUSINESS LEASES (SPECIFIC)

Some specific business leases are excluded from the LTA 1954 provisions, including:

- agricultural tenancies;
- mining tenancies;
- service tenancies;
- farm business leases;
- leases of railways property;
- leases of military establishments; and
- leases of dockyards.

23.3.3.2 The premises must be occupied by the tenant

The tenant must occupy the premises. This can mean that the tenant personally occupies the premises or occupies them through an agent, manager, or company owned by the tenant. If the tenant has sub-let the whole of the premises, then the tenant will not have security of tenure as they are not in occupation (but the sub-tenant will); however, if only part of the premises is sub-let, then the tenant and the sub-tenant will each have security of tenure over the respective parts of the premises that each of them occupies.

23.3.3.3 The premises must be occupied for business purposes

The tenant must occupy for the purposes of a business carried on by them.

'Business' purposes include trade, profession or employment, or any activity carried on by a 'body of persons', whether commercial or otherwise.

The tenant's business use does not need to be the sole purpose for occupying the premises, as long as it is the main purpose and is not incidental to a residential or other purpose – working from home occasionally will not constitute a business use.

The business use must be permitted by the tenancy.

23.3.4 Procedures under the LTA 1954

There are two key procedures under the LTA 1954:

1. the landlord wishes to terminate the lease; or
2. the tenant requests a new lease.

We introduced in Section 23.3.2 the circumstances in which these might arise.

23.3.4.1 Landlord wants to terminate the current lease: section 25

This is the situation where the landlord wants to bring the current lease to an end and stop the tenant from holding over. There are two possible reasons for this:

- the landlord wants to renegotiate the terms of the lease and grant a new lease on more favourable terms (e.g. perhaps under the current lease the tenant is paying less than market rate for rent); or
- the landlord wants the tenant to vacate the premises.

The landlord can commence this process at any point after the expiration of the contractual end date under the original lease. The process is noted in what follows, and illustrated in Figure 23.3.

23.3.4.1.1 THE LANDLORD MUST SERVE A NOTICE

The landlord must first serve a notice on the tenant, which complies with section 25 of the LTA 1954. This notice must specify a ***date of termination*** of the lease: this must be more than six months and less than 12 months from the date of the notice. To illustrate, a notice served on 1 January must contain a termination date between 1 July and 31 December.

The landlord must specify in the notice whether they are willing to grant the tenant a new lease, and if not, they must give the reason.[9] A notice in which the landlord is willing to grant a new lease is known as a ***'friendly' section 25 notice***,

9 See Section 23.3.5.1 for a discussion of the possible valid reasons.

and a notice in which the landlord is not willing to grant a new lease is known as a ***'hostile' section 25 notice***.

23.3.4.1.2 OPTIONS FOR THE TENANT

Upon receipt of a section 25 notice from the landlord, the tenant has the right to apply for a new lease or vacate the premises.

23.3.4.1.2.1 IF THE TENANT DOESN'T WANT A NEW LEASE

If the tenant does not want a new lease, then they can simply vacate the premises by the termination date specified in the section 25 notice.

23.3.4.1.2.2 IF THE TENANT WANTS A NEW LEASE

If the tenant wants a new lease, then the process varies depending on whether the landlord's section 25 notice was 'friendly' or 'hostile'.

23.3.4.1.2.2.1 THE LANDLORD IS HAPPY TO GRANT A NEW LEASE TO THE TENANT

The landlord may be terminating the current lease so that a new tenancy can be granted on different terms, for example, to increase the rent. If this is the case, the landlord will specify it in the section 25 notice.

Parties negotiate the new lease. Where both parties want to enter into a new lease, they enter negotiations for the new lease. They can agree amongst themselves and complete the lease by the relevant date.

The tenant applies to the court for a new lease. Alternatively, the tenant can apply to the court for a new lease and have the court determine the matter. This must be done before the expiry of the notice, and so if negotiations are slow and there's a possibility that the lease will not be agreed and completed by the termination date in the section 25 notice, the tenant should make this application to ensure they do not lose their right to do so.

The landlord applies to the court for a new lease. The landlord can also apply to the court for a new lease.

If either party applies to court, the court will determine the issues (e.g. advise on the terms of the new lease).

23.3.4.1.2.2.2 THE LANDLORD DOESN'T WANT TO GRANT A NEW LEASE TO THE TENANT

As we saw above, if the landlord does not want to grant a new lease to the tenant, then this will have been specified in the section 25 notice that the landlord intended to oppose an application for a new tenancy, and the statutory ground of opposition will have been stated.

The tenant applies to court for a new lease. Even if the landlord opposes the grant of a new lease, the tenant still has the right to apply to court for one, provided the application is made before the expiry date in the section 25 notice.

The landlord applies to court to terminate lease. The landlord can apply to court for an order to terminate the lease, but he must do this before the tenant applies for a new lease.

If either party applies to court, the court will determine the issues.

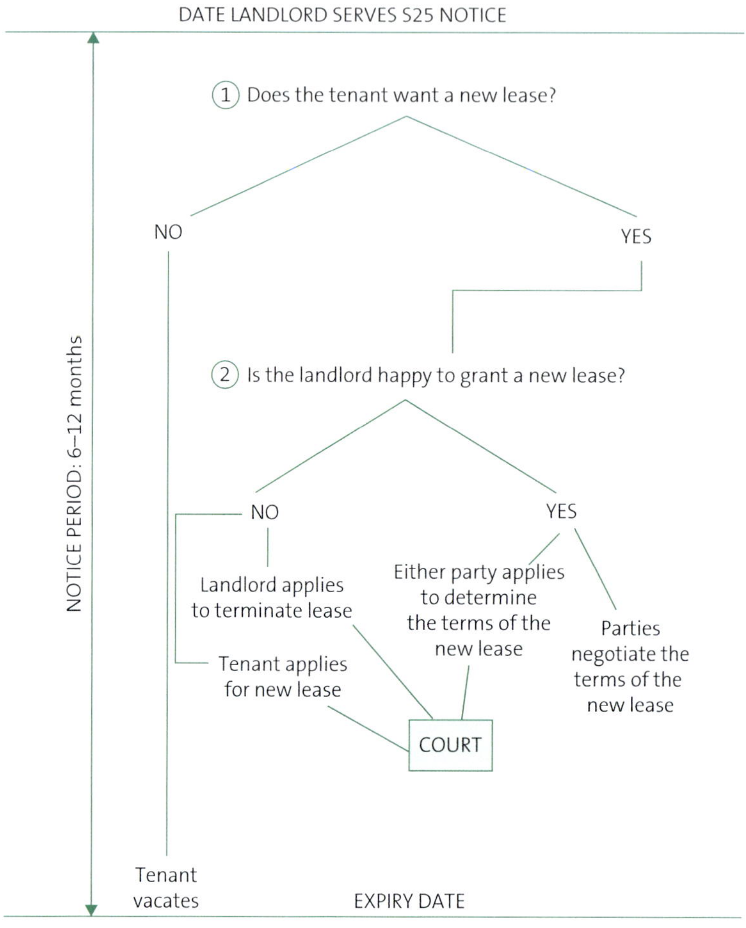

Figure 23.3 The section 25 process.

23.3.4.2 Tenant wants to apply for a new lease: section 26

This is the situation where the tenant wants to bring the current lease to an end and request a new one on different (presumably, more favourable) terms. This option is only available for tenants on a fixed term of more than one year and is not available for periodic tenants. This process is noted in what follows, and illustrated in Figure 23.4.

The tenant must serve a notice on the landlord in compliance with section 26 of the LTA 1954. The notice must propose a start date for the new lease which is more than six months and less than 12 months from the date of service of the notice.

Upon receipt of a section 26 notice, there are two possible responses from the landlord:

- the landlord is happy to grant a new lease; or
- the landlord does not want to grant a new lease. Instead, the landlord wants the tenant to vacate the premises.

23.3.4.2.1 THE LANDLORD IS HAPPY TO GRANT A NEW LEASE

Parties can negotiate terms. Upon receipt of a section 26 notice from the tenant, if a landlord is happy to grant a new lease, then the parties can negotiate and agree the terms of that lease between them.

Alternatively, either party can apply to the court for a new tenancy, provided the application is made before the start date of the new tenancy as specified in the section 26 notice.

23.3.4.2.2 THE LANDLORD DOESN'T WANT TO GRANT A NEW LEASE

If the landlord does not wish to grant a new lease to the tenant, they can serve a counter-notice on the tenant within two months of service of the section 26 request. This counter-notice must state the statutory ground upon which they are opposing the grant of a new lease.

Clearly, the parties are not going to negotiate a new lease between them if the landlord doesn't want to grant one. The tenant can, at this point, give up and vacate the premises, or if the tenant still wants a new lease, they must apply to the court for it. This application must be made before the start date of the new tenancy as noted in the section 26 notice, and if the tenant does not make this application in time, then they lose their right to apply to the court.

The landlord is also entitled to apply to the court for an order to terminate the lease, but only if the tenant hasn't yet applied for a new lease with the court.

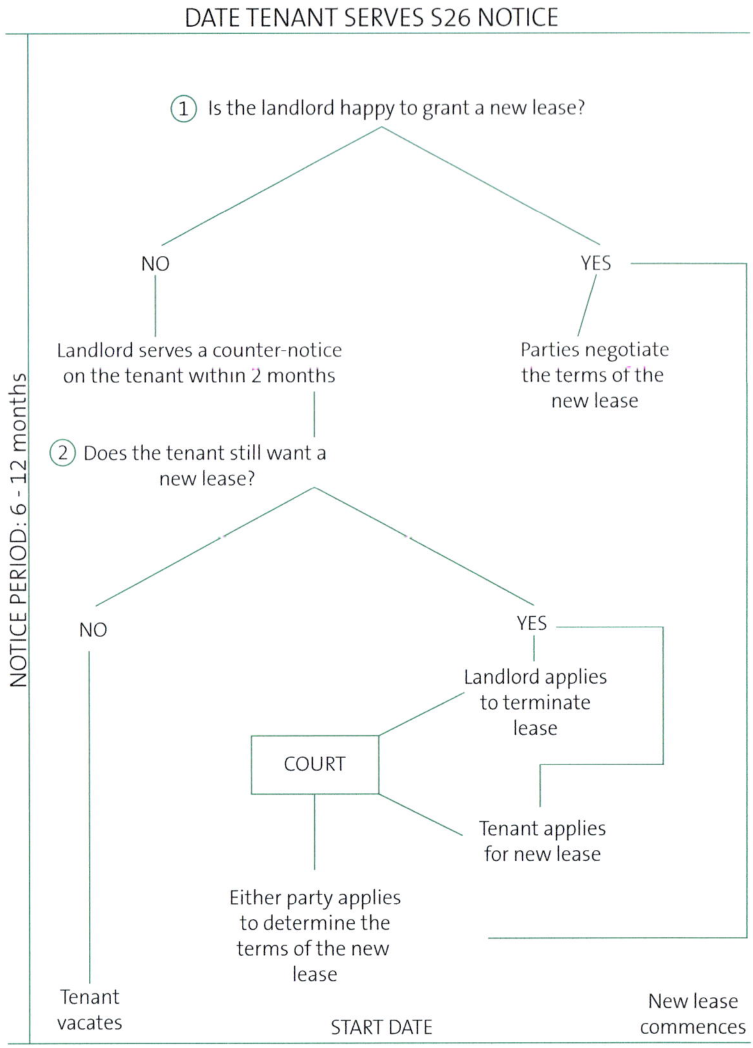

Figure 23.4 The section 26 process.

23.3.5 The court

Upon receipt of an application from either party, the court will determine whether a new lease should be granted and, if so, the terms of that lease.

23.3.5.1 Determining whether a new lease should be granted: the section 30 grounds

As noted above, there are only certain grounds upon which the landlord is permitted to oppose the grant of a new lease. These are contained within section 30 of the LTA 1954.

Some of these grounds are ***mandatory***; this means that if the ground is established by the landlord, the court will find in favour of the landlord. Some grounds are ***discretionary***; the landlord must establish the ground, but this is not determinative – the landlord must also show that the tenant shouldn't be granted a new lease. Ultimately, the court has discretion to find in favour of either party.

23.3.5.1.1 MANDATORY GROUNDS

If the landlord relies upon and establishes any of these grounds, the court must find in favour of the landlord.

23.3.5.1.1.1 GROUND (D): THE LANDLORD HAS OFFERED AND CAN PROVIDE ALTERNATIVE SUITABLE ACCOMMODATION TO THE TENANT.

If the landlord has offered alternative accommodation to the tenant, then the court must find in favour of the landlord and refuse to grant the new lease to the tenant.

There are some provisos:

- the terms of this accommodation must be reasonable when compared to the terms of the current tenancy; and
- the accommodation must be suitable for the tenant having regard to the tenant's business, including in respect of location and facilities.

23.3.5.1.1.2 GROUND (F): THE LANDLORD TENDS TO DEMOLISH OR RECONSTRUCT THE PREMISES AND CANNOT REASONABLY DO SO WITHOUT OBTAINING POSSESSION.

If the landlord needs the premises vacant in order to undertake demolition or reconstruction works, then the court must find in favour of the landlord and refuse to grant the new lease to the tenant.

The landlord must be able to demonstrate a firm and settled intention to undertake works:[10]

- That the intended works involve demolition, reconstruction, or substantial construction, and such works are to take place to the whole of the premises or to a substantial part of the premises.
- That the works cannot be undertaken without obtaining possession from the tenant. If they could do the work whilst the tenant is in situ and the tenant is willing to give the landlord the required access to facilitate this and the works would not interfere with the tenant's business, then this limb will not be satisfied.

10 What the court is looking for here is a genuine intention, even if the landlord subsequently changes its mind. See *Fisher v Taylor's Furnishings* [1956] 2 QB 78.

23.3.5.1.1.3 GROUND (G): THE LANDLORD INTENDS TO OCCUPY THE PREMISES FOR THEIR OWN BUSINESS OR AS A RESIDENCE.

If the landlord requires the premises to be vacated so that the landlord itself can either live in the premises or occupy it for business purposes, then the court must find in favour of the landlord and refuse to grant the new lease to the tenant.

There are some provisos:

- the landlord must have a firm and settled intention to occupy the premises; and
- the landlord must not have purchased their interest in the property (e.g. the reversion) in the last five years, unless the landlord purchased their interest with vacant possession and subsequently let it to the tenant.

23.3.5.1.2 DISCRETIONARY GROUNDS

If the landlord establishes one of these grounds, then the court has the discretion to find in favour of the landlord and refuse to grant a new lease, but only if the court determines that the tenant ought not to be granted a new lease.

23.3.5.1.2.1 GROUND (A): THE TENANT HAS BREACHED ITS REPAIR AND MAINTENANCE OBLIGATIONS UNDER THE CURRENT LEASE.

If the landlord establishes that the tenant has breached its repair and maintenance obligations under the current lease, the court will assess the seriousness of the breach and use its discretion to decide whether or not a new lease should be granted to the tenant.

23.3.5.1.2.2 GROUND (B): THE TENANT HAS DELAYED PAYING RENT UNDER THE CURRENT LEASE.

If the landlord establishes that the tenant has not paid its rent on time under the current lease, the court will assess the seriousness of the breach and use its discretion to decide whether or not a new lease should be granted to the tenant.

23.3.5.1.2.3 GROUND (C): THE TENANT HAS BREACHED OTHER OBLIGATIONS UNDER THE CURRENT LEASE.

If the landlord establishes that the tenant has breached other obligations under the current lease, the court will assess the seriousness of the breach and use its discretion to decide whether or not a new lease should be granted to the tenant.

23.3.5.1.2.4 GROUND (E): THE CURRENT TENANCY IS A SUB-LET OF PART OF THE PREMISES, AND A HIGHER RENT CAN BE ACHIEVED BY RENTING THE PREMISES AS A WHOLE.

If the landlord establishes that the current tenancy was created by sub-letting part of a larger property and that higher rents could be obtained by letting the property out as a whole than by way of a number of sub-lets of part, then the court will assess the difference in financial potential between disposing of the property as a whole and multiple disposals of part and use its discretion to decide whether or not a new lease should be granted to the tenant.

23.3.5.1.3 THE COMPENSATION GROUNDS

If the court refuses to grant a new tenancy on the basis of grounds (e), (f), or (g), the tenant may be entitled to compensation equivalent to the rateable value[11] of the premises, or twice the rateable value if the tenant has occupied the premises for more than 14 years.

23.3.5.2 *Terms of the new lease*

In addition to determining whether a new lease should be granted, the court will also determine the terms of that lease.

23.3.5.2.1 THE PREMISES

The premises in the new tenancy will be those premises which the tenant is currently occupying. However, if the tenant has sub-let part of the original premises, then the landlord can insist that a new tenancy include those parts currently sub-let, which the tenant is not currently occupying.[12]

23.3.5.2.2 DURATION

The duration of the new tenancy cannot exceed 15 years (commencing upon expiry of the current tenancy) and will be whatever the court determines is reasonable in the circumstances, having regard to any agreement between the parties.[13]

23.3.5.2.3 RENT

The court will direct that the rent payable under the new tenancy should reflect the amount agreed between the parties.[14] If there is no agreement, it will reflect the market rate for a tenancy on these terms, disregarding any effect on rent which is attributable to:

- the fact that the tenant has been in occupation;
- goodwill attributable to the tenant's business;
- voluntary improvements to the premises made by the tenant; and
- (for licensed premises) the fact that the tenant holds a license.

The court can impose a rent review clause even if there isn't one in the current tenancy agreement.

11 The rateable value is a particular valuation of the property. The rateable value is most commonly used for calculating business rates (a tax which businesses must pay).

12 s32 LTA 1954.

13 s33 LTA 1954.

14 s34 LTA 1954.

23.3.5.2.4 OTHER TERMS

Unless agreed between the parties, the other terms of the new tenancy will largely reflect the current tenancy agreement.

23.3.6 The new lease

Once the terms have been determined by the court, there is a period of four weeks during which the parties can appeal if they are unhappy with the terms. The tenant additionally has a right to have the court order revoked.

After this appeal period, there is a break of three months, after which the new lease will commence.

During this period from the expiry of the relevant notice, through the court proceedings and the subsequent appeal and 3-month break, the original tenancy continues on the same terms. If either party is unhappy with this, they can apply for an interim rent to apply from the expiry of the relevant notice through to the start date of the new lease.

Where both parties are in favour of a new tenancy, this interim rent will be set at the amount of the new rent, unless the new rent is very different from the current rent or the terms of the new tenancy are substantially different from the terms of the current tenancy. In this case, the court will determine what level of interim rent would be 'reasonable', having regard to the rent under the original tenancy.

Chapter 23 revision points

- A tenancy can end by effluxion of time, surrender, merger, a notice to quit, or a break clause.
- Some business tenancies are protected by the provisions of the Landlord and Tenant Act 1954.
- If a tenancy is protected by the 1954 Act, the tenant can hold over at the end of the lease term and can request a new lease on different terms. The landlord is only permitted to require the tenant to leave the property or to deny the tenant a new lease of the premises on certain specific grounds.
- Some of the grounds are mandatory, and the court must find in favour of the landlord provided the landlord has evidenced the ground. Others are discretionary, and the court can find in favour of either party.
- The court may award a tenant compensation if they find in favour of the landlord under certain grounds.
- A court will be guided by the current lease when deciding the terms of a new lease, although the term of that new lease cannot exceed 15 years.

Revision Summary

PHASE 6 Leasehold management

Alienation

- Alienation can take the form of ***assignment***, ***sub-letting***, and sharing occupation.
- Alienation covenants will be contained within the lease and will either be:
  - an ***absolute prohibition***;
  - a ***qualified covenant***; or
  - a ***fully qualified covenant***.
- Where the covenant is a qualified covenant, a landlord must act reasonably when deciding whether to grant consent.
- A 'reasonable' reason for refusing consent must be related to the premises or to the landlord/tenant relationship.
- Leases created before 1 January 1996 can contain pre-conditions to the landlord's consent.
- Leases created on or after 1 January 1995 can include a list of reasons upon which the landlord is permitted to withhold consent to an assignment or preconditions to consent. The landlord must agree to exercise any discretion reasonably or permit the exercise of this discretion to be reviewed by an independent third party.
- The landlord must provide written notice of their decision within a reasonable time, commonly 28 days, and must give reasons for a refusal.
- The process for assigning or sub-letting a lease is as follows:
  - First, the current tenant must ascertain whether the landlord's consent is required.
  - Then, the transaction follows Phases 1–5, with the consent being documented in the form of a licence.

Alterations

- Alteration covenants will be contained within the lease and will either be:
  - an absolute prohibition;
  - a qualified covenant; or
  - a fully qualified covenant.
- A landlord cannot unreasonably withhold consent under a qualified covenant.
- A 'reasonable' reason for refusing consent will be one which is related to the premises or to the landlord/tenant relationship.
- The landlord can impose conditions on his consent to be included as a covenant in the licence, including payment of compensation, expenses, and reinstatement of the premises.
- There is no requirement in the statute that the landlord provide their consent within a reasonable timeframe, nor that they give reasons for a refusal.
- The process for making alterations is as follows:
  - First, the current tenant must ascertain whether the landlord's consent is required under the lease and, if so, obtain the landlord's consent in the form of a licence for alterations.
  - Then, the tenant should:
    - check the title register for covenants likely to be interfered with when undertaking the works; and
    - check the planning permission and building regulations position.

Enforcing leasehold covenants

All leases

- Where the original landlord and tenant are still the landlord and tenant under the lease (e.g. neither the lease nor the reversion has been assigned), these parties remain liable to each other under ***privity of contract***.

Leases created before 1 January 1996

- On assignment of the lease by the original tenant (see also Figure R6.1):
  - *Privity of contract*. The original tenant remains liable to the landlord for breaches of tenant covenants committed by the assignee.
  - ***Privity of estate***. The landlord and the assignee are liable to each other for breaches of leasehold covenant.
- On assignment of the reversion by the original landlord (see also Figure R6.2):
  - *Section 141 LPA 1925*. The tenant is liable to the assignee for breaches of tenant covenants which pre-date the assignment.
  - *Privity of estate*. The tenant and the assignee are liable to each other for breaches of leasehold covenant post-assignment.

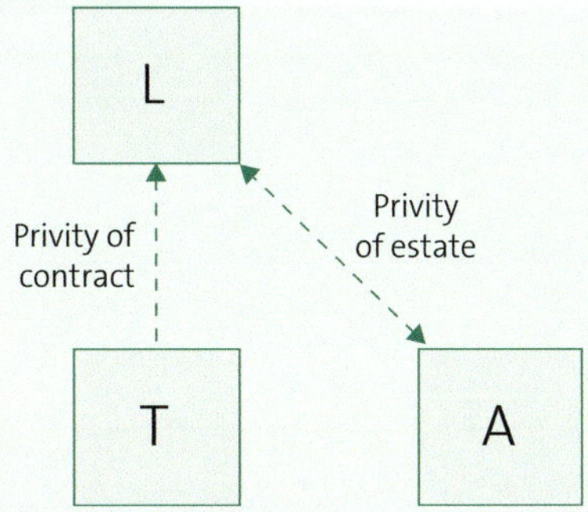

Figure R6.1 The liability position for leases pre–1 January 1996, where the lease has been assigned.

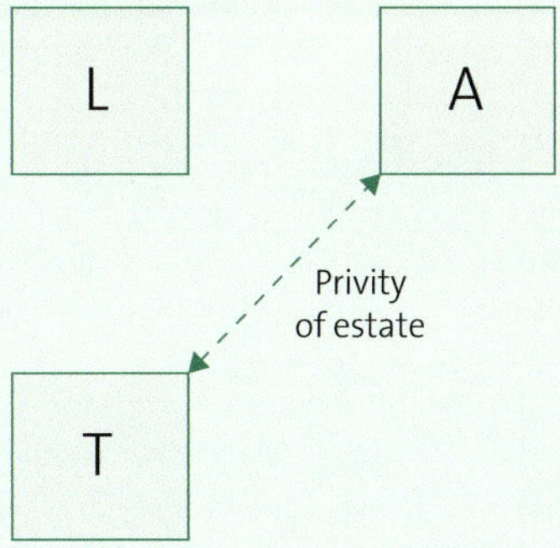

Figure R6.2 The liability position for leases pre–1 January 1996 where the reversion has been assigned.

Leases created on or after 1 January 1996

- On assignment of the lease (see also Figure R6.3):
  - *Privity of estate*. The landlord and the assignee are liable to each other for breaches of leasehold covenant.
  - *AGA*. The original tenant is liable to the landlord for breaches of tenant covenants committed by the assignee if there is an AGA in place.
- On assignment of the reversion (see also Figure R6.4):
  - *Section 141 LPA 1925*. The tenant is liable to the assignee for breaches of tenant covenants which pre-date the assignment.
  - *Privity of estate*. The tenant and the assignee are liable to each other for breaches of leasehold covenant post-assignment.
  - *Privity of contract*. The landlord remains liable to the tenant for breaches of landlord covenant by the assignee unless expressly released.

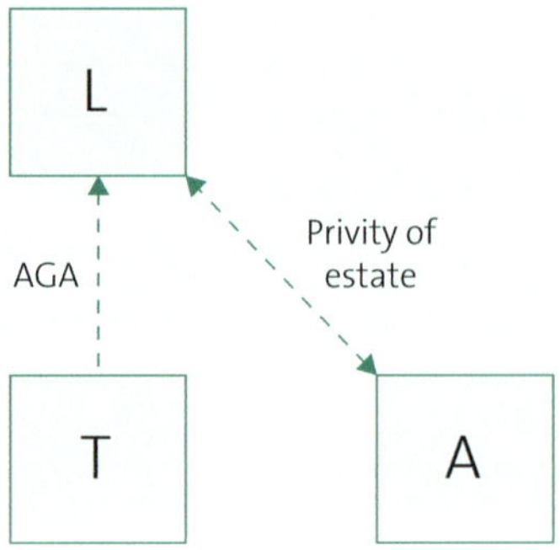

Figure R6.3 The liability position for leases on or after 1 January 1996 where the lease has been assigned.

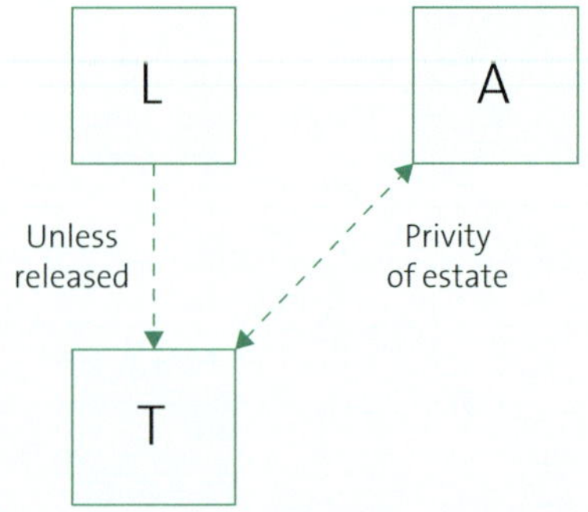

Figure R6.4 The liability position for leases on or after 1 January 1996 where the reversion has been assigned.

Landlord's remedy for tenant's breach of the covenant to pay rent

- **Forfeiture of the lease**
  - This enables the landlord to terminate the lease early and gain possession of the property.
  - ***Forfeiture*** can be exercised by physical re-entry or obtaining a court order.
  - The requirements to exercise forfeiture for non-payment of rent are that:
    - forfeiture is expressly permitted by the lease;
    - the rent is unpaid for the duration specified in the forfeiture clause;
    - there is compliance with any requirement to make formal demand;
    - there are no restrictions on forfeiture; and
    - the right to forfeit has not been waived.

- If the requirements are satisfied, the landlord can re-enter or seek a court order.
- The tenant can apply to have the lease reinstated.

- ***Commercial Rent Arrears Recovery* scheme**
  - The scheme is governed by the Taking Control of Goods Regulations 2013.
  - It is available for commercial premises only.
  - Rent arrears must be outstanding for at least seven days.
  - The landlord must serve an ***enforcement notice*** and give seven clear days' notice of entry.
  - The tenant can apply to set aside the enforcement notice.
  - After the relevant notice periods, an enforcement agent enters the premises and seizes goods to sell.
- **Debt action**
  - This is often preferable to a common law damages claim.
  - Action must be commenced within six years of the rent falling due.
- **Draw upon a rent deposit**
  - The landlord may be able to draw upon a deposit paid by the tenant.
  - A rent deposit deed sets out when a ***rent deposit*** can be kept by the landlord.
- **Pursue other parties for the sum**
  - Those parties may include:
    - the current tenant's guarantor;
    - a former tenant of a lease granted before 1 January 1996, under privity of contract, provided a default notice has been served within six months of the sum falling due; and
    - a former tenant's guarantor, provided their liability isn't restricted to the former tenant's ownership.

Landlord's remedy for tenant's breach of the repair covenant

- **Forfeiture**
  - This enables the landlord to terminate the lease early and gain possession of the property.
  - Forfeiture can be exercised by physical re-entry or obtaining a court order.
  - The requirements to exercise forfeiture for breach of a repair covenant are that:
    - Forfeiture is expressly permitted by the lease.
    - A section 146– and section 1 LP(R)A 1938–compliant notice has been served.

- The tenant has failed to:
  - serve a counter-notice;
  - remedy the breach; or
  - pay compensation.
- Where the tenant has served a counter-notice, the landlord requires a court order in order to take possession.

- **Common law damages**
  - These are capped at the diminution in value to the landlord's reversion.
  - There is a requirement to serve a section 146–compliant notice on the tenant if the lease is subject to LP(R)A 1938.
- **Self-help**
  - The landlord can make the repairs himself and claim any costs as a debt.

Landlord's remedies for tenant's breach of all other leasehold covenants

- **Forfeiture**
  - This enables the landlord to terminate the lease early and gain possession of the property.
  - Forfeiture can be exercised by physical re-entry or obtaining a court order.
  - The requirements to exercise forfeiture for breach of a repair covenant are that:
    - forfeiture is expressly permitted by the lease;
    - a section 146-compliant notice has been served; and
    - the tenant has failed to remedy the breach and pay compensation.
  - The tenant can apply to the court to reinstate the lease.
- **Common law damages.**
- **An *injunction* to stop the breach.**
- ***Specific performance* to stop the breach.**

Methods of ending a lease

- Expiry of the contractual term, for fixed-term leases.
- The tenant ***surrenders*** their lease to the landlord by deed.
- The leasehold interest and reversion come into the same ownership, are ***merged***, and extinguished.
- Either party serves a ***notice to quit*** on the other party.
  - This is only applicable for periodic tenancies.
  - The notice period is determined by the lease.
  - If a notice period is not specified in the lease, the common law will imply a notice period of:
    - (for yearly tenancies) at least half a year expiring on the last day of the tenancy; or
    - (for other periods) at least one period, expiring at the end of a completed period.
- In accordance with a ***break clause*** contained within the lease.

Security of tenure

- Section 24 of the Landlord and Tenant Act 1954 gives ***security of tenure*** to certain tenancies.
- The LTA 1954 applies to tenancies which are occupied by the tenant for business purposes.
- The LTA 1954 enables a tenant to ***hold over*** in the premises after a fixed-term lease has expired and/or to request a new lease of the same premises on different terms.
- If the landlord wants to terminate the current lease, the landlord can serve a ***section 25 notice*** specifying an end date for the current lease dated between 6 and 12 months from the date of the notice. This can be 'friendly' or 'hostile'. The tenant can choose to vacate the premises, negotiate a new lease with the landlord, or apply to the court to determine the matter.
- If the tenant wishes to apply for a new lease, the tenant can serve a ***section 26 notice*** on the landlord specifying a start date for the new lease dated between 6 and 12 months from the date of the notice. The landlord must serve a counter-notice if he isn't willing to grant a new lease. The tenant can vacate the premises or apply to the court to determine the matter.
- Where a landlord isn't willing to grant a new lease (either in a hostile s25 notice or a counter-notice to a s26 notice), he must specify a ***statutory ground for opposition***, under s30.

- The court must find in the landlord's favour and refuse to grant a new lease if:
  - the landlord can provide suitable alternative accommodation;
  - the landlord intends to demolish the premises; or
  - the landlord intends to occupy the premises.
- The court has discretion to find for either party when deciding whether to grant a new lease if:
  - the tenant has breached obligations under the lease; or
  - the tenancy is a sub-let of part and a higher rent can be achieved by letting the whole.
- The court will determine the terms of the new lease. The court has discretion over the terms but will be guided as follows:
  - the premises should be the same as under the current lease;
  - the duration cannot exceed 15 years;
  - the rent must be as agreed between the parties, or market rate; and
  - other terms should match the current lease where appropriate and possible.

PHASE 6

Multiple-choice practice questions

Question 1

The freeholder of a commercial building ('the Landlord') granted a lease of the whole building to a tenant.

The tenant wishes to create two new apertures in an external wall of the building to accommodate windows.

The alternations covenant in the lease is as follows:

> *The Tenant may not make alterations to the Building save for non-structural alterations, which are permitted with the consent of the Landlord.*

What advice should the tenant's solicitor give?

A. There is an absolute prohibition against structural alternations.
B. There is an absolute prohibition against non-structural alterations.
C. The tenant requires the Landlord's consent, and he can refuse consent for any reason.
D. The tenant requires the Landlord's consent, and he can refuse consent if the work is likely to affect the structural integrity of the rest of the building.
E. The tenant does not require the Landlord's consent.

Question 2

A freeholder ('the Landlord') has granted a commercial lease of a property to a tenant.

The lease provides that the property may not be used other than for retail purposes.

The tenant is an independent chemist and requests the Landlord's consent to assign the lease to a national chemist. The proposed assignee is operated by a highly profitable national chain.

The Landlord wishes to withhold consent to the assignment.

The relevant wording of the alienation covenant in the lease is as follows:

> *The Tenant shall not assign underlet or charge the Property without the prior written consent of the Landlord.*

Can the Landlord lawfully withhold consent to the assignment?

A. Yes, because there is an absolute prohibition on alienation in the lease.
B. No, because the Landlord cannot unreasonably withhold consent.
C. Yes, because covenant strength of the tenant is a reasonable reason to withhold consent.
D. Yes, because the Landlord can refuse consent for any reason.
E. No, because the proposed assignee will comply with the user provisions in the lease.

Question 3

A freeholder ('the Landlord') granted a commercial lease of a property to a Tenant on 7 May 1997.

The Tenant requests the Landlord's consent to assign the lease.

The Landlord wishes to withhold consent to the assignment on the basis of poor covenant strength of the proposed assignee.

The relevant wording of the alienation covenant in the lease is as follows:

> *The Tenant shall not assign underlet or charge the Property without the prior written consent of the Landlord. The Landlord shall be permitted to withhold consent if it is not satisfied as to the covenant strength of the Tenant.*

Can the Landlord lawfully withhold consent to the assignment?

A. Yes, because covenant strength is an automatically reasonable reason to withhold consent because it is drafted into the lease.
B. Yes, because covenant strength of the proposed assignee is a reasonable reason to withhold consent.
C. Yes, because the lease does not contain a requirement for the Landlord to act reasonably when withholding consent.
D. Yes, because there is an absolute prohibition on alienation in the lease.
E. No, because the Landlord cannot unreasonably withhold consent.

Question 4

A solicitor acts for a commercial landlord under a 40-year lease dated 1 January 2000.

The tenant is two months behind with the rent. The landlord wishes to re-enter the premises and change the locks.

The lease expressly permits forfeiture provided the rent is unpaid for 21 days after falling due. It does not contain any further provisions relating to forfeiture.

What advice should the landlord's solicitor give to the landlord?

A. The landlord must serve a notice on the tenant which complies with section 146 of the LPA 1925 and give the tenant the opportunity to remedy the breach.
B. The landlord must serve a notice on the tenant which complies with section 146 of the LPA 1925 and section 1 of the LP(R)A 1938 and give the tenant the opportunity to remedy the breach.
C. The landlord must serve a notice on the tenant which complies with section 1 of the LP(R)A 1938 and give the tenant the opportunity to remedy the breach.
D. The landlord must serve a formal demand on the tenant.
E. The landlord does not need to serve a notice on the tenant before re-entering the premises.

Question 5

A solicitor acts for a commercial landlord under a 40-year lease dated 1 January 2000.

The tenant has breached the repair covenant in the lease. The landlord wishes to re-enter the premises and change the locks.

The lease expressly permits forfeiture.

What advice should the landlord's solicitor give to the landlord?

A. The landlord must serve a notice on the tenant which complies with section 146 of the LTCA and give the tenant the opportunity to remedy the breach.
B. The landlord must serve a notice on the tenant which complies with section 146 of the LPA 1925 and section 1 of the LP(R)A 1938 and give the tenant the opportunity to remedy the breach.
C. The landlord must serve a notice on the tenant which complies with section 1 of the LP(R)A 1938 and give the tenant the opportunity to remedy the breach.
D. The landlord must serve a formal demand on the tenant.
E. The landlord does not need to serve a notice on the tenant as the lease permits forfeiture.

Question 6

A freeholder granted a 15-year commercial lease of a property in 2012 to a supermarket.

The supermarket subsequently assigned the lease to a clothing retailer. The clothing retailer assigned the lease to a chemist.

All the assignments were made with the landlord's consent. For the assignment to the clothing retailer, the freeholder required an authorised guarantee agreement from the supermarket.

The chemist has failed to pay the latest quarter's rent.

From whom can the freeholder recover the outstanding rent?

A. The chemist, under the doctrine of privity of estate.
B. The clothing retailer under the authorised guarantee agreement.
C. The supermarket under the doctrine of privity of contract.
D. The supermarket under the authorised guarantee agreement.
E. The supermarket under the authorised guarantee agreement and the chemist under privity of estate.

Question 7

A freeholder granted a 35-year commercial lease of a property in 1992 to a supermarket.

The supermarket subsequently assigned the lease to a clothing retailer. The clothing retailer assigned the lease to a chemist.

All the assignments were made with the landlord's consent. For the assignment to the clothing retailer, the freeholder required an authorised guarantee agreement from the supermarket.

The chemist has failed to pay the latest quarter's rent.

From whom can the freeholder recover the outstanding rent?

A. The chemist only.
B. The clothing retailer.
C. The supermarket only.
D. The supermarket, the clothing retailer, and the chemist.
E. The supermarket and the chemist.

Question 8

A solicitor is acting for a tenant of business premises in connection with an application for the grant of a new tenancy following service by the tenant of a request under s.26 of the Landlord and Tenant Act 1954.

The landlord has served a counter-claim indicating that it opposes the grant of a new tenancy on the basis that the landlord intends to occupy the premises to run its own business.

What advice should the solicitor give to the tenant?

A. The court must find in favour of the landlord, but the tenant may be entitled to compensation.
B. The court has discretion over whether to order the grant of a new lease, and the tenant may be entitled to compensation if the court finds against it.
C. The court must find in favour of the landlord.
D. The court has discretion over whether to order the grant of a new lease.
E. The court must order the grant of a new lease.

Question 9

A solicitor is acting for a tenant of business premises.

The tenant has received a notice from the landlord under s.25 of the Landlord and Tenant Act 1954 ending the current lease and indicating that it would not be amenable to granting a new lease to the tenant, who is behind with the rent payments.

What advice should the solicitor give to the tenant?

A. The tenant should immediately vacate the premises.
B. The tenant should vacate the premises on the date specified in the notice from the landlord.
C. The tenant can apply to the court for a new lease, who have discretion over whether to order it.
D. The tenant can apply to the court for a new lease, who must find in favour of the landlord.
E. The tenant can apply to the court for a new lease, who have discretion over whether to order it, and the tenant will be entitled to compensation if the court finds against it.

Appendix 1: André's purchase of the House

Accompanying Documents

Document 1

Heads of terms – The Old Bakery	
Seller	Michael Tomlinson's estate
Seller's solicitor	Thompson & Thompson LLP of 27 High Street, Barnford, Westshire, EX82 7YK (contact Paul Thompson)
Buyer	André Gomez
Buyer's solicitor	David Cob Solicitors LLP, 18 Woodlands Road, Torton, Westshire, EX79 2FT
Property	Freehold property: The Old Bakery, Cob Lane, Torton, Westshire, EX79 1AP registered with title number EG132465
Price	£350,000
Deposit	£35,000
Finance	Cash: £35,000
	Associated sale: £150,000
	Mortgage from Country Funding Building Society: £165,000
Proposed use	Primary residence
Chain	Buyer is in a chain

Land Registry

Official copy of register of title

Title number EG132465

Edition date 01.01.2025

- This official copy shows the entries in the register of title on 1 September 2025 at 10:33:06.
- This date must be quoted as the "search from date" in any official search application based on this copy.
- The date at the beginning of an entry is the date on which the entry was made in the register.
- Issued on 1 September 2025.
- Under s.67 of the Land Registration Act 2002, this copy is admissible in evidence to the same extent as the original.
- For information about the register of title see Land Registry website www.landregistry.gov.uk or Land Registry Public Guide 1 – *A guide to the information we keep and how you can obtain it.*

A: Property register

This register describes the land and estate comprised in the title

Westshire : Torton

1. (7.11.1991) The Freehold land shown edged with thick black on the plan of the above Title filed at the Registry and being The Old Bakery, Cob Lane, Torton, Westshire, EX79 1AP.

B: Proprietorship register

This register specifies the class of title and identifies the owner. It contains any entries that affect the right of disposal.

Title absolute

1. (12.08.1994) Proprietor(s): Michael Tomlinson of The Old Bakery, Cob Lane, Torton, EX79 1AP.

2. (12.08.1994) Restriction: no disposition of the registered estate by the proprietor of the registered estate is to be registered without a certificate signed by a conveyancer that the provisions of clause 11.1 of the Transfer dated 1 November 1991 made between (1) Joanne Bates and (2) Alan Wright have been complied with.

C: Charges register

This register contains any charges and other matters that affect the land.

1. (7.11.1991) A Conveyance of the land in this title dated 27 January 1929 made between (1) Richard Edward Jones (Vendor) and (2) Peter John Bates and Marie Evelyn Bates

(Purchaser) contains rights and covenants but neither the original nor a certified copy was produced on first registration.

2. (7.11.1991) A transfer of the land in this title dated 1 November 1991 made between (1) Joanne Bates (Vendor) and (2) Alan Wright (Purchaser) contains the following covenants:

   "11.1 The Purchaser with the intent to bind (so far as practicable) the property hereby conveyed (the Property) and to benefit and protect the retained land of the Vendor (the Retained Land) hereby covenants with the Vendor that he and his successors in title will at all times observe and perform the stipulations and conditions set out in Schedule 1.

   SCHEDULE 1

   1. The Purchaser shall, upon demand by the Vendor or his successors in title, contribute financially towards the maintenance of any boundary features along the boundary lines marked 'T' on the plan, to the maximum value of 25 per cent per annum of all costs reasonably incurred by the Vendor or his successors in title.
   2. The Purchaser will not make any disposal of the whole or any part of the Property without first procuring that the disponee enters into a Deed of Covenant with, and supplies the same to, the owner or owners from time to time of the Retained Land or any part of it.
   3. The Purchaser consents to the entry of the following restriction against the Purchaser's title to the Property at HM Land Registry following the registration of this transfer and shall provide the Transferor with all necessary assistance and documentation to permit entry of the restriction:

      "No disposition of the registered estate by the proprietor of the registered estate is to be registered without a certificate signed by a conveyancer that the provisions of clause 11.1 of the Transfer dated 1 November 1991 made between (1) Joanne Bates and (2) Alan Wright have been complied with."

End of register

Land Registry
Official copy of
Title plan

Title number **EG132465**
Ordnance Survey map reference **EG 1234 NN**
Scale **1:2500**
Administrative area **Westshire: Torton**

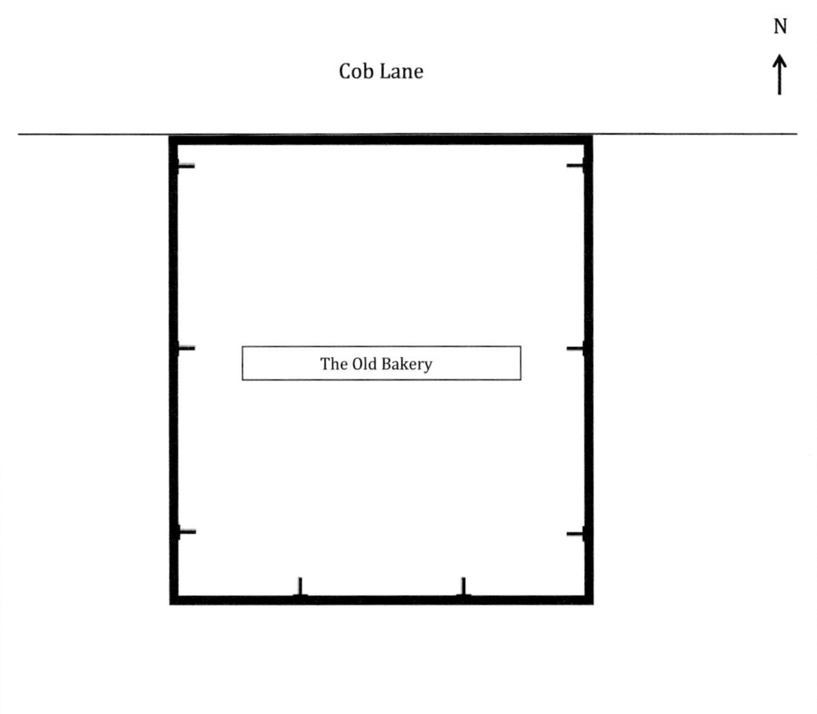

This official copy issued on 1 September 2025 shows the state of this title plan on 1 September 2025 at 10:33:06
It is admissible in evidence to the same extent as the original (s. 67 Land Registration Act 2002).
This title plan shows the general position, not the exact line, of the boundaries. It may be subject to distortions in scale.
Measurements scaled from this plan may not match measurements between the same points on the ground.
See Land Registry Public Guide 19 – Title Plans and Boundaries.

Document 3

SIMR

Official certificate of the result of search of the index map

Land Registry
Land Registration Rules 2003

Certificate Date: 8 September 2025
Certificate Time: 10:33:03
Certificate Ref: XYD/EXH02

Property	THE OLD BAKERY, COB LANE, TORTON, WESTSHIRE, EX79 1AP AND NEIGHBOURING PROPERTIES

Result

The index map has been searched in respect of the Property with the following result:

Plan reference	**Title No.**	**Registered Estate or Caution**	**Notes**
Edged with thick black line (excluding all hatched areas)	EG132465	Freehold	
Areas hatched and cross-hatched with thin black line	EG135265	Freehold	

No registered estate, caution against first registration, application for first registration or application for a caution against first registration is shown on the index map in relation to the remainder of the property.

******

The plan attached to this result is prepared for the sole purpose of showing the area in respect of which an official search has been made. The information has been taken from the index map. It is illustrative only and does not define the extent of the land in any individual title. For information about the general boundaries of a title please refer to the individual register and title plan.

******

Verbal descriptions of registered relating franchises and registered manors, and of pending applications and cautions against first registrations in respect of relating franchises, are kept in the index of relating franchises and manors. The application form for a search of the index is form SIF.

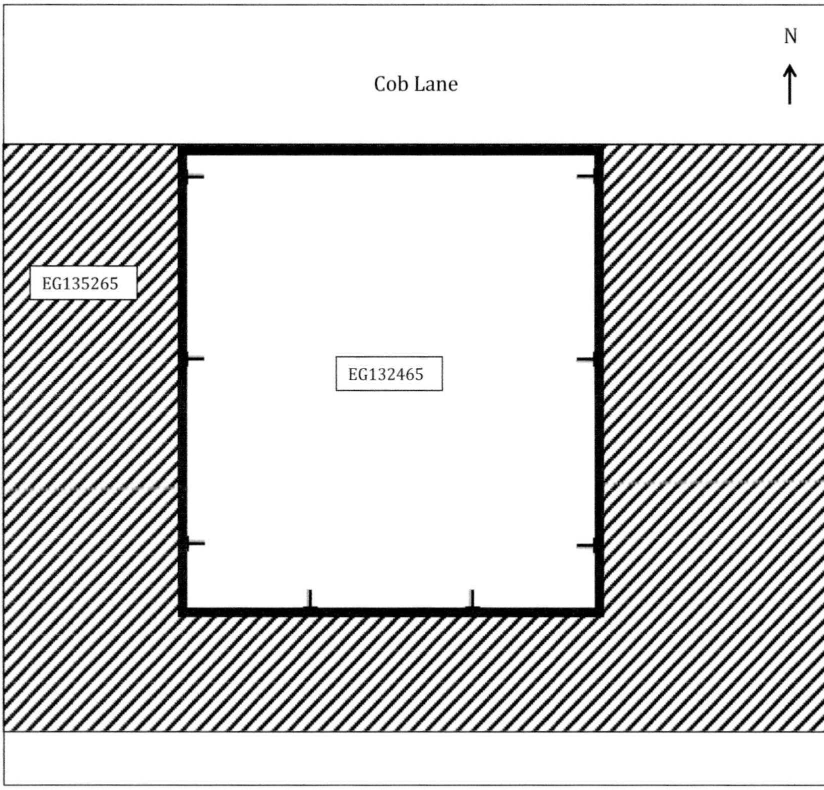
N
Cob Lane
EG135265
EG132465

Document 4

Westshire District Council Offices
Council House,
Exton,
Westshire
(DX 765567 Exton 7)

Westshire
District Council

REGISTER OF LOCAL LAND CHARGES
OFFICIAL CERTIFICATE OF SEARCH

Search Reference:	ZYX/EXH02
Date:	4 September 2025
Applicant:	David Cob Solicitors LLP

Official search required in all parts of the Register of Local Land Charges for subsisting registrations against the land described and the plan submitted.

Land:	The Old Bakery, Cob Lane, Torton, Westshire, EX79 1AP.

It is hereby certified that the search requested above reveals 2 registrations described in the Schedule(s) hereto up to and including the date of this certificate.

Westshire District Council

Register of Local Land Charges
Schedule to Official Certificate of Search

Part 4: Miscellaneous Charges

Description of charge (including reference to appropriate statutory provision)	Originating Authority	Place where relevant documents may be inspected	Date of Registration
This property is affected by a Tree Preservation Order pursuant to the Town and Country Planning (Tree Preservation) (England) Regulations 2012. If you require more precise information please apply to the Environmental Services Department	Westshire District Council	Council House, Exton, Westshire	01/03/2015
This property is affected by one of the various smoke control orders made between 1 December 1960 and 1 October 1991. If you require more precise information please apply to the Environmental Services Department	Westshire District Council	Council House, Exton, Westshire	17/07/1988

Document 5

NB: In practice, the local authority provides answers to all of the questions raised in the CON 29. Many of the questions are not relevant to André's purchase of the House so we have only reproduced answers to those questions which could be relevant to this property. Missing answers are indicated with [...]

Westshire District Council Offices
Council House,
Exton,
Westshire
(DX 765567 Exton 7)

Westshire
District Council

CON29 ENQUIRIES OF LOCAL AUTHORITY
(2016)

Applicant: David Cob Solicitors LLP

Search Reference: ZYX/EXH02

Date: 4 September 2025

Property: The Old Bakery, Cob Lane, Torton, Westshire, EX79 1AP

I refer to your Standard Enquiries relating to the above property. These replies relate to that property as shown on the location plan where supplied. The replies are given subject to the Notes to the Standard Enquiries.

All correspondence relating to these answers should quote the official Search Reference.

Standard Enquiries of Local Authority

PLANNING AND BUILDING REGULATIONS
1.1. Planning and building decisions and pending applications
Which of the following relating to the property have been granted, issued or refused or (where applicable) are the subject of pending applications or agreements?
(a) a planning permission
none

(j) building regulations approval
Reference: BR777/PJG
Description: installation of ground floor toilet
Application date: 1 June 2020
Decision: GRANTED on 1 July 2020

(k) a building regulation completion certificate and

Reference: BRCC777/PJG
Description: installation of ground floor toilet
Date of certificate: 1 July 2020

[...]

Informatives:

(1) Copy documents available from Planning and Building Control Services, Westshire District Council.

(2) This reply does not cover other properties in the vicinity of the property.

(3) As from 1 April 2002 the installation of a replacement window, rooflight or roof window or specified type of glazed door must either have building regulation approval or be carried out and certified by a person who is registered under the Fenestration Self-Assessment Scheme by the Glass and Glazing Federation. The owner or occupier of the property should be asked to produce any such certificate.

ROADS AND PUBLIC RIGHTS OF WAY

Roadways, footways and footpaths

2.1 Which of the roads, footways and footpaths named in the application for this search (via boxes B and C) are:

(a) highways maintainable at public expense

2.1.(a) Cob Lane

(b) subject to adoption and supported by a bond or bond waiver

2.1.(b) None

(c) to be made up by a local authority who will reclaim the cost from the frontagers

2.1.(c) None

(d) to be adopted by a local authority without reclaiming the cost from the frontagers

2.1.(d) None

Informative: If a road, footway or footpath is not a highway, there may be no right to use it and the local authority cannot express an opinion without seeing the title plan and carrying out a site inspection.

Public rights of way

2.2 Is any public right of way which abuts on, or crosses, the property shown in a definitive map or revised definitive map?

2.2. No

[...]

2.5 If so, please attach a plan showing the approximate route.

2.5. Not applicable

Informative: A definitive map for Westshire District Council has now been published. However, a survey of all paths has not been completed and whilst this does not preclude the existence of unrecorded rights of way, the local authority is unaware of any claimed rights of way existing over the search site.

OTHER MATTERS:
Apart from matters entered on the registers of local land charges, do any of the following matters apply to the property? If so, how can copies of relevant documents be obtained?

> **Note:** Matters entered onto the Local Land Charges Register, or visible by property/site inspection, will not be referred to (where relevant) in answer to the enquiries 3.1 to 3.15 below.

Informative: In some circumstances, road closures can be obtained by third parties from magistrate's courts, or can be made by the Secretary of State for Transport without involving the local authority. This enquiry is designed to reveal matters that are yet to be implemented and could not therefore be ascertained by a visual inspection. Schemes that have been, or are currently being, implemented will not be referred to in answer to this enquiry.

[...]

3.5. Nearby railway schemes
(a) Is the property (or will it be) within 200 metres of the centre line of a proposed railway, tramway, light railway or monorail?

> 3.5.(a) No

[...]

3.6 Traffic schemes
Has a local authority approved but not yet implemented any of the following for the roads, footways and footpaths which are named in Boxes B and C and are within 200 metres of the boundaries of the property?

[...]

(e) pedestrianisation

> 3.6(e) No

[...]

3.8. Contravention of building regulations
Has a local authority authorised in relation to the property any proceedings for the contravention of any provision contained in building regulations?

> 3.8. No

3.9. Notices, orders, directions and proceedings under Planning Acts
Do any of the following subsist in relation to the property, or has a local authority decided to issue, serve, make or commence any of the following?
(a) an enforcement notice

> 3.9.(a) No

(b) a stop notice

> 3.9.(b) No

[...]

(d) a breach of condition notice

3.9.(d) No

(e) a planning contravention notice

3.9.(e) No

[...]

(j) a direction restricting permitted development

3.9.(j) No

[...]

3.11. Conservation area
Do the following apply in relation to the property?
(a) the making of the area a conservation area before 31 August 1974

3.11.(a) No

(b) an unimplemented resolution to designate the area a Conservation Area

3.11.(b) No

[...]

3.13. Contaminated land
Do any of the following apply (including any relating to land adjacent to or adjoining the property which has been identified as contaminated land because it is in such a condition that harm or pollution of controlled waters might be caused on the property)?
(a) a contaminated land notice

3.13.(a) No

(b) in relation to a register maintained under section 78R of the Environmental Protection Act 1990

(i) a decision to make an entry
3.13.(b)(i) No

(ii) an entry
3.13.(b)(ii) No

(c) consultation with the owner or occupier of the property conducted under section 78G(3) of the Environmental Protection Act 1990 before the service of a remediation notice

3.13.(c) No

Informative: A negative reply does not imply that the property or any adjoining or adjacent land is free from contamination or from the risk of it and the reply may not disclose steps taken by another local authority in whose area adjacent or adjoining land is situated.

[...]

Document 6

Highways Division
Westshire District Council Offices
Council House,
Exton,
Westshire
(DX 765567 Exton 7)

Westshire
District Council

Date: 25 September 2025

Dear Sirs

The Old Bakery, Cob Lane, Torton, Westshire, EX79 1AP

Please find below the plan; showing by black shading the extent of the publicly maintainable highway in the immediate vicinity of the property, as far as can be ascertained from existing records.

If you have any further queries please do not hesitate to contact us.

Yours faithfully

Highway Records Manager

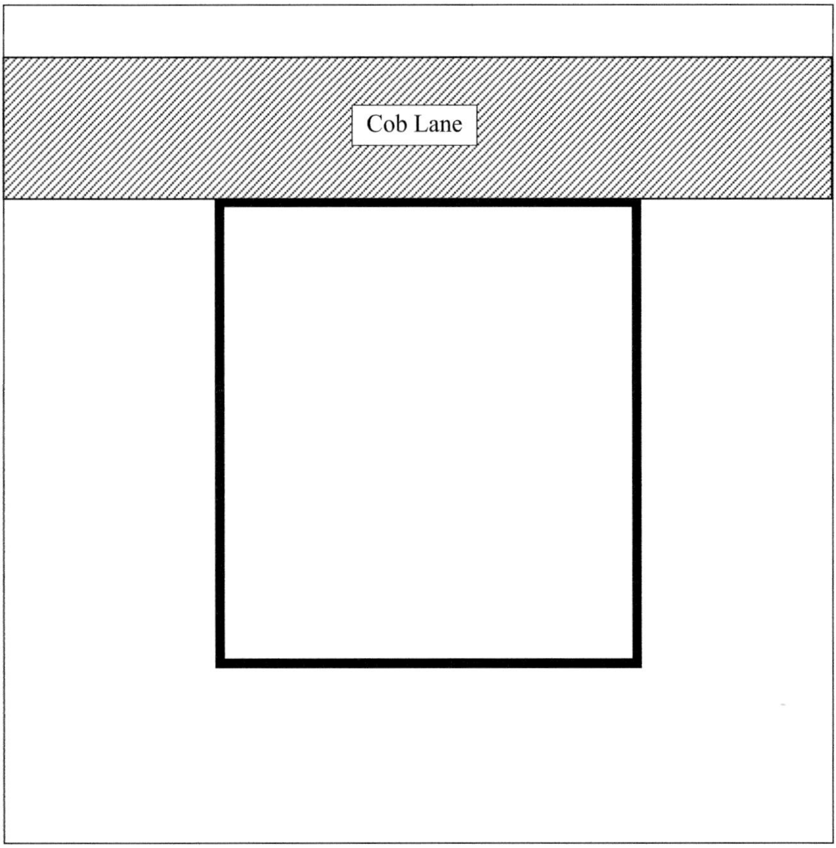
Cob Lane

Document 7

WESTSHIRE WATER

Drainage and Water search

Date: 25 September 2025

Property: The Old Bakery, Cob Lane, Torton, Westshire, EX79 1AP

Results:

Mains water: connected

Foul water: connected

Surface water sewer: connected

Sewer pipe within boundary: no

Water pipe within boundary: no

WESTSHIRE ENVIRO-CHECK

Date: 25 September 2025

Type of report: Homebuyers

Property: The Old Bakery, Cob Lane, Torton, Westshire, EX79 1AP

RESULTS:

Professional opinion: PASS

Environmental search results:

Contaminated Land: passed
No significant concerns have been identified as a result of the contaminated land searches.

Flood risk: low
The property's overall risk assessment for river, coastal, surface water and groundwater flooding is low.

Ground stability: passed
No significant concerns have been identified as a result of the ground stability searches. No action required.

Radon: passed
Local levels of radon are considered normal.

Westshire Enviro-check

Document 9

CHANCEL REPAIR SEARCH

Report details

Report number: CC/877/EXH02

Issue date: 4 September 2025

Address: The Old Bakery, Cob Lane, Torton, EX79 1AP

Result

The above address is located within the historical boundary of a tithe district within a parish which continues to have a potential chancel repair liability based upon historical parish data and the relevant inland Revenue Indices held by The National Archives.

www.lawsociety.org.uk

The Law Society

Law Society Property Information Form (4th edition 2020 – second revision)

Address of the property	The Old Bakery, Cob Lane, Torton, Westshire Postcode E X 7 9 1 A P
Full names of the seller	Paul Thompson (on behalf of Michael Tomlinson's estate)
Seller's solicitor Name of solicitor's firm	Thompson & Thompson LLP
Address	27 High Street Barnford Westshire
Email	mpt@thompsons.com
Reference number	MPT/EX79/2025

About this form

This form is completed by the seller to supply the detailed information and documents which may be relied upon for the conveyancing process.

Definitions

- 'Seller' means all sellers together where the property is owned by more than one person.
- 'Buyer' means all buyers together where the property is being bought by more than one person.
- 'Property' includes all buildings and land within its boundaries.

Instructions to the seller

- The answers should be prepared by the person or persons who are named as owner on the deeds or Land Registry title or by the owner's legal representative(s) if selling under a power of attorney or grant of probate or representation. If there is more than one seller, you should prepare the answers together or, if only one seller prepares the form, the other(s) should check the answers given and all sellers should sign the form.
- If you do not know the answer to any question, you must say so. If you are unsure of the meaning of any questions or answers, please ask your solicitor. Completing this form is not mandatory, but omissions or delay in providing some information may delay the sale.
- If you later become aware of any information which would alter any replies you have given, you must inform your solicitor immediately. This is as important as giving the right answers in the first place. Do not change any arrangements concerning the property with anyone (such as a tenant or neighbour) without first consulting your solicitor.
- It is very important that your answers are accurate. If you give incorrect or incomplete information to the buyer (on this form or otherwise in writing or in conversation, whether through your estate agent or solicitor or directly to the buyer), the buyer may make a claim for compensation from you or refuse to complete the purchase.
- You should answer the questions based upon information known to you (or, in the case of legal representatives, you or the owner). You are not expected to have expert knowledge of legal or technical matters, or matters that occurred prior to your ownership of the property.
- Please give your solicitor any letters, agreements or other papers which help answer the questions. If you are aware of any which you are not supplying with the answers, tell your solicitor. If you do not have any documentation you may need to obtain copies at your own expense. Also pass to your solicitor any notices you have received concerning the property and any which arrive at any time before completion of the sale.

Instructions to the buyer

- If the seller gives you, separately from this form, any information concerning the property (in writing or in conversation, whether through an estate agent or solicitor or directly to you) on which you wish to rely when buying the property, you should tell your solicitor.
- You are entitled to rely on the replies given to enquiries but in relation to the physical condition of the property, the replies should not be treated as a substitute for undertaking your own survey or making your own independent enquiries, which you are recommended to do.
- The seller is only obliged to give answers based on their own information. They may not have knowledge of legal or technical matters. You should not expect the seller to have knowledge of, or give information about, matters prior to their ownership of the property.

1. Boundaries

If the property is leasehold this section, or parts of it, may not apply.

1.1 Looking towards the property from the road, who owns or accepts responsibility to maintain or repair the boundary features:

(a) on the left?	☐ Seller ☐ Shared	☑ Neighbour ☐ Not known
(b) on the right?	☐ Seller ☐ Shared	☑ Neighbour ☐ Not known
(c) at the rear?	☐ Seller ☐ Shared	☑ Neighbour ☐ Not known
(d) at the front?	☑ Seller ☐ Shared	☐ Neighbour ☐ Not known

1.2 If the boundaries are irregular please indicate ownership by written description or by reference to a plan:

1.3 Is the seller aware of any boundary feature having been moved in the last 10 years or during the seller's period of ownership if longer? If Yes, please give details:

☐ Yes ☑ No

1.4 During the seller's ownership, has any adjacent land or property been purchased by the seller? If Yes, please give details:

☐ Yes ☑ No

1.5 Does any part of the property or any building on the property overhang, or project under, the boundary of the neighbouring property or road, for example cellars under the pavement, overhanging eaves or covered walkways? If Yes, please give details:

☐ Yes ☑ No

1.6 Has any notice been received under the Party Wall etc. Act 1996 in respect of any shared/party boundaries? If Yes, please supply a copy, and give details of any works carried out or agreed:

☐ Yes ☑ No
☐ Enclosed ☐ To follow

2. Disputes and complaints

2.1 Have there been any disputes or complaints regarding this property or a property nearby? If Yes, please give details:

☐ Yes ☑ No

2.2 Is the seller aware of anything which might lead to a dispute about the property or a property nearby? If Yes, please give details:

☐ Yes ☑ No

3. Notices and proposals

3.1 Have any notices or correspondence been received or sent (e.g. from or to a neighbour, council or government department), or any negotiations or discussions taken place, which affect the property or a property nearby? If Yes, please give details:

☐ Yes ☑ No

3.2 Is the seller aware of any proposals to develop property or land nearby, or of any proposals to make alterations to buildings nearby?
If Yes, please give details:

☐ Yes ☑ No

---

4. Alterations, planning and building control

Note to seller: All relevant approvals and supporting paperwork referred to in section 4 of this form, such as listed building consents, planning permissions, Building Regulations consents and completion certificates should be provided. If the seller has had works carried out the seller should produce the documentation authorising this. Copies may be obtained from the relevant local authority website. Competent Persons Certificates may be obtained from the contractor or the scheme provider (e.g. FENSA or Gas Safe Register). Further information about Competent Persons Certificates can be found at: **https://www.gov.uk/guidance/competent-person-scheme-current-schemes-and-how-schemes-are-authorised**

Note to buyer: If any alterations or improvements have been made since the property was last valued for council tax, the sale of the property may trigger a revaluation. This may mean that following completion of the sale, the property will be put into a higher council tax band. Further information about council tax valuation can be found at:
http://www.gov.uk/government/organisations/valuation-office-agency

4.1 Have any of the following changes been made to the whole or any part of the property (including the garden)?

(a) Building works (e.g. extension, loft or garage conversion, removal of internal walls). If Yes, please give details including dates of all work undertaken:

☑ Yes ☐ No

Conversion of space under the stairs into downstairs toilet. Completed in 2020

(b) Change of use (e.g. from an office to a residence)

☐ Yes ☑ No
Year:

(c) Installation of replacement windows, roof windows, roof lights, glazed doors since 1 April 2002

☐ Yes ☑ No
Year:

(d) Addition of a conservatory

☐ Yes ☑ No
Year:

4.2 If Yes to any of the questions in 4.1 and if the work was undertaken during the seller's ownership of the property:

(a) please supply copies of the planning permissions, Building Regulations approvals and Completion Certificates, OR:

(b) if none were required, please explain why these were not required – e.g. permitted development rights applied or the work was exempt from Building Regulations:

(a) Building Regulations Completion Certificate enclosed. (b) Planning permission not required because work is excluded under s55(2).

Further information about permitted development can be found at:
https://www.planningportal.co.uk/info/200126/applications

4.3 Are any of the works disclosed in 4.1 above unfinished? If Yes, please give details:

☐ Yes ☑ No

4.4 Is the seller aware of any breaches of planning permission conditions or Building Regulations consent conditions, unfinished work or work that does not have all necessary consents? If Yes, please give details:

☐ Yes ☑ No

4.5 Are there any planning or building control issues to resolve? If Yes, please give details:

☐ Yes ☑ No

4.6 Have solar panels been installed?

☐ Yes ☑ No

If Yes:

(a) In what year were the solar panels installed?

☐ Year

(b) Are the solar panels owned outright?

☐ Yes ☐ No

(c) Has a long lease of the roof/air space been granted to a solar panel provider? If Yes, please supply copies of the relevant documents e.g. copies of electricity bills for feed in tariffs.

☐ Yes ☐ No
☐ Enclosed ☐ To follow

4.7 Is the property or any part of it:

(a) a listed building? — [ ] Yes [✓] No [ ] Not known

(b) in a conservation area? — [ ] Yes [✓] No [ ] Not known

If Yes, please supply copies of any relevant documents. — [ ] Enclosed [ ] To follow

4.8 Are any of the trees on the property subject to a Tree Preservation Order? — [✓] Yes [ ] No [ ] Not known

If Yes:

(a) Have the terms of the Order been complied with? — [✓] Yes [ ] No [ ] Not known

(b) Please supply a copy of any relevant documents. — [✓] Enclosed [ ] To follow

5. Guarantees and warranties

Note to seller: All available guarantees, warranties and supporting paperwork should be supplied before exchange of contracts.

Note to buyer: Some guarantees only operate to protect the person who had the work carried out or may not be valid if their terms have been breached. You may wish to contact the company to establish whether it is still trading and if so, whether the terms of the guarantee will apply to you.

5.1 Does the property benefit from any of the following guarantees or warranties? If Yes, please supply a copy.

(a) New home warranty (e.g. NHBC or similar) — [ ] Yes [✓] No [ ] Enclosed [ ] To follow

(b) Damp proofing — [✓] Yes [ ] No [✓] Enclosed [ ] To follow

(c) Timber treatment — [ ] Yes [✓] No [ ] Enclosed [ ] To follow

(d) Windows, roof lights, roof windows or glazed doors — [✓] Yes [ ] No [✓] Enclosed [ ] To follow

(e) Electrical work — [✓] Yes [ ] No [✓] Enclosed [ ] To follow

(f) Roofing	☑ Yes ☐ No	☑ Enclosed ☐ To follow
(g) Central heating	☑ Yes ☐ No	☑ Enclosed ☐ To follow
(h) Underpinning	☐ Yes ☑ No	☐ Enclosed ☐ To follow
(i) Other (please state):	☐ Yes ☑ No	☐ Enclosed ☐ To follow

5.2 Have any claims been made under any of these guarantees or warranties? If Yes, please give details: ☐ Yes ☑ No

6. Insurance

6.1 Does the seller insure the property? ☑ Yes ☐ No

6.2 If not, why not?

6.3 If the property is a flat, does the landlord insure the building? ☐ Yes ☐ No

6.4 Has any buildings insurance taken out by the seller ever been:

(a) subject to an abnormal rise in premiums? ☐ Yes ☑ No

(b) subject to high excesses? ☐ Yes ☑ No

(c) subject to unusual conditions? ☐ Yes ☑ No

(d) refused? ☐ Yes ☑ No

If Yes, please give details:

6.5 Has the seller made any buildings insurance claims? If Yes, please give details: ☐ Yes ☑ No

7. Environmental matters

Flooding

Note: Flooding may take a variety of forms: it may be seasonal or irregular or simply a one-off occurrence. The property does not need to be near a sea or river for flooding to occur. Further information about flooding can be found at: **www.gov.uk/government/organisations/department-for-environment-food-rural-affairs**. The flood risk check can be found at: **www.gov.uk/check-flood-risk.**

Read our updated Flood Risk Practice Note at **https://www.lawsociety.org.uk/support-services/advice/practice-notes/flood-risk/**

7.1 Has any part of the property (whether buildings or surrounding garden or land) ever been flooded? If Yes, please state when the flooding occurred and identify the parts that flooded: ☐ Yes ☑ No

If No to question 7.1 please continue to 7.3 and do not answer 7.2 below.

7.2 What type of flooding occurred?

(a) Ground water ☐ Yes ☐ No

(b) Sewer flooding ☐ Yes ☐ No

(c) Surface water ☐ Yes ☐ No

(d) Coastal flooding ☐ Yes ☐ No

(e) River flooding ☐ Yes ☐ No

(f) Other (please state):

7.3 Has a Flood Risk Report been prepared? If Yes, please supply a copy. ☐ Yes ☑ No ☐ Enclosed ☐ To follow

Further information about the types of flooding and Flood Risk Reports can be found at: **www.gov.uk/government/organisations/environment-agency.**

Radon

Note: Radon is a naturally occurring inert radioactive gas found in the ground. Some parts of England and Wales are more adversely affected by it than others. Remedial action is advised for properties with a test result above the 'recommended action level'. Further information about Radon can be found at: **www.gov.uk/government/organisations/public-health-england** and **www.publichealthwales.wales.nhs.uk**.

7.4 Has a Radon test been carried out on the property? ☐ Yes ☑ No

If Yes:

(a) please supply a copy of the report ☐ Enclosed ☐ To follow

(b) was the test result below the 'recommended action level'? ☐ Yes ☐ No

7.5 Were any remedial measures undertaken on construction to reduce Radon gas levels in the property? ☐ Yes ☐ No ☐ Not known

Energy efficiency

Note: An Energy Performance Certificate (EPC) is a document that gives information about a property's energy usage. Further information about EPCs can be found at: **https://www.gov.uk/buy-sell-your-home/energy-performance-certificates**

7.6 Please supply a copy of the EPC for the property. ☑ Enclosed ☐ To follow ☐ Already supplied

7.7 Have any installations in the property been financed under the Green Deal scheme? If Yes, please give details of all installations and supply a copy of your last electricity bill.

☐ Yes ☑ No
☐ Enclosed ☐ To follow

Further information about the Green Deal can be found at:
www.gov.uk/green-deal-energy-saving-measures

Japanese knotweed

Note: Japanese knotweed is an invasive non-native plant that can cause damage to property if left untreated. The plant consists of visible above ground growth and an invisible rhizome (root) below ground in the soil. It can take several years to control and manage through a management and treatment plan and rhizomes may remain alive below the soil even after treatment.

7.8 Is the property affected by Japanese knotweed?

☐ Yes ☑ No
☐ Not known

If Yes, please state whether there is a Japanese knotweed management and treatment plan in place and supply a copy with any insurance cover linked to the plan.

☐ Yes ☐ No
☐ Not known
☐ Enclosed ☐ To follow

8. Rights and informal arrangements

Note: Rights and arrangements may relate to access or shared use. They may also include leases of less than seven years, rights to mines and minerals, manorial rights, chancel repair and similar matters. If you are uncertain about whether a right or arrangement is covered by this question, please ask your solicitor.

8.1 Does ownership of the property carry a responsibility to contribute towards the cost of any jointly used services, such as maintenance of a private road, a shared driveway, a boundary or drain?
If Yes, please give details:

☑ Yes ☐ No

Obligation to contribute financially towards maintenance of boundary features - see official copies. Deed of Covenant with Joanne Bates or successors required.

8.2 Does the property benefit from any rights or arrangements over any neighbouring property (this includes any rights of way)?
If Yes, please give details:

☐ Yes ☑ No

8.3 Has anyone taken steps to prevent access to the property, or to complain about or demand payment for access to the property? If Yes, please give details:

☐ Yes ☑ No

8.4 Does the seller know if any of the following rights benefit the property:

(a) Rights of light — ☐ Yes ☑ No

(b) Rights of support from adjoining properties — ☐ Yes ☑ No

(c) Customary rights (e.g. rights deriving from local traditions) — ☐ Yes ☑ No

8.5 Does the seller know if any of the following arrangements affect the property:

(a) Other people's rights to mines and minerals under the land — ☐ Yes ☑ No

(b) Chancel repair liability — ☐ Yes ☑ No

(c) Other people's rights to take things from the land (such as timber, hay or fish) — ☐ Yes ☑ No

If Yes, please give details:

Seller does not know. Buyer should rely on their own searches and enquiries

8.6 Are there any other rights or arrangements affecting the property? This includes any rights of way. If Yes, please give details:

☑ Yes ☐ No

Unknown rights and covenants on title - see official copies

Services crossing the property or neighbouring property

8.7 Do any drains, pipes or wires serving the property cross any neighbour's property?

☐ Yes ☐ No
☑ Not known

8.8 Do any drains, pipes or wires leading to any neighbour's property cross the property?

☐ Yes ☐ No
☑ Not known

8.9 Is there any agreement or arrangement about drains, pipes or wires?

☐ Yes ☐ No
☑ Not known

If Yes, please supply a copy or give details:

☐ Enclosed ☐ To follow

9. Parking

9.1 What are the parking arrangements at the property?

Own parking - driveway

9.2 Is the property in a controlled parking zone or within a local authority parking scheme?

☐ Yes ☑ No
☐ Not known

10. Other charges

Note: If the property is leasehold, details of lease expenses such as service charges and ground rent should be set out on the separate TA7 Leasehold Information Form. If the property is freehold, there may still be charges: for example, payments to a management company or for the use of a private drainage system.

10.1 Does the seller have to pay any charges relating to the property (excluding any payments such as council tax, utility charges, etc.), for example payments to a management company? If Yes, please give details:

☑ Yes ☐ No

Financial contribution towards maintenance of boundary features - see question 8.1

11. Occupiers

11.1 Does the seller live at the property? ☐ Yes ☑ No

11.2 Does anyone else, aged 17 or over, live at the property? ☐ Yes ☑ No

If No to question 11.2, please continue to section 12 'Services' and do not answer 11.3–11.5 below.

11.3 Please give the full names of any occupiers (other than the sellers) aged 17 or over:

11.4 Are any of the occupiers (other than the sellers), aged 17 or over, tenants or lodgers? ☐ Yes ☐ No

11.5 Is the property being sold with vacant possession? ☐ Yes ☐ No

If Yes, have all the occupiers aged 17 or over:

(a) agreed to leave prior to completion? ☐ Yes ☐ No

(b) agreed to sign the sale contract? If No, please supply other evidence that the property will be vacant on completion. ☐ Yes ☐ No ☐ Enclosed ☐ To follow

12. Services

Note: If the seller does not have a certificate requested below this can be obtained from the relevant Competent Persons Scheme. Further information about Competent Persons Schemes can be found at: **https://www.gov.uk/guidance/competent-person-scheme-current-schemes-and-how-schemes-are-authorised**

Electricity

12.1 Has the whole or any part of the electrical installation been tested by a qualified and registered electrician? ☑ Yes ☐ No

If Yes, please state the year it was tested and provide a copy of the test certificate. 2022 Year ☑ Enclosed ☐ To follow

12.2 Has the property been rewired or had any electrical installation work carried out since 1 January 2005? ☐ Yes ☑ No ☐ Not known

If Yes, please supply one of the following:

(a) a copy of the signed BS7671 Electrical Safety Certificate ☐ Enclosed ☐ To follow

(b) the installer's Building Regulations Compliance Certificate ☐ Enclosed ☐ To follow

(c) the Building Control Completion Certificate ☐ Enclosed ☐ To follow

Central heating

12.3 Does the property have a central heating system? ☑ Yes ☐ No

If Yes:

(a) What type of system is it (e.g. mains gas, liquid gas, oil, electricity, etc.)? mains gas

(b) When was the heating system installed? If on or after 1 April 2005 please supply a copy of the 'completion certificate' (e.g. CORGI or Gas Safe Register) or the 'exceptional circumstances' form.
17/6/1995 Date
☐ Not known
☐ Enclosed ☐ To follow

(c) Is the heating system in good working order? ☑ Yes ☐ No

(d) In what year was the heating system last serviced/ maintained? Please supply a copy of the inspection report.
2022 Year
☐ Not known
☑ Enclosed ☐ To follow
☐ Not available

Drainage and sewerage

Note: Further information about drainage and sewerage can be found at:
www.gov.uk/government/organisations/environment-agency

12.4 Is the property connected to mains:

(a) foul water drainage? ☑ Yes ☐ No ☐ Not known

(b) surface water drainage? ☑ Yes ☐ No ☐ Not known

If Yes to both questions in 12.4, please continue to section 13 'Connection to utilities and services' and do not answer 12.5–12.10 below.

12.5 Is sewerage for the property provided by:

(a) a septic tank? ☐ Yes ☐ No

If the property is in England and you answered Yes to question 12.5 and your septic tank discharges directly into surface water, you must do one of the following as soon as possible:

- **connect to mains sewer**
- **install a drainage field (also known as an infiltration system) so the septic tank can discharge to ground instead**
- **replace your septic tank with a small sewage treatment plant**

You must have plans in place to carry out this work within a reasonable timescale, typically 12 months.

12.5.1 When was the septic tank last replaced or upgraded?
Month
Year

(b) a sewage treatment plant? ☐ Yes ☐ No

(c) cesspool? ☐ Yes ☐ No

12.6 Is the use of the septic tank, sewage treatment plant or cesspool shared with other properties? If Yes, how many properties share the system? ☐ Yes ☐ No ☐ Properties share

12.7 When was the system last emptied? ☐ Year

12.8 If the property is served by a sewage treatment plant, when was the treatment plant last serviced? ☐ Year

12.9 When was the system installed? ☐ Year

Note: Some systems installed after 1 January 1991 require Building Regulations approval, environmental permits or registration. Further information about permits and registration can be found at: **www.gov.uk/government/organisations/environment-agency**

12.10 Is any part of the septic tank, sewage treatment plant (including any soakaway or outfall) or cesspool, or the access to it, outside the boundary of the property? If Yes, please supply a plan showing the location of the system and how access is obtained. ☐ Yes ☐ No ☐ Enclosed ☐ To follow

Specific information about permits and general binding rules can be found at **www.gov.uk/permits-you-need-for-septic-tanks**

13. Connection to utilities and services

Please mark the Yes or No boxes to show which of the following utilities and services are connected to the property and give details of any providers.

Mains electricity ☑ Yes ☐ No

Provider's name Octopus Energy

Location of meter under stairs

Mains gas ☑ Yes ☐ No

Provider's name Octopus Energy

Location of meter under stairs

Mains water ☑ Yes ☐ No

Provider's name Westshire

Location of stopcock utility room

Location of meter, if any

Mains sewerage ☑ Yes ☐ No

Provider's name Westshire

Telephone ☑ Yes ☐ No

Provider's name BT

Cable ☑ Yes ☐ No

Provider's name BT

14. Transaction information

14.1 Is this sale dependent on the seller completing the purchase of another property on the same day?

☐ Yes ☑ No

14.2 Does the seller have any special requirements about a moving date? If Yes, please give details:

☐ Yes ☑ No

14.3 Will the sale price be sufficient to repay all mortgages and charges secured on the property?

☐ Yes ☐ No
☑ No mortgage

14.4 Will the seller ensure that:

(a) all rubbish is removed from the property (including from the loft, garden, outbuildings, garages and sheds) and that the property will be left in a clean and tidy condition?

☑ Yes ☐ No

(b) if light fittings are removed, the fittings will be replaced with ceiling rose, flex, bulb holder and bulb?

☑ Yes ☐ No

(c) reasonable care will be taken when removing any other fittings or contents?

☑ Yes ☐ No

(d) keys to all windows and doors and details of alarm codes will be left at the property or with the estate agent?

☑ Yes ☐ No

Signed: Paul Thompson Dated: 01/09/2025

Signed: Dated:

Each seller should sign this form.

The Law Society

The Law Society is the representative body for solicitors in England and Wales.

Type	Enquiry from André's solicitor	Response from Michael's estate's solicitor
Documentation	Please provide a copy of the grant of probate	Enclosed
	Please provide a copy of the transfer dated 1 November 1991 between Joanne Bates and Alan Wright	Enclosed
Title queries	Due diligence has revealed unknown rights and covenants contained in a conveyance dated 27 January 1929. Please provide a copy of the conveyance. Please confirm: - what these rights and covenants are; - who has the benefit of these rights and covenants; and - whether they have been breached; - whether the rights and covenants have been enforced.	The seller does not have a copy of this conveyance, nor any information about the rights or covenants mentioned.
	There is a covenant on the title in respect of the contribution towards the maintenance of boundary features. Please confirm: - whether the covenant has been breached; - whether there are outstanding costs; - how much has this charge been, on average, annually?	The seller confirms: - there are outstanding costs amounting to £57 which are due to be paid by 1 September 2025; and - the average annual charge is £40.
Searches	The property is subject to a TPO. Please identify the relevant tree.	The relevant tree is the willow tree on the southern edge of the garden.
Use	Please confirm the current use of the property.	The property has been used as a residence since purchase by Michael Tomlinson in 1994. It is currently unoccupied as Michael has passed away.
Overriding interests	Please confirm whether there are any overriding interests affecting the property	Confirmed none to the seller's knowledge.

Document 12

Acquisition of The Old Bakery

Summary of due diligence for inclusion in a report on title

1. Key details of the transaction

- The property is being purchased for the buyer to live in.
- Seller: Michael Tomlinson is the registered proprietor according to the title deeds. We have been informed that Michael has passed away and the House is being sold by his personal representative, Paul Thompson. We have viewed the grant of probate. Actions:
    - contract: Paul Thompson will need to be listed as the 'seller' in the contract;
    - transfer: Paul Thompson will need to be listed as the 'seller' in the transfer deed;
    - post-completion: the death certificate and grant of probate must be sent to HMLR when registering André as the new proprietor.
- Buyer: André Gomez
- Property: The Old Bakery, Cob Lane, Torton, Westshire, EX79 1AP. A SIM search over the land noted that it was registered with title number EG132465.
- Price: £350,000
- Deposit: 10% of purchase price.
- Finance: £185,000 will be funded in cash (£35,000 deposit and £150,000 from ar associated sale) and £165,000 which will be funded by way of mortgage. Actions:
    - the mortgage will need to be arranged;
    - completion: the mortgage deed must be completed immediately after completion of the transfer;
    - post-completion: the mortgage will need to be registered with HMLR immediately after completion.
- André will need to pay £7,500 in SDLT for the acquisition of the House.
- The House is being sold with vacant possession. Actions:
    - contract: this will need to be included as a special condition in the contract.

2. Title investigation

- Investigation of the title revealed unknown rights and covenants. HMLR does not have a copy of these, and the seller has not been able to provide any information about these. These rights and covenants will burden André. We recommend obtaining title defect insurance.

- Investigation of the title revealed a positive covenant requiring the payment of costs contributing towards maintaining the boundary between the House and the neighbouring land. We have done a SIM search which confirms that the land benefitting from this is still owned by Joanne Bates. The seller has confirmed that this is an average annual cost of around £40 and that there are outstanding costs of £57. This positive covenant and restriction will remain on the title. Actions:
  - contract:
    - include a special condition requiring the seller to pay the outstanding costs before completion;
    - include a special condition requiring the TR1 to include a covenant requiring Andre to comply with the positive covenant and enter into a deed of covenant with Joanne Bates;
  - transfer: will need to include a covenant that Andre to comply with the positive covenant and enter into a deed of covenant with Joanne Bates; Andre will need to sign the TR1 as he is giving this covenant;
  - completion: Andre will need to enter into a deed of covenant with Joanne Bates;
  - post-completion: a certificate needed from a conveyancer, confirming that the restriction has been complied with.
- The seller does not know of any overriding interests affecting the House. We recommend a physical inspection of the property, as Andre will be bound by these if any do exist and are discoverable.

3 Searches

- The local search revealed a Smoke Control Order. Andre will only be able to burn certain fuels at the House.
- The local search revealed a Tree Preservation Order. The seller has confirmed that this relates to the willow tree on the southern edge of the garden. The seller has confirmed they have not breached this Order, and has supplied a copy. Andre will not be able to remove this tree.
- The highways search has confirmed that the House is accessed directly from Cob Lane, which is an adopted highway.
- The drainage and water search confirmed that Westshire Water are responsible for maintaining the drains and sewers and for the quality of the water supplied to the House.
- The risk of contaminants on the land is low and we do not recommend any further environmental surveys.
- The flood risk to the House is low and we do not recommend further flood surveys.

- The House is in a potential chancel repair liability area. We recommend obtaining insurance for this.
- The House is connected to mains electricity and gas provided by Octopus Energy, and receives telephone and cable from BT.

Planning and building regulations

- A toilet was installed downstairs in 2020. It did not require planning permission. It was approved by building control, and a building regulations certificate has been supplied by the seller.
- The House is being purchased as a residence. The local authority searches have not confirmed the current use of the House. However, the enquiries of the seller have confirmed that it is currently being used as residence and has been since 1994. André will not change the use, and so planning permission is not required.

5 Other practicalities

- The buyer is in a chain. Actions:
    - contract: the completion time will need to be amended to 12pm to enable the sale of André's other property to complete;
    - exchange: this must occur after the exchange of André's other property;
    - completion: this must occur after the exchange of André's other property.

NB: the authors have included dates in this contract in square brackets – in practice these would be entered at the relevant moment (e.g. on exchange).

CONTRACT	**For conveyancer's use only** Buyer's conveyancer David Cob Solicitors LLP Seller's conveyancer Thompson & Thompson LLP Law Society Formula C Time: 2:15pm **The information above does not form part of the Contract**

(Incorporating the Standard Conditions of Sale (Fifth Edition – 2018 Revision))

Date	:	*[14 November 2025]*
Seller	:	Paul Thompson
Buyer	:	André Gomez
Property (freehold/~~leasehold~~)	:	The Old Bakery, Cob Lane, Torton, Westshire, EX79 1AP
Title Number/~~Root of title~~	:	EG132465
Specified Encumbrances	:	The matters contained in or referred to in the property, proprietorship and charges register of title number EG132465
Title guarantee (full/~~limited~~)	:	Full
Completion Date	:	*[4 December 2025]*
Contract Rate	:	4% above the base lending rate of Barclays Bank plc from time to time in force
Purchase Price	:	£350,000
Deposit	:	£35,000
Content price (if separate)	:	n/a
Balance	:	£315,000

The Seller will sell and the Buyer will buy the Property for the Purchase Price.

WARNING This is a formal document, designed to create legal rights and legal obligations. Take advice before using it.	**Signed** ***André Gomez*** Buyer

SPECIAL CONDITIONS

1. (a) This contract incorporates the Standard Conditions of Sale (Fifth Edition – 2018 Revision).
   (b) The terms used in this contract have the same meaning when used in the Conditions.

2. Subject to the terms of this contract and to the Standard Conditions of Sale, the seller is to transfer the property with either full title guarantee or limited title guarantee, as specified on the front page.

3. (a) The sale includes those contents which are indicated on the attached list as included in the sale and the buyer is to pay the contents price for them.

   (b) The sale excludes those fixtures which are at the property and are indicated on the attached list as excluded from the sale.

4. The property is sold with vacant possession

5. Conditions 6.1.2 and 6.1.3 shall take effect as if the time specified in them were 12:00 pm rather than 2.00 pm

6. **Representations**

   Neither party can rely on any representation made by the other, unless made in writing by the other or his conveyancer, but this does not exclude liability for fraud or recklessness.

7. The Seller will, by the Completion Date, ensure that all outstanding sums referred to in covenant 1 of the Schedule 1 contained in entry 2 of the Charges Register of title number EG132465 are paid to Joanne Bates.

8. The transfer to the Buyer will contain the following provision:

   "The Transferee covenants with the Transferor to observe and perform the covenants contained or referred to in entry number 2 in the Charges Register of title number EG132465."

Notices may be sent to:

Seller's Conveyancer's name: Thompson & Thompson LLP of 27 High Street, Barnford, Westshire, EX82 7YK

Buyer's Conveyancer's name: David Cob Solicitors LLP, 18 Woodlands Road, Torton, Westshire, EX79 2FT

NB: the authors have included dates in this deed in square brackets – in practice these would be entered at the relevant moment (e.g. on completion).

HM Land Registry

Transfer of whole of registered title(s)

TR1

Any parts of the form that are not typed should be completed in black ink and in block capitals.

If you need more room than is provided for in a panel, and your software allows, you can expand any panel in the form. Alternatively use continuation sheet CS and attach it to this form.

For information on how HM Land Registry processes your personal information, see our Personal Information Charter.

Leave blank if not yet registered.	1 Title number(s) of the property: EG132465
Insert address including postcode (if any) or other description of the property, for example 'land adjoining 2 Acacia Avenue'.	2 Property: The Old Bakery, Cob Lane, Torton, Westshire, EX79 1AP
Remember to date this deed with the day of completion, but not before it has been signed and witnessed.	3 Date: [*4 December 2025*]
Give full name(s) of **all** the persons transferring the property. Complete as appropriate where the transferor is a company. Enter the overseas entity ID issued by Companies House for the transferor pursuant to the Economic Crime (Transparency and Enforcement) Act 2022. If the ID is not required, you may instead state 'not required'. Further details on overseas entities can be found in practice guide 78: overseas entities.	4 Transferor: Paul Thompson For UK incorporated companies/LLPs Registered number of company or limited liability partnership including any prefix: For overseas entities (a) Territory of incorporation or formation: (b) Overseas entity ID issued by Companies House, including any prefix: (c) Where the entity is a company with a place of business in the United Kingdom, the registered number, if any, issued by Companies House, including any prefix:

Give full name(s) of **all** the persons to be shown as registered proprietors. Complete as appropriate where the transferee is a company. Also, for an overseas company, unless an arrangement with HM Land Registry exists, lodge either a certificate in Form 7 in Schedule 3 to the Land Registration Rules 2003 or a certified copy of the constitution in English or Welsh, or other evidence permitted by rule 183 of the Land Registration Rules 2003. Enter the overseas entity ID issued by Companies House for the transferee pursuant to the Economic Crime (Transparency and Enforcement) Act 2022. If the ID is not required, you may instead state 'not required'. Further details on overseas entities can be found in practice guide 78: overseas entities.	5 Transferee for entry in the register: André Gomez For UK incorporated companies/LLPs Registered number of company or limited liability partnership including any prefix: For overseas entities (a) Territory of incorporation or formation: (b) Overseas entity ID issued by Companies House, including any prefix: (c) Where the entity is a company with a place of business in the United Kingdom, the registered number, if any, issued by Companies House, including any prefix:
Each transferee may give up to three addresses for service, one of which must be a postal address whether or not in the UK (including the postcode, if any). The others can be any combination of a postal address, a UK DX box number or an email address.	6 Transferee's intended address(es) for service for entry in the register: The Old Bakery, Cob Lane, Torton, Westshire, EX79 1AP
	7 The transferor transfers the property to the transferee
Place 'X' in the appropriate box. State the currency unit if other than sterling. If none of the boxes apply, insert an appropriate memorandum in panel 11.	8 Consideration ☒ The transferor has received from the transferee for the property the following sum (in words and figures): £350,000 ☐ The transfer is not for money or anything that has a monetary value ☐ Insert other receipt as appropriate:
Place 'X' in any box that applies. Add any modifications.	9 The transferor transfers with ☒ full title guarantee ☐ limited title guarantee

Where the transferee is more than one person, place 'X' in the appropriate box.

Complete as necessary.

The registrar will enter a Form A restriction in the register *unless*:
- an 'X' is placed:
  - in the first box, or
  - in the third box and the details of the trust or of the trust instrument show that the transferees are to hold the property on trust for themselves alone as joint tenants, *or*
- it is clear from completion of a form JO lodged with this application that the transferees are to hold the property on trust for themselves alone as joint tenants.

Please refer to *Joint property ownership* and *practice guide 24: private trusts of land* for further guidance. These are both available on the GOV.UK website.

Insert here any required or permitted statement, certificate or application and any agreed covenants, declarations and so on.

10 Declaration of trust. The transferee is more than one person and

☐ they are to hold the property on trust for themselves as joint tenants

☐ they are to hold the property on trust for themselves as tenants in common in equal shares

☐ they are to hold the property on trust:

11 Additional provisions

11.1 The Transferee covenants with the Transferor to observe and perform the covenants contained or referred to in entry number 2 in the Charges Register of title number EG132465.

The transferor must execute this transfer as a deed using the space opposite. If there is more than one transferor, all must execute. Forms of execution are given in Schedule 9 to the Land Registration Rules 2003. If the transfer contains transferee's covenants or declarations or contains an application by the transferee (such as for a restriction), it must also be executed by the transferee.

If there is more than one transferee and panel 10 has been completed, each transferee must also execute this transfer to comply with the requirements in section 53(1)(b) of the Law of Property Act 1925 relating to the declaration of a trust of land. Please refer to *Joint property ownership* and practice guide *24: private trusts of land* for further guidance.

Examples of the correct form of execution are set out in practice guide 8: execution of deeds. Execution as a deed usually means that a witness must also sign, and add their name and address.

Remember to date this deed in panel 3.

12 Execution

Seller
Signed as a deed by Paul Thompson
Paul Thompson

In the presence of:
Michelle March
MICHELLE MARCH
27 High Street, Barnford, Westshire, EX82 7YK

Buyer
Signed as a deed by André Gomez
André Gomez

In the presence of:
David Cob
DAVID COB
18 Woodlands Road, Torton, Westshire, EX79 2FT

WARNING
If you dishonestly enter information or make a statement that you know is, or might be, untrue or misleading, and intend by doing so to make a gain for yourself or another person, or to cause loss or the risk of loss to another person, you may commit the offence of fraud under section 1 of the Fraud Act 2006, the maximum penalty for which is 10 years' imprisonment or an unlimited fine, or both.

Failure to complete this form with proper care may result in a loss of protection under the Land Registration Act 2002 if, as a result, a mistake is made in the register.

Under section 66 of the Land Registration Act 2002 most documents (including this form) kept by the registrar relating to an application to the registrar or referred to in the register are open to public inspection and copying. If you believe a document contains prejudicial information, you may apply for that part of the document to be made exempt using Form EX1, under rule 136 of the Land Registration Rules 2003.

HM Land Registry
Legal charge of a registered estate

CH1

This form should be accompanied by either Form AP1 or Form FR1

Any parts of the form that are not typed should be completed in black ink and in block capitals.

If you need more room than is provided for in a panel, and your software allows, you can expand any panel in the form. Alternatively use continuation sheet CS and attach it to this form.

Conveyancer is a term used in this form. It is defined in rule 217A, Land Registration Rules 2003 and includes persons authorised under the Legal Services Act 2007 to provide reserved legal services relating to land registration and includes solicitors and licensed conveyancers.

For information on how HM Land Registry processes your personal information, see our Personal Information Charter.

Guidance	Panel	
Leave blank if not yet registered.	1	Title number(s) of the property: EG132465
Insert address including postcode (if any) or other description of the property, for example 'land adjoining 2 Acacia Avenue'.	2	Property: The Old Bakery, Cob Lane, Torton, Westshire, EX79 1AP
	3	Date: [*4 December 2025*]
Give full name(s). Complete as appropriate where the borrower is a company. Enter the overseas entity ID issued by Companies House for the borrower pursuant to the Economic Crime (Transparency and Enforcement) Act 2022. If the ID is not required, you may instead state 'not required'. Further details on overseas entities can be found in practice guide 78: overseas entities.	4	Borrower: André Gomez For UK incorporated companies/LLPs Registered number of company or limited liability partnership including any prefix: For overseas entities (a) Territory of incorporation or formation: (b) Overseas entity ID issued by Companies House, including any prefix: (c) Where the entity is a company with a place of business in the United Kingdom, the registered number, if any, issued by Companies House, including any prefix:

Give full name(s).	5 Lender for entry in the register: Country Funding Building Society
Complete as appropriate where the lender is a company. Also, for an overseas company, unless an arrangement with HM Land Registry exists, lodge either a certificate in Form 7 in Schedule 3 to the Land Registration Rules 2003 or a certified copy of the constitution in English or Welsh, or other evidence permitted by rule 183 of the Land Registration Rules 2003.	<u>For UK incorporated companies/LLPs</u> Registered number of company or limited liability partnership including any prefix: 7774590 <u>For overseas companies</u> (a) Territory of incorporation: (b) Where the entity is a company with a place of business in the United Kingdom, the registered number, if any, issued by Companies House, including any prefix:
Each proprietor may give up to three addresses for service, one of which must be a postal address whether or not in the UK (including the postcode, if any). The others can be any combination of a postal address, a UK DX box number or an email address.	6 Lender's intended address(es) for service for entry in the register: Finance House, Torton, Westshire, EX79 2AB
Place 'X' in any box that applies. Add any modifications.	7 The borrower with ☒ full title guarantee ☐ limited title guarantee charges the property by way of legal mortgage as security for the payment of the sums detailed in panel 9
Place 'X' in the appropriate box(es). You must set out the wording of the restriction in full. Standard forms of restriction are set out in Schedule 4 to the Land Registration Rules 2003.	8 ☐ The lender is under an obligation to make further advances and applies for the obligation to be entered in the register ☒ The borrower applies to enter the following standard form of restriction in the proprietorship register of the registered estate: Except under an order of the Registrar no disposition by the proprietor of the land is to be registered without the consent of the proprietor of the charge dated 4 December 2025 in favour of Country Funding Building Society referred to in the Charges Register.
Insert details of the sums to be paid (amount and dates) and so on.	9 Additional provisions [not reproduced]

The borrower must execute this charge as a deed using the space opposite. If there is more than one borrower, all must execute. Forms of execution are given in Schedule 9 to the Land Registration Rules 2003. If a note of an obligation to make further advances has been applied for in panel 8 this document must be signed by the lender or its conveyancer. Examples of the correct form of execution are set out in practice guide 8: execution of deeds. Execution as a deed usually means that a witness must also sign, and add their name and address.	10 Execution Signed as a deed by André Gomez *André Gomez* In the presence of: *David Cob* DAVID COB 18 Woodlands Road, Torton, Westshire, EX79 2FT

WARNING
If you dishonestly enter information or make a statement that you know is, or might be, untrue or misleading, and intend by doing so to make a gain for yourself or another person, or to cause loss or the risk of loss to another person, you may commit the offence of fraud under section 1 of the Fraud Act 2006, the maximum penalty for which is 10 years' imprisonment or an unlimited fine, or both.

Failure to complete this form with proper care may result in a loss of protection under the Land Registration Act 2002 if, as a result, a mistake is made in the register.

Under section 66 of the Land Registration Act 2002 most documents (including this form) kept by the registrar relating to an application to the registrar or referred to in the register are open to public inspection and copying. If you believe a document contains prejudicial information, you may apply for that part of the document to be made exempt using Form EX1, under rule 136 of the Land Registration Rules 2003.

Document 16

Memorandum of exchange: The Old Bakery

14 November 2025

Part 1:

1. Solicitors agreed on 14 November 2025 at 9:30am to use formula C.
2. Deposit already transferred to seller's solicitor via CHAPS on 12 November 2025 so the sentence requiring the purchaser's solicitor to send a banker's draft or client account cheque is deleted from the formula.
3. Final time for exchange is 4pm.
4. Agreed completion date: 4 December 2025.
5. No deposit is to be paid – see 2. Above.
6. David Cob solicitors LLP – solicitor for the buyer.
   Thompson & Thompson LLP – solicitor for the seller.

Part 2:

7. Request received at 2pm on 14 November 2025 from seller's solicitor. Part 2 activated.
8. Exchange occurred on 14 November 2025 at 2:15pm.

Official search certificate of search of whole with priority

Land Registry

Land Registration Rules 2003

Form **OS1R**

Official Search No. OB/EXH02	Certificate Date: **14 November 2025** Priority Period began at: **15:33:33**	Priority Period expires on: **30 December 2025** at midnight but see the note below

Particulars of Search as Supplied

Title Number	EG132465
Applicant	André Gomez

Result

It is certified that the official search applied for has been made with the following result:

Since 1 September 2025 at 10:33:06 no adverse entries have been made.

****

END OF RESULT

Note: To be sure to obtain priority for your application you should deliver it to the proper office by 12:00 (noon) on the date when priority expires.

Document 18

HM Land Registry

Application to change the register

AP1

Any parts of the form that are not typed should be completed in black ink and in block capitals.

If you need more room than is provided for in a panel, and your software allows, you can expand any panel in the form. Alternatively use continuation sheet CS and attach it to this form.

HM Land Registry is unable to give legal advice, but you can find guidance on HM Land Registry applications (including our practice guides for conveyancers) at www.gov.uk/land-registry.

Conveyancer is a term used in this form. It is defined in rule 217A, Land Registration Rules 2003 and includes persons authorised under the Legal Services Act 2007 to provide reserved legal services relating to land registration and includes solicitors and licensed conveyancers.

For information on how HM Land Registry processes your personal information, see our Personal Information Charter.

HM LAND REGISTRY USE ONLY
Record of fees paid
Particulars of under/over payments
Reference number Fees debited £

Where there is more than one local authority serving an area, enter the one to which council tax or business rates are normally paid.

1 Local authority serving the property: *Westshire*

Full postcode of property (if any): *EX79 1AP*

Enter the title number of each title that requires an entry to be made in that register.

2 Title number(s) of the property:
EG132465

3 The application affects

Place 'X' in the appropriate box.

☒ the whole of the title(s)

Give a brief description of the part affected, for example 'edged red on the plan to the transfer dated ....'.

☐ part of the title(s) as shown:

4 Application, priority and fees

To find out more about our fees visit www.gov.uk/government/collections/fees-land-registry-guides

Remember restrictions in deeds may apply to other deeds of lower priority in this list, unless you specify otherwise.

Applications in priority order	Price paid/Value (£)	Fees paid (£)
Transfer of whole	*350,000*	*150*
Registration of charge	*165,000*	*30*
	Total fees (£)	*180*

Fee payment method

Place 'X' in the appropriate box.

☐ cheque made payable to 'Land Registry'

☒ direct debit, under an agreement with Land Registry

Where the application is sent to HM Land Registry by a private individual, payment must be by way of postal order or cheque made payable to HM Land Registry.

The fee will be charged to the account specified in panel 7.

List the documents lodged with this form. We only need certified copies of deeds or documents you send to us with HM Land Registry application forms. Once we have made a copy of the documents you send to us, they will be destroyed, this applies to both originals and certified copies

5 Documents lodged with this form:

Certified copy of Transfer dated 4 December 2025 and made between (1) Paul Thompson and (2) André Gomez, executed by Paul Thompson

Certified copy of Transfer dated 4 December 2025 and made between (1) Paul Thompson and (2) André Gomez, executed by André Gomez

Certified copy of SDLT5 dated 5 December 2025

Certified copy of death certificate of Michael Tomlinson

Certified copy of grant of probate appointing Paul Thompson as the executor of Michael Tomlinson's estate

Form RXC dated 8 December 2025 relating to entry B2 of the register of title of the property identified in panel 2

Certified copy of mortgage deed using Form CH1, dated 4 December 2025 made between (1) Country Funding Building Society and (2) André Gomez, executed by André Gomez

Provide the full name(s) of the person(s) applying to change the register. Where a conveyancer lodges the application, this must be the name(s) of the client(s), not the conveyancer.

Complete as appropriate where the applicant is a company. Also, for an overseas company, unless an arrangement with HM Land Registry exists, lodge either a certificate in Form 7 in Schedule 3 to the Land Registration Rules 2003 or a certified copy of the constitution in English or Welsh, or other evidence permitted by rule 183 of the Land Registration Rules 2003.

Enter the overseas entity ID issued by Companies House for the applicant pursuant to the Economic Crime (Transparency and Enforcement) Act 2022. If the ID is not required, you may instead state 'not required'.

Further details on overseas entities can be found in practice guide 78: overseas entities.

6 The applicant:

André Gomez

For UK incorporated companies/LLPs
Registered number of company or limited liability partnership including any prefix:

For overseas entities
(a) Territory of incorporation or formation:

(b) Overseas entity ID issued by Companies House, including any prefix:

(c) Where the entity is a company with a place of business in the United Kingdom, the registered number, if any, issued by Companies House, including any prefix:

This panel must always be completed.

This panel must always be completed with the details of the person sending the application to HM Land Registry. However, a key number is only available to professional customers, such as solicitors, and so a key number cannot be entered where the application is sent to HM Land Registry by a private individual.

If you are paying by direct debit, this will be the account charged.

This is the address to which we will normally send requisitions. However if you insert an email address, we will use this whenever possible.

An acknowledgement of receipt of this

7 This application is sent to Land Registry by

Key number (if applicable): n/a

Name: *David Cob Solicitors LLP*
Address or UK DX box number:

18 Woodlands Road, Torton, Westshire, EX79 2FT

Email address: *David@davidcob.com*
Reference: *555933/DXC01*

application, if lodged by post, will be sent by email if one is available. We will only issue warning of cancellation letters to conveyancers if an email address is inserted.	Phone no: *0000 123456* | Fax no: n/a
When completing this panel please refer to Guidance: completing form AP1.	8 Third party notification Name: Address or UK DX box number: Email address: Reference:
When completing this panel please refer to Guidance: completing form AP1. Place 'X' in the appropriate box. In this and panel 10, each proprietor may give up to three addresses for service, one of which must be a postal address whether or not in the UK (including the postcode, if any). The others can be any combination of a postal address, a UK DX box number or an email address.	9 The address(es) for service for each proprietor of the registered estate(s) to be entered in the register is ☒ the address of the property (where this is a single postal address) ☐ the address(es) for service from the transfer/assent ☐ (for existing proprietors who are remaining in the register) the current address(es) for service in the register ☐ the following address(es):
Where a charge has an MD reference we will ignore an address given in this panel unless the charge is in favour of a United Kingdom bank and neither the charge form nor any agreement we have with the lender specifies an address for service. For permitted addresses see note to panel 9. Complete as appropriate where the lender is a company. Also, for an overseas company, unless an arrangement with HM Land Registry exists, lodge either a certificate in Form 7 in Schedule 3 to the Land Registration Rules 2003 or a certified copy of the constitution in English or Welsh, or other evidence permitted by rule 183 of the Land Registration Rules 2003.	10 Name and address(es) for service of the proprietor of any new charge to be entered in the register: *Country Funding Building Society, Finance House, Torton, Westshire, EX79 2AB* For UK incorporated companies/LLPs Registered number of company or limited liability partnership including any prefix: *7774590* For overseas companies (a) Territory of incorporation: (b) Where the entity is a company with a place of business in the United Kingdom, the registered number, if any, issued by Companies House, including any prefix:
If this statement applies (i) place 'X' in the box and (ii) enclose Form DI. Section 27 of the Land Registration Act 2002 lists the registrable dispositions. Rule 57 of the Land Registration Rules 2003 sets out the disclosable overriding interests that you must tell us about.	11 Disclosable overriding interests ☐ This application relates to a registrable disposition and disclosable overriding interests affect the registered estate.

12	Confirmation of identity

When registering transfers, charges, leases and other dispositions of land, or giving effect to a discharge or release of a registered charge, Land Registry relies on the steps that conveyancers take, where appropriate, to verify the identity of their clients. These checks reduce the risk of property fraud.

Full details of the evidence of identity that is required can be found in Practice Guide 67 and in 'Completing the evidence of identity panels on forms AP1, FR1, and DS2' both of which can be found on the GOV.UK website.

Where a person was not represented by a conveyancer, Land Registry requires 'evidence of identity' in respect of that person, except where the first alternative in panel 13(2) applies.

'Evidence of identity' is evidence provided in accordance with any current direction made by the Chief Land Registrar under section 100(4) of the Land Registration Act 2002 for the purpose of confirming a person's identity.

If this application is to register a transfer, lease or charge, or to give effect to a discharge in Form DS1 or a release in Form DS3 complete one of the following

Place 'X' in the appropriate box.

Conveyancer is defined in rule 217A, Land Registration Rules 2003 and includes persons authorised under the Legal Services Act 2007 to provide reserved legal services relating to land registration and includes solicitors and licensed conveyancers.

☒ I am a conveyancer, and I have completed panel 13

☐ I am not a conveyancer, and I have completed panel 14

13	Where the application is sent to Land Registry by a conveyancer

(1) Details of conveyancer acting

If you are sending an application to register a transfer, lease or charge, for each party to each disposition that is to be registered state in the table below the details of the conveyancer (if any) who represented them.

Where a party is not represented by a conveyancer you must also complete (2) below.

Place 'X' in the box in the second column if the person or firm who is sending the application to HM Land Registry represented that party in the transaction. Otherwise complete the details in the third column. If the party is not represented insert 'none' in the third column.

A separate box is provided, or can be added, for each party, as required by panel 13(1). That includes separate boxes for attorneys and donors where appropriate.

Name of transferor, landlord, transferee, tenant, borrower or lender		Conveyancer's name, address and reference
Paul Thompson (Transferor)	☐	*Thompson & Thompson LLP of 27 High Street, Barnford, Westshire, EX82 7YK* *Reference: FAO Paul Thompson*
André Gomez (Transferee and Borrower)	☒	*Reference: 555933/DXC01*
Country Funding Building Society (Lender)	☒	*Reference: 555933/DXC01*

If you are sending an application to give effect to a discharge in Form DS1 or release in Form DS3 for each lender, state in the table below the details of the conveyancer (if any) who represented them.

Where a lender is not represented by a conveyancer you must also complete (2) below.

Place 'X' in the box in the second column if the person or firm who is sending the application to HM Land Registry represented that party in the transaction. Otherwise complete the details in the third column. If the party is not represented insert 'none' in the third column.

A separate box is provided, or can be added, for each party, as required by panel 13(1). That includes separate boxes for attorneys and donors where appropriate.

Name of lender		Conveyancer's name, address and reference
	☐	Reference:
	☐	Reference:

(2) Evidence of identity

Where any transferor, landlord, transferee, tenant, borrower or lender listed in (1) was not represented by a conveyancer

Place 'X' in the appropriate box(es).

☐ I confirm that I am satisfied that sufficient steps have been taken to verify the identity of

Insert the name of each unrepresented transferor, landlord, transferee, tenant, borrower or lender for whom you give this confirmation.

----

and that they are the registered proprietor or have the right to be registered as the registered proprietor

Evidence of identity is defined in panel 12. Full details of the evidence of identity that is required can be found in Practice Guide 67 available on the GOV.UK website.

☐ I enclose evidence of identity in respect of each unrepresented transferor, landlord, transferee, tenant, borrower or lender for whom I have not provided the confirmation above

14 Where the application is sent to Land Registry by someone who is not a conveyancer

(1) Details of conveyancer acting

If you are sending an application to register a transfer, lease or charge (ie a mortgage), for each party to each disposition that is to be registered, state in the table below the details of the conveyancer (if any) who represented them.

You must also complete (2) below.

If the party is not represented insert 'none' in the second column.

A separate box is provided, or can be added, for each party, as required by panel 14(1). That includes separate boxes for attorneys and donors where appropriate.

Name of transferor, landlord, transferee, tenant, borrower or lender	Conveyancer's name, address and reference
	Reference:

	Reference:
	Reference:
	Reference:
	Reference:

If you are sending an application to give effect to a discharge in Form DS1 or release in Form DS3, for each lender state in the table below the details of the conveyancer (if any) who represented them.

You must also complete (2) below.

If the party is not represented insert 'none' in the second column.

A separate box is provided, or can be added, for each party, as required by panel 14(1). That includes separate boxes for attorneys and donors where appropriate.

Name of lender	Conveyancer's name, address and reference
	Reference:
	Reference:

(2) Evidence of identity

Place 'X' in the appropriate box(es).

Evidence of identity is defined in panel 12. Full details of the evidence of identity that is required can be found in 'Completing the evidence of identity panels on forms AP1, FR1, and DS2' available on the GOV.UK website.

☐ for each applicant named in panel 6 is enclosed

☐ for each unrepresented transferor, landlord, transferee, tenant, borrower or lender listed in (1) is enclosed

If a conveyancer is acting for the applicant, that conveyancer must sign. If no conveyancer is acting, the applicant (and if the applicant is more than one person then each of them) must sign.	15 Signature of conveyancer: *David Cob Solicitors* Date: *8 December 2025*

WARNING
If you dishonestly enter information or make a statement that you know is, or might be, untrue or misleading, and intend by doing so to make a gain for yourself or another person, or to cause loss or the risk of loss to another person, you may commit the offence of fraud under section 1 of the Fraud Act 2006, the maximum penalty for which is 10 years' imprisonment or an unlimited fine, or both.

Failure to complete this form with proper care may result in a loss of protection under the Land Registration Act 2002 if, as a result, a mistake is made in the register.

Under section 66 of the Land Registration Act 2002 most documents (including this form) kept by the registrar relating to an application to the registrar or referred to in the register are open to public inspection and copying. If you believe a document contains prejudicial information, you may apply for that part of the document to be made exempt using Form EX1, under rule 136 of the Land Registration Rules 2003.

HM Land Registry
Restriction – consent or certificate

RXC

IMPORTANT – PLEASE READ

- **Use Form RXC as part of an application to register a disposition. It is not a standalone application form.**
- **You can use the form in all situations where a restriction on the register requires a consent or a certificate to be provided – this includes a certificate to comply with a Form LL restriction.**
- **For guidance as to how to use the form in respect of Form LL restrictions, please see Practice Guide 19.**
- **You cannot use a single RXC form to provide consents or certificates in respect of multiple titles.**

Any parts of the form that are not typed should be completed in black ink and in block capitals.

If you need more room than is provided for in a panel, and your software allows, you can expand any panel in the form. Alternatively use continuation sheet CS and attach it to this form.

HM Land Registry is unable to give legal advice, but you can find guidance on HM Land Registry applications (including our practice guides for conveyancers) at www.gov.uk/land-registry. You may find it useful to refer to Practice Guide 19, which addresses compliance with restrictions.

For information on how HM Land Registry processes your personal information, see our Personal Information Charter.

Insert HM Land Registry title number and the address of the property affected by the restriction.

1 Title number:

EG132465

Property:

The Old Bakery, Cob Lane, Torton, Westshire, EX79 1AP

Each restriction will usually start with a date in brackets. This is the date the restriction was added to the register. Each restriction will also be numbered. Insert the date shown in brackets, if one appears, and the entry number.

An official copy of the register contains an edition date. Insert this date or, if you access the register via Register View in My Portal, insert the date you are given as the date of the register showing the entries subsisting.

2 The restriction:

(i) was registered on 12.8.1994

and

(ii) is at entry number 2 in the

☒ B (Proprietorship) Register ☐ C (Charges) Register

on *(insert register edition date OR date shown in 'Register View')*

OR *(where the restriction is not yet registered)*

☐ Is contained in the following document submitted for registration:

Document:

Date:

Place 'X' in the box(es) that apply. You must complete this panel fully and accurately with the details of the individual(s) signing panel 4 or 5.

See rule 217A Land Registration Rules 2003 for the definition of conveyancer.

An individual is "personally named" when their own name (as opposed to, for example, their employer's name) appears in the restriction.

"Acting on behalf of someone else" includes a conveyancer representing a restrictioner, an employee or agent of a corporation, or an attorney of an individual or corporation.

You will need to provide further evidence of your authority to provide the consent or certificate with this form if this is not otherwise clear.

Examples of appropriate evidence may include a power of attorney or grant of probate.

An employee of a conveyancer can only give a certificate for a form LL restriction if the employee is an individually regulated conveyancer. Please see Practice Guide 19.

Only certain individuals can give a consent or certificate on behalf of a corporation – see rule 91B of the Land Registration Rules 2003.

Where a Right to Manage Company has been appointed please see Practice Guide 27.

If one or more individuals are the registered proprietors of the title referred to in the restriction, insert "Registered Proprietor(s) of title..." under "Status".

If the registered proprietor of the title is a company, provide details of the position of the individual(s) within the company who are giving the consent or certificate under "Status".

If a consent or certificate is given by an employee or agent of a company, please provide the postal address of the company or agent and the work e-mail address of the person giving the consent or certificate under "Address".

3

*If you are **personally named** in the restriction, tick the first box in Part A. There is no need to complete Part B.*

*If your **status is described in the restriction**, but you are not personally named (for example the restriction requires a consent or certificate from 'a conveyancer' or 'the registered proprietor' of a specific title without naming them), tick the first box in part A and complete part B.*

*If you are acting **on behalf** of someone else (for example as their conveyancer, or as an employee or agent) tick the second box in Part A, select **one** of the three options and complete Part B.*

Part A - Choose one of the following two statements:

EITHER

☒ I confirm that I am/we are described in the restriction as being able to give the consent or certificate.

OR

☐ I can consent or give the required certificate on behalf of

(insert details) because:

*Choose **one** of the following three options:*

☐ I am an individually regulated conveyancer acting on their behalf
I am signing this form in my own name
I have provided my details in Part B.

☐ I am employed by the regulated conveyancer acting on their behalf
I am signing this form and acting on behalf of my employer
I have provided my details in Part B.

Select the option below if you are an agent, attorney or an employee of a corporation.

☐ My status (described in Part B), and/or the additional evidence I have lodged, establishes that I am duly authorised to sign this form on their behalf in my own name.

Part B – Provide details of the individual signing the consent or certificate:

Name: David Cob

Status: Solicitor
(e.g. authorised employee / officer of a company, solicitor, paralegal, agent, attorney etc.)

Address: David Cob Solicitors LLP, 18 Woodlands Road, Torton, Westshire, EX79 2FT

		Roll Number and Approved Regulator details *(if applicable)*: 55678 SRA **You must now complete <u>either:</u>** • **panel 4 if the restriction requires a <u>consent</u>; or** • **panel 5 if the restriction requires a <u>certificate</u>**
Insert details of all dispositions the consent relates to which accompany this application – for example, transfer, lease, grant or release of easements, legal charge or mortgage. You may wish to specify the date of the disposition and the parties, for example "transfer dated [insert] made between [insert]". If you are providing a bulk consent in respect of a developing estate, you may wish to identify the specific plot numbers the consent applies to, for example "Transfer of plots 1-7 Bluebell Green." Continuation sheet CS can be used if more than two persons are providing the consent.	4	I/We **consent** to the following disposition(s) and to their registration: 1. 2. 3. **Signature:** ____________________ *(of individual or firm, as applicable)* **Name of individual signing:** **Date:** **Signature:** ____________________ *(of individual or firm, as applicable)* **Name of individual signing:** **Date:**

Insert details of all dispositions the certificate relates to which accompany this application – for example, transfer, lease, grant or release of easements, legal charge or mortgage. You may wish to specify the date of the disposition and the parties, for example "transfer dated [insert] made between [insert]".

If you are providing a bulk certificate in respect of a developing estate, you may wish to identify the specific plot numbers the certificate applies to, for example "Transfer of plots 1-7 Bluebell Green."

If you are sending form RXC to a third party to sign, you may prefer to select option C and set out the wording of the certificate required in full. The certificate must never be qualified.

When providing a certificate OE1 or OE2 to comply with a restriction entered under the provisions of Schedule 4A of the Land Registration Act 2002, you must select Option C and insert the full wording of the certificate.

If the wording of the certificate allows you to certify that specific provisions have been complied with or that they do not apply to a particular disposition, you do not have to specify which alternative applies.

The details given as to the individual signing panel 5 must match those given in part B of panel 3.

A certificate to comply with a Form LL restriction must be signed in wet ink in the name of an individual conveyancer.

Please see Practice Guide 19 for further information on complying with Form LL restrictions.

Continuation sheet CS can be used if more than two persons are providing the certificate.

5 This certificate relates to the following disposition(s):

1. Transfer dated 4 December 2025 made between (1) Paul Thompson and (2) André Gomez

*Select **either** Option A, Option B or Option C below and add your signature where indicated to provide the certificate required by the restriction.*

A ☒ I/we have read the terms of the restriction identified in panel 2 of this form. By selecting this Option A and signing this form, I am/ we are providing the certificate required by that restriction. **(Do not use this option for a Form LL restriction).**

OR – ***if you are a conveyancer giving a certificate to comply with a Form LL restriction***

B ☐ I certify that I am satisfied that the person who executed the document submitted for registration as disponor is the same person as the proprietor **(individual conveyancer to sign below IN WET INK).**

OR – ***choose the following option if you prefer to set out the terms of the certificate required by the restriction.***

C ☐ The certificate that I/we give, as required by the terms of the restriction is as follows:

Signature: *David Cob Solicitors*
(*of individual or firm, as applicable*)

Name of individual signing: David Cob

Date: 8 December 2025

WARNING
If you dishonestly enter information or make a statement that you know is, or might be, untrue or misleading, and intend by doing so to make a gain for yourself or another person, or to cause loss or the risk of loss to another person, you may commit the offence of fraud under section 1 of the Fraud Act 2006, the maximum penalty for which is 10 years' imprisonment or an unlimited fine, or both.

Failure to complete this form with proper care may result in a loss of protection under the Land Registration Act 2002 if, as a result, a mistake is made in the register.

Under section 66 of the Land Registration Act 2002 most documents (including this form) kept by the registrar relating to an application to the registrar or referred to in the register are open to public inspection and copying. If you believe a document contains prejudicial information, you may apply for that part of the document to be made exempt using Form EX1, under rule 136 of the Land Registration Rules 2003.

Land Registry

Official copy of register of title

Title number EG132465

Edition date 01.01.2025

- This official copy shows the entries in the register of title on 4 January 2026 at 11:36:26.
- This date must be quoted as the "search from date" in any official search application based on this copy.
- The date at the beginning of an entry is the date on which the entry was made in the register.
- Issued on 4 January 2026.
- Under s.67 of the Land Registration Act 2002, this copy is admissible in evidence to the same extent as the original.
- For information about the register of title see Land Registry website www.landregistry.gov.uk or Land Registry Public Guide 1 – *A guide to the information we keep and how you can obtain it.*

A: Property register

This register describes the land and estate comprised in the title

Westshire : Torton

1. (7.11.1991) The Freehold land shown edged with thick black on the plan of the above Title filed at the Registry and being The Old Bakery, Cob Lane, Torton, Westshire, EX79 1AP.

B: Proprietorship register

This register specifies the class of title and identifies the owner. It contains any entries that affect the right of disposal.

Title absolute

1. (04.01.2026) Proprietor(s): André Gomez of The Old Bakery, Cob Lane, Torton, EX79 1AP.

2. (12.08.1994) Restriction: no disposition of the registered estate by the proprietor of the registered estate is to be registered without a certificate signed by a conveyancer that the provisions of clause 11.1 of the Transfer dated 1 November 1991 made between (1) Joanne Bates and (2) Alan Wright have been complied with.

3. (04.01.2026) Restriction: except under an order of the Registrar no disposition by the proprietor of the land is to be registered without the consent of the proprietor of the charge dated 4 December 2025 in favour of Country Funding Building Society referred to in the Charges Register.

C: Charges register

This register contains any charges and other matters that affect the land.

1. (07.11.1991) A Conveyance of the land in this title dated 27 January 1929 made between (1) Richard Edward Jones (Vendor) and (2) Peter John Bates and Marie Evelyn Bates (Purchaser) contains rights and covenants but neither the original nor a certified copy was produced on first registration.

2. (07.11.1991) A transfer of the land in this title dated 1 November 1991 made between (1) Joanne Bates (Vendor) and (2) Alan Wright (Purchaser) contains the following covenants:

   "11.1 The Purchaser with the intent to bind (so far as practicable) the property hereby conveyed (the Property) and to benefit and protect the retained land of the Vendor (the Retained Land) hereby covenants with the Vendor that he and his successors in title will at all times observe and perform the stipulations and conditions set out in Schedule 1.

   SCHEDULE 1

   1. The Purchaser shall, upon demand by the Vendor or his successors in title, contribute financially towards the maintenance of any boundary features along the boundary lines marked 'T' on the plan, to the maximum value of 25 per cent per annum of all costs reasonably incurred by the Vendor or his successors in title.
   2. The Purchaser will not make any disposal of the whole or any part of the Property without first procuring that the disponee enters into a Deed of Covenant with, and supplies the same to, the owner or owners from time to time of the Retained Land or any part of it.
   3. The Purchaser consents to the entry of the following restriction against the Purchaser's title to the Property at HM Land Registry following the registration of this transfer and shall provide the Transferor with all necessary assistance and documentation to permit entry of the restriction:

      "No disposition of the registered estate by the proprietor of the registered estate is to be registered without a certificate signed by a conveyancer that the provisions of clause 11.1 of the Transfer dated 1 November 1991 made between (1) Joanne Bates and (2) Alan Wright have been complied with."

3. (04.01.26) REGISTERED CHARGE dated 4 December 2025.

4. (04.01.26) Proprietor: Country Funding Building Society (Co. Regn. No. 7774590) of Finance House, Torton, Westshire, EX79 2AB.

End of register

Land Registry
Official copy of
Title plan

Title number EG132465
Ordnance Survey map reference **EG 1234 NN**
Scale **1:2500**
Administrative area **Westshire: Torton**

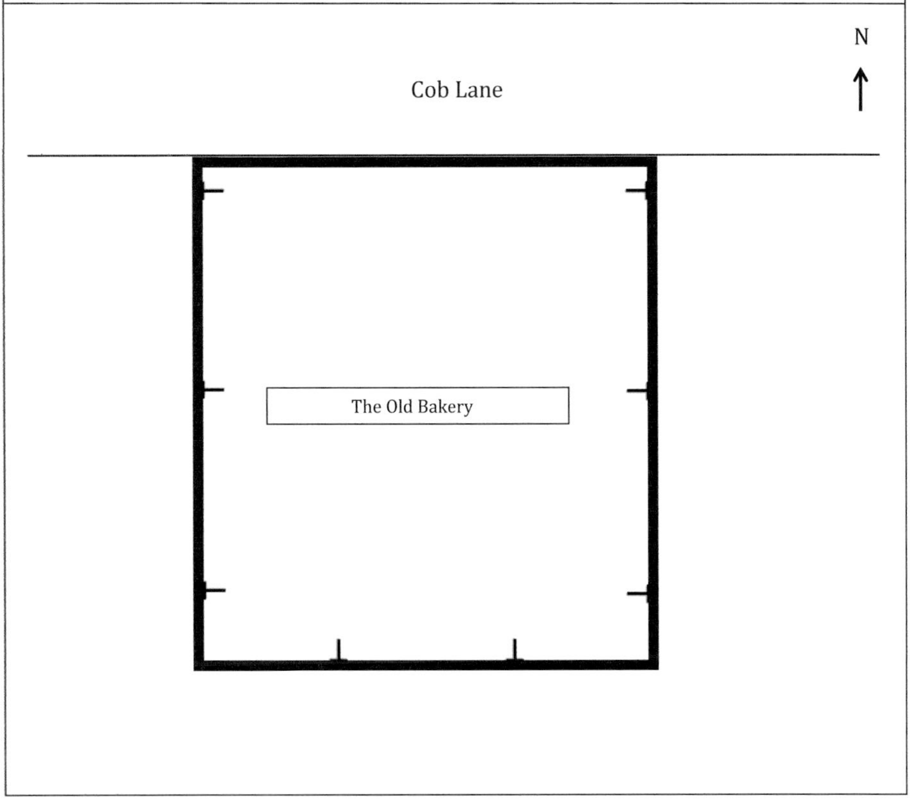

This official copy issued on 4 January 2026 shows the state of this title plan on 4 January 2026 at 11:36:26
It is admissible in evidence to the same extent as the original (s. 67 Land Registration Act 2002).
This title plan shows the general position, not the exact line, of the boundaries. It may be subject to distortions in scale.
Measurements scaled from this plan may not match measurements between the same points on the ground.
See Land Registry Public Guide 19 – Title Plans and Boundaries.

Appendix 2: Style&Go Ltd's purchase of the Salon

Accompanying documents

Document 1

Heads of terms – 17 High Street, Barnford	
Seller	Mrs Neeta Mukhtar
Seller's solicitor	Chantry Richardson solicitors, 17 The Quay, Barnford, EX81 9JP
Buyer	Style&Go Ltd registered with company number 00127976 c/o Blackhurst&Sons LLP of 22 High Street, Barnford, Westshire, EX82 7YK
Buyer's solicitor	Blackhurst & Sons LLP of 22 High Street, Barnford, Westshire, EX82 7YK
Property	Freehold property: 17 High Street, Barnford, Westshire, EX82 7YK registered with title number EG576798
Price	£525,000
Deposit	£52,500
Finance	Cash: £525,000
Proposed use	Hair salon

Land Registry

Official copy of register of title

Title number EG576798

Edition date 5.02.2025

- This official copy shows the entries in the register of title on 6 January 2026 at 15:03:27.
- This date must be quoted as the "search from date" in any official search application based on this copy.
- The date at the beginning of an entry is the date on which the entry was made in the register.
- Issued on 6 January 2026.
- Under s.67 of the Land Registration Act 2002, this copy is admissible in evidence to the same extent as the original.
- For information about the register of title see Land Registry website www.landregistry.gov.uk or Land Registry Public Guide 1 – *A guide to the information we keep and how you can obtain it.*

A: Property register

This register describes the land and estate comprised in the title

Westshire : Barnford

1. (17.07.1993) The Freehold land shown edged with thick black on the plan of the above Title filed at the Registry and being 17 High Street, Barnford, Westshire, EX82 7YK.

B: Proprietorship register

This register specifies the class of title and identifies the owner. It contains any entries that affect the right of disposal.

Title absolute

1. (17.07.1993) Proprietor(s): Ansar Mukhtar and Neeta Mukhtar of 17 High Street, Barnford, Westshire, EX82 7YK.

2. (17.07.1993) Restriction: no disposition by a sole proprietor of the registered estate (except a trust corporation) under which capital money arises is to be registered unless authorised by an order of the court.

3. (17.07.1993) Restriction: Except under an order of the Registrar no disposition by the proprietor of the land is to be registered without the consent of the proprietor of the charge dated 10 July 1993 in favour of Secure Trust Bank referred to in the Charges Register.

4. (17.07.1993) The transfer to the proprietor contains a covenant to observe and perform the covenants referred to at entry C2 the Charges Register and of indemnity in respect thereof.

C: Charges register

This register contains any charges and other matters that affect the land.

1. (17.07.1993) A conveyance of the land in this title dated 4 March 1959 made between (1) Vince Francis Moon (Vendor) and (2) Norman Jones (Purchaser) the land in this title is subject the following rights in favour of 19 High Street:

   "A right of way to pass and repass day or night by foot only over the land coloured brown".

   *Note: the land coloured brown is shown hatched grey on the filed plan.

2. (17.07.1993) A conveyance of the land in this title dated 4 March 1959 made between (1) Vince Francis Moon (Vendor) and (2) Norman Jones (Purchaser) contains the following covenant:

   "And the Purchaser for itself and its assigns with the intent to bind the Property hereby covenants with the Vendor his heirs executors administrators and assigns to keep in good repair the land coloured brown in order that it remains safely passable on foot."

   *Note: the land coloured brown is shown hatched grey on the filed plan

3. (17.07.1993) A conveyance of the land in this title dated 10 July 1993 made between (1) Charles Bainbridge (Vendor) and (2) Ansar Mukhtar and Anita Mukhtar (Purchaser) contains the following covenant:

   "11.1 And the Purchaser for itself and its assigns with the intent to bind the Property hereby covenants with the Vendor his heirs executors administrators and assigns not to build any structure on the Property."

4. (17.07.1993) REGISTERED CHARGE dated 10 July 1993.

5. (17.07.1993) Proprietor: Secure Trust Bank (Co. Regn. No. 747443) of 14 King Edward Street, Barnford, EX83 4PJ.

End of register

Land Registry Official copy of Title plan

Title number **EG576798**
Ordnance Survey map reference **EG 5432 SS**
Scale **1:2500**
Administrative area **Westshire : Barnford**

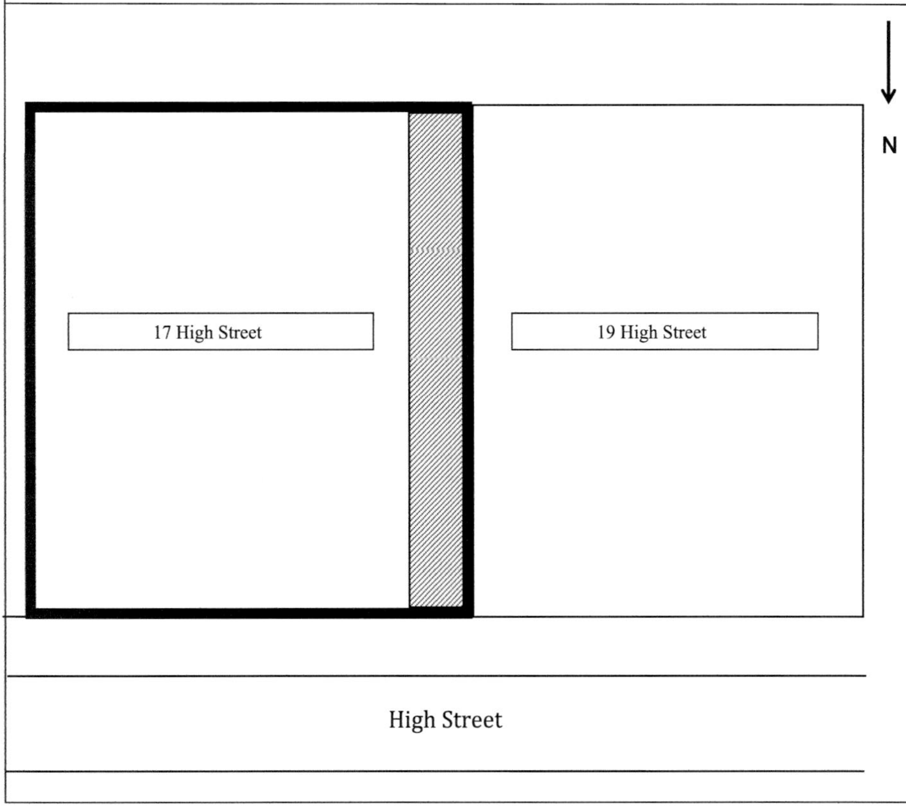

This official copy issued on 6 January 2026 shows the state of this title plan on 6 January 2026 at 15:03:27.
It is admissible in evidence to the same extent as the original (s. 67 Land Registration Act 2002).
This title plan shows the general position, not the exact line, of the boundaries. It may be subject to distortions in scale.
Measurements scaled from this plan may not match measurements between the same points on the ground.
See Land Registry Public Guide 19 – Title Plans and Boundaries.

Document 3

Official certificate of the result of search of the index map

Land Registry
Land Registration Rules 2003

SIMR

Certificate Date: 6 January 2026
Certificate Time: 16:03:27
Certificate Ref: FFG/EXH02

Property	17 HIGH STREET, BARNFORD, WESTSHIRE, EX82 7YK

Result

The index map has been searched in respect of the Property with the following result:

Plan reference	Title No.	Registered Estate or Caution	Notes
Edged with thick black line	EG576798	Freehold	

No registered estate, caution against first registration, application for first registration or application for a caution against first registration is shown on the index map in relation to the remainder of the property.

******

The plan attached to this result is prepared for the sole purpose of showing the area in respect of which an official search has been made. The information has been taken from the index map. It is illustrative only and does not define the extent of the land in any individual title. For information about the general boundaries of a title please refer to the individual register and title plan.

******

Verbal descriptions of registered relating franchises and registered manors, and of pending applications and cautions against first registrations in respect of relating franchises, are kept in the index of relating franchises and manors. The application form for a search of the index is form SIF.

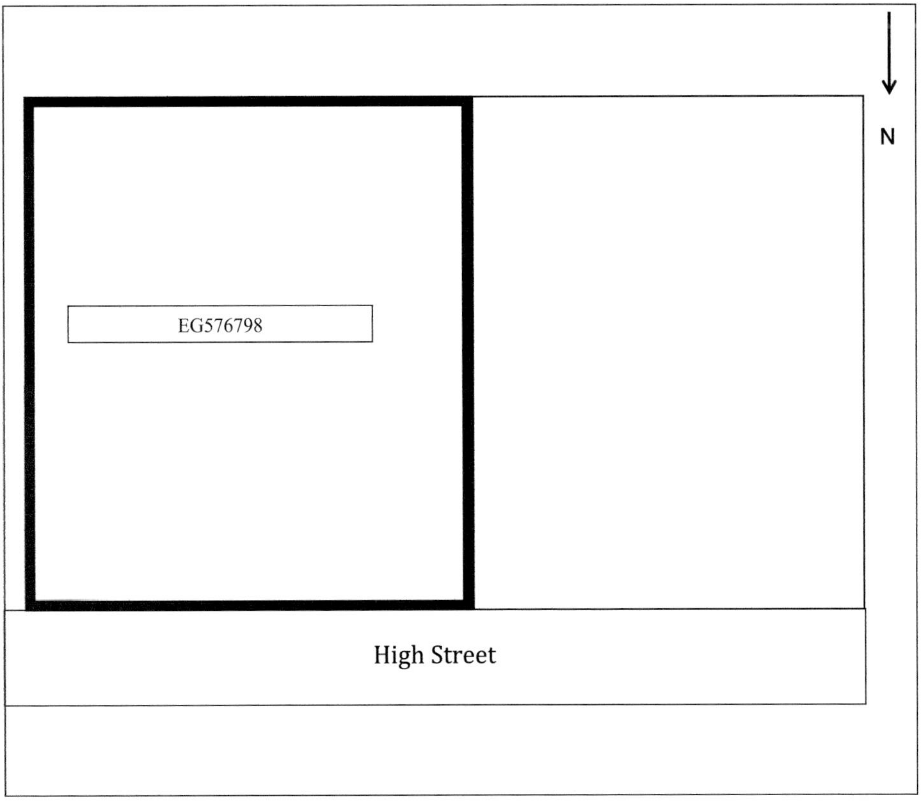
N
EG576798
High Street

Document 4

Westshire District Council Offices
Council House,
Exton,
Westshire
(DX 765567 Exton 7)

Westshire
District Council

REGISTER OF LOCAL LAND CHARGES
OFFICIAL CERTIFICATE OF SEARCH

Search Reference: HHG/EXH02

Date: 6 January 2026

Applicant: Blackhurst & Sons LLP

Official search required in all parts of the Register of Local Land Charges for subsisting registrations against the land described and the plan submitted.

Land: 17 High Street, Barnford, Westshire, EX82 7YK

It is hereby certified that the search requested above reveals 2 registrations described in the Schedule(s) hereto up to and including the date of this certificate.

LLC1: Search Reference HHG/EXH02 Date: 6 January 2026

Westshire District Council Register of Local Land Charges Schedule to Official Certificate of Search			
Part 3: Planning Charges			
Description of charge (including reference to appropriate statutory provision)	**Originating Authority**	**Place where relevant documents may be inspected**	**Date of Registration**
PP/UC/774/91 Permission for change of use from Class A1 to Class C3(a)	Westshire District Council	Council House, Exton, Westshire	08/08/1991
PP/W/774/95 Conditional permission for erection of single storey rear extension	Westshire District Council	Council House, Exton, Westshire	17/09/1995

Document 5

Westshire District Council Offices
Council House,
Exton,
Westshire
(DX 765567 Exton 7)

Westshire District Council

CON29 ENQUIRIES OF LOCAL AUTHORITY
(2016)

Applicant: Blackhurst & Sons LLP

Search Reference: BBC/EXH02

Date: 6 January 2026

Property: 17 High Street, Barnford, Westshire, EX82 7KY

I refer to your Standard Enquiries relating to the above property. These replies relate to that property as shown on the location plan where supplied. The replies are given subject to the Notes to the Standard Enquiries.

All correspondence relating to these answers should quote the official Search Reference.

Standard Enquiries of Local Authority

PLANNING AND BUILDING REGULATIONS
1.1. Planning and building decisions and pending applications
Which of the following relating to the property have been granted, issued or refused or (where applicable) are the subject of pending applications or agreements?
(a) a planning permission

1.1.(a) Reference: PP/UC/774/91
Description: Change of use from Class A1 to Class C3(a)
Application date: 20/7/1991
Decision: GRANTED on 8/8/1991

1.1.(a) Reference: PP/W/774/95
Description: Erection of single storey rear extension
Application date: 1/9/1995
Decision: GRANTED SUBJECT TO CONDITIONS on 17/9/1995

[...]

(j) building regulations approval
none

(k) a building regulation completion certificate
none

[...]

Informatives:

(1) Copy documents available from Planning and Building Control Services, Westshire District Council.

(2) This reply does not cover other properties in the vicinity of the property.

(3) As from 1 April 2002 the installation of a replacement window, rooflight or roof window or specified type of glazed door must either have building regulation approval or be carried out and certified by a person who is registered under the Fenestration Self-Assessment Scheme by the Glass and Glazing Federation. The owner or occupier of the property should be asked to produce any such certificate.

ROADS AND PUBLIC RIGHTS OF WAY
Roadways, footways and footpaths
2.1 Which of the roads, footways and footpaths named in the application for this search (via boxes B and C) are:
(a) highways maintainable at public expense
2.1.(a) High Street

(b) subject to adoption and supported by a bond or bond waiver
2.1.(b) None

(c) to be made up by a local authority who will reclaim the cost from the frontagers
2.1.(c) None

(d) to be adopted by a local authority without reclaiming the cost from the frontagers
2.1.(d) None

Informative: If a road, footway or footpath is not a highway, there may be no right to use it and the local authority cannot express an opinion without seeing the title plan and carrying out a site inspection.

Public rights of way
2.2 Is any public right of way which abuts on, or crosses, the property shown in a definitive map or revised definitive map?
2.2. No

[...]

2.5 If so, please attach a plan showing the approximate route.
2.5. Not applicable

Informative: A definitive map for Westshire District Council has now been published. However, a survey of all paths has not been completed and whilst this does not preclude the existence of unrecorded rights of way, the local authority is unaware of any claimed rights of way existing over the search site.

OTHER MATTERS:
Apart from matters entered on the registers of local land charges, do any of the following matters apply to the property? If so, how can copies of relevant documents be obtained?

Note: Matters entered onto the Local Land Charges Register, or visible by property/site inspection, will not be referred to (where relevant) in answer to the enquiries 3.1 to 3.15 below.

Informative: In some circumstances, road closures can be obtained by third parties from magistrate's courts, or can be made by the Secretary of State for Transport without involving the local authority. This enquiry is designed to reveal matters that are yet to be implemented and could not therefore be ascertained by a visual inspection. Schemes that have been, or are currently being, implemented will not be referred to in answer to this enquiry.

[...]

3.5. Nearby railway schemes
(a) Is the property (or will it be) within 200 metres of the centre line of a proposed railway, tramway, light railway or monorail?
3.5.(a) Yes – proposed railway scheme at Barnford Central. Please see details at westshirerailwayredevelopment.co.uk.

[...]

3.6 Traffic schemes
Has a local authority approved but not yet implemented any of the following for the roads, footways and footpaths which are named in Boxes B and C and are within 200 metres of the boundaries of the property?

[...]

(e) pedestrianisation
3.6(e) Yes – Main Street, which is within 200 metres of the boundaries of the property, is to be pedestrianised.

[...]

3.8. Contravention of building regulations
Has a local authority authorised in relation to the property any proceedings for the contravention of any provision contained in building regulations?
3.8. No

3.9. Notices, orders, directions and proceedings under Planning Acts
Do any of the following subsist in relation to the property, or has a local authority decided to issue, serve, make or commence any of the following?
(a) an enforcement notice
3.9.(a) No

(b) a stop notice
3.9.(b) No

...

(d) a breach of condition notice
3.9.(d) No

(e) a planning contravention notice
3.9.(e) No

[...]

(j) a direction restricting permitted development
3.9.(j) No

[...]

3.11. Conservation area
Do the following apply in relation to the property?
(a) the making of the area a conservation area before 31 August 1974
3.11.(a) No

(b) an unimplemented resolution to designate the area a Conservation Area
3.11.(b) No

[...]
3.13. Contaminated land
Do any of the following apply (including any relating to land adjacent to or adjoining the property which has been identified as contaminated land because it is in such a condition that harm or pollution of controlled waters might be caused on the property)?
(a) a contaminated land notice
3.13.(a) No

(b) in relation to a register maintained under section 78R of the Environmental Protection Act 1990

(i) a decision to make an entry
3.13.(b)(i) No

(ii) an entry
3.13.(b)(ii) No

(c) consultation with the owner or occupier of the property conducted under section 78G(3) of the Environmental Protection Act 1990 before the service of a remediation notice
3.13.(c) No

Informative: A negative reply does not imply that the property or any adjoining or adjacent land is free from contamination or from the risk of it and the reply may not disclose steps taken by another local authority in whose area adjacent or adjoining land is situated.

[...]

Document 6

Highways Division
Westshire District Council Offices
Council House,
Exton,
Westshire
(DX 765567 Exton 7)

Westshire
District Council

Date 6 January 2026

Dear Sirs

17 High Street and land adjoining Sheep Street, Barnford, Westshire, EX82 7YK

Please find below the plan; showing by black shading the extent of the publicly maintainable highway in the immediate vicinity of the property, as far as can be ascertained from existing records.

If you have any further queries please do not hesitate to contact us.

Yours faithfully

Highway Records Manager

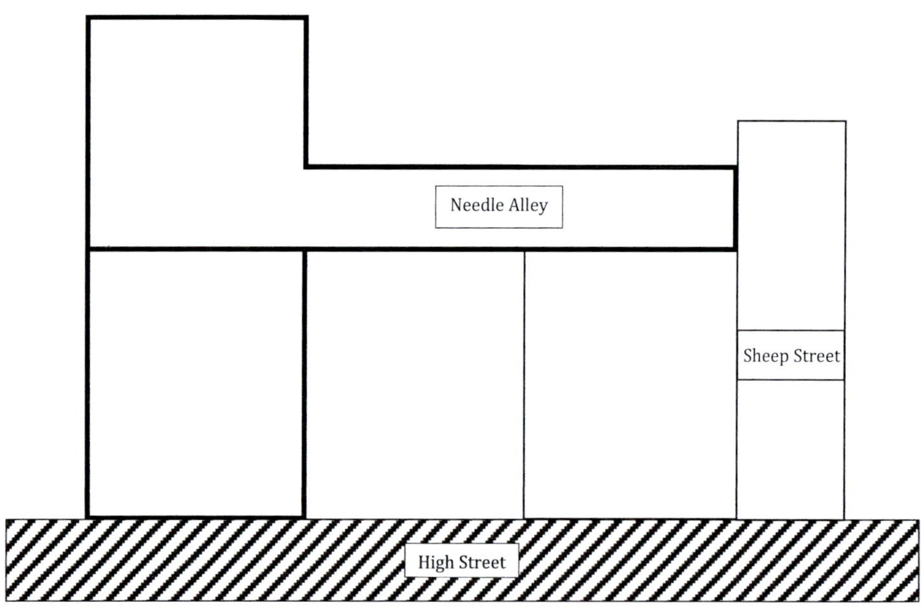

WESTSHIRE WATER

Drainage and Water search

Date: 6 January 2026

Property: 17, High Street, Barnford, Westshire, EX82 7YK

Results:

Mains water: connected

Foul water: connected

Surface water sewer: connected

Sewer pipe within boundary: no

Water pipe within boundary: no

Document 8

WESTSHIRE ENVIRO-CHECK

Date: 6 January 2026

Type of report: Homebuyers

Property: 17 High Street and land adjoining Sheep Street, Barnford, Westshire, EX82 7YK

RESULTS:

Professional opinion: PASS

Environmental search results:

Contaminated Land: passed
No significant concerns have been identified as a result of the contaminated land searches.

Flood risk: low
The village of Barnford suffered flooding in 1994, but the property was unaffected and the property's overall risk assessment for river, coastal, surface water and groundwater flooding is low.

Ground stability: passed
No significant concerns have been identified as a result of the ground stability searches. No action required.

Radon: passed
Local levels of radon are considered normal.

Westshire Enviro-check

CHANCEL REPAIR SEARCH

Report details

Report number: CC/994/EXH02

Issue date: 6 January 2026

Address: 17 High Street and land adjoining Sheep Street, Barnford, Westshire, EX82 7YK

Result

The above address is not located within the historical boundary of a tithe district within a parish which continues to have a potential chancel repair liability based upon historical parish data and the relevant inland Revenue Indices held by The National Archives.

Document 10

www.lawsociety.org.uk

The Law Society

Law Society Property Information Form (4th edition 2020 – second revision)

Address of the property	17 High Street, Barnford, Westshire Postcode E X 8 2 7 Y K
Full names of the seller	Mrs Neeta Mukhtar
Seller's solicitor Name of solicitor's firm	Chantry R'son
Address	17 The Quay Barnford EX81 9JP
Email	Enquiries@CR.co
Reference number	CR5445

About this form

This form is completed by the seller to supply the detailed information and documents which may be relied upon for the conveyancing process.

Definitions

- 'Seller' means all sellers together where the property is owned by more than one person.
- 'Buyer' means all buyers together where the property is being bought by more than one person.
- 'Property' includes all buildings and land within its boundaries.

Instructions to the seller

- The answers should be prepared by the person or persons who are named as owner on the deeds or Land Registry title or by the owner's legal representative(s) if selling under a power of attorney or grant of probate or representation. If there is more than one seller, you should prepare the answers together or, if only one seller prepares the form, the other(s) should check the answers given and all sellers should sign the form.
- If you do not know the answer to any question, you must say so. If you are unsure of the meaning of any questions or answers, please ask your solicitor. Completing this form is not mandatory, but omissions or delay in providing some information may delay the sale.
- If you later become aware of any information which would alter any replies you have given, you must inform your solicitor immediately. This is as important as giving the right answers in the first place. Do not change any arrangements concerning the property with anyone (such as a tenant or neighbour) without first consulting your solicitor.
- It is very important that your answers are accurate. If you give incorrect or incomplete information to the buyer (on this form or otherwise in writing or in conversation, whether through your estate agent or solicitor or directly to the buyer), the buyer may make a claim for compensation from you or refuse to complete the purchase.
- You should answer the questions based upon information known to you (or, in the case of legal representatives, you or the owner). You are not expected to have expert knowledge of legal or technical matters, or matters that occurred prior to your ownership of the property.
- Please give your solicitor any letters, agreements or other papers which help answer the questions. If you are aware of any which you are not supplying with the answers, tell your solicitor. If you do not have any documentation you may need to obtain copies at your own expense. Also pass to your solicitor any notices you have received concerning the property and any which arrive at any time before completion of the sale.

Instructions to the buyer

- If the seller gives you, separately from this form, any information concerning the property (in writing or in conversation, whether through an estate agent or solicitor or directly to you) on which you wish to rely when buying the property, you should tell your solicitor.
- You are entitled to rely on the replies given to enquiries but in relation to the physical condition of the property, the replies should not be treated as a substitute for undertaking your own survey or making your own independent enquiries, which you are recommended to do.
- The seller is only obliged to give answers based on their own information. They may not have knowledge of legal or technical matters. You should not expect the seller to have knowledge of, or give information about, matters prior to their ownership of the property.

1. Boundaries

If the property is leasehold this section, or parts of it, may not apply.

1.1 Looking towards the property from the road, who owns or accepts responsibility to maintain or repair the boundary features:

(a) on the left?	☐ Seller ☐ Shared	☐ Neighbour ☑ Not known
(b) on the right?	☐ Seller ☐ Shared	☐ Neighbour ☑ Not known
(c) at the rear?	☐ Seller ☐ Shared	☐ Neighbour ☑ Not known
(d) at the front?	☐ Seller ☐ Shared	☐ Neighbour ☑ Not known

1.2 If the boundaries are irregular please indicate ownership by written description or by reference to a plan:

1.3 Is the seller aware of any boundary feature having been moved in the last 10 years or during the seller's period of ownership if longer? If Yes, please give details:

☐ Yes ☑ No

1.4 During the seller's ownership, has any adjacent land or property been purchased by the seller? If Yes, please give details:

☐ Yes ☑ No

1.5 **Does any part of the property or any building on the property overhang, or project under, the boundary of the neighbouring property or road, for example cellars under the pavement, overhanging eaves or covered walkways? If Yes, please give details:**

☐ Yes ☑ No

1.6 **Has any notice been received under the Party Wall etc. Act 1996 in respect of any shared/party boundaries? If Yes, please supply a copy, and give details of any works carried out or agreed:**

☐ Yes ☑ No
☐ Enclosed ☐ To follow

2. Disputes and complaints

2.1 **Have there been any disputes or complaints regarding this property or a property nearby? If Yes, please give details:**

☐ Yes ☑ No

2.2 **Is the seller aware of anything which might lead to a dispute about the property or a property nearby? If Yes, please give details:**

☐ Yes ☑ No

3. Notices and proposals

3.1 **Have any notices or correspondence been received or sent (e.g. from or to a neighbour, council or government department), or any negotiations or discussions taken place, which affect the property or a property nearby? If Yes, please give details:**

☐ Yes ☑ No

3.2 Is the seller aware of any proposals to develop property or land nearby, or of any proposals to make alterations to buildings nearby? If Yes, please give details:

☐ Yes ☑ No

4. Alterations, planning and building control

Note to seller: All relevant approvals and supporting paperwork referred to in section 4 of this form, such as listed building consents, planning permissions, Building Regulations consents and completion certificates should be provided. If the seller has had works carried out the seller should produce the documentation authorising this. Copies may be obtained from the relevant local authority website. Competent Persons Certificates may be obtained from the contractor or the scheme provider (e.g. FENSA or Gas Safe Register). Further information about Competent Persons Certificates can be found at: **https://www.gov.uk/guidance/competent-person-scheme-current-schemes-and-how-schemes-are-authorised**

Note to buyer: If any alterations or improvements have been made since the property was last valued for council tax, the sale of the property may trigger a revaluation. This may mean that following completion of the sale, the property will be put into a higher council tax band. Further information about council tax valuation can be found at:
http://www.gov.uk/government/organisations/valuation-office-agency

4.1 Have any of the following changes been made to the whole or any part of the property (including the garden)?

(a) Building works (e.g. extension, loft or garage conversion, removal of internal walls). If Yes, please give details including dates of all work undertaken:

☑ Yes ☐ No

Ground floor extension completed in 1996

(b) Change of use (e.g. from an office to a residence)

☑ Yes ☐ No
1991 Year

(c) Installation of replacement windows, roof windows, roof lights, glazed doors since 1 April 2002

☐ Yes ☑ No
Year

(d) Addition of a conservatory

☐ Yes ☑ No
Year

4.2 If Yes to any of the questions in 4.1 and if the work was undertaken during the seller's ownership of the property:

(a) please supply copies of the planning permissions, Building Regulations approvals and Completion Certificates, OR:

(b) if none were required, please explain why these were not required – e.g. permitted development rights applied or the work was exempt from Building Regulations:

Planning permission for extension and change of use enclosed.

Further information about permitted development can be found at:
https://www.planningportal.co.uk/info/200126/applications

4.3 Are any of the works disclosed in 4.1 above unfinished? If Yes, please give details:

☐ Yes ☑ No

4.4 Is the seller aware of any breaches of planning permission conditions or Building Regulations consent conditions, unfinished work or work that does not have all necessary consents? If Yes, please give details:

☑ Yes ☐ No

Extension was not completed in accordance with planning permission condition re window style, but this cannot be enforced as the deadline for doing so has passed.

4.5 Are there any planning or building control issues to resolve? If Yes, please give details:

☑ Yes ☐ No

Missing building regulations approval or certificate in respect of extension.

4.6 Have solar panels been installed?

☐ Yes ☑ No

If Yes:

(a) In what year were the solar panels installed? ☐ Year

(b) Are the solar panels owned outright? ☐ Yes ☐ No

(c) Has a long lease of the roof/air space been granted to a solar panel provider? If Yes, please supply copies of the relevant documents e.g. copies of electricity bills for feed in tariffs.

☐ Yes ☐ No
☐ Enclosed ☐ To follow

4.7 Is the property or any part of it:

(a) a listed building? — ☐ Yes ☑ No ☐ Not known

(b) in a conservation area? — ☐ Yes ☑ No ☐ Not known

If Yes, please supply copies of any relevant documents. — ☐ Enclosed ☐ To follow

4.8 Are any of the trees on the property subject to a Tree Preservation Order? — ☐ Yes ☑ No ☐ Not known

If Yes:

(a) Have the terms of the Order been complied with? — ☐ Yes ☐ No ☐ Not known

(b) Please supply a copy of any relevant documents. — ☐ Enclosed ☐ To follow

5. Guarantees and warranties

Note to seller: All available guarantees, warranties and supporting paperwork should be supplied before exchange of contracts.

Note to buyer: Some guarantees only operate to protect the person who had the work carried out or may not be valid if their terms have been breached. You may wish to contact the company to establish whether it is still trading and if so, whether the terms of the guarantee will apply to you.

5.1 Does the property benefit from any of the following guarantees or warranties? If Yes, please supply a copy.

(a) New home warranty (e.g. NHBC or similar) — ☐ Yes ☑ No ☐ Enclosed ☐ To follow

(b) Damp proofing — ☐ Yes ☑ No ☐ Enclosed ☐ To follow

(c) Timber treatment — ☐ Yes ☑ No ☐ Enclosed ☐ To follow

(d) Windows, roof lights, roof windows or glazed doors — ☐ Yes ☑ No ☐ Enclosed ☐ To follow

(e) Electrical work — ☐ Yes ☑ No ☐ Enclosed ☐ To follow

(f) Roofing — ☐ Yes ☑ No ☐ Enclosed ☐ To follow

(g) Central heating — ☐ Yes ☑ No ☐ Enclosed ☐ To follow

(h) Underpinning — ☐ Yes ☑ No ☐ Enclosed ☐ To follow

(i) Other (please state): — ☐ Yes ☐ No ☐ Enclosed ☐ To follow

5.2 Have any claims been made under any of these guarantees or warranties? If Yes, please give details: — ☐ Yes ☑ No

6. Insurance

6.1 Does the seller insure the property? — ☑ Yes ☐ No

6.2 If not, why not?

6.3 If the property is a flat, does the landlord insure the building? — ☐ Yes ☐ No

6.4 Has any buildings insurance taken out by the seller ever been:

(a) subject to an abnormal rise in premiums? — ☐ Yes ☑ No

(b) subject to high excesses? — ☐ Yes ☑ No

(c) subject to unusual conditions? ☐ Yes ☑ No

(d) refused? ☐ Yes ☑ No

If Yes, please give details:

6.5 Has the seller made any buildings insurance claims? ☐ Yes ☐ No
If Yes, please give details:

7. Environmental matters

Flooding

Note: Flooding may take a variety of forms: it may be seasonal or irregular or simply a one-off occurrence. The property does not need to be near a sea or river for flooding to occur. Further information about flooding can be found at: **www.gov.uk/government/organisations/department-for-environment-food-rural-affairs**. The flood risk check can be found at: **www.gov.uk/check-flood-risk.**

Read our updated Flood Risk Practice Note at **https://www.lawsociety.org.uk/support-services/advice/practice-notes/flood-risk/**

7.1 Has any part of the property (whether buildings or surrounding garden or land) ever been flooded? If Yes, please state when the flooding occurred and identify the parts that flooded: ☐ Yes ☑ No

If No to question 7.1 please continue to 7.3 and do not answer 7.2 below.

7.2 What type of flooding occurred?

(a) Ground water ☐ Yes ☐ No

(b) Sewer flooding ☐ Yes ☐ No

(c) Surface water ☐ Yes ☐ No

(d) Coastal flooding ☐ Yes ☐ No

(e) River flooding ☐ Yes ☐ No

(f) Other (please state):

7.3 Has a Flood Risk Report been prepared? If Yes, please supply a copy. ☐ Yes ☐ No ☐ Enclosed ☐ To follow

Further information about the types of flooding and Flood Risk Reports can be found at: **www.gov.uk/government/organisations/environment-agency**.

Radon

Note: Radon is a naturally occurring inert radioactive gas found in the ground. Some parts of England and Wales are more adversely affected by it than others. Remedial action is advised for properties with a test result above the 'recommended action level'. Further information about Radon can be found at: **www.gov.uk/government/organisations/public-health-england** and **www.publichealthwales.wales.nhs.uk**.

7.4 Has a Radon test been carried out on the property? ☐ Yes ☑ No

If Yes:

(a) please supply a copy of the report ☐ Enclosed ☐ To follow

(b) was the test result below the 'recommended action level'? ☐ Yes ☐ No

7.5 Were any remedial measures undertaken on construction to reduce Radon gas levels in the property? ☐ Yes ☐ No ☐ Not known

Energy efficiency

Note: An Energy Performance Certificate (EPC) is a document that gives information about a property's energy usage. Further information about EPCs can be found at: **https://www.gov.uk/buy-sell-your-home/energy-performance-certificates**

7.6 Please supply a copy of the EPC for the property. ☑ Enclosed ☐ To follow ☐ Already supplied

7.7 Have any installations in the property been financed under the Green Deal scheme? If Yes, please give details of all installations and supply a copy of your last electricity bill.

☐ Yes ☑ No
☐ Enclosed ☐ To follow

Further information about the Green Deal can be found at:
www.gov.uk/green-deal-energy-saving-measures

Japanese knotweed

Note: Japanese knotweed is an invasive non-native plant that can cause damage to property if left untreated. The plant consists of visible above ground growth and an invisible rhizome (root) below ground in the soil. It can take several years to control and manage through a management and treatment plan and rhizomes may remain alive below the soil even after treatment.

7.8 Is the property affected by Japanese knotweed?

☐ Yes ☑ No
☐ Not known

If Yes, please state whether there is a Japanese knotweed management and treatment plan in place and supply a copy with any insurance cover linked to the plan.

☐ Yes ☐ No
☐ Not known
☐ Enclosed ☐ To follow

8. Rights and informal arrangements

Note: Rights and arrangements may relate to access or shared use. They may also include leases of less than seven years, rights to mines and minerals, manorial rights, chancel repair and similar matters. If you are uncertain about whether a right or arrangement is covered by this question, please ask your solicitor.

**8.1 Does ownership of the property carry a responsibility to contribute towards the cost of any jointly used services, such as maintenance of a private road, a shared driveway, a boundary or drain?
If Yes, please give details:**

☐ Yes ☑ No

**8.2 Does the property benefit from any rights or arrangements over any neighbouring property (this includes any rights of way)?
If Yes, please give details:**

☐ Yes ☑ No

8.3 Has anyone taken steps to prevent access to the property, or to complain about or demand payment for access to the property? If Yes, please give details:

☐ Yes ☑ No

8.4 Does the seller know if any of the following rights benefit the property:

(a) Rights of light — ☐ Yes ☑ No

(b) Rights of support from adjoining properties — ☐ Yes ☑ No

(c) Customary rights (e.g. rights deriving from local traditions) — ☐ Yes ☑ No

8.5 Does the seller know if any of the following arrangements affect the property:

(a) Other people's rights to mines and minerals under the land — ☐ Yes ☑ No

(b) Chancel repair liability — ☐ Yes ☑ No

(c) Other people's rights to take things from the land (such as timber, hay or fish) — ☐ Yes ☑ No

If Yes, please give details:

Not known

8.6 Are there any other rights or arrangements affecting the property? This includes any rights of way. If Yes, please give details:

☑ Yes ☐ No

Right of way over the alleyway alongside the Property is enjoyed by the adjoining property (19 High Street)

Services crossing the property or neighbouring property

8.7 Do any drains, pipes or wires serving the property cross any neighbour's property?

☐ Yes ☐ No
☑ Not known

8.8 Do any drains, pipes or wires leading to any neighbour's property cross the property?

☐ Yes ☐ No
☑ Not known

8.9 Is there any agreement or arrangement about drains, pipes or wires?

☐ Yes ☐ No
☑ Not known

If Yes, please supply a copy or give details:

☐ Enclosed ☐ To follow

9. Parking

9.1 What are the parking arrangements at the property?

None

9.2 Is the property in a controlled parking zone or within a local authority parking scheme?

☐ Yes ☑ No
☐ Not known

10. Other charges

Note: If the property is leasehold, details of lease expenses such as service charges and ground rent should be set out on the separate TA7 Leasehold Information Form. If the property is freehold, there may still be charges: for example, payments to a management company or for the use of a private drainage system.

10.1 Does the seller have to pay any charges relating to the property (excluding any payments such as council tax, utility charges, etc.), for example payments to a management company? If Yes, please give details:

☐ Yes ☑ No

11. Occupiers

11.1 Does the seller live at the property? ☑ Yes ☐ No

11.2 Does anyone else, aged 17 or over, live at the property? ☐ Yes ☑ No

If No to question 11.2, please continue to section 12 'Services' and do not answer 11.3–11.5 below.

11.3 Please give the full names of any occupiers (other than the sellers) aged 17 or over:

11.4 Are any of the occupiers (other than the sellers), aged 17 or over, tenants or lodgers? ☐ Yes ☐ No

11.5 Is the property being sold with vacant possession? ☐ Yes ☐ No

If Yes, have all the occupiers aged 17 or over:

(a) agreed to leave prior to completion? ☐ Yes ☐ No

(b) agreed to sign the sale contract? If No, please supply other evidence that the property will be vacant on completion. ☐ Yes ☐ No ☐ Enclosed ☐ To follow

12. Services

Note: If the seller does not have a certificate requested below this can be obtained from the relevant Competent Persons Scheme. Further information about Competent Persons Schemes can be found at: **https://www.gov.uk/guidance/competent-person-scheme-current-schemes-and-how-schemes-are-authorised**

Electricity

12.1 Has the whole or any part of the electrical installation been tested by a qualified and registered electrician? ☑ Yes ☐ No

If Yes, please state the year it was tested and provide a copy of the test certificate. 2022 Year ☑ Enclosed ☐ To follow

12.2 Has the property been rewired or had any electrical installation work carried out since 1 January 2005? ☐ Yes ☑ No ☐ Not known

If Yes, please supply one of the following:

(a) a copy of the signed BS7671 Electrical Safety Certificate ☐ Enclosed ☐ To follow

(b) the installer's Building Regulations Compliance Certificate ☐ Enclosed ☐ To follow

(c) the Building Control Completion Certificate ☐ Enclosed ☐ To follow

Central heating

12.3 Does the property have a central heating system? ☑ Yes ☐ No

If Yes:

(a) What type of system is it (e.g. mains gas, liquid gas, oil, electricity, etc.)? mains gas

(b) When was the heating system installed? If on or after 1 April 2005 please supply a copy of the 'completion certificate' (e.g. CORGI or Gas Safe Register) or the 'exceptional circumstances' form.

Date ☑ Not known ☐ Enclosed ☐ To follow

(c) Is the heating system in good working order? ☑ Yes ☐ No

(d) In what year was the heating system last serviced/ maintained? Please supply a copy of the inspection report.

2024 Year ☐ Not known ☑ Enclosed ☐ To follow ☐ Not available

Drainage and sewerage

Note: Further information about drainage and sewerage can be found at: **www.gov.uk/government/organisations/environment-agency**

12.4 Is the property connected to mains:

(a) foul water drainage? ☑ Yes ☐ No ☐ Not known

(b) surface water drainage? ☑ Yes ☐ No ☐ Not known

If Yes to both questions in 12.4, please continue to section 13 'Connection to utilities and services' and do not answer 12.5–12.10 below.

12.5 Is sewerage for the property provided by:

(a) a septic tank? ☐ Yes ☐ No

If the property is in England and you answered Yes to question 12.5 and your septic tank discharges directly into surface water, you must do one of the following as soon as possible:

- **connect to mains sewer**
- **install a drainage field (also known as an infiltration system) so the septic tank can discharge to ground instead**
- **replace your septic tank with a small sewage treatment plant**

You must have plans in place to carry out this work within a reasonable timescale, typically 12 months.

12.5.1 When was the septic tank last replaced or upgraded? Month Year

(b) a sewage treatment plant? ☐ Yes ☐ No

(c) cesspool? ☐ Yes ☐ No

12.6 Is the use of the septic tank, sewage treatment plant or cesspool shared with other properties? If Yes, how many properties share the system? ☐ Yes ☐ No ☐ Properties share

12.7 When was the system last emptied? ☐ Year

12.8 If the property is served by a sewage treatment plant, when was the treatment plant last serviced? ☐ Year

12.9 When was the system installed? ☐ Year

Note: Some systems installed after 1 January 1991 require Building Regulations approval, environmental permits or registration. Further information about permits and registration can be found at: **www.gov.uk/government/organisations/environment-agency**

12.10 Is any part of the septic tank, sewage treatment plant (including any soakaway or outfall) or cesspool, or the access to it, outside the boundary of the property? If Yes, please supply a plan showing the location of the system and how access is obtained. ☐ Yes ☐ No ☐ Enclosed ☐ To follow

Specific information about permits and general binding rules can be found at **www.gov.uk/permits-you-need-for-septic-tanks**

13. Connection to utilities and services

Please mark the Yes or No boxes to show which of the following utilities and services are connected to the property and give details of any providers.

Mains electricity ☑ Yes ☐ No

Provider's name Scottish Power

Location of meter under stairs

Mains gas ☑ Yes ☐ No

Provider's name Scottish Power

Location of meter under stairs

Mains water ☑ Yes ☐ No

Provider's name Westshire Water

Location of stopcock under kitchen sink

Location of meter, if any

Mains sewerage ☑ Yes ☐ No

Provider's name Westshire Water

Telephone ☑ Yes ☐ No

Provider's name Virgin Media

Cable ☑ Yes ☐ No

Provider's name Virgin Media

14. Transaction information

14.1 Is this sale dependent on the seller completing the purchase of another property on the same day?

☐ Yes ☑ No

14.2 Does the seller have any special requirements about a moving date? If Yes, please give details:

☐ Yes ☑ No

14.3 Will the sale price be sufficient to repay all mortgages and charges secured on the property?

☑ Yes ☐ No
☐ No mortgage

14.4 Will the seller ensure that:

(a) all rubbish is removed from the property (including from the loft, garden, outbuildings, garages and sheds) and that the property will be left in a clean and tidy condition?

☑ Yes ☐ No

(b) if light fittings are removed, the fittings will be replaced with ceiling rose, flex, bulb holder and bulb?

☑ Yes ☐ No

(c) reasonable care will be taken when removing any other fittings or contents?

☑ Yes ☐ No

(d) keys to all windows and doors and details of alarm codes will be left at the property or with the estate agent?

☑ Yes ☐ No

Signed: Neeta Mukhtar Dated: 02/02/2026

Signed: Samir Mukhtar Dated: 02/02/2026

Each seller should sign this form.

The Law Society

The Law Society is the representative body for solicitors in England and Wales.

Document 11

	Enquiry from Style&Go Ltd's solicitor	Response from Neeta's solicitor
Title queries	The registered proprietors are Ansar Mukhtar and Neeta Mukhtar, and there is a restriction preventing the disposal by a sole trustee. Please confirm why Ansar is not a seller and the arrangements for sale by a sole trustee.	Ansar Mukhtar has passed away. Copy of death certificate enclosed. The second trustee to the contract and transfer (to comply with the restriction) will be Samir Mukhtar.
	There is a restrictive covenant prohibiting building any structure on the property. An extension has been built in breach of that covenant. Please confirm that your client will obtain and pay for a restrictive covenant insurance policy to cover my client in respect of the risk of enforcement action.	Confirmed – my client is willing to obtain and pay for a restrictive covenant insurance policy for the benefit of your client.
	There is a positive covenant at entry C2 and an indemnity in respect thereof. Please confirm: - whether there have been any breaches of this covenant to date; - what work has been done to ensure compliance with this covenant; and - the average annual cost of maintaining the land referred to.	The seller confirms: - the covenant has not been breached during the seller's ownership. The seller has no knowledge about any breaches before her ownership commenced; - the seller does not store anything in the alleyway and sweeps it regularly to ensure it is free from debris. The seller pressure-washes the alleyway once per year to ensure it is not slippery underfoot; - the average annual cost is less than £10.
	The property is subject to a right of way. Please provide the following details: - the nature of the right of way; - who uses it; and - how regularly is it used.	The neighbours at 19 High St have a right of way over the alleyway. The seller only knows of Sally and Neil Jackson who live at number 19 using the alleyway. As far as the seller is aware the right of way is only used once per week to take refuse from the back of the property to the front.
Mortgage	There is a mortgage registered against the property and an associated restriction.	We undertake to pay any completion monies we receive from our client towards the mortgage with Secure Trust

	Please provide an undertaking that you will: - pay the completion monies towards the mortgage; and - immediately send a DS1 to us.	Bank, and to send a Form DS1 to you once we have received it from the lender.
Planning and building regs	There is no building regulations certificate in respect of the extension. Please confirm that your client will obtain and pay for a building regulations insurance policy to cover my client in respect of the risk of enforcement action.	Confirmed - my client is willing to obtain and pay for a building regulations insurance policy for the benefit of your client.
Overriding interests	Please confirm whether there are any overriding interests affecting the property	Confirmed none to the seller's knowledge.

Document 12

Acquisition of 17 High Street, Barnford

Summary of due diligence for inclusion in a report on title

1. Key details of the transaction

- The property is being purchased alongside a second site (land adjoining Sheep Street, Barnford) for the buyer to run as a hair salon with on-site parking for staff and customers.
- Seller: Ansar Mukhtar and Neeta Mukhtar are the registered proprietors according to the title deeds. The seller has confirmed that Ansar Mukhtar has passed away and has provided a copy of the death certificate. There is a restriction on the title preventing Neeta from disposing of the property alone. Actions:
    - contract: a second trustee will need to be party to the contract with Neeta – the seller has confirmed this will be Samir Mukhtar;
    - transfer: a second trustee will need to be party to the TR1 with Neeta – the seller has confirmed this will be Samir Mukhtar;
    - post-completion: on registration of the transfer to Style&Go Ltd, HMLR will automatically remove this restriction.
- Buyer: Style&Go Ltd
- Property: 17 High Street, Barnford, Westshire, EX82 7YK. A SIM search over the land confirmed that it is registered with title number EG576798.
- Price: £525,000 to be funded in cash
- Deposit: 10% of purchase price
- As the buyer is a corporate entity, £89,250 in SDLT will be payable on the transaction.
- The Salon is being sold with vacant possession. It is currently occupied by Neeta. Actions:
    - contract: this will need to be included as a special condition in the contract.

2. Title investigation

- Title investigation revealed a restrictive covenant preventing building on the property. The buyer will not be able to build structures on the property. The extension was built in breach of this covenant and the seller has agreed to pay for restrictive covenant insurance policy. Actions:

  - contract: include a special condition requiring Neeta to obtain the insurance policy.
- There is a mortgage registered against the property. The seller's solicitors have provided an undertaking that they will apply the completion monies to discharge this mortgage and will send a DS1 form to enable us to remove the mortgage from the title. Actions:
  - post-completion: apply to discharge this mortgage.
- The neighbours at 19 High St have a right of way over the alleyway at the side of the property. The seller has confirmed that Sally and Neil Jackson currently live at number 19 and use the alleyway to take the bins out.
- There is a positive covenant requiring Style&Go Ltd to maintain the alleyway so that it is safe to walk down.
  - The seller has confirmed that she has complied with this during her ownership; she keeps the alleyway clear of items, sweeps it regularly and pressure washes it once a year. She estimates it costs less than £10 per year to maintain it.
  - Style&Go Ltd will be responsible for this once they own the property and will need to provide an indemnity to the seller. I understand that their plans for using the Salon will not interfere with this covenant. Actions:
    - contract: include special condition which requires the TR1 to include a covenant requiring Style&Go Ltd to comply with the positive covenant and indemnify the seller;
    - transfer: include covenant that Style&Go Ltd will comply with the positive covenant and indemnify the seller. Style&Go Ltd will need to sign the TR1 as they are giving this covenant;
    - post-completion: HMLR will automatically register the indemnity covenant on the proprietorship register.
- The seller does not know of any overriding interests affecting the property. We recommend a physical inspection of the property as Style&Go Ltd will be bound by these if any do exist and are discoverable.

3. Searches

- The local search revealed that there is going to be a new railway close-by and that Main Street is going to be pedestrianised.
- The drainage and water search confirmed that Westshire Water are responsible for maintaining the drains and sewers and for the quality of the water supplied to the property.
- The environmental search confirmed that the risk of contaminants being on the property is low and we do not recommend any further environmental surveys.

- The flood search confirmed that the surrounding village has been affected by flooding previously, but that the property was unaffected. We do not recommend any further flood surveys.
- The properties are not located within the boundary of a parish which has chancel repair liability, and insurance is not required.
- The Salon benefits from mains electricity and gas supplied by Scottish Power, and telephone and cable from Virgin Media.

4. Planning permission and building regulations

- The property was extended in 1996. The local searches confirm that planning permission was granted for this extension, but an inspection confirms that the conditions were not complied with; the time-limit for the local planning authority to enforce this breach has expired. No buildings regulation approval was given for the extension – this is still enforceable, and so the seller has confirmed that she is willing to pay for insurance to cover the risk of enforcement. Actions:
  - contract: include a special condition requiring Neeta to pay for insurance.
- We deal with future planning permission for the Salon and the additional site together as they will constitute one planning unit:
  - the Salon currently has planning permission for residential use, and the Car Park has planning permission for the sale and display for sale of motor vehicles. Style&Go Ltd will require planning permission to change the use of the land. We will assist in making an application for planning permission to use the land as Class E, designating some of the space as ancillary parking;
  - Style&Go Ltd will not need planning permission for the fit-out works to the Salon, but may require planning permission to do the works to the Car Park. Our searches confirmed that an Article 4 Direction is in place in respect of the Car Park and therefore an express application for planning permission for these works will need to be made – we can assist with this.

5. Accessing the property

- Pedestrian access to the property is via the High Street, which is an adopted highway directly abutting the Salon.
- Style&Go Ltd intend for their staff and customers to park in the additional site, the Car Park. Vehicular access is via Sheep Street, which is a private road. An easement already exists over Sheep Street for the benefit of the Car Park, and so anyone they allow to use the Car Park will be permitted to pass over Sheep Street in order to access it.

NB: the authors have included dates in this contract in square brackets – in practice these would be entered at the relevant moment (e.g. on exchange).

For conveyancer's use only
Buyer's conveyancer Blackhurst & Sons LLP
Seller's conveyancer: Chantry Richardson solicitors
Law Society Formula B
Time: 12:05pm
The information above does not form part of the Contract

CONTRACT

(Incorporating the Standard Conditions of Sale (Fifth Edition – 2018 Revision))

Date	:	*[1 May 2026]*
Seller	:	Mrs Neeta Mukhtar and Mr Samir Mukhtar
Buyer	:	Style&Go Ltd
Property (freehold/~~leasehold~~)	:	17 High Street, Barnford, Westshire, EX82 7YK
Title Number/~~Root of title~~	:	EG576798
Specified Encumbrances	:	The matters contained or referred to in the property, proprietorship and charges registers of title number EG576798 except any subsisting financial charges
Title guarantee (full/~~limited~~)	:	Full
Completion Date	:	*[18 May 2026]*
Contract Rate	:	4% above the base lending rate of Barclays Bank plc from time to time in force
Purchase Price	:	£525,000 exclusive of any VAT
Deposit	:	£52,500
Content price (if separate)	:	n/a
Balance	:	£472,500

The Seller will sell and the Buyer will buy the Property for the Purchase Price.

WARNING This is a formal document, designed to create legal rights and legal obligations. Take advice before using it.	**Signed** ***André Gomez*** Director Authorised to sign on behalf of Buyer

SPECIAL CONDITIONS

1. (a) This contract incorporates the Standard Conditions of Sale (Fifth Edition – 2018 Revision).
   (b) The terms used in this contract have the same meaning when used in the Conditions.

2. Subject to the terms of this contract and to the Standard Conditions of Sale, the seller is to transfer the property with either full title guarantee or limited title guarantee, as specified on the front page.

3. (a) The sale includes those contents which are indicated on the attached list as included in the sale and the buyer is to pay the contents price for them.

   (b) The sale excludes those fixtures which are at the property and are indicated on the attached list as excluded from the sale.

4. The property is sold with vacant possession

5. **Representations**

   Neither party can rely on any representation made by the other, unless made in writing by the other or his conveyancer, but this does not exclude liability for fraud or recklessness.

6. The Seller will, at its own expense, obtain a restrictive covenant insurance policy in a form agreed between the parties in relation to the Seller's past breach of covenant referred to at entry 3 of the Charges Register of title number EG576798 and will provide the Buyer with the original policy by the Completion Date. The Seller will pay the cost of the premium for this insurance policy.

7. The Seller will, at its own expense, obtain a building regulations indemnity insurance policy in a form agreed between the parties in relation to the Seller's construction of an extension without obtaining building regulations certification, and will provide the Buyer with the original policy by the Completion Date. The Seller will pay the cost of the premium for this insurance policy.

8. The transfer to the Buyer will contain the following provision:

"The Transferee covenants with the Transferor to observe and perform the covenants contained or referred to in entry number 2 in the Charges Register of title number EG576798 and to indemnify the Transferor against any liability for any future breach or non-observance thereof."

Notices may be sent to:

Seller's Conveyancer's name: Chantry Richardson solicitors, 17 The Quay, Barnford, EX81 9JP

Buyer's Conveyancer's name: Blackhurst & Sons LLP of 22 High Street, Barnford, Westshire, EX82 7YK

NB: the authors have included dates in this deed in square brackets – in practice these would be entered at the relevant moment (e.g. on completion).

HM Land Registry
Transfer of whole of registered title(s)

TR1

Any parts of the form that are not typed should be completed in black ink and in block capitals.

If you need more room than is provided for in a panel, and your software allows, you can expand any panel in the form. Alternatively use continuation sheet CS and attach it to this form.

For information on how HM Land Registry processes your personal information, see our Personal Information Charter.

Guidance	No.	Panel
Leave blank if not yet registered.	1	Title number(s) of the property: EG576798
Insert address including postcode (if any) or other description of the property, for example 'land adjoining 2 Acacia Avenue'.	2	Property: 17 High Street, Barnford, Westshire, EX82 7YK
Remember to date this deed with the day of completion, but not before it has been signed and witnessed.	3	Date: [*18 May 2026*]
Give full name(s) of **all** the persons transferring the property. Complete as appropriate where the transferor is a company. Enter the overseas entity ID issued by Companies House for the transferor pursuant to the Economic Crime (Transparency and Enforcement) Act 2022. If the ID is not required, you may instead state 'not required'. Further details on overseas entities can be found in practice guide 78: overseas entities.	4	Transferor: Mrs Anita Mukhtar Mr Samir Mukhtar For UK incorporated companies/LLPs Registered number of company or limited liability partnership including any prefix: For overseas entities (a) Territory of incorporation or formation: (b) Overseas entity ID issued by Companies House, including any prefix: (c) Where the entity is a company with a place of business in the United Kingdom, the registered number, if any, issued by Companies House, including any prefix:

Give full name(s) of **all** the persons to be shown as registered proprietors. Complete as appropriate where the transferee is a company. Also, for an overseas company, unless an arrangement with HM Land Registry exists, lodge either a certificate in Form 7 in Schedule 3 to the Land Registration Rules 2003 or a certified copy of the constitution in English or Welsh, or other evidence permitted by rule 183 of the Land Registration Rules 2003. Enter the overseas entity ID issued by Companies House for the transferee pursuant to the Economic Crime (Transparency and Enforcement) Act 2022. If the ID is not required, you may instead state 'not required'. Further details on overseas entities can be found in practice guide 78: overseas entities.	5	Transferee for entry in the register: Style&Go Ltd For UK incorporated companies/LLPs Registered number of company or limited liability partnership including any prefix: 00127976 For overseas entities (a) Territory of incorporation or formation: (b) Overseas entity ID issued by Companies House, including any prefix: (c) Where the entity is a company with a place of business in the United Kingdom, the registered number, if any, issued by Companies House, including any prefix:
Each transferee may give up to three addresses for service, one of which must be a postal address whether or not in the UK (including the postcode, if any). The others can be any combination of a postal address, a UK DX box number or an email address.	6	Transferee's intended address(es) for service for entry in the register: c/o Blackhurst&Sons LLP of 22 High Street, Barnford, Westshire, EX82 7YK
	7	The transferor transfers the property to the transferee
Place 'X' in the appropriate box. State the currency unit if other than sterling. If none of the boxes apply, insert an appropriate memorandum in panel 11.	8	Consideration ☒ The transferor has received from the transferee for the property the following sum (in words and figures): £525,000 ☐ The transfer is not for money or anything that has a monetary value ☐ Insert other receipt as appropriate:
Place 'X' in any box that applies. Add any modifications.	9	The transferor transfers with ☒ full title guarantee ☐ limited title guarantee

Where the transferee is more than one person, place 'X' in the appropriate box.

Complete as necessary.

The registrar will enter a Form A restriction in the register *unless*:

- an 'X' is placed:
  - in the first box, or
  - in the third box and the details of the trust or of the trust instrument show that the transferees are to hold the property on trust for themselves alone as joint tenants, *or*
- it is clear from completion of a form JO lodged with this application that the transferees are to hold the property on trust for themselves alone as joint tenants.

Please refer to *Joint property ownership* and *practice guide 24: private trusts of land* for further guidance. These are both available on the GOV.UK website.

10 Declaration of trust. The transferee is more than one person and

☐ they are to hold the property on trust for themselves as joint tenants

☐ they are to hold the property on trust for themselves as tenants in common in equal shares

☐ they are to hold the property on trust:

Insert here any required or permitted statement, certificate or application and any agreed covenants, declarations and so on.

11 Additional provisions

11.1 So that the Transferor can give a good receipt for the purchase price, Neeta Mukhtar in exercise of her statutory power appoints Samir Mukhtar to be a trustee of the property with Neeta Mukhtar in place of Ansar Mukhtar.

11.2 The Transferee covenants with the Transferor to observe and perform the covenants contained or referred to in entry number 2 in the Charges Register of title number EG576798 and to indemnify the Transferor against any liability for any future breach or non-observance thereof.

The transferor must execute this transfer as a deed using the space opposite. If there is more than one transferor, all must execute. Forms of execution are given in Schedule 9 to the Land Registration Rules 2003. If the transfer contains transferee's covenants or declarations or contains an application by the transferee (such as for a restriction), it must also be executed by the transferee.

If there is more than one transferee and panel 10 has been completed, each transferee must also execute this transfer to comply with the requirements in section 53(1)(b) of the Law of Property Act 1925 relating to the declaration of a trust of land. Please refer to *Joint property ownership* and practice guide *24: private trusts of land* for further guidance.

Examples of the correct form of execution are set out in practice guide 8: execution of deeds. Execution as a deed usually means that a witness must also sign, and add their name and address.

Remember to date this deed in panel 3.

12 Execution

Seller

Signed as a deed by Neeta Mukhtar
Neeta Mukhtar

in the presence of
Pauline Jones
PAULINE JONES
21 High Street, Barnford, Westshire, EX82 7YK

Signed as a deed by Samir Mukhtar
Samir Mukhtar

in the presence of
Pauline Jones
PAULINE JONES
21 High Street, Barnford, Westshire, EX82 7YK

Buyer

Executed as a deed by Style&Go Ltd acting by a director and its secretary

André Gomez
Director

Karen Chester
Secretary

WARNING
If you dishonestly enter information or make a statement that you know is, or might be, untrue or misleading, and intend by doing so to make a gain for yourself or another person, or to cause loss or the risk of loss to another person, you may commit the offence of fraud under section 1 of the Fraud Act 2006, the maximum penalty for which is 10 years' imprisonment or an unlimited fine, or both.

Failure to complete this form with proper care may result in a loss of protection under the Land Registration Act 2002 if, as a result, a mistake is made in the register.

Under section 66 of the Land Registration Act 2002 most documents (including this form) kept by the registrar relating to an application to the registrar or referred to in the register are open to public inspection and copying. If you believe a document contains prejudicial information, you may apply for that part of the document to be made exempt using Form EX1, under rule 136 of the Land Registration Rules 2003.

Memorandum of exchange: 17 High Street, Barnford

1 May 2026

1. Exchange occurred on 1 May 2026 at 12:05pm.
2. Formula B. Deposit already transferred to seller's solicitor via CHAPS on 29 April 2026, so the sentence requiring the purchaser's solicitor to send a banker's draft or client account cheque is deleted from the formula.
3. Agreed completion date: 18 May 2026.
4. No deposit to be paid – see 2. Above
5. Blackhurst & Sons LLP – solicitor for the buyer
   Chantry Richardson solicitors LLP – solicitor for the seller.

Document 16

Official search certificate of search of whole with priority

Land Registry
Land Registration Rules 2003

Form **OS1R**

Official Search No. SA/EXH02	Certificate Date: **1 May 2026** Priority Period began at: **13:32:27**	Priority Period expires on: **12 June 2026** at midnight but see the note below

Particulars of Search as Supplied

Title Number	EG576798
Applicant	Style&Go Ltd

Result

It is certified that the official search applied for has been made with the following result:

Since 6 January 2026 at 15:03:27 no adverse entries have been made.

****

END OF RESULT

Note: To be sure to obtain priority for your application you should deliver it to the proper office by 12:00 (noon) on the date when priority expires.

HM Land Registry
Cancellation of entries relating to a registered charge

DS1

This form should be accompanied by either Form AP1 or Form DS2

Any parts of the form that are not typed should be completed in black ink and in block capitals.

If you need more room than is provided for in a panel, and your software allows, you can expand any panel in the form. Alternatively use continuation sheet CS and attach it to this form.

For information on how HM Land Registry processes your personal information, see our Personal Information Charter.

	1	Title number(s) of the property: EG576798
Insert address including postcode (if any) or other description of the property, for example 'land adjoining 2 Acacia Avenue'.	2	Property: 17 High Street, Barnford, Westshire, EX82 7YK
	3	Date: 19 May 2026
Include register entry number, if more than one charge of same date to same lender.	4	Date of charge: 10 July 1993
Complete as appropriate where the lender is a company.	5	Lender: Secure Trust Bank For UK incorporated companies/LLPs Registered number of company or limited liability partnership including any prefix: 747443 For overseas companies (a) Territory of incorporation: (b) Registered number in the United Kingdom including any prefix:
	6	The lender acknowledges that the property identified in panel 2 is no longer charged as security for the payment of sums due under the charge
	7	Date of Land Registry facility letter (if any):
The lender must execute this as a deed using the space opposite. If there is more than one lender, all must execute. Forms of execution are given in Schedule 9 to the Land Registration Rules 2003. Examples of the correct form of execution are set out in practice guide 8: execution of deeds. Execution as a deed usually means that a witness must also sign, and add their name and address. Alternatively the lender may sign in accordance with the facility letter referred to in panel 7.	8	Execution Executed as a deed by SECURE TRUST BANK acting by Mai Ting, a director — *Mai Ting* Director and Sara Dolvolo its secretary — *Sara Dolvolo* Secretary

WARNING
If you dishonestly enter information or make a statement that you know is, or might be, untrue or misleading, and intend by doing so to make a gain for yourself or another person, or to cause loss or the risk of loss to another person, you may commit the offence of fraud under section 1 of the Fraud Act 2006, the maximum penalty for which is 10 years' imprisonment or an unlimited fine, or both.

Failure to complete this form with proper care may result in a loss of protection under the Land Registration Act 2002 if, as a result, a mistake is made in the register.

Under section 66 of the Land Registration Act 2002 most documents (including this form) kept by the registrar relating to an application to the registrar or referred to in the register are open to public inspection and copying. If you believe a document contains prejudicial information, you may apply for that part of the document to be made exempt using Form EX1, under rule 136 of the Land Registration Rules 2003.

HM Land Registry

Application to change the register

AP1

Any parts of the form that are not typed should be completed in black ink and in block capitals.

If you need more room than is provided for in a panel, and your software allows, you can expand any panel in the form. Alternatively use continuation sheet CS and attach it to this form.

HM Land Registry is unable to give legal advice, but you can find guidance on HM Land Registry applications (including our practice guides for conveyancers) at www.gov.uk/land-registry.

Conveyancer is a term used in this form. It is defined in rule 217A, Land Registration Rules 2003 and includes persons authorised under the Legal Services Act 2007 to provide reserved legal services relating to land registration and includes solicitors and licensed conveyancers.

For information on how HM Land Registry processes your personal information, see our Personal Information Charter.

HM LAND REGISTRY USE ONLY
Record of fees paid
Particulars of under/over payments
Reference number Fees debited £

Where there is more than one local authority serving an area, enter the one to which council tax or business rates are normally paid.

1 Local authority serving the property: Westshire

Full postcode of property (if any): EX82 7YK

Enter the title number of each title that requires an entry to be made in that register.

2 Title number(s) of the property:
EG576798

3 The application affects

Place 'X' in the appropriate box.

☒ the whole of the title(s)

☐ part of the title(s) as shown:

Give a brief description of the part affected, for example 'edged red on the plan to the transfer dated ....'.

4 Application, priority and fees

To find out more about our fees visit www.gov.uk/government/collections/fees-land-registry-guides

Remember restrictions in deeds may apply to other deeds of lower priority in this list, unless you specify otherwise.

Applications in priority order	Price paid/Value (£)	Fees paid (£)
Discharge a registered charge	n/a	0
Transfer of whole	525,000	295
	Total fees (£)	295

Fee payment method

Place 'X' in the appropriate box.

Where the application is sent to HM Land Registry by a private individual, payment must be by way of postal order or cheque made payable to HM Land Registry.

☐ cheque made payable to 'Land Registry'

☒ direct debit, under an agreement with Land Registry

The fee will be charged to the account specified in panel 7.

List the documents lodged with this form. We only need certified copies of deeds or documents you send to us with HM Land Registry application forms. Once we have made a copy of the documents you send to us, they will be destroyed, this applies to both originals and certified copies	5	Documents lodged with this form: *Form DS1 dated 19 May 2026, executed by Secure Trust Bank* *Certified copy of Transfer dated 18 May 2026 and made between (1) Neeta Mukhtar and Samir Mukhtar and (2) Style&Go Ltd, executed by Neeta Mukhtar and Samir Mukhtar* *Certified copy of Transfer dated 18 May 2026 and made between (1) Neeta Mukhtar and Samir Mukhtar and (2) Style&Go Ltd, executed by Style&Go Ltd* *Certified copy of SDLT5 dated 19 May 2026* *Certified copy of death certificate of Ansar Mukhtar*
Provide the full name(s) of the person(s) applying to change the register. Where a conveyancer lodges the application, this must be the name(s) of the client(s), not the conveyancer. Complete as appropriate where the applicant is a company. Also, for an overseas company, unless an arrangement with HM Land Registry exists, lodge either a certificate in Form 7 in Schedule 3 to the Land Registration Rules 2003 or a certified copy of the constitution in English or Welsh, or other evidence permitted by rule 183 of the Land Registration Rules 2003. Enter the overseas entity ID issued by Companies House for the applicant pursuant to the Economic Crime (Transparency and Enforcement) Act 2022. If the ID is not required, you may instead state 'not required'. Further details on overseas entities can be found in practice guide 78: overseas entities.	6	The applicant: Style&Go Ltd For UK incorporated companies/LLPs Registered number of company or limited liability partnership including any prefix: 00127976 For overseas entities (a) Territory of incorporation or formation: (b) Overseas entity ID issued by Companies House, including any prefix: (c) Where the entity is a company with a place of business in the United Kingdom, the registered number, if any, issued by Companies House, including any prefix:
This panel must always be completed. This panel must always be completed with the details of the person sending the application to HM Land Registry. However, a key number is only available to professional customers, such as solicitors, and so a key number cannot be entered where the application is sent to HM Land Registry by a private individual. If you are paying by direct debit, this will be the account charged. This is the address to which we will normally send requisitions. However if you insert an email address, we will use this whenever possible. An acknowledgement of receipt of this application, if lodged by post, will be sent by email if one is available. We will only issue warning of cancellation letters to conveyancers if an email address is inserted.	7	This application is sent to Land Registry by Key number (if applicable): Name: Blackhurst & Sons LLP Address or UK DX box number: 22 High Street, Barnford, Westshire, EX82 7YK Email address: Blackhursts@blackhursts.com Reference: 17/BH Phone no: 0000 543212 — Fax no: n/a

When completing this panel please refer to Guidance: completing form AP1.

8 Third party notification
Name:
Address or UK DX box number:

Email address:
Reference:

When completing this panel please refer to Guidance: completing form AP1.

Place 'X' in the appropriate box.

In this and panel 10, each proprietor may give up to three addresses for service, one of which must be a postal address whether or not in the UK (including the postcode, if any). The others can be any combination of a postal address, a UK DX box number or an email address.

9 The address(es) for service for each proprietor of the registered estate(s) to be entered in the register is

☐ the address of the property (where this is a single postal address)

☒ the address(es) for service from the transfer/assent

☐ (for existing proprietors who are remaining in the register) the current address(es) for service in the register

☐ the following address(es):

Where a charge has an MD reference we will ignore an address given in this panel unless the charge is in favour of a United Kingdom bank and neither the charge form nor any agreement we have with the lender specifies an address for service.

For permitted addresses see note to panel 9.

Complete as appropriate where the lender is a company. Also, for an overseas company, unless an arrangement with HM Land Registry exists, lodge either a certificate in Form 7 in Schedule 3 to the Land Registration Rules 2003 or a certified copy of the constitution in English or Welsh, or other evidence permitted by rule 183 of the Land Registration Rules 2003.

10 Name and address(es) for service of the proprietor of any new charge to be entered in the register:

For UK incorporated companies/LLPs
Registered number of company or limited liability partnership including any prefix:

For overseas companies
(a) Territory of incorporation:

(b) Where the entity is a company with a place of business in the United Kingdom, the registered number, if any, issued by Companies House, including any prefix:

If this statement applies (i) place 'X' in the box and (ii) enclose Form DI.

Section 27 of the Land Registration Act 2002 lists the registrable dispositions.

Rule 57 of the Land Registration Rules 2003 sets out the disclosable overriding interests that you must tell us about.

11 Disclosable overriding interests

☐ This application relates to a registrable disposition and disclosable overriding interests affect the registered estate.

12 Confirmation of identity

When registering transfers, charges, leases and other dispositions of land, or giving effect to a discharge or release of a registered charge, Land Registry relies on the steps that conveyancers take, where appropriate, to verify the identity of their clients. These checks reduce the risk of property fraud.

Full details of the evidence of identity that is required can be found in Practice Guide 67 and in 'Completing the evidence of identity panels on forms AP1, FR1, and DS2' both of which can be found on the GOV.UK website.

Where a person was not represented by a conveyancer, Land Registry requires 'evidence of identity' in respect of that person, except where the first alternative in panel 13(2) applies.

'Evidence of identity' is evidence provided in accordance with any current direction made by the Chief Land Registrar under section 100(4) of the Land Registration Act 2002 for the purpose of confirming a person's identity.

If this application is to register a transfer, lease or charge, or to give effect to a discharge in Form DS1 or a release in Form DS3 complete one of the following

Place 'X' in the appropriate box.

Conveyancer is defined in rule 217A, Land Registration Rules 2003 and includes persons authorised under the Legal Services Act 2007 to provide reserved legal services relating to land registration and includes solicitors and licensed conveyancers.

☒ I am a conveyancer, and I have completed panel 13

☐ I am not a conveyancer, and I have completed panel 14

13 Where the application is sent to Land Registry by a conveyancer

(1) Details of conveyancer acting

If you are sending an application to register a transfer, lease or charge, for each party to each disposition that is to be registered state in the table below the details of the conveyancer (if any) who represented them.

Where a party is not represented by a conveyancer you must also complete (2) below.

Place 'X' in the box in the second column if the person or firm who is sending the application to HM Land Registry represented that party in the transaction. Otherwise complete the details in the third column. If the party is not represented insert 'none' in the third column.

A separate box is provided, or can be added, for each party, as required by panel 13(1). That includes separate boxes for attorneys and donors where appropriate.

Name of transferor, landlord, transferee, tenant, borrower or lender		Conveyancer's name, address and reference
Neeta Mukhtar and Samir Mukhtar (Transferor)	☐	Chantry Richardson solicitors, 17 The Quay, Barnford, EX81 9JP Reference: FAO Finnegan Hale
Style&Go Ltd (Transferee)	☒	Reference: 17/BH
	☐	Reference:

	☐	Reference:
	☐	Reference:

If you are sending an application to give effect to a discharge in Form DS1 or release in Form DS3 for each lender, state in the table below the details of the conveyancer (if any) who represented them.

Where a lender is not represented by a conveyancer you must also complete (2) below.

Place 'X' in the box in the second column if the person or firm who is sending the application to HM Land Registry represented that party in the transaction. Otherwise complete the details in the third column. If the party is not represented insert 'none' in the third column.

A separate box is provided, or can be added, for each party, as required by panel 13(1). That includes separate boxes for attorneys and donors where appropriate.

Name of lender		Conveyancer's name, address and reference
Secure Trust Bank	☐	Chantry Richardson solicitors, 17 The Quay, Barnford, EX81 9JP Reference: FAO Finnegan Hale
	☐	Reference:

(2) Evidence of identity

Where any transferor, landlord, transferee, tenant, borrower or lender listed in (1) was not represented by a conveyancer

Place 'X' in the appropriate box(es).

Insert the name of each unrepresented transferor, landlord, transferee, tenant, borrower or lender for whom you give this confirmation.

☐ I confirm that I am satisfied that sufficient steps have been taken to verify the identity of

____

____

and that they are the registered proprietor or have the right to be registered as the registered proprietor

Evidence of identity is defined in panel 12. Full details of the evidence of identity that is required can be found in Practice Guide 67 available on the GOV.UK website.

☐ I enclose evidence of identity in respect of each unrepresented transferor, landlord, transferee, tenant, borrower or lender for whom I have not provided the confirmation above

14 Where the application is sent to Land Registry by someone who is not a conveyancer

(1) Details of conveyancer acting

If you are sending an application to register a transfer, lease or charge (ie a mortgage), for each party to each disposition that is to be registered, state in the table below the details of the conveyancer (if any) who represented them.

You must also complete (2) below.

If the party is not represented insert 'none' in the second column.

A separate box is provided, or can be added, for each party, as required by panel 14(1). That includes separate boxes for attorneys and donors where appropriate.

Name of transferor, landlord, transferee, tenant, borrower or lender	Conveyancer's name, address and reference
	Reference:
	Reference:
	Reference:
	Reference:
	Reference:

If you are sending an application to give effect to a discharge in Form DS1 or release in Form DS3, for each lender state in the table below the details of the conveyancer (if any) who represented them.

You must also complete (2) below.

If the party is not represented insert 'none' in the second column.

A separate box is provided, or can be added, for each party, as required by panel 14(1). That includes separate boxes for attorneys and donors where appropriate.

Name of lender	Conveyancer's name, address and reference
	Reference:
	Reference:

(2) Evidence of identity

Place 'X' in the appropriate box(es).

Evidence of identity is defined in panel 12. Full details of the evidence of identity that is required can be found in 'Completing the evidence of identity panels on forms AP1, FR1, and DS2' available on the GOV.UK website.

☐ for each applicant named in panel 6 is enclosed

☐ for each unrepresented transferor, landlord, transferee, tenant, borrower or lender listed in (1) is enclosed

If a conveyancer is acting for the applicant, that conveyancer must sign. If no conveyancer is acting, the applicant (and if the applicant is more than one person then each of them) must sign.	15 Signature of conveyancer: *Blackhurst &Sons LLP* Date: 19 May 2026

WARNING

If you dishonestly enter information or make a statement that you know is, or might be, untrue or misleading, and intend by doing so to make a gain for yourself or another person, or to cause loss or the risk of loss to another person, you may commit the offence of fraud under section 1 of the Fraud Act 2006, the maximum penalty for which is 10 years' imprisonment or an unlimited fine, or both.

Failure to complete this form with proper care may result in a loss of protection under the Land Registration Act 2002 if, as a result, a mistake is made in the register.

Under section 66 of the Land Registration Act 2002 most documents (including this form) kept by the registrar relating to an application to the registrar or referred to in the register are open to public inspection and copying. If you believe a document contains prejudicial information, you may apply for that part of the document to be made exempt using Form EX1, under rule 136 of the Land Registration Rules 2003.

Document 19

Land Registry

Official copy of register of title

Title number EG576798

Edition date 5.02.2025

- This official copy shows the entries in the register of title on 6 June 2026 at 09:03:57.
- This date must be quoted as the "search from date" in any official search application based on this copy.
- The date at the beginning of an entry is the date on which the entry was made in the register.
- Issued on 6 June 2026.
- Under s.67 of the Land Registration Act 2002, this copy is admissible in evidence to the same extent as the original.
- For information about the register of title see Land Registry website www.landregistry.gov.uk or Land Registry Public Guide 1 – *A guide to the information we keep and how you can obtain it.*

A: Property register

This register describes the land and estate comprised in the title

Westshire : Barnford

1. (17.07.1993) The Freehold land shown edged with thick black on the plan of the above Title filed at the Registry and being 17 High Street, Barnford, Westshire, EX82 7YK.

B: Proprietorship register

This register specifies the class of title and identifies the owner. It contains any entries that affect the right of disposal.

Title absolute

1. (06.06.2026) Proprietor(s): Style&Go Ltd of c/o Blackhurst&Sons LLP of 22 High Street, Barnford, Westshire, EX82 7YK.

2. (06.06.2026) The transfer to the proprietor contains a covenant to observe and perform the covenants referred to at entry C2 the Charges Register and of indemnity in respect thereof.

C: Charges register

This register contains any charges and other matters that affect the land.

1. (17.07.1993) A conveyance of the land in this title dated 4 March 1959 made between (1) Vince Francis Moon (Vendor) and (2) Norman Jones (Purchaser) the land in this title is subject the following rights in favour of 19 High Street:

"A right of way to pass and repass day or night by foot only over the land coloured brown".

*Note: the land coloured brown is shown hatched grey on the filed plan.

2. (17.07.1993) A conveyance of the land in this title dated 4 March 1959 made between (1) Vince Francis Moon (Vendor) and (2) Norman Jones (Purchaser) contains the following covenant:

   "And the Purchaser for itself and its assigns with the intent to bind the Property hereby covenants with the Vendor his heirs executors administrators and assigns to keep in good repair the land coloured brown in order that it remains safely passable on foot."

   *Note: the land coloured brown is shown hatched grey on the filed plan

3. (17.07.1993) A conveyance of the land in this title dated 10 July 1993 made between (1) Charles Bainbridge (Vendor) and (2) Ansar Mukhtar and Anita Mukhtar (Purchaser) contains the following covenant:

   "11.1 And the Purchaser for itself and its assigns with the intent to bind the Property hereby covenants with the Vendor his heirs executors administrators and assigns not to build any structure on the Property."

End of register

Land Registry
Official copy of
Title plan

Title number **EG576798**
Ordnance Survey map reference **EG 5432 SS**
Scale **1:2500**
Administrative area **Westshire : Barnford**

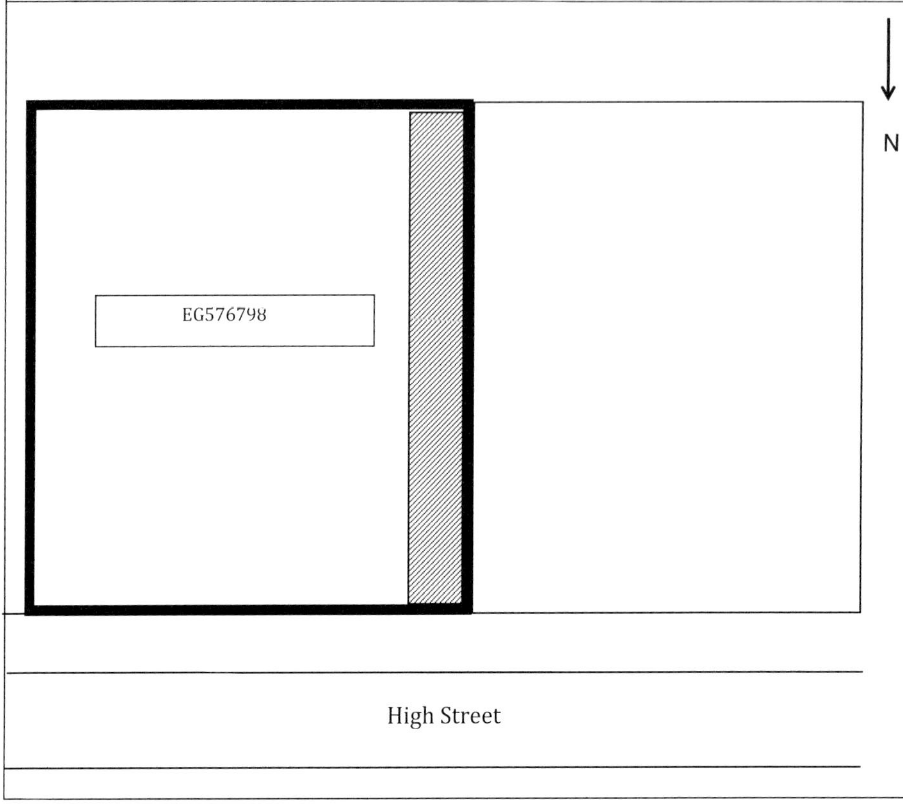

This official copy issued on 6 June 2026 shows the state of this title plan on 6 June 2026 at 09:03:57.
It is admissible in evidence to the same extent as the original (s. 67 Land Registration Act 2002).
This title plan shows the general position, not the exact line, of the boundaries. It may be subject to distortions in scale. Measurements scaled from this plan may not match measurements between the same points on the ground.
See Land Registry Public Guide 19 – Title Plans and Boundaries.

Appendix 3: Style&Go Ltd's purchase of the Car Park

Accompanying documents

Document 1

Heads of terms – land adjoining Sheep Street	
Seller	Urban Spaces Ltd, co. number 22135687
Seller's solicitor	Stoney Mace LLP, 94 The Quay, Barnford, EX81 9JQ
Buyer	Style&Go Ltd registered with company number 00127976 c/o Blackhurst&Sons LLP of 22 High Street, Barnford, Westshire, EX82 7YK
Buyer's solicitor	Blackhurst & Sons LLP of 22 High Street, Barnford, Westshire, EX82 7YK
Property	Freehold property: land adjoining Sheep Street, Barnford, Westshire, EX82 7YK
Price	£85,000
Deposit	5% of purchase price (£4,250)
Finance	Cash: £85,000
Proposed use	Onsite car park for additional site at 17 High Street, Barnford
VAT	The seller is registered for VAT under number GB987654321. Seller is not opting to tax.

EPITOME OF TITLE

of Urban Spaces Ltd
to freehold premises known as
land adjoining Sheep Street, Barnford, Westshire, EX82 7YK

No of Document	Date	Description of document including parties or event	Evidence now supplied	Whether original or certified copy will be handed over on completion
1.	29 September 1989	Conveyance (1) FBC Storage Ltd (2) Urban Developments Ltd	Photocopy	Original
2.	4 September 1989	Central Land Charges Search result	Photocopy	Original
3.	1 June 1956	Conveyance (1) Kristjan Norris and Miranda Norris (2) Regener8 Ltd	Photocopy	Original
4.	30 Sept 1989	Lease between (1) Urban Developments Ltd and (2) Revolution Autos Ltd	Photocopy	Original
5.	20 May 2020	Change of name certificate	Photocopy	Original
6.	29 September 1989	Mortgage deed	Photocopy	Certified copy

Document 3

INLAND REVENUE
07 JULY 1990
FINANCE ACT 1931

£100 £100 £100

£20

THIS CONVEYANCE is made the 29 day of September One thousand nine hundred and eighty nine **BETWEEN** FPC Storage Ltd of 27 The Unit, Bidtown, EX93 1AW (hereinafter referred to as 'the Vendors') of the one part and Urban Developments Ltd of 3 Snow Towers, Barnford, EX83 2HT (hereinafter referred to as 'the Purchaser') of the other part.

Whereas the Vendors are seised in fee simple in possession free from encumbrances of the piece or parcel of freehold land hereinafter described and have agreed to sell the same to the Purchaser for the like estate and subject as hereinafter referred to at the price of thirty thousand pounds (£30,000).

NOW THIS DEED WITNESSETH as follows

1. In pursuance of the said agreement and in consideration of the sum of thirty thousand pounds (£30,000) paid to the Vendors by the Purchaser (the receipt of which sum the Vendors hereby acknowledge) the Vendors as beneficial owners **HEREBY CONVEY UNTO** the Purchaser **ALL THAT** land known as land adjoining Sheep Street, Barnford, Westshire, EX82 7YK shown more particularly edged in thick black on the plan annexed to the conveyance dated 1 day of June One thousand nine hundred and fifty six **BETWEEN** Kristjan Norris and Miranda Norris of Riverside Cottage, Fremville EX81 7PH of the one part and Regener8 Ltd of 2, The Quay, Fremville, EX81 6JK of the other part (hereinafter referred to as 'the Conveyance') (hereinafter referred to as 'the Property') **TO HOLD** the same **UNTO** the Purchasers in fee simple **TOGETHER WITH** the benefit of the right of way referred to in the Conveyance but **SUBJECT** to the covenants contained or referred to in the Conveyance.

IN WITNESS whereof the parties hereto have hereunto set their hands and seals the day and year first written.

Executed as a deed by affixing the
common seal of FPC Storage Ltd in
the presence of:

Hamish Stone
Director

John Crick
Secretary

Executed as a deed by affixing the common seal of Urban Developments Ltd in the presence of:

William Peat
Director

Jade Wong
Secretary

Document 4

LAND CHARGES ACT 1972

Form K18 **CERTIFICATE OF THE RESULT OF THE SEARCH**

CERTIFICATE NO.	CERTIFICATE DATE	PROTECTION ENDS ON
1324354	4/9/1989	25/9/1989

It is hereby certified that an official search in respect of the undermentioned particulars has been made in the index to the registers which are kept pursuant to the Land Charges Act 1972. The result of the search is shown below.

PARTICULARS SEARCHED			
COUNTY OR COUNTIES	WESTSHIRE		
NAME(S)	Particulars of Charge	PERIOD	FEES
KRISTJAN *NORRIS* NO SUBSISTING ENTRY ***************		1926 - 1956	2.00
MIRANDA *NORRIS* NO SUBSISTING ENTRY ***************		1926 - 1956	2.00
REGENER8 LTD (1) D(II) NO 7577 REGISTERED ON 1 JUNE 1956 (2) 2 THE QUAY (3) FREMVILLE (4) WESTSHIRE (5) URBAN DEVELOPMENTS LTD (6) 3 SNOW TOWERS, BARNFORD, EX83 2HT ***************		1956 - 1976	2.00
FPC STORAGE LTD (1) D(II) NO.8644 REGISTERED ON 29 AUGUST 1983 (2) 27 THE UNIT (3) BIDTOWN (4) WESTSHIRE (5) URBAN DEVELOPMENTS LTD (6) 3 SNOW TOWERS, BARNFORD, EX83 2HT ***************		1980 - 1989	2.00
---------------------------END OF SEARCH -----------------------			

APPLICANT'S REFERENCE	SM361/MP	APPLICANT'S KEY NUMBER	239814	AMOUNT DEBITED £	8.00

INLAND REVENUE

07 JULY 1990
FINANCE ACT 1931

THIS CONVEYANCE is made the 1 day of June One thousand nine hundred and fifty six **BETWEEN** Kristjan Norris and Miranda Norris of 21 High Street, Barnford, EX82 7YK (hereinafter referred to as 'the Vendors') of the one part and Regener8 Ltd of 2, The Quay, Fremville, EX81 6JK (hereinafter referred to as 'the Purchaser') of the other part.

Whereas the Vendors are seised in fee simple in possession free from encumbrances of the piece or parcel of freehold land hereinafter described and have agreed to sell the same to the Purchaser for the like estate and subject as hereinafter referred to at the price of two thousand seven hundred and fifty pounds (£2,750).

NOW THIS DEED WITNESSETH as follows

1. In pursuance of the said agreement and in consideration of the sum of two thousand seven hundred and fifty pounds (£2,750) paid to the Vendors by the Purchaser (the receipt of which sum the Vendors hereby acknowledge) the Vendors as beneficial owners **HEREBY CONVEY UNTO** the Purchaser **ALL THAT** part of the land known as land adjoining Sheep Street, Barnford, Westshire, EX82 7YK shown more particularly edged in thick black on the plan annexed hereto (hereinafter referred to as 'the Property') **TOGETHER WITH** a right of way with or without vehicles over Sheep Street (such right benefiting each and every part of the Property) shown hatched black on the attached plan **TO HOLD** the same **UNTO** the Purchasers in fee simple.
2. The Purchasers with the intent and so that this covenant shall be binding on each and every part of the Property into whosoever hands the same may come and for the benefit of the remainder of the Vendors' property (the 'Retained Land') hereby for themselves and their successors in title covenant with the Vendors and their successors in title and assigns that the Purchasers and their successors in title will at all times hereafter observe and perform the conditions and restrictions and stipulations set out below:
   a) Not to use the Property or any part for any purpose which may be or grow to be a nuisance to the Vendors or to the owner or owners of any adjoining or neighbouring property.
   b) Not to erect any building or other structure on the Property without the previous written consent of the Vendors.
3. The Purchasers shall not by implication or otherwise become entitled to any rights whatsoever in on over or under the Retained Land save as shall have been expressly granted by this Conveyance and without prejudice to the generality of this provision the Purchasers shall not become entitled to any rights of light or air which would restrict or interfere with the free use of the Retained Land for building or other purposes.

4. It is hereby certified that the transaction hereby effected does not form part of a larger transaction or of a series of transactions in respect of which the amount or value or the aggregate amount or value of the consideration exceeds thirty thousand pounds.

IN WITNESS whereof the parties hereto have hereunto set their hands and seals the day and year first written.

SIGNED SEALED AND DELIVERED
by Kristjan
Norris

Kristjan Norris

in the presence of:
Maurice McGraw
Maurice McGraw
MMK Solicitors LLP, 89 Barnford Lane, Barnford, Westshire, EX83 3QT Solicitor

SIGNED SEALED AND DELIVERED
by Miranda
Norris

Miranda Norris

in the presence of:
Maurice McGraw
Maurice McGraw
MMK Solicitors LLP, 89 Barnford Lane, Barnford, Westshire, EX83 3QT Solicitor

Executed as a deed by affixing the common seal of Regener8 Ltd in the presence of:

J. Holmes
Director

S. Dixon
Director

Document 6

LEASE OF LAND ADJOINING SHEEP STREET

This lease is dated *30 September 1989*

PARTIES

(1)

URBAN DEVELOPMENTS LTD incorporated and registered in England and Wales with company number 22135687 whose registered office is at 3 Snow Towers, Barnford, EX83 2HT (**Landlord**)

(2)

REVOLUTION AUTOS LTD incorporated and registered in England and Wales with company number 25891137 whose registered office is at 5 Temple Rise, Exton, EX44 3PJ (**Tenant**)

RECITALS

(A)

The Landlord is the freehold owner of the Property.

(B)

The Landlord has agreed to grant a lease of the Property to the Tenant on the terms set out in this lease.

DEFINITIONS

Annual Rent: rent at a rate of £7,500 per annum

Contractual Term: a term of years from and including the date of this lease to and including 29 September 2004.

Property: land adjoining Sheep Street, Barnford, Westshire, EX82 7YK

TERMS

1. The Landlord lets the Property to the Tenant for the Contractual Term.
2. The grant in clause 1 is made with the Tenant paying the Annual Rent to the Landlord.
3. The parties agree that the provisions of sections 24 to 28 of the LTA 1954 are excluded in relation to the tenancy created by this lease.

EXECUTION

Executed as deed by URBAN DEVELOPMENTS LTD acting by ANOUSKA DAY a director, in the presence of:	*Anouska Day* Director

Greta Konig
Greta Konig, Secretary, Urban Developments Ltd, 3 Snow Towers, Barnford, EX83 2HT

Executed as deed by REVOLUTION AUTOS LTD acting by ANDREW MITCHELL a director, in the presence of:

Andrew Mitchell
Director

James Mitchell
James Mitchell, Director, 5 Temple Rise, Exton, EX44 3PJ

Document 7

CERTIFICATE OF INCOPORATION

ON CHANGE OF NAME

Company number 22135687

The Registrar of Companies for England and Wales hereby certifies that under the Companies Act 2006:

URBAN DEVELOPMENTS LTD

a company incorporated as private limited by shares, having its registered office situated in England and Wales, has changed its name to:

URBAN SPACES LTD

Given at Companies House on **20th May 2020.**

The above information was communicated by electronic means and authenticated by the Registrar of Companies under section 1115 of the Companies Act 2006.

Companies House   Official Seal of the Registrar of Companies

BARNFORD BANK

MORTGAGE DEED

This deed is dated *29 September 1989*

PARTIES

(1) Urban Developments Ltd incorporated and registered in England and Wales with company number 22135687 whose registered office is at 3 Snow Towers, Barnford, EX83 2HT (**Borrower**)

(2) Barnford Bank incorporated and registered in England and Wales whose registered office is at 1 The Quay, Barnford, EX81 8HH (**Lender**)

RECITALS

(A) The Lender has agreed to provide the Borrower with the Loan on a secured basis.

(B) The Borrower owns the Property.

(C) Under this deed, the Borrower provides the Property as security to the Lender for the Loan.

DEFINITIONS

Loan: the sum of twenty two thousand pounds (£22,000)

Property: Land adjoining Sheet Street, Barnford, Westshire, EX82 7YK

TERMS

[not reproduced]

EXECUTION

Executed as a deed by Urban Developments Ltd acting by ANOUSKA DAY, a director, and GRETA KONIG, its secretary	*Anouska Day* Director *Greta Konig* Secretary
Executed as a deed by Barnford Bank acting by Tony Twain, a director, and Sebastian Schon, a director	*Tony Twain* Director *Sebastian Schon* Director

Document 9

LAND CHARGES ACT 1972

Form K18 CERTIFICATE OF THE RESULT OF THE SEARCH

CERTIFICATE NO.	CERTIFICATE DATE	PROTECTION ENDS ON
885/EXH02	6/1/2026	27/1/2026

It is hereby certified that an official search in respect of the undermentioned particulars has been made in the index to the registers which are kept pursuant to the Land Charges Act 1972. The result of the search is shown below.

PARTICULARS SEARCHED			
COUNTY OR COUNTIES	WESTSHIRE		
NAME(S)	Particulars of Charge	PERIOD	FEES

KRISTJAN *NORRIS* NO SUBSISTING ENTRY ***************	1926 - 1956	2.00
KRIS NORRIS NO SUBSISTING ENTRY ***************	1926 – 1956	2.00
KRISTIAN NORRIS NO SUBSISTING ENTRY ***************	1926 - 1956	2.00
CHRISTIAN NORRIS NO SUBSISTING ENTRY ***************	1926 - 1956	2.00
MIRANDA *NORRIS* NO SUBSISTING ENTRY ***************	1926 - 1956	2.00
REGENER8 LTD (1) D(II) NO 7577 REGISTERED ON 1 JUNE 1956 (2) 2 THE QUAY (3) FREMVILLE (4) WESTSHIRE (5) STYLE&GO LTD (6) BLACKHURST & SONS LLP OF 22 HIGH STREET, BARNFORD, WESTSHIRE, EX82 7YK ***************	1956 – 1989	2.00
FPC STORAGE LTD (1) D(II) NO.8644 REGISTERED ON 29 AUGUST 1983 (2) 27 THE UNIT (3) BIDTOWN (4) WESTSHIRE (5) STYLE&GO LTD (6) BLACKHURST & SONS LLP OF 22 HIGH STREET, BARNFORD, WESTSHIRE, EX82 7YK ***************	1956 – 1989	2.00
URBAN DEVELOPMENTS LTD (1) D(II), NO. 9965, REGISTERED ON 29 SEPTEMBER 1989 (2) 3 SNOW TOWERS (3) BARNFORD (4) WESTSHIRE (5) STYLE&GO LTD (6) BLACKHURST & SONS LLP OF 22 HIGH STREET, BARNFORD, WESTSHIRE, EX82 7YK ***************	1989 – 2020	2.00
URBAN SPACES LTD (1) D(II), NO. 9965, REGISTERED ON 20 MAY 2020 (2) 3 SNOW TOWERS (3) BARNFORD (4) WESTSHIRE (5) STYLE&GO LTD (6) BLACKHURST & SONS LLP OF 22 HIGH STREET, BARNFORD, WESTSHIRE, EX82 7YK ***************	2020 – 2026	2.00
---------------------------END OF SEARCH -----------------------		

APPLICANT'S REFERENCE	BS77577	APPLICANT'S KEY NUMBER	75689	AMOUNT DEBITED £	18.00

Document 10

SIMR

Official certificate of the result of search of the index map

Land Registry
Land Registration Rules 2003

Certificate Date: 6 January 2026
Certificate Time: 16:28:44
Certificate Ref: BFG/EXH02

Property	LAND AT SHEEP STREET, BARNFORD, WESTSHIRE, EX82 7YK

Result

The index map has been searched in respect of the Property with the following result:

Plan reference	Title No.	Registered Estate or Caution	Notes

No registered estate, caution against first registration, application for first registration or application for a caution against first registration is shown on the index map in relation to the property.

******

The plan attached to this result is prepared for the sole purpose of showing the area in respect of which an official search has been made. The information has been taken from the index map. It is illustrative only and does not define the extent of the land in any individual title. For information about the general boundaries of a title please refer to the individual register and title plan.

******

Verbal descriptions of registered relating franchises and registered manors, and of pending applications and cautions against first registrations in respect of relating franchises, are kept in the index of relating franchises and manors. The application form for a search of the index is form SIF.

High Street

Document 11

Westshire District Council Offices
Council House,
Exton,
Westshire
(DX 765567 Exton 7)

Westshire
District Council

REGISTER OF LOCAL LAND CHARGES
OFFICIAL CERTIFICATE OF SEARCH

Search Reference: BCG/ECH02

Date: 6 January 2026

Applicant: Blackhurst & Sons LLP

Official search required in all parts of the Register of Local Land Charges for subsisting registrations against the land described and the plan submitted.

Land: Land adjoining Sheep Street, Barnford, Westshire, EX82 7YK

It is hereby certified that the search requested above reveals 2 registrations described in the Schedule(s) hereto up to and including the date of this certificate.

LLC1: Search Reference BCG/EXH02 Date: 6 January 2026

Westshire District Council

Register of Local Land Charges
Schedule to Official Certificate of Search

Part 3: Planning Charges

Description of charge (including reference to appropriate statutory provision)	**Originating Authority**	**Place where relevant documents may be inspected**	**Date of Registration**
PP/UC/737/89 Permission for change of use from Class B1 to the use for the sale or display for sale of motor vehicles	Westshire District Council	Council House, Exton, Westshire	6/11/1989
Direction made 3 March 1996 under Article 4 of the GENERAL PERMITTED DEVELOPMENT ORDER 1995 that type of Permitted Development (being development comprised within Part 7 in Schedule 2 of the said order) shall not be carried out unless express planning permission is granted.	Westshire District Council	Council House, Exton, Westshire	03/03/1996

Document 12

Westshire District Council Offices
Council House,
Exton,
Westshire
(DX 765567 Exton 7)

Westshire District Council

CON29 ENQUIRIES OF LOCAL AUTHORITY
(2016)

Applicant: Blackhurst & Sons LLP

Search Reference: KLF/EXH02

Date: 6 January 2026

Property: Land adjoining Sheep Street, Barnford, Westshire, EX82 7KY

I refer to your Standard Enquiries relating to the above property. These replies relate to that property as shown on the location plan where supplied. The replies are given subject to the Notes to the Standard Enquiries.

All correspondence relating to these answers should quote the official Search Reference.

Standard Enquiries of Local Authority

PLANNING AND BUILDING REGULATIONS
1.1. Planning and building decisions and pending applications
Which of the following relating to the property have been granted, issued or refused or (where applicable) are the subject of pending applications or agreements?
(a) a planning permission

1.1.(a) Reference: PP/UC/737/89
Description: Change of use from Class B1 to use for the sale or display for sale of motor vehicles
Application date: 10/10/1989
Decision: GRANTED on 6/11/1989

[...]

(j) building regulations approval
none

(k) a building regulation completion certificate
none

[...]

Informatives:
(1) Copy documents available from Planning and Building Control Services, Westshire District Council.

(2) This reply does not cover other properties in the vicinity of the property.

(3) As from 1 April 2002 the installation of a replacement window, rooflight or roof window or specified type of glazed door must either have building regulation approval or be carried out and certified by a person who is registered under the Fenestration Self-Assessment Scheme by the Glass and Glazing Federation. The owner or occupier of the property should be asked to produce any such certificate.

ROADS AND PUBLIC RIGHTS OF WAY
Roadways, footways and footpaths
2.1 Which of the roads, footways and footpaths named in the application for this search (via boxes B and C) are:
(a) highways maintainable at public expense
2.1.(a) High Street

(b) subject to adoption and supported by a bond or bond waiver
2.1.(b) None

(c) to be made up by a local authority who will reclaim the cost from the frontagers
2.1.(c) None

(d) to be adopted by a local authority without reclaiming the cost from the frontagers
2.1.(d) None

Informative: If a road, footway or footpath is not a highway, there may be no right to use it and the local authority cannot express an opinion without seeing the title plan and carrying out a site inspection.

Public rights of way
2.2 Is any public right of way which abuts on, or crosses, the property shown in a definitive map or revised definitive map?
2.2. No

[...]

2.5 If so, please attach a plan showing the approximate route.
2.5. Not applicable

Informative: A definitive map for Westshire District Council has now been published. However, a survey of all paths has not been completed and whilst this does not preclude the existence of unrecorded rights of way, the local authority is unaware of any claimed rights of way existing over the search site.

OTHER MATTERS:

Apart from matters entered on the registers of local land charges, do any of the following matters apply to the property? If so, how can copies of relevant documents be obtained?

> **Note:** Matters entered onto the Local Land Charges Register, or visible by property/site inspection, will not be referred to (where relevant) in answer to the enquiries 3.1 to 3.15 below.

Informative: In some circumstances, road closures can be obtained by third parties from magistrate's courts, or can be made by the Secretary of State for Transport without involving the local authority. This enquiry is designed to reveal matters that are yet to be implemented and could not therefore be ascertained by a visual inspection. Schemes that have been, or are currently being, implemented will not be referred to in answer to this enquiry.

[...]

3.5. Nearby railway schemes

(a) Is the property (or will it be) within 200 metres of the centre line of a proposed railway, tramway, light railway or monorail?

> 3.5.(a) Yes – proposed railway scheme at Barnford Central. Please see details at westshirerailwayredevelopment.co.uk.

[...]

3.6 Traffic schemes

Has a local authority approved but not yet implemented any of the following for the roads, footways and footpaths which are named in Boxes B and C and are within 200 metres of the boundaries of the property?

[...]

(e) pedestrianisation

> 3.6(e) Yes – Main Street, which is within 200 metres of the boundaries of the property, is to be pedestrianised.

[...]

3.8. Contravention of building regulations

Has a local authority authorised in relation to the property any proceedings for the contravention of any provision contained in building regulations?

> 3.8. No

3.9. Notices, orders, directions and proceedings under Planning Acts

Do any of the following subsist in relation to the property, or has a local authority decided to issue, serve, make or commence any of the following?

(a) an enforcement notice

> 3.9.(a) No

(b) a stop notice

> 3.9.(b) No

...

(d) a breach of condition notice

3.9.(d) No

(e) a planning contravention notice

3.9.(e) No

[...]

(j) a direction restricting permitted development

3.9.(j) Yes, Direction made 3 March 1996 under Article 4 of the GENERAL PERMITTED DEVELOPMENT ORDER 1995 that type of Permitted Development (being development comprised within Part 7 in Schedule 2 of the said order) shall not be carried out unless express planning permission is granted.

[...]

3.11. Conservation area
Do the following apply in relation to the property?
(a) the making of the area a conservation area before 31 August 1974

3.11.(a) No

(b) an unimplemented resolution to designate the area a Conservation Area

3.11.(b) No

[...]

3.13. Contaminated land
Do any of the following apply (including any relating to land adjacent to or adjoining the property which has been identified as contaminated land because it is in such a condition that harm or pollution of controlled waters might be caused on the property)?
(a) a contaminated land notice

3.13.(a) No

(b) in relation to a register maintained under section 78R of the Environmental Protection Act 1990

(i) a decision to make an entry

3.13.(b)(i) No

(ii) an entry

3.13.(b)(ii) No

(c) consultation with the owner or occupier of the property conducted under section 78G(3) of the Environmental Protection Act 1990 before the service of a remediation notice

3.13.(c) No

Informative: A negative reply does not imply that the property or any adjoining or adjacent land is free from contamination or from the risk of it and the reply may not disclose steps taken by another local authority in whose area adjacent or adjoining land is situated.

[...]

Document 13

Highways Division
Westshire District Council Offices
Council House,
Exton,
Westshire
(DX 765567 Exton 7)

Westshire
District Council

Date: 6 January 2026

Dear Sirs

17 High Street and land adjoining Sheep Street, Barnford, Westshire, EX82 7YK

Please find below the plan; showing by black shading the extent of the publicly maintainable highway in the immediate vicinity of the property, as far as can be ascertained from existing records.

If you have any further queries please do not hesitate to contact us.

Yours faithfully

Highway Records Manager

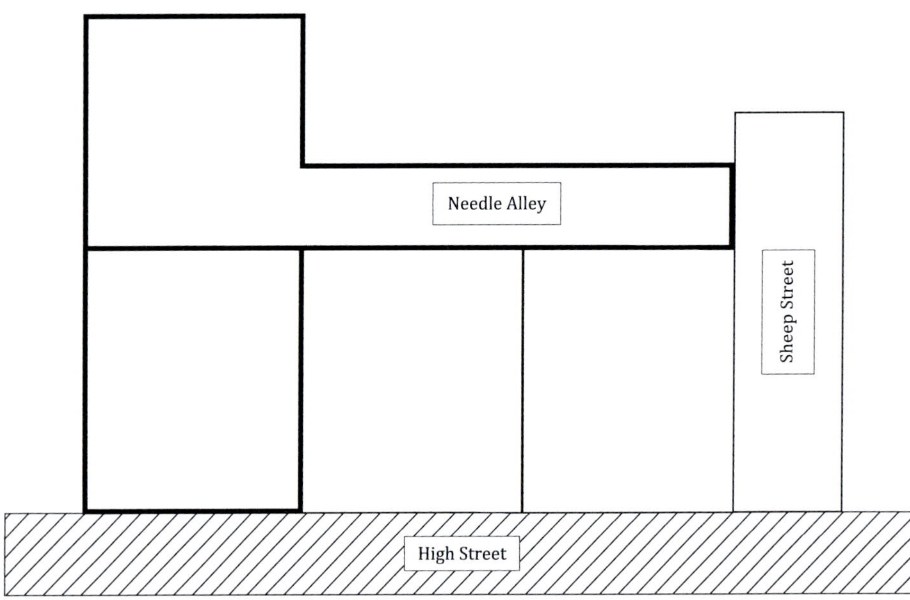

WESTSHIRE WATER

Drainage and Water search

Date: 6 January 2026

Property: Land at Sheep Street, Barnford, Westshire, EX82 7YK

Results:

Mains water: connected

Foul water: connected

Surface water sewer: connected

Sewer pipe within boundary: no

Water pipe within boundary: no

Document 15

WESTSHIRE ENVIRO-CHECK

Date: 6 January 2026

Type of report: Homebuyers

Property land adjoining Sheep Street, Barnford, Westshire, EX82 7YK

RESULTS:

Professional opinion: PASS

Environmental search results:

Contaminated Land: passed
No significant concerns have been identified as a result of the contaminated land searches.

Flood risk: low
The village of Barnford suffered flooding in 1994, but the property was unaffected and the property's overall risk assessment for river, coastal, surface water and groundwater flooding is low.

Ground stability: passed
No significant concerns have been identified as a result of the ground stability searches. No action required.

Radon: passed
Local levels of radon are considered normal.

Westshire Enviro-check

CHANCEL REPAIR SEARCH

Report details

Report number: CC/994/EXH02

Issue date: 6 January 2026

Address: land adjoining Sheep Street, Barnford, Westshire, EX82 7YK

Result

The above address is not located within the historical boundary of a tithe district within a parish which continues to have a potential chancel repair liability based upon historical parish data and the relevant inland Revenue Indices held by The National Archives.

Document 17

EXTRACT OF COMPANY SEARCH REPORT

Urban Spaces Ltd

Company Number:	22135687
Date of Incorporation:	3 May 1985
Registered Office:	3 Snow Towers, Barnford, EX83 2HT
Change(s) of Name:	Urban Developments Ltd to Urban Spaces Ltd, in 2020
Charges:	Barnford Bank holds a Debenture including fixed charges over the assets of the Company following the loan of £22,000 provided by Barnford Bank.

WESTSHIRE UTILITIES

Utilities search

Date: 6 January 2026

Property: Land at Sheep Street, Barnford, Westshire, EX82 7YK

Summary:

- Westshire utilities has equipment in the vicinity.
- Electricity connection: High Street, marked 'A' on the plan.
- Gas connection: High Street, marked 'B' on the plan.
- Cables: run underneath 17 High Street, route marked 'Y-Z' on the plan.

Plan:

[*not reproduced*]

Document 19

WESTSHIRE COMMUNICATIONS

Telecoms search

Date: 6 January 2026

Property: Land at Sheep Street, Barnford, Westshire, EX82 7YK

Summary:

- No telecommunications equipment is located within the boundaries of the site.
- Telecommunications equipment in the vicinity is marked on the attached plan.

Plan:

[not reproduced]

Commercial Property Standard Enquiries

CPSE.7 (version 1.3.2) General short form pre-contract enquiries for all property transactions

Conditions

This document may be used free of charge subject to the Conditions set out in *GN/CPSE (version 3.3) Guidance notes on the Commercial Property Standard Enquiries*.

Particulars

Seller: Urban Spaces Ltd

Buyer: Style&Go Ltd

Property: land adjoining Sheep Street, Barnford, Westshire, EX82 7YK

Seller's solicitors: Stoney Mace LLP

Buyer's solicitors: Blackhurst & Sons LLP of 22 High Street, Barnford, Westshire, EX82 7YK

Date: 6 January 2026

Interpretation

1. In interpreting these enquiries, the terms set out in the Particulars have the meanings given to them in the Particulars and the following interpretation also applies:

- **Buyer:** includes tenant and prospective tenant.
- **Conduits:** means the pipes, wires and cables through which utilities and other services are carried.
- **Property:** includes any part of it and all buildings and other structures on it.
- **Rights:** means any covenants, agreements, rights, restrictions, or informal arrangements of any kind (including any which are in the course of being acquired).

Practical Law

BPF
BRITISH PROPERTY FEDERATION

- **SDLT:** includes Land Transaction Tax where the Property is in Wales, and references to HMRC include the Welsh Revenue Authority where relevant.

- **Seller:** includes landlord and prospective landlord.

2. The replies to the enquiries will be given by the Seller and addressed to the Buyer. Unless otherwise agreed in writing, only the Buyer and those acting for it may rely on them.

- References in these enquiries to "**you**" mean the Seller and to "**we**" and "**us**" mean the Buyer.

- In replies to the enquiries, references to "**you**" will be taken to mean the Buyer and to "**we**" and "**us**" will be taken to mean the Seller.

3. The replies are given without liability on the part of the Seller's solicitors, its members, partners, employees, consultants or other staff.

4. The Buyer acknowledges that even though the Seller will be giving replies to the enquiries, the Buyer should still inspect the Property, have the Property surveyed, investigate title and make all appropriate searches and enquiries of third parties.

5. In replying to each of these enquiries and any supplemental enquiries, the Seller acknowledges that it is required to provide the Buyer with copies of all documents and correspondence and to supply all details relevant to the replies, whether or not specifically requested to do so.

6. The Seller confirms that pending exchange of contracts or, where there is no prior contract, pending completion of the Transaction, it will notify the Buyer on becoming aware of anything which may cause any reply that it has given to these or any supplemental enquiries to be incorrect.

Practical Law

Contents

CLAUSE

ENQUIRIES

1. BOUNDARIES AND EXTENT

In this enquiry, "**Boundary Features**" means all walls, fences, ditches, hedges or other features that form the physical boundary of the Property.

1.1 Are you aware of any discrepancies between the boundaries referred to in the title deeds and the Boundary Features?

No, but the buyer must rely on its own searches and enquiries

1.2 Have any alterations been made to the position of any Boundary Features during your ownership or, to your knowledge, earlier?

Not to the knowledge of the seller

1.3 In relation to each of the Boundary Features:

(a) Which of them have you maintained or regarded as your responsibility?

(b) Which of them has someone else maintained or regarded as their responsibility?

(c) Which of them have you treated as a party structure or jointly repaired or maintained with someone else?

(d) Are there any agreements for their maintenance?

(e) Are any of them subject to a party wall award or agreement?

(a)	All
(b)	None
(c)	None
(d)	No
(e)	No

1.4 Does any part of the Property lie beneath or above adjoining premises, roads or footpaths?

No

1.5 Are there any adjoining or nearby premises or land which you use or occupy in connection with the Property?

Sheep Street is a private road which is required for access to and from the Property. See replies to question 2 below.

2. RIGHTS BENEFITING THE PROPERTY

2.1 What Rights does the Property benefit from, other than those which are apparent from the copy documents supplied?

> Other than as disclosed in the title deeds, none of which the seller is aware but the buyer must rely on its own searches and enquiries

2.2 Please confirm that all terms and conditions relating to the exercise of any Rights which benefit the Property have been complied with.

> Confirmed so far as the seller is aware

2.3 Have you (or, to your knowledge, has any predecessor in title) registered any notices, cautions against first registration or other entries against any other titles at the Land Registry in relation to any Rights which benefit the Property?

> The seller believes the Right is registered against a title at the Land Registry but the buyer must rely on its own searches and enquiries

2.4 What are the pedestrian and vehicular access routes to and from the Property?

> Via Sheep Street.

2.5 Have you, or to your knowledge has anyone else, applied to modify or discharge any Rights benefitting the Property?

> Not so far as the seller is aware but the buyer must rely on its own searches and enquiries

3. ADVERSE RIGHTS AFFECTING THE PROPERTY

3.1 What Rights is the Property subject to, other than those which are apparent from the copy documents supplied?

> The seller is aware of covenants affecting the Property – see documents supplied.

3.2 Please confirm that all terms and conditions relating to the exercise of any Rights to which the Property is subject have been complied with.

> The seller has not breached the covenant contained in the Conveyance dated 1 June 1956 between Kristjan Norris and Miranda Norris and Regener8 Ltd but the buyer must rely on its own searches and enquiries in respect of others.

3.3 Are there any overriding interests to which the Property is subject?

Not so far as the seller is aware but the buyer must rely on its own searches and enquiries

3.4 Does the Property, or any property over which Rights are enjoyed, include any land that is currently used or has in the past ten years been used by members of the public for recreational purposes, whether with or without your permission?

Not so far as the seller is aware but the buyer must rely on its own searches and enquiries

3.5 Have you, or to your knowledge has anyone else, applied to modify or discharge any Rights to which the Property is subject?

Not so far as the seller is aware but the buyer must rely on its own searches and enquiries

4. PHYSICAL CONDITION

4.1 Is the Property now, or has it ever been, affected by any of the following:

(a) structural or inherent defects;

(b) subsidence, settlement, landslip or heave;

(c) defective Conduits, fixtures, plant or equipment;

(d) rising damp, rot, or any fungal or other infection;

(e) Japanese knotweed;

(f) any other infestation; or

(g) flooding?

(a) – (f) n/a so far as the seller is aware (g) the village of Barnford has flooded during the seller's ownership of the Property. The Property was not affected. The buyer must rely on its own searches and inspections for further information.

4.2 Is there any Green Deal Plan affecting the Property?

Not to the knowledge of the seller but the buyer must rely on its own searches and enquiries

4.3 Has asbestos, or any other substance known or suspected to be unsuitable for its purpose, unstable or hazardous, been used in, or removed from, the Property including Conduits, fixtures, plant and equipment?

Not to the knowledge of the seller but the buyer must rely on its own searches and enquiries

4.4 Please supply copies of the most recent asbestos survey and asbestos management plan for the Property, together with any other relevant information you hold.

There are none so far as the seller is aware.

4.5 Please supply copies of any subsisting guarantees, warranties and/or insurance policies relating to any buildings erected on or major alterations or engineering works carried out at the Property within the last 12 years.

There are none so far as the seller is aware.

4.6 Please confirm that all Conduits, fixtures, plant or equipment in or serving the Property have been regularly tested and maintained and that all recommended work has been carried out.

Confirmed

5. CONTENTS

5.1 Please list any fixtures and fittings that will be removed from the Property before completion.

None

5.2 Other than those belonging to an occupational tenant, please confirm that you own all fixtures and fittings that will remain on the Property free from third party rights.

None

6. UTILITIES AND SERVICES

6.1 Please list the services available at the Property and confirm which (if any) are connected to the mains and which are metered.

Electricity Gas Broadband and telephone Water Connections are direct to a mains supply. Connections are not metered.

6.2 Do any parts of the services pass over, under or through any land which is not part of the Property?

Services pass from the High Street under 17 High Street, which adjoins the Property.

6.3 Does the Property have a communal heating, cooling or hot water system?

no

6.4 Please provide:

(a) Copies of the most recent bills for the services referred to at enquiry 6.1;

(b) The name and contact details of the individual within your organisation who deals with energy supplies relating to the Property and confirm that we may make contact in order to obtain information about the services supplied.

Enclosed.

7. FIRE SAFETY AND MEANS OF ESCAPE

7.1 What are the current means of escape from the Property in case of emergency?

n/a – property is outside

7.2 Have you experienced any difficulty in completing the fire risk assessment for the Property or when co-operating with anybody else in order to comply with fire safety regulations?

Not so far as the seller is aware

7.3 Has there been any fire risk recommendation that has not been implemented?

Not so far as the seller is aware

8. PLANNING AND BUILDING REGULATIONS

8.1 Are you aware of any breach of planning law in relation to the construction, use or occupation of the Property?

None so far as the seller is aware

8.2 Is any building or structure on the Property listed under planning law?

Not so far as the seller is aware

8.3 What works have been carried out at the Property during the last 10 years?

None so far as the seller is aware

8.4 What changes of use have taken place at the Property during the last 10 years?

Change of use in 1989 from class B1 to use for sale or display of motor vehicles.

8.5 What is the existing use of the Property and how is it authorised under planning legislation?

The Property is currently used for the sale of cars – has planning permission

8.6 Where you or your solicitor have them, please supply copies of all planning documents and all building regulations consents relating to the Property.

Enclosed

8.7 Have you made an application for planning permission which has not yet been determined by the local authority or are there any other planning proceedings currently taking place in relation to the Property?

Not so far as the seller is aware

8.8 What information do you have about any proposals for the development of any adjoining or neighbouring property?

The buyer must rely on its own enquiries

8.9 Are you aware of any existing or future Community Infrastructure Levy liability relating to the Property?

The buyer must rely on its own enquiries

9. STATUTORY AGREEMENTS AND INFRASTRUCTURE

9.1 Are you aware of any outstanding obligations relating to the construction or adoption of the highway, Conduits or any other infrastructure that supplies the Property?

Not so far as the seller is aware

9.2 Are you required to enter into any agreement or obligation with any planning, highway or other public authority or utilities provider?

Not so far as the seller is aware

9.3 Are you aware of anything affecting the Property that is capable of being registered on the Local Land Charges Register but is not so registered?

Not so far as the seller is aware

10. STATUTORY AND OTHER REQUIREMENTS

10.1 Are you aware of any breach of statutory requirements that relate to the Property or its use or occupation?

Not so far as the seller is aware

10.2 Do you have a health and safety file for the Property?

Yes

10.3 If the answer to enquiry 10.2 is yes

(a) Is the file at the Property and available for us to inspect?

(b) In what form will the file be provided to us upon completion?

(a) Yes (b) Hard copy

10.4 Please supply a valid Energy Performance Certificate (**EPC**) for the Property.

Enclosed

10.5 Where the Property has an EPC rating of F or G, please supply a copy of any information or evidence used to support any registration in the Exemptions Register established under the Energy Efficiency (Private Rented Property) (England and Wales) Regulations 2015.

n/a

10.6 Please confirm when the air conditioning at the Property was last inspected and provide a copy of that inspection report.

n/a

10.7 Please supply details of any grant made or claimed in respect of the Property including circumstances in which it may have to be repaid.

n/a

11. Environmental

11.1 Where you or your solicitor have them, please supply copies of all environmental and flood risk reports that have been prepared in relation to the Property.

None

11.2 Please supply a copy of all statutory authorisations under all environmental law for the current uses of the Property (if applicable).

N/a

11.3 Are there, or have there ever been, any above or below ground bulk storage tanks at the Property? If so, please confirm the contents and age of those tanks (or estimate the age as accurately as possible).

None so far as the seller is aware but the buyer must rely on its own enquiries

11.4 Please confirm that you are not aware of any breach of any environmental law relating to the past or present use or occupation of the Property or for substances in, on, at or under the Property.

None so far as the seller is aware but the buyer must rely on its own enquiries

11.5 Please confirm that you are not aware of any environmental incidents including the leaking or discharging of any substances at the Property or on or at any nearby properties.

None so far as the seller is aware but the buyer must rely on its own enquiries

12. Occupiers

12.1 Does anyone apart from you have any right to use or occupy the Property?

Not so far as the seller is aware.

12.2 If the Property is vacant, when and why did it become vacant?

Lease expired on 29 September 2004 and Property has been vacant since then.

13. INSURANCE

13.1 Have you ever experienced any difficulty in obtaining insurance cover for the Property at normal rates and subject to normal exclusions?

Not so far as the seller is aware.

13.2 Please give details of any outstanding insurance claims in relation to the Property.

None so far as the seller is aware.

13.3 If the buildings insurance policy is to remain in place after exchange of contracts, please supply a copy of the policy and schedule of insurance cover.

n/a

13.4 Please provide a copy of any other insurance policies relating to the Property (together with the proposal form and other material correspondence with the insurers) including any title indemnity insurance policies.

n/a

13.5 Please provide details of any breaches of any insurance policies relating to the Property.

n/a

14. RATES AND OTHER OUTGOINGS

14.1 Have any works been carried out to the Property which may cause the rateable value of the Property to be reviewed?

Not so far as the seller is aware.

14.2 Have you or any occupier of the Property, made any claim for void period allowance or for exemption from liability from business rates? Is any claim pending/outstanding?

Not so far as the seller is aware.

14.3 Are there any other outgoings relating to the Property not referred to elsewhere in these enquiries?

Not so far as the seller is aware.

14.4 Please supply the most recent bills for business rates and all other outgoings relating to the Property.

Enclosed

14.5 If the Property is subject to a Business Improvement District Arrangement, please give details of any levy currently payable.

n/a

15. NOTICES

Please supply a copy of any notices affecting the Property that you or your predecessors or any tenant or occupier have given or received and confirm that those notices have been complied with.

None except as disclosed.

16. DISPUTES

Please provide details of any outstanding complaints or past, current or likely disputes affecting the Property its use and occupation.

None to the seller's knowledge.

17. SDLT ON ASSIGNMENT OF A LEASE

In this enquiry, Lease is any lease under which the Property is held and which is to be assigned by you in the Transaction.

17.1 Where the Lease or the substantial performance of the agreement to grant the Lease or any event since the grant of the Lease constitutes a transaction notifiable for SDLT purposes, including the payment of a premium for the grant of the Lease or any assignment of it, please provide copies of all land transaction returns and certificates issued by HMRC certifying notification.

n/a

17.2 Is there any potential or actual outstanding SDLT liability, including any resulting from the settlement or determination of any rent reviews or other provision for varying the rent or settlement or determination of any contingent, uncertain or unascertained rents?

n/a

17.3 Were any SDLT reliefs claimed on the grant of the Lease and, if applicable, on the assignment of the Lease to you that would result in the assignment of the Lease by you being deemed to be the grant of a new lease?

n/a

18. DEFERRED PAYMENT OF SDLT

Please give details of any deferred payment of SDLT which is outstanding in respect of the Property, together with copies of the original land transaction and all relevant correspondence with HMRC.

None so far as the seller is aware

19. VAT

19.1 If you are registered for VAT, please supply your VAT registration number.

GB987654321

19.2 Please state whether the Transaction is to be treated as a transfer of a business as a going concern ('**TOGC**') and therefore outside the scope of VAT.

No

19.3 If enquiry 19.2 does not apply, is the Transaction standard-rated for VAT purposes as a result of either:

(a) the exercise of an option to tax in relation to the Property; or

(b) compulsory standard-rating?

no

19.4 If the answer to enquiry 19.3 is yes, please provide a copy of either:

(a) the option notice given to HMRC, together with a copy of HMRC's acknowledgement; or

(b) evidence of the reason that compulsory standard-rating applies to this transaction.

n/a

19.5 If the Transaction is not standard-rated for VAT purposes, please state if it is zero-rated, exempt or outside the scope of VAT other than by reason of being a TOGC.

Exempt supply

20. CAPITAL ALLOWANCES

20.1 Is there anything in the Property upon which a capital allowances claim can be based?

no

20.2 If the answer to enquiry 20.1 is yes, please give details and copy documents including the name and contact details of your capital allowances advisor and confirm that we may make contact direct to ascertain any required capital allowances information.

n/a

Document 21

Type	Enquiry from Style&Go Ltd's solicitor	Response from Urban Spaces Ltd's solicitor
Title	Please confirm there has not been a breach of the restrictive covenants (D(ii) land charges) registered against Urban Spaces Ltd.	Confirmed.
	Please confirm whether there are any overriding interests affecting the property	Confirmed none to the seller's knowledge.
	A company search has revealed that Barnford Bank has a fixed charge against the property. Please provide an undertaking that you will: - pay the completion monies towards the mortgage; and - send a copy of the receipted mortgage deed to us as evidence that the charge has been discharged.	We undertake to pay any completion monies we receive from our client towards the mortgage with Barnford Bank, and to send a copy of the receipted mortgage deed to you once it has been received from Barnford Bank.
Access	We note the property is accessed via Sheep Street, which we understand is private. Please confirm: • how much the right of way is used; • whether there are any restrictions on access; and • whether there are any maintenance requirements or obligations to contribute towards maintenance costs.	The right of way is very regularly exercised. In particular, when the land was used for the sale of motor vehicles, there was near-constant usage throughout the day by employees and customers of Revolution Autos, including taking vehicles on and off the forecourt for test drives. There are no restrictions on access nor maintenance requirements or costs.
	We understand that a private road (Needle Alley) forms part of the property. Please confirm the current maintenance arrangements and costs for this.	No work has been done since the seller acquired the property.

Acquisition of land adjoining Sheep Street, Barnford

Summary of due diligence for inclusion in a report on title

1. Key details of the transaction

2. The property is being purchased alongside a second site (17 High Street, Barnford) for the buyer to run as a hair salon with on-site parking for staff and customers.

- Seller: Urban Spaces Ltd. The title deeds are in the name of Urban Developments Ltd and we have obtained a certificate confirming that Urban Developments Ltd changed their name to Urban Spaces Ltd in 2020.
- Buyer: Style&Go Ltd
- Property: freehold property known as land adjoining Sheep Street, Barnford. A SIM search has confirmed this property is unregistered.
- Price: £85,000 cash
- Deposit: 5% of the purchase price. Actions:
  - contract: include the deposit in the particulars of sale.
- The purchase price falls below the SDLT threshold so no SDLT will be payable.
- The seller is not opting to tax the property, so no VAT is payable on top of the purchase price. Actions:
  - contract: this will need to be included as a special condition in the contract.
- The property is being sold with vacant possession. The seller has confirmed that it is currently unoccupied. Actions:
  - contract: this will need to be included as a special condition in the contract.

2. Title investigation

- The property benefits from a right of way over Sheep Street which was granted in 1956. This access is necessary to get to the property. Our highways search has confirmed that Sheep Street is private, and title investigations have revealed that it is currently registered; the easement is registered against the title. The Car Park will continue to benefit from this easement once Style&Go Ltd own it. The seller has confirmed there are no restrictions on access and no maintenance responsibilities or costs associated with the right of way. Actions:
  - post-completion: the benefit of the easement will automatically be registered against the title to the Car Park.
- Title investigations revealed a covenant restricting the use of the land (anything creating nuisance) and preventing building any structure on the land. The seller has confirmed these covenants have not been breached in the past. These will

automatically be entered onto the title register to the land and Style&Go Ltd will need to comply with them.

- The seller does not know of any overriding interests affecting the Car Park. We recommend a physical inspection of the property as Style&Go Ltd will be bound by these if any do exist and are discoverable.

3. Searches

- A company search against the seller revealed that there is a fixed charge over the property held by Barnford Bank. The seller's solicitor has provided an undertaking that they will apply the completion monies to discharge this mortgage, and supply a receipted mortgage deed from the lender.
- Needle Alley is a private road forming part of the property – there are no plans for it to be adopted by the local authority. The seller has not done any maintenance works to this since acquiring the property in 1989. Style&Go Ltd will be responsible for maintaining this road.
- Style&Go Ltd wish to install lighting and a charging point for electric vehicles in the Car Park. The utilities search confirms that the nearest electricity connection is located under the high Street. Connecting cables run under the Salon.
- A telecoms search has confirmed that resurfacing works will not interfere with any telecommunications equipment.

4. Planning permission and building regulations

We deal with future planning permission for the Salon and the Car Park together as they will constitute one planning unit:

- the Salon currently has planning permission for residential use, and the Car Park has planning permission for the sale and display for sale of motor vehicles. Style&Go Ltd will require planning permission to change the use of the land. We will assist in making an application for planning permission to use the land as Class E, designating some of the space as ancillary parking;
- Style&Go Ltd will not need planning permission for the fit-out works to the Salon, but may require planning permission to do the works to the Car Park. Our searches confirmed that an Article 4 Direction is in place in respect of the Car Park and therefore an express application for planning permission for these works will need to be made – we can assist with this.

NB: the authors have included dates in this contract in square brackets – in practice these would be entered at the relevant moment (e.g. on exchange).

CONTRACT
(Incorporating the Standard Commercial Property Conditions (Third Edition – 2018 Revision))

For conveyancer's use only
Buyer's conveyancer Blackhurst & Sons LLP
Seller's conveyancer Stoney Mace LLP
Law Society Formula B
Time: 12:35pm
The information above does not form part of the Contract

Date	:	*[1 May 2026]*
Seller	:	Urban Spaces Ltd
Buyer	:	Style&Go Ltd
Property (freehold/~~leasehold~~)	:	Land adjoining Sheep Street, Barnford, Westshire, EX82 7YK
~~Title Number/~~Root of title	:	Conveyance dated 29 September 1989 made between (1) FBC Storage Ltd and (2) Urban Developments Ltd
Specified Encumbrances	:	The covenants referred to in a conveyance dated 1 June 1956 and made between (1) Kristjan Norris and (2) Regener8 Ltd
Completion Date	:	*[18 May 2026]*
Contract Rate	:	4% above the base lending rate of Barclays Bank plc from time to time in force
Purchase Price	:	£85,000 exclusive of any VAT
Deposit	:	5%
Balance	:	£80,750

The Seller will sell and the Buyer will buy the Property for the Purchase Price.

WARNING
This is a formal document, designed to create legal rights and legal obligations. Take advice before using it.

Signed
André Gomez
Director
Authorised to sign on behalf of Buyer

SPECIAL CONDITIONS

1. (a) This contract incorporates the Standard Commercial Property Conditions (Third Edition – 2018 Revision).

   (b) The terms used in this contract have the same meaning when used in the Standard Commercial Property Conditions.

2. Neither party can rely on any representation made by the other, unless made in writing by the other or its conveyancer, but this does not exclude liability for fraud or recklessness.

If the box next to any of Special Conditions 3 to 8 is checked, that Special Condition applies, provided that (in the case of Special Conditions 6 and 7 and the second alternative for 8) the gaps in the printed text have been filled in.

3. [ ] ~~The Property is sold with limited title guarantee, which replaces the reference to full title guarantee in condition 7.6.2.~~

4. [X] The Property is sold with vacant possession on completion.

(or) 4. [ ] ~~The Property is sold subject to the leases or tenancies set out on the attached list but otherwise with vacant possession on completion.~~

5. [ ] ~~(a) The sale includes those contents which are indicated on the attached list as included in the sale.~~

   ~~(b) The sale excludes those fixtures which are at the Property and are indicated on the attached list as excluded from the sale.~~

6. [ ] ~~In conditions 3.2.2 and 9.7, as an alternative to payment from a conveyancer's account, the payment may be made from an account held by ______ at~~

7. [ ] ~~Conditions 9.1.2 and 9.1.3 are to have effect as if the time specified in them were am/pm rather than 2:00pm.~~

8. [ ] ~~Where after the transfer the Seller will be retaining the land near the Property, the transfer is to be in the form of the attached draft transfer.~~

(or) 8. [ ] ~~Where after the transfer the Seller will be retaining land near the Property, the transfer is to contain the following additional express terms:~~

   ~~(a)~~

   ~~(b)~~

Standard Commercial Property Conditions Part 2

9. The conditions in Part 2 shown against the boxes checked below are included in the contract.

[X] Condition A1 (VAT: not a taxable supply)

[or] [ ] Condition A2 (VAT: transfer of a going concern)

[ ] Condition B (capital allowances). The amount of the Purchase Price apportioned to plant and machinery that are fixtures for the purposes of the Capital Allowances Act Capital Allowances Act 2001 is £

[ ] Condition C1 (flats: no tenants' rights of first refusal)

[or] [ ] Condition C2 (flats: with tenants' rights of first refusal in auction sales)

Further additional special conditions:

Notices may be sent to:

Seller's Conveyancer's name: Stoney Mace LLP

Buyer's Conveyancer's name: Blackhurst & Sons LLP

Document 24

NB: the authors have included dates in this deed in square brackets – in practice these would be entered at the relevant moment (e.g. on completion).

HM Land Registry

Transfer of whole of registered title(s)

TR1

Any parts of the form that are not typed should be completed in black ink and in block capitals.

If you need more room than is provided for in a panel, and your software allows, you can expand any panel in the form. Alternatively use continuation sheet CS and attach it to this form.

For information on how HM Land Registry processes your personal information, see our Personal Information Charter.

Leave blank if not yet registered.	1	Title number(s) of the property:
Insert address including postcode (if any) or other description of the property, for example 'land adjoining 2 Acacia Avenue'.	2	Property: Land adjoining Sheep Street, Barnford, Westshire, EX82 7YK
Remember to date this deed with the day of completion, but not before it has been signed and witnessed.	3	Date: [*18 May 2026*]
Give full name(s) of **all** the persons transferring the property. Complete as appropriate where the transferor is a company. Enter the overseas entity ID issued by Companies House for the transferor pursuant to the Economic Crime (Transparency and Enforcement) Act 2022. If the ID is not required, you may instead state 'not required'. Further details on overseas entities can be found in practice guide 78: overseas entities.	4	Transferor: Urban Spaces Ltd For UK incorporated companies/LLPs Registered number of company or limited liability partnership including any prefix: 22135687 For overseas entities (a) Territory of incorporation or formation: (b) Overseas entity ID issued by Companies House, including any prefix: (c) Where the entity is a company with a place of business in the United Kingdom, the registered number, if any, issued by Companies House, including any prefix:

Give full name(s) of **all** the persons to be shown as registered proprietors. Complete as appropriate where the transferee is a company. Also, for an overseas company, unless an arrangement with HM Land Registry exists, lodge either a certificate in Form 7 in Schedule 3 to the Land Registration Rules 2003 or a certified copy of the constitution in English or Welsh, or other evidence permitted by rule 183 of the Land Registration Rules 2003. Enter the overseas entity ID issued by Companies House for the transferee pursuant to the Economic Crime (Transparency and Enforcement) Act 2022. If the ID is not required, you may instead state 'not required'. Further details on overseas entities can be found in practice guide 78: overseas entities.	5	Transferee for entry in the register: Style&Go Ltd For UK incorporated companies/LLPs Registered number of company or limited liability partnership including any prefix: 00127976 For overseas entities (a) Territory of incorporation or formation: (b) Overseas entity ID issued by Companies House, including any prefix: (c) Where the entity is a company with a place of business in the United Kingdom, the registered number, if any, issued by Companies House, including any prefix:
Each transferee may give up to three addresses for service, one of which must be a postal address whether or not in the UK (including the postcode, if any). The others can be any combination of a postal address, a UK DX box number or an email address.	6	Transferee's intended address(es) for service for entry in the register: c/o Blackhurst&Sons LLP of 22 High Street, Barnford, Westshire, EX82 7YK
	7	The transferor transfers the property to the transferee
Place 'X' in the appropriate box. State the currency unit if other than sterling. If none of the boxes apply, insert an appropriate memorandum in panel 11.	8	Consideration ☒ The transferor has received from the transferee for the property the following sum (in words and figures): £85,000 ☐ The transfer is not for money or anything that has a monetary value ☐ Insert other receipt as appropriate:
Place 'X' in any box that applies. Add any modifications.	9	The transferor transfers with ☒ full title guarantee ☐ limited title guarantee

Where the transferee is more than one person, place 'X' in the appropriate box.	10 Declaration of trust. The transferee is more than one person and ☐ they are to hold the property on trust for themselves as joint tenants ☐ they are to hold the property on trust for themselves as tenants in common in equal shares ☐ they are to hold the property on trust:

Complete as necessary.
 	
The registrar will enter a Form A restriction in the register *unless*:
– an 'X' is placed:
  – in the first box, or
  – in the third box and the details of the trust or of the trust instrument show that the transferees are to hold the property on trust for themselves alone as joint tenants, *or*
– it is clear from completion of a form JO lodged with this application that the transferees are to hold the property on trust for themselves alone as joint tenants.
 	
Please refer to *Joint property ownership* and practice guide *24: private trusts of land* for further guidance. These are both available on the GOV.UK website.	

Insert here any required or permitted statement, certificate or application and any agreed covenants, declarations and so on.	11 Additional provisions

The transferor must execute this transfer as a deed using the space opposite. If there is more than one transferor, all must execute. Forms of execution are given in Schedule 9 to the Land Registration Rules 2003. If the transfer contains transferee's covenants or declarations or contains an application by the transferee (such as for a restriction), it must also be executed by the transferee.

If there is more than one transferee and panel 10 has been completed, each transferee must also execute this transfer to comply with the requirements in section 53(1)(b) of the Law of Property Act 1925 relating to the declaration of a trust of land. Please refer to *Joint property ownership* and practice guide *24: private trusts of land* for further guidance.

Examples of the correct form of execution are set out in practice guide 8: execution of deeds. Execution as a deed usually means that a witness must also sign, and add their name and address.

Remember to date this deed in panel 3.

12 Execution

Seller

Executed as a deed by Urban Spaces Ltd acting by a director and its secretary

William Peat
Director

Geoffrey Wong
Secretary

Buyer

Executed as a deed by Style&Go Ltd acting by a director and its secretary

André Gomez
Director

Karen Chester
Secretary

WARNING
If you dishonestly enter information or make a statement that you know is, or might be, untrue or misleading, and intend by doing so to make a gain for yourself or another person, or to cause loss or the risk of loss to another person, you may commit the offence of fraud under section 1 of the Fraud Act 2006, the maximum penalty for which is 10 years' imprisonment or an unlimited fine, or both.

Failure to complete this form with proper care may result in a loss of protection under the Land Registration Act 2002 if, as a result, a mistake is made in the register.

Under section 66 of the Land Registration Act 2002 most documents (including this form) kept by the registrar relating to an application to the registrar or referred to in the register are open to public inspection and copying. If you believe a document contains prejudicial information, you may apply for that part of the document to be made exempt using Form EX1, under rule 136 of the Land Registration Rules 2003.

Document 25

Memorandum of exchange: land adjoining Sheep Street, Barnford

1 May 2026

1. Exchange occurred on 1 May 2026 at 12:35pm.
2. Formula B. Deposit already transferred to seller's solicitor via CHAPS on 29 April 2026 so the sentence requiring the purchaser's solicitor to send a banker's draft or client account cheque is deleted from the formula.
3. Agreed completion date: 18 May 2026.
4. No deposit to be paid – see 2. Above.
5. Blackhurst & Sons LLP – solicitor for the buyer
   Stoney Mace LLP – solicitor for the seller.

LAND CHARGES ACT 1972

Form K18 CERTIFICATE OF THE RESULT OF THE SEARCH

CERTIFICATE NO.	CERTIFICATE DATE	PROTECTION ENDS ON
88510129/EXH02	1/5/2026	22 May 2026

It is hereby certified that an official search in respect of the undermentioned particulars has been made in the index to the registers which are kept pursuant to the Land Charges Act 1972. The result of the search is shown below.

PARTICULARS SEARCHED			
COUNTY OR COUNTIES	WESTSHIRE		
NAME(S)	Particulars of Charge	PERIOD	FEES
URBAN SPACES LTD NO SUBSISTING ENTRY *************** ---------------------------END OF SEARCH -----------------------		2026 – 2026	2.00

APPLICANT'S REFERENCE	BS77577	APPLICANT'S KEY NUMBER	75689	AMOUNT DEBITED £	2.00

Document 27

HM Land Registry

Application for first registration

FR1

Any parts of the form that are not typed should be completed in black ink and in block capitals.

You must lodge the documents of title with this application; these must be listed on Form DL.

If you need more room than is provided for in a panel, and your software allows, you can expand any panel in the form. Alternatively use continuation sheet CS and attach it to this form.

HM Land Registry is unable to give legal advice, but you can find guidance on HM Land Registry applications (including our practice guides for conveyancers) at www.gov.uk/land-registry.

Conveyancer is a term used in this form. It is defined in rule 217A, Land Registration Rules 2003 and includes persons authorised under the Legal Services Act 2007 to provide reserved legal services relating to land registration and includes solicitors and licensed conveyancers.

For information on how HM Land Registry processes your personal information, see our Personal Information Charter.

HM LAND REGISTRY USE ONLY
Record of fees paid
Particulars of under/over payments
Reference number Fees debited £

Guidance	No.	Panel
Where there is more than one local authority serving an area, enter the one to which council tax or business rates are normally paid.	1	Local authority serving the property: Westshire
Insert address including postcode (if any) or other description of the property, for example 'land adjoining 2 Acacia Avenue'. On registering a rentcharge, profit a prendre in gross or franchise, insert a description, for example 'Rentcharge (or as appropriate) over 2 Acacia Avenue'.	2	Property: land adjoining Sheep Street, Barnford, Westshire, EX82 7YK
Place 'X' in the appropriate box. Only use the third option where the property has an address and is fenced on the ground. Only use the first option if the plan is attached to the FR1 form. Enter reference, for example 'edged red'. Enter nature and date of document. Failure to complete this panel accurately is likely to result in the rejection of the application.	3	The extent of the land to be registered can be clearly identified on the current edition of the Ordnance Survey map from ☐ the attached plan and shown: ☒ the plan attached to the: Conveyance dated 1 June 1956 and made between (1) Kristjan Norris and Miranda Norris and (2) Regener8 Ltd ☐ the address shown in panel 2
Place 'X' in the appropriate box.	4	The class of title applied for is ☒ absolute freehold ☐ possessory freehold ☐ absolute leasehold ☐ good leasehold ☐ possessory leasehold

5	Application, priority and fees		

Applications in priority order	Price paid/Value (£)	Fees paid (£)
First registration of the freehold estate	85,000	95
	Total fees (£)	95

To find out more about our fees visit www.gov.uk/government/collections/fees-land-registry-guides

Failure to enter the current market value of the land in this panel and/or to include a fee based on Scale 1 will result in a requisition being raised or rejection of the application.

Remember restrictions in deeds may apply to other deeds of lower priority in this list, unless you specify otherwise.

Fee payment method

Place 'X' in the appropriate box.

☐ cheque made payable to 'Land Registry'

☒ direct debit, under an agreement with Land Registry

The fee will be charged to the account specified in panel 7.

6 The applicant:

Provide the full name(s) of the person(s) applying for first registration. Where a conveyancer lodges the application, this must be the name(s) of the client(s), not the conveyancer.

Style&Go Ltd

If the application is based on adverse possession or lost deeds, you may add a telephone number and/or email address for the applicant that we can use for arranging any survey which may be needed.

Complete as appropriate where the applicant is a company. Also, for an overseas company, unless an arrangement with HM Land Registry exists, lodge either a certificate in Form 7 in Schedule 3 to the Land Registration Rules 2003 or a certified copy of the constitution in English or Welsh, or other evidence permitted by rule 183 of the Land Registration Rules 2003.

Enter the overseas entity ID issued by Companies House for the applicant pursuant to the Economic Crime (Transparency and Enforcement) Act 2022. If the ID is not required, you may instead state 'not required'.

Further details on overseas entities can be found in practice guide 78: overseas entities.

For UK incorporated companies/LLPs
Registered number of company or limited liability partnership including any prefix: 00127976

For overseas entities
(a) Territory of incorporation or formation:

(b) Overseas entity ID issued by Companies House, including any prefix:

(c) Where the entity is a company with a place of business in the United Kingdom, the registered number, if any, issued by Companies House, including any prefix:

This panel must always be completed. A key number is only available to professional customers, such as solicitors. If you are paying by direct debit, this will be the account charged. This is the address to which we will normally send requisitions and return documents. However if you insert an email address, we will use this whenever possible. An acknowledgement of receipt of this application will be sent by email if one is available. We will only issue warning of cancellation letters to conveyancers if an email address is inserted.	7	This application is sent to Land Registry by Key number (if applicable): Name: Blackhurst & Sons LLP Address or UK DX box number: 22 High Street, Barnford, Westshire, EX82 7YK Email address: Blackhursts@blackhursts.com Reference: 18/BH
		Phone no: 0000 543212 Fax no: n/a
Place 'X' in the appropriate box. In this and panel 10, each proprietor may give up to three addresses for service, one of which must be a postal address whether or not in the UK (including the postcode, if any). The others can be any combination of a postal address, a UK DX box number or an email address.	8	The address(es) for service for each proprietor of the estate to be entered in the register is ☐ the address of the property (where this is a single postal address) ☒ the following address(es): c/o Blackhurst & Sons LLP, 22 High Street, Barnford, Westshire, EX82 7YK

Where the applicant is more than one person, place 'X' in the appropriate box.
 	
Complete as necessary.
 	
The registrar will enter a Form A restriction in the register *unless*:
– an 'X' is placed:
  – in the first box, or
  – in the third box and the details of the trust or of the trust instrument show that the applicants are to hold the property on trust for themselves alone as joint tenants, *or*
– it is clear from completion of a form JO lodged with this application that the applicants are to hold the property on trust for themselves alone as joint tenants.
 	
Please refer to *Joint property ownership* and practice guide *24: private trusts of land* for further guidance. These are both available on the GOV.UK website.
	9	Where the applicant is more than one person
		
		☐ they hold the property on trust for themselves as joint tenants
		
		☐ they hold the property on trust for themselves as tenants in common in equal shares
		
		☐ they hold the property on trust:

Where a charge has an MD reference we will ignore an address given in this panel unless the charge is in favour of a United Kingdom bank and neither the charge form nor any agreement we have with the lender specifies an address for service.

For permitted addresses see note to panel 8.

Complete as appropriate where the proprietor of the charge is a company. Also, for an overseas company, unless an arrangement with HM Land Registry exists, lodge either a certificate in Form 7 in Schedule 3 to the Land Registration Rules 2003 or a certified copy of the constitution in English or Welsh, or other evidence permitted by rule 183 of the Land Registration Rules 2003.

10 Name and address(es) for service for the proprietor of any charge to be entered in the register:

For UK incorporated companies/LLPs
Registered number of company or limited liability partnership including any prefix:

For overseas companies
(a) Territory of incorporation:

(b) Where the entity is a company with a place of business in the United Kingdom, the registered number, if any, issued by Companies House, including any prefix:

If this statement applies (i) place 'X' in the box and (ii) enclose Form DI.

Rule 28 of the Land Registration Rules 2003 sets out the disclosable overriding interests that you must tell us about.

11 Disclosable overriding interests

☐ Disclosable overriding interests affect the estate.

This panel must be completed for all applications for first registration regardless of whether you are relying on title documents or only on a statutory declaration or statement of truth. Failure to complete this panel is likely to result in the rejection of the application.

If you are lodging certified copy deeds only, have you remembered to include the separate certificate?

Place 'X' in the appropriate box.

If applicable complete the second statement with details of the interest(s); for interests disclosed only by searches do not include those shown on local land charge searches. Certify any interests disclosed by searches that do not affect the estate being registered.

12 Certificate

The title is based on the title documents listed in Form DL which are all those under the control of the applicant.

Details of rights, interests and claims affecting the estate (other than non-disclosable interests falling within rule 28(2) of the Land Registration Rules 2003) known to the applicant are, where applicable, disclosed in the title documents and Form DI if accompanying this application.

☒ The applicant knows of no other such rights, interests and claims. Only the applicant is in actual possession of the property or in receipt of the rent and profits from the property.

☐ The applicant knows only of the following additional such rights, interests and claims, including those of any person (other than the applicant) in actual possession of the property or in receipt of the rent and profits from the property:

If you do not place 'X' in the box we will assume that you have examined the applicant's title or are satisfied that it has been examined in the usual way.

13 Examination of title

☐ I/we have not fully examined the applicant's title to the estate, including any appurtenant rights, or satisfied myself/ourselves that it has been fully examined by a conveyancer in the usual way prior to this application.

14 Confirmation of identity

When registering transfers, charges, leases and other dispositions of land, Land Registry relies on the steps that conveyancers take,

Full details of the evidence of identity that is required can be found in Practice Guide 67 and in 'Completing the evidence of identity panels on forms AP1, FR1, and DS2' both of which can be found on the GOV.UK website. The requirement of registration is contained in section 4, Land Registration Act 2002. Further guidance is contained in Practice Guide 1. Place 'X' in the appropriate box. Conveyancer is defined in rule 217A, Land Registration Rules 2003 and includes persons authorised under the Legal Services Act 2007 to provide reserved legal services relating to land registration and includes solicitors and licensed conveyancers.		where appropriate, to verify the identity of their clients. These checks reduce the risk of property fraud. Where a person was not represented by a conveyancer, Land Registry requires 'evidence of identity' in respect of that person, except where the first alternative in panel 15(2) applies. 'Evidence of identity' is evidence provided in accordance with any current direction made by the Chief Land Registrar under section 100(4) of the Land Registration Act 2002 for the purpose of confirming a person's identity. If this application is to register a transfer, lease or charge, dated on or after 10 November 2008 **and** the requirement of registration applies, complete one of the following ☒ I am a conveyancer, and I have completed panel 15 ☐ I am not a conveyancer, and I have completed panel 16
Place 'X' in the box in the second column if the person or firm who is sending the application to HM Land Registry represented that party in the transaction. Otherwise complete the details in the third column. If the party is not represented insert 'none' in the third column. A separate box is provided, or can be added, for each party, as required by panel 15(1). That includes separate boxes for attorneys and donors where appropriate.	15	Where the application is sent to Land Registry by a conveyancer (1) Details of conveyancer acting If you are sending an application to register a transfer, lease or charge, for each party to each disposition that is to be registered, state in the table below the details of the conveyancer (if any) who represented them. Where a party is not represented by a conveyancer you must also complete (2) below.

Name of transferor, landlord, transferee, tenant, borrower or lender		Conveyancer's name, address and reference
Urban Spaces Ltd (Transferor)	☐	Stoney Mace LLP, 94 The Quay, Barnford, EX81 9JQ Reference: FAO Jennifer Burt
Style&Go Ltd (Transferee)	☒	Reference: 18/BH
	☐	Reference:
	☐	Reference:

	☐	Reference:

(2) Evidence of identity

Where any transferor, landlord, transferee, tenant, borrower or lender listed in (1) was not represented by a conveyancer

Place 'X' in the appropriate box(es).

Insert the name of each unrepresented transferor, landlord, transferee, tenant, borrower or lender for whom you give this confirmation.

☐ I confirm that I am satisfied that sufficient steps have been taken to verify the identity of

----

----

and that they are the transferor, landlord, transferee, tenant, borrower or lender listed in (1) (as appropriate)

Evidence of identity is defined in panel 14. Full details of the evidence of identity that is required can be found in Practice Guide 67 available on the GOV.UK website.

☐ I enclose evidence of identity in respect of each unrepresented transferor, landlord, transferee, tenant, borrower or lender for whom I have not provided the confirmation above

16 Where the application is sent to Land Registry by someone who is not a conveyancer

(1) Details of conveyancer acting

If you are sending an application to register a transfer, lease or charge (ie a mortgage), for each party to each disposition that is to be registered, state in the table below the details of the conveyancer (if any) who represented them.

You must also complete (2) below.

If the party is not represented insert 'none' in the second column.

A separate box is provided, or can be added, for each party, as required by panel 16(1). That includes separate boxes for attorneys and donors where appropriate.

Name of transferor, landlord, transferee, tenant, borrower or lender	Conveyancer's name, address and reference
	Reference:
	Reference:
	Reference:
	Reference:

			Reference:
Place 'X' in the appropriate box(es). **Evidence of identity is defined in panel 14. Full details of the evidence of identity that is required can be found in 'Completing the evidence of identity panels on forms AP1, FR1, and DS2' available on the GOV.UK website.**		(2) Evidence of identity ☐ for each applicant named in panel 6 is enclosed ☐ for each unrepresented transferor, landlord, transferee, tenant, borrower or lender listed in (1) is enclosed	
If a conveyancer is acting for the applicant, that conveyancer must sign. If you are lodging certified copy deeds only, have you remembered to include the separate certificate? If no conveyancer is acting, the applicant (and if the applicant is more than one person then each of them) must sign.	17	Signature of conveyancer: *Blackhurst &Sons LLP* Date: 19 May 2026	

WARNING
If you dishonestly enter information or make a statement that you know is, or might be, untrue or misleading, and intend by doing so to make a gain for yourself or another person, or to cause loss or the risk of loss to another person, you may commit the offence of fraud under section 1 of the Fraud Act 2006, the maximum penalty for which is 10 years' imprisonment or an unlimited fine, or both.

Failure to complete this form with proper care may result in a loss of protection under the Land Registration Act 2002 if, as a result, a mistake is made in the register.

Under section 66 of the Land Registration Act 2002 most documents (including this form) kept by the registrar relating to an application to the registrar or referred to in the register are open to public inspection and copying. If you believe a document contains prejudicial information, you may apply for that part of the document to be made exempt using Form EX1, under rule 136 of the Land Registration Rules 2003.

HM Land Registry

List of documents

DL

- **Any parts of the form that are not typed should be completed in black ink and in block capitals.**
- Please complete and lodge this form in duplicate.
- If the application is a first registration application and you supply the original and a certified copy of a statutory declaration, stamp duty land tax certificate or land transaction tax certificate, subsisting lease, subsisting charge or the latest document of title (for example any conveyance to the applicant) we will return the original; if a certified copy is not supplied, we may retain the original document and it may be destroyed.
- If the application is not a first registration then we only need certified copies of deeds or documents you send to us with HM Land Registry application forms. Once we have made a copy of the documents you send to us, they will be destroyed, this applies to both originals and certified copies.
- For information on how HM Land Registry processes your personal information, see our Personal Information Charter.

1	Property address including postcode (if any): Land adjoining Sheet Street, Barnford, Westshire, EX82 7YK
2	Documents lodged with this form — The first column is for Land Registry use only. If Land Registry places an asterisk '*' in this column, it shows that we have kept that document. — Please number the documents in sequence; copies should also be numbered and listed as separate documents. — You need not list the names on land charges searches. Simply enter the search number.

Land Registry use only	Item no	Date	Document type	Parties

	1	29 September 1989	Conveyance (original)	(1) FPC Storage Ltd (2) Urban Developments Ltd
	2	29 September 1989	Conveyance (certified copy)	(1) FPC Storage Ltd (2) Urban Developments Ltd
	3	1 June 1956	Conveyance (original)	(1) Kristjan Norris and Miranda Norris (2) Regener8 Ltd
	4	1 June 1956	Conveyance (certified copy)	(1) Kristjan Norris and Miranda Norris (2) Regener8 Ltd
	5	20 May 2020	Change of name certificate (certified copy)	Issued by Companies House
	6	6 January 2026	Land Charges Search result	Certificate number 885/EXH02
	7	1 May 2026	Land Charges Search result	Certificate number 88510129/EXH02
	8	1 May 2026	Contract (original)	(1) Urban Spaces Ltd (2) Style&Go Ltd
	9	1 May 2026	Contract (certified copy)	(1) Urban Spaces Ltd (2) Style&Go Ltd
	10	18 May 2026	TR1 (original)	(1) Urban Spaces Ltd (2) Style&Go Ltd
	11	18 May 2026	TR1 (certified copy)	(1) Urban Spaces Ltd (2) Style&Go Ltd
	12	18 May 2026	Mortgage deed (receipted) (original)	(1) Urban Developments Ltd (2) Barnford Bank
	13	18 May 2026	Mortgage deed (receipted) (certified copy)	(1) Urban Developments Ltd (2) Barnford Bank
	14	19 May 2026	SDLT5 certificate (original)	Issued by HMRC
	15	19 May 2026	SDLT5 certificate (certified copy)	Issued by HMRC
	16	undated	Seller responses to enquiries on title	Provided by Urban Spaces Ltd

WARNING
If you dishonestly enter information or make a statement that you know is, or might be, untrue or misleading, and intend by doing so to make a gain for yourself or another person, or to cause loss or the risk of loss to another person, you may commit the offence of fraud under section 1 of the Fraud Act 2006, the maximum penalty for which is 10 years' imprisonment or an unlimited fine, or both.

Failure to complete this form with proper care may result in a loss of protection under the Land Registration Act 2002 if, as a result, a mistake is made in the register.

Under section 66 of the Land Registration Act 2002 most documents (including this form) kept by the registrar relating to an application to the registrar or referred to in the register are open to public inspection and copying. If you believe a document contains prejudicial information, you may apply for that part of the document to be made exempt using Form EX1, under rule 136 of the Land Registration Rules 2003.

Document 29

BARNFORD BANK

MORTGAGE DEED

This deed is dated *29 September 1989*

PARTIES

(1) Urban Developments Ltd incorporated and registered in England and Wales with company number 22135687 whose registered office is at 3 Snow Towers, Barnford, EX83 2HT (**Borrower**)
(2) Barnford Bank incorporated and registered in England and Wales whose registered office is at 1 The Quay, Barnford, EX81 8HH **(Lender**)

RECITALS

(A) The Lender has agreed to provide the Borrower with the Loan on a secured basis.
(B) The Borrower owns the Property.
(C) Under this deed, the Borrower provides the Property as security to the Lender for the Loan.

DEFINITIONS

Loan: the sum of twenty two thousand pounds (£22,000)

Property: Land adjoining Sheet Street, Barnford, Westshire, EX82 7YK

TERMS

[not reproduced]

EXECUTION

Executed as a deed by Urban Developments Ltd acting by ANOUSKA DAY, a director, and GRETA KONIG, its secretary	*Anouska Day* Director *Greta Konig* Secretary
Executed as a deed by Barnford Bank acting by Tony Twain, a director, and Sebastian Schon, a director	*Tony Twain* Director *Sebastian Schon* Director

RECEIPT

Date: [*18 May 2026*]

Barnford Bank hereby acknowledges receipt of the Loan secured by this mortgage.

BARNFORD BANK acting by Tony Twain, a director, and Sebastian Schon, a director	*Tony Twain* Director *Sebastian Schon* Director

Document 30

Land Registry

Official copy of register of title

Title number EG994587

Edition date 5.02.2025

- This official copy shows the entries in the register of title on 10 June 2026 at 10:02:37.
- This date must be quoted as the "search from date" in any official search application based on this copy.
- The date at the beginning of an entry is the date on which the entry was made in the register.
- Issued on 10 June 2026.
- Under s.67 of the Land Registration Act 2002, this copy is admissible in evidence to the same extent as the original.
- For information about the register of title see Land Registry website www.landregistry.gov.uk or Land Registry Public Guide 1 – *A guide to the information we keep and how you can obtain it.*

A: Property register

This register describes the land and estate comprised in the title

Westshire : Barnford

1. (10.06.2026) The Freehold land shown edged with thick black on the plan of the above Title filed at the Registry and being land adjoining Sheep Street, Barnford, Westshire, EX82 7YK.

2. (10.06.2026) A conveyance dated 1 June 1956 made between (1) Kristjan Norris and Miranda Norris and (2) Regener8 Ltd granted rights which benefit the land in this title:

   "a right of way with or without vehicles over Sheep Street (such right benefiting each and every part of the Property) shown hatched black on the attached plan."

   *Note: the land hatched black is shown hatched grey on the filed plan.

B: Proprietorship register

This register specifies the class of title and identifies the owner. It contains any entries that affect the right of disposal.

Title absolute

1. (10.06.2026) Proprietor(s): Style&Go Ltd of c/o Blackhurst&Sons LLP of 22 High Street, Barnford, Westshire, EX82 7YK

C: Charges register

This register contains any charges and other matters that affect the land.

1. (10.06.2026) A conveyance dated 1 June 1956 made between (1) Kristjan Norris and Miranda Norris and (2) Regener8 Ltd contained covenants affecting the land in this title:

"The Purchasers with the intent and so that this covenant shall be binding on each and every part of the Property into whosoever hands the same may come and for the benefit of the remainder of the Vendors' property (the 'Retained Land') hereby for themselves and their successors in title covenant with the Vendors and their successors in title and assigns that the Purchasers and their successors in title will at all times hereafter observe and perform the conditions and restrictions and stipulations set out below:

a) Not to use the Property or any part for any purpose which may be or grow to be a nuisance to the Vendors or to the owner or owners of any adjoining or neighbouring property.
b) Not to erect any building or other structure on the Property without the previous written consent of the Vendors."

End of register

Land Registry
Official copy of
Title plan

Title number **EG994587**
Ordnance Survey map reference **EG 5432 SS**
Scale **1:2500**
Administrative area **Westshire : Barnford**

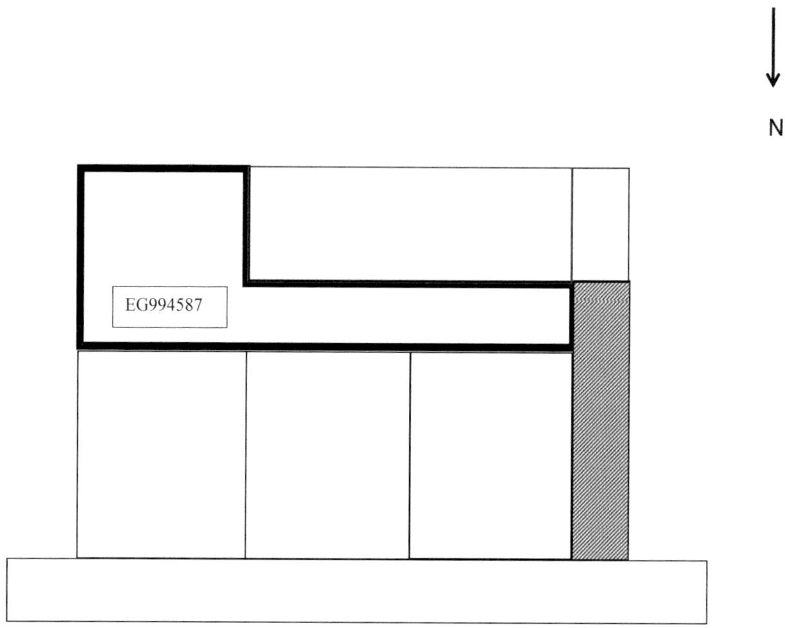

This official copy issued on 10 June 2026 shows the state of this title plan on 10 June 2026 at 10:02:37.
It is admissible in evidence to the same extent as the original (s. 67 Land Registration Act 2002).
This title plan shows the general position, not the exact line, of the boundaries. It may be subject to distortions in scale.
Measurements scaled from this plan may not match measurements between the same points on the ground.
See Land Registry Public Guide 19 – Title Plans and Boundaries.

Appendix 4: Grant of the Nail Bar Lease to Polished Perfection Ltd

Accompanying documents

Document 1

Heads of terms – Lease of First Floor, 17 High Street	
Landlord	Style&Go Ltd (Director André Gomez) registered with company number 00127976 c/o Blackhurst&Sons LLP of 22 High Street, Barnford, Westshire, EX82 7YK
Landlord's solicitor	Blackhurst & Sons LLP of 22 High Street, Barnford, Westshire, EX82 7YK
Tenant	Polished Perfection Ltd (Director Meena Kasih), co. number 22375943, address c/o Talbot & Wick LLP, 47B Vale Road, Torton, Westshire, EX79 4PJ
Tenant's solicitor	Talbot & Wick LLP, 47B Vale Road, Torton, Westshire, EX79 4PJ
Property	First floor, 17 High Street, Barnford, Westshire, EX82 7YK
Term	Ten years commencing on the completion date
VAT	The seller is registered for VAT under number GB654567814. Seller intends to exercise option to tax.
Deposit	None
Premium	None
Finance	Cash: monthly rent
Proposed use	Nail salon
Break clause	None
Rent	£10,000 per annum exclusive of VAT.
Rent deposit	None
Rent review	Upwards-only open market rent review every five years of the term.
Rates and outgoings	Tenant to pay utility costs.
Insurance	Landlord responsible for insurance.
User	Class E
Alienation	Assignment, underletting and charging of whole permitted with landlord's consent.
Repair	Tenant to repair

Heads of terms – Lease of First Floor, 17 High Street	
Alterations	Internal non-structural alterations require landlord's consent. No other alterations permitted.
Service charge	None
Rights	Right over ground floor and stairs to access the premises. Right to use common areas (toilets and kitchen). Right to park in car park at the rear of the premises.
Security of tenure	The lease will be contracted out of the security of tenure provisions of the Landlord & Tenant Act 1954.
Costs	Each party to pay their own legal costs.

Document 2

Land Registry

Official copy of register of title

Title number EG576798

Edition date 05.02.2025

- This official copy shows the entries in the register of title on 29 June 2026 at 13:06:15.
- This date must be quoted as the "search from date" in any official search application based on this copy.
- The date at the beginning of an entry is the date on which the entry was made in the register.
- Issued on 29 June 2026.
- Under s.67 of the Land Registration Act 2002, this copy is admissible in evidence to the same extent as the original.
- For information about the register of title see Land Registry website www.landregistry.gov.uk or Land Registry Public Guide 1 – *A guide to the information we keep and how you can obtain it.*

A: Property register

This register describes the land and estate comprised in the title

Westshire : Barnford

1. (17.07.1993) The Freehold land shown edged with thick black on the plan of the above Title filed at the Registry and being 17 High Street, Barnford, Westshire, EX82 7YK.

B: Proprietorship register

This register specifies the class of title and identifies the owner. It contains any entries that affect the right of disposal.

Title absolute

1. (06.06.2026) Proprietor(s): Style & Go Ltd of c/o Blackhurst&Sons LLP of 22 High Street, Barnford, Westshire, EX82 7YK.

2. (06.06.2026) The transfer to the proprietor contains a covenant to observe and perform the covenants referred to at entry C2 the Charges Register and of indemnity in respect thereof.

C: Charges register

This register contains any charges and other matters that affect the land.

1. (17.07.1993) A conveyance of the land in this title dated 4 March 1959 made between (1) Vince Francis Moon (Vendor) and (2) Norman Jones (Purchaser) the land in this title is subject the following rights in favour of 19 High Street:

"A right of way to pass and repass day or night by foot only over the land coloured brown".

*Note: the land coloured brown is shown hatched grey on the filed plan.

2. (17.07.1993) A conveyance of the land in this title dated 4 March 1959 made between (1) Vince Francis Moon (Vendor) and (2) Norman Jones (Purchaser) contains the following covenant:

   "And the Purchaser for itself and its assigns with the intent to bind the Property hereby covenants with the Vendor his heirs executors administrators and assigns to keep in good repair the land coloured brown in order that it remains safely passable on foot."

   *Note: the land coloured brown is shown hatched grey on the filed plan

3. (17.07.1993) A conveyance of the land in this title dated 10 July 1993 made between (1) Charles Bainbridge (Vendor) and (2) Ansar Mukhtar and Anita Mukhtar (Purchaser) contains the following covenant:

   "11.1 And the Purchaser for itself and its assigns with the intent to bind the Property hereby covenants with the Vendor his heirs executors administrators and assigns not to build any structure on the Property."

End of register

Land Registry
Official copy of
Title plan

Title number **EG576798**
Ordnance Survey map reference **EG 5432 SS**
Scale **1:2500**
Administrative area **Westshire: Barnford**

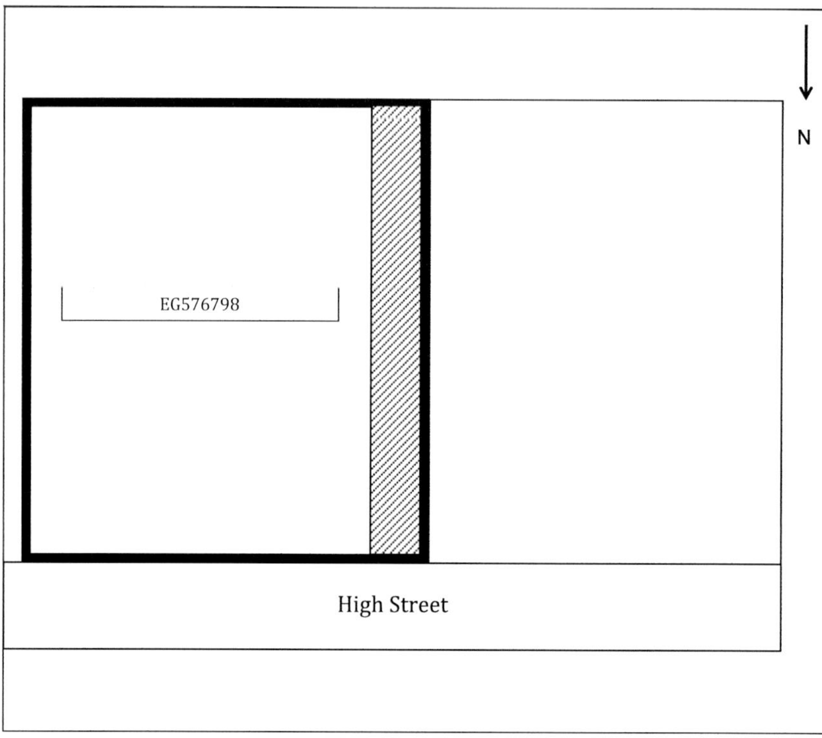

This official copy issued on 29 June 2026 shows the state of this title plan on 29 June 2026 at 13:06:15.
It is admissible in evidence to the same extent as the original (s. 67 Land Registration Act 2002).
This title plan shows the general position, not the exact line, of the boundaries. It may be subject to distortions in scale.
Measurements scaled from this plan may not match measurements between the same points on the ground.
See Land Registry Public Guide 19 – Title Plans and Boundaries.

SIMR

Official certificate of the result of search of the index map

Land Registry
Land Registration Rules 2003

Certificate Date:29 June 2026
Certificate Time: 14:59:59
Certificate Ref: BFG/EXH02

Property	17 HIGH STREET, BARNFORD, WESTSHIRE, EX82 7YK

Result

The index map has been searched in respect of the Property with the following result:

Plan reference	Title No.	Registered Estate or Caution	Notes
Edged with thick black line	EG576798	Freehold	

No registered estate, caution against first registration, application for first registration or application for a caution against first registration is shown on the index map in relation to the remainder of the property.

******

The plan attached to this result is prepared for the sole purpose of showing the area in respect of which an official search has been made. The information has been taken from the index map. It is illustrative only and does not define the extent of the land in any individual title. For information about the general boundaries of a title please refer to the individual register and title plan.

******

Verbal descriptions of registered relating franchises and registered manors, and of pending applications and cautions against first registrations in respect of relating franchises, are kept in the index of relating franchises and manors. The application form for a search of the index is form SIF.

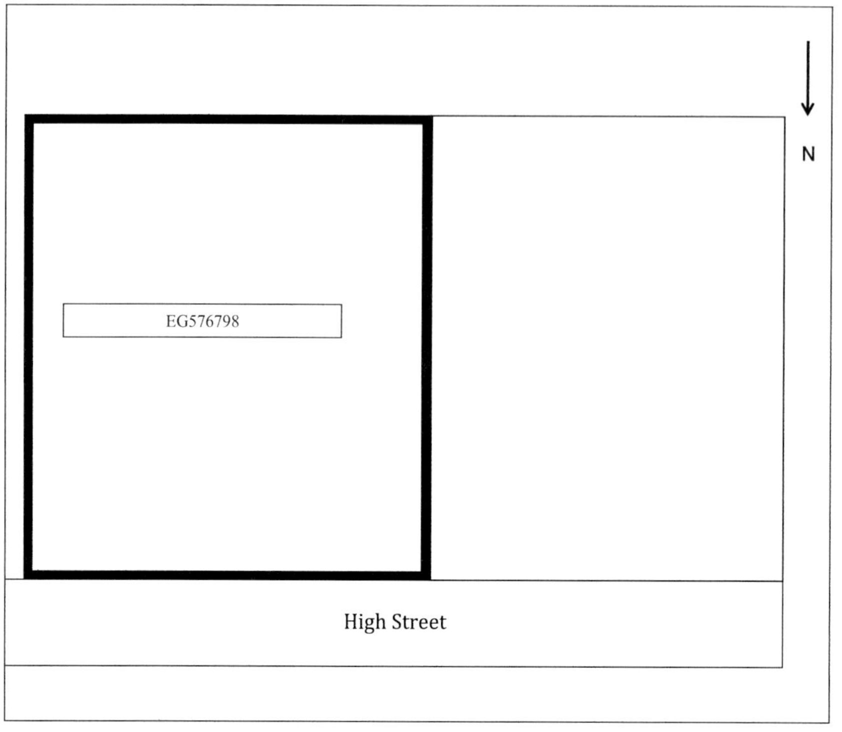
N
EG576798
High Street

Westshire District Council Offices
Council House,
Exton,
Westshire
(DX 765567 Exton 7)

Westshire
District Council

REGISTER OF LOCAL LAND CHARGES
OFFICIAL CERTIFICATE OF SEARCH

Search Reference: PLM/EXH02

Date: 29 June 2026

Applicant: Talbot & Wick LLP

Official search required in all parts of the Register of Local Land Charges for subsisting registrations against the land described and the plan submitted.

Land: First Floor, 17 High Street, Barnford, Westshire, EX82 7YK

It is hereby certified that the search requested above reveals 3 registrations described in the Schedule(s) hereto up to and including the date of this certificate.

LLC1: Search Reference PLM/EXH02

Date: 29 June 2026

Westshire District Council

Register of Local Land Charges
Schedule to Official Certificate of Search

Part 3: Planning Charges

Description of charge (including reference to appropriate statutory provision)	**Originating Authority**	**Place where relevant documents may be inspected**	**Date of Registration**
PP/UC/774/91 Permission for change of use from Class A1 to Class C3(a)	Westshire District Council	Council House, Exton, Westshire	08/08/1991
PP/W/774/95 Conditional permission for erection of single storey rear extension	Westshire District Council	Council House, Exton, Westshire	17/09/1995
PP/UC/774/26 Permission for change of use from Class C3(a) to Class E	Westshire District Council	Council House, Exton, Westshire	29/05/2026

Westshire District Council Offices
Council House,
Exton,
Westshire
(DX 765567 Exton 7)

Westshire District Council

CON29 ENQUIRIES OF LOCAL AUTHORITY
(2016)

Applicant: Talbot & Wick LLP

Search Reference: PLM/EXH02

Date: 29 June 2026

Property: First floor, 17 High Street, Barnford, Westshire, EX82 7KY

I refer to your Standard Enquiries relating to the above property. These replies relate to that property as shown on the location plan where supplied. The replies are given subject to the Notes to the Standard Enquiries.

All correspondence relating to these answers should quote the official Search Reference.

Standard Enquiries of Local Authority

PLANNING AND BUILDING REGULATIONS
1.1. Planning and building decisions and pending applications
Which of the following relating to the property have been granted, issued or refused or (where applicable) are the subject of pending applications or agreements?
(a) a planning permission

1.1.(a) Reference: PP/UC/774/91
Description: Change of use from Class A1 to Class C3(a)
Application date: 20/7/1991
Decision: GRANTED on 8/8/1991

1.1.(a) Reference: PP/W/774/95
Description: Erection of single storey rear extension
Application date: 1/9/1995
Decision: GRANTED SUBJECT TO CONDITIONS on 17/9/1995

1.1.(a) Reference: PP/UC/774/26
Description: Change of use from Class C3(a) to E
Application date: 29/5/2026
Decision: GRANTED on 29/5/2026

[...]

(j) building regulations approval
none

(k) a building regulation completion certificate
none

[...]

Informatives:

(1) Copy documents available from Planning and Building Control Services, Westshire District Council.

(2) This reply does not cover other properties in the vicinity of the property.

(3) As from 1 April 2002 the installation of a replacement window, rooflight or roof window or specified type of glazed door must either have building regulation approval or be carried out and certified by a person who is registered under the Fenestration Self-Assessment Scheme by the Glass and Glazing Federation. The owner or occupier of the property should be asked to produce any such certificate.

ROADS AND PUBLIC RIGHTS OF WAY
Roadways, footways and footpaths
2.1 Which of the roads, footways and footpaths named in the application for this search (via boxes B and C) are:
(a) highways maintainable at public expense
2.1.(a) High Street

(b) subject to adoption and supported by a bond or bond waiver
2.1.(b) None

(c) to be made up by a local authority who will reclaim the cost from the frontagers
2.1.(c) None

(d) to be adopted by a local authority without reclaiming the cost from the frontagers
2.1.(d) None

Informative: If a road, footway or footpath is not a highway, there may be no right to use it and the local authority cannot express an opinion without seeing the title plan and carrying out a site inspection.

Public rights of way
2.2 Is any public right of way which abuts on, or crosses, the property shown in a definitive map or revised definitive map?
2.2. No

[...]

2.5 If so, please attach a plan showing the approximate route.

2.5. Not applicable

Informative: A definitive map for Westshire District Council has now been published. However, a survey of all paths has not been completed and whilst this does not preclude the existence of unrecorded rights of way, the local authority is unaware of any claimed rights of way existing over the search site.

OTHER MATTERS:

Apart from matters entered on the registers of local land charges, do any of the following matters apply to the property? If so, how can copies of relevant documents be obtained?

Note: Matters entered onto the Local Land Charges Register, or visible by property/site inspection, will not be referred to (where relevant) in answer to the enquiries 3.1 to 3.15 below.

Informative: In some circumstances, road closures can be obtained by third parties from magistrate's courts, or can be made by the Secretary of State for Transport without involving the local authority. This enquiry is designed to reveal matters that are yet to be implemented and could not therefore be ascertained by a visual Inspection. Schemes that have been, or are currently being, implemented will not be referred to in answer to this enquiry.

[...]

3.5. Nearby railway schemes

(a) Is the property (or will it be) within 200 metres of the centre line of a proposed railway, tramway, light railway or monorail?

3.5.(a) Yes – proposed railway scheme at Barnford Central. Please see details at westshirerailwayredevelopment.co.uk.

[...]

3.6 Traffic schemes

Has a local authority approved but not yet implemented any of the following for the roads, footways and footpaths which are named in Boxes B and C and are within 200 metres of the boundaries of the property?

[...]

(e) pedestrianisation

3.6(e) Yes – Main Street, which is within 200 metres of the boundaries of the property, is to be pedestrianised.

[...]

3.8. Contravention of building regulations

Has a local authority authorised in relation to the property any proceedings for the contravention of any provision contained in building regulations?

3.8. No

3.9. Notices, orders, directions and proceedings under Planning Acts

Do any of the following subsist in relation to the property, or has a local authority decided to issue, serve, make or commence any of the following?

(a) an enforcement notice

3.9.(a) No

(b) a stop notice
3.9.(b) No

...

(d) a breach of condition notice
3.9.(d) No

(e) a planning contravention notice
3.9.(e) No

[...]

(j) a direction restricting permitted development
3.9.(j) No

[...]

3.11. Conservation area
Do the following apply in relation to the property?
(a) the making of the area a conservation area before 31 August 1974
3.11.(a) No

(b) an unimplemented resolution to designate the area a Conservation Area
3.11.(b) No

[...]
3.13. Contaminated land
Do any of the following apply (including any relating to land adjacent to or adjoining the property which has been identified as contaminated land because it is in such a condition that harm or pollution of controlled waters might be caused on the property)?
(a) a contaminated land notice
3.13.(a) No

(b) in relation to a register maintained under section 78R of the Environmental Protection Act 1990

> **(i) a decision to make an entry**
> 3.13.(b)(i) No
>
> **(ii) an entry**
> 3.13.(b)(ii) No

(c) consultation with the owner or occupier of the property conducted under section 78G(3) of the Environmental Protection Act 1990 before the service of a remediation notice
3.13.(c) No

Informative: A negative reply does not imply that the property or any adjoining or adjacent land is free from contamination or from the risk of it and the reply may not disclose steps taken by another local authority in whose area adjacent or adjoining land is situated.

[...]

Highways Division
Westshire District Council Offices
Council House,
Exton,
Westshire
(DX 765567 Exton 7)

Westshire
District Council

Date: 29 June 2026

Dear Sirs

First floor, 17 High Street, Barnford, Westshire, EX82 7YK

Please find below the plan; showing by black shading the extent of the publicly maintainable highway in the immediate vicinity of the property, as far as can be ascertained from existing records.

If you have any further queries please do not hesitate to contact us.

Yours faithfully

Highway Records Manager

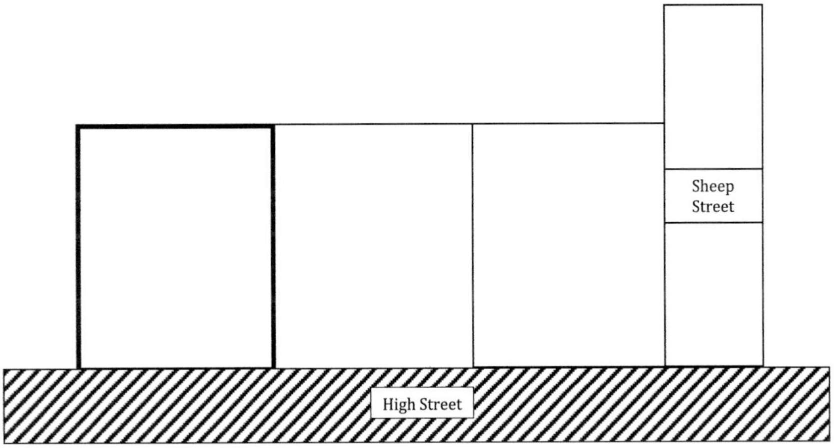

Document 7

WESTSHIRE WATER

Drainage and Water search

Date: 29 June 2026

Property: First floor, 17, High Street, Barnford, Westshire, EX82 7YK

Results:

Mains water: connected

Foul water: connected

Surface water sewer: connected

Sewer pipe within boundary: no

Water pipe within boundary: no

WESTSHIRE ENVIRO-CHECK

Date: 29 June 2026

Type of report: Homebuyers

Property: First floor, 17 High Street, Barnford, Westshire, EX82 7YK

RESULTS:

Professional opinion: PASS

Environmental search results:

Contaminated Land: passed
No significant concerns have been identified as a result of the contaminated land searches.

Flood risk: low
The village of Barnford suffered flooding in 1994, but the property was unaffected and the property's overall risk assessment for river, coastal, surface water and groundwater flooding is low.

Ground stability: passed
No significant concerns have been identified as a result of the ground stability searches. No action required.

Radon: passed
Local levels of radon are considered normal.

Westshire Enviro-check

Document 9

CHANCEL REPAIR SEARCH

Report details

Report number: BB/774/EXH02

Issue date: 29 June 2026

Address: First floor, 17 High Street, Barnford, Westshire, EX82 7YK

The above address is not located within the historical boundary of a tithe district within a parish which continues to have a potential chancel repair liability based upon historical parish data and the relevant inland Revenue Indices held by The National Archives.

EXTRACT OF COMPANY SEARCH REPORT:

Style&Go Ltd

Company Number:	00127976
Date of Incorporation:	5 January 2026
Registered Office:	c/o Blackhurst&Sons LLP of 22 High Street, Barnford, Westshire, EX82 7YK
Change(s) of Name:	none
Charges:	none

Document 11

Practical Law

BPF

BRITISH PROPERTY FEDERATION

Commercial Property Standard Enquiries

CPSE.7 (version 1.3.2) General short form pre-contract enquiries for all property transactions

Conditions

This document may be used free of charge subject to the Conditions set out in *GN/CPSE (version 3.3) Guidance notes on the Commercial Property Standard Enquiries*.

Particulars

Seller: Style&Go Ltd

Buyer: Polished Perfection Ltd

Property: First floor, 17 High St, Barnford, Westshire, EX82 7YK

Seller's solicitors: Blackhurst & Sons LLP

Buyer's solicitors: Talbot & Wick LLP

Date: 2 September 2026

Interpretation

1. In interpreting these enquiries, the terms set out in the Particulars have the meanings given to them in the Particulars and the following interpretation also applies:

- **Buyer:** includes tenant and prospective tenant.
- **Conduits:** means the pipes, wires and cables through which utilities and other services are carried.
- **Property:** includes any part of it and all buildings and other structures on it.
- **Rights:** means any covenants, agreements, rights, restrictions, or informal arrangements of any kind (including any which are in the course of being acquired).

Practical Law

BPF

BRITISH PROPERTY FEDERATION

- **SDLT:** includes Land Transaction Tax where the Property is in Wales, and references to HMRC include the Welsh Revenue Authority where relevant.

- **Seller:** includes landlord and prospective landlord.

2. The replies to the enquiries will be given by the Seller and addressed to the Buyer. Unless otherwise agreed in writing, only the Buyer and those acting for it may rely on them.

- References in these enquiries to "**you**" mean the Seller and to "**we**" and "**us**" mean the Buyer.

- In replies to the enquiries, references to "**you**" will be taken to mean the Buyer and to "**we**" and "**us**" will be taken to mean the Seller.

3. The replies are given without liability on the part of the Seller's solicitors, its members, partners, employees, consultants or other staff.

4. The Buyer acknowledges that even though the Seller will be giving replies to the enquiries, the Buyer should still inspect the Property, have the Property surveyed, investigate title and make all appropriate searches and enquiries of third parties.

5. In replying to each of these enquiries and any supplemental enquiries, the Seller acknowledges that it is required to provide the Buyer with copies of all documents and correspondence and to supply all details relevant to the replies, whether or not specifically requested to do so.

6. The Seller confirms that pending exchange of contracts or, where there is no prior contract, pending completion of the Transaction, it will notify the Buyer on becoming aware of anything which may cause any reply that it has given to these or any supplemental enquiries to be incorrect.

Practical Law

Contents

CLAUSE

Enquiries

1. Boundaries and extent

In this enquiry, "**Boundary Features**" means all walls, fences, ditches, hedges or other features that form the physical boundary of the Property.

1.1 Are you aware of any discrepancies between the boundaries referred to in the title deeds and the Boundary Features?

No, but the buyer must rely on its own searches and enquiries

1.2 Have any alterations been made to the position of any Boundary Features during your ownership or, to your knowledge, earlier?

Not to the knowledge of the seller

1.3 In relation to each of the Boundary Features:

(a) Which of them have you maintained or regarded as your responsibility?

(b) Which of them has someone else maintained or regarded as their responsibility?

(c) Which of them have you treated as a party structure or jointly repaired or maintained with someone else?

(d) Are there any agreements for their maintenance?

(e) Are any of them subject to a party wall award or agreement?

(a)	All
(b)	None
(c)	None
(d)	No
(e)	No

1.4 Does any part of the Property lie beneath or above adjoining premises, roads or footpaths?

Above ground floor, 17 High St

1.5 Are there any adjoining or nearby premises or land which you use or occupy in connection with the Property?

Ground floor, 17 High St. The lease will contain access rights over ground floor and stairs

to reach first floor.

2. Rights benefiting the property

2.1 What Rights does the Property benefit from, other than those which are apparent from the copy documents supplied?

The lease will contain a right to park in car park behind premises

2.2 Please confirm that all terms and conditions relating to the exercise of any Rights which benefit the Property have been complied with.

n/a

2.3 Have you (or, to your knowledge, has any predecessor in title) registered any notices, cautions against first registration or other entries against any other titles at the Land Registry in relation to any Rights which benefit the Property?

No

2.4 What are the pedestrian and vehicular access routes to and from the Property?

Vehicular directly via High St. If using right in 2.1, access is via Sheep Street. Pedestrian through Ground floor premises 17 High St

2.5 Have you, or to your knowledge has anyone else, applied to modify or discharge any Rights benefitting the Property?

Not so far as the seller is aware but the buyer must rely on its own searches and enquiries

3. Adverse rights affecting the Property

3.1 What Rights is the Property subject to, other than those which are apparent from the copy documents supplied?

The seller is aware of covenants affecting the Property – see documents supplied.

3.2 Please confirm that all terms and conditions relating to the exercise of any Rights to which the Property is subject have been complied with.

Seller has not breached any covenants. Buyer must rely on its own searches and enquiries in respect of others.

3.3 Are there any overriding interests to which the Property is subject?

Not so far as the seller is aware but the buyer must rely on its own searches and enquiries

3.4 Does the Property, or any property over which Rights are enjoyed, include any land that is currently used or has in the past ten years been used by members of the public for recreational purposes, whether with or without your permission?

Not so far as the seller is aware but the buyer must rely on its own searches and enquiries

3.5 Have you, or to your knowledge has anyone else, applied to modify or discharge any Rights to which the Property is subject?

Not so far as the seller is aware but the buyer must rely on its own searches and enquiries

4. PHYSICAL CONDITION

4.1 Is the Property now, or has it ever been, affected by any of the following:

(a) structural or inherent defects;

(b) subsidence, settlement, landslip or heave;

(c) defective Conduits, fixtures, plant or equipment;

(d) rising damp, rot, or any fungal or other infection;

(e) Japanese knotweed;

(f) any other infestation; or

(g) flooding?

(a) – (g) n/a so far as the seller is aware The buyer must rely on its own searches and inspections for further information.

4.2 Is there any Green Deal Plan affecting the Property?

Not to the knowledge of the seller but the buyer must rely on its own searches and enquiries

4.3 Has asbestos, or any other substance known or suspected to be unsuitable for its purpose, unstable or hazardous, been used in, or removed from, the Property including Conduits, fixtures, plant and equipment?

Not to the knowledge of the seller but the buyer must rely on its own searches and enquiries

4.4 Please supply copies of the most recent asbestos survey and asbestos management plan for the Property, together with any other relevant information you hold.

None so far as the seller is aware. Extension to ground floor of building but doesn't affect Property.

8.4 What changes of use have taken place at the Property during the last 10 years?

Change of use in 2026 from C3(a) to E.

8.5 What is the existing use of the Property and how is it authorised under planning legislation?

The Property is currently used for Class E – has planning permission

8.6 Where you or your solicitor have them, please supply copies of all planning documents and all building regulations consents relating to the Property.

Enclosed

8.7 Have you made an application for planning permission which has not yet been determined by the local authority or are there any other planning proceedings currently taking place in relation to the Property?

Not so far as the seller is aware

8.8 What information do you have about any proposals for the development of any adjoining or neighbouring property?

The buyer must rely on its own enquiries

8.9 Are you aware of any existing or future Community Infrastructure Levy liability relating to the Property?

The buyer must rely on its own enquiries

9. STATUTORY AGREEMENTS AND INFRASTRUCTURE

9.1 Are you aware of any outstanding obligations relating to the construction or adoption of the highway, Conduits or any other infrastructure that supplies the Property?

Not so far as the seller is aware

9.2 Are you required to enter into any agreement or obligation with any planning, highway or other public authority or utilities provider?

Not so far as the seller is aware

9.3 Are you aware of anything affecting the Property that is capable of being registered on the Local Land Charges Register but is not so registered?

Not so far as the seller is aware

10. STATUTORY AND OTHER REQUIREMENTS

10.1 Are you aware of any breach of statutory requirements that relate to the Property or its use or occupation?

Not so far as the seller is aware

10.2 Do you have a health and safety file for the Property?

Yes

10.3 If the answer to enquiry 10.2 is yes

(a) Is the file at the Property and available for us to inspect?

(b) In what form will the file be provided to us upon completion?

(a) Yes (b) Digital copy

10.4 Please supply a valid Energy Performance Certificate (**EPC**) for the Property.

Enclosed

10.5 Where the Property has an EPC rating of F or G, please supply a copy of any information or evidence used to support any registration in the Exemptions Register established under the Energy Efficiency (Private Rented Property) (England and Wales) Regulations 2015.

n/a

10.6 Please confirm when the air conditioning at the Property was last inspected and provide a copy of that inspection report.

2025 - enclosed

10.7 Please supply details of any grant made or claimed in respect of the Property including circumstances in which it may have to be repaid.

n/a

11. ENVIRONMENTAL

11.1 Where you or your solicitor have them, please supply copies of all environmental and flood risk reports that have been prepared in relation to the Property.

The buyer must rely on its own enquiries

11.2 Please supply a copy of all statutory authorisations under all environmental law for the current uses of the Property (if applicable).

N/a

11.3 Are there, or have there ever been, any above or below ground bulk storage tanks at the Property? If so, please confirm the contents and age of those tanks (or estimate the age as accurately as possible).

None so far as the seller is aware but the buyer must rely on its own enquiries

11.4 Please confirm that you are not aware of any breach of any environmental law relating to the past or present use or occupation of the Property or for substances in, on, at or under the Property.

None so far as the seller is aware but the buyer must rely on its own enquiries

11.5 Please confirm that you are not aware of any environmental incidents including the leaking or discharging of any substances at the Property or on or at any nearby properties.

None so far as the seller is aware but the buyer must rely on its own enquiries

12. OCCUPIERS

12.1 Does anyone apart from you have any right to use or occupy the Property?

Not so far as the seller is aware.

12.2 If the Property is vacant, when and why did it become vacant?

n/a

13. INSURANCE

13.1 Have you ever experienced any difficulty in obtaining insurance cover for the Property at normal rates and subject to normal exclusions?

Not so far as the seller is aware.

13.2 Please give details of any outstanding insurance claims in relation to the Property.

None so far as the seller is aware.

13.3 If the buildings insurance policy is to remain in place after exchange of contracts, please supply a copy of the policy and schedule of insurance cover.

Enclosed

13.4 Please provide a copy of any other insurance policies relating to the Property (together with the proposal form and other material correspondence with the insurers) including any title indemnity insurance policies.

n/a

13.5 Please provide details of any breaches of any insurance policies relating to the Property.

n/a

14. RATES AND OTHER OUTGOINGS

14.1 Have any works been carried out to the Property which may cause the rateable value of the Property to be reviewed?

Not so far as the seller is aware.

14.2 Have you or any occupier of the Property, made any claim for void period allowance or for exemption from liability from business rates? Is any claim pending/outstanding?

Not so far as the seller is aware.

14.3 Are there any other outgoings relating to the Property not referred to elsewhere in these enquiries?

Not so far as the seller is aware.

14.4 Please supply the most recent bills for business rates and all other outgoings relating to the Property.

Enclosed

14.5 If the Property is subject to a Business Improvement District Arrangement, please give details of any levy currently payable.

n/a

15. NOTICES

Please supply a copy of any notices affecting the Property that you or your predecessors or any tenant or occupier have given or received and confirm that those notices have been complied with.

None except as disclosed.

16. DISPUTES

Please provide details of any outstanding complaints or past, current or likely disputes affecting the Property its use and occupation.

None to the seller's knowledge.

17. SDLT ON ASSIGNMENT OF A LEASE

In this enquiry, Lease is any lease under which the Property is held and which is to be assigned by you in the Transaction.

17.1 Where the Lease or the substantial performance of the agreement to grant the Lease or any event since the grant of the Lease constitutes a transaction notifiable for SDLT purposes, including the payment of a premium for the grant of the Lease or any assignment of it, please provide copies of all land transaction returns and certificates issued by HMRC certifying notification.

n/a

17.2 Is there any potential or actual outstanding SDLT liability, including any resulting from the settlement or determination of any rent reviews or other provision for varying the rent or settlement or determination of any contingent, uncertain or unascertained rents?

n/a

17.3 Were any SDLT reliefs claimed on the grant of the Lease and, if applicable, on the assignment of the Lease to you that would result in the assignment of the Lease by you being deemed to be the grant of a new lease?

n/a

18. DEFERRED PAYMENT OF SDLT

Please give details of any deferred payment of SDLT which is outstanding in respect of the Property, together with copies of the original land transaction and all relevant correspondence with HMRC.

None so far as the seller is aware

19. VAT

19.1 If you are registered for VAT, please supply your VAT registration number.

GB654567814

19.2 Please state whether the Transaction is to be treated as a transfer of a business as a going concern ('**TOGC**') and therefore outside the scope of VAT.

No

19.3 If enquiry 19.2 does not apply, is the Transaction standard-rated for VAT purposes as a result of either:

(a) the exercise of an option to tax in relation to the Property; or

(b) compulsory standard-rating?

(a) yes

19.4 If the answer to enquiry 19.3 is yes, please provide a copy of either:

(a) the option notice given to HMRC, together with a copy of HMRC's acknowledgement; or

(b) evidence of the reason that compulsory standard-rating applies to this transaction.

Enclosed

19.5 If the Transaction is not standard-rated for VAT purposes, please state if it is zero-rated, exempt or outside the scope of VAT other than by reason of being a TOGC.

n/a

20. CAPITAL ALLOWANCES

20.1 Is there anything in the Property upon which a capital allowances claim can be based?

no

20.2 If the answer to enquiry 20.1 is yes, please give details and copy documents including the name and contact details of your capital allowances advisor and confirm that we may make contact direct to ascertain any required capital allowances information.

n/a

Practical Law

BPF

BRITISH PROPERTY FEDERATION

Commercial Property Standard Enquiries

CPSE.3 (version 3.1) Supplemental pre-contract enquiries for commercial property on the grant of a new lease (with integrated guidance notes)

Conditions

This document may be used free of charge subject to the Conditions set out in *GN/CPSE (version 3.3) Guidance notes on the Commercial Property Standard Enquiries: Conditions (www.practicallaw.com/3-628-1672)*.

Particulars

Seller: Style&Go Ltd

Buyer: Polished Perfection Ltd

Property: First floor, 17 High St, Barnford, Westshire, EX82 7YK

Seller's solicitors: Blackhurst & Sons LLP

Buyer's solicitors: Talbot & Wick LLP

Date: 2 September 2026

Interpretation

The section on Interpretation in CPSE.1 is incorporated in this document and the following interpretation also applies:

- **Lease:** means the lease proposed to be granted by the Seller to the Buyer on completion of the Transaction.

Instructions

Where the Particulars do not specify a Development, please disregard the parts of any enquiries that refer to the Development.

CONTENTS

CLAUSE

ENQUIRIES

1. SERVICE CHARGES

1.1 Unless apparent from the Lease, what is the service charge accounting period?

n/a

1.2 What is the estimated amount due for the first period under the Lease and how is this amount calculated?

n/a

1.3 What proportion of the service charge will be attributable to the Property under the Lease?

n/a

1.4 How is that proportion calculated and can it be varied?

n/a

1.5 Please give details of planned maintenance programmes and projected expenditure.

n/a

1.6 Will the service charge accounts be:

(a) certified;

(b) audited; or

(c) covered by an independent accountant's report?

In each case, please state by whom.

n/a

1.7 Is each tenant of the Development under an obligation to contribute to the service charge costs of the Development? Are there any capping or weighting provisions agreed with any tenant?

n/a

1.8 Will there be a reserve or sinking fund? If so, please give details including:

(a) the amount to be paid into it;

(b) the name and type of account in which it will be held;

(c) what arrangements are to be made to deal with any interest accruing on money in the fund;

(d) the expenditure which it is intended to cover; and

(e) the arrangements for apportioning any money in the fund on assignment or termination of the Lease.

n/a

Enquiries 1.9-1.12 apply only where the service charge is already in operation.

1.9 Please supply details of the annual service charge for the Development for the last three years (or longer if available) including copies of all certified or audited service charge accounts.

n/a

1.10 Except as already disclosed, has there been any dispute relating to the service charge costs for the Development and the proportions payable?

n/a

1.11 Please give details of any expenditure that has been incurred but which has not yet been included in the service charge for the Development.

n/a

1.12 Are you aware of any circumstances arising since the preparation of the service charge estimates provided which might result in a departure from those estimates?

n/a

2. MANAGEMENT

2.1 Please supply the name and address of any managing agents employed for the management of the Property or of the Development. Please give details of their responsibilities and charges.

None

2.2 What regulations have been made or are proposed for the use and management of the Property that are not set out in the Lease?

None

2.3 Please give details of any management company and/or tenants' association and what our participation in it will be.

None

2.4 If no managing agents are to be employed, do you intend to charge any management fee yourself?

No

2.5 Are you resident in the United Kingdom for taxation purposes?

Yes

3. INSURANCE

3.1 If you are to insure the Property then, to the extent that the following information has not already been given in response to CPSE.1, please state:

(a) the insurer's name and address;

(b) the policy number;

(c) details of all the premises to which the insurance relates, the risks covered and the exclusions and the excesses payable;

(d) the sums insured (showing separately, where applicable, the sums for buildings, plant and machinery, professionals' fees, loss of rent and public liability);

(e) the name(s) of the insured(s) and of all other persons whose interests are, or on completion of the Transaction will be, noted on the policy;

(f) the current premium, what proportion will be attributed to the Property and how this is calculated;

(g) the next renewal date;

(h) the name and address of the brokers; and

(i) details of any separate terrorism insurance arrangements.

See enclosed

3.2 Have you arranged for any subrogation rights that the insurers may have against any tenant to be waived?

Yes

3.3 Will our interest be noted on the policy?

Yes

4. DISPUTES, COMPLAINTS AND ENFORCEMENT

4.1 Except as already disclosed in replies to CPSE.1, please give details of:

(a) any disputes or complaints relating to the Property or to the Development;

(b) any breaches of covenants in any tenancies of any part of the Development that might affect our use of the Property; and

(c) any dispute or breach of covenant alleged in respect of any superior lease or the freehold.

None

4.2 Has any previous lease of the Property been forfeited during the last three years?

No

	Enquiry from Polished Perfection Ltd's solicitor	Response from Style&Go Ltd's solicitor
Title	There is a restrictive covenant prohibiting building any structure on the property. An extension has been built. Please confirm that this structure does not overlap with the demised premises.	Confirmed.
	There is a positive covenant at entry C2 and an indemnity in respect thereof. Please confirm this does not affect the demised premises.	Confirmed.
	The property is subject to a right of way. Please confirm that this does not affect the demised premises.	Confirmed.
Vacant possession	Please confirm that vacant possession of the first floor premises will be provided on completion of the lease.	Confirmed

Document 14

Grant of lease over First floor premises, 17 High Street, Barnford

Summary of due diligence for inclusion in a report on title

1. Key details of the transaction

- The buyer plans to take a lease over the premises to use as a nail bar.
- Seller/Landlord: Style&Go Ltd
- Buyer/Tenant: Polished Perfection Ltd
- Property: First floor, 17 High Street, Barnford, Westshire, EX82 7YK. The property forms part of the freehold property registered under title number EG576798. The lease has not yet been granted and so there is no leasehold title yet.
- Price:
    - Premium: none
    - Rent: £10,000 per annum plus VAT
- No SDLT is payable on the premium (as there is not one) nor on the rent, because the value is too low.
- The seller is opting to tax the property, meaning that VAT at 20% is payable on top of the rent.
- Term of lease: 10 years
- The premises will be provided with vacant possession. The seller has confirmed it is currently occupied by the seller.

2. Title investigation

- There is a restrictive covenant preventing Polished Perfection Ltd from building on the property. This has been breached when a previous owner constructed a ground floor extension, but this does not overlap with the premises being demised.
- The seller does not know of any overriding interests affecting the premises. We recommend a physical inspection of the property, as Polished Perfection Ltd will be bound by these if any do exist and are discoverable.

3. Searches

- The highways search confirms that the High Street is an adopted highway and directly abuts the salon, through which you will reach the first floor premises.
- The drainage and water search confirmed that Westshire Water are responsible for maintaining the drains and sewers and for the quality of the water supplied to the property.

- The environmental search confirmed that the risk of contaminants being present on the land is low and we do not recommend any further environmental surveys.
- The flood search confirmed that the risk of flooding to the property is low and we do not recommend any further flood surveys.
- A company search against the seller revealed no charges, nor insolvency or administration events.
- The property benefits from mains electricity and gas (not metered) and broadband connections.
- The seller has confirmed that heating and hot water are shared with the rest of the building.
- The seller has confirmed they will continue to insure the whole building. The tenant's interest will be noted on the policy and insurers have waived their subrogation rights.

4. Planning permission

- The property has planning permission E. This will be sufficient for the proposed use of the property as a nail bar.
- Proposed fit-out works will not require planning permission.

5. Access

- Access to the premises is through the ground floor of the building. The lease will contain rights over this part of the building.
- The lease will contain a right to use the Car Park behind the building, for staff and customers.

Document 15

NB: the authors have included dates in this lease in square brackets – in practice these would be entered at the relevant moment (e.g. on completion).

DATED

[*21 September 2026*]

LEASE

relating to

First Floor, 17 High Street, Barnford, Westshire, EX82 7YK

between

Style&Go Ltd

and

Polished Perfection Ltd

CONTENTS

CLAUSE

SCHEDULE

ANNEX

LR1. Date of lease

[*21 September 2026*]

LR2. Title number(s)

LR2.1 Landlord's title number

EG576798

LR2.2 Other title numbers

EG994587

LR3. Parties to this lease

Landlord

Style&Go Ltd
c/o Blackhurst&Sons LLP of 22 High Street, Barnford, Westshire, EX82 7YK

00127976

Tenant

Polished Perfection Ltd

c/o Talbot & Wick LLP, 47B Vale Road, Torton, Westshire, EX79 4PJ

22375943

Other parties

None

LR4. Property

In the case of a conflict between this clause and the remainder of this lease then, for the purposes of registration, this clause shall prevail.

See the definition of "Property" in Clause 1.1 and Schedule 1 of this lease.

The Property is let without the benefit of any existing easements or other rights which are appurtenant to the whole or any part of the Building

LR5. Prescribed statements etc.

LR5.1 Statements prescribed under rules 179 (dispositions in favour of a charity), 180 (dispositions by a charity) or 196 (leases under the Leasehold Reform, Housing and Urban Development Act 1993) of the Land Registration Rules 2003.

None.

LR5.2 This lease is made under, or by reference to, provisions of:

None.

LR6. Term for which the Property is leased

The term specified in the definition of "Contractual Term" in Clause 1.1 of this lease.

LR7. Premium

None.

LR8. Prohibitions or restrictions on disposing of this lease

This lease contains a provision that prohibits or restricts dispositions.

LR9. Rights of acquisition etc.

LR9.1 Tenant's contractual rights to renew this lease, to acquire the reversion or another lease of the Property, or to acquire an interest in other land

None.

LR9.2 Tenant's covenant to (or offer to) surrender this lease

None.

LR9.3 Landlord's contractual rights to acquire this lease

None.

LR10. Restrictive covenants given in this lease by the Landlord in respect of land other than the Property

None.

LR11. Easements

LR11.1 Easements granted by this lease for the benefit of the Property

The easements set out in paragraph 1 of Schedule 2 to this lease are granted by this lease for the benefit of the Property.

LR11.2 Easements granted or reserved by this lease over the Property for the benefit of other property

The easements set out in paragraph 1 of Schedule 3 to this lease are granted or reserved over the Property for the benefit of other property.

LR12. Estate rentcharge burdening the Property

None.

LR13. Application for standard form of restriction

None

LR14. Declaration of trust where there is more than one person comprising the Tenant

N/A

This lease is dated [*21 September 2026*]

PARTIES

(1) STYLE&GO LTD incorporated and registered in England and Wales with company number 00127976 whose registered office is at c/o Blackhurst&Sons LLP of 22 High Street, Barnford, Westshire, EX82 7YK **(Landlord)**

(2) POLISHED PERFECTION LTD incorporated and registered in England and Wales with company number 22375943 whose registered office is at c/o Talbot & Wick LLP, 47B Vale Road, Torton, Westshire, EX79 4PJ **(Tenant)**

BACKGROUND

(A) The Landlord is the freehold owner of the Building.

(B) The Property forms part of the Building.

(C) The Landlord has agreed to grant a lease of the Property to the Tenant on the terms set out in this lease.

AGREED TERMS

1. Interpretation

The following definitions and rules of interpretation apply in this lease.

1.1 Definitions:

Annual Rent: rent at an initial rate of £10,000 per annum and then as revised under Schedule 4.

Authorised Person: any:

a) undertenant or person deriving title under the Tenant;

b) workers, contractors or agents of the Tenant or of any person referred to in paragraph (a) of this definition; or

c) person at the Property or the Building with the actual or implied authority of the Tenant or any person referred to in paragraph (a) or paragraph (b) of this definition.

Building: is the land and buildings known as 17 High Street, Barnford, Westshire, EX82 7YK registered under title number EG576798 and shown edged thick black on the Building Plan.

Building Damage: damage to or destruction of the Building (excluding the Excluded Insurance Items) that makes the Property wholly or partially unfit for occupation and use or inaccessible.

Building Plan: the plan annexed to this lease at ANNEX B and marked "Building Plan".

Car Park: the parking area at the rear of the Building outlined in green on the Plan.

Common Areas: the Toilet and the Kitchen.

Contractual Term: a term of years from and including the date of this lease to and including 20 September 2036.

Excluded Insurance Items: the tenant's fixtures that are installed by or for the tenant or any undertenant and that form part of the Building.

Expert: an independent surveyor:

a) who is a Member or Fellow of the Royal Institution of Chartered Surveyors;

b) with relevant experience in the subject matter of the dispute; and

c) appointed in accordance with paragraph 2 of Part 5 of Schedule 4.

Insolvency Event: [not reproduced]

Insurance Rent: the aggregate in each year of:

a) a fair proportion of the gross cost of any premiums that the Landlord expends (after any discount or commission is allowed or paid to the Landlord) and any fees and other expenses that the Landlord reasonably incurs in insuring the Building (excluding the Excluded Insurance Items) against the Insured Risks for the Reinstatement Cost in accordance with this lease;

b) a fair proportion of the gross cost of the premium that the Landlord expends in effecting public liability insurance in relation to the Retained Parts in accordance with this lease (after any discount or commission is allowed or paid to the Landlord);

c) the gross cost of the premium after any discount or commission for insurance for loss of Annual Rent from the Property for three years; and

d) any VAT (except to the extent that the Landlord obtains credit for such VAT as input tax or otherwise recovers it) payable on any sum set out in paragraphs (a) to (c) of this definition.

Insured Risks: (except to the extent any of the following are not insured against at the date of the relevant damage or destruction because of an exclusion imposed by the insurers or insurance for such risks was not available in the London insurance market on reasonable terms acceptable to the Landlord at the time the insurance policy was entered into) fire, explosion, lightning, earthquake, tempest, storm, flood, bursting and overflowing of water tanks, apparatus or pipes, damage to underground water, oil or gas pipes or electricity wires or cables, impact by aircraft and aerial devices and articles dropped from them, impact by vehicles, subsidence, ground slip, heave, riot, civil commotion, strikes, labour or political disturbances, malicious damage, and any other risks against which the Landlord decides to insure against from time to time and **Insured Risk** means any one of the Insured Risks.

Interest Rate: the base rate from time to time of Westshire Bank plc or, if that base rate stops being used or published, a comparable commercial rate specified by the Landlord (acting reasonably).

Kitchen: the kitchen area marked cross-hatched grey on the Plan.

LTA 1927: Landlord and Tenant Act 1927.

LTA 1954: Landlord and Tenant Act 1954.

LTCA 1995: Landlord and Tenant (Covenants) Act 1995.

Permitted Use: use for the provision of commercial beauty services within Use Class E of the Town and Country Planning (Use Classes) Order 2020 (as it applied in England at the date this lease was granted)

President: the president for the time being of the Royal Institution of Chartered Surveyors or a person acting on their behalf.

Property: the property described in Schedule 1.

Property Plan: the plan annexed to this lease at ANNEX A and marked "Property Plan".

Reinstatement Cost: the full cost of reinstatement of the Building (excluding the Excluded Insurance Items) taking into account inflation of building costs and including any costs of demolition, site clearance, site protection, shoring up, professionals' and statutory fees and incidental expenses and any other work to the Building that may be required by law and any VAT on all such costs, fees and expenses.

Rents: the rents set out in clause 2.3.

Rent Commencement Date: the date of this lease.

Rent Payment Dates: 25 March, 24 June, 29 September and 25 December .

Reservations: the rights excepted and reserved in paragraph 1 of Schedule 3.

Retained Parts: all parts of the Building including (but not limited to) all of:

a) the structural parts of the Building; and

b) the Service Media.

Rights: the rights granted in paragraph 1 of Schedule 2.

Service Media: all media for the supply or removal of Utilities and all structures, machinery and equipment ancillary to those media.

Term: the Contractual Term.

Termination Date: the date on which this lease determines (however it determines).

Toilet: the Toilet marked hatched grey on the Plan.

Utilities: electricity, gas, water, sewage, air-conditioning, heating, energy, telecommunications, data and all other services and utilities.

Utility Costs: all costs in connection with the supply or removal of Utilities to or from the Property (or a fair proportion of the total cost if any of those costs are payable in respect of the Property together with any other property).

VAT: value added tax chargeable in the UK.

1.2 A reference to this **lease**, except a reference to the date of this lease or to the grant of this lease, is a reference to this deed and any deed, licence, consent, approval or other instrument supplemental or collateral to it.

1.3 The Schedules form part of this lease and shall have effect as if set out in full in the body of this lease. Any reference to **this lease** includes the Schedules.

1.4 Unless the context otherwise requires, references to clauses, Schedules and Annexes are to the clauses, Schedules and Annexes of this lease and references to paragraphs are to paragraphs of the relevant Schedule.

1.5 Clause, Schedule and paragraph headings shall not affect the interpretation of this lease.

1.6 A reference to:

(a) the **Landlord** includes a reference to the person entitled to the immediate reversion to this lease; and

(b) the **Tenant** includes a reference to its successors in title and assigns.

1.7 In relation to any payment, a reference to a **fair proportion** is to a fair proportion of the total amount payable, determined conclusively (except as to questions of law) by the Landlord.

1.8 A **person** includes a natural person, corporate or unincorporated body (whether or not having separate legal personality).

1.9 Unless the context otherwise requires, a reference to one gender shall include a reference to the other genders.

1.10 The expressions **authorised guarantee agreement**, **landlord covenant** and **tenant covenant** each has the meaning given to it by the LTCA 1995.

1.11 Any obligation on the Tenant not to do something includes an obligation not to allow that thing to be done and an obligation to use best endeavours to prevent that thing being done by another person.

1.12 Unless the context otherwise requires, references to the **Building**, the **Property** and the **Retained Parts** are to the whole and any part of them or it.

1.13 Unless the context otherwise requires, any words following the terms **including**, **include**, **in particular**, **for example** or any similar expression shall be construed as illustrative and shall not limit the sense of the words, description, definition, phrase or term preceding those terms.

1.14 A reference to **writing** or **written** excludes fax and email.

1.15 Unless the context otherwise requires, words in the singular shall include the plural and in the plural shall include the singular.

1.16 A **working day** is any day which is not a Saturday, a Sunday, a bank holiday or a public holiday in England.

1.17 Unless expressly provided otherwise in this lease, a reference to legislation or a legislative provision is a reference to it as amended, extended or re-enacted from time to time.

1.18 Unless expressly provided otherwise in this lease, a reference to legislation or a legislative provision shall include all subordinate legislation made from time to time under that legislation or legislative provision.

2. Grant

2.1 If any provision or part-provision of this lease is or becomes invalid, illegal or unenforceable, it shall be deemed deleted, but that shall not affect the validity and enforceability of the rest of this lease.

2.2 The Landlord lets the Property to the Tenant:

(a) for the Contractual Term;

(b) with full title guarantee;

(c) together with the Rights; and

(d) excepting and reserving the Reservations.

2.3 The grant in clause 2.1 is made with the Tenant paying as rent to the Landlord:

(a) the Annual Rent;

(b) the Insurance Rent;

(c) all interest payable under this lease; and

(d) all VAT chargeable on the other rents set out in this clause 2.3.

3. Tenant covenants

The Tenant covenants with the Landlord to observe and perform the tenant covenants of this lease during the Term or (if earlier) until the Tenant is released from the tenant covenants of this lease by virtue of the LTCA 1995.

4. **Payment of Annual Rent**

The Tenant must pay the Annual Rent by four equal instalments in advance on or before the Rent Payment Dates except that:

(a) the Tenant must pay the first instalment of Annual Rent on the Rent Commencement Date; and

(b) that first instalment of Annual Rent shall be the proportion of the Annual Rent calculated on a daily basis for the period from and including the Rent Commencement Date to and including the day before the next Rent Payment Date after the Rent Commencement Date.

5. **Utilities**

5.1 The Tenant must pay all Utility Costs.

5.2 The Tenant must comply with all laws and with any recommendations of the relevant suppliers relating to the supply and removal of Utilities to or from the Property.

6. **Prohibition of dealings**

Except as expressly permitted by clause 7, clause 8 or clause 9, the Tenant must not assign, underlet, charge, part with or share possession or occupation of the whole or part of either this lease or the Property.

7. **Assignments**

7.1 The Tenant may assign the whole of this lease with the consent of the Landlord.

7.2 The Landlord and the Tenant agree that, for the purposes of section 19(1A) of the LTA 1927, the Landlord may give its consent to an assignment subject to all or any of the following conditions:

(a) a condition that the assignor enters into an authorised guarantee agreement in favour of the Landlord which:

(i) is in respect of all the tenant covenants of this lease;

(ii) is in respect of the period beginning with the date the assignee becomes bound by those covenants and ending on the date when the assignee is released from those covenants by virtue of section 5 of the LTCA 1995; and

(iii) is otherwise in a form reasonably required by the Landlord;

(b) a condition that the assignee enters into a rent deposit deed with the Landlord in a form reasonably required by the Landlord and for an initial deposit of six months' Annual Rent (as at the date of assignment) plus a sum equivalent to VAT on that Annual Rent.

7.3 The Landlord and the Tenant agree that, for the purposes of section 19(1A) of the LTA 1927, the Landlord may refuse its consent to an assignment if any of the following circumstances exist:

(a) the Annual Rent or any other sum due under this lease is outstanding;

(b) there is a material breach of covenant by the Tenant that has not been remedied; or

(c) in the Landlord's reasonable opinion the assignee is not of sufficient financial standing to enable it to comply with the Tenant's covenants and conditions contained in this lease.

7.4 Nothing in this clause shall prevent the Landlord from giving consent subject to any other reasonable condition nor from refusing consent to an assignment in any other circumstance where it is reasonable to do so.

8. Underletting

8.1 The Tenant may underlet the whole of the Property in accordance with this clause 8 and with the consent of the Landlord.

8.2 The Tenant must not underlet the whole of the Property:

(a) together with any property, or any right over property, that is not included within this lease;

(b) unless the underlease has first been validly excluded from the provisions of the LTA 1954 (where it is a lease that might otherwise acquire security of tenure under Part II of the LTA 1954);

(c) for a term that will expire by effluxion of time later than three days before the Contractual Term expires by effluxion of time; and

(d) unless the undertenant has first entered into a direct covenant in favour of the Landlord to observe and perform the tenant covenants in the underlease and any document that is collateral or supplemental to it.

8.3 Any underletting by the Tenant must include:

(a) an agreement between the Tenant and the undertenant that the provisions of sections 24 to 28 of the LTA 1954 are excluded from applying to the tenancy created by the underlease (where the underlease was required to be contracted out under clause 8.2(b));

(b) the reservation of a rent which is not less than the open market rental value of the Property at the date on which the Landlord grants consent to the underletting and which is payable at the same times as the Annual Rent under this lease;

(c) provisions for the review of rent at the same dates and on the same basis as the review of the Annual Rent in this lease unless the term of the underlease is five years or less;

(d) a covenant by the undertenant not to:

(i) assign or charge the whole or any part of the underlease;

(ii) part with, share possession or share occupation of the whole or any part of the underlet property;

(iii) underlet the whole or part only of the underlet property;

(iv) (if the underlease permits the undertenant to assign the underlease) assign the underlease without first procuring a direct covenant in favour of the Landlord to observe and perform the covenants in the underlease and any document that is collateral or supplemental to it;

(e) a covenant by the undertenant to comply with the terms of this lease except the covenant to pay the Annual Rent; and

(f) provisions requiring the consent or approval of the Landlord to be obtained in respect of any matter for which the consent or approval of the Landlord is required under this lease.

8.4 Any underletting by the Tenant must otherwise be:

(a) by deed;

(b) consistent with and include tenant covenants no less onerous than those in this lease excluding the covenant in this lease to pay the Annual Rent; and

(c) in a form approved by the Landlord (such approval not to be unreasonably withheld).

8.5 In relation to any underlease granted by the Tenant, the Tenant must:

(a) not vary the terms of the underlease nor accept a surrender of the underlease without the consent of the Landlord (such consent not to be unreasonably withheld);

(b) enforce the tenant covenants in the underlease and not waive any of them nor allow any reduction in the rent payable under the underlease; and

(c) ensure that in relation to any rent review the revised rent is not agreed without the approval of the Landlord (such approval not to be unreasonably withheld).

9. Charging

The Tenant may charge the whole of this lease with the consent of the Landlord (such consent not to be unreasonably withheld).

10. Repair

10.1 The Tenant must:

(a) subject to clause 10.2, keep the Property in good repair and condition;

(b) keep the Property clean, tidy and clear of rubbish.

10.2 The Tenant shall not be liable to repair the Property (excluding any Excluded Insurance Items forming part of the Property) to the extent that any disrepair has been caused by an Insured Risk unless and to the extent that:

(a) the policy of insurance of the Property has been vitiated or any insurance proceeds withheld in consequence of any act or omission of the Tenant or any Authorised Person (except where the Tenant has paid an amount equal to any insurance money that the insurers refuse to pay in accordance with paragraph 3.2(f) of Schedule 5); or

(b) thc insurance cover in relation to that disrepair is limited as referred to in paragraph 1.3 of Schedule 5.

11. Decoration

The Tenant must:

(a) decorate the Property once per five years of the Contractual Term and also in the last twelve months before the Termination Date;

(b) carry out all decoration (including all appropriate preparatory work) in a good and proper manner using good quality materials that are appropriate to the Property and the Permitted Use; and

(c) carry out the decoration required in the last three months before the Termination Date to the reasonable satisfaction of the Landlord and using materials, designs and colours approved by the Landlord (acting reasonably).

12. Alterations

12.1 Except as permitted by this clause 12, the Tenant must not make any alteration or addition to the Property.

12.2 The Tenant may make internal non-structural alterations to the Property with the consent of the Landlord (such consent not to be unreasonably withheld or delayed).

12.3 With the consent of the Landlord (such consent not to be unreasonably withheld or delayed), the Tenant may:

(a) install any Service Media at the Property; or

(b) alter the route of any Service Media at the Property.

13. Returning the Property to the Landlord

13.1 The Tenant must return the Property to the Landlord on the Termination Date with vacant possession and in the repair and condition required by this lease.

14. Use

14.1 The Tenant must not use the Property for any purpose other than the Permitted Use.

14.2 The Tenant must not:

(a) use the Property for any illegal purposes nor for any purpose or in a manner that would cause loss, damage, injury, nuisance or inconvenience to the Landlord, the other tenants or occupiers of the Building or any property that neighbours the Building;

(b) allow any noise, music, flashing lights, fumes or smells to emanate from the Property so as to cause a nuisance or annoyance to any other tenants or occupiers of the Building or any property that neighbours the Building;

(c) overload any part of the Building nor overload or block any Service Media at or serving the Property;

(d) store, sell or display any offensive, dangerous, illegal, explosive or highly flammable items at the Property;

(e) (except as permitted by the Rights and clause 12.3) interfere with any Service Media at the Building.

15. Exercise of the Rights

15.1 The Tenant must exercise the Rights:

(a) only in connection with the Tenant's use of the Property for the Permitted Use;

(b) in compliance with all laws relating to the Tenant's use of the Building.

16. Allow entry

16.1 The Tenant must allow all those entitled to exercise any right to enter the Property to enter the Property:

(a) except in the case of an emergency (when no notice shall be required), after having given reasonable notice (which need not be in writing) to the Tenant;

(b) at any reasonable time (whether or not during usual business hours); and

(c) with their workers, contractors, agents and professional advisers.

17. Compliance with laws

17.1 The Tenant must comply with all laws relating to:

(a) the Property and the occupation and use of the Property by the Tenant;

(b) the use or operation of all Service Media and any other machinery and equipment at or serving the Property whether or not used or operated;

(c) any works carried out at the Property; and

(d) all materials kept at or disposed of from the Property.

18. Indemnity

The Tenant must keep the Landlord indemnified against all liabilities, expenses, costs (including, but not limited to, any solicitors' or other professionals' costs and expenses), claims, damages and losses (including, but not limited to, any diminution in the value of the Landlord's interest in the Building and loss of amenity of the Building) suffered or incurred by the Landlord arising out of or in connection with:

(a) any breach of any tenant covenants in this lease;

(b) any use or occupation of the Property or the carrying out of any works permitted or required to be carried out under this lease; or

(c) any act or omission of the Tenant or any Authorised Person.

19. Landlord covenants

The Landlord covenants with the Tenant to observe and perform the landlord covenants of this lease during the Term.

20. Quiet enjoyment

The Landlord covenants with the Tenant that the Tenant shall have quiet enjoyment of the Property without any interruption by the Landlord or any person claiming under the Landlord except as otherwise permitted by this lease.

21. Exercise of right of entry

In exercising any right of entry on to the Property pursuant to paragraph 1.2 of Schedule 3, the Landlord must:

(a) except in case of emergency, give reasonable notice of its intention to exercise that right to the Tenant;

(b) where reasonably required by the Tenant, exercise that right only if accompanied by a representative of the Tenant;

(c) cause as little damage as possible to the Property and to any property belonging to or used by the Tenant;

(d) cause as little inconvenience as reasonably possible to the Tenant; and

(e) promptly make good any physical damage caused to the Property by reason of the Landlord exercising that right.

22. Re-entry and forfeiture

22.1 The Landlord may re-enter the Property (or any part of the Property in the name of the whole) at any time after any of the following occurs:

(a) the whole or any part of the Rents is unpaid 21 days after becoming payable (whether it has been formally demanded or not);

(b) any breach of any condition of, or tenant covenant in, this lease; or

(c) an Insolvency Event.

22.2 If the Landlord re-enters the Property (or any part of the Property in the name of the whole) pursuant to this clause, this lease shall immediately end but without prejudice to any right or remedy of the Landlord in respect of any breach of covenant by the Tenant or any guarantor.

23. Exclusion of sections 24 to 28 of the LTA 1954

The parties:

(a) confirm that:

(i) the Landlord served a notice on the Tenant, as required by section 38A(3)(a) of the LTA 1954, applying to the tenancy created by this lease, not less than 14 days before this lease was entered into;

(ii) the Tenant made a statutory declaration dated 4 September 2026 in accordance with the requirements of section 38A(3)(b) of the LTA 1954; and

(b) agree that the provisions of sections 24 to 28 of the LTA 1954 are excluded in relation to the tenancy created by this lease.

24. Limitation of liability

The Landlord shall not be liable to the Tenant for any failure of the Landlord to perform any landlord covenant in this lease unless the Landlord knows it has failed to perform the covenant (or reasonably should know this) and has not remedied that failure within a reasonable time.

25. Breach of repair and maintenance obligation

25.1 The Landlord may enter the Property to inspect its condition and state of repair and give the Tenant a notice of any breach of any of the tenant covenants in this lease relating to the condition or repair of the Property.

25.2 Following the service of a notice pursuant to clause 25.1, the Landlord may enter the Property and carry out the required works if the Tenant:

(a) has not begun any works required to remedy any breach specified in that notice within two months of the notice or, if works are required as a matter of emergency, immediately; or

(b) is not carrying out the required works with all due speed.

25.3 The costs incurred by the Landlord in carrying out any works pursuant to clause 25.2 (and any professional fees and any VAT in respect of those costs) shall be a debt due from the Tenant to the Landlord and payable on demand.

25.4 Any action taken by the Landlord pursuant to this clause 25 shall be without prejudice to the Landlord's other rights (including those under clause 22).

26. Consents and approvals

26.1 Where the consent of the Landlord is required under this lease, a consent shall only be valid if it is given by deed unless:

(a) it is given in writing and signed by the Landlord or a person duly authorised on its behalf; and

(b) it expressly states that the Landlord waives the requirement for a deed in that particular case.

26.2 If the Landlord gives a consent or approval under this lease, the giving of that consent or approval shall not:

(a) imply that any consent or approval required from a third party has been obtained; or

(b) obviate the need to obtain any consent or approval from a third party.

27. VAT

27.1 All sums payable by either party under or in connection with this lease are exclusive of any VAT that may be chargeable.

27.2 A party to this lease must pay VAT in respect of all taxable supplies made to that party in connection with this lease on the due date for making any payment or, if earlier, the date on which that supply is made for VAT purposes.

27.3 Every obligation on either party, under or in connection with this lease, to pay any sum by way of a refund or indemnity, includes an obligation to pay an amount equal to any VAT incurred on that sum by the receiving party (except to the extent that the receiving party obtains credit for such VAT).

This document has been executed as a deed and is delivered and takes effect on the date stated at the beginning of it.

Schedule 1 Property

1. The premises known as first floor, 17 High Street, Barnford, Westshire, EX82 7YK situated on the first floor of the Building and shown edged red on the Property Plan:

1.1 Including:

(a) the whole of any non-structural walls and columns wholly within those premises;

(b) the interior plaster and other interior surface finishes on the:

(i) exterior non-structural walls and columns bounding those premises;

(ii) interior non-structural walls and columns separating those premises from any adjoining Retained Parts; and

(iii) structural walls and columns within or bounding those premises;

(c) the interior plaster and other interior surface finishes on the ceilings within those premises;

(d) the floor screed and other interior surface finishes on the floors within those premises;

(e) the doors, door frames and fittings within all the walls within and bounding those premises;

(f) the windows, window frames and fittings within all the walls within and bounding those premises (except the exterior walls);

(g) all Service Media and any other media, plant, machinery and equipment within and exclusively serving those premises;

(h) all landlord's fixtures and fittings within those premises; and

(i) all additions and improvements to those premises.

1.2 Excluding:

(a) subject to paragraph 1.1(b), paragraph 1.1(e) and paragraph 1.1(f) of this Schedule, the whole of the:

(i) exterior non-structural walls and columns bounding those premises;

(ii) interior non-structural walls and columns separating those premises from any adjoining Retained Parts; and

(iii) structural walls and columns within or bounding those premises;

(b) the windows, window frames and fittings within the exterior walls bounding those premises;

(c) subject to paragraph 1.1(c) and paragraph 1.1(d) of this Schedule, the floors and ceilings within those premises;

(d) all Service Media and any other media, plant, machinery and equipment within but not exclusively serving those premises; and

(e) all structural parts of the Building (except any set out in paragraph 1.1 of this Schedule).

Schedule 2 Rights

1. In common with the Landlord and any other person authorised by the Landlord, the Landlord grants to the Tenant the following easements (for the benefit of the Property) and the following other rights:

1.1 A right of access for the Tenant and any person authorised by the Tenant over the Retained Land for the purpose of accessing the Property.

1.2 A right to use the Common Areas for the Tenant and its employees, and a right for any person who is a customer of the Tenant to use the Toilet.

1.3 The right to support and protection for the Property from the other parts of the Building to the extent that those parts of the Building provide support and protection to the Property at the date of this lease.

1.4 The right to use and to connect into any Service Media at the Building that belong to the Landlord and serve (but do not form part of) the Property which are in existence at the date of this lease or are installed or constructed during the Term. Provided that the Landlord may, at its discretion and at any time, re-route or replace any Service Media at the Building pursuant to paragraph 1.3(c) of Schedule 3 and this right shall then apply in relation to the Service Media as re-routed or replaced.

1.5 A right to use the Car Park for the Tenant, its employees and any person who is a customer of the Tenant, for the purpose of parking a car whilst visiting the Property.

Schedule 3 Reservations

1. Subject to paragraph 2 and paragraph 3 of this Schedule, the Landlord excepts and reserves from this lease the following easements (for the benefit of the Building (excluding the Property)) and the following other rights:

1.1 Rights of light, air, support and protection to the extent those rights are capable of being enjoyed at any time during the Term.

1.2 Subject to the Landlord complying with clause 21, the right to enter the Property:

(a) to repair, maintain, install, construct, re-route or replace any Service Media or structure relating to any of the Reservations;

(b) to carry out any works to any other part of the Building; and

(c) for any other purpose mentioned in or connected with:

(i) this lease;

(ii) the Reservations; or

(iii) the Landlord's interest in the Building.

1.3 The right to:

(a) use and connect into Service Media at, but not forming part of, the Property which are in existence at the date of this lease or which are installed or constructed during the Term;

(b) install and construct Service Media at the Property to serve any other part of the Building; and

(c) re-route and replace any Service Media referred to in this paragraph.

1.4 At any time during the Term, the full and free right to build, rebuild, alter or develop the Building as the Landlord may think fit.

2. The Reservations:

2.1 Are excepted and reserved notwithstanding that the exercise of any of the Reservations or the works carried out pursuant to them result in a reduction in the flow of light or air to the Property or loss of amenity for the Property.

2.2 May be exercised by:

(a) the Landlord;

(b) anyone else who is or becomes entitled to exercise them; and

(c) anyone authorised by the Landlord.

3. No party exercising any of the Reservations, nor its workers, contractors, agents and professional advisers, shall be liable to the Tenant or to any undertenant or other occupier of or person at the Property for any loss, damage, injury, nuisance

or inconvenience arising by reason of its exercising any of the Reservations except for:

3.1 Physical damage to the Property.

3.2 Any loss, damage, injury, nuisance or inconvenience in relation to which the law prevents the Landlord from excluding liability.

Schedule 4 Rent review

Part 1 Definitions

1. Definitions

The following definitions apply in this Schedule 4.

Assumptions: the assumptions set out in Part 2 of this Schedule 4.

Disregards: the disregards set out in Part 3 of this Schedule 4.

Hypothetical Lease: the lease described in Part 4 of this Schedule 4.

Open Market Rent: the best annual rent (exclusive of VAT) at which the Property could reasonably be expected to be let:

a) in the open market;

b) at the Review Date; and

c) applying the Assumptions and Disregards.

Review Dates: 21 September 2031

Shortfall Payment Date: the date that the revised Annual Rent is agreed or determined.

Part 2 Assumptions

1. The matters to be assumed are:

1.1 The Property is available to let in the open market:

(a) on the terms of the Hypothetical Lease;

(b) by a willing landlord to a willing tenant;

(c) with vacant possession.

1.2 The Property may lawfully be used, and is in a physical state to enable it to be lawfully used, by the willing tenant (or any potential undertenant or assignee of the willing tenant) for any use permitted by this lease.

1.3 The Tenant has fully complied with their obligations in this lease.

1.4 If the Property or any means of access to it or any Service Media serving the Property has been destroyed or damaged, it has been fully restored.

1.5 No work has been carried out on the Property that has diminished its rental value other than work carried out in compliance with clause 17.

1.6 Any fixtures, fittings, machinery or equipment supplied to the Property by the Landlord that have been removed by or at the request of the Tenant, or any undertenant or their respective predecessors in title (otherwise than to comply with any law) remain at the Property.

Part 3 Disregards

1. The matters to be disregarded are:

1.1 Any effect on rent of the fact that the Tenant or any authorised undertenant has been in occupation of the Property.

1.2 Any goodwill attached to the Property by reason of any business carried out there by the Tenant or by any authorised undertenant or by any of their predecessors in business.

1.3 Any effect on rent attributable to any physical improvement to the Property carried out before or after the date of this lease (including any physical improvement to any Service Media servicing the Property), by or at the expense of the Tenant or any authorised undertenant with all necessary consents, approvals and authorisations and not pursuant to an obligation to the Landlord (other than an obligation to comply with any law).

1.4 Any statutory restriction on rents or the right to recover them.

Part 4 Hypothetical Lease

1. A lease:

1.1 Of the whole of the Property.

1.2 For a term equal to the unexpired residue of the Contractual Term at the Review Date.

1.3 With rent review dates every 5 years from the Review Date.

1.4 Otherwise on the terms of this lease (other than the amount of the Annual Rent).

Part 5 Review of the Annual Rent

1. Review

1.1 The Annual Rent shall be reviewed on the Review Date to equal:

(a) the amount agreed between the Landlord and Tenant at any time (whether or not that amount is the Open Market Rent); or

(b) in the absence of such agreement, the greater of:

(i) the Annual Rent payable immediately before the Review Date (or which would then be payable but for any abatement, suspension, concession or reduction of the Annual Rent or restriction on the right to collect it); and

(ii) the Open Market Rent agreed or determined pursuant to this Schedule 4.

1.2 The Landlord and Tenant may agree the revised Annual Rent at any time before it is determined by the Expert.

1.3 As soon as practicable after the amount of the revised Annual Rent has been agreed or determined, a memorandum recording the amount shall be signed by or on behalf of the Landlord, the Tenant and the guarantor. The parties shall each bear their own costs in connection with the memorandum.

2. Determination by the Expert

2.1 If the Landlord and Tenant have not agreed the revised Annual Rent by the date three months before the Review Date, then either party may at any time refer the revised Annual Rent for determination by the Expert in accordance with this paragraph 2 of this Part of this Schedule. The Expert can be appointed in accordance with the terms of this lease irrespective of whether the Landlord and Tenant have tried to first reach an agreement on the revised Annual Rent.

2.2 The Landlord and Tenant shall agree on the appointment of an Expert and shall agree with the Expert the terms of their appointment.

2.3 If the Landlord and Tenant are unable to agree on an Expert or the terms of their appointment within 10 working days of either party serving details of a suggested expert on the other, either party shall then be entitled to request the President to appoint an Expert and agree with the Expert the terms of appointment.

2.4 The Expert shall be required to prepare a written decision including reasons and give notice (including a copy) of the decision to the parties within a maximum of 15 working days of the matter being referred to the Expert.

2.5 The parties are entitled to make submissions to the Expert and must provide (or procure that others provide) the Expert with such assistance and documents as the Expert reasonably requires for the purpose of reaching a decision.

2.6 The Expert shall act as an expert and not as an arbitrator. The Expert shall determine the matter referred to the Expert under this lease. The Expert may award interest as part of their decision. The Expert's written decision on the matters referred to them shall be final and binding on the parties in the absence of manifest error or fraud.

2.7 The Landlord and Tenant must bear their own costs in relation to the reference to the Expert.

2.8 The Landlord and Tenant must bear the Expert's fees and any costs properly incurred by them in arriving at their determination (including any fees and costs of any advisers appointed by the Expert) equally or in such other proportions as the Expert shall direct.

2.9 The Landlord and Tenant must act reasonably and co-operate to give effect to the provisions of this paragraph 2 of this Part of this Schedule and otherwise do nothing to hinder or prevent the Expert from reaching their determination.

3. Late review of Annual Rent

3.1 If the revised Annual Rent has not been agreed or determined on or before the Review Date, the Tenant must:

(a) continue to pay the Annual Rent at the rate payable immediately before that Review Date; and

(b) on the Shortfall Payment Date, pay:

(i) the shortfall (if any) between the amount of Annual Rent that the Tenant has paid for the period from and including that Review Date and the amount of Annual Rent for that period that would have been payable had the revised Annual Rent been agreed or determined on or before that Review Date; and

(ii) interest at the Interest Rate on that shortfall. That interest shall be calculated on a daily basis by reference to the Rent Payment Dates on which parts of the shortfall would have been payable if the revised Annual Rent had been agreed or determined on or before that Review Date and the Shortfall Payment Date.

4. Time not of the essence

4.1 Time is not of the essence for the purposes of this Schedule 4.

Schedule 5 Insurance

1. Landlord's obligation to insure

1.1 Subject to paragraph 1.2 and paragraph 1.3 of this Schedule, the Landlord must insure (and keep insured):

(a) the Building on normal market terms against loss or damage by the Insured Risks for the Reinstatement Cost;

(b) against public liability of the Landlord in relation to the Retained Parts in such amount and on such terms as the Landlord shall reasonably consider appropriate; and

(c) loss of Annual Rent from the Property for three years.

1.2 The Landlord shall not be obliged to insure:

(a) the Excluded Insurance Items or repair any damage to or destruction of the Excluded Insurance Items. References to the Property and the Building in this Schedule 5 shall exclude the Excluded Insurance Items;

(b) the Building when the insurance is vitiated by any act or omission of the Tenant or any Authorised Person.

1.3 The Landlord's obligation to insure is subject to any limitations, excesses and conditions that may be imposed by the insurers.

2. Landlord to provide insurance details

2.1 In relation to any insurance effected by the Landlord under this Schedule 5, the Landlord must:

(a) at the request of the Tenant supply the Tenant with:

(i) full details of the insurance policy;

(ii) evidence of payment of the current year's premiums; and

(iii) details of any commission paid to the Landlord by the Landlord's insurer;

(b) procure that the Tenant is informed of any change in the scope, level or terms of cover as soon as reasonably practicable after the Landlord or its agents becoming aware of the change.

3. Tenant's obligations

3.1 The Tenant must pay to the Landlord on demand:

(a) the Insurance Rent;

(b) a fair proportion of any amount that is deducted or disallowed by the insurers pursuant to any excess provision in the insurance policy; and

(c) a fair proportion of any costs that the Landlord incurs in obtaining a valuation of the Building for insurance purposes.

3.2 The Tenant must:

(a) immediately inform the Landlord if any matter occurs in relation to the Tenant or the Property that any insurer or underwriter may treat as material in deciding whether or on what terms to insure or to continue to insure the Building and must also give the Landlord notice of that matter;

(b) not do or omit to do anything as a result of which:

(i) any insurance policy for the Building may become void or voidable or otherwise prejudiced;

(ii) the payment of any policy money may be withheld; or

(iii) any increased or additional insurance premium may become payable (unless the Tenant has previously notified the Landlord and has paid any increased or additional premium (including any IPT due on that amount));

(c) comply at all times with the requirements and recommendations of the insurers relating to the Property and the use by the Tenant of any other part of the Building where written details of those requirements or recommendations have first been given to the Tenant;

(d) give the Landlord immediate notice of the occurrence of:

(i) any damage or loss relating to the Property arising from an Insured Risk; or

(ii) any other event that might affect any insurance policy relating to the Property;

(e) except for the Excluded Insurance Items forming part of the Property, not effect any buildings insurance of the Property but, if the Tenant becomes entitled to the benefit of any buildings insurance proceeds in respect of the Property, pay those proceeds or cause them to be paid to the Landlord;

(f) pay the Landlord an amount equal to any insurance money that the insurers of the Building refuse to pay in relation to the Building by reason of any act or omission of the Tenant or any Authorised Person.

4. Rent suspension

4.1 Subject to paragraph 4.2 of this Schedule, if any Building Damage by an Insured Risk occurs, payment of the Annual Rent (or a fair proportion of it according to the nature and extent of that Building Damage) shall be suspended until the earlier of:

(a) the date on which the Building has been reinstated so as to make the Property fit for occupation and use and accessible; and

(b) the date which is three years from and including the date on which that Building Damage occurred.

4.2 The Annual Rent shall not be suspended under paragraph 4.1 of this Schedule if the Building Damage is caused by an Insured Risk and:

(a) the policy of insurance in relation to the Building has been vitiated in whole or in part as a result of any act or omission of the Tenant or any Authorised Person; and

(b) the Tenant has not complied with paragraph 3.2(f) of this Schedule.

5. Landlord's obligation to reinstate following damage or destruction by an Insured Risk

5.1 Following any damage to or destruction of the Building by an Insured Risk, the Landlord must:

(a) use reasonable endeavours to obtain all necessary planning and other consents to enable the Landlord to reinstate the relevant parts of the Building; and

(b) reinstate the relevant parts of the Building except that the Landlord shall not be obliged to:

(i) reinstate unless all necessary planning and other consents are obtained;

(ii) reinstate unless the Tenant has paid the sums due under paragraph 3.1(b) and paragraph 3.2(f) of this Schedule;

(iii) provide accommodation or facilities identical in layout or design so long as accommodation reasonably equivalent to that previously at the Property and its access, services and amenities is provided; or

(iv) reinstate after a notice to terminate has been served pursuant to this Schedule 5.

5.2 If the Landlord is obliged to reinstate the relevant parts of the Building pursuant to paragraph 5.1(b) of this Schedule, the Landlord must:

(a) use all insurance money received (other than for loss of rent) and all sums received under paragraph 3.1(b) and paragraph 3.2(f) of this Schedule for the purposes of that reinstatement; and

(b) make up any shortfall out of its own funds.

6. Termination if reinstatement impossible or impractical following Building Damage by an Insured Risk

6.1 Following Building Damage by an Insured Risk, if the Landlord (acting reasonably) considers that it is impossible or impractical to reinstate the relevant parts of the

Building, the Landlord may terminate this lease by giving notice to the Tenant within six months from and including the date on which that Building Damage occurred.

7. Termination if reinstatement not complete by expiry of rent suspension

7.1 If Building Damage by an Insured Risk occurs and the relevant parts of the Building have not been reinstated so as to make the Property fit for occupation and use and accessible by the date which is three years after the date on which that Building Damage occurred, either party may at any time thereafter terminate this lease by giving notice to the other provided that:

(a) such notice is served before the relevant parts of the Building have been reinstated so as to make the Property fit for occupation and use and accessible; and

(b) where the Tenant serves the notice, the failure to reinstate so that the Property is fit for occupation and use is not caused by a breach of the Tenant's obligations under clause 10 or this Schedule 5.

8. Consequences of termination

8.1 If either party gives a notice to terminate this lease in accordance with this Schedule 5:

(a) this lease shall terminate with immediate effect from the date of the notice;

(b) none of the parties shall have any further rights or obligations under this lease except for the rights of any party in respect of any earlier breach of this lease; and

(c) any proceeds of the insurance for the Building shall belong to the Landlord.

Executed as deed by Style&Go Ltd (**Landlord)** acting by André Gomez a director, in the presence of:	*André Gomez*
Karen Chester	Director
Karen Chester, 29 Woodgrove Close, Barnford, Westshire, EX79 5PJ	
Secretary	
Executed as deed by Polished Perfection Ltd (**Tenant**) acting by Meena Kasih a director, in the presence of:	*Aminah Kasih*
Fatimah Hiraney	Director
Fatimah Hiraney, Flat 3b, Windridge Heights, Barnford, EX78 9JK	
Accountant	

ANNEX A Property Plan

[not reproduced]

ANNEX B Building Plan

[not reproduced]

Document 16

Official search certificate of search of whole with priority

Land Registry
Land Registration Rules 2003

Form **OS1R**

Official Search No. SANB/EXH02	Certificate Date: **4 September 2026** Priority Period began at: **15:17:17**	Priority Period expires on: **16 October 2026** at midnight but see the note below

Particulars of Search as Supplied

Title Number	EG576798
Applicant	Polished Perfection Ltd

Result

It is certified that the official search applied for has been made with the following result:

Since 29 June 2026 at 13:06:15 no adverse entries have been made.

****

END OF RESULT

Note: To be sure to obtain priority for your application you should deliver it to the proper office by 12:00 (noon) on the date when priority expires.

HM Land Registry

Application to change the register

AP1

Any parts of the form that are not typed should be completed in black ink and in block capitals.

If you need more room than is provided for in a panel, and your software allows, you can expand any panel in the form. Alternatively use continuation sheet CS and attach it to this form.

HM Land Registry is unable to give legal advice, but you can find guidance on HM Land Registry applications (including our practice guides for conveyancers) at www.gov.uk/land-registry.

Conveyancer is a term used in this form. It is defined in rule 217A, Land Registration Rules 2003 and includes persons authorised under the Legal Services Act 2007 to provide reserved legal services relating to land registration and includes solicitors and licensed conveyancers.

For information on how HM Land Registry processes your personal information, see our Personal Information Charter.

HM LAND REGISTRY USE ONLY
Record of fees paid
Particulars of under/over payments
Reference number Fees debited £

Where there is more than one local authority serving an area, enter the one to which council tax or business rates are normally paid.

1 Local authority serving the property: Westshire

Full postcode of property (if any): EX82 7YK

Enter the title number of each title that requires an entry to be made in that register.

2 Title number(s) of the property:
EG576798

3 The application affects

Place 'X' in the appropriate box.

Give a brief description of the part affected, for example 'edged red on the plan to the transfer dated ....'.

☐ the whole of the title(s)

☒ part of the title(s) as shown: edged red in the Property Plan, at Annex A in the Lease dated 21 September 2026

4 Application, priority and fees

To find out more about our fees visit www.gov.uk/government/collections/fees-land-registry-guides

Remember restrictions in deeds may apply to other deeds of lower priority in this list, unless you specify otherwise.

Applications in priority order	Price paid/Value (£)	Fees paid (£)
Grant of a lease	10,000	45
	Total fees (£)	45

Fee payment method

Place 'X' in the appropriate box.

Where the application is sent to HM Land Registry by a private individual, payment must be by way of postal order or cheque made payable to HM Land Registry.

The fee will be charged to the account specified in panel 7.

☐ cheque made payable to 'Land Registry'

☒ direct debit, under an agreement with Land Registry

List the documents lodged with this form. We only need certified copies of deeds or documents you send to us with HM Land Registry application forms. Once we have made a copy of the documents you send to us, they will be destroyed, this applies to both originals and certified copies	5	Documents lodged with this form: *Certified copy Lease dated 21 September 2026 and made between (1) Style&Go Ltd and (2) Polished Perfection Ltd, executed by Style&Go Ltd* *Certified copy Lease dated 21 September 2026 and made between (1) Style&Go Ltd and (2) Polished Perfection Ltd, executed by Polished Perfection Ltd* *Certified copy of SDLT5 dated 22 September 2026*
Provide the full name(s) of the person(s) applying to change the register. Where a conveyancer lodges the application, this must be the name(s) of the client(s), not the conveyancer. Complete as appropriate where the applicant is a company. Also, for an overseas company, unless an arrangement with HM Land Registry exists, lodge either a certificate in Form 7 in Schedule 3 to the Land Registration Rules 2003 or a certified copy of the constitution in English or Welsh, or other evidence permitted by rule 183 of the Land Registration Rules 2003. Enter the overseas entity ID issued by Companies House for the applicant pursuant to the Economic Crime (Transparency and Enforcement) Act 2022. If the ID is not required, you may instead state 'not required'. Further details on overseas entities can be found in practice guide 78: overseas entities.	6	The applicant: Polished Perfection Ltd For UK incorporated companies/LLPs Registered number of company or limited liability partnership including any prefix: 22375943 For overseas entities (a) Territory of incorporation or formation: (b) Overseas entity ID issued by Companies House, including any prefix: (c) Where the entity is a company with a place of business in the United Kingdom, the registered number, if any, issued by Companies House, including any prefix:
This panel must always be completed. This panel must always be completed with the details of the person sending the application to HM Land Registry. However, a key number is only available to professional customers, such as solicitors, and so a key number cannot be entered where the application is sent to HM Land Registry by a private individual. If you are paying by direct debit, this will be the account charged. This is the address to which we will normally send requisitions. However if you insert an email address, we will use this whenever possible. An acknowledgement of receipt of this application, if lodged by post, will be sent by email if one is available. We will only issue warning of cancellation letters to conveyancers if an email address is inserted.	7	This application is sent to Land Registry by Key number (if applicable): Name: Talbot & Wick LLP Address or UK DX box number: 47B Vale Road, Torton, Westshire, EX79 4PJ Email address: enquiries@talbotwick.com Reference: 9234/JXR Phone no: 0000 62723 — Fax no: n/a
When completing this panel please refer to Guidance: completing form AP1.	8	Third party notification Name: Address or UK DX box number: Email address: Reference:

When completing this panel please refer to Guidance: completing form AP1. Place 'X' in the appropriate box. In this and panel 10, each proprietor may give up to three addresses for service, one of which must be a postal address whether or not in the UK (including the postcode, if any). The others can be any combination of a postal address, a UK DX box number or an email address.	9	The address(es) for service for each proprietor of the registered estate(s) to be entered in the register is ☒ the address of the property (where this is a single postal address) ☐ the address(es) for service from the transfer/assent ☐ (for existing proprietors who are remaining in the register) the current address(es) for service in the register ☐ the following address(es):
Where a charge has an MD reference we will ignore an address given in this panel unless the charge is in favour of a United Kingdom bank and neither the charge form nor any agreement we have with the lender specifies an address for service. For permitted addresses see note to panel 9. Complete as appropriate where the lender is a company. Also, for an overseas company, unless an arrangement with HM Land Registry exists, lodge either a certificate in Form 7 in Schedule 3 to the Land Registration Rules 2003 or a certified copy of the constitution in English or Welsh, or other evidence permitted by rule 183 of the Land Registration Rules 2003.	10	Name and address(es) for service of the proprietor of any new charge to be entered in the register: For UK incorporated companies/LLPs Registered number of company or limited liability partnership including any prefix: For overseas companies (a) Territory of incorporation: (b) Where the entity is a company with a place of business in the United Kingdom, the registered number, if any, issued by Companies House, including any prefix:
If this statement applies (i) place 'X' in the box and (ii) enclose Form DI. Section 27 of the Land Registration Act 2002 lists the registrable dispositions. Rule 57 of the Land Registration Rules 2003 sets out the disclosable overriding interests that you must tell us about.	11	Disclosable overriding interests ☐ This application relates to a registrable disposition and disclosable overriding interests affect the registered estate.

12 Confirmation of identity

When registering transfers, charges, leases and other dispositions of land, or giving effect to a discharge or release of a registered charge, Land Registry relies on the steps that conveyancers take, where appropriate, to verify the identity of their clients. These checks reduce the risk of property fraud.

Full details of the evidence of identity that is required can be found in Practice Guide 67 and in 'Completing the evidence of identity panels on forms AP1, FR1, and DS2' both of which can be found on the GOV.UK website.

Where a person was not represented by a conveyancer, Land Registry requires 'evidence of identity' in respect of that person, except where the first alternative in panel 13(2) applies.

'Evidence of identity' is evidence provided in accordance with any current direction made by the Chief Land Registrar under section 100(4) of the Land Registration Act 2002 for the purpose of confirming a person's identity.

If this application is to register a transfer, lease or charge, or to give effect to a discharge in Form DS1 or a release in Form DS3 complete one of the following

Place 'X' in the appropriate box.

Conveyancer is defined in rule 217A, Land Registration Rules 2003 and includes persons authorised under the Legal Services Act 2007 to provide reserved legal services relating to land registration and includes solicitors and licensed conveyancers.

☒ I am a conveyancer, and I have completed panel 13

☐ I am not a conveyancer, and I have completed panel 14

13 Where the application is sent to Land Registry by a conveyancer

(1) Details of conveyancer acting

If you are sending an application to register a transfer, lease or charge, for each party to each disposition that is to be registered state in the table below the details of the conveyancer (if any) who represented them.

Where a party is not represented by a conveyancer you must also complete (2) below.

Place 'X' in the box in the second column if the person or firm who is sending the application to HM Land Registry represented that party in the transaction. Otherwise complete the details in the third column. If the party is not represented insert 'none' in the third column.

A separate box is provided, or can be added, for each party, as required by panel 13(1). That includes separate boxes for attorneys and donors where appropriate.

Name of transferor, landlord, transferee, tenant, borrower or lender		Conveyancer's name, address and reference
Style&Go Ltd (Landlord)	☐	Blackhurst & Sons LLP of 22 High Street, Barnford, Westshire, EX82 7YK Reference: FAO June Day
Polished Perfection Ltd (Tenant)	☒	Reference: 9234/JXR

If you are sending an application to give effect to a discharge in Form DS1 or release in Form DS3 for each lender, state in the table below the details of the conveyancer (if any) who represented them.

Where a lender is not represented by a conveyancer you must also complete (2) below.

Place 'X' in the box in the second column if the person or firm who is sending the application to HM Land Registry represented that party in the transaction. Otherwise complete the details in the third column. If the party is not represented insert 'none' in the third column.

A separate box is provided, or can be added, for each party, as required by panel 13(1). That includes separate boxes for attorneys and donors where appropriate.

Name of lender		Conveyancer's name, address and reference
	☐	Reference:

(2) Evidence of identity

Where any transferor, landlord, transferee, tenant, borrower or lender listed in (1) was not represented by a conveyancer

Place 'X' in the appropriate box(es).

☐ I confirm that I am satisfied that sufficient steps have been taken to verify the identity of

Insert the name of each unrepresented transferor, landlord, transferee, tenant, borrower or lender for whom you give this confirmation.

----

and that they are the registered proprietor or have the right to be registered as the registered proprietor

Evidence of identity is defined in panel 12. Full details of the evidence of identity that is required can be found in Practice Guide 67 available on the GOV.UK website.

☐ I enclose evidence of identity in respect of each unrepresented transferor, landlord, transferee, tenant, borrower or lender for whom I have not provided the confirmation above

14 Where the application is sent to Land Registry by someone who is not a conveyancer

(1) Details of conveyancer acting

If you are sending an application to register a transfer, lease or charge (ie a mortgage), for each party to each disposition that is to be registered, state in the table below the details of the conveyancer (if any) who represented them.

You must also complete (2) below.

If the party is not represented insert 'none' in the second column.

A separate box is provided, or can be added, for each party, as required by panel 14(1). That includes separate boxes for attorneys and donors where appropriate.

Name of transferor, landlord, transferee, tenant, borrower or lender	Conveyancer's name, address and reference
	Reference:
	Reference.
	Reference:

	Reference:
	Reference:

If you are sending an application to give effect to a discharge in Form DS1 or release in Form DS3, for each lender state in the table below the details of the conveyancer (if any) who represented them.

You must also complete (2) below.

If the party is not represented insert 'none' in the second column.

A separate box is provided, or can be added, for each party, as required by panel 14(1). That includes separate boxes for attorneys and donors where appropriate.

Name of lender	Conveyancer's name, address and reference
	Reference:
	Reference:

(2) Evidence of identity

Place 'X' in the appropriate box(es).

Evidence of identity is defined in panel 12. Full details of the evidence of identity that is required can be found in 'Completing the evidence of identity panels on forms AP1, FR1, and DS2' available on the GOV.UK website.

☐ for each applicant named in panel 6 is enclosed

☐ for each unrepresented transferor, landlord, transferee, tenant, borrower or lender listed in (1) is enclosed

If a conveyancer is acting for the applicant, that conveyancer must sign.

If no conveyancer is acting, the applicant (and if the applicant is more than one person then each of them) must sign.

15

Signature of conveyancer: *Talbot&Wick LLP*

Date: 22 September 2026

WARNING
If you dishonestly enter information or make a statement that you know is, or might be, untrue or misleading, and intend by doing so to make a gain for yourself or another person, or to cause loss or the risk of loss to another person, you may commit the offence of fraud under section 1 of the Fraud Act 2006, the maximum penalty for which is 10 years' imprisonment or an unlimited fine, or both.

Failure to complete this form with proper care may result in a loss of protection under the Land Registration Act 2002 if, as a result, a mistake is made in the register.

Under section 66 of the Land Registration Act 2002 most documents (including this form) kept by the registrar relating to an application to the registrar or referred to in the register are open to public inspection and copying. If you believe a document contains prejudicial information, you may apply for that part of the document to be made exempt using Form EX1, under rule 136 of the Land Registration Rules 2003.

Document 18

Land Registry

Official copy of register of title

Title number WX727338

Edition date 01.03.2025

- This official copy shows the entries in the register of title on 28 October 2026 at 13:26:27.
- This date must be quoted as the "search from date" in any official search application based on this copy.
- The date at the beginning of an entry is the date on which the entry was made in the register.
- Issued on 28 October 2026.
- Under s.67 of the Land Registration Act 2002, this copy is admissible in evidence to the same extent as the original.
- For information about the register of title see Land Registry website www.landregistry.gov.uk or Land Registry Public Guide 1 – *A guide to the information we keep and how you can obtain it.*

A: Property register

This register describes the land and estate comprised in the title

Westshire : Barnford

1. (28.10.2026) The leasehold land shown edged with thick black on the plan of the above Title filed at the Registry and being First Floor, 17 High Street, Barnford, Westshire, EX82 7YK.

B: Proprietorship register

This register specifies the class of title and identifies the owner. It contains any entries that affect the right of disposal.

Title absolute

1. (28.10.26) Proprietor(s): Polished Perfection Ltd of First Floor, 17 High Street, Barnford, Westshire, EX82 7YK

2. (28.10.26) Short particulars of the leases under which the land is held:

Date:	21 September 2026
Term:	10 years
Rent:	as therein mentioned
Parties	(1) Style&Go Ltd (2) Polished Perfection Ltd

C: Charges register

This register contains any charges and other matters that affect the land.

1. (28.10.2026) A conveyance of the land in this title dated 10 July 1993 made between (1) Charles Bainbridge (Vendor) and (2) Ansar Mukhtar and Anita Mukhtar (Purchaser) contains the following covenant:

   "11.1 And the Purchaser for itself and its assigns with the intent to bind the Property hereby covenants with the Vendor his heirs executors administrators and assigns not to build any structure on the Property."

End of register

Land Registry
Official copy of
Title plan

Title number **WX727338**
Ordnance Survey map reference **EG 4231 SS**
Scale **1:2500**
Administrative area **Westshire: Barnford**

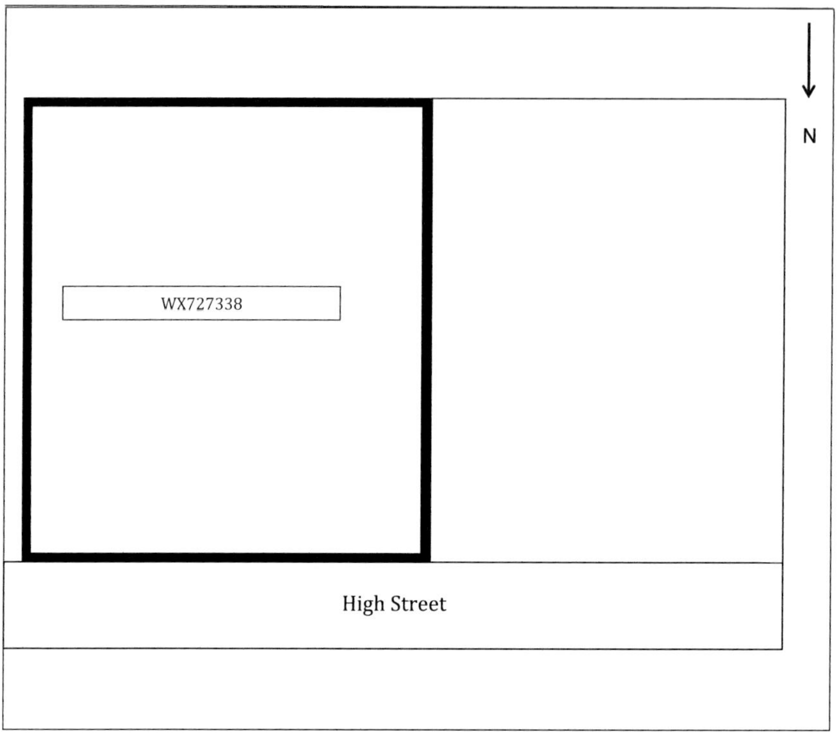

This official copy issued on 28 October 2026 shows the state of this title plan on 28 October 2026 at 13:26:27.
It is admissible in evidence to the same extent as the original (s. 67 Land Registration Act 2002).
This title plan shows the general position, not the exact line, of the boundaries. It may be subject to distortions in scale.
Measurements scaled from this plan may not match measurements between the same points on the ground.
See Land Registry Public Guide 19 – Title Plans and Boundaries.

Appendix 5: Assignment of the Nail Bar Lease to Gemma's Gels Ltd

Accompanying documents

Document 1

Heads of terms – assignment of Nail Bar Lease	
Seller	Polished Perfection Ltd (Director Meena Kasih), co. number 22375943, address c/o Talbot & Wick LLP, 47B Vale Road, Torton, Westshire, EX79 4PJ
Seller's solicitor	Talbot & Wick LLP, 47B Vale Road, Torton, Westshire, EX79 4PJ
Buyer	Gemma's Gels Ltd (Director Gemma Gray) registered with company number 01276917 c/o MMK Solicitors LLP, 89 Barnford Lane, Barnford, Westshire, EX83 3QT
Buyer's solicitor	MMK Solicitors LLP, 89 Barnford Lane, Barnford, Westshire, EX83 3QT
Property	Leasehold: Nail Bar, First floor, 17 High Street, Barnford, Westshire, EX82 7YK registered at HMLR with title number WX727338
Premium	£1
Deposit	None
Finance	Cash
Proposed use	Nail bar
VAT	Seller will not exercise option to tax
Lease	10 year lease dated 21 September 2026 with 9 years and 8 months remaining

Land Registry

Official copy of register of title

Title number WX727338

Edition date 01.03.2025

- This official copy shows the entries in the register of title on 4 January 2027 at 13:26:27.
- This date must be quoted as the "search from date" in any official search application based on this copy.
- The date at the beginning of an entry is the date on which the entry was made in the register.
- Issued on 4 January 2027.
- Under s.67 of the Land Registration Act 2002, this copy is admissible in evidence to the same extent as the original.
- For information about the register of title see Land Registry website www.landregistry.gov.uk or Land Registry Public Guide 1 – *A guide to the information we keep and how you can obtain it.*

A: Property register

This register describes the land and estate comprised in the title

Westshire : Barnford

1. (28.10.2026) The leasehold land shown edged with thick black on the plan of the above Title filed at the Registry and being First Floor, 17 High Street, Barnford, Westshire, EX82 7YK.

B: Proprietorship register

This register specifies the class of title and identifies the owner. It contains any entries that affect the right of disposal.

Title absolute

1. (28.10.26) Proprietor(s): Polished Perfection Ltd of First Floor, 17 High Street, Barnford, Westshire, EX82 7YK.

2. (28.10.26) Short particulars of the leases under which the land is held:

Date:	21 September 2026
Term:	10 years
Rent:	as therein mentioned
Parties	(1) Style&Go Ltd
	(2) Polished Perfection Ltd

C: Charges register

This register contains any charges and other matters that affect the land.

1. (28.10.2026) A conveyance of the land in this title dated 10 July 1993 made between (1) Charles Bainbridge (Vendor) and (2) Ansar Mukhtar and Anita Mukhtar (Purchaser) contains the following covenant:

   "11.1 And the Purchaser for itself and its assigns with the intent to bind the Property hereby covenants with the Vendor his heirs executors administrators and assigns not to build any structure on the Property."

End of register

Land Registry
Official copy of
Title plan

Title number **WX727338**
Ordnance Survey map reference **EG 4231 SS**
Scale **1:2500**
Administrative area **Westshire: Barnford**

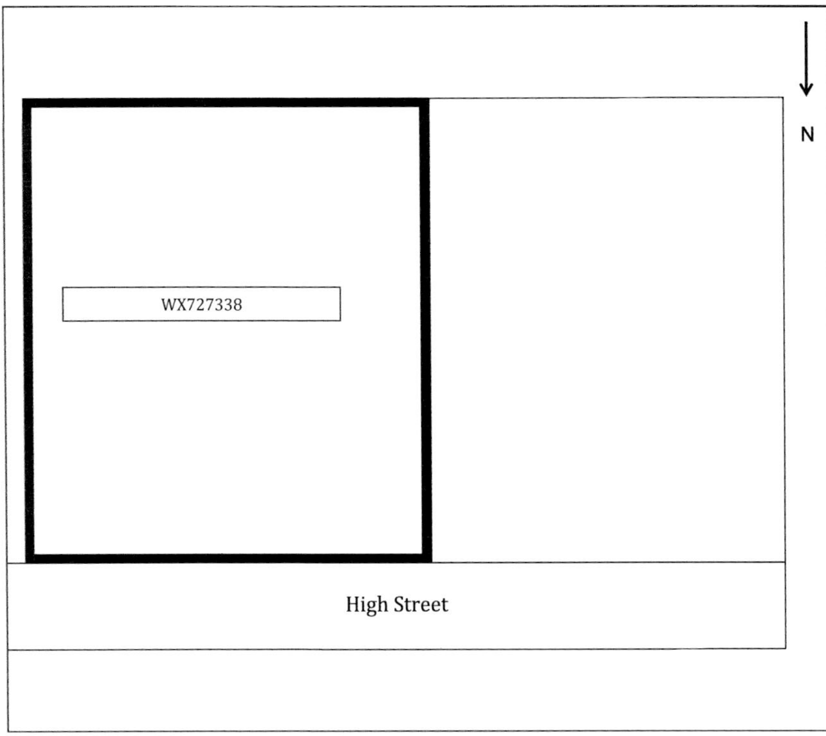

This official copy issued on 4 January 2027 shows the state of this title plan on 4 January 2027 at 13:26:27.
It is admissible in evidence to the same extent as the original (s. 67 Land Registration Act 2002).
This title plan shows the general position, not the exact line, of the boundaries. It may be subject to distortions in scale.
Measurements scaled from this plan may not match measurements between the same points on the ground.
See Land Registry Public Guide 19 – Title Plans and Boundaries.

Document 4

SIMR

Official certificate of the result of search of the index map

Land Registry
Land Registration Rules 2003

Certificate Date: 4 January 2027
Certificate Time: 17:27:37
Certificate Ref: FFR/EXH02

Property	FIRST FLOOR, 17 HIGH STREET, BARNFORD, WESTSHIRE, EX82 7YK

Result

The index map has been searched in respect of the Property with the following result:

Plan reference	**Title No.**	**Registered Estate or Caution**	**Notes**
Edged with thick black line	EG576798	Freehold	
Edged with thick black line	WX727338	Leasehold	

No registered estate, caution against first registration, application for first registration or application for a caution against first registration is shown on the index map in relation to the remainder of the property.

******

The plan attached to this result is prepared for the sole purpose of showing the area in respect of which an official search has been made. The information has been taken from the index map. It is illustrative only and does not define the extent of the land in any individual title. For information about the general boundaries of a title please refer to the individual register and title plan.

******

Verbal descriptions of registered relating franchises and registered manors, and of pending applications and cautions against first registrations in respect of relating franchises, are kept in the index of relating franchises and manors. The application form for a search of the index is form SIF.

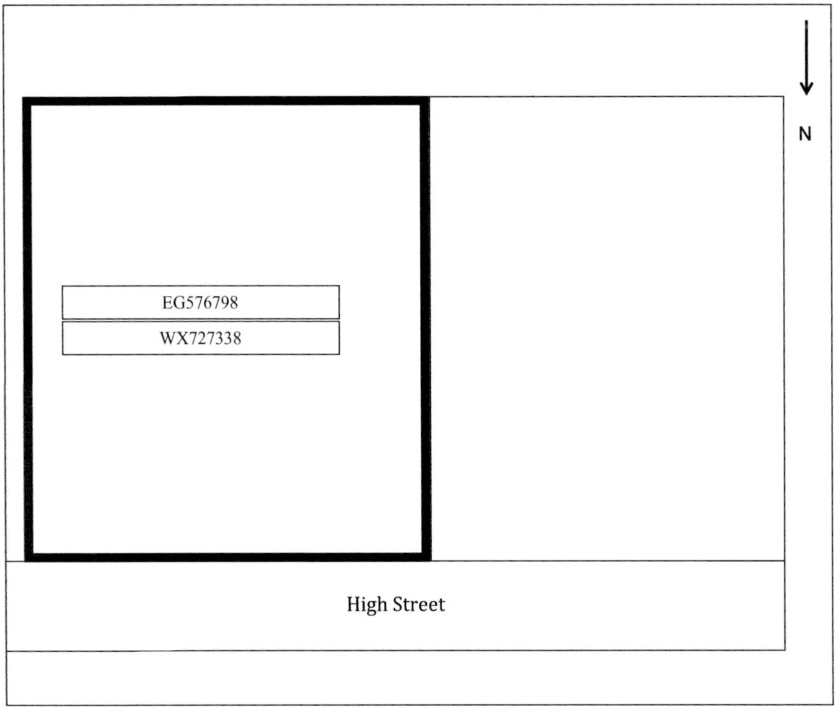
N
EG576798
WX727338
High Street

Document 5

Westshire District Council Offices
Council House,
Exton,
Westshire
(DX 765567 Exton 7)

Westshire
District Council

REGISTER OF LOCAL LAND CHARGES
OFFICIAL CERTIFICATE OF SEARCH

Search Reference: LPG/EXH02

Date: 4 January 2027

Applicant: MMK Solicitors LLP

Official search required in all parts of the Register of Local Land Charges for subsisting registrations against the land described and the plan submitted.

Land: First Floor, 17 High Street, Barnford, Westshire, EX82 7YK

It is hereby certified that the search requested above reveals 3 registrations described in the Schedule(s) hereto up to and including the date of this certificate.

LLC1: Search Reference LPG/EXH02

Date: 4 January 2027

Westshire District Council

Register of Local Land Charges
Schedule to Official Certificate of Search

Part 3: Planning Charges

Description of charge (including reference to appropriate statutory provision)	Originating Authority	Place where relevant documents may be inspected	Date of Registration
PP/UC/774/91 Permission for change of use from Class A1 to Class C3(a)	Westshire District Council	Council House, Exton, Westshire	08/08/1991
PP/W/774/95 Conditional permission for erection of single storey rear extension	Westshire District Council	Council House, Exton, Westshire	17/09/1995
PP/UC/774/26 Permission for change of use from Class C3(a) to Class E	Westshire District Council	Council House, Exton, Westshire	29/05/2026

Document 6

Westshire District Council Offices
Council House,
Exton,
Westshire
(DX 765567 Exton 7)

Westshire District Council

CON29 ENQUIRIES OF LOCAL AUTHORITY
(2016)

Applicant: MMK Solicitors LLP

Search Reference: LLR/EXH02

Date: 4 January 2027

Property: First floor, 17 High Street, Barnford, Westshire, EX82 7KY

I refer to your Standard Enquiries relating to the above property. These replies relate to that property as shown on the location plan where supplied. The replies are given subject to the Notes to the Standard Enquiries.

All correspondence relating to these answers should quote the official Search Reference.

Standard Enquiries of Local Authority

PLANNING AND BUILDING REGULATIONS
1.1. Planning and building decisions and pending applications
Which of the following relating to the property have been granted, issued or refused or (where applicable) are the subject of pending applications or agreements?
(a) a planning permission

1.1.(a) Reference: PP/UC/774/91
Description: Change of use from Class A1 to Class C3(a)
Application date: 20/7/1991
Decision: GRANTED on 8/8/1991

1.1.(a) Reference: PP/W/774/95
Description: Erection of single storey rear extension
Application date: 1/9/1995
Decision: GRANTED SUBJECT TO CONDITIONS on 17/9/1995

1.1.(a) Reference: PP/UC/774/26
Description: Change of use from Class C3(a) to E
Application date: 29/5/2026
Decision: GRANTED on 29/5/2026

[...]

(j) building regulations approval
none

(k) a building regulation completion certificate
none

[...]

Informatives:
(1) Copy documents available from Planning and Building Control Services, Westshire District Council.

(2) This reply does not cover other properties in the vicinity of the property.

(3) As from 1 April 2002 the installation of a replacement window, rooflight or roof window or specified type of glazed door must either have building regulation approval or be carried out and certified by a person who is registered under the Fenestration Self-Assessment Scheme by the Glass and Glazing Federation. The owner or occupier of the property should be asked to produce any such certificate.

ROADS AND PUBLIC RIGHTS OF WAY
Roadways, footways and footpaths
2.1 Which of the roads, footways and footpaths named in the application for this search (via boxes B and C) are:
(a) highways maintainable at public expense
2.1.(a) High Street

(b) subject to adoption and supported by a bond or bond waiver
2.1.(b) None

(c) to be made up by a local authority who will reclaim the cost from the frontagers
2.1.(c) None

(d) to be adopted by a local authority without reclaiming the cost from the frontagers
2.1.(d) None

Informative: If a road, footway or footpath is not a highway, there may be no right to use it and the local authority cannot express an opinion without seeing the title plan and carrying out a site inspection.

Public rights of way
2.2 Is any public right of way which abuts on, or crosses, the property shown in a definitive map or revised definitive map?
2.2. No

[...]

2.5 If so, please attach a plan showing the approximate route.

2.5. Not applicable

Informative: A definitive map for Westshire District Council has now been published. However, a survey of all paths has not been completed and whilst this does not preclude the existence of unrecorded rights of way, the local authority is unaware of any claimed rights of way existing over the search site.

OTHER MATTERS:

Apart from matters entered on the registers of local land charges, do any of the following matters apply to the property? If so, how can copies of relevant documents be obtained?

Note: Matters entered onto the Local Land Charges Register, or visible by property/site inspection, will not be referred to (where relevant) in answer to the enquiries 3.1 to 3.15 below.

Informative: In some circumstances, road closures can be obtained by third parties from magistrate's courts, or can be made by the Secretary of State for Transport without involving the local authority. This enquiry is designed to reveal matters that are yet to be implemented and could not therefore be ascertained by a visual inspection. Schemes that have been, or are currently being, implemented will not be referred to in answer to this enquiry.

[...]

3.5. Nearby railway schemes

(a) Is the property (or will it be) within 200 metres of the centre line of a proposed railway, tramway, light railway or monorail?

3.5.(a) Yes – proposed railway scheme at Barnford Central. Please see details at westshirerailwayredevelopment.co.uk.

[...]

3.6 Traffic schemes

Has a local authority approved but not yet implemented any of the following for the roads, footways and footpaths which are named in Boxes B and C and are within 200 metres of the boundaries of the property?

[...]

(e) pedestrianisation

3.6(e) Yes – Main Street, which is within 200 metres of the boundaries of the property, is to be pedestrianised.

[...]

3.8. Contravention of building regulations

Has a local authority authorised in relation to the property any proceedings for the contravention of any provision contained in building regulations?

3.8. No

3.9. Notices, orders, directions and proceedings under Planning Acts

Do any of the following subsist in relation to the property, or has a local authority decided to issue, serve, make or commence any of the following?

(a) an enforcement notice

3.9.(a) No

(b) a stop notice
3.9.(b) No

...

(d) a breach of condition notice
3.9.(d) No

(e) a planning contravention notice
3.9.(e) No

[...]

(j) a direction restricting permitted development
3.9.(j) No

[...]

3.11. Conservation area
Do the following apply in relation to the property?
(a) the making of the area a conservation area before 31 August 1974
3.11.(a) No

(b) an unimplemented resolution to designate the area a Conservation Area
3.11.(b) No

[...]
3.13. Contaminated land
Do any of the following apply (including any relating to land adjacent to or adjoining the property which has been identified as contaminated land because it is in such a condition that harm or pollution of controlled waters might be caused on the property)?
(a) a contaminated land notice
3.13.(a) No

(b) in relation to a register maintained under section 78R of the Environmental Protection Act 1990

(i) a decision to make an entry
3.13.(b)(i) No

(ii) an entry
3.13.(b)(ii) No

(c) consultation with the owner or occupier of the property conducted under section 78G(3) of the Environmental Protection Act 1990 before the service of a remediation notice
3.13.(c) No

Informative: A negative reply does not imply that the property or any adjoining or adjacent land is free from contamination or from the risk of it and the reply may not disclose steps taken by another local authority in whose area adjacent or adjoining land is situated.

[...]

Document 7

Highways Division
Westshire District Council Offices
Council House,
Exton,
Westshire
(DX 765567 Exton 7)

Westshire
District Council

Date: 4 January 2027

Dear Sirs

First floor, 17 High Street, Barnford, Westshire, EX82 7YK

Please find below the plan; showing by black shading the extent of the publicly maintainabl highway in the immediate vicinity of the property, as far as can be ascertained from existin records.

If you have any further queries please do not hesitate to contact us.

Yours faithfully

Highway Records Manager

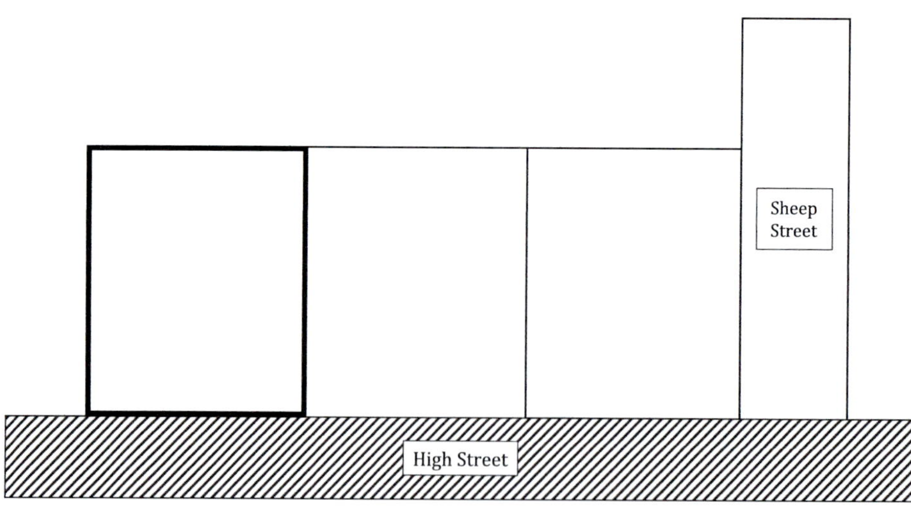

WESTSHIRE WATER

Drainage and Water search

Date: 4 January 2027

Property: First floor, 17, High Street, Barnford, Westshire, EX82 7YK

Results:

Mains water: connected

Foul water: connected

Surface water sewer: connected

Sewer pipe within boundary: no

Water pipe within boundary: no

Document 9

WESTSHIRE ENVIRO-CHECK

Date: 4 January 2027

Type of report: Homebuyers

Property: First floor, 17 High Street, Barnford, Westshire, EX82 7YK

RESULTS:

Professional opinion: PASS

Environmental search results:

Contaminated Land: passed
No significant concerns have been identified as a result of the contaminated land searches.

Flood risk: low
The village of Barnford suffered flooding in 1994, but the property was unaffected and the property's overall risk assessment for river, coastal, surface water and groundwater flooding is low.

Ground stability: passed
No significant concerns have been identified as a result of the ground stability searches. No action required.

Radon: passed
Local levels of radon are considered normal.

Westshire Enviro-check

CHANCEL REPAIR SEARCH

Report details

Report number: GR/767/EXH02

Issue date: 4 January 2027

Address: First floor, 17 High Street, Barnford, Westshire, EX82 7YK

The above address is not located within the historical boundary of a tithe district within a parish which continues to have a potential chancel repair liability based upon historical parish data and the relevant inland Revenue Indices held by The National Archives.

Document 11

EXTRACT OF COMPANY SEARCH REPORT:

Polished Perfection Ltd

Company Number:	22375943
Date of Incorporation:	1 June 2007
Registered Office:	c/o Talbot & Wick LLP, 47B Vale Road, Torton, Westshire, EX79 4PJ
Change(s) of Name:	none
Charges:	none

Practical Law

BPF

BRITISH PROPERTY FEDERATION

Commercial Property Standard Enquiries

CPSE.7 (version 1.3.2) General short form pre-contract enquiries for all property transactions

Conditions

This document may be used free of charge subject to the Conditions set out in *GN/CPSE (version 3.3) Guidance notes on the Commercial Property Standard Enquiries*.

Particulars

Seller: Polished Perfection Ltd

Buyer: Gemma's Gels Ltd

Property: First floor, 17 High St, Barnford, EX82 7YK

Seller's solicitors: Talbot & Wick LLP

Buyer's solicitors: MMK Solicitors LLP

Date: 4 January 2027

Interpretation

1. In interpreting these enquiries, the terms set out in the Particulars have the meanings given to them in the Particulars and the following interpretation also applies:

- **Buyer:** includes tenant and prospective tenant.
- **Conduits:** means the pipes, wires and cables through which utilities and other services are carried.
- **Property:** includes any part of it and all buildings and other structures on it.
- **Rights:** means any covenants, agreements, rights, restrictions, or informal arrangements of any kind (including any which are in the course of being acquired).

Practical Law

BPF

- **SDLT:** includes Land Transaction Tax where the Property is in Wales, and references to HMRC include the Welsh Revenue Authority where relevant.

- **Seller:** includes landlord and prospective landlord.

2. The replies to the enquiries will be given by the Seller and addressed to the Buyer. Unless otherwise agreed in writing, only the Buyer and those acting for it may rely on them.

- References in these enquiries to "**you**" mean the Seller and to "**we**" and "**us**" mean the Buyer.

- In replies to the enquiries, references to "**you**" will be taken to mean the Buyer and to "**we**" and "**us**" will be taken to mean the Seller.

3. The replies are given without liability on the part of the Seller's solicitors, its members, partners, employees, consultants or other staff.

4. The Buyer acknowledges that even though the Seller will be giving replies to the enquiries, the Buyer should still inspect the Property, have the Property surveyed, investigate title and make all appropriate searches and enquiries of third parties.

5. In replying to each of these enquiries and any supplemental enquiries, the Seller acknowledges that it is required to provide the Buyer with copies of all documents and correspondence and to supply all details relevant to the replies, whether or not specifically requested to do so.

6. The Seller confirms that pending exchange of contracts or, where there is no prior contract, pending completion of the Transaction, it will notify the Buyer on becoming aware of anything which may cause any reply that it has given to these or any supplemental enquiries to be incorrect.

Practical Law

CONTENTS

CLAUSE

Enquiries

1. Boundaries and extent

In this enquiry, "**Boundary Features**" means all walls, fences, ditches, hedges or other features that form the physical boundary of the Property.

1.1 Are you aware of any discrepancies between the boundaries referred to in the title deeds and the Boundary Features?

No, but the buyer must rely on its own searches and enquiries

1.2 Have any alterations been made to the position of any Boundary Features during your ownership or, to your knowledge, earlier?

Not to the knowledge of the seller

1.3 In relation to each of the Boundary Features:

(a) Which of them have you maintained or regarded as your responsibility?

(b) Which of them has someone else maintained or regarded as their responsibility?

(c) Which of them have you treated as a party structure or jointly repaired or maintained with someone else?

(d) Are there any agreements for their maintenance?

(e) Are any of them subject to a party wall award or agreement?

(a)	All
(b)	None
(c)	None
(d)	No
(e)	No

1.4 Does any part of the Property lie beneath or above adjoining premises, roads or footpaths?

Above ground floor, 17 High St

1.5 Are there any adjoining or nearby premises or land which you use or occupy in connection with the Property?

Ground floor, 17 High St. Lease contains access rights over ground floor and stairs to reach

first floor.

2. **RIGHTS BENEFITING THE PROPERTY**

2.1 What Rights does the Property benefit from, other than those which are apparent from the copy documents supplied?

Lease contains right to park in car park behind premises

2.2 Please confirm that all terms and conditions relating to the exercise of any Rights which benefit the Property have been complied with.

Confirmed by seller.

2.3 Have you (or, to your knowledge, has any predecessor in title) registered any notices, cautions against first registration or other entries against any other titles at the Land Registry in relation to any Rights which benefit the Property?

Right is noted against title to car park

2.4 What are the pedestrian and vehicular access routes to and from the Property?

Vehicular directly via High St. If using right in 2.1, access is via Sheep Street. Pedestrian through Ground floor premises 17 High St

2.5 Have you, or to your knowledge has anyone else, applied to modify or discharge any Rights benefitting the Property?

Not so far as the seller is aware but the buyer must rely on its own searches and enquiries

3. **ADVERSE RIGHTS AFFECTING THE PROPERTY**

3.1 What Rights is the Property subject to, other than those which are apparent from the copy documents supplied?

The seller is aware of covenants affecting the Property – see documents supplied.

3.2 Please confirm that all terms and conditions relating to the exercise of any Rights to which the Property is subject have been complied with.

Seller has not breached any covenants. Buyer must rely on its own searches and enquiries in respect of others.

3.3 Are there any overriding interests to which the Property is subject?

Not so far as the seller is aware but the buyer must rely on its own searches and enquiries

3.4 Does the Property, or any property over which Rights are enjoyed, include any land that is currently used or has in the past ten years been used by members of the public for recreational purposes, whether with or without your permission?

Not so far as the seller is aware but the buyer must rely on its own searches and enquiries

3.5 Have you, or to your knowledge has anyone else, applied to modify or discharge any Rights to which the Property is subject?

Not so far as the seller is aware but the buyer must rely on its own searches and enquiries

4. PHYSICAL CONDITION

4.1 Is the Property now, or has it ever been, affected by any of the following:

(a) structural or inherent defects;

(b) subsidence, settlement, landslip or heave;

(c) defective Conduits, fixtures, plant or equipment;

(d) rising damp, rot, or any fungal or other infection;

(e) Japanese knotweed;

(f) any other infestation; or

(g) flooding?

(a) – (g) n/a so far as the seller is aware The buyer must rely on its own searches and inspections for further information.

4.2 Is there any Green Deal Plan affecting the Property?

Not to the knowledge of the seller but the buyer must rely on its own searches and enquiries

4.3 Has asbestos, or any other substance known or suspected to be unsuitable for its purpose, unstable or hazardous, been used in, or removed from, the Property including Conduits, fixtures, plant and equipment?

Not to the knowledge of the seller but the buyer must rely on its own searches and enquiries

4.4 Please supply copies of the most recent asbestos survey and asbestos management plan for the Property, together with any other relevant information you hold.

There are none so far as the seller is aware.

4.5 Please supply copies of any subsisting guarantees, warranties and/or insurance policies relating to any buildings erected on or major alterations or engineering works carried out at the Property within the last 12 years.

There are none so far as the seller is aware.

4.6 Please confirm that all Conduits, fixtures, plant or equipment in or serving the Property have been regularly tested and maintained and that all recommended work has been carried out.

Confirmed

5. CONTENTS

5.1 Please list any fixtures and fittings that will be removed from the Property before completion.

None

5.2 Other than those belonging to an occupational tenant, please confirm that you own all fixtures and fittings that will remain on the Property free from third party rights.

Confirmed

6. UTILITIES AND SERVICES

6.1 Please list the services available at the Property and confirm which (if any) are connected to the mains and which are metered.

Electricity Gas Broadband and telephone Water Connections are direct to a mains supply. Connections are not metered.

6.2 Do any parts of the services pass over, under or through any land which is not part of the Property?

Services pass from the High Street via 17 High Street

6.3 Does the Property have a communal heating, cooling or hot water system?

Heating and hot water supplied to entire building – 17 High St

6.4 Please provide:

(a) Copies of the most recent bills for the services referred to at enquiry 6.1;

(b) The name and contact details of the individual within your organisation who deals with energy supplies relating to the Property and confirm that we may make contact in order to obtain information about the services supplied.

Enclosed.

7. FIRE SAFETY AND MEANS OF ESCAPE

7.1 What are the current means of escape from the Property in case of emergency?

Main staircase and exit rear of building

7.2 Have you experienced any difficulty in completing the fire risk assessment for the Property or when co-operating with anybody else in order to comply with fire safety regulations?

Not so far as the seller is aware

7.3 Has there been any fire risk recommendation that has not been implemented?

Not so far as the seller is aware

8. PLANNING AND BUILDING REGULATIONS

8.1 Are you aware of any breach of planning law in relation to the construction, use or occupation of the Property?

None so far as the seller is aware

8.2 Is any building or structure on the Property listed under planning law?

Not so far as the seller is aware

8.3 What works have been carried out at the Property during the last 10 years?

None so far as the seller is aware. Extension to ground floor of building but doesn't affect Property.

8.4 What changes of use have taken place at the Property during the last 10 years?

Change of use in 2026 from C3(a) to E.

8.5 What is the existing use of the Property and how is it authorised under planning legislation?

The Property is currently used for Class E – has planning permission

8.6 Where you or your solicitor have them, please supply copies of all planning documents and all building regulations consents relating to the Property.

Enclosed

8.7 Have you made an application for planning permission which has not yet been determined by the local authority or are there any other planning proceedings currently taking place in relation to the Property?

Not so far as the seller is aware

8.8 What information do you have about any proposals for the development of any adjoining or neighbouring property?

The buyer must rely on its own enquiries

8.9 Are you aware of any existing or future Community Infrastructure Levy liability relating to the Property?

The buyer must rely on its own enquiries

9. STATUTORY AGREEMENTS AND INFRASTRUCTURE

9.1 Are you aware of any outstanding obligations relating to the construction or adoption of the highway, Conduits or any other infrastructure that supplies the Property?

Not so far as the seller is aware

9.2 Are you required to enter into any agreement or obligation with any planning, highway or other public authority or utilities provider?

Not so far as the seller is aware

9.3 Are you aware of anything affecting the Property that is capable of being registered on the Local Land Charges Register but is not so registered?

Not so far as the seller is aware

10. STATUTORY AND OTHER REQUIREMENTS

10.1 Are you aware of any breach of statutory requirements that relate to the Property or its use or occupation?

Not so far as the seller is aware

10.2 Do you have a health and safety file for the Property?

Yes

10.3 If the answer to enquiry 10.2 is yes

(a) Is the file at the Property and available for us to inspect?

(b) In what form will the file be provided to us upon completion?

(a) Yes (b) Digital copy

10.4 Please supply a valid Energy Performance Certificate (**EPC**) for the Property.

Enclosed

10.5 Where the Property has an EPC rating of F or G, please supply a copy of any information or evidence used to support any registration in the Exemptions Register established under the Energy Efficiency (Private Rented Property) (England and Wales) Regulations 2015.

n/a

10.6 Please confirm when the air conditioning at the Property was last inspected and provide a copy of that inspection report.

2025 - enclosed

10.7 Please supply details of any grant made or claimed in respect of the Property including circumstances in which it may have to be repaid.

n/a

11. ENVIRONMENTAL

11.1 Where you or your solicitor have them, please supply copies of all environmental and flood risk reports that have been prepared in relation to the Property.

The buyer must rely on its own enquiries

11.2 Please supply a copy of all statutory authorisations under all environmental law for the current uses of the Property (if applicable).

N/a

11.3 Are there, or have there ever been, any above or below ground bulk storage tanks at the Property? If so, please confirm the contents and age of those tanks (or estimate the age as accurately as possible).

None so far as the seller is aware but the buyer must rely on its own enquiries

11.4 Please confirm that you are not aware of any breach of any environmental law relating to the past or present use or occupation of the Property or for substances in, on, at or under the Property.

None so far as the seller is aware but the buyer must rely on its own enquiries

11.5 Please confirm that you are not aware of any environmental incidents including the leaking or discharging of any substances at the Property or on or at any nearby properties.

None so far as the seller is aware but the buyer must rely on its own enquiries

12. OCCUPIERS

12.1 Does anyone apart from you have any right to use or occupy the Property?

Not so far as the seller is aware.

12.2 If the Property is vacant, when and why did it become vacant?

n/a

13. INSURANCE

13.1 Have you ever experienced any difficulty in obtaining insurance cover for the Property at normal rates and subject to normal exclusions?

Not so far as the seller is aware.

13.2 Please give details of any outstanding insurance claims in relation to the Property.

None so far as the seller is aware.

13.3 If the buildings insurance policy is to remain in place after exchange of contracts, please supply a copy of the policy and schedule of insurance cover.

Enclosed

13.4 Please provide a copy of any other insurance policies relating to the Property (together with the proposal form and other material correspondence with the insurers) including any title indemnity insurance policies.

n/a

13.5 Please provide details of any breaches of any insurance policies relating to the Property.

n/a

14. RATES AND OTHER OUTGOINGS

14.1 Have any works been carried out to the Property which may cause the rateable value of the Property to be reviewed?

Not so far as the seller is aware.

14.2 Have you or any occupier of the Property, made any claim for void period allowance or for exemption from liability from business rates? Is any claim pending/outstanding?

Not so far as the seller is aware.

14.3 Are there any other outgoings relating to the Property not referred to elsewhere in these enquiries?

Not so far as the seller is aware.

14.4 Please supply the most recent bills for business rates and all other outgoings relating to the Property.

Enclosed

14.5 If the Property is subject to a Business Improvement District Arrangement, please give details of any levy currently payable.

n/a

15. NOTICES

Please supply a copy of any notices affecting the Property that you or your predecessors or any tenant or occupier have given or received and confirm that those notices have been complied with.

None except as disclosed.

16. DISPUTES

Please provide details of any outstanding complaints or past, current or likely disputes affecting the Property its use and occupation.

None to the seller's knowledge.

17. SDLT ON ASSIGNMENT OF A LEASE

In this enquiry, Lease is any lease under which the Property is held and which is to be assigned by you in the Transaction.

17.1 Where the Lease or the substantial performance of the agreement to grant the Lease or any event since the grant of the Lease constitutes a transaction notifiable for SDLT purposes, including the payment of a premium for the grant of the Lease or any assignment of it, please provide copies of all land transaction returns and certificates issued by HMRC certifying notification.

n/a

17.2 Is there any potential or actual outstanding SDLT liability, including any resulting from the settlement or determination of any rent reviews or other provision for varying the rent or settlement or determination of any contingent, uncertain or unascertained rents?

n/a

17.3 Were any SDLT reliefs claimed on the grant of the Lease and, if applicable, on the assignment of the Lease to you that would result in the assignment of the Lease by you being deemed to be the grant of a new lease?

n/a

18. DEFERRED PAYMENT OF SDLT

Please give details of any deferred payment of SDLT which is outstanding in respect of the Property, together with copies of the original land transaction and all relevant correspondence with HMRC.

None so far as the seller is aware

19. VAT

19.1 If you are registered for VAT, please supply your VAT registration number.

n/a

19.2 Please state whether the Transaction is to be treated as a transfer of a business as a going concern ('**TOGC**') and therefore outside the scope of VAT.

No

19.3 If enquiry 19.2 does not apply, is the Transaction standard-rated for VAT purposes as a result of either:

(a) the exercise of an option to tax in relation to the Property; or

(b) compulsory standard-rating?

(a) No (b) no

19.4 If the answer to enquiry 19.3 is yes, please provide a copy of either:

(a) the option notice given to HMRC, together with a copy of HMRC's acknowledgement; or

(b) evidence of the reason that compulsory standard-rating applies to this transaction.

n/a

19.5 If the Transaction is not standard-rated for VAT purposes, please state if it is zero-rated, exempt or outside the scope of VAT other than by reason of being a TOGC.

exempt

20. CAPITAL ALLOWANCES

20.1 Is there anything in the Property upon which a capital allowances claim can be based?

no

20.2 If the answer to enquiry 20.1 is yes, please give details and copy documents including the name and contact details of your capital allowances advisor and confirm that we may make contact direct to ascertain any required capital allowances information.

n/a

Document 13

Practical Law

BPF
BRITISH PROPERTY FEDERATION

Commercial Property Standard Enquiries

CPSE.4 (version 3.3) Supplemental pre-contract enquiries for commercial leasehold property on the assignment of the lease

Conditions of use

This document may be used free of charge subject to the Conditions set out in *GN/CPSE (version 3.3) Guidance notes on the Commercial Property Standard Enquiries (www.practicallaw.com/3-628-1672)*.

Particulars

Seller: Polished Perfection Ltd

Buyer: Gemma's Gels Ltd

Property: First floor, 17 High St, Barnford, EX82 7YK

Seller's solicitors: Talbot & Wick LLP

Buyer's solicitors: MMK Solicitors LLP

Date: 4 January 2027

Interpretation

The section on Interpretation in CPSE.1 is incorporated in this document and the following interpretation also applies:

- **1954 Act:** means the Landlord and Tenant Act 1954.
- **1995 Act:** means the Landlord and Tenant (Covenants) Act 1995.
- **Consent:** refers to an approval, a licence or a permission (whether of the landlord, any superior landlord or any other person).
- **Lease:** means the lease under which the Property is held and which is to be assigned by the Seller to the Buyer.
- **Tenancy Documents:** refers to the Lease, and to any of the following that relate to it: charges, mortgages, surrenders, variations, side letters, undertakings, applications,

Practical Law

BPF

BRITISH PROPERTY FEDERATION

Consents, memoranda, registrations, notices, rent deposit deeds, orders, guarantees, concessions, franchise agreements, counsel's opinions, arbitrators' or experts' decisions.

Instructions

Where the Particulars do not specify a Development, please disregard the parts of any enquiries that refer to the Development.

Contents

Enquiries

ENQUIRIES

1. LEASE

1.1 Please provide the names and current addresses of:

(a) the current landlord and its solicitors;

(b) all superior landlords and their solicitors; and

(c) any continuing guarantor.

(a) Style&Go Ltd registered with company number 00127976 c/o Blackhurst&Sons LLP of 22 High Street, Barnford, Westshire, EX82 7YK (b) None (c) none

1.2 Have there been any variations of the terms of the Tenancy Documents or have any terms been waived?

No

2. CONSENTS

2.1 Were all requisite Consents obtained for:

(a) any past alterations and additions to the Property; and

(b) any changes to the use of the Property?

n/a

2.2 Has any application for Consent been refused within the past three years? If so, please provide details.

N/a

2.3 Please supply details of any tenant's applications for Consents that are presently outstanding.

n/a

3. LANDLORD LIABILITY

3.1 Has any former landlord been released from liability under the Lease?

No former landlords

3.2 Is there any pending application by a former landlord for a release from liability?

n/a

4. SCOPE OF DEMISE

4.1 Please identify by reference to a plan the extent of any adjoining property (including the Development if any) which to your knowledge is owned by the current landlord.

See enclosed plans

4.2 Unless apparent from the Lease, are there any car parking facilities available for the use of the tenant? If so, please describe them and explain the basis on which they can be used.

Lease contains right for staff and customers to park on car park behind 17 High st

4.3 Apart from car parking, are there any other facilities available for use by the tenant either alone or shared with others and which are not apparent from the Lease? Please describe them and:

(a) explain the basis on which they can be used; and

(b) give details of other users and explain the basis of their use.

Common areas – kitchen and toilet. See lease for details.

4.4 Do you have uninterrupted use of all facilities necessary for the use and enjoyment of the Property?

Yes, but kitchen and toilet are shared with hair salon on ground floor

4.5 Please supply a list of the landlord's fixtures and fittings which form part of the Property.

See enclosed schedule

5. HISTORY OF THE LEASE

5.1 If the Transaction includes the sale of a business carried on at the Property:

(a) when was the Property first occupied for the purposes of that business; and

(b) if you are yourself a successor in title to that business, when was the Property first occupied for the purposes of that business by any predecessor?

n/a

5.2 Have any works been carried out to the Property:

(a) during the term of the Lease; or

(b) if not more than 21 years ago, during any previous tenancy?

Fit-out works carried out in October 2026

5.3 In respect of any works identified in the reply to enquiry 5.2, please:

(a) supply details of the works;

(b) state whether they were carried out under an obligation to the landlord under the Lease or any previous tenancy; and

(c) supply copies of all notices given or received in connection with the works under the Landlord and Tenant Act 1927 or the 1954 Act.

(a)	Fit-out works
(b)	No
(c)	n/a

5.4 When was redecoration last carried out:

(a) externally;

(b) internally?

(a)	n/a – landlord's responsibility;
(b)	October 2026

5.5 Please supply a copy of any agreement relating to the treatment on rent review of any works carried out to the Property by you or your predecessors.

See lease

5.6 Please supply copies of all notices given or received by you under the 1954 Act and all court applications and proceedings.

See enclosed

5.7 Are there any informal arrangements with the landlord that are not disclosed by the Tenancy Documents supplied?

No

5.8 Are there any outstanding obligations on the part of either the landlord or the tenant under any agreement for lease under which the Lease was granted?

no

5.9 Please supply copies of any correspondence between you and the landlord (whether the current landlord or any previous landlord) in relation to the Control of Asbestos Regulations 2006 or the Control of Asbestos at Work Regulations 2002, together with copies of any surveys or assessments carried out by the landlord in compliance with those regulations that have been supplied to the Seller.

N/a

6. **Rent and Rent review**

6.1 In respect of the rent currently payable:

(a) how much is it;

(b) has it been paid in accordance with the terms of the Lease;

(c) to whom is it paid; and

(d) is the landlord resident in the UK for taxation purposes?

(a)	£10,000 per annum plus VAT
(b)	Yes
(c)	Style&Go Ltd
(d)	Yes

6.2 Please confirm that:

(a) all rent reviews have taken place strictly in accordance with the terms of the Lease;

(b) all review settlements are satisfactorily evidenced in accordance with the terms of the Lease; and

(c) in respect of any current review, all notices and applications for arbitration or for determination by an expert have been served or made on time.

Confirmed

6.3 Unless otherwise disclosed, please tell us whether there has been any discussion with the landlord as to the amount of rent payable in the future.

no

7. SERVICE CHARGE

7.1 Unless apparent from the Lease, what is the service charge accounting period and the estimated annual service charge for the current period?

n/a

7.2 Please give details of the annual service charge for the last three years (or longer if available) including copies of all certificates, auditors' reports, accounts and other documents relating to its calculation and apportionment.

n/a

7.3 Please supply:

(a) a schedule of the services which the landlord provides and a breakdown of the costs of each service;

(b) details of any sinking fund or reserve account;

(c) details of the landlord's planned maintenance programme and projected expenditure, if any; and

(d) details of any unusual or exceptionally large expenditure which the landlord intends to incur.

n/a

7.4 If the Property is part of a Development:

(a) what proportion of the service charge is attributable to the Property;

(b) how is that proportion calculated;

(c) is any variation of the proportion contemplated;

(d) is each tenant of the Development under an obligation to contribute to the service charge costs of the Development; and

(e) are there any agreed capping or weighting provisions in any other leases of parts of the Development?

n/a

7.5 Except as already disclosed, have there been any disputes relating to the services or the service charge?

n/a

8. MANAGEMENT

8.1 Please supply the name and address of any managing agents employed for the management of the Property or of the Development. Please give details of their responsibilities and charges.

n/a

8.2 What regulations have been made for the use and management of the Property that are not set out in the Tenancy Documents supplied?

n/a

8.3 Please give details of any management company and/or tenants' association and what your participation is in it.

n/a

9. ARREARS

9.1 Are there any payments of rent, service charge, insurance premiums or other payments under the Lease:

(a) demanded but not yet paid; or

(b) that should have been due for payment but that have not yet been demanded?

If so, please give details.

None

9.2 If you are aware that the landlord has served a notice under section 17 of the 1995 Act on any former tenant or guarantor in respect of any arrears, please give details including details of any payment made in response.

n/a

10. INSURANCE

10.1 If the landlord insures the Property then, to the extent that the following information has not already been given in response to CPSE.1, please state:

(a) the insurer's name and address;

(b) the policy number;

(c) details of all the premises to which the insurance relates, the risks covered and the exclusions and the excesses payable;

(d) the sums insured (showing separately, where applicable, the sums for buildings, plant and machinery, professionals' fees, loss of rent and public liability);

(e) the name(s) of the insured(s) and of all other persons whose interests are, or on completion of the Transaction will be, noted on the policy;

(f) the current premium, what proportion will be attributed to the Property and how this is calculated;

(g) the next renewal date;

(h) the name and address of the brokers; and

(i) details of any separate terrorism insurance arrangements.

See enclosed

10.2 Have any subrogation rights that the insurers may have against the tenant been waived?

See documentation supplied

11. BREACHES, COMPLAINTS AND ENFORCEMENT

Except as already disclosed in replies to CPSE.1, please confirm that:

(a) all covenants, conditions and obligations in the Tenancy Documents, whether on the part of the landlord or the tenant, have been observed, performed and fulfilled;

(b) there have been no proceedings before any court, tribunal, arbitrator or expert relating to the Lease;

(c) the landlord has never exercised any right of re-entry under the Lease; and

(d) you are not aware of any dispute or breach of covenant alleged in respect of any superior lease or the freehold.

Confirmed

Type	Enquiry from Gemma's Gels Ltd's solicitor	Response from Polished Perfection Ltd's solicitor
Title	Please confirm whether the property is currently occupied and whether vacant possession will be provided on completion.	Confirmed - the seller occupies the property and vacant possession will be provided on completion.
	There is a restrictive covenant prohibiting building any structure on the property. Please confirm this has not been breached.	Confirmed
Security of tenure	Please confirm that the notice procedure required under the LTA 1954 was properly followed.	Confirmed. Notice documentation enclosed.

Document 15

Assignment of lease over first floor premises, 17 High Street, Barnford

Summary of due diligence for inclusion in a report on title

1. Key details of the transaction

- The buyer plans to purchase the lease over the Nail Bar.
- Seller: Polished Perfection Ltd
- Buyer: Gemma's Gels Ltd
- Property: leasehold of first floor premises, 17 High Street, Barnford, Westshire, EX82 7YK, registered with title number WX727338
- Lease: dated 21 September 2026 between Style&Go Ltd and Polished Perfection Ltd
- Landlord's consent is required under the lease.
    - contract: make completion date conditional upon the seller obtaining the landlord's consent.
- Price:
    - Premium: £1
    - Rent: £10,000 plus VAT per annum
- No SDLT is payable on the rent, and the premium is too low in value to attract SDLT.
- The seller is not opting to tax the premium, but VAT at 20% is payable on top of the rent. Actions:
    - contract: include a special condition re no option to tax.
- Term: there is 9 years and 8 months remaining on the lease
- The premises will be provided with vacant possession. The seller has confirmed it is currently occupied by the seller. Actions:
    - contract: include a special condition re vacant possession.

2. Title investigation

- There is a restrictive covenant on the title preventing building on the premises. The seller has confirmed this has not been breached. Gemma's Gels Ltd will not be permitted to build any structure on the premises.

- The seller does not know of any overriding interests affecting the premises. We recommend a physical inspection of the property, as Gemma's Gels Ltd will be bound by these if any do exist and are discoverable.

3. Searches

- The highways search confirms that the High Street is an adopted highway and directly abuts the salon, through which you will reach the first floor premises.
- The drainage and water search confirmed that Westshire Water are responsible for maintaining the drains and sewers and for the quality of the water supplied to the property.
- The environmental search confirmed that the risk of contaminants being present on the land is low and we do not recommend any further environmental surveys.
- The flood search confirmed that the risk of flooding to the property is low and we do not recommend any further flood surveys.
- A company search against the seller revealed no charges, nor insolvency or administration events.
- The property benefits from mains electricity and gas (not metered) and broadband connections.
- The seller has confirmed that heating and hot water are shared with the rest of the building.
- The seller has confirmed they will continue to insure the whole building. The tenant's interest is noted on the policy and insurers have waived their subrogation rights.

4. Planning permission

- The property has planning permission for use class E. This will be sufficient for the proposed use of the property as a nail bar.
- The premises have already recently been fitted out and the buyer will not be doing any additional works.

5. Access

- Access to the premises is through the ground floor of the building. The lease will contain rights over this part of the building.
- The lease will contain a right to use the Car Park behind the building, for staff and customers.

Document 16

DATED

[27 February 2027]

LICENCE TO ASSIGN

relating to

Lease of Nail Bar, First Floor, 17 High Street, Barnford, Westshire, EX82 7YK

between

Style&Go Ltd

and

Polished Perfection Ltd

and

Gemma's Gels Ltd

CONTENTS

CLAUSE

SCHEDULE

ANNEX

This deed is dated [*27 February 2027*]

HM Land Registry

Landlord's title number: EG576798

Tenant's title number: WX727338

Parties

(1) STYLE&GO LTD incorporated and registered in England and Wales with company number 00127976 whose registered office is at c/a Blackhurst&Sons LLP of 22 High Street, Barnford, Westshire, EX82 7YK **(Landlord)**

(2) POLISHED PERFECTION LTD incorporated and registered in England and Wales with company number 22375943 whose registered office is c/o Talbot & Wick LLP, 47B Vale Road, Torton, Westshire, EX79 4PJ **(Tenant)**

(3) GEMMA'S GELS LTD incorporated and registered in England and Wales with company number 01276917whose registered office is at c/o MMK Solicitors LLP, 89 Barnford Lane, Barnford, Westshire, EX83 3QT **(Assignee)**

BACKGROUND

(A) This licence is supplemental and collateral to the Lease.

(B) The Landlord is entitled to the immediate reversion to the Lease.

(C) The residue of the term granted by the Lease is vested in the Tenant.

(D) The Tenant intends to assign the Lease to the Assignee and, under the terms of the Lease, requires the consent of the Landlord to that assignment.

AGREED TERMS

1. Interpretation

The following definitions and rules of interpretation apply in this licence.

1.1 Definitions:

Assignee's Solicitors: MMK Solicitors LLP of 89 Barnford Lane, Barnford, Westshire, EX83 3QT DX 324586 97 (reference 30088MXK).

Authorised Guarantee Agreement: the authorised guarantee agreement in Schedule 1 and incorporated into this licence

Electronic Payment: payment by electronic means in same day cleared funds from an account held in the name of the Assignee's Solicitors at a clearing bank to an account in the name of the Landlord's Solicitors.

Landlord's Solicitors: Blackhurst and Sons LLP of 22 High Street, Barnford, Westshire, EX82 7YK DX 313505 Westshire 79 (reference 29384BHS02).

Lease: a lease of First Floor Premises, 17 High Street, Barnford, Westshire, EX82 7YK dated 21 September 2026 made between the Landlord and the Tenant and all documents supplemental or collateral to that lease.

LTA 1954: Landlord and Tenant Act 1954.

LTCA 1995: Landlord and Tenant (Covenants) Act 1995.

Property: First Floor Premises, 17 High Street, Barnford, Westshire, EX82 7YK as more particularly described in and demised by the Lease.

Rent Deposit Deed: a rent deposit deed in the form attached to this licence at Annex A.

Term: has the same meaning as in the Lease

1.2 The expression **tenant covenants** has the meaning given to it by the LTCA 1995.

1.3 References to **completion of the assignment** (and similar expressions) are to the date on which the deed of assignment to the Assignee is dated and not to the registration of that deed at HM Land Registry.

1.4 Clause, Schedule and paragraph headings shall not affect the interpretation of this licence.

1.5 A **person** includes a natural person, corporate or unincorporated body (whether or not having separate legal personality).

1.6 The Schedule forms part of this licence and shall have effect as if set out in full in the body of this licence. Any reference to this licence includes the Schedule.

1.7 Unless the context otherwise requires, words in the singular shall include the plural and in the plural shall include the singular.

1.8 Unless the context otherwise requires, a reference to one gender shall include a reference to the other genders.

1.9 Unless otherwise specified, reference to legislation or a legislative provision is a reference to it as amended, extended or re-enacted from time to time.

1.10 A reference to legislation or a legislative provision shall include all subordinate legislation made from time to time under that legislation or legislative provision.

1.11 A reference to laws in general is a reference to all local, national and directly applicable supra-national laws as amended, extended or re-enacted from time to time and shall include all subordinate laws made from time to time under them and all orders, notices, codes of practice and guidance made under them.

1.12 Unless otherwise specified, a reference to **writing** or **written** includes fax but not email.

1.13 Any obligation on a party not to do something includes an obligation not to allow that thing to be done.

1.14 A reference to **this licence** or to any other agreement or document referred to in this licence is a reference to this licence or such other agreement or document as varied or novated (in each case, other than in breach of the provisions of this licence) from time to time.

1.15 Unless the context otherwise requires, references to clauses and the Schedule is to the clauses and the Schedule of this licence and references to paragraphs are to paragraphs of the Schedule.

1.16 Any words following the terms **including**, **include**, **in particular**, **for example** or any similar expression shall be construed as illustrative and shall not limit the sense of the words, description, definition, phrase or term preceding those terms.

1.17 A **working day** is any day, other than a Saturday, a Sunday, a bank holiday or a public holiday in England.

2. Consent to assign

2.1 Subject to clause 2.2, clause 2.3, and clause 2.4, the Landlord consents to the Tenant assigning the Lease to the Assignee.

2.2 The consent given by clause 2.1 is valid for three months from (and including) the date of this licence. If that consent ceases to be valid before the assignment is completed, all the terms of this licence (except clause 2.1) shall remain in force.

2.3 Simultaneously with completion of this licence, the Tenant shall execute and deliver the Authorised Guarantee Agreement to the Landlord as a deed.

2.4 On completion of the assignment the Assignee shall execute and deliver to the Landlord the Rent Deposit Deed as a deed and pay the Initial Deposit (as defined in the Rent Deposit Deed) by Electronic Payment to the Landlord.

2.5 Nothing in this licence shall operate to waive or be deemed to waive any subsisting breach of any of the tenant covenants of the Lease.

2.6 Any sum which becomes due under the Lease after completion of the assignment but which relates to any period before completion of the assignment shall be payable in full by the Assignee.

2.7 The consent given by clause 2.1 does not obviate the need for the consent or licence of any person other than the Landlord that may be required for the assignment.

3. Obligations relating to the assignment

3.1 The Assignee shall not occupy, and the Tenant shall not allow the Assignee to occupy, the Property or any part of it before completion of the assignment.

3.2 Immediately following completion of the assignment and thereafter throughout the Term the Assignee shall:

(a) observe and perform the terms, covenants and conditions contained in the Lease and on the part of the Tenant to be observed and performed;

(b) pay all the rents and other monies due under the Lease as if the Assignee were the Tenant named in the Lease;

3.3 Immediately following completion of the assignment, the Assignee shall notify the Landlord (or its managing agents) of the name and address of the person to whom demands for rent should be sent.

3.4 Within one month after completion of the assignment, the Assignee shall:

(a) notify the Landlord of completion;

(b) send the Landlord a certified copy of the assignment; and

(c) pay the Landlord's registration fee of £40 plus value added tax.

4. Authorised Guarantee Agreement

4.1 The Authorised Guarantee Agreement is an authorised guarantee agreement for the purposes of section 16 of the LTCA 1995.

4.2 The Authorised Guarantee Agreement shall take effect on the date the Tenant is released from the tenant covenants of the Lease by virtue of the LTCA 1995.

5. Costs

On completion of this licence the Tenant shall pay the reasonable costs and disbursements of the Landlord's solicitors and its managing agents in connection with this licence. This obligation extends to costs and disbursements assessed on a full indemnity basis and to any value added tax in respect of those costs and disbursements except to the extent that the Landlord is able to recover that value added tax.

6. The right of re-entry in the Lease

The right of re-entry in the Lease shall be exercisable if any covenant or condition of this licence is breached as well as if any of the events stated in the provision for re-entry in the Lease occurs.

7. Indemnity

The Tenant and the Assignee shall indemnify the Landlord against all liabilities, costs, expenses, damages and losses suffered or incurred by the Landlord arising out of or in connection with any breach of their respective obligations in this licence.

8. Notices

8.1 Any notice given to a party under or in connection with this licence shall be in writing and shall be delivered by hand or sent by pre-paid first-class post or other next working day delivery service, at the address given for that party in this licence or as otherwise notified in writing to each other party.

8.2 A notice shall be deemed to have been received:

(a) if delivered by hand, on signature of a delivery receipt or otherwise at the time the notice is left at the proper address; or

(b) if sent by pre-paid first-class post or other next working day delivery service, at 9.00 am on the second working day after posting or at the time recorded by the delivery service.

8.3 A notice given under this licence is not valid if sent by fax or email.

8.4 This clause does not apply to the service of any proceedings or other documents in any legal action or, where applicable, any arbitration or other method of dispute resolution.

9. Liability

9.1 The obligations of each of the Tenant and the Assignee in this licence are owed to the Landlord.

10. Third party rights

This licence does not give rise to any rights under the Contracts (Rights of Third Parties) Act 1999 to enforce any term of this licence.

11. Registration at the Land Registry

The Assignee shall:

(a) apply for registration of the assignment at HM Land Registry within one month following completion of the assignment;

(b) ensure that any requisitions raised by HM Land Registry in connection with its registration application are responded to promptly and properly; and

(c) send the Landlord official copies of its title within one month after the registration has been completed.

12. Governing Law

This licence and any dispute or claim (including non-contractual disputes or claims) arising out of or in connection with it or its subject matter or formation shall be governed by and construed in accordance with the law of England and Wales.

13. Jurisdiction

Each party to this licence irrevocably agrees that the courts of England and Wales shall have exclusive jurisdiction to settle any dispute or claim (including non-contractual disputes or claims) arising out of or in connection with this licence or its subject matter or formation.

This document has been executed as a deed and is delivered and takes effect on the date stated at the beginning of it.

Schedule 1 Authorised guarantee agreement

1. Guarantee and indemnity

1.1 The Tenant guarantees to the Landlord that the Assignee shall pay the rents reserved by the Lease and observe and perform the tenant covenants of the Lease and that, if the Assignee fails to pay any of those rents or to observe or perform any of those tenant covenants, the Tenant shall pay or observe and perform them.

1.2 The Tenant covenants with the Landlord as principal obligor and as a separate and independent obligation and liability from its obligations and liabilities under paragraph 1.1 to indemnify and keep indemnified the Landlord against any failure by the Assignee either:

(a) to pay any of the rents reserved by the Lease; or

(b) to observe or perform any of the tenant covenants of the Lease.

2. Tenant's liability

2.1 The liability of the Tenant under paragraph 1 shall continue until the end of the term of the Lease (however it may end), or until the Assignee is released from the tenant covenants of the Lease by virtue of the LTCA 1995, if earlier.

2.2 The liability of the Tenant shall not be reduced, discharged or otherwise adversely affected by any of the following:

(a) any time or indulgence granted by the Landlord to the Assignee (or to any person to whom the Assignee has assigned the Lease pursuant to an assignment that is an excluded assignment under section 11 of the LTCA 1995);

(b) any delay or forbearance by the Landlord in enforcing the payment of any of the rents or the observance or performance of any of the tenant covenants of the Lease or in making any demand in respect of any of them;

(c) any refusal by the Landlord to accept any rent or other payment due under the Lease where the Landlord believes that the acceptance of such rent or payment may prejudice its ability to re-enter the Property;

(d) the Landlord exercising any right or remedy against the Assignee for any failure to pay the rents reserved by the Lease or to observe or perform the tenant covenants of the Lease;

(e) the Landlord taking any action or refraining from taking any action in connection with any other security held by the Landlord in respect of the Assignee's liability to pay the rents reserved by the Lease and observe and perform the tenant covenants of the Lease, including the release of any such security;

(f) a release or compromise of the liability of any one of the persons who is the Tenant, or the grant of any time or concession to any one of them;

(g) any legal limitation on or disability of the Assignee or any invalidity or irregularity of any of the tenant covenants of the Lease or any unenforceability of any of them against the Assignee;

(h) the Assignee being dissolved or being struck off the register of companies or otherwise ceasing to exist or, if the Assignee is an individual, by the Assignee dying or becoming incapable of managing its affairs;

(i) without prejudice to paragraph 4, the disclaimer of the liability of the Assignee under the Lease;

(j) the surrender of the Lease in respect of part only of the Property, except that the Tenant shall not be under any liability in relation to the surrendered part in respect of any period after the surrender; or

(k) any other act or omission except an express written release of the Tenant by the Landlord.

2.3 Any sum payable by the Tenant under this Authorised Guarantee Agreement shall be paid without any deduction, set-off or counter-claim against the Landlord or the Assignee.

3. Variations and supplemental documents

3.1 The Tenant shall, at the request of the Landlord, join in and give its consent to the terms of any licence, consent, approval, variation or other document that may be entered into by the Assignee in connection with the Lease.

3.2 The liability of the Tenant shall not be released by any variation of the rents reserved by, or the tenant covenants of, the Lease, whether or not:

(a) the variation is material or prejudicial to the Tenant;

(b) the variation is made in any document; or

(c) the Tenant has consented, in writing or otherwise, to the variation.

3.3 Except to the extent that its liability is affected by section 18 of the LTCA 1995, the Tenant's liability under this Authorised Guarantee Agreement shall apply to:

(a) the rents reserved by the Lease as varied; and

(b) the tenant covenants of the Lease as varied.

4. Tenant to take a new lease

4.1 If the liability of the Assignee under the Lease is disclaimed and the Landlord gives the Tenant written notice not later than six months after the Landlord receives notice of the disclaimer, the Tenant shall enter into a new lease of the Property on the terms set out in paragraph 4.2.

4.2 The rights and obligations under the new lease shall take effect from the date of the disclaimer and the new lease shall:

(a) be granted subject to the right of any person to have the Lease vested in them by the court and to the terms on which any such order may be made and subject to the rights of any third party existing at the date of grant;

(b) be for a term that expires at the same date as the end of the [contractual] term granted by the Lease had there been no disclaimer;

(c) reserve as an initial annual rent an amount equal to the rent which is reserved under the Lease at the date of disclaimer or which would be payable but for any abatement or suspension of such annual rent or restriction on the right to collect it and which is subject to review on the same terms and dates provided by the Lease;

(d) be excluded from sections 24 to 28 of the LTA 1954; and

(e) otherwise be on the same terms as the Lease (as varied, save to the extent that the Tenant is not bound by any such variation by virtue of section 18 of the LTCA 1995).

4.3 The parties confirm that:

(a) the Landlord served a notice on the Tenant, as required by section 38A(3)(a) of the LTA 1954, applying to the tenancy to be entered into by the Tenant pursuant to paragraph 4.1 not less than 14 days before this Authorised Guarantee Agreement was entered into; and

(b) the Tenant made a statutory declaration dated [DATE] in accordance with the requirements of section 38A(3)(b) of the LTA 1954.

4.4 The Tenant shall pay the Landlord's solicitors' costs and disbursements (on a full indemnity basis) and any value added tax on them in relation to the new lease and shall execute and deliver to the Landlord a counterpart of the new lease within one month after service of the Landlord's notice under paragraph 4.1.

4.5 The grant of a new lease and its acceptance by the Tenant shall be without prejudice to any other rights which the Landlord may have against the Tenant or against any other person or in respect of any other security that the Landlord may have in connection with the Lease.

5. Payments in gross and restrictions on the Tenant

5.1 Any payment or dividend that the Landlord receives from the Assignee (or its estate) or any other person in connection with any insolvency proceedings or arrangement involving the Assignee shall be taken and applied as a payment in gross and shall not prejudice the right of the Landlord to recover from the Tenant to the full extent of the obligations that are the subject of this Authorised Guarantee Agreement.

5.2 The Tenant shall not claim in competition with the Landlord in any insolvency proceedings or arrangement of the Assignee in respect of any payment made by the Tenant pursuant to this Authorised Guarantee Agreement. If it otherwise receives any money in such proceedings or arrangement, it shall hold that money on trust for the Landlord to the extent of its liability to the Landlord.

5.3 The Tenant shall not, without the consent of the Landlord, exercise any right or remedy that it may have (whether against the Assignee or any other person) in respect of any amount paid or other obligation performed by the Tenant under this Authorised Guarantee Agreement unless and until all the obligations of the Tenant under this Authorised Guarantee Agreement have been fully performed.

6. Other securities

6.1 The Tenant warrants that it has not taken and covenants that it shall not take any security from or over the assets of the Assignee in respect of any liability of the Assignee to the Tenant. If it does take or hold any such security it shall hold it for the benefit of the Landlord.

6.2 This Authorised Guarantee Agreement is in addition to and independent of any other security that the Landlord may from time to time hold from the Tenant, or the Assignee or any other person in respect of the liability of the Assignee to pay the rents reserved by the Lease and to observe and perform the tenant covenants of the Lease. It shall not merge in or be affected by any other security.

6.3 The Tenant shall not be entitled to claim or participate in any other security held by the Landlord in respect of the liability of the Assignee to pay the rents reserved by the Lease or to observe and perform the tenant covenants of the Lease.

Executed as deed by Style&Go Ltd (**Landlord**) acting by André Gomez a director, in the presence of:	*André Gomez* Director

Karen Chester

Karen Chester, 29 Woodgrove Close, Barnford, Westshire, EX79 5PJ

Secretary

Executed as deed by Polished Perfection Ltd (**Tenant**) acting by Meena Kasih a director, in the presence of:	*Aminah Kasih* Director

Fatimah Hiraney

Fatimah Hiraney, Flat 3b, Windridge Heights, Barnford, EX78 9JK

Accountant

Executed as deed by Gemma's Gels Ltd (**Assignee**) acting by Gemma Gray a director, in the presence of:	*Gemma Gray* Director

Leon Hart

Leon Hart, 20, Metchbrook Road, Barnford, EX69 1QV,

Nail Technician

ANNEX A FORM OF RENT DEPOSIT DEED

[not reproduced]

Document 17

NB: the authors have included dates in this contract in square brackets – in practice these would be entered at the relevant moment (e.g. on exchange).

CONTRACT

(Incorporating the Standard Commercial Property Conditions (Third Edition – 2018 Revision))

For conveyancer's use only
Buyer's conveyancer: MMK Solicitors LLP
Seller's conveyancer: Talbot&Wick LLP
Law Society Formula B
Time 1:30pm
The information above does not form part of the Contract

Date	:	*[20 Feb 2027]*
Seller	:	Polished Perfection Ltd
Buyer	:	Gemma's Gels Ltd
Property (freehold/~~leasehold~~)	:	First floor premises, 17 High Street, Barnford, Westshire, EX82 7YK
Title Number/~~Root of title~~	:	WX727338
Specified Encumbrances	:	The matters contained or referred to in the property, proprietorship and charges registers of title number WX727338 except any subsisting financial charges
Completion Date	:	[*27 February 2027*]
Contract Rate	:	4% above the base lending rate of Barclays Bank plc from time to time in force
Purchase Price	:	£1 exclusive of any VAT
Deposit	:	0%
Balance	:	£1

The Seller will sell and the Buyer will buy the Property for the Purchase Price.

WARNING
This is a formal document, designed to create legal rights and legal obligations. Take advice before using it.

Signed
Gemma Gray
Director
Authorised to sign on behalf of Buyer

SPECIAL CONDITIONS

1. (a) This contract incorporates the Standard Commercial Property Conditions (Third Edition – 2018 Revision).

   (b) The terms used in this contract have the same meaning when used in the Standard Commercial Property Conditions.

2. Neither party can rely on any representation made by the other, unless made in writing by the other or its conveyancer, but this does not exclude liability for fraud or recklessness.

If the box next to any of Special Conditions 3 to 8 is checked, that Special Condition applies, provided that (in the case of Special Conditions 6 and 7 and the second alternative for 8) the gaps in the printed text have been filled in.

3. ☐ ~~The Property is sold with limited title guarantee, which replaces the reference to full title guarantee in condition 7.6.2.~~

4. ☒ The Property is sold with vacant possession on completion.

(or) 4. ☐ ~~The Property is sold subject to the leases or tenancies set out on the attached list but otherwise with vacant possession on completion.~~

5. ☐ ~~(a) The sale includes those contents which are indicated on the attached list as included in the sale.~~

   ~~(b) The sale excludes those fixtures which are at the Property and are indicated on the attached list as excluded from the sale.~~

6. ☐ ~~In conditions 3.2.2 and 9.7, as an alternative to payment from a conveyancer's account, the payment may be made from an account held by at~~

7. ☐ ~~Conditions 9.1.2 and 9.1.3 are to have effect as if the time specified in them were ________ am/pm rather than 2:00pm.~~

8. ☐ ~~Where after the transfer the Seller will be retaining the land near the Property, the transfer is to be in the form of the attached draft transfer.~~

(or) 8. ☐ ~~Where after the transfer the Seller will be retaining land near the Property, the transfer is to contain the following additional express terms:~~

   ~~(a)~~

   ~~(b)~~

Standard Commercial Property Conditions Part 2

9. The conditions in Part 2 shown against the boxes checked below are included in the contract.

	[X]	Condition A1 (VAT: not a taxable supply)
[or]	[ ]	Condition A2 (VAT: transfer of a going concern)
	[ ]	Condition B (capital allowances). The amount of the Purchase Price apportioned to plant and machinery that are fixtures for the purposes of the Capital Allowances Act Capital Allowances Act 2001 is £
	[ ]	Condition C1 (flats: no tenants' rights of first refusal)
[or]	[ ]	Condition C2 (flats: with tenants' rights of first refusal in auction sales)

Further additional special conditions:

1. The Completion Date is conditional upon the Seller obtaining the consent of the Landlord.
2. The covenants set out in section 4 of the Law of Property (Miscellaneous Provisions) Act 1994 will not extend to any breach of the tenant's covenants in the lease relating to the physical state of the property and so clauses 4.2.2 and 7.6.4 of the conditions in Part 1 do not apply to this contract.

Notices may be sent to:

Seller's Conveyancer's name: Talbot & Wick LLP

Buyer's Conveyancer's name: MMK Solicitors LLP

NB: the authors have included dates in this deed in square brackets – in practice these would be entered at the relevant moment (e.g. on completion).

HM Land Registry
Transfer of whole of registered title(s)

TR1

Any parts of the form that are not typed should be completed in black ink and in block capitals.

If you need more room than is provided for in a panel, and your software allows, you can expand any panel in the form. Alternatively use continuation sheet CS and attach it to this form.

For information on how HM Land Registry processes your personal information, see our Personal Information Charter.

Leave blank if not yet registered.	1	Title number(s) of the property: WX727338
Insert address including postcode (if any) or other description of the property, for example 'land adjoining 2 Acacia Avenue'.	2	Property: First floor premises, 17 High Street, Barnford, Westshire, EX82 7YK
Remember to date this deed with the day of completion, but not before it has been signed and witnessed.	3	Date: [*27 February 2027*]
Give full name(s) of **all** the persons transferring the property. Complete as appropriate where the transferor is a company. Enter the overseas entity ID issued by Companies House for the transferor pursuant to the Economic Crime (Transparency and Enforcement) Act 2022. If the ID is not required, you may instead state 'not required'. Further details on overseas entities can be found in practice guide 78: overseas entities.	4	Transferor: Polished Perfection Ltd For UK incorporated companies/LLPs Registered number of company or limited liability partnership including any prefix: 22375943 For overseas entities (a) Territory of incorporation or formation: (b) Overseas entity ID issued by Companies House, including any prefix: (c) Where the entity is a company with a place of business in the United Kingdom, the registered number, if any, issued by Companies House, including any prefix:

Guidance	No.	Panel
Give full name(s) of **all** the persons to be shown as registered proprietors. Complete as appropriate where the transferee is a company. Also, for an overseas company, unless an arrangement with HM Land Registry exists, lodge either a certificate in Form 7 in Schedule 3 to the Land Registration Rules 2003 or a certified copy of the constitution in English or Welsh, or other evidence permitted by rule 183 of the Land Registration Rules 2003. Enter the overseas entity ID issued by Companies House for the transferee pursuant to the Economic Crime (Transparency and Enforcement) Act 2022. If the ID is not required, you may instead state 'not required'. Further details on overseas entities can be found in practice guide 78: overseas entities.	5	Transferee for entry in the register: Gemma's Gels Ltd For UK incorporated companies/LLPs Registered number of company or limited liability partnership including any prefix: 01276917 For overseas entities (a) Territory of incorporation or formation: (b) Overseas entity ID issued by Companies House, including any prefix: (c) Where the entity is a company with a place of business in the United Kingdom, the registered number, if any, issued by Companies House, including any prefix:
Each transferee may give up to three addresses for service, one of which must be a postal address whether or not in the UK (including the postcode, if any). The others can be any combination of a postal address, a UK DX box number or an email address.	6	Transferee's intended address(es) for service for entry in the register: First Floor, 17 High Street, Barnford, Westshire, EX82 7YK
	7	The transferor transfers the property to the transferee
Place 'X' in the appropriate box. State the currency unit if other than sterling. If none of the boxes apply, insert an appropriate memorandum in panel 11.	8	Consideration ☒ The transferor has received from the transferee for the property the following sum (in words and figures): £1 ☐ The transfer is not for money or anything that has a monetary value ☐ Insert other receipt as appropriate:
Place 'X' in any box that applies. Add any modifications.	9	The transferor transfers with ☒ full title guarantee ☐ limited title guarantee The covenants set out in section 4 of the Law of Property (Miscellaneous Provisions) Act 1994 will not extend to any breach of the tenant's covenants in the lease relating to the physical state of the property.

Where the transferee is more than one person, place 'X' in the appropriate box.
 	
Complete as necessary.
 	
The registrar will enter a Form A restriction in the register *unless*:
– an 'X' is placed:
  – in the first box, or
  – in the third box and the details of the trust or of the trust instrument show that the transferees are to hold the property on trust for themselves alone as joint tenants, *or*
– it is clear from completion of a form JO lodged with this application that the transferees are to hold the property on trust for themselves alone as joint tenants.
 	
Please refer to *Joint property ownership* and *practice guide 24: private trusts of land* for further guidance. These are both available on the GOV.UK website.
	10 Declaration of trust. The transferee is more than one person and
	☐ they are to hold the property on trust for themselves as joint tenants
	☐ they are to hold the property on trust for themselves as tenants in common in equal shares
	☐ they are to hold the property on trust:

Insert here any required or permitted statement, certificate or application and any agreed covenants, declarations and so on.	11 Additional provisions

The transferor must execute this transfer as a deed using the space opposite. If there is more than one transferor, all must execute. Forms of execution are given in Schedule 9 to the Land Registration Rules 2003. If the transfer contains transferee's covenants or declarations or contains an application by the transferee (such as for a restriction), it must also be executed by the transferee.

If there is more than one transferee and panel 10 has been completed, each transferee must also execute this transfer to comply with the requirements in section 53(1)(b) of the Law of Property Act 1925 relating to the declaration of a trust of land. Please refer to *Joint property ownership* and practice guide *24: private trusts of land* for further guidance.

Examples of the correct form of execution are set out in practice guide 8: execution of deeds. Execution as a deed usually means that a witness must also sign, and add their name and address.

Remember to date this deed in panel 3.

12 Execution

Seller

Executed as a deed by Polished Perfection Ltd acting by a director and its secretary

Meena Kasih
Director

Lucius Ho
Secretary

WARNING
If you dishonestly enter information or make a statement that you know is, or might be, untrue or misleading, and intend by doing so to make a gain for yourself or another person, or to cause loss or the risk of loss to another person, you may commit the offence of fraud under section 1 of the Fraud Act 2006, the maximum penalty for which is 10 years' imprisonment or an unlimited fine, or both.

Failure to complete this form with proper care may result in a loss of protection under the Land Registration Act 2002 if, as a result, a mistake is made in the register.

Under section 66 of the Land Registration Act 2002 most documents (including this form) kept by the registrar relating to an application to the registrar or referred to in the register are open to public inspection and copying. If you believe a document contains prejudicial information, you may apply for that part of the document to be made exempt using Form EX1, under rule 136 of the Land Registration Rules 2003.

Memorandum of exchange: acquisition of lease at Nail Bar, 17 High Street, Barnford

19 February 2027

1. Exchange occurred on 19 February 2027 at 1:30pm.
2. Formula B. No deposit to be paid, so the sentence requiring the purchaser's solicitor to send a banker's draft or client account cheque is deleted from the formula.
3. Agreed completion date: 27 February 2027.
4. No deposit to be paid – see 2. Above.
5. MMK solicitors – solicitor for the buyer
   Talbot&Wick LLP – solicitor for the seller

Document 20

Official search certificate of search of whole with priority

Land Registry

Land Registration Rules 2003

Form **OS1R**

Official Search No. NB/EXH02	Certificate Date: **19 February 2027** Priority Period began at: **14:12:17**	Priority Period expires on: **2 April 2027** at midnight but see the note below

Particulars of Search as Supplied

Title Number	WX727338
Applicant	Gemma's Gels Ltd

Result

It is certified that the official search applied for has been made with the following result:

Since 4 January 2027 at 13:26:27 no adverse entries have been made.

****

END OF RESULT

Note: To be sure to obtain priority for your application you should deliver it to the proper office by 12:00 (noon) on the date when priority expires.

HM Land Registry

Application to change the register

AP1

Any parts of the form that are not typed should be completed in black ink and in block capitals.

If you need more room than is provided for in a panel, and your software allows, you can expand any panel in the form. Alternatively use continuation sheet CS and attach it to this form.

HM Land Registry is unable to give legal advice, but you can find guidance on HM Land Registry applications (including our practice guides for conveyancers) at www.gov.uk/land-registry.

Conveyancer is a term used in this form. It is defined in rule 217A, Land Registration Rules 2003 and includes persons authorised under the Legal Services Act 2007 to provide reserved legal services relating to land registration and includes solicitors and licensed conveyancers.

For information on how HM Land Registry processes your personal information, see our Personal Information Charter.

HM LAND REGISTRY USE ONLY
Record of fees paid
Particulars of under/over payments
Reference number Fees debited £

Where there is more than one local authority serving an area, enter the one to which council tax or business rates are normally paid.

1 Local authority serving the property: Westshire

Full postcode of property (if any): EX82 7YK

Enter the title number of each title that requires an entry to be made in that register.

2 Title number(s) of the property:
WX727338

Place 'X' in the appropriate box.

Give a brief description of the part affected, for example 'edged red on the plan to the transfer dated ....'.

3 The application affects

☒ the whole of the title(s)

☐ part of the title(s) as shown:

To find out more about our fees visit www.gov.uk/government/collections/fees-land-registry-guides

Remember restrictions in deeds may apply to other deeds of lower priority in this list, unless you specify otherwise.

4 Application, priority and fees

Applications in priority order	Price paid/Value (£)	Fees paid (£)
Transfer of whole	1	20
	Total fees (£)	20

Place 'X' in the appropriate box.

Where the application is sent to HM Land Registry by a private individual, payment must be by way of postal order or cheque made payable to HM Land Registry.

The fee will be charged to the account specified in panel 7.

Fee payment method

☐ cheque made payable to 'Land Registry'

☒ direct debit, under an agreement with Land Registry

List the documents lodged with this form. We only need certified copies of deeds or documents you send to us with HM Land Registry application forms. Once we have made a copy of the documents you send to us, they will be destroyed, this applies to both originals and certified copies	5	Documents lodged with this form: *Certified copy Transfer dated 27 February 2027 and made between (1) Polished Perfection Ltd and (2) Gemma's Gels Ltd, executed by Polished Perfection Ltd* *Certified copy Transfer dated 27 February 2027 and made between (1) Polished Perfection Ltd and (2) Gemma's Gels Ltd, executed by Gemma's Gels Ltd*
Provide the full name(s) of the person(s) applying to change the register. Where a conveyancer lodges the application, this must be the name(s) of the client(s), not the conveyancer. Complete as appropriate where the applicant is a company. Also, for an overseas company, unless an arrangement with HM Land Registry exists, lodge either a certificate in Form 7 in Schedule 3 to the Land Registration Rules 2003 or a certified copy of the constitution in English or Welsh, or other evidence permitted by rule 183 of the Land Registration Rules 2003. Enter the overseas entity ID issued by Companies House for the applicant pursuant to the Economic Crime (Transparency and Enforcement) Act 2022. If the ID is not required, you may instead state 'not required'. Further details on overseas entities can be found in practice guide 78: overseas entities.	6	The applicant: Gemma's Gels Ltd For UK incorporated companies/LLPs Registered number of company or limited liability partnership including any prefix: 01276917 For overseas entities (a) Territory of incorporation or formation: (b) Overseas entity ID issued by Companies House, including any prefix: (c) Where the entity is a company with a place of business in the United Kingdom, the registered number, if any, issued by Companies House, including any prefix:
This panel must always be completed. This panel must always be completed with the details of the person sending the application to HM Land Registry. However, a key number is only available to professional customers, such as solicitors, and so a key number cannot be entered where the application is sent to HM Land Registry by a private individual. If you are paying by direct debit, this will be the account charged. This is the address to which we will normally send requisitions. However if you insert an email address, we will use this whenever possible. An acknowledgement of receipt of this application, if lodged by post, will be sent by email if one is available. We will only issue warning of cancellation letters to conveyancers if an email address is inserted.	7	This application is sent to Land Registry by Key number (if applicable): Name: MMK Solicitors LLP Address or UK DX box number: 89 Barnford Lane, Barnford, Westshire, EX83 3QT Email address: enquiries@mmk.com Reference: 7273/GR Phone no: 0000 633256 — Fax no: n/a
When completing this panel please refer to Guidance: completing form AP1.	8	Third party notification Name: Address or UK DX box number: Email address: Reference:

When completing this panel please refer to Guidance: completing form AP1. Place 'X' in the appropriate box. In this and panel 10, each proprietor may give up to three addresses for service, one of which must be a postal address whether or not in the UK (including the postcode, if any). The others can be any combination of a postal address, a UK DX box number or an email address.	9	The address(es) for service for each proprietor of the registered estate(s) to be entered in the register is ☒ the address of the property (where this is a single postal address) ☐ the address(es) for service from the transfer/assent ☐ (for existing proprietors who are remaining in the register) the current address(es) for service in the register ☐ the following address(es):
Where a charge has an MD reference we will ignore an address given in this panel unless the charge is in favour of a United Kingdom bank and neither the charge form nor any agreement we have with the lender specifies an address for service. For permitted addresses see note to panel 9. Complete as appropriate where the lender is a company. Also, for an overseas company, unless an arrangement with HM Land Registry exists, lodge either a certificate in Form 7 in Schedule 3 to the Land Registration Rules 2003 or a certified copy of the constitution in English or Welsh, or other evidence permitted by rule 183 of the Land Registration Rules 2003.	10	Name and address(es) for service of the proprietor of any new charge to be entered in the register: For UK incorporated companies/LLPs Registered number of company or limited liability partnership including any prefix: For overseas companies (a) Territory of incorporation: (b) Where the entity is a company with a place of business in the United Kingdom, the registered number, if any, issued by Companies House, including any prefix:
If this statement applies (i) place 'X' in the box and (ii) enclose Form DI. Section 27 of the Land Registration Act 2002 lists the registrable dispositions. Rule 57 of the Land Registration Rules 2003 sets out the disclosable overriding interests that you must tell us about.	11	Disclosable overriding interests ☐ This application relates to a registrable disposition and disclosable overriding interests affect the registered estate.

12 Confirmation of identity

When registering transfers, charges, leases and other dispositions of land, or giving effect to a discharge or release of a registered charge, Land Registry relies on the steps that conveyancers take, where appropriate, to verify the identity of their clients. These checks reduce the risk of property fraud.

Full details of the evidence of identity that is required can be found in Practice Guide 67 and in 'Completing the evidence of identity panels on forms AP1, FR1, and DS2' both of which can be found on the GOV.UK website.

Where a person was not represented by a conveyancer, Land Registry requires 'evidence of identity' in respect of that person, except where the first alternative in panel 13(2) applies.

'Evidence of identity' is evidence provided in accordance with any current direction made by the Chief Land Registrar under section 100(4) of the Land Registration Act 2002 for the purpose of confirming a person's identity.

If this application is to register a transfer, lease or charge, or to give effect to a discharge in Form DS1 or a release in Form DS3 complete one of the following

Place 'X' in the appropriate box.

Conveyancer is defined in rule 217A, Land Registration Rules 2003 and includes persons authorised under the Legal Services Act 2007 to provide reserved legal services relating to land registration and includes solicitors and licensed conveyancers.

☒ I am a conveyancer, and I have completed panel 13

☐ I am not a conveyancer, and I have completed panel 14

13 Where the application is sent to Land Registry by a conveyancer

(1) Details of conveyancer acting

If you are sending an application to register a transfer, lease or charge, for each party to each disposition that is to be registered state in the table below the details of the conveyancer (if any) who represented them.

Where a party is not represented by a conveyancer you must also complete (2) below.

Place 'X' in the box in the second column if the person or firm who is sending the application to HM Land Registry represented that party in the transaction. Otherwise complete the details in the third column. If the party is not represented insert 'none' in the third column.

A separate box is provided, or can be added, for each party, as required by panel 13(1). That includes separate boxes for attorneys and donors where appropriate.

Name of transferor, landlord, transferee, tenant, borrower or lender		Conveyancer's name, address and reference
Polished Perfection Ltd (Transferor)	☐	Talbot & Wick LLP, 47B Vale Road, Torton, Westshire, EX79 4PJ Reference: 9234/JXR
Gemma's Gels Ltd (Transferee)	☒	Reference: 7273/GR

If you are sending an application to give effect to a discharge in Form DS1 or release in Form DS3 for each lender, state in the table below the details of the conveyancer (if any) who represented them.

Where a lender is not represented by a conveyancer you must also complete (2) below.

Place 'X' in the box in the second column if the person or firm who is sending the application to HM Land Registry represented that party in the transaction. Otherwise complete the details in the third column. If the party is not represented insert 'none' in the third column.

A separate box is provided, or can be added, for each party, as required by panel 13(1). That includes separate boxes for attorneys and donors where appropriate.

Name of lender		Conveyancer's name, address and reference
	☐	Reference:

(2) Evidence of identity

Where any transferor, landlord, transferee, tenant, borrower or lender listed in (1) was not represented by a conveyancer

Place 'X' in the appropriate box(es).

☐ I confirm that I am satisfied that sufficient steps have been taken to verify the identity of

Insert the name of each unrepresented transferor, landlord, transferee, tenant, borrower or lender for whom you give this confirmation.

----

and that they are the registered proprietor or have the right to be registered as the registered proprietor

Evidence of identity is defined in panel 12. Full details of the evidence of identity that is required can be found in Practice Guide 67 available on the GOV.UK website.

☐ I enclose evidence of identity in respect of each unrepresented transferor, landlord, transferee, tenant, borrower or lender for whom I have not provided the confirmation above

14 Where the application is sent to Land Registry by someone who is not a conveyancer

(1) Details of conveyancer acting

If you are sending an application to register a transfer, lease or charge (ie a mortgage), for each party to each disposition that is to be registered, state in the table below the details of the conveyancer (if any) who represented them.

You must also complete (2) below.

If the party is not represented insert 'none' in the second column.

A separate box is provided, or can be added, for each party, as required by panel 14(1). That includes separate boxes for attorneys and donors where appropriate.

Name of transferor, landlord, transferee, tenant, borrower or lender	Conveyancer's name, address and reference
	Reference:
	Reference:
	Reference:

	Reference:
	Reference:

If you are sending an application to give effect to a discharge in Form DS1 or release in Form DS3, for each lender state in the table below the details of the conveyancer (if any) who represented them.

You must also complete (2) below.

If the party is not represented insert 'none' in the second column.

A separate box is provided, or can be added, for each party, as required by panel 14(1). That includes separate boxes for attorneys and donors where appropriate.

Name of lender	Conveyancer's name, address and reference
	Reference:
	Reference:

(2) Evidence of identity

Place 'X' in the appropriate box(es).

Evidence of identity is defined in panel 12. Full details of the evidence of identity that is required can be found in 'Completing the evidence of identity panels on forms AP1, FR1, and DS2' available on the GOV.UK website.

☐ for each applicant named in panel 6 is enclosed

☐ for each unrepresented transferor, landlord, transferee, tenant, borrower or lender listed in (1) is enclosed

If a conveyancer is acting for the applicant, that conveyancer must sign.

If no conveyancer is acting, the applicant (and if the applicant is more than one person then each of them) must sign.

15

Signature of conveyancer: *MMK LLP*

Date: 1 March 2027

WARNING
If you dishonestly enter information or make a statement that you know is, or might be, untrue or misleading, and intend by doing so to make a gain for yourself or another person, or to cause loss or the risk of loss to another person, you may commit the offence of fraud under section 1 of the Fraud Act 2006, the maximum penalty for which is 10 years' imprisonment or an unlimited fine, or both.

Failure to complete this form with proper care may result in a loss of protection under the Land Registration Act 2002 if, as a result, a mistake is made in the register.

Under section 66 of the Land Registration Act 2002 most documents (including this form) kept by the registrar relating to an application to the registrar or referred to in the register are open to public inspection and copying. If you believe a document contains prejudicial information, you may apply for that part of the document to be made exempt using Form EX1, under rule 136 of the Land Registration Rules 2003.

Document 22

Land Registry

Official copy of register of title

Title number WX727338

Edition date 01.03.2025

- This official copy shows the entries in the register of title on 29 March 2027 at 13:24:57.
- This date must be quoted as the "search from date" in any official search application based on this copy.
- The date at the beginning of an entry is the date on which the entry was made in the register.
- Issued on 29 March 2027.
- Under s.67 of the Land Registration Act 2002, this copy is admissible in evidence to the same extent as the original.
- For information about the register of title see Land Registry website www.landregistry.gov.uk or Land Registry Public Guide 1 – *A guide to the information we keep and how you can obtain it.*

A: Property register

This register describes the land and estate comprised in the title

Westshire : Barnford

1. (28.10.2026) The leasehold land shown edged with thick black on the plan of the above Title filed at the Registry and being First Floor, 17 High Street, Barnford, Westshire, EX82 7YK.

B: Proprietorship register

This register specifies the class of title and identifies the owner. It contains any entries that affect the right of disposal.

Title absolute

1. (29.03.27) Proprietor(s): Gemma's Gels Ltd of First Floor, 17 High Street, Barnford, Westshire, EX82 7YK.

2. (28.10.26) Short particulars of the leases under which the land is held:

Date:	21 September 2026
Term:	10 years
Rent:	as therein mentioned
Parties	(1) Style&Go Ltd
	(2) Polished Perfection Ltd

C: Charges register

This register contains any charges and other matters that affect the land.

1. (28.10.2026) A conveyance of the land in this title dated 10 July 1993 made between (1) Charles Bainbridge (Vendor) and (2) Ansar Mukhtar and Anita Mukhtar (Purchaser) contains the following covenant:

   "11.1 And the Purchaser for itself and its assigns with the intent to bind the Property hereby covenants with the Vendor his heirs executors administrators and assigns not to build any structure on the Property."

End of register

Land Registry
Official copy of
Title plan

Title number **WX727338**
Ordnance Survey map reference **EG 4231 SS**
Scale **1:2500**
Administrative area **Westshire: Barnford**

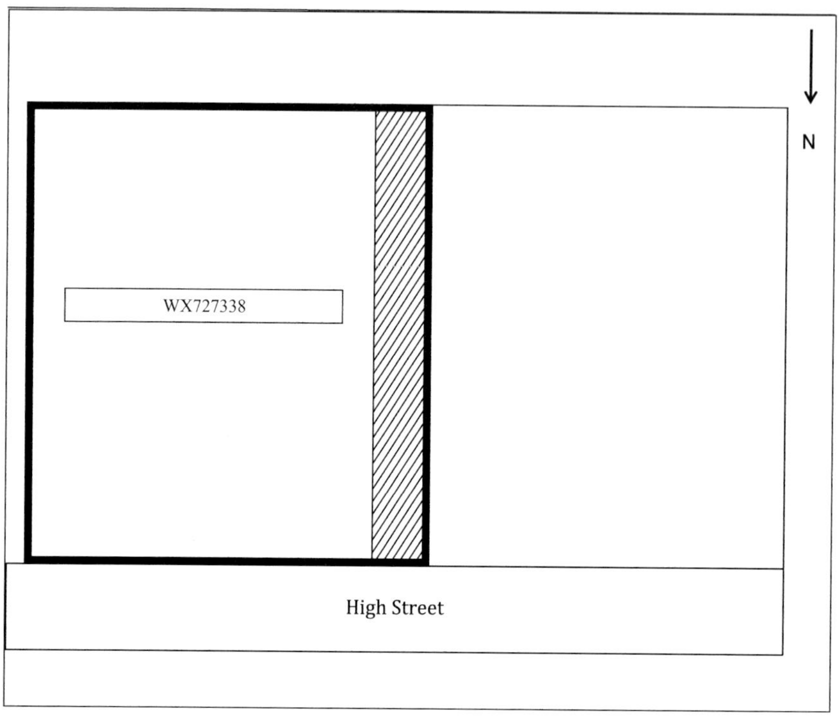

This official copy issued on 29 March 2027 shows the state of this title plan on 29 March 2027 at 13:24:57.
It is admissible in evidence to the same extent as the original (s. 67 Land Registration Act 2002).
This title plan shows the general position, not the exact line, of the boundaries. It may be subject to distortions in scale.
Measurements scaled from this plan may not match measurements between the same points on the ground.
See Land Registry Public Guide 19 – Title Plans and Boundaries.

Appendix 6: External documents

STANDARD CONDITIONS OF SALE (FIFTH EDITION)
(NATIONAL CONDITIONS OF SALE 25TH EDITION, LAW SOCIETY'S CONDITIONS OF SALE 2011)

1. GENERAL

1.1 **Definitions**

1.1.1 In these conditions:

(a) 'accrued interest' means:

(i) if money has been placed on deposit or in a building society share account, the interest actually earned

(ii) otherwise, the interest which might reasonably have been earned by depositing the money at interest on seven days' notice of withdrawal with a clearing bank

less, in either case, any proper charges for handling the money

(b) 'clearing bank' means a bank which is a shareholder in CHAPS Clearing Co. Limited

(c) 'completion date' has the meaning given in condition 6.1.1

(d) 'contents price' means any separate amount payable for contents included in the contract

(e) 'contract rate' means the Law Society's interest rate from time to time in force

(f) 'conveyancer' means a solicitor, barrister, duly certified notary public, licensed conveyancer or recognised body under sections 9 or 23 of the Administration of Justice Act 1985

(g) 'lease' includes sub-lease, tenancy and agreement for a lease or sub-lease

(h) 'mortgage' means a mortgage or charge securing the repayment of money

(i) 'notice to complete' means a notice requiring completion of the contract in accordance with condition 6

(j) 'public requirement' means any notice, order or proposal given or made (whether before or after the date of the contract) by a body acting on statutory authority

(k) 'requisition' includes objection

(l) 'transfer' includes conveyance and assignment

(m) 'working day' means any day from Monday to Friday (inclusive) which is not Christmas Day, Good Friday or a statutory Bank Holiday.

1.1.2 In these conditions the terms 'absolute title' and 'official copies' have the special meanings given to them by the Land Registration Act 2002.

1.1.3 A party is ready, able and willing to complete:

(a) if he could be, but for the default of the other party, and

(b) in the case of the seller, even though the property remains subject to a mortgage, if the amount to be paid on completion enables the property to be transferred freed of all mortgages (except any to which the sale is expressly subject).

1.1.4 These conditions apply except as varied or excluded by the contract.

1.2 **Joint parties**

If there is more than one seller or more than one buyer, the obligations which they undertake can be enforced against them all jointly or against each individually.

1.3 **Notices and documents**

1.3.1 A notice required or authorised by the contract must be in writing.

1.3.2 Giving a notice or delivering a document to a party's conveyancer has the same effect as giving or delivering it to that party.

1.3.3 Where delivery of the original document is not essential, a notice or document is validly given or sent if it is sent:

(a) by fax, or

(b) by e-mail to an e-mail address for the intended recipient given in the contract.

1.3.4 Subject to conditions 1.3.5 to 1.3.7, a notice is given and a document is delivered when it is received.

1.3.5 (a) A notice or document sent through a document exchange is received when it is available for collection.

(b) A notice or document which is received after 4.00pm on a working day, or on a day which is not a working day, is to be treated as having been received on the next working day.

(c) An automated response to a notice or document sent by e-mail that the intended recipient is out of the office is to be treated as proof that the notice or document was not received.

1.3.6 Condition 1.3.7 applies unless there is proof:

(a) that a notice or document has not been received, or

(b) of when it was received.

1.3.7 A notice or document sent by the following means is treated as having been received as follows:

(a) by first-class post:	before 4.00pm on the second working day after posting
(b) by second-class post:	before 4.00pm on the third working day after posting
(c) through a document exchange:	before 4.00pm on the first working day after the day on which it would normally be available for collection by the addressee
(d) by fax:	one hour after despatch
(e) by e-mail:	before 4.00pm on the first working day after despatch.

1.4 VAT

1.4.1 The purchase price and the contents price are inclusive of any value added tax.

1.4.2 All other sums made payable by the contract are exclusive of any value added tax and where a supply is made which is chargeable to value added tax, the recipient of the supply is to pay the supplier (in addition to any other amounts payable under the contract) a sum equal to the value added tax chargeable on that supply.

1.5 **Assignment and sub-sales**

1.5.1 The buyer is not entitled to transfer the benefit of the contract.

1.5.2 The seller cannot be required to transfer the property in parts or to any person other than the buyer.

1.6 **Third party rights**

Unless otherwise expressly stated nothing in this contract will create rights pursuant to the Contracts (Rights of Third Parties) Act 1999 in favour of anyone other than the parties to the contract.

2. FORMATION

2.1 **Date**

2.1.1 If the parties intend to make a contract by exchanging duplicate copies by post or through a document exchange, the contract is made when the last copy is posted or deposited at the document exchange.

2.1.2 If the parties' conveyancers agree to treat exchange as taking place before duplicate copies are actually exchanged, the contract is made as so agreed.

2.2 **Deposit**

2.2.1 The buyer is to pay or send a deposit of 10 per cent of the purchase price no later than the date of the contract.

2.2.2 If a cheque tendered in payment of all or part of the deposit is dishonoured when first presented, the seller may, within seven working days of being notified that the cheque has been dishonoured, give notice to the buyer that the contract is discharged by the buyer's breach.

2.2.3 Conditions 2.2.4 to 2.2.6 do not apply on a sale by auction.

2.2.4 The deposit is to be paid:

(a) by electronic means from an account held in the name of a conveyancer at a clearing bank to an account in the name of the seller's conveyancer or (in a case where condition 2.2.5 applies) a conveyancer nominated by him and maintained at a clearing bank,

or

(b) to the seller's conveyancer or (in a case where condition 2.2.5 applies) a conveyancer nominated by him by cheque drawn on a solicitor's or licensed conveyancer's client account.

2.2.5 If before completion date the seller agrees to buy another property in England and Wales for his residence, he may use all or any part of the deposit as a deposit in that transaction to be held on terms to the same effect as this condition and condition 2.2.6.

2.2.6 Any deposit or part of a deposit not being used in accordance with condition 2.2.5 is to be held by the seller's conveyancer as stakeholder on terms that on completion it is paid to the seller with accrued interest.

2.3 **Auctions**

2.3.1 On a sale by auction the following conditions apply to the property and, if it is sold in lots, to each lot.

2.3.2 The sale is subject to a reserve price.

2.3.3 The seller, or a person on his behalf, may bid up to the reserve price.

2.3.4 The auctioneer may refuse any bid.

2.3.5 If there is a dispute about a bid, the auctioneer may resolve the dispute or restart the auction at the last undisputed bid.

2.3.6 The deposit is to be paid to the auctioneer as agent for the seller.

3. MATTERS AFFECTING THE PROPERTY

3.1 **Freedom from incumbrances**

3.1.1 The seller is selling the property free from incumbrances, other than those mentioned in condition 3.1.2.

3.1.2 The incumbrances subject to which the property is sold are:

(a) those specified in the contract

(b) those discoverable by inspection of the property before the date of the contract

(c) those the seller does not and could not reasonably know about

(d) those, other than mortgages, which the buyer knows about

(e) entries made before the date of the contract in any public register except those maintained by the Land Registry or its Land Charges Department or by Companies House

(f) public requirements.

3.1.3 After the contract is made, the seller is to give the buyer written details without delay of any new public requirement and of anything in writing which he learns about concerning a matter covered by condition 3.1.2.

3.1.4 The buyer is to bear the cost of complying with any outstanding public requirement and is to indemnify the seller against any liability resulting from a public requirement.

3.2 **Physical state**

3.2.1 The buyer accepts the property in the physical state it is in at the date of the contract unless the seller is building or converting it.

3.2.2 A leasehold property is sold subject to any subsisting breach of a condition or tenant's obligation relating to the physical state of the property which renders the lease liable to forfeiture.

3.2.3 A sub-lease is granted subject to any subsisting breach of a condition or tenant's obligation relating to the physical state of the property which renders the seller's own lease liable to forfeiture.

3.3 **Leases affecting the property**

3.3.1 The following provisions apply if any part of the property is sold subject to a lease.

3.3.2 (a) The seller having provided the buyer with full details of each lease or copies of the documents embodying the lease terms, the buyer is treated as entering into the contract knowing and fully accepting those terms.

(b) The seller is to inform the buyer without delay if the lease ends or if the seller learns of any application by the tenant in connection with the lease; the seller is then to act as the buyer reasonably directs, and the buyer is to indemnify him against all consequent loss and expense.

(c) Except with the buyer's consent, the seller is not to agree to any proposal to change the lease terms nor to take any step to end the lease.

(d) The seller is to inform the buyer without delay of any change to the lease terms which may be proposed or agreed.

(e) The buyer is to indemnify the seller against all claims arising from the lease after actual completion; this includes claims which are unenforceable against a buyer for want of registration.

(f) The seller takes no responsibility for what rent is lawfully recoverable, nor for whether or how any legislation affects the lease.

(g) If the let land is not wholly within the property, the seller may apportion the rent.

4. TITLE AND TRANSFER

4.1 **Proof of title**

4.1.1 Without cost to the buyer, the seller is to provide the buyer with proof of the title to the property and of his ability to transfer it, or to procure its transfer.

4.1.2 Where the property has a registered title the proof is to include official copies of the items referred to in rules 134(1)(a) and (b) and 135(1)(a) of the Land Registration Rules 2003, so far as they are not to be discharged or overridden at or before completion.

4.1.3 Where the property has an unregistered title, the proof is to include:

(a) an abstract of title or an epitome of title with photocopies of the documents, and

(b) production of every document or an abstract, epitome or copy of it with an original marking by a conveyancer either against the original or an examined abstract or an examined copy.

4.2 **Requisitions**

4.2.1 The buyer may not raise requisitions:

(a) on any title shown by the seller before the contract was made

(b) in relation to the matters covered by condition 3.1.2.

4.2.2 Notwithstanding condition 4.2.1, the buyer may, within six working days of a matter coming to his attention after the contract was made, raise written requisitions on that matter. In that event, steps 3 and 4 in condition 4.3.1 apply.

4.2.3 On the expiry of the relevant time limit under condition 4.2.2 or condition 4.3.1, the buyer loses his right to raise requisitions or to make observations.

4.3 **Timetable**

4.3.1 Subject to condition 4.2 and to the extent that the seller did not take the steps described in condition 4.1.1 before the contract was made, the following are the steps for deducing and investigating the title to the property to be taken within the following time limits:

Step	Time Limit
1. The seller is to comply with condition 4.1.1	Immediately after making the contract
2. The buyer may raise written requisitions	Six working days after either the date of the contract or the date of delivery of the seller's evidence of title on which the requisitions are raised, whichever is the later
3. The seller is to reply in writing to any requisitions raised	Four working days after receiving the requisitions
4. The buyer may make written observations on the seller's replies	Three working days after receiving the replies

The time limit on the buyer's right to raise requisitions applies even where the seller supplies incomplete evidence of his title, but the buyer may, within six working days from delivery of any further evidence, raise further requisitions resulting from that evidence.

4.3.2 The parties are to take the following steps to prepare and agree the transfer of the property within the following time limits:

Step	Time Limit
A. The buyer is to send the seller a draft transfer	At least twelve working days before completion date
B. The seller is to approve or revise that draft and either return it or retain it for use as the actual transfer	Four working days after delivery of the draft transfer
C. If the draft is returned the buyer is to send an engrossment to the seller	At least five working days before completion date

4.3.3 Periods of time under conditions 4.3.1 and 4.3.2 may run concurrently.

4.3.4 If the period between the date of the contract and completion date is less than 15 working days, the time limits in conditions 4.2.2, 4.3.1 and 4.3.2 are to be reduced by the same proportion as that period bears to the period of 15 working days. Fractions of a working day are to be rounded down except that the time limit to perform any step is not to be less than one working day.

4.4 **Defining the property**

The seller need not:

(a) prove the exact boundaries of the property

(b) prove who owns fences, ditches, hedges or walls

(c) separately identify parts of the property with different titles further than he may be able to do from information in his possession.

4.5 **Rents and rentcharges**

The fact that a rent or rentcharge, whether payable or receivable by the owner of the property, has been, or will on completion be, informally apportioned is not to be regarded as a defect in title.

4.6 **Transfer**

4.6.1 The buyer does not prejudice his right to raise requisitions, or to require replies to any raised, by taking any steps in relation to preparing or agreeing the transfer.

4.6.2 Subject to condition 4.6.3, the seller is to transfer the property with full title guarantee.

4.6.3 The transfer is to have effect as if the disposition is expressly made subject to all matters covered by condition 3.1.2 and, if the property is leasehold, is to contain a statement that the covenants set out in section 4 of the Law of Property (Miscellaneous Provisions) Act 1994 will not extend to any breach of the tenant's covenants in the lease relating to the physical state of the property.

4.6.4 If after completion the seller will remain bound by any obligation affecting the property which was disclosed to the buyer before the contract was made, but the law does not imply any covenant by the buyer to indemnify the seller against liability for future breaches of it:
(a) the buyer is to covenant in the transfer to indemnify the seller against liability for any future breach of the obligation and to perform it from then on, and
(b) if required by the seller, the buyer is to execute and deliver to the seller on completion a duplicate transfer prepared by the buyer.

4.6.5 The seller is to arrange at his expense that, in relation to every document of title which the buyer does not receive on completion, the buyer is to have the benefit of:
(a) a written acknowledgement of his right to its production, and
(b) a written undertaking for its safe custody (except while it is held by a mortgagee or by someone in a fiduciary capacity).

4.7 **Membership of company**
Where the seller is, or is required to be, a member of a company that has an interest in the property or has management responsibilities for the property or the surrounding areas, the seller is, without cost to the buyer, to provide such documents on completion as will enable the buyer to become a member of that company.

5. RISK, INSURANCE AND OCCUPATION PENDING COMPLETION
5.1.1 The property is at the risk of the buyer from the date of the contract.
5.1.2 The seller is under no obligation to the buyer to insure the property unless:
(a) the contract provides that a policy effected by or for the seller and insuring the property or any part of it against liability for loss or damage is to continue in force, or
(b) the property or any part of it is let on terms under which the seller (whether as landlord or as tenant) is obliged to insure against loss or damage.
5.1.3 If the seller is obliged to insure the property under condition 5.1.2, the seller is to:
(a) do everything necessary to maintain the policy
(b) permit the buyer to inspect the policy or evidence of its terms
(c) if before completion the property suffers loss or damage:
(i) pay to the buyer on completion the amount of the policy monies which the seller has received, so far as not applied in repairing or reinstating the property, and
(ii) if no final payment has then been received, assign to the buyer, at the buyer's expense, all rights to claim under the policy in such form as the buyer reasonably requires and pending execution of the assignment hold any policy monies received in trust for the buyer
(d) cancel the policy on completion.
5.1.4 Where the property is leasehold and the property, or any building containing it, is insured by a reversioner or other third party, the seller is to use reasonable efforts to ensure that the insurance is maintained until completion and if, before completion, the property or building suffers loss or damage the seller is to assign to the buyer on completion, at the buyer's expense, such rights as the seller may have in the policy monies, in such form as the buyer reasonably requires.
5.1.5 If payment under a policy effected by or for the buyer is reduced, because the property is covered against loss or damage by an insurance policy effected by or on behalf of the seller, then, unless the seller is obliged to insure the property under condition 5.1.2, the purchase price is to be abated by the amount of that reduction.
5.1.6 Section 47 of the Law of Property Act 1925 does not apply.

5.2 **Occupation by buyer**
5.2.1 If the buyer is not already lawfully in the property, and the seller agrees to let him into occupation, the buyer occupies on the following terms.
5.2.2 The buyer is a licensee and not a tenant. The terms of the licence are that the buyer:
(a) cannot transfer it
(b) may permit members of his household to occupy the property
(c) is to pay or indemnify the seller against all outgoings and other expenses in respect of the property
(d) is to pay the seller a fee calculated at the contract rate on a sum equal to the purchase price (less any deposit paid) for the period of the licence
(e) is entitled to any rents and profits from any part of the property which he does not occupy
(f) is to keep the property in as good a state of repair as it was in when he went into occupation (except for fair wear and tear) and is not to alter it
(g) if the property is leasehold, is not to do anything which puts the seller in breach of his obligations in the lease,
and
(h) is to quit the property when the licence ends.
5.2.3 The buyer is not in occupation for the purposes of this condition if he merely exercises rights of access given solely to do work agreed by the seller.
5.2.4 The buyer's licence ends on the earliest of: completion date, rescission of the contract or when five working days' notice given by one party to the other takes effect.
5.2.5 If the buyer is in occupation of the property after his licence has come to an end and the contract is subsequently completed he is to pay the seller compensation for his continued occupation calculated at the same rate as the fee mentioned in condition 5.2.2(d).
5.2.6 The buyer's right to raise requisitions is unaffected.

6. COMPLETION
6.1 **Date**
6.1.1 Completion date is twenty working days after the date of the contract but time is not of the essence of the contract unless a notice to complete has been served.
6.1.2 If the money due on completion is received after 2.00pm, completion is to be treated, for the purposes only of conditions 6.3 and 7.2, as taking place on the next working day as a result of the buyer's default.
6.1.3 Condition 6.1.2 does not apply and the seller is treated as in default if:
(a) the sale is with vacant possession of the property or any part of it, and
(b) the buyer is ready, able and willing to complete but does not pay the money due on completion until after 2.00 pm because the seller has not vacated the property or that part by that time.

6.2 **Arrangements and place**
6.2.1 The buyer's conveyancer and the seller's conveyancer are to co-operate in agreeing arrangements for completing the contract.
6.2.2 Completion is to take place in England and Wales, either at the seller's conveyancer's office or at some other place which the seller reasonably specifies.

6.3 **Apportionments**
6.3.1 On evidence of proper payment being made, income and outgoings of the property are to be apportioned between the parties so far as the change of ownership on completion will affect entitlement to receive or liability to pay them.
6.3.2 If the whole property is sold with vacant possession or the seller exercises his option in condition 7.2.4, apportionment is to be made with effect from the date of actual completion; otherwise, it is to be made from completion date.
6.3.3 In apportioning any sum, it is to be assumed that the seller owns the property until the end of the day from which apportionment is made and that the sum accrues from day to day at the rate at which it is payable on that day.
6.3.4 For the purpose of apportioning income and outgoings, it is to be assumed that they accrue at an equal daily rate throughout the year.
6.3.5 When a sum to be apportioned is not known or easily ascertainable at completion, a provisional apportionment is to be made according to the best estimate available. As soon as the amount is known, a final apportionment is to be made and notified to the other party. Any resulting balance is to be paid no more than ten working days later, and if not then paid the balance is to bear interest at the contract rate from then until payment.
6.3.6 Compensation payable under condition 5.2.5 is not to be apportioned.

6.4 **Amount payable**
The amount payable by the buyer on completion is the purchase price and the contents price (less any deposit already paid to the seller or his agent) adjusted to take account of:
(a) apportionments made under condition 6.3
(b) any compensation to be paid or allowed under condition 7.2
(c) any sum payable under condition 5.1.3.

6.5 **Title deeds**
6.5.1 As soon as the buyer has complied with all his obligations under this contract on completion the seller must hand over the documents of title.
6.5.2 Condition 6.5.1 does not apply to any documents of title relating to land being retained by the seller after completion.

6.6 **Rent receipts**
The buyer is to assume that whoever gave any receipt for a payment of rent or service charge which the seller produces was the person or the agent of the person then entitled to that rent or service charge.

6.7 **Means of payment**
The buyer is to pay the money due on completion by a direct transfer of cleared funds from an account held in the name of a conveyancer at a clearing bank and, if appropriate, an unconditional release of a deposit held by a stakeholder.

6.8 **Notice to complete**
6.8.1 At any time after the time applicable under condition 6.1.2 on completion date, a party who is ready, able and willing to complete may give the other a notice to complete.
6.8.2 The parties are to complete the contract within ten working days of giving a notice to complete, excluding the day on which the notice is given. For this purpose, time is of the essence of the contract.
6.8.3 On receipt of a notice to complete:
(a) if the buyer paid no deposit, he is forthwith to pay a deposit of 10 per cent
(b) if the buyer paid a deposit of less than 10 per cent, he is forthwith to pay a further deposit equal to the balance of that 10 per cent.

7. REMEDIES
7.1 **Errors and omissions**
7.1.1 If any plan or statement in the contract, or in the negotiations leading to it, is or was misleading or inaccurate due to an error or omission by the seller, the remedies available to the buyer are as follows.
(a) When there is a material difference between the description or value of the property, or of any of the contents included in the contract, as represented and as it is, the buyer is entitled to damages.
(b) An error or omission only entitles the buyer to rescind the contract:
(i) where it results from fraud or recklessness, or
(ii) where he would be obliged, to his prejudice, to accept property differing substantially (in quantity, quality or tenure) from what the error or omission had led him to expect.
7.1.2 If either party rescinds the contract:
(a) unless the rescission is a result of the buyer's breach of contract the deposit is to be repaid to the buyer with accrued interest
(b) the buyer is to return any documents he received from the seller and is to cancel any registration of the contract.

7.2 **Late completion**
7.2.1 If there is default by either or both of the parties in performing their obligations under the contract and completion is delayed, the party whose total period of default is the greater is to pay compensation to the other party.
7.2.2 Compensation is calculated at the contract rate on an amount equal to the purchase price, less (where the buyer is the paying party) any deposit paid, for the period by which the paying party's default exceeds that of the receiving party, or, if shorter, the period between completion date and actual completion.
7.2.3 Any claim for loss resulting from delayed completion is to be reduced by any compensation paid under this contract.
7.2.4 Where the buyer holds the property as tenant of the seller and completion is delayed, the seller may give notice to the buyer, before the date of actual completion, that he intends to take the net income from the property until completion. If he does so, he cannot claim compensation under condition 7.2.1 as well.

7.3 **After completion**
Completion does not cancel liability to perform any outstanding obligation under this contract.

7.4 **Buyer's failure to comply with notice to complete**
7.4.1 If the buyer fails to complete in accordance with a notice to complete, the following terms apply.
7.4.2 The seller may rescind the contract, and if he does so:
(a) he may:
(i) forfeit and keep any deposit and accrued interest
(ii) resell the property and any contents included in the contract
(iii) claim damages
(b) the buyer is to return any documents he received from the seller and is to cancel any registration of the contract.
7.4.3 The seller retains his other rights and remedies.

7.5 **Seller's failure to comply with notice to complete**
7.5.1 If the seller fails to complete in accordance with a notice to complete, the following terms apply.
7.5.2 The buyer may rescind the contract, and if he does so:
(a) the deposit is to be repaid to the buyer with accrued interest
(b) the buyer is to return any documents he received from the seller and is, at the seller's expense, to cancel any registration of the contract.
7.5.3 The buyer retains his other rights and remedies.

8. LEASEHOLD PROPERTY
8.1 **Existing leases**
8.1.1 The following provisions apply to a sale of leasehold land.
8.1.2 The seller having provided the buyer with copies of the documents embodying the lease terms, the buyer is treated as entering into the contract knowing and fully accepting those terms.

8.2 **New leases**
8.2.1 The following provisions apply to a contract to grant a new lease.
8.2.2 The conditions apply so that:
'seller' means the proposed landlord
'buyer' means the proposed tenant
'purchase price' means the premium to be paid on the grant of a lease.
8.2.3 The lease is to be in the form of the draft attached to the contract.
8.2.4 If the term of the new lease will exceed seven years, the seller is to deduce a title which will enable the buyer to register the lease at the Land Registry with an absolute title.
8.2.5 The seller is to engross the lease and a counterpart of it and is to send the counterpart to the buyer at least five working days before completion date.
8.2.6 The buyer is to execute the counterpart and deliver it to the seller on completion.

8.3 **Consent**
8.3.1 (a) The following provisions apply if a consent to let, assign or sub-let is required to complete the contract.
(b) In this condition 'consent' means consent in the form which satisfies the requirement to obtain it.
8.3.2 (a) The seller is to apply for the consent at his expense, and to use all reasonable efforts to obtain it.
(b) The buyer is to provide all information and references reasonably required.
8.3.3 Unless he is in breach of his obligation under condition 8.3.2, either party may rescind the contract by notice to the other party if three working days before completion date (or before a later date on which the parties have agreed to complete the contract):
(a) the consent has not been given, or
(b) the consent has been given subject to a condition to which a party reasonably objects. In that case, neither party is to be treated as in breach of contract and condition 7.1.2 applies.

9. CONTENTS
9.1 The following provisions apply to any contents which are included in the contract, whether or not a separate price is to be paid for them.
9.2 The contract takes effect as a contract for sale of goods.
9.3 The buyer takes the contents in the physical state they are in at the date of the contract.
9.4 Ownership of the contents passes to the buyer on actual completion.

STANDARD COMMERCIAL PROPERTY CONDITIONS (THIRD EDITION - 2018 REVISION)

PART 1

1. GENERAL

1.1 Definitions

1.1.1 In these conditions:

(a) "accrued interest" means:

(i) if money has been placed on deposit or in a building society share account, the interest actually earned

(ii) otherwise, the interest which might reasonably have been earned by depositing the money at interest on seven days' notice of withdrawal with a clearing bank

less, in either case, any proper charges for handling the money

(b) "apportionment day" has the meaning given in condition 9.3.2

(c) "clearing bank" means a bank admitted by the Bank of England as a direct participant in its CHAPS system

(d) "completion date" has the meaning given in condition 9.1.1

(e) "contract rate" means the Law Society's interest rate from time to time in force

(f) "conveyancer" has the meaning given by rule 217A of the Land Registration Rules 2003

(g) "lease" includes sub-lease, tenancy and agreement for a lease or sub-lease

(h) "mortgage" means a mortgage or charge securing the performance of any obligation (whether or not for the payment of money)

(i) "notice to complete" means a notice requiring completion of the contract in accordance with condition 9.8

(j) "option to tax" means an option to tax any land having effect under Part 1 of Schedule 10 to the Value Added Tax Act 1994 and references to exercising the option to tax include electing to waive exemption under previous legislation and option in this context includes such an election

(k) "post" includes postal services provided by a postal operator and "postal services" has the meaning given to it by section 27(1)(a) and (c) of the Postal Services Act 2011 and "postal operator" has the meaning given by section 27(3) and (4) of that Act

(l) "public requirement" means any notice, order or proposal given or made (whether before or after the date of the contract) by a body acting on statutory authority

(m) "requisition" includes objection

(n) "transfer" includes conveyance and assignment

(o) "VAT" means value added tax

(p) "working day" means any day from Monday to Friday (inclusive) which is not Christmas Day, Good Friday or a statutory Bank Holiday.

1.1.2 In these conditions the terms "absolute title" and "official copies" have the special meanings given to them by the Land Registration Act 2002.

1.1.3 A party is ready, able and willing to complete:

(a) if it would be, but for the default of the other party, and

(b) in the case of the seller, even though the property remains subject to a mortgage, if the amount to be paid on completion enables the property to be transferred freed of all mortgages (except those to which the sale is expressly subject).

1.1.4 (a) The conditions in Part 1 apply subject to any variations or exclusions in the contract.

(b) A condition in Part 2 only applies if expressly incorporated into the contract.

1.2 Joint parties

If there is more than one seller or more than one buyer, the obligations which they undertake can be enforced against them all jointly or against each individually.

1.3 Notices and documents

1.3.1 A notice required or authorised by the contract is to be in writing.

1.3.2 Giving a notice or delivering a document to a party's conveyancer has the same effect as giving or delivering it to that party.

1.3.3 Where delivery of the original document is not essential, a notice or document is validly given or sent if it is sent by:

(a) fax to a fax number for the intended recipient expressly given in the contract for that purpose, or

(b) e-mail to an e-mail address for the intended recipient expressly given in the contract for that purpose.

1.3.4 Subject to conditions 1.3.5 to 1.3.7, a notice is given and a document delivered when it is received.

1.3.5 (a) A notice or document sent through the document exchange is received when it is available for collection.

(b) A notice or document which is received after 4.00 p.m. on a working day, or on a day which is not a working day, is to be treated as having been received on the next working day.

(c) An automated response to a notice or document sent by e-mail that the intended recipient is out of the office is to be treated as proof that the notice or document was not received.

1.3.6 Condition 1.3.7 applies unless there is proof:

(a) that a notice or document has not been received, or

(b) of the actual time of receipt.

1.3.7 A notice or document sent by the following means is treated as having been received as follows:

(a) by first class post:	before 4.00 pm on the second working day after posting
(b) by second class post:	before 4.00 pm on the third working day after posting
(c) through a document exchange:	before 4.00 pm on the first working day after the day on which it would normally be available for collection by the addressee
(d) by fax:	one hour after despatch
(e) by e-mail:	one hour after despatch

1.3.8 In condition 1.3.7, "first class post" means a postal service which seeks to deliver posted items no later than the next working day in all or the majority of cases.

1.4 Assignment and sub-sales

1.4.1 The buyer is not entitled to transfer the benefit of the contract.

1.4.2 The seller cannot be required to transfer the property in parts or to any person other than the buyer.

1.5 Third party rights

Nothing in this contract creates rights under the Contracts (Rights of Third Parties) Act 1999 intended to be enforceable by third parties.

2. VAT STANDARD RATED SUPPLY

2.1 The seller warrants that the sale of the property will constitute a supply chargeable to VAT at the standard rate.

2.2 The buyer is to pay to the seller on completion an additional amount equal to the VAT in exchange for a VAT invoice from the seller.

3. FORMATION

3.1 Date

3.1.1 If the parties intend to make a contract by exchanging duplicate copies by post or through a document exchange, the contract is made when the last copy is posted or deposited at the document exchange.

3.1.2 If the parties' conveyancers agree to treat exchange as taking place before duplicate copies are actually exchanged, the contract is made as so agreed.

3.2 Deposit

3.2.1 Unless otherwise agreed, the buyer is to pay a deposit of 10 per cent of the purchase price no later than the date of the contract. Where the agreed deposit is less than 10 per cent of the purchase price, condition 9.8.3 applies.

3.2.2 Except on a sale by auction the deposit is to be paid by electronic means from an account held in the name of a conveyancer at a clearing bank to an account in the name of the seller's conveyancer and is to be held by the seller's conveyancer as stakeholder on terms that on completion it is to be paid to the seller with accrued interest.

3.3 Auctions

3.3.1 On a sale by auction the following conditions apply to the property and, if it is sold in lots, to each lot.

3.3.2 The sale is subject to a reserve price.

3.3.3 The seller, or a person on its behalf, may bid up to the reserve price.

3.3.4 The auctioneer may refuse any bid.

3.3.5 If there is a dispute about a bid, the auctioneer may resolve the dispute or restart the auction at the last undisputed bid.

3.3.6 The auctioneer is to hold the deposit as agent for the seller.

3.3.7 If any cheque tendered in payment of all or part of the deposit is dishonoured when first presented, the seller may, within seven working days of being notified that the cheque has been dishonoured, give notice to the buyer that the contract is discharged by the buyer's breach.

4. MATTERS AFFECTING THE PROPERTY

4.1 Freedom from incumbrances

4.1.1 The seller is selling the property free from incumbrances, other than those mentioned in condition 4.1.2.

4.1.2 The incumbrances subject to which the property is sold are:

(a) those specified in the contract

(b) those discoverable by inspection of the property before the date of the contract

(c) those the seller does not and could not reasonably know about

(d) matters, other than mortgages, disclosed or which would have been disclosed by the searches and enquiries which a prudent buyer would have made before entering into the contract

(e) public requirements.

4.1.3 After the contract is made, the seller is to give the buyer written details without delay of any new public requirement and of anything in writing which it learns about concerning a matter covered by condition 4.1.2.

4.1.4 The buyer is to bear the cost of complying with any outstanding public requirement and is to indemnify the seller against any liability resulting from a public requirement.

4.2 Physical state

4.2.1 The buyer accepts the property in the physical state it is in at the date of the contract unless the seller is building or converting it.

4.2.2 A leasehold property is sold subject to any subsisting breach of a condition or tenant's obligation relating to the physical state of the property which renders the lease liable to forfeiture.

4.2.3 A sub-lease is granted subject to any subsisting breach of a condition or tenant's obligation relating to the physical state of the property which renders the seller's own lease liable to forfeiture.

5. LEASES AFFECTING THE PROPERTY

5.1 General

5.1.1 This condition applies if any part of the property is sold subject to a lease.

5.1.2 The seller having provided the buyer with full details of each lease or copies of documents embodying the lease terms, the buyer is treated as entering into the contract knowing and fully accepting those terms.

5.1.3 The seller is not to serve a notice to end the lease nor to accept a surrender.

5.1.4 The seller is to inform the buyer without delay if the lease ends.

5.1.5 The buyer is to indemnify the seller against all claims arising from the lease after actual completion; this includes claims which are unenforceable against a buyer for want of registration.

5.1.6 If the property does not include all the land let, the seller may apportion the rent and, if the lease is a new tenancy, the buyer may require the seller to apply under section 10 of the Landlord and Tenant (Covenants) Act 1995 for the apportionment to bind the tenant.

5.2 Property management

5.2.1 The seller is promptly to give the buyer full particulars of:

(a) any court or arbitration proceedings in connection with the lease, and

(b) any application for a licence, consent or approval under the lease.

5.2.2 Conditions 5.2.3 to 5.2.8 do not apply to a rent review process to which condition 6.1 applies or any negotiations or proceedings to which condition 6.2 applies.

5.2.3 Subject to condition 5.2.4, the seller is to conduct the proceedings in accordance with written directions given by the buyer from time to time (for which the seller is to apply), unless to do so might place the seller in breach of an obligation to the tenant or a statutory duty.

5.2.4 If the seller applies for directions from the buyer in relation to a proposed step in the proceedings and the buyer does not give such directions within 10 working days, the seller may take or refrain from taking that step as it thinks fit.

5.2.5 The buyer is to indemnify the seller against all loss and expense resulting from the seller's conduct of the proceedings in accordance with the buyer's directions.

5.2.6 Unless the buyer gives written consent, the seller is not to:
(a) grant or formally withhold any licence, consent or approval under the lease, or
(b) serve any notice or take any action (other than action in court or arbitration proceedings) as landlord under the lease.

5.2.7 When the seller applies for the buyer's consent under condition 5.2.6:
(a) the buyer is not to withhold its consent or attach conditions to the consent where to do so might place the seller in breach of an obligation to the tenant or a statutory duty
(b) the seller may proceed as if the buyer has consented when:
(i) in accordance with paragraph (a), the buyer is not entitled to withhold its consent, or
(ii) the buyer does not refuse its consent within 10 working days.

5.2.8 If the buyer withholds or attaches conditions to its consent, the buyer is to indemnify the seller against all loss and expense resulting from such withholding or attachment of conditions.

5.2.9 In all other respects, the seller is to manage the property in accordance with the principles of good estate management until completion.

5.3 **Continuing liability**
At the request and cost of the seller, the buyer is to support any application by the seller to be released from the landlord covenants in a lease to which the property is sold subject.

6. RENT REVIEWS AND PENDING LEASE RENEWALS

6.1 **Rent reviews**

6.1.1 Subject to condition 6.1.3, this condition 6.1 applies if:
(a) the rent reserved by a lease of all or part of the property is to be reviewed
(b) the seller is either the landlord or the tenant
(c) the rent review process starts before actual completion, and
(d) no reviewed rent has been agreed or determined at the date of the contract.

6.1.2 The seller is to conduct the rent review process until actual completion, after which the buyer is to conduct it.

6.1.3 Conditions 6.1.4 and 6.1.5 cease to apply on actual completion if the reviewed rent will only be payable in respect of a period after that date or if the rent review date precedes the completion date by more than two years.

6.1.4 In the course of the rent review process, the seller and the buyer are each to:
(a) act promptly with a view to achieving the best result obtainable
(b) consult with and have regard to the views of the other
(c) provide the other with copies of all material correspondence and papers
(d) ensure that its representations take account of matters put forward by the other, and
(e) keep the other informed of progress.

6.1.5 Neither the seller nor the buyer is to agree a rent figure unless it has been approved in writing by the other (such approval not to be unreasonably withheld).

6.1.6 The seller and the buyer are each to bear their own costs of the rent review process.

6.1.7 Unless the rent review date precedes the apportionment day, the buyer is to pay the costs of a third party appointed to determine the rent.

6.1.8 Where the rent review date precedes the apportionment day, those costs are to be divided as follows:
(a) the seller is to pay the proportion that the number of days from the rent review date to the apportionment day bears to the number of days from that rent review date until either the following rent review date or, if none, the expiry of the term, and
(b) the buyer is to pay the balance.

6.2 **Pending lease renewals**

6.2.1 This condition 6.2 applies if:
(a) the tenancy created by a lease of all or part of the property is continuing under Part II of the Landlord and Tenant Act 1954 at the date of the contract or at actual completion
(b) the seller is the competent landlord, and
(c) any of the following have been neither agreed nor determined at the date of the contract: an interim rent, the termination of the tenancy or the terms of a new tenancy.

6.2.2 Until actual completion the seller is to conduct any negotiations or proceedings relating to the matters mentioned in condition 6.2.1(c), after which the buyer is to conduct those negotiations or proceedings and is to apply without delay to be substituted for the seller as a party in any such proceedings.

6.2.3 In the course of those negotiations or proceedings, the buyer and the seller are each to act as described in condition 6.1.4(a) to (e).

6.2.4 Neither the seller nor the buyer is to agree an interim rent or any of the terms of the new tenancy without the written approval of the other (such approval not to be unreasonably withheld).

6.2.5 As from actual completion conditions 6.2.3 and 6.2.4 apply only to negotiations or proceedings relating to or affecting the amount of any rent (including any interim rent) payable from a date before actual completion.

6.2.6 The seller and the buyer are each to bear their own costs of the negotiations or proceedings.

7. TITLE AND TRANSFER

7.1 **Proof of title**

7.1.1 Without cost to the buyer, the seller is to provide the buyer with proof of the title to the property and of the seller's ability to transfer it or to procure its transfer.

7.1.2 Where the property has a registered title the proof is to include official copies of the items referred to in rules 134(1)(a) and (b) and 135(1)(a) of the Land Registration Rules 2003, so far as they are not to be discharged or overridden at or before completion.

7.1.3 Where the property has an unregistered title, the proof is to include:
(a) an abstract of title or an epitome of title with photocopies of the documents, and
(b) production of every document or an abstract, epitome or copy of it with an original marking by a conveyancer either against the original or an examined abstract or an examined copy.

7.2 **Requisitions**

7.2.1 The buyer may not raise requisitions:
(a) on any title shown by the seller taking the steps described in condition 7.1.1 before the contract was made
(b) in relation to the matters covered by condition 4.1.2.

7.2.2 Notwithstanding condition 7.2.1, the buyer may, within six working days of a matter coming to its attention after the contract was made, raise written requisitions on that matter. In that event steps 3 and 4 in condition 7.3.1 apply.

7.2.3 On the expiry of the relevant time limit under condition 7.2.2 or condition 7.3.1, the buyer loses its right to raise requisitions or to make observations.

7.3 **Timetable**

7.3.1 Subject to condition 7.2 and to the extent that the seller did not take the steps described in condition 7.1.1 before the contract was made, the following are the steps for deducing and investigating the title to the property to be taken within the following time limits:

Step	Time limit
1. The seller is to comply with condition 7.1.1	Immediately after making the contract
2. The buyer may raise written requisitions	Six working days after either the date of the contract or the date of delivery of the seller's evidence of title on which the requisitions are raised whichever is the later
3. The seller is to reply in writing to any requisitions raised	Four working days after receiving the requisitions
4. The buyer may make written observations on the seller's replies	Three working days after receiving the replies

The time limit on the buyer's right to raise requisitions applies even where the seller supplies incomplete evidence of its title, but the buyer may, within six working days from delivery of any further evidence, raise further requisitions resulting from that evidence.

7.3.2 The parties are to take the following steps to prepare and agree the transfer of the property within the following time limits:

Step	Time limit
A. The buyer is to send the seller a draft transfer	At least twelve working days before completion date
B. The seller is to approve or revise that draft and either return it or retain it for use as the actual transfer	Four working days after delivery of the draft transfer
C. If the draft is returned the buyer is to send an engrossment to the seller	At least five working days before completion date

7.3.3 Periods of time under conditions 7.3.1 and 7.3.2 may run concurrently.

7.3.4 If the period between the date of the contract and completion date is less than 15 working days, the time limits in conditions 7.2.2, 7.3.1 and 7.3.2 are to be reduced by the same proportion as that period bears to the period of 15 working days. Fractions of a working day are to be rounded down except that the time limit to perform any step is not to be less than one working day.

7.4 **Defining the property**

7.4.1 The seller need not:
(a) prove the exact boundaries of the property
(b) prove who owns fences, ditches, hedges or walls
(c) separately identify parts of the property with different titles further than it may be able to do from information in its possession.

7.4.2 The buyer may, if to do so is reasonable, require the seller to make or obtain, pay for and hand over a statutory declaration about facts relevant to the matters mentioned in condition 7.4.1. The form of the declaration is to be approved by the buyer (such approval not to be unreasonably withheld).

7.5 **Rents and rentcharges**
The fact that a rent or rentcharge, whether payable or receivable by the owner of the property, has been, or will on completion be, informally apportioned is not to be regarded as a defect in title.

7.6 **Transfer**

7.6.1 The buyer does not prejudice its right to raise requisitions, or to require replies to any raised, by taking steps in relation to the preparation or agreement of the transfer.

7.6.2 Subject to conditions 7.6.3 and 7.6.4, the seller is to transfer the property with full title guarantee.

7.6.3 The transfer is to have effect as if the disposition is expressly made subject to all matters covered by condition 4.1.2.

7.6.4 If the property is leasehold, the transfer is to contain a statement that the covenants set out in section 4 of the Law of Property (Miscellaneous Provisions) Act 1994 will not extend to any breach of the tenant's covenants in the lease relating to the physical state of the property.

7.6.5 If after completion the seller will remain bound by any obligation affecting the property which was disclosed to the buyer before the contract was made, but the law does not imply any covenant by the buyer to indemnify the seller against liability for future breaches of it:
(a) the buyer is to covenant in the transfer to indemnify the seller against liability for any future breach of the obligation and to perform it from then on, and
(b) if required by the seller, the buyer is to execute and deliver to the seller on completion a duplicate transfer prepared by the buyer.

7.6.6 Where the seller's title to the property is not registered at Land Registry, the seller is to arrange at its expense that, in relation to every document of title which the buyer does not receive on completion, the buyer is to have the benefit of:

(a) a written acknowledgement of the buyer's right to its production, and

(b) a written undertaking for its safe custody (except while it is held by a mortgagee or by someone in a fiduciary capacity).

8. RISK AND INSURANCE

8.1 **Risk**

The property is at the risk of the buyer from the date of the contract.

8.2 **Responsibility for insuring**

8.2.1 Conditions 8.2.2 and 8.2.3 apply if:

(a) the contract provides that the policy effected by or for the seller and insuring the property or any part of it against loss or damage is to continue in force after the exchange of contracts, or

(b) the property or any part of it is let on terms under which the seller (whether as landlord or as tenant) is obliged to insure against loss or damage.

8.2.2 The seller is to:

(a) do everything required to continue to maintain the policy, including the prompt payment of any premium which falls due

(b) increase the amount or extent of the cover as requested by the buyer if the insurers agree and the buyer pays the additional premium

(c) permit the buyer to inspect the policy, or evidence of its terms, at any time

(d) if the policy does not cover a contractual purchaser's interest in the property, extend the cover accordingly at the buyer's request and expense, if the insurers agree, for the period until completion

(e) pay to the buyer, immediately on receipt, any part of an additional premium which the buyer paid and which is returned by the insurers

(f) if before completion the property suffers loss or damage:

(i) pay to the buyer on completion the amount of policy monies which the seller has received, so far as not applied in repairing or reinstating the property, and

(ii) if no final payment has then been received, assign to the buyer, at the buyer's expense, all rights to claim under the policy in such form as the buyer reasonably requires and pending execution of the assignment, hold any policy monies received in trust for the buyer

(g) on completion:

(i) cancel the insurance policy

(ii) apply for a refund of the premium and pay the buyer, immediately on receipt, any amount received which relates to a part of the premium which was paid or reimbursed by a tenant or third party. The buyer is to hold the money paid subject to the rights of that tenant or third party.

8.2.3 The buyer is to pay the seller a proportionate part of the premium which the seller paid in respect of the period from the date when the contract is made to the date of actual completion, except so far as the seller is entitled to recover it from a tenant.

8.2.4 Unless condition 8.2.2 or 8.2.5 applies:

(a) the seller is under no obligation to the buyer to insure the property

(b) if payment under a policy effected by or for the buyer is reduced, because the property is covered against loss or damage by an insurance policy effected by or for the seller, the purchase price is to be abated by the amount of that reduction.

8.2.5 Where the property is leasehold and the property, or any building containing it, is insured by a reversioner or other third party

(a) the seller is to use reasonable efforts to ensure that the insurance is maintained until completion

(b) if, before completion, the property or building suffers loss or damage the seller is to assign to the buyer on completion, at the buyer's expense, such rights as the seller may have in the policy monies, in such form as the buyer reasonably requires.

8.2.6 Section 47 of the Law of Property Act 1925 does not apply.

8.2.7 If the policy does not extend cover to a contractual purchaser's loss of rent from the property following completion, the seller has no responsibility to arrange for it to do so.

9. COMPLETION

9.1 **Date**

9.1.1 Completion date is twenty working days after the date of the contract but time is not of the essence of the contract unless a notice to complete has been served.

9.1.2 If the money due on completion is received after 2.00 p.m., completion is to be treated, for the purposes only of conditions 9.3 and 10.3, as taking place on the next working day as a result of the buyer's default.

9.1.3 Condition 9.1.2 does not apply and the seller is treated as in default if:

(a) the sale is with vacant possession of the property or part of it, and

(b) the buyer is ready, able and willing to complete but does not pay the money due on completion until after 2.00 p.m. because the seller has not vacated the property or that part by that time.

9.2 **Arrangements and place**

9.2.1 The buyer's conveyancer and the seller's conveyancer are to co-operate in agreeing arrangements for completing the contract.

9.2.2 Completion is to take place in England and Wales, either at the seller's conveyancer's office or at some other place which the seller reasonably specifies.

9.3 **Apportionments**

9.3.1 Subject to condition 9.3.6 income and outgoings of the property are to be apportioned between the parties so far as the change of ownership on completion will affect entitlement to receive or liability to pay them.

9.3.2 The day from which the apportionment is to be made ('apportionment day') is:

(a) if the whole property is sold with vacant possession or the seller exercises its option in condition 10.3.4, the date of actual completion, or

(b) otherwise, completion date.

9.3.3 In apportioning any sum, it is to be assumed that the buyer owns the property from the beginning of the day on which the apportionment is to be made.

9.3.4 A sum to be apportioned is to be treated as:

(a) payable for the period which it covers, except that if it is an instalment of an annual sum the buyer is to be attributed with an amount equal to 1/365th of the annual sum for each day from and including the apportionment day to the end of the instalment period

(b) accruing:

(i) from day to day, and

(ii) at the rate applicable from time to time.

9.3.5 When a sum to be apportioned, or the rate at which it is to be treated as accruing, is not known or easily ascertainable:

(a) at completion, a provisional apportionment is to be made according to the best estimate available

(b) if the sum to be provisionally apportioned is rent or service charge subject to review, final determination or adjustment, the provisional apportionment is to be made according to the amount payable on account

(c) as soon as the amount is known, a final apportionment is to be made and notified to the other party

(d) subject to condition 9.3.8, any resulting balance is to be paid no more than ten working days later, and if not then paid, so much of the balance as is from time to time unpaid is to bear interest at the contract rate from then until payment.

9.3.6 Where a lease of the property requires the tenant to reimburse the landlord for expenditure on goods or services, on completion:

(a) the buyer is to pay the seller the amount of any expenditure already incurred by the seller but not yet due from the tenant and in respect of which the seller provides the buyer with the information and vouchers required for its recovery from the tenant, and

(b) the seller is to credit the buyer with payments already recovered from the tenant but not yet incurred by the seller.

9.3.7 Condition 9.3.8 has effect if any part of the property is sold subject to a lease and Case 1 or Case 2 below applies:

(a) Case 1 is that:

(i) on completion any rent or other sum payable under the lease is due but not paid,

(ii) the contract does not provide that the buyer is to assign to the seller the right to collect any arrears due to the seller under the terms of the contract, and

(iii) the seller is not entitled to recover any arrears from the tenant

(b) Case 2 is that:

(i) a reviewed rent or interim rent is agreed or determined after actual completion as a result either of a review to which condition 6.1 applies or of negotiations or proceedings to which condition 6.2 applies, and

(ii) an additional sum then becomes payable or an allowance becomes due in respect of a period before the apportionment day.

9.3.8 (a) The buyer is to seek to collect all sums due from the tenant in the circumstances referred to in condition 9.3.7 in the ordinary course of management, but need not take legal proceedings or exercise the commercial rent arrears recovery (CRAR) procedure.

(b) A payment made on account of those sums is to be apportioned between the parties in the ratio of the amounts owed to each, notwithstanding that the tenant exercises its right to appropriate the payment in some other manner.

(c) Any part of a payment on account received by one party but due to the other is to be paid no more than ten working days after the receipt of cash or cleared funds and, if not then paid, the sum is to bear interest at the contract rate until payment.

(d) Any allowance due to the tenant is to be apportioned between the parties in the ratio of the amounts owed by each of them.

9.4 **Amount payable**

The amount payable by the buyer on completion is the purchase price (less any deposit already paid to the seller or its agent) adjusted to take account of:

(a) apportionments made under condition 9.3

(b) any compensation to be paid or allowed under condition 10.3

(c) any sum payable under condition 8.2.2 or 8.2.3.

9.5 **Title deeds**

9.5.1 As soon as the buyer has complied with all its obligations under this contract on completion the seller is to hand over the documents of title.

9.5.2 Condition 9.5.1 does not apply to any documents of title relating to land being retained by the seller after completion.

9.6 **Rent receipts**

The buyer is to assume that whoever gave any receipt for a payment of rent or service charge which the seller produces was the person or the agent of the person then entitled to that rent or service charge.

9.7 **Means of payment**

The buyer is to pay the money due on completion by electronic means in same day cleared funds from an account held in the name of a conveyancer at a clearing bank to an account in the name of the seller's conveyancer and, if appropriate, by an unconditional release of a deposit held by a stakeholder.

9.8 **Notice to complete**

9.8.1 At any time after the time applicable under condition 9.1.2 on completion date, a party who is ready, able and willing to complete may give the other a notice to complete.

9.8.2 The parties are to complete the contract within ten working days of giving a notice to complete, excluding the day on which the notice is given. For this purpose, time is of the essence of the contract.

9.8.3 On receipt of a notice to complete:

(a) if the buyer paid no deposit, it is without delay to pay a deposit of 10 per cent of the purchase price

(b) if the buyer paid a deposit of less than 10 per cent of the purchase price, it is without delay to pay a further deposit equal to the balance of that 10 per cent.

10. REMEDIES

10.1 Errors and omissions

If any plan or statement in the contract, or in the negotiations leading to it, is or was misleading or inaccurate due to an error or omission by the seller, the remedies available to the buyer are as follows:

(a) when there is a material difference between the description or value of the property, or any of the contents included in the contract, as represented and as it is, the buyer is entitled to damages

(b) an error or omission only entitles the buyer to rescind the contract:

(i) where it results from fraud or recklessness, or

(ii) where the buyer would be obliged, to its prejudice, to accept property differing substantially (in quantity, quality or tenure) from what the error or omission had led it to expect.

10.2 Rescission

If either party rescinds the contract:

(a) unless the rescission is a result of the buyer's breach of contract the deposit is to be repaid to the buyer with accrued interest

(b) the buyer is to return any documents it received from the seller and is to cancel any registration of the contract

(c) the seller's duty to pay any returned premium under condition 8.2.2(e) (whenever received) is not affected.

10.3 Late completion

10.3.1 If the buyer defaults in performing its obligations under the contract and completion is delayed, the buyer is to pay compensation to the seller.

10.3.2 Compensation is calculated at the contract rate on an amount equal to the purchase price (less any deposit paid) for the period between completion date and actual completion, but ignoring any period during which the seller was in default.

10.3.3 Any claim by the seller for loss resulting from delayed completion is to be reduced by any compensation paid under this contract.

10.3.4 Where the sale is not with vacant possession of the whole property and completion is delayed, the seller may give notice to the buyer, before the date of actual completion, that it will take the net income from the property until completion as well as compensation under condition 10.3.1.

10.4 After completion

Completion does not cancel liability to perform any outstanding obligation under the contract.

10.5 Buyer's failure to comply with notice to complete

10.5.1 If the buyer fails to complete in accordance with a notice to complete, the following terms apply.

10.5.2 The seller may rescind the contract, and if it does so:

(a) it may

(i) forfeit and keep any deposit and accrued interest

(ii) resell the property and any contents included in the contract

(iii) claim damages

(b) the buyer is to return any documents it received from the seller and is to cancel any registration of the contract.

10.5.3 The seller retains its other rights and remedies.

10.6 Seller's failure to comply with notice to complete

10.6.1 If the seller fails to complete in accordance with a notice to complete, the following terms apply.

10.6.2 The buyer may rescind the contract, and if it does so:

(a) the deposit is to be repaid to the buyer with accrued interest

(b) the buyer is to return any documents it received from the seller and is, at the seller's expense, to cancel any registration of the contract.

10.6.3 The buyer retains its other rights and remedies.

11. LEASEHOLD PROPERTY

11.1 Existing leases

11.1.1 The following provisions apply to a sale of leasehold land.

11.1.2 The seller having provided the buyer with copies of the documents embodying the lease terms, the buyer is treated as entering into the contract knowing and fully accepting those terms.

11.2 New leases

11.2.1 The following provisions apply to a contract to grant a new lease.

11.2.2 The conditions apply so that:

(a) "seller" means the proposed landlord

(b) "buyer" means the proposed tenant

(c) "purchase price" means the premium to be paid on the grant of a lease.

11.2.3 The lease is to be in the form of the draft attached to the contract.

11.2.4 If the term of the new lease will exceed seven years, the seller is to deduce a title which will enable the buyer to register the lease at Land Registry with an absolute title.

11.2.5 The seller is to engross the lease and a counterpart of it and is to send the counterpart to the buyer at least five working days before completion date.

11.2.6 The buyer is to execute the counterpart and deliver it to the seller on completion.

11.3 Consents

11.3.1 (a) The following provisions apply if a consent to let, assign or sub-let is required to complete the contract

(b) In this condition "consent" means consent in the form which satisfies the requirement to obtain it.

11.3.2 (a) The seller is to:

(i) apply for the consent at its expense, and to use all reasonable efforts to obtain it

(ii) give the buyer without delay a copy of all correspondence with a reversioner (whether or not immediate) in relation to obtaining the consent

(iii) give the buyer notice without delay on obtaining the consent

(b) The buyer is to comply with all reasonable requirements, including requirements for the provision of information and references.

11.3.3 Where the consent of a reversioner (whether or not immediate) is required to an assignment or sub-letting, then so far as the reversioner lawfully imposes such a condition:

(a) the buyer is to:

(i) covenant directly with the reversioner to perform and observe the tenant's covenants and the conditions in the seller's lease or (in the case of a sub-letting by the seller) in the new sub-lease

(ii) use reasonable endeavours to provide guarantees of the performance and observance of the tenant's covenants and the conditions in the seller's lease or (in the case of a sub-letting by the seller) in the new sub-lease

(iii) execute or procure the execution of the licence

(b) the seller, in the case of an assignment, is to enter into an authorised guarantee agreement.

11.3.4 Neither party may object to a reversioner's consent given subject to a condition:

(a) which under section 19(1A) of the Landlord and Tenant Act 1927 is not regarded as unreasonable, and

(b) which is lawfully imposed under an express term of the lease.

11.3.5 If any required consent has not been obtained by the original completion date:

(a) the time for completion is to be postponed until five working days after the seller gives written notice to the buyer that the consent has been given or a court has declared that consent has been unreasonably withheld

(b) the postponed date is to be treated as the completion date.

11.3.6 At any time after six months from the original completion date, either party may rescind the contract by notice to the other, if:

(a) consent has still not been given, and

(b) no declaration has been obtained from the court that consent has been unreasonably withheld.

11.3.7 If the contract is rescinded under condition 11.3.6 the seller is to remain liable for any breach of condition 11.3.2(a) or 11.3.3(b) and the buyer is to remain liable for any breach of condition 11.3.2(b) or 11.3.3(a) but condition 10.2 is to apply as if neither party is in breach of contract.

11.3.8 A party in breach of its obligations under condition 11.3.2 or 11.3.3 cannot rescind under condition 11.3.6 for so long as its breach is a cause of the consent being withheld.

12. CONTENTS

12.1 The following provisions apply to any contents which are included in the contract, whether or not a separate price is to be paid for them.

12.2 The contract takes effect as a contract for the sale of goods.

12.3 The buyer takes the contents in the physical state they are in at the date of the contract.

12.4 Ownership of the contents passes to the buyer on actual completion but they are at the buyer's risk from the contract date.

PART 2*

A. VAT

A1 Not a taxable supply

A1.1 Condition 2 does not apply.

A1.2 The seller:

(a) warrants that the sale of the property does not constitute a supply that is taxable for VAT purposes

(b) agrees not to exercise the option to tax in relation to the property, and

(c) cannot require the buyer to pay any amount in respect of any liability to VAT arising in respect of the sale of the property, unless condition A1.3 applies.

A1.3 If, solely as a result of a change in law made and coming into effect between the date of the contract and completion, the sale of the property will constitute a supply chargeable to VAT, the buyer is to pay to the seller on completion an additional amount equal to that VAT in exchange for a VAT invoice from the seller.

A1.4 The buyer is to pay to the seller on completion an additional amount equal to any VAT charged on the supply of any contents included in the sale in exchange for a VAT invoice from the seller.

A2 Transfer of a going concern

A2.1 Condition 2 does not apply.

A2.2 In this condition "TOGC" means a transfer of a business as a going concern treated as neither a supply of goods nor a supply of services by virtue of article 5 of the Value Added Tax (Special Provisions) Order 1995.

A2.3 The seller warrants that it is using the property for the business of letting to produce rental income.

A2.4 The buyer is to comply with the conditions to be met by a transferee under article 5(1) and 5(2) for the sale to constitute a TOGC.

A2.5 The buyer is, on or before the earlier of:

(a) completion date, and

(b) the earliest date on which a supply of the property could be treated as made by the seller under this contract if the sale does not constitute a TOGC,

to notify the seller that paragraph (2B) of article 5 of the Value Added Tax (Special Provisions) Order 1995 does not apply to the buyer.

A2.6 The parties are to treat the sale as a TOGC at completion if the buyer provides written evidence to the seller before completion that it is a taxable person and that it has exercised an option to tax in relation to the property and has given a written notification of the exercise of such option in conformity with article 5(2A) and has given the notification referred to in condition A2.5.

A2.7 The buyer may not revoke its option to tax in relation to the property at any time.

A2.8 If the parties treat the sale at completion as a TOGC but it is later determined that the sale was not a TOGC, then within five working days of that determination the buyer is to pay to the seller:

(a) an amount equal to the VAT chargeable in respect of the supply of the property, in exchange for a VAT invoice from the seller, and

(b) except where the sale is not a TOGC because of an act or omission of the seller, an amount equal to any interest or penalty for which the seller is liable to account to HM Revenue and Customs in respect of or by reference to that VAT.

A2.9 If the seller obtains the consent of HM Revenue and Customs to retain its VAT records relating to the property, it is to make them available to the buyer for inspection and copying at reasonable times on reasonable request during the six years following completion.

B. CAPITAL ALLOWANCES

B1 In this condition "the Act" means the Capital Allowances Act 2001.

B2 To enable the buyer to make and substantiate claims under the Act in respect of the property, the seller is to use its reasonable endeavours to provide, or to procure that its agents provide:

(a) copies of all relevant information in its possession or that of its agents, and

(b) whatever co-operation and assistance the buyer may reasonably require.

B3 If the seller has claimed capital allowances under Chapter 14 of the Act in respect of expenditure on plant and machinery that is a fixture:

(a) the seller is to take such steps and provide such information and written statements as the buyer may reasonably require to enable the buyer to meet the requirements of section 187A and section 187B of the Act

(b) the buyer is to use the information provided only for the stated purpose

(c) the buyer may not without the consent of the seller disclose the information which the seller expressly provides on a confidential basis

(d) on completion, the seller and the buyer are jointly to make an election under section 198 of the Act which is consistent with the apportionment in the Special Conditions

(e) the seller and the buyer are each promptly to submit the amount fixed by that election to HM Revenue and Customs for the purposes of their respective capital allowance computations

(f) the seller is to bring into account the disposal value of the fixtures fixed by the election in its tax return for the chargeable period in which completion takes place.

B4 If the seller is not entitled to claim allowances under Chapter 14 of the Act in respect of expenditure on plant and machinery that is a fixture but the buyer wishes to make such a claim:

(a) the seller is to use its reasonable endeavours to trace information about the historic expenditure from a predecessor in title of the seller by whom the expenditure was most recently incurred to enable the buyer to claim any available allowance in respect of the historic expenditure and to assist the buyer to do so

(b) the buyer is to indemnify the seller for the reasonable professional costs it properly incurs in complying with its obligations under (a).

C. REVERSIONARY INTERESTS IN FLATS

C1 **No tenants' rights of first refusal**

C1.1 In this condition, sections refer to sections of the Landlord and Tenant Act 1987 and expressions have the special meanings given to them in that Act.

C1.2 The seller warrants that:

(a) it gave the notice required by section 5

(b) no acceptance notice was served on the landlord or no person was nominated for the purposes of section 6 during the protected period, and

(c) that period ended less than 12 months before the date of the contract.

C2 **Tenants' rights of first refusal in auction sales**

C2.1 In this condition, sections refer to sections of the Landlord and Tenant Act 1987 and expressions have the special meanings given to them in that Act.

C2.2 The seller warrants that:

(a) it gave the notice required by section 5B, and

(b) it has given the buyer a copy of:

(i) any acceptance notice served on the landlord

(ii) any nomination of a person duly nominated for the purposes of section 6 and

(iii) any notice served on the landlord electing that section 8B shall apply.

C2.3 The following additional provisions shall apply:

(a) condition 9.1.1 applies as if "thirty working days" were substituted for "twenty working days"

(b) the seller is to send a copy of the contract to the nominated person as required by section 8B(3), and

(c) if the nominated person serves notice under section 8B(4):

(i) the seller is to give the buyer a copy of the notice, and

(ii) condition 10.2 is to apply as if the contract had been rescinded.

*The conditions in Part 2 do not apply unless expressly incorporated. See condition 1.1.4(b).

Practical Law

BPF
BRITISH PROPERTY FEDERATION

Commercial Property Standard Enquiries

SCR (version 3.5) Solicitor's completion requirements

Conditions

This document may be used free of charge subject to the Conditions set out in *GN/CPSE (version 3.3) Guidance notes on the Commercial Property Standard Enquiries (www.practicallaw.com/3-628-1672)*.

Particulars

Seller:

Buyer:

Property:

Transaction:

Seller's solicitors:

Buyer's solicitors:

Date:

Notes

1. This document is designed for use with pre-contract enquiries in CPSE.1 and deals with arrangements, as between solicitors, for completion.

Interpretation

The section on Interpretation in CPSE.1 is incorporated in this document and the following interpretation also applies save that:

- "**we**" refers to the Buyer's solicitors and "**you**" refers to the Seller's solicitors; and
- the following interpretation also applies:
  - **Lease:** means the lease proposed to be granted by the Seller to the Buyer or, as the case may be, the lease under which the Property is held and which is to be assigned by the Seller to the Buyer.

Practical Law

BPF
BRITISH PROPERTY FEDERATION

- **Tenancy Documents:** refers to the Lease (or, where the Transaction is the sale of a property subject to tenancies, the instrument creating each tenancy), and to any of the following that relate to it: charges, mortgages, surrenders, variations, side letters, undertakings, applications, consents, memoranda, registrations, notices, rent deposit deeds, orders, guarantees, concessions, franchise agreements, counsel's opinions and arbitrators' or experts' decisions.

CONTENTS

ENQUIRIES

SCHEDULE

COMPLETION REQUIREMENTS

1. COMPLETION BY POST

1.1 We wish to complete by post. Please confirm:

(a) you will adopt the Law Society's code for completion by post (2019 version) (2019 Completion Code);

(b) the mortgages and financial charges listed in Schedule 1 to this form are those specified for the purpose of paragraph 7 of the 2019 Completion Code; and

(c) you will mark the copies of those documents listed in Schedule 2 to this form (the originals of which are not to be handed over on completion) as examined against the originals.

[Insert answer to question here]

1.2 If you will not be adopting the 2019 Completion Code, please provide copies of the following authorities:

(a) from the Seller authorising you to receive the purchase money; and

(b) from the proprietor of each mortgage or other financial charge listed in Schedule 1 to this form authorising you to receive the sum needed to repay it.

[Insert answer to question here]

1.3 If you will not be adopting the 2019 Completion Code, please confirm that you will act as our agent (without fee) in marking the copies of those documents listed in Schedule 2 to this form (the originals of which are not to be handed over on completion) as examined against the originals.

[Insert answer to question here]

2. COMPLETION STATEMENT

2.1 Please supply a completion statement, showing how any apportionments have been calculated.

[Insert answer to question here]

2.2 Where any payments are being apportioned, please supply copies of the most recent receipts for them.

[Insert answer to question here]

3. **UNDERTAKINGS**

3.1 In relation to each of the mortgages and financial charges listed in Schedule 1 to this form will you:

(a) hand over DS1 (or DS3, as the case may be) on completion;

(b) be giving an undertaking for DS1 (or DS3, as the case may be);

(c) be giving an undertaking for an ED; or

(d) be giving an undertaking for an e-DS1?

[Insert answer to question here]

3.2 Where an undertaking will be given, please provide a draft for our approval.

[Insert answer to question here]

4. **OTHER MATTERS**

4.1 Where the Property is subject to Tenancies, please provide a draft rent authority for our approval.

[Insert answer to question here]

4.2 What arrangements will be made:

(a) to hand over keys; and

(b) where there is a security system at the Property, to supply codes etc?

[Insert answer to question here]

5. **METHOD OF SIGNING COMPLETION DOCUMENTS**

In this enquiry:

"Conveyancer-certified electronic signatures", "Mercury" and "Option 1" have the same meaning as in Land Registry Practice Guide 82;

"mortgagee" means any mortgagee or chargee discharging a mortgage or financial charge on completion.

5.1 How will your client and any mortgagee sign the completion documents, i.e. will they be using wet ink, Mercury or electronic signatures?

[Insert answer to question here]

5.2 Unless we are controlling the signature process, if electronic signatures are to be used by your client or any mortgagee for any completion document, please state which e-signing platform will be used.

[Insert answer to question here]

5.3 Unless we are controlling the signature process, if electronic signatures are to be used by your client or any mortgagee for any completion document where use of a conveyancer-certified electronic signature is mandatory under Land Registry Practice Guide 82:

(a) please list the documents to which this applies;

(b) please confirm that the signature process will comply with the requirements for conveyancer-certified electronic signatures set out in Land Registry Practice Guide 82;

(c) please confirm that at the same time as supplying the relevant documents on completion, you undertake to supply a conveyancer's certificate in the form set out in appendix 2 to that Practice Guide relating to each conveyancer-certified electronic signature; and

(d) please provide a draft of the conveyancer's certificate referred to in 5.3(c) for our approval before completion.

[Insert answer to question here]

5.4 If Mercury signatures are to be used on any document at completion, please confirm that the signature process will comply with Option 1.

[Insert answer to question here]

5.5 Where any completion document is to be executed by an attorney, please also respond to 5.1-5.4 inclusive in relation to the power of attorney.

[Insert answer to question here]

6. CONFIRMATION

Please confirm that the Seller is not aware of anything which would change or make incorrect the reply given to any pre-contract enquiry.

[Insert answer to question here]

Schedule 1 Mortgages and financial charges to be discharged on completion

Schedule 2 Title documents the originals of which will not be handed over on completion

Appendix 7: Answers to multiple-choice practice questions

In this appendix you will find the answers to the multiple-choice practice questions at the end of each phase. You can find a further set of questions and answers at www.routledge.com/cw/sqe.

Phase 0: commercial considerations

Question 1

The correct answer is A because LTT is the tax due on the acquisition of properties in Wales.

B is not correct because SDLT is only chargeable on the acquisition of properties in England.

C and E are not correct because VAT is not chargeable on a residential property.

D is not correct because CGT liability arises on the disposal of property, not the acquisition.

Question 2

The correct answer is D because the seller has used the property as their main residence throughout their ownership.

A is not correct because interests in land are chargeable assets.

B is not correct because individuals are chargeable persons.

C is not correct because the property has increased in value since it was acquired.

E is not correct because CGT liability arises on the disposal of property, not the acquisition.

Question 3

The correct answer is B because the acquisition of a lease is an exempt supply, but the seller may exercise an option to tax and add VAT to the purchase price. The construction supplies and works and the professional services will attract VAT at the standard rate.

A is correct, but it is not the best answer because it does not advise that VAT may also be chargeable on the price of the property and the professional fees.

C is incorrect because the seller may exercise an option to tax and add VAT to the purchase price.

D is incorrect because the supply is exempt, not zero-rated.

E is correct, but it is not the best answer because it does not advise that VAT may also be chargeable on the construction supplies and works.

Phase 1: due diligence

Question 1

Answer

The correct answer is E because the conveyance is over 15 years old and pre-dates compulsory registration.

A is not correct because, although the conveyance is 15 years old, it does not pre-date compulsory registration, and so the conveyance would have triggered first registration of the land.

B is not correct because the document is not 15 years old.

C and D are not correct because neither document is 15 years old, and both dispositions would have triggered first registration of the land.

Question 2

Answer

The correct answer is C because the conveyance contains a certificate of value relating to ad valorem duty and an exemption certificate instead of a PD stamp.

A is not correct because the stamp or certificate of value relating to ad valorem stamp duty is missing. Leases of less than seven years did not require a particulars delivered stamp.

B is not correct because it is missing a particulars delivered stamp or certificate.

D is not correct because the conveyance contained no stamps or certificates relating to either ad valorem stamp duty or particulars delivered.

E is not correct because the conveyance is missing a stamp or certificate of value relating to ad valorem stamp duty.

Question 3

Answer

The correct answer is A. The easement and lease are legal interests, and the restrictive covenant has been registered as a land charge, all of which bind a purchaser for valuable consideration.

B is not correct because the contract for sale is an equitable interest.

C is not the best answer because, whilst the easement and restrictive covenant will bind the purchaser, so will the lease.

D is not the best answer because, whilst the restrictive covenant will bind the purchaser, so will the lease and the easement.

E is not the best answer because, whilst the restrictive covenant and the lease will bind the purchaser, so will the easement.

Question 4

Answer

The correct answer is C because the common seal of the company has been applied in the presence of two directors.

A is not correct because the seal needed to be applied in the presence of two directors or one director and a secretary.

B is not correct because the deed was executed in 1990; it was not possible for one director to sign a deed until 6 April 2008.

D and E are not correct because an individual has executed the deed rather than the company.

Question 5

Answer

The correct answer is C because a right of way is an easement, and it is the Charges Register which details charges and matters burdening the land such as easements.

A is not correct because the Property Register describes the land and estate comprised in the title, including rights benefitting the property. The question tells us that the property is *subject* to a right of way; this easement, therefore, burdens the property.

B is not correct because the Proprietorship Register specifies the class of title, identifies the proprietor, and details any restrictions on the proprietor's ability to dispose of the property. It does not detail easements.

D is not correct because there is no suggestion that the easement affects the right of disposal.

E is not correct because a right of way is an easement, not a restrictive covenant.

Question 6

Answer

The best answer is D because this promise is a positive covenant; positive covenants can be enforced by way of an indemnity covenant noted on the Proprietorship Register.

A is not correct because a covenant is not usually noted on the Property Register, which describes the property and estate comprised in the title, including rights benefitting the property.

B and E are not correct because this is a positive covenant, not a restrictive covenant.

C is not the best answer. A positive covenant can be noted on the Charges Register, but this is not the mechanism by which it can bind a purchaser.

Question 7

Answer

The correct answer is B. In cases where the legal title to property is owned by tenants-in-common, HMLR will automatically add a restriction to the Proprietorship Register preventing disposal of the property by one owner, to ensure that overreaching occurs.

A is not the best answer because HMLR automatically enters a restriction on the Proprietorship Register when the legal title is owned by tenants-in-common.

C is not correct because the restriction referred to is the wrong type of restriction.

D and E are not correct because it is not possible to note trust interests on the title register.

Question 8

Answer

The correct answer is D because the change of use occurred in January 2021, which falls within the transitional period; this means that planning permission is not required if under *either* of the versions of the Order the change was not considered to be material.

A is not correct because the change *was* material under the 1987 version of the Order.

B is not correct because the change was not material under the 2020 version of the Order.

C is not correct because planning permission is not required as the change was not material under the 2020 version of the Order; for changes falling within the transitional period, planning permission is not required if under either version of the Order the change was not considered to be material.

E is not correct because the change was *not* material under the 2020 version of the Order.

Question 9

Answer

The correct answer is B because the extension constitutes 'development' and therefore requires planning permission, but the change of use from a library to a museum is not a material change of use because these both fall within the same use class.

A is not correct because the change of use does not require planning permission.

C is not correct: the change of use does not require planning permission, and the extension does constitute 'development'.

D is not correct because the extension does constitute 'development'.

E is not correct because the extension is not 'permitted development'.

Question 10

Answer

The correct answer is A because the internal works do not constitute 'development' and the change of use, whilst material, is 'permitted development' according to Part 3 of Schedule 2 GPDO.

B and C are not correct because the change of use still constitutes 'development' even though it is permitted under Schedule 2.

D is not correct because the internal works do not require planning permission and the change of use does not require an application for planning permission.

E is not correct because the change of use is material.

Question 11

Answer

The best answer is D because it is a planning condition which has not been complied with.

A is not correct because the building works have already been completed and, in any event, a stop notice cannot be served without service of an enforcement notice.

B and E are not the best answer because the building works have already been completed.

C is not correct. Building works carried out in breach of a planning condition can be enforced up to ten years from the breach of the condition which occurred five years ago.

Phase 2: the documentation

Question 1

Answer

The correct answer is D because this requires the Subtenant to give a direct covenant to the Landlord and ensures the Landlord can pursue the Subtenant for any breaches of covenant throughout the entire duration of the lease.

E is an acceptable answer because it requires the Subtenant to give a direct covenant to the Landlord, but this only lasts until the lease is assigned and is therefore a less secure position for the Landlord than under **D**.

A, B and C all provide the Landlord with some security as the Landlord can pursue the Tenant if the Subtenant breaches a covenant, but it is better to require the Subtenant to covenant directly with the Landlord. In addition, **C** provides a more limited security than **B** because it only lasts until the lease is assigned, as opposed to the entire term.

Question 2

Answer

The correct answer is B because the SCSs automatically assume that a deposit of 10% will be paid by the buyer, and that the deposit will be held as stakeholder for the seller.

A and B are not correct because it does not need to be noted in the particulars of sale or as a special condition.

C is not correct because the SCPCs do not govern residential transactions.

E is not correct because it is the sale contract not the transfer deed which details the payment of a deposit.

Question 3

Answer

The correct answer is D because any change to how the deposit is to be held must be incorporated as a special condition.

A is not correct because the particulars of sale only allow for changes to the amount of deposit to be paid, not how this deposit is to be held.

B is not correct because the SCSs state that the deposit will be held as stake-holder for the seller.

C is not correct because the SCPCs do not govern residential transactions.

E is not correct because it is the sale contract not the transfer deed which details the payment of a deposit.

Question 4

Answer

C is the correct answer because the SCPCs already state that full guarantee will be provided by the seller.

A and D are not correct because the SCPCs already cover the position and so amendment via the particulars of sale or special condition is not required.

B is not correct because the SCSs do not apply to commercial transactions.

E is not correct because it is the sale contract not the transfer deed which details the title guarantee.

Question 5

Answer

The correct answer is A. Encumbrances appearing on the title register should be specifically disclosed in the particulars of sale.

B is not correct. The SCSs do not automatically disclose matters contained on the title register.

C is not correct because the SCPCs do not govern residential transactions.

D is not correct because specified encumbrances should be listed in the particulars of sale.

E is not correct because it is the sale contract not the transfer deed which details the encumbrances affecting a property.

Question 6

Answer

The correct answer is A. Encumbrances appearing on the title register should be specifically disclosed in the particulars of sale.

B is not correct. the SCSs do not govern commercial transactions.

C is not correct because the SCPCs do not automatically disclose matters contained in the Land Charges Register.

D is not correct because specified encumbrances should be listed in the particulars of sale.

E is not correct because it is the sale contract not the transfer deed which details the encumbrances affecting a property.

Question 7

Answer

The correct answer is C because under the SCPCs, the buyer is not entitled to compensation for late completion.

A and B are not correct because under the SCPCs the buyer is not entitled to compensation for late completion.

D is not correct because the reason for which the buyer is not entitled to compensation is not correct – completion *is* delayed, but this is not something which entitles the buyer to compensation under the SCPCs.

E is not correct because it does not reflect the sale contract.

Question 8

Answer

The correct answer is C.

(1) and (2) are not correct because these are obligations which must be complied with *upon or before* completion; the TR1 deals with things affecting the property or its proprietors *after* completion. This means that **A, D, and E** cannot be correct.

(3) is correct because this affects the scope of the ongoing tenant covenants under the lease. This means that **B** cannot be correct.

Question 9

Answer

The correct answer is A. Upon rent review, goodwill generated by the tenant, improvements made by the tenant, and the tenant's occupation of the premises will all make the hypothetical lease more valuable, and therefore the hypothetical rent higher. The tenant should not be penalised by paying a higher rent for benefits they have created. This means that **C** cannot be the best answer.

An assumption that the tenant covenants and landlord covenants have been complied with will make the hypothetical lease more attractive, with higher rent. A disregard will have the opposite effect. The best position is to ensure that the hypothetical lease reflects the reality. This means that **B and D** are not the best answers because we cannot be sure how closely each is to the real position.

An assumption that the tenant paid a premium for the lease would likely make the hypothetical rent under the hypothetical lease lower than it is in reality. This is unlikely to be acceptable to the landlord, and therefore, **E** is not the best answer even though it secures a lower rent for the client.

Question 10

Answer

The correct answer is D. The alienation clause is a qualified prohibition – meaning, the tenant requires the landlord's consent to an assignment; section 19(1)(a) LTA 1927 requires the landlord to act reasonably when deciding whether to consent.

A is not correct because the clause is not an absolute prohibition.

Although the clause is a qualified prohibition, the landlord cannot refuse consent for any reason at all – it must act reasonably, under section 19(1)(a) LTA 1927; this means that **B** is not correct.

C is not correct because the clause is not a fully qualified prohibition.

E is not correct because the clause is a qualified prohibition; the landlord can refuse consent provided it acts reasonably in deciding to do so.

Question 11

Answer

The correct answer is C. When an individual grants a mortgage over their house, the mortgage deed is usually on the bank's standard T&Cs and will contain clauses requiring the borrower to repay the loan and keep the property in good repair.

A, B, and E are not correct because facility agreements and debentures are used for commercial mortgages, not residential mortgages.

D is not correct because a lender cannot take a floating charge over the assets of an individual, only a company, and there is nothing to suggest this borrower is a company.

Phase 3: preparing for completion

Question 1

Answer

The correct answer is A; the solicitor must ensure that the title queries are resolved and that they have their client's authority to exchange.

B is not the best answer; whilst it is correct that the solicitor must ensure that the title queries are resolved and that they have their client's authority to exchange, we already know that the solicitor is holding the signed contract.

We are not told that the purchaser is granting a mortgage, and we know that no deposit is to be paid. Therefore, **C** cannot be correct.

The Landlord is required to insure the premises, so **D and E** cannot be correct.

Question 2

Answer

The correct answer is E because this accurately depicts exchange using Formula B.

A is not correct because this describes Formula C.

B is not correct because this describes Formula A.

C is not correct because this describes postal exchange.

D is not correct because it is not possible to exchange via email.

Question 3

Answer

The correct answer is A because an OS1 will reveal encumbrances registered against the whole of a registered title since the initial title investigation.

B is not the best answer because an OS2 is used for searching encumbrances against part of a registered title; we have no indication that the purchaser is only purchasing part of the property.

C is not correct because a Land Charges Search is not of relevance to registered land. This means that **E** also cannot be correct.

D is not the best answer because a bankruptcy search against an individual seller is not usually required. This means that **E** also cannot be the best answer.

Question 4

Answer

The correct answer is E. The property is unregistered, and so a Land Charges Search against the seller will reveal encumbrances affecting the property, and a company search against the seller will reveal any charges registered against the assets of the company.

A, B, and D are not correct because OS1 and OS2 are searches of registered land. Further, a bankruptcy search is a search against an individual; the seller is a company.

C is not the best answer because it will only reveal land charges, not charges registered against the assets of the company (for which a company search is required).

Question 5

Answer

The correct answer is B. In order to ensure that the client's purchase takes priority over any other dispositions, the application to register the transfer to the purchaser must be submitted to HMLR within 30 working days of the date of the OS1.

A is not correct because it is an application to register, which must be made within the priority period, not the completion of the transfer.

C is not correct for two reasons: the priority period is 30 working days, not 15, and it is an application to register which must be made within the priority period, not the completion of the transfer.

D is not the best answer. Whilst the date of the OS1 search result may well be the same as the date the OS1 search was undertaken, this is not necessarily the case. Therefore, this answer is less accurate than **B**.

E is not correct because the expiry date specified on the OS1 is the end of the priority period, not the beginning of it.

Phase 4: completion

Question 1

Answer

In order to complete on time, the Standard Conditions of Sale require completion monies to have been sent by 2:00 p.m. on 1 May, and for completion to have occurred on that day. The buyer sent the completion monies after 2:00 p.m., at which point one day's worth of compensation accrued. Completion then did not occur until the following day, incurring a further day's worth of compensation. The compensation is calculated at 4% of the outstanding funds, being the price minus the deposit, which is £315,000. Therefore, **the correct answer is C.**

A and B are not correct because they have only charged one day's worth of compensation. In addition, **B** has calculated the compensation on the full purchase price.

D is not correct because it has calculated the compensation on the full purchase price.

E is not correct because under the Standard Conditions of Sale the seller is entitled to compensation.

Question 2

Answer

The correct answer is D; recission becomes available to the buyer once a notice to complete has been served and the seller has failed to comply with the completion date specified within it.

A is not correct because the SCPCs do not entitle the buyer to compensation for late completion.

B is not correct; the buyer *can* pursue a claim for damages for breach of contract, but this is not the only option, and it is not mandatory.

C is not correct because the buyer cannot rescind the contract without non-compliance with a notice to complete.

E is not correct. Recission becomes available upon non-compliance with a notice to complete; the notice will specify a date within 10 working days. Therefore, the recission date is likely to be before 1 November.

Phase 5: post-completion

Question 1

Answer

The correct answer is C; for a disposition which triggers first registration, legal title is passed to the purchaser upon completion of the transfer, but this legal title reverts back to the seller if the transfer is not registered within two months.

A is not correct because it is the submission of the SDLT return and payment of SDLT to HMRC which would avoid penalties and interest in respect of SDLT; it is unrelated to the registration at HMLR.

B is not correct because registration at HMLR would not affect interest on completion monies as this is a contractual matter between the buyer and the seller.

D is not correct because the land is currently unregistered; therefore, there is no register upon which entries can be made.

E is not correct because we have no information about what events trigger the mortgagee's power of sale.

Question 2

Answer

The correct answer is A because the transaction is notifiable and is likely to give rise to an SDLT liability; the purchaser has 14 days from completion to comply with these obligations.

B is not correct; the deadline noted relates to the deadline for applying for first registration with HMLR.

C is not correct because the deadline noted relates to the deadline for applying for registration of a disposition of registered land.

D is not correct – returns are required in some situations even where no SDLT is payable.

E is not correct because this transaction does not fall within the list of exceptions to the requirement to notify HMRC.

Question 3

Answer

The correct answer is E; the transaction is not notifiable because it is the assignment of a lease of more than seven years for less than £40,000. This necessarily means that **A, B, and C** are not correct.

D is incorrect because the reason for not requiring a land transaction return is wrong; it is not related to whether SDLT is payable.

Phase 6: leasehold management

Question 1

Answer

The correct answer is A. The lease prohibits all structural alterations, and creating apertures in an external wall constitutes a structural alteration. This necessarily means that **E** is incorrect.

B is incorrect because the lease contains a qualified prohibition against *non-structural* alterations.

C and D are incorrect because the work is structural and falls under an absolute prohibition; therefore, considerations as to what might constitute 'reasonable refusal of consent' are not relevant.

Question 2

Answer

The correct answer is B; the lease contains a qualified prohibition on alienation. Section 19(1)(a) LTA1927 requires the Landlord to act reasonably when deciding whether to withhold consent. This necessarily means that **D** is incorrect.

A is incorrect because the alienation covenant is a qualified prohibition, not an absolute prohibition.

C is not the best answer; whilst tenant covenant strength is a reasonable reason for the Landlord to withhold consent, the proposed tenant's covenant strength does not appear to be a concern here as they are 'a highly profitable national chain'.

E is not the best answer because the user covenant is not the only covenant that the proposed assignee will be required to comply with; there may be other reasonable grounds upon which the Landlord withholds consent to the assignment.

Question 3

Answer

The correct answer is A; the parties have agreed that covenant strength of the assignee will be a valid reason for the Landlord to withhold consent; this is permitted under section 19(1A) LTA 1927 because this is a new lease.

B is correct in that covenant strength is usually a valid reason for withholding consent but is not as strong an answer as A because it misses the point that s19(1A) LTA 1927 permits the parties to include a list of 'reasonable' reasons in the lease itself.

C is incorrect because the lease does not need to require the Landlord to act reasonably – this is implied by statute.

D is incorrect because the lease does not contain an *absolute* prohibition on alienation; it contains a *qualified* prohibition.

It is correct in **E** that the Landlord cannot unreasonably withhold consent, but this answer fails to appreciate that covenant strength is a valid reason for withholding consent.

Question 4

Answer

The correct answer is E; a section 146 notice is not required where the covenant breached is the covenant to pay rent.

A and B are not correct because the requirement to serve a notice under section 146 does not apply in cases of non-payment of rent where the lease has removed the requirement to serve a notice on the tenant.

B and C are not correct because the LP(R)A 1938 applies to breaches of repair covenants, not rent.

D is not correct because the lease has removed the requirement to serve a formal demand ('it does not contain any further provisions relating to forfeiture').

Question 5

Answer

The correct answer is B; in cases of a breach of repair covenant, the landlord must serve a notice which complies with section 146 LPA 1925 and section 1 LP(R)A 1938, giving the tenant the opportunity to remedy the breach before forfeiture is permitted.

A is not the best answer; it is correct that in cases of a breach of repair covenant the landlord must serve a notice which complies with section 146 LPA 1925, but this answer misses the requirement for that notice to also comply with section 1 LP(R)A 1938.

C is not the best answer; it is correct that in cases of a breach of repair covenant the landlord must serve a notice which complies with section 1 LP(R)A 1938, but this answer misses the requirement for that notice to also comply with section 146 LPA 1925.

D is not correct; a formal demand relates to the non-payment of rent.

E is not correct; the lease must permit forfeiture, but this is not sufficient. A notice must also be served.

Question 6

Answer

The correct answer is A; the freeholder has privity of estate with the chemist, as the chemist is the current tenant of the freeholder, the current landlord.

B is not correct because there is no AGA in place, under which the clothing retailer acts as guarantor for the chemist.

C is not correct because this is a new lease, and so the original tenant is not liable for breaches by the assignee.

D is not the best answer because it is likely that the AGA under which the supermarket acted as guarantor for the clothing retailer would only cover breaches of covenant by the clothing retailer.

E is not the best answer; whilst part of it is correct, part of it is incorrect as it is likely that the AGA under which the supermarket acted as guarantor for the clothing retailer would only cover breaches of covenant by the clothing retailer.

Question 7

Answer

The correct answer is E; the freeholder has privity of contract with the supermarket, and so, as this is an old lease, the freeholder can pursue the original tenant for breaches of covenant by subsequent tenants, and the freeholder has privity of estate with the chemist and so can pursue the chemist directly.

A is not the best answer because it misses the freeholder's ability to pursue the supermarket under privity of contract.

B is not correct because the freeholder does not have privity of contract or estate with the clothing retailer.

C is not the best answer because it misses the freeholder's ability to pursue the chemist under privity of estate.

D is not correct because the clothing retailer cannot be pursued.

Question 8

Answer

The correct answer is A because it recognises that this is a mandatory ground under which the court does not have discretion over whether to grant a new lease, and that the tenant may be entitled to compensation.

C is not the best answer; it recognises that this is a mandatory ground, but it misses that the tenant may be entitled to compensation.

B, D, and E are incorrect because they fail to recognise that this is a mandatory ground under which the court does not have discretion over whether to grant a new lease.

Question 9

Answer

The correct answer is C as it recognises that this is a discretionary ground.

A and B are not correct because they do not recognise that the tenant can apply to the court for a new lease.

D is not correct because it fails to recognise that this is a discretionary ground.

E is not correct because, whilst it recognises that this is a discretionary ground, it incorrectly states that compensation is available under the discretionary grounds.

Index

For Product Safety Concerns and Information please contact our EU representative GPSR@taylorandfrancis.com Taylor & Francis Verlag GmbH, Kaufingerstraße 24, 80331 München, Germany